The Paradox of a Suffering God
On the Classical, Modern-Western and Third World
Struggles to harmonise the incompatible Attributes of the Trinitarian God

STUDIEN ZUR INTERKULTURELLEN GESCHICHTE DES CHRISTENTUMS
ETUDES D' HISTOIRE INTERCULTURELLE DU CHRISTIANISME
STUDIES IN THE INTERCULTURAL HISTORY OF CHRISTIANITY

begründet von / fondé par / founded by
Hans Jochen Margull†, Hamburg

herausgegeben von / édité par / edited by

Richard Friedli
Université de Fribourg

Walter J. Hollenweger
University of Birmingham

Theo Sundermeier
Universität Heidelberg

Jan A. B. Jongeneel
Universiteit Utrecht

Volume 95

PETER LANG
Frankfurt am Main · Berlin · Bern · New York · Paris · Wien

Amuluche Gregory Nnamani

The Paradox of a Suffering God

On the Classical, Modern-Western and Third World Struggles to harmonise the incompatible Attributes of the Trinitarian God

PETER LANG
Europäischer Verlag der Wissenschaften

Die Deutsche Bibliothek - CIP-Einheitsaufnahme

Nnamani, Amuluche Gregory:

The paradox of a suffering God : on the classical, modern
Western and Third World struggles to harmonise the
incompatible attributes of the Trinitarian God / Amuluche
Gregory Nnamani. - Frankfurt am Main ; Berlin ; Bern ; New
York ; Paris ; Wien : Lang, 1995
    (Studien zur interkulturellen Geschichte des Christentums ;
    Bd. 95)
    Zugl.: Innsbruck, Univ., Diss., 1994
    ISBN 3-631-49032-1

NE: GT

ISSN 0170-9240
ISBN 3-631-49032-1
US-ISBN 0-8204-2935-X

© Peter Lang GmbH
Europäischer Verlag der Wissenschaften
Frankfurt am Main 1995
All rights reserved.

Printed in Germany 1 2   4 5 6 7

In Memory of
my dear father, the late Mr. Alexander Nnamani Ugwu and
my dear nephew, the late Chika Gregory Nnamani,
I dedicate this study to
my beloved Mother, Agnes Nnamani Ugwu, and to
my sisters and brothers

TABLE OF CONTENTS

ACKNOWLEDGEMENT

Thanks be to God for the health and strength He gave me to accomplish this study. In His special providence, He offered me the opportunity to encounter people, friends and colleagues who immensely inspired my work with enriching ideas and through their prayers. While thanking them heartily, I ask God to reward them abundantly.

Some outstanding sources of inspiration need to be acknowledged here. I therefore wish to express my special gratitude to my former bishop, Rt. Rev. Dr. Michael Eneja for sending me to further studies prior to my priestly ordination, and to my bishop, Rt. Rev. Dr. Francis Okobo for allowing me finish this study. My moderator, Univ.-Prof. DDr.Walter Kern, who conceived the idea of this research and fatherly guided it until its completion particularly deserves my thanks. I appreciate his assistance in the collection of literature and his effort towards the publication of this dissertation after it had been accepted by the faculty of Catholic theology of the University of Innsbruck, Austria, in 1994, as partial fulfilment of the requirements for the acquisition of a doctorate degree in theology. I am grateful to him for allowing me to change the title of the original version, which earlier read "The Trinitarian (Im)passibility of God".

This study would not have been undertaken, if friends and organisations had not offered me their financial assistance. To that effect, my thanks go to Collegium Canisianum in Innsbruck, Kaplan Emil Bonetti and the "Missionskreis" of St. Christopher's parish in Dornbirn, Austria, for the initial scholarship they offered me for my studies in Innsbruck. I am also indebted to the Church Council of St. Pius parish in Meggen, Switzerland, and to the "Bischöfliches Ordinariat - Referat Weltkirchliche Aufgaben" of the diocese of Rottenburg-Stuttgart for their supplementary scholarship to finish my studies in Tübingen.

Finally, I wish to thank my parents, sisters, brothers and relations for their patience during my long stay in Europe. I missed them as much as they missed me. May the pains of our labour and deprivation yield good fruits.

K'furt / Tübingen, May 18, 1995   Amuluche G. Nnamani

INTRODUCTION

The twentieth century will go into the annals of history as a period characterised by theological pluralism. The last three decades alone have witnessed the development of five major theological trends: the political, liberation, feminist, process and inculturation theologies. In addition to being theologies from the perspective of the oppressed, all but one of these theologies emerged to fulfil various cultural, political and social expectations. It should not be surprising therefore that they differ among themselves in terms of methodologies and emphasis.

But despite their differences, they share some features in common: they generally discredit the absolutism characteristic of the monolithic cultures in which classical theologies were conceived. Unlike the latter they are intrinsically disposed to tolerate divergent views. This explains why all the major theologies of this century appeared within a short period of time, almost simultaneously, and are now existing side by side on the same theological landscape, without any of them making the slightest claim to exclusiveness or singular legitimacy.

The provision for diversity evident in the modern theologies makes them peculiarly pluralistic. Let it be observed, however, that pluralism is more an issue of *tolerance* than of multiplicity. For, even though a multiple of theological trends existed in the past, we cannot, in reference to that period, speak of pluralism, since the theological atmosphere at that time was less tolerant of divergent views. Undoubtedly, therefore, tolerance, and not multiplicity, is the main pillar of a pluralistic structure and indeed the major distinguishing feature of modern and pluralistic theologies.

This point becomes clearer if it is seen in the context of the ongoing changes in values in modern societies. Earlier in the feudalistic era, and even later in the flourishing period of the communist system, uniformity of thought and action, as well as conformity to the group used to be prime goods. But now, as freedom becomes a major principle of life and the individual increasingly receives the position he deserves in society, these values seem to have become secondary to the art of being authentic to oneself. Thus, in modern society, personal feelings and experiences have become as influential in decision-making as public expectations used to be in the past. Nowadays people feel more obliged to let their actions and statements reflect their inner dispositions than to let them conform to the views of the rest of the world.

This phenomenon can equally be observed in the domain of religion, where faithfulness to one's own conviction increasingly appears to rank higher than conformity to religious conventions. Particularly in matters of spirituality, many believers consider personal religious experiences to be more important than any

15

sort of supposedly universal truths or inherited dogmas. In recent times, this development has led to the demand that every theological substance should reflect the needs of the present day believers. To this effect, an ever increasing number of theologians now insist that the ancient doctrines and the assumptions underlying them should be updated. In their view, abstract theological truths should be discarded once they become irrelevant to the religious experiences of any given time. This means in effect that every ancient doctrine can become dispensable once it fails to pass the test of relevance.

Does this fact not amount to making the issue of *relevance* the determining factor for theological inquiry? Unfortunately, most modern theologians are as quick at giving this impression as they are unable to allay the fear that today's theological temperament might unjustifiably become the measure of truth. Be that as it may, it would be wrong to understand the current appeal for the reinterpretation of ancient doctrines as a plea for the relativity of truth. Far from that, the question of relevance in theological language arises out of the aspiration to contextualise, and not to relativise, theological truth. In spite of the unavoidable tendency towards relativism in today's multi-cultural and changing world, the actual objective of pluralistic theologies is contextualisation, the endeavour to reflect on Christ's message from the perspective of the believer himself.

Thus, for most modern theologians, the contextualisation of theology should necessarily begin with a reinterpretation of supposedly inapplicable doctrines, so that they can reflect the prevalent feelings of believers. At times, this preliminary work of contextualisation often entails a review of earlier heresies. Theologians now summon courage to review heresies, since it is suspected that the classical theologies unduly neglected and sometimes misrepresented certain aspects of Christ's message. Amazingly, the re-examination of heresies has exposed certain basic truths and lost articles of faith which now appeal to modern believers and enrich the main body of theological understanding. Through this exercise, it has therefore become abundantly clear that some of the stones rejected by the early builders of Christianity could become the corner stone for today's theologies.

This awareness has obviously sparked off widespread anxieties about the inadequacy of some ancient attributes of God, which presuppose values that are relatively alien to modern believers. It could be observed, for example, that although the image of God as the eternal judge was very useful in the attempt to represent His royal power to people in the feudalistic period, it now has the reputation of making Him look like the communist "Big Brother" watching and waiting vigilantly for an occasion to catch and punish culprits. Often, the conception of God as the king-judge practically amounted to visualising Him as "a punishing God",[1] whose nearness generates more fear than a sense of protection. At that time God was mainly conceived as a detached Being, whose aseity, immutability and impassibility counted more than His pathos. Even though God was believed to have been involved in the world and to have allowed the crucifixion of His Son on the Cross, the idea that He might have equally suffered sympathetically had always seemed heretical to the classical theologies.

Today, the situation looks different: people readily conceive Him as a God of love and mercy, a God who reveals Himself, not in His aseity, but in His involvement in the world. To many modern theologians and believers, a God who becomes involved is a God who can suffer. In their view, God's involvement in the world makes His suffering very probable, just as His ability to suffer with His creatures demonstrates the radical nature of His love. In this light, the idea that God suffered with Jesus Christ on the Cross seems to have dropped its heretical import. It has become, not only a widely tolerable motif for theological inquiry but also something like the very core of modern Christianity.

The affirmation of divine suffering apparently occurs in all recent theological approaches either overtly or covertly. It has been variously observed both as "a kind of open secret", and as a "doctrinal revolution" that "occurred without a widespread awareness that it was happening".[2] Now, as the idea of a suffering God grows day by day both in importance and popularity, keen observers of the theological environment are puzzled. People are uncertain whether to understand this development as an accidental phenomenon or indeed as something significant of an important and epochal change in Church and theology. In any case, this issue undoubtedly represents the general change taking place in our God-talk.

The renewed claim that God can suffer is certainly indicative of a new theological bearing, whose exact contours are not yet visible. In terms of what is apparent, it is now widely believed that this development perhaps signifies a change of paradigm in the Christian God-talk. However, it remains a matter of conjecture, whether the rehabilitation of this heresy is part of the tendency in our time to see humankind as a victim and not as an agent of the evil in the world or whether it presupposes a new conception of perfection, a new philosophical orientation. The truth in this case is definitely far-fetched; but the mere fact that what used to be a heresy has turned to be a basic theological motif obliges us to make a theological inquiry.

---

[1]   For the impact such an image of God could have on believers see T. Moser, *Gottesvergiftung*.

[2]   R. Goetz, The Suffering God: The Rise of a New Orthodoxy.

Such a research must not so much seek to validate as to ascertain the reasons for this development. Therefore, for the study in hand, the primary aim is not to build up arguments with which divine passibility or impassibility could be proved or disproved. The objective of this research is much more modest; for if it is assumed that both claims are legitimate, it would suffice to examine the background, the significance and the prospects of the various claims about divine passibility and impassibility. Moreover, given the scope of the topic in question, it would be both unnecessary and impossible to attempt a comprehensive examination of every theology of divine suffering.[3] For the same reason, this investigation cannot claim to be a monographic treatment of all the various views of every individual theologian and school of thought.[4] Nevertheless, some theologies of divine suffering that typify the major trends, will be elaborately treated.[5] To all intents and purposes, therefore, this study seeks to expose the *shift* in the conception of God and in the theological presuppositions, which the issue of divine suffering signifies.

The method of our inquiry is thus historical, systematic and empirical at the same time. By doing so, it is hoped that this study can attain three goals at the same time: to outline a short history of the problem, to point out the basic features of the debate, and to state the significance of this development for today's pluralistic theologies. The whole inquiry has accordingly been organised in three sections, each with a slightly different methodology, corresponding to the project in question.

The first section, which embraces the first three chapters, seeks to situate and work out the contour of the problem in its historical context, from the Hellenistic Judaism down to the contemporary time. Emphasis, however, is laid on what might be called the classical theologies. The different stages of the development of this debate are noted.

The second section, which stretches from the fourth to the sixth chapter, pursues a detailed exposé of three authors whose views typify the Western contributions to the topic in question. Since this problem has received much more atten-

---

3   For more details see F. Meessen, *Unveränderlichkeit und Menschwerdung Gottes. Eine theologiegeschichtlich-systematische Untersuchung*; W. McWilliams, *The Passion of God. Divine Suffering in Contemporary Protestant Theology*.

4   For such methodologies see Thomas R. Krenski, *Passio Caritatis. Trinitarische Passiologie im Werk Hans Urs von Balthasars*; G. F. O'Hanlon, *The Immutability of God in the Theology of Hans Urs von Balthasar*;

5   Some others shall be omitted. For instance, the contributions of the process, feminist and Asian theologians shall not be treated exhaustively.

tion in the West, an attempt will be made at this stage to make a systematic presentation of the basic features of the theme of divine suffering.

The third section, consisting of chapters seven, eight and nine, is dedicated to the Third World liberation theologies. In this section, the endeavour to demonstrate how the issue of divine suffering is already presupposed in the emergent and much more pragmatic theologies of the oppressed is paramount. In contrast to the modern Western approach, which uses speculative arguments to prove its point, the methods of the liberation theologies are less reflective. They appeal more to the experience of the sufferer than to the logic of their claims. This section is accordingly more empirical and comparative than the two earlier sections. Thus, rather than trying to build up arguments for divine suffering, the primary aim here is to show that the affirmation of divine suffering is implicit in the very structure of the Third World theologies. As a result, a large part of the chapters in this section is to be dedicated to introducing and delineating the traits of these theologies.

Taken together, therefore, the three parts could be seen as a comparative presentation of the classical, Western and Third World approaches to the reality of God and particularly to the issue of divine suffering. In the concluding chapter, the findings will be streamlined and the basic features and prospects of a theology of divine suffering shown.

To avoid unnecessary repetition, the citations of literature-sources in the footnote-references are abbreviated. The full quotations are to be found in the bibliography. For the purpose of easy identification, book-titles in the references are italicised, while the article-appellations are not.

SECTION ONE:

THE ISSUE OF DIVINE (IM)PASSIBILITY IN ITS HISTORICAL PERSPECTIVE: FROM ANCIENT TO PRESENT TIMES

... Chapters One, Two and Three ...

1. THE HELLENISTIC ORIGIN OF THE AXIOM OF DIVINE IMPASSIBILITY (APATHEIA TOU THEOU)

1.1 The Impassibility of God as a Theological Dilemma

The Christian world has inherited two apparently conflicting ideas of God. On the one hand, it has been bequeathed with the image of Yahweh, the God of the Old Testament Jews, who, by virtue of His activities in history, is known as a pathetic and sympathetic lover of His people. Yahweh can be angry, jealous, sorrowful and regretful when His love is not reciprocated.[1] On the other hand, Christianity has also adopted a notion of God from the philosophers and theologians of Greek antiquity. Unlike the God of the Bible, the "God of the philosophers"[2] is, among other things, impassible, that is to say, beyond the influence of any external force or agent.

The issue of harmonising these two prevalent conceptions of God has plagued theology since the onset of Christianity. There is the awareness that dropping one and taking the other would not offer a reasonable solution, especially as it is obvious that both Judaic and Greek traditions equally contributed toward the formulation of Christian principles in the early Church. Christianity is to that effect committed to both cultures. Most theologians would of course agree and also want to grant the Jewish heritage more authenticity, but the realisation of that concern has always been evasive in practical terms. In terms of precise conceptualisation, however, philosophical principles have always proved to be more advantageous and have thus given the philosophical tradition an undue predominance in theology. The recognition of this fact today makes some theologians perceive the adoption of the Greek metaphysical concept of God in general and the axiom of

---

1   Cf. J. Scharbert, *Der Schmerz im Alten Testament,* esp. pp. 216-225. P. Kuhn, *Gottes Selbsterniedrigung in der Theologie der Rabbinen,* who makes the same point by referring to the self-renunciation of God in the rabbinical theology. J. Jeremias, *Die Reue Gottes,* who concludes that God's passionate care for His people effects a change of will (*Willenswandel*) and self-limitation in Him (p. 110). A. J. Heschel, *The Prophets,* who makes a plea for the recognition of the God's pathos in the theology of the prophets. T. E. Fretheim, *The suffering of God,* who contends that the God of the Bible is revealed, "not as one who remains coolly unaffected, by the rejection of His people, but as one who is deeply wounded by the broken relationship" (p. 123).

2   By using this terminology, we do not intend to suggest that there are two Gods, but to indicate that there are two fundamentally different approaches to the same God. See for instance, W. Weischeldel, *Der Gott der Philosophen.*

divine impassibility in particular as the main problem in the history of Church Dogma.[3]

The axiom of the divine impassibility is considered plausible nevertheless, but in the face of the reality of the Christ-event, its truth has consistently appeared negotiable in history. It has always "been keenly disputed in the Christian tradition".[4] And now the doubt continues whether the image of an impassible God, as propagated by philosophers, can ever be compatible with the image of God in Jesus Christ. In any case, with the adoption of these two varied notions of God, the early Church was confronted with a theological dilemma: if God is passible as the events in Jesus Christ suggest, how can His perfection be defended? And if He is impassible as the logic of philosophy postulates, how can the divine involvement in Jesus Christ be accounted for? This dilemma continued to characterise - and better still, dictate and to a great extent determine - the trend of the Christological discussions from the earliest stages of the Christian Church[5] till today.[6]

The gravity of this dilemma moves into focus better, if one bears in mind that much is at stake in every discussion concerning the axioms of divine impassibility and passibility. This issue raises general questions about the Hellenisation of theology and the use of anthropomorphic expressions and symbols in the Bible. Furthermore, it also focuses on the paradoxes of Incarnation, *kenosis*, divine mutability and immutability, transcendence and immanence, omnipotence and love, wrath and compassion, and in fact on everything that concerns God's involvement and independence. Thus, the issues of God's involvement in history, theodicy,[7]

---

3 W. Pannenberg, *Grundfragen Systematischer Theologie*, pp. 296-346. Pannenberg attributes the dogmatic problem of the early Christian theology to the adoption of philosophical concept of God, without, however, failing to show the merits of such an adoption. For T. E. Pollard, The impassibility of God, p. 1, "the doctrine of God in particular, have suffered because of the lack of caution which theologians in every age have shown in their too ready acceptance of the gifts which the Greeks have brought" .

4 R. E. Creel, *Divine Impassibility*, p. 1.

5 Cf. W. Elert, Die Theopaschitische Formel, p. 196. Here, Elert calls the contradiction between the axioms of apatheia and the theopaschite question the engine of the whole Christological dialectic, which was at first latent, but later overtly operational in the old Church. Recently, it has also been argued that the intractability of the passibility-impassibility dilemma helped in no minor way to induce the Christological problems of Ebionism, Docetism and the Christian Gnosticism. See H. Frohnhofen, *Apatheia tou theou*, p. 18.

6 Later Chapters will show how this debate continues both in overt and covert forms even in contemporary and Third World theologies.

7 Attempts to view divine passibility as a solution to the problem of theodicy abound. Cf. K. Surin, The Impassibility of God and the Problem of Evil, pp. 97-115. R. Goetz, The Di-

God-world-relationship and the practical relevance of petition prayers also arise in discussions of this type.

As a result of its wide scope, a shift of emphasis in the approach to this problem affects almost every other issue in the doctrine of God. It is for this reason, that some theologians see the contemporary emphasis on the divine passibility as a signal for a paradigm shift in the conception of God.[8] And it is precisely from this point of view that the issue of divine passibility appears to be well received in today's Third World liberation theologies,[9] where theologians are ready to risk every theory that tends to deny God's involvement in the situation of the poor. To this effect, the problem of divine impassibility in contemporary theology could be seen as the test ground, not only for the authenticity of the adoption of the Hellenistic conception of God,[10] but also for the relevance of the contextualisation and inculturation of theology today.

---

vine Burden, pp. 298-302. G. MacGregor, *He Who Lets Us Be.* J. Moltmann, *The Crucified God.*

[8] Cf. R. Goetz, The Suffering of God, pp. 385-389. Goetz sees the renewed affirmation of divine suffering as a clear sign of a paradigm shift (386) in theology, which in his view is founded on some global cultural and religious transformation. The rejection of divine impassibility today is based on three major factors - a) the rise of democratic aspirations, which makes people resist the image of an immutable and impassible God in the name of human freedom; b) divine passibility as a workable solution to the problem of theodicy; c) the need to make our belief reflect the image of the God of the Bible has led to increased scholarly reappraisal of the Bible. The tendency to see the issue of divine suffering as a sort of paradigm shift in theology becomes once more evident in the title of a symposium which took place in the Katholische Akademie Rabanus Maurus - Wiesbaden (Germany) from 9th to 11th March 1992: "*Das Leiden Gottes. Ein neues Paradigma der Theologie*"?

[9] We defer detailed reference until we come to the third section, where the liberation theologies will be discussed. It suffices here to mention that even in feminist theology, the issue of divine suffering is being discussed in the context of a new conception of God. Cf. D. Sölle, Leiden / Opfer, p. 242. Sölle argues for the importance of the belief in the passibility of God in the context of a feminist attack on the patriarchal conception of God. She also criticises her colleague M. Daly particularly for not recognising the significance of divine passibility for the feminist course. See also H. Pissarek-Hudelist, Trinität, p. 422. Pissarek affirms, not only the affinity of the feminist Trinitarian theology to Moltmann's Trinitarian theology of the Cross, but also that the axiom of divine passibility grows in the consciousness of the suffering of women in the Church and society. Pissarek concludes her article on the Trinity with the appeal for a redefinition of the concept of transcendence in the light of the infinite wealth of the human relationality.

[10] H. Frohnhofen, *Apatheia tou theou*, p, 15.

1.2   The Etymology of Apatheia (Impassibilitas)

The exact scope of the problem of divine impassibility becomes definitely more understandable when it is perceived in the light of the historical development of the concept of apatheia, out of which it arose.[11] Being a concept of negation, the root meaning of *apatheia* (impassibilitas) is perceivable in its opposite concept *pathos* (passibilitas). Both concepts are derived from the root of the Greek verb *paschein*. The dictionary meaning of paschein is "to suffer, endure, undergo, experience".[12] Since its first noted usage by Homer (Iliad),[13] Greeks have used paschein to express various feelings or movements of the soul, mind, spirit or heart, whose occurrence were induced by an external agent. Common to all the various applications of the term paschein in the Greek antiquity is therefore the connotation of an external influence on a personal subject. While in its limited and earliest sense, paschein means merely having a negative feeling (pain, suffering), in its later and more general usage, it stands for any sort of influence on a personal being caused by an external force.[14]

Similarly, the corresponding substantive *pathos* is mostly conceived and applied in its broad sense in the writings of the Greeks of antiquity.[15] It is mainly used to denote a negative[16] or positive, short-lived or ongoing inner feeling or condition of the soul, which was initiated by an external force. Unlike the Apostolic Fathers, who use pathos solely to denote suffering, the Greeks of antiquity rarely use it in such a restricted sense.[17] Thus, in its earliest appearance, pathos connotes the experience of being befallen and influenced. The related adjectives

---

[11]   Our sketch of the history of this concept shall be based predominantly on the very reliable study made by H. Frohnhofen, *Apatheia tou theou*, pp. 27-115 on the foundation of the idea of divine apatheia.

[12]   Cf. *A Concise Greek Dictionary of the New Testament*, prepared by B. M. Newman, Jr., United Bible Societies 1971

[13]   Cf. *pascho*, in: H. Frisk, *Griechisches Etymologisches Wörterbuch II* p. 478 f.

[14]   Cf. H. Frohnhofen, *Apatheia tou theou*, pp. 30-40.

[15]   Plato and Aristotle for instance used pathos or *pathe* to denote change, alteration and process; in some of their writings it stood for "accidence" in contrast to *ousia*. Cf. H. Frohnhofen, *Apatheia tou theou*, p. 32 as well as Aristotle, *Met.* I 985b 29 & 986a and Plato, *Rep.* III 389c, to cite but a few.

[16]   This was common among the Stoa, who conceived pathos as irrational and unnatural excitement of the soul (passions). For the other feelings which the Stoics considered positive, like pleasure, pain, fear and desire, they used the expression *eupatheiai*. See H. Frohnhofen, *Apatheia tou theou*, p. 41 and Diogenes Laetius, *Vitae philosophorum* (H. S. Long) 2 Bde, Oxford 1964, VII 116.

[17]   H. Frohnhofen, *Apatheia tou theou*, p. 39.

pathetikos and *pathetos*, are used accordingly to qualify the state of being beyond influence or being able to feel *pathe* and suffering.

To contrast everything paschein, pathos and pathetikos stand for, the Greek thinkers employ the abstract and antonymous substantive *apatheia*. In the manner in which this term is used in ancient Greek writings, it qualifies, in a thing or a personal subject, that characteristic of being beyond influence, that is, of not being subject to any internal or external force. Four various senses of apatheia have been identified in the history of its application in the Greek writings. It is used in denoting the momentary or lasting "noninfluenceability"[18] (a) of any entity through an external agent - this represents the most general meaning of the word. In most cases however, it is used in describing the momentary or lasting "noninfluenceability" of personal beings (b) through feelings of the soul, (c) through learned sovereignty over suffering arising from negatively experienced feelings of the soul, and (d) through acquired passionlessness or freedom from passions.

While in the first sense, it is applied generally to entities, in the other three senses of the concept, it is used only on personal beings. And except for the Stoics, who put emphasis on the fourth sense of apatheia, namely on the sense of being free from passions, a majority of the Greeks of antiquity used the (b) sense of the word, which denotes an intrinsic or acquired "noninfluenceability" of a personal being to feelings of the soul. The use of apatheia to indicate intrinsic or acquired sovereignty over suffering is however minimal among the Greeks.[19]

A close look at these four meanings of apatheia reveals that they all connote "noninfluenceability". "Noninfluenceability" could thus be seen as constituting the basic meaning of apatheia, and is as such conceived in two forms, as *intrinsic* and as *acquired* "noninfluenceability" of personal beings.[20] The Greeks perceive apatheia either as an essential characteristic belonging to the very nature of a personal being, or as an acquired mode of sovereignty over pathos. In the history of this concept, intrinsic apatheia is however attributed mainly to God and the divinities, while learned or acquired apatheia is visualised as a moral ideal, necessary for the human attainment of moral perfection (the Stoics). The attribution of intrinsic apatheia to the divinity leads implicitly to the confirmation of divine immutability, simplicity/indivisibility, incorporeality/invisibility, self-sufficiency and

---

18 We shall use "noninfluenceability" to denote the state of being beyond influence.

19 For more details on their use in the Greek literature consult H. Frohnhofen, *Apatheia tou theou*, pp. 33, 36, 39, 41 & 42.

20 *Ibid.*, p. 37.

transcendence. For, when a being is simple, immutable, incorporeal and self-sufficient the ancient Greeks usually attribute intrinsic apatheia to it.[21]

As the above facts suggest, it is evident that the words pathos and apatheia are predominantly used in their broad meaning in the Greek antiquity. The same thing, however, cannot be said of the Latin translation of these concepts. By virtue of the abundance of Latin expressions, the Latin authors tend to make use of many terminologies in explaining the one concept pathos. Cicero, for instance, uses "passio", "perturbatio", "affectio/affectus" and even "dolor" and "morbus" in translating the different forms of pathos.[22] But despite the abundance of words - passion, perturbation, affection, pain and sickness - only the one sense of pathos as suffering could be adequately represented. Paradoxically, therefore, it is through the use of varied Latin equivalents, which is meant to demonstrate the wealth of Latin language, that the synthetic meaning of the Greek word pathos - in the broad sense of being beyond influence - gets lost. The same thing applies to the translation of apatheia as "impassibilitas" and apathes as "impassibilis". Consequently, with the adoption of the term "impassibilitas", the later non-Christian and Patristic Latin world took over the narrow sense of this concept and continued to render it mainly as freedom from passions, emotions and suffering.

In summary, therefore, it can be observed that apatheia, as an antonym of pathos, is a later derivative concept from the root Greek verb paschein, which in itself has a synthetic meaning. Accordingly, it could be used in both narrow and broad sense. Whereas its broad meaning is predominantly used in the Greek antiquity, its narrow meaning prevails in the later theologies, especially after it had been rendered in Latin language as impassibilitas.[23]

1.3   The Doctrine of Divine Apatheia in the Greek Philosophy

In the pre-philosophic Greek literature pathos is attributed to all the gods. The situation changes however when we come to the writings of the philosophers. For, right from the dawn of philosophical reflections, it was the custom to attribute pathos to the lower gods and apatheia to the supreme God. With the maturity of monotheistic thought, philosophers tended to make apatheia the main attribute

---

21   *Ibid.*, p. 48. See also W. Maas, *Unveränderlichkeit Gottes*, p. 68.

22   Cicero was convinced that the concept of pathos found better expression in Latin than in Greek. Cf. Cicero, *Tusc.* III 5,10 (passio); *Tusc.* IV 28,60 (perturbatio) and *Tusc.* III 10, 23 (morbus). See also H. Frohnhofen, *Apatheia tou theou*, pp. 55 ff.

23   In this study, we shall use impassibility in its widest sense, as "noninfluenceability"; i.e. as "the condition of being acted upon, and being affected, receptive" to use the words of R. S. Frank, *Passibility and Impassibility*, p. 658.

of God. This phenomenon occurred, not only among the Greeks, but also among the Romans influenced by Greek philosophy. For although the attribution of pathos to the gods was common in the ancient Roman religions, that practise was stopped as soon as they came into contact with the Greek philosophy.[24]

In the light of the above the following question might arise: was the development of the concept of apatheia dependent on philosophy as such or particularly on the Greek mode of thought? While we leave this question open, we should bear it in mind as we proceed.

1.3.1   The Development of the Doctrine of Apatheia

In the etymological data given above, it is evident that the concept of apatheia witnessed a gradual development in the Hellenistic tradition. At first, only the verb paschein was known in the Greek vocabulary; later, the substantive *pathos* was introduced; and only much later did its antonym *apatheia* come into use. As an idea, apatheia had existed among the Pre-Socratic thinkers,[25] but as a terminology, it first appeared in the writings of Aristotle.[26] This should not be surprising, for given its abstract nature, an exact conceptualisation and application of apatheia would have been practically impossible prior to the development of philosophical language and thought-pattern.[27]

Plato, for instance, ascribes incorporeality, simplicity, immutability and perfection to the highest divinity in the hierarchy of divinities,[28] and is sceptical about the anthropomorphic characterisation of the lower divinities in the Olympic pantheon. Yet he neither uses the term "apatheia" in the predication of the divine en-

---

24   Cf. H. Frohnhofen, *Apatheia tou theou*, p. 95.

25   Cf. *ibid.*, p. 62 ff. The ideas which the concept of apatheia expresses, especially the possibility of the noninfluenceability of a being, the author contends, were held in different forms in the pre-Socratic era. It was already entailed in Homer's idea of the immortality of the gods, which he applied parallel to other anthropomorphic characteristics of the divinity (64). The pre-Socratic philosophers (Xenophanes, Empedocles and Melisos of Samos) ascribed apatheia to God both in the broad and strict sense of the concept without using the term apatheia (68 ff.). The idea also resonates in the Socratic tradition, though only in the narrow sense, as sovereignty over suffering (72). See also W. Kroll, Apathy, p. 603.

26   H. Frohnhofen, *Apatheia tou theou*, p. 29. See also W. Michaelis, *páscho ktl*, pp. 903. Cf. also Aristotle, *Phys.* IV 217b 26 & *Met.* IX 1046a 13.

27   Ostensibly, as Frohnhofen observes, an abstract terminus like apatheia could not have been conceivable outside the context of a matured philosophical mode of expression. See *Op. cit.* p. 30.

28   See Plato, *Tim.* 41d-42e, 69c-d & *Phdr.* 246c (on incorporeality); *Rep.* II 381c (on simplicity); *Rep.* II 380d-3381e (on immutability); see also W. Maas, *op. cit.* p. 45) .

tities,[29] nor does he develop an explicit theology of divine apatheia. However, the attribution of an intrinsic apatheia (in its general sense of "noninfluenceability" and imperturbability) to the highest ranking Deity is implicit in his writings. What differentiates the highest Deity from the Homeric gods (which occupy the lowest rank in hierarchy of divine entities) is, according to Plato, its simplicity and immutability. Similarly, the idea of a God who cannot be acted upon is also echoed in his theory of the soul's immortality. It is in fact his theories of the Soul and the Idea of the Good that gave impulse to the development of a full-fledged doctrine of divine apatheia in the theologies of later centuries.

Aristotle, despite his elaborate criticisms of Plato's theory of Ideas,[30] adopts the latter's "Idea of the Good" and reformulates it into a doctrine of God as the "Unmoved Mover".[31] To him, God is the *purpose* of all existing beings, the *final* cause of every reality - He is the object of desire and thought, who, though immutable in Himself, produces motion in the creatures that desire and depend on Him (*Metaphysics*, 1072b). He thinks, in this connection, that God is "impassive and unalterable" (1073a), suffers no change and is apathetic[32] in the broad sense of being "noninfluenceable" and imperturbable. Divine immutability is thus identical to divine impassibility in Aristotle's metaphysics. This means by implication, as Russell contends, that the God of Aristotle does not show any feeling of love to His creatures; in His static perfection, God "moves the world only through the love that finite beings feel for Him". Aristotle's view here, Russell further maintains, inevitably leads to the logical conclusion in his ethics: that we cannot be friends with God, since He cannot love us as we love Him.[33]

Yet, the concept of apatheia in Aristotelian philosophy does not exclude the possibility of the positive feeling of happiness in God - His blessedness is the highest good. If Aristotle envisaged feeling in God, he does that only on the condition that divine feeling must be eternal so as not to entail any change. Hence, God's bliss surpasses human happiness, exactly because it is eternal.[34]

---

29   Cf. H. Frohnhofen, *Apatheia tou theou*, p. 76.

30   Cf. Aristotle, *Metaphy.*, 990 b 8-11; 990 a 34-b 8; 991 a 12-13; 991 a 8-10; 997 b 5-12, just to indicate a few. In the last cited passage, however, Aristotle criticises the theory of Ideas, on the ground of its anthropomorphic connotation. For if the Ideas are Forms or Copies of the sensible world, as Plato contended, they do not differ much from their duplicates in the sensible world except that they are eternal.

31   *Ibid.*, 1051 a 20-1. For more details consult, H. von Arnim, *Die Entwicklung der aristotelischen Gotteslehre*.

32   *De Caelo*, I 270b 2. See also *De anima* III 430a 23 about the apatheia of the divine Nous.

33   B. Russell, *History of Western Philosophy*, pp. 182 & 191.

34   Cf. *Metaphy.* 1072b 29f.

After Aristotle had made explicit use of the concept of apatheia for the predication of God, one would have expected the term apatheia to appear in subsequent writings. It did not however become immediately popular. For, in the writings of *Xenocrates*, the Platonist, the terminology of apatheia has not been found. He, however, indirectly refers to the divine apatheia, at the very point where he speaks about the excitement of the soul.[35] If Xenocrates avoids or is unaware of the terminology of apatheia, it is not because he does not propagate this idea, but perhaps because he does not get his impulse from Aristotle, but from Plato's "theory of Idea".

The doctrine of divine apatheia takes a different and interesting dimension as one comes to the *Epicureans*. To them, apparently, apatheia does not exclude the attribution of human characteristics to God. For on the one hand, human-like "corporeality" is attributed to the divinity, with the conviction that happiness, which is an intrinsic feeling in God, must presuppose corporeality in Him.[36] On the other hand, suffering and negative emotions of any sort are denied the divine being: neither pain, nor wrath is considered worthy of the divinity, since such disturbances of the soul would obstruct the perfect happiness due to his essence.[37] In the light of the above, it is observable that the Epicureans do not perceive any contradiction between anthropomorphism and the doctrine of divine apatheia. Accordingly, they conceive apatheia in its restricted sense and attribute emotions to God, if they are not negative.

Likewise, the *Stoics* advance a materialistic image of God side by side with the doctrine of apatheia. In their theology and cosmology, God is conceived as the soul of the world, as the fine stuff of which the world is made.[38] And in their ethic, a moral doctrine of apatheia is propagated, which enjoins people to ultimately renounce all passions. Their materialistic image of God, that is to say, anthropomorphic representation of God seems all the more inexplicable, when one recalls that they are opposed to the anthropomorphic image of the Homeric gods.[39] Their aversion to the Homeric gods is however not motivated by any anti-

---

35 See R. Heinze, *Xenokrates. Darstellung der Lehre und Sammlung der Fragmente*, p. 164 f.

36 As a matter of fact, the Epicureans believe that emotions are an essential part of corporeality. This is an issue which Thomas Aquinas, as we shall see later in the second chapter, tries to settle.

37 Cf. R. Philipson, *Studien zur Epikur und den Epikureern*, p. 597 Anm. 112; Laktanz, *De ira Dei / Vom Zorne Gottes*, 4, 1 f; H. Frohnhofen, *Apatheia tou theou*, p. 83.

38 F. Copleston, *A History of Philosophy*, Vol. 1 part II, p. 133.

39 The Homeric gods were so contingent and corrupt that they deserved no reverence. According to B. Russell, *History of Western Philosophy*, p. 32, these gods differed "from

anthropomorphic temperament, but by their distaste for the immoral conduct usually attributed to these gods.[40] In other words, immorality, and not anthropomorphism, is what they consider unworthy of God.

Be that as it may, "inherent contradictions" in the Stoic theology and ethics are evident.[41] Given the long history of Stoicism,[42] a shift in emphasis was bound to occur. For while early Stoics were materialistic and disliked Platonism, later Stoics adopted it. From the middle Stoics (esp. Panaetius and Posidonius) down to the Roman Stoics (Seneca Aurelius), when Platonism displaced materialism, a moral idealism conceived after the example of the Socratic asceticism shaped the whole Stoic theology. It is in the later system, that virtue becomes synonymous with the will to self-conquest and to sovereignty over all affections and passions.[43] For the Stoics, apatheia, understood as the negation of all passions, is the ideal of human morality. And although divine apatheia is not denied in the Stoic theology, emphasis is laid on human apatheia.[44]

The *Sceptics*, known for their "dogmatic doubt", could not overlook the ambivalence of the Stoic theology.[45] The Stoic materialistic conception of God is their beloved target of attack. Carneades, a celebrated Sceptic, criticises the Stoic doctrine of God because in his view, if God is conceived as part of the world, as the soul that harmonises and animates the world, as the Stoics do, it would inevitably lead to the one logical conclusion that God has feelings, that is

---

men only in being immortal and possessed of superhuman powers". And as W. Pannenberg affirms, they were so much a part the natural order of the world that they needed no special revelation to make their nature known. Cf. *Op. cit.*, p. 299 f. The Stoics' notion of God was different. See Cicero, *De natura Deorum* (A. S. Pease), Cambridge / Mass. 1958, vol. II p. 70.

40 Cf. A. J. Heschel, *The Prophets*, p. 268. Heschel rightly argues that the "aversion to anthropomorphism among ... Greeks was, first of all, a reaction against conceptions offensive to their moral sensibilities". Similarly, what Xenophanes and Plato criticised most was the shabby moral of the gods of Homer and Hesiod.

41 B. Russell, *History of Western Philosophy*, p. 272.

42 Stoicism stretches from the time of Zeno (336-263 BC.) to Marcus Aurelius (161-180 AD.). Like no other Hellenistic school Stoicism has a cross-cultural background, while some of its proponents were Syrian Greeks (early and middle Stoics), the later Stoics were mostly Romans (like Seneca and Marcus Aurelius).

43 Cf. *Ibid.*, pp. 260-276.

44 See section 1.3.2. below for more details on Stoics' understanding of appatheia as the elimination of all passions.

45 *Ibid.*, p. 243 ff.

to say, that He can suffer.[46] This criticism is of course no proof that the Stoics attribute pathos to God; it merely points to the logical conclusion of the Stoic materialism. By implication however, it affirms that the Sceptics opt for divine apatheia. This, and not human apatheia, preoccupied them more. Carneades is even said to have preached a "morality that was too lax" and scorned Socrates' asceticism and understanding of virtue.[47] Accordingly, to the Sceptics apatheia is more an attribute of God - underlining his transcendence - than it is a principle of human morality.

Among the Middle-Platonists, one meets the endeavour (made especially by *Plutarch*) to achieve a purer conception of a God. For him, God is the eternal, true, immutable and apathetic being. Only human souls that have become incorporeal and free from pathos arrive in His kingdom.[48] Plutarch uses apatheia in its widest sense, as the general "noninfluenceability", and considers desire and wrath as unworthy attributes of God.[49] On the concrete nature of the concept of human apatheia, and on matters concerning the relationship between body and soul, Plutarch is under the influence of Aristotle's golden mean (metriopathy).[50] He appeals accordingly, for the control of passions through reason, but not for their elimination. Thus, he argues, it is neither desirable nor possible to get rid of passions.[51] Similarly, *Albinus*, another Middle Platonist, is also influenced by Aristotle in this respect. Like Plutarch, he denounces the Stoic understanding of apatheia, and takes to the Aristotelian-Platonic "metriopathy" (that is to say, to the conviction that one should control passions with reason, but not eliminate them).

Plotinus, known as the founder of Neo-Platonism and as the last of the great philosophers of antiquity,[52] conceives an absolute transcendence for God. God, the ONE, is so transcendent that the attribution of positive qualities should be discouraged, except in an analogous sense. For Plotinus, God could be called "the Good" and "the One", but we cannot legitimately say that He is "one" or "good. That would amount to a "predication" of God, which, in his view, means making

---

46 Cf. Sextus Empiricus, *Adv. Math.*, 9, 23 ff.; Cicero, *De Nat. Deorum*, 3, 17, 44; 3, 29 ff.; See also F. Copleston, *A History of Philosophy*, pp. 159-162.

47 Cf. B. Russell, *History of Western Philosophy*, pp. 245-248.

48 Cf. Plutarch, *Moralia*, 382f-383a.

49 Cf. O. Dreyer, *Begriff des Gottgeziemenden in der Antike*, p. 57 f.

50 Cf. *Ibid.*, 199.

51 Cf. F. Copleston, *A History of Philosophy*, p. 198.

52 B. Russell, *History of Western Philosophy*, p. 289.

a distinction, placing God beside other beings. God is beyond every being and every distinction.[53]

It is in this sense that Plotinus uses apatheia, as a measure for guaranteeing the absolute divine transcendence. Since for him the divine transcendence, indivisibility, immutability, impassibility and non-relationality are closely interconnected, the assertion of one is believed to lead to the confirmation of the other.[54] Plotinus, like Plato, attributes immutability and apatheia only to the highest Deity in the hierarchy of divine entities. The apatheia of the soul depends similarly on its nearness to the intellectual and divine domain, where intrinsic "noninfluenceability" prevails. Only when the soul is entangled in the material world, does it become divisible and pathetic.[55]

The tendency to reduce apatheia to an ethical requirement is however absent in the theology of Plotinus. As a Neo-Platonist, he does of course consider nature (the abode of the soul) inferior to the *Nous* (the intellectual domain), but that notwithstanding, he perceives the world positively, and not as something intrinsically evil. In actual fact, he admires the sensible world and considers it relatively beautiful.[56]

Summarising the above points about the development of the concept of apatheia, one can justifiably arrive at the following conclusions: The doctrine of apatheia is developed in the Greek antiquity as a philosophical requirement for the description of the divine and human perfection. It is used more in the predication of God than in the description of human morality. Whilst the Greeks used apatheia in its wide sense when they apply it to God, they conceived it in a narrow sense when it refers to the human morality.[57] In most cases, however, anti-anthropomorphism and an exclusive view of divine transcendence accompany the use of divine apatheia. So, it can be generally said, that a negative attitude to the world predominates in the Greek thought,[58] and that an over-all tendency to predicate God by way of negation forms the background of their philosophies.

---

53 Cf. F. Copleston, *A History of Philosophy*, p. 209.

54 Cf. W. Maas, *Op. cit.*, pp. 80-86, esp. pp. 83 & 85.

55 Cf. PLotinus, *Enneads*, III, 9,1; IV, 1,1 and also H. Frohnhofen, *Apatheia tou theou*, p. 90.

56 Cf. Plotinus, *Enneads*, II, 9, 16. See also B. Russell, *Op. cit.*, p. 295 f.

57 Sextus Empiricus, *Pyrrh.* 1,162 rightly called divine apatheia the "dogma of philosophers".

58 As B. Russell contends in this regard, "Aristotle is the last Greek philosopher who faces the world cheerfully; after him, all have, in one form or another, a philosophy of retreat." *Op. cit.*, p. 242.

1.3.2   Apatheia and the Disparagement of Passions
          in Hellenistic Philosophy

The tendency to disparage passions and emotions, and to conceive apatheia as the ultimate elimination of feelings is often associated with the Stoics. Contrary to popular assumption, however, it did not begin with them. It goes back to *Socrates*, whose heroic attitude to death in 399 BC (at the age of seventy) proves to be an exceptional demonstration of an effective control of reason over feelings and passions. According to Plato, Socrates' indifference to death demonstrates a singular triumph of the heavenly soul over the earthly body in a human life.[59] It is not certain, however, whether everything that is said about the Socratic asceticism corresponds to the historical life of Socrates himself. For it is most probable that the Socratic asceticism reflects more of Plato's own imaginative mind[60] than facts about Socrates. This becomes apparent through the fact that Plato is the main source of the story about Socrates. For this reason, one can justifiably assume that Platonism lies at the background of the Socratic asceticism, if not historically, at least in its literary presentation. Thus, the Socratic asceticism, which tends toward the negation of passions, is closely connected with the duality of the soul in Plato's philosophy.

According to *Plato,* the soul is composite, consisting of rational faculty on the one hand, and of appetitive and impulsive faculties on the other hand. The *rational soul*, constituting the divine aspect of man, is imprisoned, so to say, in the bodily domain of the *appetitive soul.* The former is painstakingly trying to liberate itself from the latter, which by embodying the passions and desires, is constantly trying to frustrate the lofty attempt of the rational soul to return to the world of ideas. Plato correspondingly characterises the composite nature of man with the image of an "unruly monster".[61] The passions cause disharmony in human beings and make them imperfect. To attain perfection therefore, reason must subdue them.

This Platonic view gave a push to subsequent aversion to passions in the history of Hellenistic philosophy and even beyond. *Aristotle*, despite his criticism of Plato's doctrine of the soul, does not achieve much in his endeavour to salvage the

---

[59]   Cf. Plato, *The Last Days of Socrates.*

[60]   Given the fact that the name "Socrates" appears in most Platonic dialogues - the dialogues definitely do not correspond to historical facts - it is very probable that Plato, in narrating the story of the historic Socrates, made use of his own imagination, thereby making Socrates the "mouthpiece of his own opinions". Moreover, it is evident that Plato's account does not always agree with that of his colleague Xenophon. See for instance, B. Russell, *Op. cit.* p. 103.

[61]   Plato, *Republic*, trans. by B. Jowett, bk. IX, p. 285.

image of passions. Unlike Plato, he argues that passions are neither good nor bad - they are neutral; he consequently rejects any concept of apatheia that would entail insensibility or feelinglessness. Virtuous life, he contends, does not consist in the elimination of feelings, but in the achievement of the golden mean between two extremes (of feelings or actions).[62]

In spite of his congenial views on the neutrality of feelings and his disapproval of Plato's duality of the soul, as well as his option for the attribution of "unity to the soul",[63] he does not rate emotions and passions highly, for he considers emotion inferior to reason. This is most evident in his view about God as the "Unmoved mover". God, as the first and efficient cause, the Unmoved mover, who moves others by being admired, has only reason, but no emotions.[64] Thus, even without calling emotion evil, Aristotle does disparage passions.

Judging from the above facts, Socratic, Platonic and Aristotelian attitudes to passions anticipate its disparagement in *Stoicism*, especially at its later stage. Whereas the early Stoics resent Plato's dualism of the soul and perceive the soul as a unit of force permeating the whole body,[65] the later Stoics adopting Platonism, show a keen interest for the Socratic asceticism. Both groups, however, perceive in Socrates a model of a wise and moral human being. Thus, despite the initial rejection of Plato's dualism by the early Stoics, and their continuous adherence to the singularity of the soul, Stoicism advances the Platonic view that passions are unruly, constituting the source of evil and disaster.[66]

The jump the Stoics make from a materialistic image of God to the negation of passions is puzzling. However, it becomes understandable, when one bears in mind that for the Stoics, the world is characterised by order, autonomy and harmony. God has ordered the world rationally, but he endowed only human beings and gods with His reason, that is to say, with "a spark of the very divinity that created them".[67] God is said to care providentially and benevolently for human

---

62 Cf. Aristotle, *Nic. Ethics*, II 1106b 16-28 and 1109a 20-24. In II 1104b 20 f, he criticises the philosophers, who "define virtues as forms of impassivity or tranquillity". In 1105b, 29 ff, he emphasises that we are neither good nor bad "merely because we are capable of feeling" (J. A. K. Thomson's translation).

63 Aristotle, *De Anima*, I, 411b, see also 404b, 27.

64 As A. J. Heschel rightly puts it: "Aristotle's Deity has no pathos, no needs. Ever resting in itself, its only activity is thinking, and its thinking is thinking of thinking. Indifferent to all things, it does not care to contemplate anything but itself. Things long for it and thus are set in motion, yet they are left to themselves." Cf. *The Prophets*, p. 251.

65 E. Zeller, *Die Philosophie der Griechen*, II, p. 466.

66 *Ibid.*, p. 250.

67 P. P. Hallie, Stoicism, p. 21.

beings and expects them to live in harmony with nature. Human happiness depends on the attainment of this harmony with the world, which can only occur at the level of reason. In order to live in accordance with divine benevolence and order of the world, human beings must participate rationally - i.e. naturally - in this world. Anything that minimises or deters the function of reason is considered to be an impediment to the achievement of this harmony with nature.[68] To guarantee the realisation of happiness in life, therefore, passions must not be allowed to hinder the individual *will* in its commitment to harmony with the whole nature.[69] Accordingly, the Stoics enjoin human beings to subdue and if possible extinguish all passions so as to attain happiness and serenity in life. It is in this sense, that they use the concept of apatheia to appeal for the elimination of all passions and emotions.[70]

The influence of this view of apatheia survived the end of Stoicism, and continues to be seen, not only as synonymous with "virtuous life" in most later philosophies,[71] but also as "a guiding star in the moral search, both in Christian and secular ethics".[72]

Summarising the points on the Greek conception of apatheia in terms of the disparagement of passions, we can hold to the following: The morality of God is important to the Greeks. And it is exactly the moral, and not the ontological question, that initially influenced the conception of divine apatheia. Scared by the immoral conducts of the gods in the Greek mythologies, the philosophers, especially Plato, are pushed to conceive God as the wholly other, as the very oppo-

---

[68] S. E. Stumpf, *Philosophy: History and Problems*, p. 123.

[69] Cf. B. Russell, *History of Western Philosophy*, p. 262.

[70] Cf. H. Frohnhofen, *Apatheia tou theou*, p. 51

[71] For details about the development of the doctrine of apatheia as a moral principle, see Th. Rüther, *Die Sittliche Forderung der Apatheia in den beiden ersten christlichen Jahrhunderten und bei Klemens von Alexandrien.* H. Frohnhofen, *Apatheia tou theou*, pp. 52-54. While it is true that the doctrine of apatheia as a moral principle reached its climax in the Stoic philosophy, both authors agree that this idea had appeared earlier, in the thoughts of the Pythagoreans, Democrites, Antisthenes, Socrates and his pupils, Plato and Aristotle, albeit in different forms. After it had been developed fully by the Stoics, apatheia was eminently introduced into Hellenistic Judaism as a moral ideal by Philo of Alexandria. Justin, the apologist and Clement of Alexandria helped to popularise it in Christianity. There is no trace of apatheia as a moral principle in the Old Testament. And even though the New Testament doctrine of Logos and Sarx smacks of this doctrine, in the end it turned out to have a different meaning. For while the Stoic apatheia meant the elimination of pathos, the New Testament asceticism was never directed against the body, but against the sin in the body.

[72] Heschel, *The Prophets*, p. 255.

site of everything human. The concern to free the divinity from moral imperfection gives rise in turn to the need of conceiving the ontological perfection of God. Indeed, the roots of the Greek disparagement of passions and the overall tendency to negate what is worldly, are imbedded in the Hellenistic sense of morality. This fact, which is implied in all the Greek philosophies, receives its explicit expression in the Stoic' conception of the ethical dimension of apatheia. Irrespective of the fact that the Stoics pay more attention to the human than to divine apatheia, it can be observed that their conception of apatheia as a human ethical ideal arises out of the desire to imitate divine apatheia.[73] Consequently, the negation of passions in God could be seen as strengthening the urge among philosophers to suppress or eliminate all passions and emotions in human beings.

1.3.3 Apatheia and the Way of Negation (via negativa) in the Hellenistic Hermeneutics of the Doctrine of God

There is a general tendency in the philosophy of Greek antiquity to conceive God only by way of negation (*via negationis*). This approach to the ultimate reality arises out of the desire to demonstrate God's sovereignty and transcendence over and above all the creaturely contingency. God is "being qua being", the ultimate Good and the logical End and Source of every reality. Since He has His imprint in humankind, He is thought to have endowed human beings with reason, love and freedom of will. If this should perhaps suggest that God has certain qualities in common with His creatures, one is reminded immediately that He excels in all these qualities. His perfection is so infinite, that what He has in common with His creatures is nothing compared to the difference between Him and them. For the philosophers, therefore, the difference stands out more than the similarity between God and humankind. Accordingly, God is conceived invariably, in relation to human beings, as the ontologically, morally and logically wholly "other".

The negative consequence of this approach to God is that the similarity between God and human beings is either forgotten or disregarded. From the human point of view God easily becomes a reality, whose existence can only be established through negation (*via negativa*). This one-dimensional emphasis on difference is to a great extent influenced by Plato's theory of Ideas. It should not be surprising therefore, that it is Aristotle, the great critic of the Platonic Ideas, who first perceived the deficiency of the way of negation, and without denying the justification for the conception of God by way of negation, tries to conceive God

---

[73] Cf. H. Frohnhofen, *Apatheia tou theou*, p. 54.

in terms of analogy (*via analogica*),[74] albeit in a mathematical and linguistic sense.[75] With his concept of analogy, he was able to refer to the proportional similarity and difference between related things, and also between God and His creatures. Strictly speaking, the *via analogica* in the sense Aristotle uses it, means predicating with proportionality - *analogia* (Greek) = *proportio* (Latin) - and implies the recognition of both the similarity and difference between things or people. Naturally, analogy projects both similarity and difference.

Despite the availability of these two approaches to the conception of God right from the prime time of Greek philosophy, a cursory look into the history of the intellectual conception of God reveals the dominance of the way of negation. Neither then, in the era of Greek philosophy, nor later, until contemporary time, could the way of analogy receive the attention of many thinkers. Catholic theology has however never given up the attempt to correct the one-sidedness of the way of negation. The earliest attempt to confront the deficiency of the way of negation is to be found in the thoughts of Thomas Aquinas:

Following the tradition of Aristotle, Thomas Aquinas introduced the *via positiva* at a much later time to make up for the deficiencies of the *via negativa*. (The *via positiva* denotes the use of some positive human qualities as pointers to God in an exclusively pre-eminent way.)[76] But despite the corrective measures which the Aristotelian analogy and Thomistic way of positive predication bring, the inclination of theology towards the predication of God *via negationis* is enormous. Theologians often avow to use the *via analogica*, but they end up conceiving God *via negativa*, especially if the Platonic and Stoic philosophies are operating at the background.[77]

---

[74]   *Poetics*, 1459a 5.

[75]   *Rhetoric*, 1410b 12.

[76]   Cf. Articles "Via Negativa" and "Via Positiva" by E. J. Tinsley, in: *A New Dictionary of Christian Theology*, pp. 596-597.

[77]   The impact of the Hellenistic hermeneutics of divine attributes is evident, not only among the Neo-platonic philosophies and theologies, but also among the early Christian writers - the biblical writers are not excluded. According to Rudolf Bultmann, one can suspect the influence of the Greek hermeneutics in St Paul's use of negation in the predication of God. Cf. R. Bultmann, *Theology of the New Testament, Vol. I,*, p. 72. Here are some examples: invisible (Rom 1.20, Col. 1.15 f., I Tim. 1.17, Heb. 11.27); immortal, incorruptible (Rom. 1.23, I Tim. 1.17, Acts. 17.25). Moreover, it is extensively in use among the Apostolic Fathers. In his epistle to Polycarp, Ignatious called God, for instance, the "time*less*, *in*visible, *im*palpable, *im*passive". See his *Pol.* 3,2 cited in: J. B. Lightfoot, *The Apostolic Fathers, vol. II*, & Pannenberg, *Op. cit.*, p. 310

Thus, despite the efforts made to popularise the way of analogy, the way of negation continues to dominate in theology, perhaps a sign that apatheia and analogy can hardly go together. In fact, it needs to be ascertained to what extent the doctrine of apatheia can go hand in hand with the paradoxical and dialectical conceptions of God.

1.4   The Pathos of God in the Biblical and Semitic Literature

In contrast to the Hellenistic, philosophical writings, the Old Testament and the Rabbinical literature attribute pathos to God. In different forms and with different emphasis, the biblical writers use anthropomorphic language and symbols to describe both the activities and emotional life of God. The concept of apatheia, in the sense described above, is absent in the whole biblical and rabbinical literature.[78] Even the Pentateuchal passages noted for their anti-anthropomorphic expressions (like the law against making images of Yahweh) do not entail the idea of apatheia, at least not in the Hellenistic sense.[79]

1.4.1   The Wrath and Repentance of God in the Old Testament

Negative and positive anthropopathetic expressions abound in the Old Testament. Theological discourses, however, centre mostly on the negative feelings of God, especially on the issue of His wrath and repentance. The attribution of these and other negatively judged human feelings to the God of the Bible constitutes the main difference between the Semitic and Hellenistic approach to the ultimate reality.

The contrast becomes more vivid as one discovers that the Old Testament does not make an arbitrary or casual use of these anthropomorphic expressions, but that its use of them is motivated by some theological considerations.[80] The historical, prophetic and poetic books of the Old Testament abundantly testify God's

---

78   H. Frohnhofen, *op. cit.*, 96.

79   C. T. Fritsch, *The Anti-anthropomorphisms of the Greek Pentateuch*, p. 64 ff.

80   The biblical use of divine repentance is apparently theologically motivated, because, as Jeremias contends, it is a concept that never appeared in the oldest books with simple narrative tradition. The talk about divine repentance begins to appear only in the theologically conceived and reinterpreted books of the Old Testament (for example the prophetic books). Its scope and usage for evangelisation grows as one approaches the dusk of the Old Testament era. Cf. J. Jeremias, *Die Reue Gottes*, p. 14.

repenting (regretting or having remorse),[81] that is to say, changing His mind about decisions made in the past. But their references to God's repentance are neither random nor monotonous: the meaning given to divine repentance varies in accordance with the type of experience Israel makes with Yahweh. The talk about God's repentance is laden with so much theological meaning, that its scope is said to transcend the realm of anthropopathetic expressions.[82] In fact, two major forms of divine repentance can be distinguished in the Old Testament:[83] Firstly, God's repentance is understood as His remorse over His past perform-ance, that did not bring the expected result. This is the sense in which it is used in Gen. 6:6,7; 1 Sam. 15:1,35. In Gen. 6:6, God regrets having made humankind and "it grieved him to his heart"; He is angry, so to say, because humankind has betrayed His trust. Similarly, in 1 Sam 15:1,35, He regrets having made Saul king. Characteristic of this type of divine repentance is the divine anger or wrath, which invariably leads to divine punishment. For the pre-flood humankind it led to their destruction and for Saul to his dismissal. God acts out His anger immedi-ately by inflicting punishment on His erring people. According to J. Jeremias, this type of divine repentance is only used in the two places mentioned above. Hence, it is typical only of the *pre-exilic historical books*.[84]

Secondly, divine repentance denotes God's emotional withdrawal from a planned line of action, mostly threats;[85] He stops short at the execution of the threat of human perdition. Here, it is about God's change of mind (cf. Ex 32:14; 2 Sam 24:16).[86] God changes His mind not out of anger like in the first mentioned form, but out of sympathy. In other words, God's compassion for His people mo-

---

[81] The term "repentance" translates the Substantive of the Hebrew root verb *nhm* and the related word *hitp*. For more details on the etymology of the word see J. Jeremias, *Die Reue Gottes*, pp. 15-18.

[82] J. Jeremias, *Die Reue Gottes*, pp 12-13, esp. note 16. Divine repentance encompasses all the anthropopathetic expressions like compassion, love, hate, jealousy, vengeance and the wrath of God and even more: the issue of divine immutability. This makes it perhaps more theologically significant than the wrath of God.

[83] J. Jeremias, *Die Reue Gottes*, p. 17 f.

[84] Cf. J. Scharbert, "Der Schmerz Jahwes", in: idem, *Der Schmerz im Alten Testament*, p. 216 f. See also J. Jeremias, *Die Reue Gottes*, p. 19 ff.

[85] Divine repentance was used mostly in this sense: at least thirty times compared to twice in the other sense.

[86] According to Jeremias, this second sense of repentance also applies to those places in the Old Testament (Num 23:19; 1Sam 15:29; Ps 110), where repentance or change of mind is categorically denied of God. Thus, in the second sense, the affirmation or negation of re-pentance is possible. More will be said on this later.

tivates His repentance. Instead of acting out His indignation in a due punishment, like in the first form, God turns to self-limitation: He withholds His anger.

The differences between the two senses of divine repentance could be further explained this way: when God changes His mind about an act that He had performed earlier, it is usually done in the interest of His plan of salvation, but when He changes His mind about a future plan, He does that mostly to withhold a curse, or to stop a forthcoming disaster.[87] While in the first case, divine repentance is a retrospective attempt to correct the events of the past, in the other, it is a measure taken to preclude a prospective disaster.

In the *prophetic books*, the second type of divine repentance is solely applied. Here, God is still disappointed at the enormous infidelity and ingratitude of His beloved Israel. The prophets speak of God's pathetic approach to His disappointment. It pains God that His beloved one, Israel, for whom He cares most, just as a father cares for his son, and a husband for his wife,[88] continues to be unfaithful. He gets angry, but His love does not allow Him to let Israel suffer the punishment she deserves. Again and again, individuals or people who commit idolatry provoke God's anger,[89] but His anger does not last long (Ezek 15:42), partly because His love outweighs His anger, and partly because His feeling is essentially independent of His people.[90]

One thing is evident in the prophets, God is not indifferent or apathetic towards the conduct of His people.[91] Infidelity and ingratitude of His people hurts him, but the consequence of sin - in form of retribution - hurts the sinner more (Jer 7:18; Hos. 12:15). God's repentance occurs however in the prophets, when God out of mercy and compassion undertakes to liberate the errant humankind from its self-destruction through the retributive consequence of sin.[92] Out of anger, Yahweh threatens Israel with punishment, but invariably, He does not carry it out;[93] like a mother, He cannot be apathetic to the suffering of His children (Isa.

---

87 J. Jeremias, *Die Reue Gottes*, p. 18.

88 Cf. Isa 1:21; 1:2-5; 30:9; Jer 3:6-10; 3:19; Ezek 16:6-14; Hos 1-3; 11:11 f. on the infidelity and ingratitude of the beloved Israel and Jahwe's compassion and mercy.

89 Cf. Isa 63:10; 65:3; Jer 7:18 f.; 8:19; Ezek 8:17; 16:26,42; invariably, it is God's love that is turned to anger (Isa 63:10; Jer. 12:7-13; 13:14; 16:5; 21:7; 32:31).

90 Cf. J. Scharbert, *Der Schmerz Jahwes*, p. 219.

91 A. J. Heschel, *The Prophets*, pp. 221 ff.

92 Cf. J. Scharbert, "Der Schmerz Jahwes", p. 225. The bitter disappointment that sinners cause God are turned back to them as judgement and punishment. God's compassion, however, leads Him to liberate them from their pain.

93 Jer. 263,13,19; 42:10; Hos 11:8; Joel 2:13; Amos 7:3.

49:15; 66:12 f.) and His creatures (Jonah 4:11). Here, God seems to be torn apart between His anger and love.

The tendency to emphasise God's direct punishment of offences decreases in the prophetic books just as the emphasis laid on the human inclination to self-destruction and on God's effort to liberate the erring humankind from the consequence of sin increases. This fact becomes even more evident as one tries to reflect on the Old Testament's references to the *wrath of God*: While in the book of Genesis, it is depicted as leading God to the violent destruction of His creation, in the prophetic books it ends as threats and pronouncement of divine judgement. According to Abraham Heschel, divine wrath in the prophecy, must be seen in the totality of divine pathos, in its relationship to divine justice and love and as a phenomenon, whose effect and realisation were always deferred by the hope for Israel's repentance.[94]

In the *poetic books*, there is hardly any talk about divine pain. The prayers and pleas for divine mercy, however, connote the idea that God's feeling is touched.[95] Here, the expectation of divine mercy and love increases, since it has become evident that God Himself is concerned, not to see His creatures perish in their own self-destruction. God is reluctant to allow the work of His hands to be destroyed (Job 10:8-11). Moreover, the remembrance of His covenant motivates Him to show compassion (Ps 106:45).

In the *non-canonical Jewish books of the rabbinical theology*, God's concern for His people does not stop however at the suspension of punishment for their sins: He shares in their suffering, because by virtue of His indwelling, He is always in their midst. In fact, God's whole existence with Israel is suffering.[96] While jealousy is considered unworthy of God,[97] sorrow and lamentation are commonly attributed to Him.[98] God renounces His glorious position to dwell with His people. It is in this sense that Judaism expects the kingdom of God to be established here on Earth. In such a religious view, it should not be surprising that the concept of apatheia does not arise at all. Rather than deny the pathos of God, the danger of making God suffer the same fate like Israel is real.[99]

---

[94] A. J. Heschel, *The Prophets*, pp. 299 ff.

[95] Ps 6:9; 22:20-22; 31:10 ff.; 44:24-27; 74:18-23 etc. See also, J. Scharbert, *Der Schmerz Jahwes*, p. 221 f.

[96] P. Kuhn, *Gottes Selbsterniedrigung in der Theologie der Rabbinen*, p. 82. See also ---, *Gottes Trauer and Klage*, p. 440 f.

[97] H. Frohnhofen, *op. cit.* p. 104.

[98] P. Kuhn, *Gottes Trauer and Klage*, 400 f.

[99] P. Kuhn, *Gottes Selbsterniedrigung*, p. 90.

From this section, the following conclusions could be drawn: In the Old Testament, God's repentance is aroused both by human sin and also by God's own compassion and mercy. In either case it presupposes heart-felt pain, sorrow and anger in God, which are in no way signs of weakness, but signs of His determination to continue His work of salvation. God's pain is never caused by the agency of a superior power or demon, but by the resolved steadfastness of His love. His anger gives expression to the power of this steadfast love. Accordingly, His compassion stems from an infinite love and readiness to help, which subdues every resistance. In view of these facts, it is argued that God's pathos differs from that of human beings. Unlike the pathos of gods and human beings, which are invariably induced by a superior and external force against which they are mostly helpless, God's pathos is always ultimately induced by His love;[100] it is within His control and, thus, cannot overpower Him.

1.4.2   The Immutability of God in the Old Testament

It becomes clear from the previous discussions that it is characteristic of the Old Testament to suggest that God can regret His plan and action. Although this trait is predominant, it is not an unanimous view of all the books. The books of Num. 23:19 and 1 Sam 15:29 for instance, state categorically that God can neither take back His words, nor change His mind. These two passages seem to contradict all that has been said so far about divine pathos in the Old Testament.

Scholars are of the opinion, however, that the contradiction is merely apparent. The talk about divine repentance and about the immutability of His will or decision in the two mentioned passages practically say the same thing from different standpoints, contends Joseph Sharbert.[101] Apparently, his opinion finds support in 1 Sam 15, where both divine repentance and immutability are used in making the same point. Yahweh says:

---

[100] Cf. J. Scharbert, Der Schmerz Jahwes, pp. 223-225. It should be noted in this connection, that although the biblical literature use different words - anger, jealousy, sorrow and regret - to describe the passion of God, there is no word corresponding to the Greek word-group *pathos* (with its implication of being acted upon or influenced from external power. Accordingly, in all cases where the Bible speaks of divine emotion, the notion of passivity or being under the sovereign power of an external agent is excluded. This fact differentiates God's passion or suffering in the Bible from the suffering of the Homeric gods and from human suffering. On the contrary, when human beings or gods suffer, they usually stand under the influence of an external force. With Jahwe the situation is different. See esp. p. 223 and H. Frohnhofen, *op. cit.*, p. 97.

[101] J. Scharbert, Der Schmerz Jahwes, p. 217.

> I regret that I made Saul king, for he has turned back from following me and has not carried out my commands. ... And the Lord was sorry that he had made Saul king over Israel. (v. 10 & 35.)

Yet speaking of Him in the same chapter, Samuel says: "...the glory of Israel (the Lord) will not recant or change his mind; for he is not a mortal, that he should change his mind."[102]

In this context, like in Num. 23:19, the immutability of divine mind refers to Yahweh's later decision consequent to His remorse over Saul. That He changed His mind earlier is taken for granted. Following J. Jeremias' interpretation of this passage, one can identify three senses in which divine immutability is meant here: God's decision a) to dethrone Saul, b) to never again allow His repentance to determine His action in the future, and c) to uphold His new promise in David, is definite and irrevocable.[103] Though in our view, the plausibility of b) is very remote, the truth of the main point is indisputable, namely, that divine immutability means the irrevocability of divine promise for the salvation of Israel.

Indeed, it is an awareness of God's steadfastness to His promise that made the prophets emphasise divine sympathy and compassion in their view of divine repentance. God's resolute determination to salvation, and His commitment to the covenant, makes Him engage in self-limitation. Thus, rather than see His beloved Israel perish, God spares and liberates her from the entanglement of sin. In fact, God's change of mind is motivated by His not willing the death but life of the sinner (Ezek 18:23; 33:11). Even when He plans disaster for His erring people, He does it in the hope that He will never inflict it on them (Jer 26:3; 42; Joel 2; Jon 3 f.). Rather than act out His anger, or allow the evil doers to perish according to His ordinance, therefore, He controls His anger (Hos 11) and suffers the pain of His self-control.

This divine self-limitation, which takes the form of an emotional change of will in God, says Jeremias, becomes dominant in the Old Testament, from the book of Amos onwards.[104] The New Testament also takes up the idea that God's promise of salvation is irrevocable. For Paul, for instance, God's plan of salvation will be fulfilled, whether Israel breaks the covenant or not (Rom. 3:3 f.); nothing will make God drop His plan, not even when all His people loose their faith in Him (Rom. 11:29). He extends the time of grace (Lk 18:6-9), so as to spare His people; and He hastens to help them when they are in need (Lk 18:7).

---

[102] Cf. Num 23:19 "God is not a human being, that he should lie, a mortal that he should change his mind".

[103] J. Jeremias, *Die Reue Gottes*, pp. 35-38.

[104] *Ibid.*, p. 109 ff.

In summary, therefore, we can claim that divine immutability in the scriptural sense differs from the concept of immutability in Greek thought. The Old Testament conceives of divine immutability in its close connection with divine pathos. That God does not change His will is a point made just to underline His resolute promise of salvation. And when He changes His will in another instance, it is likewise necessitated by His determination not to allow sin stand in the way of the fulfilment of His promise for salvation. Divine repentance and immutability, considered from this perspective, are thus interdependent, and are at the service of each other. God's change of mind is not arbitrary; neither is His immutability totally inflexible. In order words, God suffers self-limitation, the pain of withholding His anger (pathos), in other to keep His promise (the irrevocability of His will).

1.4.3 *Anthropomorphism, Transcendence and the Jewish Hermeneutics*

What we have discussed above mainly concerns the attribution of negatively conceived human characteristics to God (anthropopathy). While this could be seen as the main problem, it forms only but a part of the anthropomorphic expressions and symbols in the biblical writings. Unlike the Greek philosophers, the biblical writers felt free to use anthropomorphism. Both the Old and New Testament make ample use of anthropomorphism. But while the Old Testament employs negative and positive emotions in the predication of God, the New Testament tends to avoid the attribution of negative emotions to God. The use of positive human emotions (love, joy and pleasure) and symbols (father, shepherd) to describe both God's relationship to humankind and the inner state of His life is common. Thus, while anthropopathy is more pronounced in the Old Testament, anthropomorphism is generally employed in both Testaments especially in the description of the divine-human relationship.

Parallel to the ample use of anthropomorphism in the Old Testament is also a slight tendency towards anti-anthropomorphism, especially in the Pentateuch.[105] How the latter got into the Pentateuch has been a source of confusion for theologians and scholars alike, because in the very least anthropomorphism is a natural feature of the Pentateuch. Scholars have no unified explanation for it yet: while

---

[105] Cf. C. T. Fritsch, *The Anti-anthropomorphisms.*

some believe that anti-anthropomorphism is inherent in Judaism itself,[106] others trace it back to Greek influence.[107]

None of these views can be conclusive; they are all partial truths, which when put together could offer an explanation for this bafflement. Apparently, the basic fact that emerges out of the multiplicity of accounts is that there are two types of anti-anthropomorphism in the biblical writings: one is of Greek origin, the other is inherent in the Jewish conception of God. The Pentateuchal anti-anthropomorphism, embodied in the laws that forbid making images of God and pronouncing His name, is different from that found in the Septuagint and in Philo. While the former stemmed from a theological development and was at the service of the rabbinical conception of a "personal God", the latter, being a sort of philosophical adjustment, led inevitably to the conception of an apathetic Absolute, represented in Philo's philosophy.[108]

The anti-anthropomorphism of the Pentateuch, unlike that of the Greek philosophy, does not entail the negation of the world; neither does it disregard the similarity between God and humankind. For while it suggests that God is unlike humankind, it does not overlook the fact that humankind is made in the image and likeness of God. This sort of anti-anthropomorphism accentuates the Jewish notion of transcendence, which differs, accordingly, from the Greek understanding of the transcendence and immanence of God. The Jews, quite unlike the Greeks, do not see the immanence of God as an immersion into a pool of imperfection. The prophets, for instance, conceive divine transcendence and immanence together;[109] and just like the psalmists and the authors of the books of Wisdom, they guard the transcendence of God "very zealously",[110] without de-emphasising divine immanence. Thus, although God's transcendence is highly prized in the Jewish religious perception, the human likeness of God is not seen

---

[106] The Advocates of the first school of thought are J. Fredenthal, Are there Traces of Greek Philosophy in the Septuagint? p. 205-222 and Frankel, *Vorstudien der Septuaginta*, pp. 175 ff.

[107] A. F. Dähne, *Geschichtliche Darstellung der jüdisch-alexandrinischen Religions-Philosphie*, Halle, II, pp. 1-72; A. F. Gförer, *Kritische Geschichte des Urchristentums*, Teil II, Stuttgart, pp. 1-18. They believe that anti-anthropomorphism began with "Philonic teachings and Alexandrian theosophy".

[108] C. T. Fritsch, *The Anti-Anthropomorphisms*, p. 64 ff. This view leads to the conclusion that the type of anti-anthropomorphism which nurtured the growth of the doctrine of impassibility in Christian tradition came, not from Judaism, but from Hellenism

[109] Cf. *ibid.*, p. 5.

[110] *Ibid.*, p. 6. According to Heschel the prophets "had no apprehension that the statements of divine pathos might impair their understanding for the one, unique, and transcendent God". *The Prophets*, p. 268 f.

as His degradation. In fact, the divine transcendence (His holiness) consists precisely in God's overwhelming presence and indwelling, i.e. in His immanence, just as the divine immanence presupposes the divine transcendence in the Semitic thought.[111]

This is so because, in Judaism, the creation of humankind in the image and likeness of God is more prominent than the difference between God and human beings. This does not, however, entail the denial of the latter. Rather, as T. E. Pollard rightly observes,

> If they (the Jews) described God in human terms, it was not because they took an anthropomorphic view of God, but because they took a theomorphic view of themselves. They knew God as 'immediately' in a personal relationship, and they knew Him as a 'Person' in whose image and likeness they had been made.[112]

Among other things, Pollard's passage explains, that the Jewish tendency to perceive more of the likeness than of the difference between humankind and God, arises out of the fact that they make their conception of God in the context of a personal relationship with Him who accompanies them through history. They see God essentially as a "partner" to be encountered in a relationship and not as an "object" of philosophical inquiry.[113] They perceive God neither as "the impersonal Absolute",[114] dwelling outside the world, nor as an object of speculation, a "working Hypothesis", employed to define "the boundary of human possibilities", to use the words of Bonhoeffer.[115]

So far, we have been able to point to the Semitic understanding of anthropomorphism and divine transcendence. If we put our findings here together with the

---

[111] It must be observed that this biblical testimony about the interdependence of the transcendence and immanence of God got lost in many theologies with Greek orientation, where the conception of God *via negationis* prevailed. Although divine immanence is never totally or officially denied in any Christian theology worth its name, divine transcendence is mostly conceived by way of negation. In fact, one of the major logical implication of the hermeneutics of *via negativa* is the monopoly of divine transcendence, that is to say, the inclination towards Docetism.

[112] T. E. Pollard, The Impassibility of God, p. 355. See also A. J. Heschel, *The Prophets*, pp. 260 & 272. According to his view: "It is perhaps more proper to describe a prophetic passion as theomorphic than to regard the divine pathos as anthropomorphic."(260) For, following the creation of man in the likeness of God (Lev. 19.2), a Jew owes his "soul, thought, feeling, even passion" to God. To them, human qualities, including passions, belong originally to God Himself. Thus, the use of human language to describe "God's unconditional concern for justice is not an anthropomorphism. Rather, man's concern for justice is a theomorphism". (272)

[113] This fact does not imply any sort of irrationalism or ametaphysical theology.

[114] Cf. T. E. Pollard, *Op. cit.* p. 356.

[115] Cf. D. Bonhoeffer, *Letters and Papers from Prison*, p. 360.

biblical views on divine repentance and immutability, we would get a picture that is full of paradoxical approaches to reality. This is unlike the Greek hermeneutics of *via negativa*; and it is definitely more subtle than the Aristotelian *via analogica*. There is a flexibility in thought here, which seems at its face value to be contradictory. By close examination however, it reveals itself to be typical of the language of relationship, defined by the "psychology" rather than by the "ontology of divine nature.[116] For instead of speaking "the language of *essence*", the Bible speaks "the language of *presence*".[117] The language of presence is the language of relationship. Conceiving God's pathos together with His transcendence is not difficult for the Jews precisely because they believe that God is a God of relationship.[118] The God of relationship, the God of history is not only the God who knows pathos, He is also the God, who can be psychologically influenced through the activities of His creatures.[119]

We can rightly say from the above, that the Semitic conception of God basically differs from the Greek notion of the Absolute, because, while the Greek philosophers conceive God speculatively, the Jews conceive Him empirically, that is to say, in the context of history and relationship. Consequently, the Semitic conception of reality entertains more flexibility than does the philosophical view.

In the view of Thorleif Boman, there is a yet more basic reason for the difference between the Greek and Semitic conceptualisation of the divinity; it has something to do with their various ways of perceiving reality.[120] Boman traces this back to the basic variations in the use of the organs of experiencing. Whereas

---

[116] J. K. Mozley, *The Impassibility of God*, p. 3. He testifies to the fact that there was an absence of metaphysical speculations in the thought of Jewish writers of the pre-Greek philosophical era

[117] Cf. A. J. Heschel, *The Prophets, p. 275*

[118] Philo, who describes God only from the point of view of His activities, does not seem to have recognised this fact. He understands God-world relationship as a quasi-relation, a non-reciprocal relation where God alone can be said to be acting and the creatures suffer. In his classic treatise on Philo, H. A. Wolfson rightly maintains, that, "in a strictly logical sense", such a non-reciprocal relation, is "not a true relation". Cf. H. A. Wolfson, *Philo, vol. II*, p. 138.

[119] R. S. Frank, Passibility and Impassibility, p. 658. According to Baldwin, as quoted by Robert Franks, passion is "the condition of being acted upon, and being affected, receptive". In this sense having passions entails the ability to be passive and to suffer action or change. From this definition's point of view, it can easily be perceived that impassibility and immutability are related concepts. The former is not subordinate to the latter as W. Maas suggests. See *Unveränderlichkeit Gottes*, p. 46). All depends on ones point of departure, because indeed, a being that changes, *suffers* change; but a being that suffers, *changes* in the process.

[120] Cf. Th. Boman, *Das hebräische Denken im Vergleich mit dem griechischen*, 1983.

the Greeks principally perceive reality *visually*, the Hebrews mainly encounter it *auditorially*.[121] The impressions gained through the ears, the author continues, have the characteristics marked with dynamism and change. They provide less room for precise objectivity. In contrast, the optic impressions are bound to give static pictures, which presuppose a higher degree of objectivity and immutability. Applying this to the thought-patterns in question, one sees immediately why the Greeks place "being" in the centre of reality, and the Hebrews emphasise "history and movement".

Boman has been accused of oversimplifying the difference between the two cultures, by calling one static and the other dynamic.[122] The difference is definitely not as simple as that. But, be that as it may, the fact remains that the God of the philosophers, especially, when conceived *via negationis*, is apathetic. In contrast, the God of the Bible is pathetic.

1.5 The Harmonisation of the Semitic and Greek Notions of God in the Hellenistic Judaism

Harmonising the Greek and the Semitic conceptions of God was already a major problem in the earliest times of the Hellenistic Judaism - first for the seventy translators of the Septuagint, and then for Philo of Alexandria. The clash between the Greek and Semitic cultures and the revolt that characterised the Maccabean era had given way to an unreserved acceptance of the Greek philosophy by the time the Septuagint was translated in the second century before Christ. Accordingly, both the translators of the Septuagint and their Hellenised Jewish readers were familiar with the Greek philosophical concepts and the philosophers conception of God. Writing out of this philosophical background, which was largely Platonic and Stoic, the translators had their reservations concerning the anthropomorphic expressions and symbols found in the Hebrew original.

Opinions differ today however as to whether these translators reinterpreted or even eliminated totally some of the anthropomorphic images and concepts to suit

---

[121] *Ibid.*, pp. 180 ff.

[122] Cf. A. Grillmeier, Hellenisierung - Judaisierung des Christentums als Deuteprinzipien der Geschichte des kirchlichen Dogmas, p. 484. Nonetheless, Boman's conclusion that each of the cultures show a genuine but one-sided conception of reality is correct. Ideally, these two visions of reality should be put together in order to gain a broader view of reality (Boman, *Op cit.*, p. 182). With reference to Christianity, both cultures made valuable contributions indeed to the formulation of Christian principles, but neither constitutes solely the Christian message, both stood "equally far and near to the Gospel" (Grillmeier, *Op. cit.*, p. 486).

their philosophical fancy,[123] or whether they faithfully translated the texts. No matter which is true, one fact is obvious, namely, that the seventy had encountered problems in the translation because of the incompatibility of the anthropopathetic language of the Bible with the popular philosophical antianthropomorphism.

Besides, if the translators rendered the words according to their exact meaning, it was definitely not because they fancied the expressions, but because they were determined to give a faithful translation. For that reason, they were the first to experience the theological dilemma - the art of using philosophical ideas without being unfaithful to the original biblical texts - which assailed later theologies. It is however scarcely credible that their bias towards such expressions never left their mark on the translation. Be that as it may, their faithfulness to the original texts is a true sign that, rather than solving the dilemma, they passed it on to their successors.

Philo of Alexandria (25 BC - 45 AD), whose writings are also directed to the Hellenised Jewish residents in Alexandria,[124] made the first conscious effort to reconcile the Greek conception of an apathetic God with the Jewish experience of a pathetic God.[125] By virtue of his being at home in both Greek and Semitic cultures, he felt free to combine ideas from the various traditions. His doctrine of God reflects this fact prominently: For although, for instance, he retains the Jewish habit of describing the "activity" rather than the "being" of God,[126] he is basically inclined towards the Greek philosophy and its characteristic conception of an apathetic God. God is accordingly the incomprehensible, simple, self-sufficient, unmixed, immortal, incorporeal, immutable, and impassible being.[127] He thus rejects the image of a God who has pathos. Wrath and repentance should not be attributed to Him since, according to him, they are incompatible with divine omniscience and immutability. The only emotions which he considers fit for

---

[123] While C. T. Fritsch, *The Anti-Anthropomorphisms* contends that some biblical ideas were Hellenised beyond recognition (chapters 1&2, pp. 9-22) and attributes the Pentateuchal anti-anthropomorphism partly to the redaction of the seventy (15 f.) - see also W. Maas, *Unveränderlichkeit Gottes*, pp. 121-124 - H. Frohnhofen, *Apatheia tou theou*, p. 102 insists that though the translators were suspicious of the anthropomorphic language, the did not manipulate the translation.

[124] C. T. Fritsch, *The Anti-Anthropomorphisms*, p. 63. The Hellenised Jews had lost intimacy with Hebrew and Aramaic.

[125] *Ibid.*, p. 64.

[126] Cf. H. Frohnhofen, *Apatheia tou theou*, p. 109.

[127] Cf. H. A. Wolfson, *Philo, vol. II*, p. 96 and Herbert Frohnhofen, *Apatheia tou theou*, p. 109 f.

God are mercy and happiness; God is free from sorrow, fear and feeling of pain; He cannot have emotions, since that would suggest that He is being acted upon; He is apathetic in the sense of being independent from external influence.[128]

How then does Philo account for the biblical use of anthropopathy? He argues that the anthropomorphic expressions do not correspond to the reality of God; they signify nothing about the ontological nature of God, whose true nature is essentially incomprehensible. The anthropomorphic expressions used in predicating the God of the Bible, he insists, serve only pedagogical purposes.[129] As such, the problem of anthropomorphism, in his view, represents an apparent contradiction that is explicable.[130] To do away with this contradiction, Philo introduces the use of allegorical method, which actually arises out of the assumption that the scriptural texts have twofold meaning, "literal" and "underlying" meaning.[131] By implication, therefore, Philo contends that the biblical passages with anthropomorphic expressions should not be taken literally, especially if they apply to God: they must be seen as possessing an underlying meaning.[132] To support his view that the anthropomorphic expressions should not be taken literally, Philo refers to two passages in the Bible (Gen 1:26 and Num 23:19) which respectively affirm the human likeness and unlikeness of God.[133] He sees it as a proof that humankind is like God but also very much unlike Him. Against this background, anthropomorphic expressions cannot be predicated to God without any qualification. They do not correspond ontologically with God's nature; they have mere pedagogical values.

Since the biblical anthropomorphic expressions reveal nothing about God's own inner disposition, Philo sees in allegorical method, a means of disclosing what the anthropomorphic expressions seem to "obscure".[134] For Philo the hidden fact is that God is eminently immutable and impassible. Consequently, he insists that the mention of divine repentance in Genesis should not be understood

---

[128] Cf. H. Frohnhofen, *Apatheia tou theou*, pp. 109-114.

[129] H. A. Wolfson, *Philo, vol. II*, p. 127. Only on this ground did Philo consider the biblical anthropomorphism justifiable.

[130] *Ibid.*, p.129.

[131] H. A. Wolfson, *Philo, vol. I, p.* 115. "The underlying meaning he describes by a variety of terms, among them also the term allegory...".

[132] H. A. Wolfson, *Philo, vol. I*, 116.

[133] Cf. H. A. Wolfson, *Philo, vol. II*, p.127

[134] H. A. Wolfson, *Philo, vol. I*, p.115.

literally. In his words, "there could be no greater impiety than to suppose that the Unchangeable changes";[135] "He is not susceptible to any passions at all".[136]

Summarising the foregoing discussions in this section, we can rightly say that the first significant attempt to harmonise the Jewish and Greek notions of God began with Philo. He reinterprets the anthropomorphic expressions of the Bible in defence of the concept of divine apatheia. Through this reinterpretation, however, he distances himself from the original meaning of some of the anthropomorphic expressions. This is particularly true with his understanding of the divine compassion, wrath and repentance. For, contrary to the biblical notion of the divine compassion, which entails repentance, Philo considers compassion worthy of God on the one hand, but wrath and repentance unworthy of Him on the other. Moreover, his allegorical method raises more questions than it answers: it does not specify the criterion for selecting the anthropomorphic expressions with   underlying meaning. Why, for instance, must only the talk about compassion be taken literally, and not also that about wrath and repentance. In the absence of such a criterion, the use of the allegorical method seems to make the biblical expressions equivocal and indefinite; their meanings would become a matter of interpretation. In fact, no one could know for certain which messages of the Bible are not ambiguous.

Excursus: The History, Problems and Prospects of Hellenisation

The history of the encounter between the Semitic and Hellenistic traditions is quite old; it began as far back as 597-538 BC., during the period of the Jewish Diaspora. Finding themselves in an alien environment that was overwhelmingly Greek, the Diaspora Jews inevitably absorbed the Greek elements of culture. And as the first and second Maccabees reveal to us, this encounter culminated soon into a clash between Judaism and Hellenism in the second century BC.

The consequent Jewish revolt against the Greek culture was however characterised by mixed feelings. For while, on the one hand, the Jews were aversive to the penetrating foreign influence - out of the deep concern to preserve their own cultural identity - on the other hand, they were eager to keep abreast with times and the new style of life.[137] The resistance to Hellenistic influence was thus weakened by the fact that it was attractive to Jews.

The seventy scholars who translated the Hebrew scriptures into Greek, were among those who found the new intellectual culture attractive. With their Greek translation, they did a lot to Hellenise the Jewish readers and spread Hellenistic Judaism. But it was Philo, who deepened and quickened the Hellenisation process, at least on the intellectual level, through the use of his celebrated allegorical

---

[135] Philo, *Quod Deus*, v, 22.

[136] *Ibid.*, xi, 52.

[137] A. Zeilinger, *Das Alte Testament verstehen II*, p. 298.

method, which rendered metaphorical, what was not compatible with the current Greek philosophy. Philo's mediation between the Hellenistic and Semitic cultures proves that Hellenism, by the time of Jesus Christ, had got itself established in the Semitic tradition, at least on the intellectual level. Philo, who lived till 45 AD was a contemporary of Jesus (c. 7 BC - 30 AD). Scholars are not sure to what extent Jesus' own life was influenced by the Hellenistic culture,[138] but the Hellenistic influence on the biblical writers (especially John and Paul) is abundantly evident.

Hellenisation reached its climax in the first century during the formulation of the Christian principles. The Fathers of the Church found the Hellenistic philosophy particularly useful, both in the articulation of the divine attributes, and in their struggle against polytheism. With its emphasis on the unity of God, Hellenistic philosophy seemed predestined to supply them with the language and logic for the defence of both the "universality" of God and the doctrine of monotheism.[139] Moreover, the Hellenistic categories were appropriate for the effective communication of the message of Christ to the educated gentiles and the Hellenised converts.[140]

The quest for intelligibility, therefore, made the adoption of Hellenistic philosophy inevitable for Christianity. Due to its foundational role in the formation of the Christian doctrines, Hellenistic philosophy has been entitled to a "permanent seat" in the Christian theology, which not only makes, Christianity without the Greek elements inconceivable, but also the attempt to separate the main content of Christianity from its Hellenistic cultural media illusory.[141] In some theologies of the past, Hellenism ran the danger of becoming synonymous with the "content" of the Christian faith. But now that the claim of Christianity to universality is in the storm of doubts, and that the cross-cultural significance of faith occupies the consciousness of a multi-cultural and pluralistic society, the inadequacy of the Hellenistic thought-pattern on certain matters has become obvious. More and more cultures are claiming to be worthy of contributing something towards the effective radiation of the revealed truth of Christianity.[142]

---

[138] F. G. Downing, Hellenism, p. 278.

[139] Cf. W. Pannenberg, *Grundfragen Systematischer Theologie*, p. 309 f.

[140] A. Grillmeier, "Christus licet uobis inuitis deus". Ein Beitrag zur Diskussion über die Hellenisierung der christlichen Botschaft, in: *Kerygma und Logos - C. Andresen-Festschrift*, p. 227

[141] R. J. Schreiter, *Constructing Local Theologies*, p. 8. In defining the relation between Christianity and the cultures that express it, Schreiter argues that the popular image of the kernel (God's message in Christ) and the husk (cultural media) has become inadequate. In its place, he suggests the "image of an onion". This should help us evade the illusion, he contends, that the content and container of Christian message could be separated from one another. In his view, they are so bound together that by separating one the other goes with it.

[142] Cf. R. E. Hood, *Must God Remain Greek?* Without denying the authenticity of the Judaisation, Hellenisation, Germanisation and Romanisation, the Third World theologies are seeking to make Christianity relevant to them through inculturation. It is hoped that a better access to the revealed truth will be gained if the message is received through ones own rather than through the mediation of a foreign culture. For details on the importance

Yet the main problem theology has with Hellenisation is not the domination of Greek philosophy, but its apparently unresolved incompatibility with the Semitic tradition. For, despite the long history of the joint venture between Semitic and Hellenistic traditions in the shaping of Christian principles, a proper integration between the two is still lacking, instituting something like a "Greek-Hebrew divide" in the Christian theology. On the issue of God and history, for instance, one encounters serious theological difficulties arising from the difference between the Greek and Semitic approach to reality.[143] The relation between the Hellenistic and Semitic tradition on some theological issues often conjures up the image of a square peg in a round hole.

Accordingly, despite the time and energy theologians have expended in defence of the heritage of Greek philosophical traditions and in establishing the monopoly of the Hellenistic matrix for casting theological truth, questions on the role and relevance of Hellenism in the Christian theology were posed immensely in the middle of this century, especially by A. von Harnack, F. Loofs and W. Elert. The question is this: Has Hellenisation contributed to the development or the degeneration of faith? Has it spelt fortune or fate for the Christian religion?

While the above mentioned theologians conclude that Hellenisation amounts to the falsification of the essence of Christianity,[144] W. Pannenberg and H. Küng[145] see Hellenisation as a positive phenomenon that deserves a positive evaluation today, especially because of the lucidity it brought to the description of the person of Christ. The positive role of Hellenisation consists, as Jaroslav Pelikan[146] and A. Grillmeier[147] claim, in its ability for self-correction. Hellenisation possessed an inner mechanism with which it checked its own excesses. It was in view of this self-regulatory mechanism, Pelikan contends, that Hellenistic thought was used in the battle against "speculations and heresies" to ward off Hellenisation. In other words, Hellenisation functioned, according to Pelikan and Grillmeier, concurrently as the assimilation and elimination of relevant and irrelevant cultural elements respectively.

In effect, Hellenisation was a necessary process of inculturation. And like any proper inculturation, it could not have been bad in itself, except when it is absolutised to an extent that its encounter with other cultures cannot lead to an inte-

---

of different cultures for the historicity of revelation and Christianity, see A. Grillmeier, Hellenisierung - Judaisierung, pp. 423-488, esp. 457 & 487.

[143] In fact, most theological deadlocks, concerning the doctrines of God, Trinity and Incarnation in the two thousand year history of Christianity, could at best be traced back to the polarity between the Semitic and Greek elements in the Christian tradition.

[144] A. v. Harnack, *Lehrbuch der Dogmengeschichte I*, pp. 20 & 55. F. Loofs, *Leitfaden zum Studium der Dogmengeschichte*, pp. 8-11. W. Elert, Die Theopaschite Formel; ----, *Der Ausgang der altkirchlichen Christologie*. pp. 71-132. See also Alois Grillmeier, Hellenisierung - Judaisierung, p. 455. According to Grillmeier, Harnack developed a positive mind to Hellenisation towards the end of his theological career.

[145] W. Pannenberg, *Op. cit.* p. 296 ff. Hans Küng, *The Incarnation of God*.

[146] J. Pelikan, *The Christian Tradition*, p. 55

[147] A. Grillmeier, Christus licet, p. 228. In his view, the council of Nicea was in itself a serious attempt to "deHellenise" the Christian faith (p. 251 ff).

gration. Whether it spelt fate or fortune for Christian theology depends on how far a working integration was achieved. This means further, that Hellenisation began to fail in history at precisely the point at which it ceased to follow the dynamism of its own inner corrective and self-regulatory mechanism - i.e. where it inhered in static permanence and failed to vote itself out in cases of its irrelevance. At such points Hellenisation was bound to produce alienation.

It should be noted however, as W. Pannenberg says, that alienation does not arise merely because one culture meets another, but because assimilation could not take place.[148] This becomes even clearer, if we agree with Grillmeier that the Christian revelation is not a "*revelatio pura*", but a historically, humanly and culturally conditioned phenomenon. That Christ's revelation of God did not take place in a cultural vacuum, is proved by Jesus himself. For not only did he not live outside his society, he also never claimed to bring a "new doctrine" but the fulfilment of the old. In view of the historical feature of revelation, therefore, it would be wrong to see Hellenisation (Judaisation) or even modern inculturation as a corruption of the Christian revelation. [149]

Consequently, Hellenisation as such was not the problem of dogma, but the apparently unfinished cultural integration between Semitic and Hellenistic traditions.[150] The task of integration, however, is often hindered by the human tendencies to polarise seemingly opposing ideas. This limitation of the human mind poses problems, especially, when we try to reconcile such apparently opposing attributes of God, like His impassibility and passibility.

1.6   Summary

We have examined the axiom of divine impassibility in the light of the Hellenistic and Semitic conceptions of God and noted that it stems from the concept of

---

[148] Cf. Pannenberg, *Op. cit.* p. 312. "Eine 'Hellenisation' im Sinne einer Überfremdung z.B. durch den philosophischen Gottesgedanken tritt nicht schon da ein, wo die Theologie das Ringen mit ihm aufnimmt, sondern erst da, wo sie in diesem Ringen versagt, indem sie ihre assimilierende, umgestaltende Kraft verliert." Reasonably, therefore, one has to differentiate between positive Hellenisation (inculturation) from negative (alienating) Hellenisation. One can justifiably speak of the latter, when the borrowed culture displaces the authentic heritage. For our purpose here, it would suffice to observe, that the Hellenisation of Christianity has two sides: on the one hand, it greatly contributed to the formulation of Christian principles, but on the other hand, it also regrettably compounded the problems of theologians, who have, to this moment, not yet effectively reconciled the philosophical conceptions of God with the experienced biblical "image" of God.

[149] Cf. A. Grillmeier, Hellenisierung - Judaisierung, pp. 457-488. For more details on this problem see also W. Maurer, "Hellenisierung - Germanisierung - Romanisierung. Bemerkung zu den Perioden der Kirchengeschichte", in: H. D. Wendland (Hrsg.), *Kosmos and Ekklesia* (Kassel 1953), pp. 55-72.

[150] Evidently, the "aggiornamento" (the adaptation process) of Pope John XXIII - which initiated the Second Vatican Council and the current process of inculturation - pursues the same aim which the Fathers of the church had, when they adopted the Greek elements of culture, namely, to situate faith into the context of the prevalent cultures.

apatheia in the ancient Greek philosophy. Apatheia is used, first, in denoting God's moral and ontological perfection, and later, in characterising human ethical ideal. It is used in the narrow and broad senses in Greek literature. The narrow sense, which denotes the freedom of a personal agent from suffering or negative emotions characterises the earliest literature, while the broad sense, in which it is understood as the absolute freedom of an entity or personal agent from all external influences, predominates in the later Greek writings. In general however, a majority of the Greeks understand divine apatheia in its broad sense.

In the light of the overall Greek tendency to conceive the world as evil, divine apatheia is often seen as being identical with anti-anthropomorphism. Only rarely does the acceptance of anthropomorphism go hand in hand with the conception of divine apatheia. In general however, divine apatheia emerges out of the Hellenistic tendency to conceive God by way of negation and through the disparagement of emotions. For that reason, apatheia invariably implies extra emphasis on the difference between God and humankind, with little or no regard for the similarity between them.

On the contrary, apatheia in the sense explained above is totally absent in the biblical and Semitic conception of God. The Jewish communities of antiquity predicate God with anthropomorphic language and symbols, speaking about His change of mind and emotional suffering. They recognise God's immutability and transcendence, albeit in a sense different from the Greek version of it. Consequently, the concept of the divine immutability occurs in the Bible only as an expression of Yahweh's resolute commitment to His promise. It is not an abstract immutability: of course, Yahweh needed to change His mind a couple of times, though only in order to remain faithful (immutable) to His promise, thereby showing that change is possible in Him despite His immutability.

Similarly, His transcendence is taken to mean ultimately His overwhelming presence and indwelling (immanence) among His people. At the background of the Jewish conception of God, therefore, is a paradoxical approach to reality, different from the Greek way of negation, and more subtle than the Aristotelian analogy. Unlike the Greeks, the Jews emphasise the human likeness of and relation with God more than the human-God-difference, so that, it has become possible to speak of their theomorphic view of themselves rather than their anthropomorphic conception of God.

Reconciling these two contrary conceptions of God - of a pathetic and an apathetic God - has been a consistent preoccupation of theology since the Hellenisation of Judaism and Christianity. The most significant attempt to harmonise the Greek and Semitic conceptions of God is to be found in the Hellenistic Judaism, which Philo of Alexandria represents. Philo's celebrated mediation, however, could not achieve a workable integration of the two cultural views. His allegorical method, with which he explains the biblical anthropomorphic expressions away, does not seem applicable to every anthropomorphic expression or symbol in the Bible. His method therefore blurs the difference between what is real and what is metaphorical. Consequently, Hellenistic Judaism passes the unsolved theological dilemma of divine impassibility on to Christianity.

(In the excursus on the history, problems and prospects of Hellenisation, we tried to negotiate the answer to a hypothetical question, namely, whether the theological dilemma can have any logical solution. The search for an integration of the two cultures through the application of the paradoxical approach in the Bible seems to be a promising way out, and perhaps even the only prospect for today's inculturation theologies.)

2. DIVINE IMPASSIBILITY IN THE PREVALENT THEOLOGIES AND CHURCH TRADITION (FROM THE FIRST TO THE SIXTEENTH CENTURY)

2.1 Divine Impassibility in the First Century Christian Church

The adoption of the Greek concept of divine apatheia[1] is characteristic of the theologies of the first three centuries of the Church. It can indeed be seen as the basic theological presupposition of the patristic Christology and the doctrine of God.[2] Of course, the nature and frequency of its application differs from writer to writer, in accordance with the time of writing. In general terms, however, the doctrine of divine impassibility occupies such a central position in the patristic theologies of the second and third centuries, and particularly in their reflections during the Christological controversies, that one can justifiably assume that it was, in their context, the distinguishing characteristic of the Christian God, in the face of which the biblical anthropomorphism must have seemed merely metaphorical or purely "fallacious"[3] and "blasphemous".[4]

A glance through some of the literature of this era, reveals that the application of this axiom is much more pronounced in the second and third than in the first century theologies. This is perhaps due to the proximity of the New Testament writers and the apostolic Fathers to the Semitic influence, which became drastically diminished in the subsequent theologies.

2.1.1 The New Testament

In the *New Testament*, there is no explicit statement about the possibility or impossibility of God. Neither is *apatheia* mentioned anywhere.[5] Only the verb

---

1   It should be noted that the conception of apatheia in the broad sense - as the noninfluenceability of an entity or of the inner soul of a personal being - which characterised its understanding in the Greek antiquity, virtually disappeared in the Christian circle, giving way to its narrow meaning understood as immunity to suffering and to the excitement of passions. But restricting it within the narrow and negative sense of apatheia, the Christians were still able to add "sinlessness" and "lack of erotic passion" (Paul) to the original Greek meaning, thereby giving it a wider meaning than it had in the Stoic ethics. Cf. W. Michaelis, *op. cit.*, p. 927 f. See also H. Frohnhofen, *Apatheia tou theou*, p. 119.

2   C. Grant, Possibilities for Divine Passibility, p. 3. T. E. Pollard, The Impassibility of God, p. 357; cf. also G. L. Prestige, *God in Patristic Thought*, p. 6.

3   A. J. Heschel, *The Prophets*, p. 273.

4   H. M. Kuitert, *Gott in Menschengestalt*, p. 56.

5   H. Frohnhofen, *Apatheia tou theou*, p. 123.

paschein is abundantly used in connection with the suffering (passion) of Jesus Christ.[6] Of course, mention is made of the "wrath" and "compassion of God", and in one instance, of His "jealousy" (2 Cor. 11:2), all in accordance with the Old Testament tradition. The predication of "repentance", "hate", "pain" and "negatively judged emotions" to God are strictly avoided. Also, not the slightest attempt is made to attribute impassibility to Jesus Christ: emotions and passions are characteristic of his person. Even in Mt. 26:42 and Lk. 23:46, where an indirect reference is made to a type of sovereignty over pain or suffering, it is referred to God Himself and not to Jesus.[7]

Thus the New Testament writers neither decry nor fully adopt the Old Testament's anthropopathic expressions. Nevertheless, the trend in the later books of the Old Testament towards emphasising divine love and compassion and speaking less about punishment as the consequence of sin finds its continuation in the New Testament.[8] The "wrath of God", for instance, is no longer seen as leading to immediate divine punishment: God is believed to often be undergoing a process of "self-limitation", deferring the realisation of His wrath to the future, containing His anger, rather than acting it out. Divine wrath is, in other words, given an "eschatological" interpretation: it is expected at a later time, namely, in the last judgement.[9] Rather than let His wrath take a violent course, God withholds it at best, and abandons the sinner at worst to his or her own self-destruction.[10]

Hence, in the New Testament, just like in the prophetic books,[11] God is experienced as the one who in His mercy always comes to rescue humankind from its self-destruction, for His wrath ends invariably in patience and mercy (Rom. 9:11-29). By implication, therefore, not only is the negativity of anger taken away

---

6   Cf. W. Michaelis, *op. cit.*, pp. 911-918.

7   H. Frohnhofen, *Apatheia tou theou*, pp. 123-126.

8   See Chapter 1, second to the last paragraph of 1.4.1.

9   M. Pohlenz, *Vom Zorne Gottes*, pp. 1-2, 10-14. It might be too presumptuous to see this shift of emphasis in NT as a sign of anti-anthropomorphism.

10   Cf. R. Schwager, *Brauchen wir einen Sündenbock?*, pp. 219-224. In his theological interpretation of René Girard's view on violence and the sacred, Schwager contends that both the apocalyptic and Pauline writings of the New Testament use the "wrath of God" to emphasise that God takes the actions of humankind seriously (224) and that he is a God of justice (219). Above all, these texts show that the "wrath of God" does not lead to a divine violent interference in human affairs. The "wrath of God" merely affects the relationship between him and humankind; it occurs at an interpersonal level, as God abandons human beings to the repercussions of their own distorted lust, emotions and thinking - i.e. to their own self-destruction (220).

11   Cf. A. J. Heschel, *The Prophets*, p. 299 ff.

from God, through this interpretation, He is, by that means, also presented as the one, who is sovereign over His anger, i.e. over His passions. Thus while the New Testament shows reservations toward the attribution of negatively judged emotions to God, it does not hesitate to emphasise the honourable ones like patience and compassion. In order words, pathos is attributed to God, but only insofar as it does not connote an external influence: God retains the initiative and sovereignty.

2.1.2   The Apostolic Fathers

The writings of the *apostolic Fathers* show abundant evidence of acquaintance with the biblical tradition. Yet the influence of Greek philosophy is undeniable. To that effect, theologies of the time depict a double commitment both to the philosophical concept of God and to the biblical notion of God, which at that time was definitely not perceived as a serious theological dilemma challenging the predication of God. It is out of this background that one can view the contribution of *St. Ignatius of Antioch*, who, in his letters, assumes the impassibility of God on the one hand, and confesses the suffering of God in Jesus Christ on the other, without any fear of contradiction.[12]

In his *Letter to Polycarp* Ignatius first speaks of

> the Eternal, the Invisible, who became visible for our sake, the Impalpable, the Impassible, who suffered for our sake, who endured in all ways for our sake;[13]

and then in his *Letter to the Ephesians*, he refers to Jesus Christ our Lord as the only physician, who is

> of flesh yet spiritual, born yet unbegotten, God incarnate, genuine life in the midst of death, sprung from Mary as well as God, first subject to suffering then beyond it.[14]

In the light of the above passages, Ignatius evidently emphasises the paradox of divine nature using both the idea of the Incarnation and the glorification of the man,[15] Jesus Christ, who was first subject to suffering (*primo passibilis*) before becoming impassible (*et tunc impassibilis*). While the second passage implies that the passible one can become impassible, it is not clear whether the impassible one can also suffer passibily.

---

12 Commenting on *ad Trall.* 7,1 and *ad Smyr.* 6,1, 10.1, both A. von Harnack, *Hist. Dogm.1*, p.189 and Lightfoot, *(The Apostolic Fathers, vol. II*, Sect.1, have reservations about believing that Ignatius really speaks of Jesus Christ as God.

13 Ignatius, *ad Polyc. 3,2*, trans. in: J. B. Lightfoot, *op cit.*

14 Ignatius, *ad Eph. 7,2*, in: Lightfoot, *op. cit.*

15 Ignatius' paradox here anticipates the tendency in the later centuries (see sect. 2.7. below) to use the kenotic motif to illuminate the mystery of God's paradoxical nature.

He does not offer any theological explanation for his paradoxical statements. This makes it practically difficult to evaluate his statements, so as to know whether they are expressions of a paradox or sheer contradiction. It does seem however that his paradoxical formulation arose out of the need to take a position on the one hand, against the Docetists[16] (who were doubting Christ's humanity and claiming that his Incarnation and suffering were unreal), and on the other hand, against the Judaists[17] (who considered the crucifixion of the Messiah a blasphemy). It was thus out of the need to affirm both humanity and the divine reality of the incarnate Christ that Ignatius was pushed to emphasise, not just Christ's suffering, but also the suffering of God in him. Since he lived prior to the turbulence of the Christological controversies over the two Natures of Christ and over the doctrine of Logos, his writings lack the precise specification of whether the suffering of Christ refers only to his human nature. In view of the historical setting of his writings, and of the explicit mention of divine suffering in his *Letter to Romans*, where he says: "permit me to be an imitator of my suffering God",[18] we can justifiably believe that he is serious about the suffering of God, and that his double-talk is no contradiction but a paradoxical representation of the divine nature.

Thus, despite his accepting the Greek concept of apatheia, Ignatius admits that God suffered in Jesus Christ. The biblical idea of a God whose nature is paradoxical must have led him to affirm that God is paradoxically passible and impassible at the same time. It is probable that he arrived at this affirmation without the rigorous philosophical reflection that characterises subsequent theologies.

2.2   Divine Impassibility in the Second Century Theologies

The predication of suffering to God is merely tolerated in the theologies of the second century. At the initial stage, a conscious attempt is made to conceive God in terms of the image of Christ and a widespread use of Theopaschite expressions is found,[19] at the background of which an undeveloped differentiation between

---

16   Evidently, the danger of Docetism was already known to Ignatius. See V. Corwin, *St. Ignatius and Christianity in Antioch*, pp. 52-57; M. Rackl, *Die Christologie des heiligen Ignatius von Antiochien*, pp. 89-133; P. Weigandt, *Der Doketismus im Urchristentum*, 1, pp. 57 ff., 109-114 & 27; H. Frohnhofen, *Apatheia tou theou*, p. 134.

17   See J. B. Lightfoot, *The Apostolic Fathers II / 1*, p. 373 ff.; M. Rackl, *Die Christologie des heiligen Ignatius von Antiochien* p. 103-108; L. W. Barnard, The Background of St. Ignatius of Antioch, p. 193-206 cited in H. Frohnhofen, *ibid.*

18   Ignatius, *Letter to Romans, 6,3.*

19   Cf. W. Elert, *Der Ausgang der altkirchlichen Christologie*, p. 72 f.; M. Slusser, *Theopaschite Expressions*; H. Frohnhofen, *Apatheia tou theou*, p. 142.

the first and second Person of the Trinity are most evident. However, in the later part of the century, especially in the theologies of the apologists, it soon becomes obvious that the Greek concept of apatheia is seen as the main distinguishing characteristic of the Christian God. And it is used not only for establishing the contrast between God and the gods of the pagan mythologies, but also in specifying the difference between the first and second Person, as well as the distinction between the humanity and divinity of Christ.[20] It is believed today, that this assumption contributed immensely to the emergence of Docetism and to the spread of Gnosticism.[21]

2.2.1   The Apologists

The Apologists helped immensely to Christianise the concept of apatheia. For, not only do they intensify its use, they also completely avoid the application of "pathos" - with the exception of compassion - to God. For *Aristeide*, the true God (whom he considers intrinsically invisible, immortal and immutable) is free from every emotion and passion. To all intents and purposes however Aristeide seems to be basing his conception of God mostly on the basic principle of divine immutability.[22]

Similarly, *Justin*, whose Platonic influence is all too evident,[23] makes the immutability of God the pivot of his conception of divine apatheia. He uses the concept of apatheia to differentiate between the Christian God and the Olympic gods (1 Apol. 25,2). But in what seems like putting aside his Platonic influence he also predicates suffering to the Christian God: God suffered, insofar as He revealed Himself in the experience of Jesus Christ (Dial., 57,3). In his answer to a question in *Dialogus cum Tryphone Judaeo*, concerning the possibility of the suffering of the immutable Christian God,[24] he speaks of the begetting of the

---

20   H. Frohnhofen, *ibid.*

21   The adoption of the Greek philosophical concept of apatheia in the early Church contributed immensely to the emergence of Docetism. Cf. J. G. Davies, The Origins of Docetism, pp. 13 ff. & 35; M. Slusser, Docetism. A Historical Definition, pp. 163-172; H. Frohnhofen, *Apatheia tou theou*, pp. 127-130.

22   *Apol.* 4, 7; 8,2 in: *Die ältesten Apologeten. Texte mit kurzen Einleitungen* (Edgar J. Goodspeed) Göttingen 1914, Neudruck Göttingen 1984. See also H. Frohnhofen, *op. cit.*, pp. 145-146. Like most Apologists, but unlike the apostolic Fathers, Aristeide considers anger, suffering, ambition, repentance and even mourning (Apol. 11,3.5 & 12,3) unworthy of God. On the view of other Apologists on this see also J. K. Mozley, *The Impassibility of God*, pp. 9-15.

23   I. M. Pfättisch, *Der Einfluß Platos auf die Theologie Justins des Märtyrers.*

24   Cf. *Dial.* 34,2 64,7; 71,2; 73,2 & 126,1f.

Logos spermatikos, (Dial. 61,1), whereby he claims that the Logos (the pre-existent Christ) was first impassible, and then became passible during the earthly life of Jesus, and again impassible after the glorification. Justin relatively differentiates his use of the concept of apatheia, which he applies to God the Father and to the pre-existent and glorified Logos.[25] Since the Logos was fully passible during the earthly life of Jesus, the divine nature of Jesus Christ was by implication also passible.

Athenagoras, who also has a Platonic influence, predicates apatheia abundantly to the Christian God. Apatheia is to him the basic divine predicate with which the difference between the Christian God and the gods of the Greek antiquity could be established.[26] The doctrine of divine suffering has little or no place in his thought. However, there are other Apologists, who, in predicating apatheia to the true God, make implicit reference to divine suffering - Tatian (*Oration ad Grecos*, 13) and Theophilus of Antioch (*Ad Autol.* 1,3.4). Basically, therefore, both Tatian and Theophilus are nearer to Justin's partial acceptance of divine suffering than to Athenagoras' outright denial of it. If through Justin the balance of the divine passibility and impassibility shifts towards the latter, it is totally lost through Athenagoras, whose thoughts exclude the divine suffering.

In the thoughts of *Melito of Sardis*, one meets yet another pronounced paradoxical expression of the axiom of divine impassibility. Not only does he predicate God with apatheia like the other Apologists, he also avoids the use of pathos while speaking about God.[27] Yet in one of his Easter sermons he speaks of the murder of God,[28] giving the impression that, though emotions and passions are unworthy of God, He experienced death nonetheless in Jesus Christ. For Melito, apatheia merely signifies the immunity from suffering or passions; accordingly, he associates pathos only with corporeality.

This narrow conception of apatheia and pathos seems to be accountable for his paradoxical interpretation of divine nature. For it is precisely because God and the pre-existent Christ are considered to be incorporeal, that he denies them the

---

25 Cf. Dial. 41,1 and 34,2. For more references see, H. Frohnhofen, *op. cit.* p. 147 f. According to Frohnhofen, it should be noted that the suffering which Justin predicates to the Logos, is not apparent, but real; like Ignatius, Justin does not say that the Logos remained impassible during the earthly life of Jesus. Again, we would not be mistaken to assume that Justin's view here anticipates the discussions of the nineteenth century kenoticists.

26 Leg. 8,2; 10,1 & 21. For details about his life and theology see L. Barnard, Athenagoras, pp. 13-18; H. Rahner, Athenagoras, p. 995; H. Frohnhofen, *op. cit.*, p. 149.

27 H. Frohnhofen, *op. cit.*, p. 151.

28 *Peri Pascha* 96

possession of passions or emotions.[29] Incarnation therefore means that the pre-existent Christ assumed flesh and with it all the bodily passions (*Peri Pascha* 66). Hence his claim that the Impassible became passible in Christ.[30] Melito tries, in this way, to work out a paradoxical distinction, not only between the divinity and humanity of Christ,[31] but also between passible and impassible states of Christ's existence. Thus it can be said of Melito's view, that although the doctrine of the two natures had not yet arrived (not until in the 5th century), his expression of the paradox of divine impassibility suggests a consequential belief in the divinity and humanity of Christ.[32]

Generally speaking, therefore, it is typical of the Apologists to use the concept of apatheia, albeit as freedom from suffering and passions, to differentiate God from the mythological gods. In the process, however, they distance themselves from the biblical image of God as much as they intensify the predication of the Christian God with the concept of apatheia.

2.2.2 The Christian Gnostics

All the leading Gnostics - *Saturinus, Carpocrates, Basilides, Valentinus* and *Marcion* - uphold the axiom of divine apatheia as a basic assumption of their doctrine of God,[33] which is invariably conceived in terms of a negative theology influenced by Middle Platonism. Understanding apatheia mainly in its narrow sense as the lack of suffering or passions, and conceiving pathos correspondingly as a characteristic feature due only to corporeal beings, the Christian Gnostics conclude that God is essentially free from all passions. The Valentinian Gnostic, Theodot, however, sees "sympathy" as the only emotion, which can be predicated of God.[34]

The approach of the Gnostics to the theological dilemma in question is two-fold: on one hand, they tend to deny the divinity of Jesus Christ; on the other, they propagate a peculiar doctrine of two Natures in Christ, which aims at sepa-

---

29 *Frgm.* XIII & XIV.

30 Cf. W. Elert, *Der Ausgang der altkirchlichen Christologie*, p. 73.

31 Cf. J. K. Mozley, *The Impassibility of God*, p. 9.

32 H. Frohnhofen, *op. cit.*, p. 154 f.

33 Cf. J. K. Mozley, *The impassibility of God*, p. 27; W. Ullmann, Die Gottesvorstellung der Gnosis, pp. 383-403, bes. 399 f; H. Frohnhofen, *op. cit.*, 160.

34 Cf. Clement of Alexandria, *Exc Theod.*, 30-31,2; see also H. Frohnhofen, *op. cit.*, pp.. 163 & 171.

rating the divine Christ from the human Jesus. These two approaches are respectively evident in the Christologies of the *Valentinians* and of *Basilides*.[35]

The Valentinians accordingly assume that the "personality" of Jesus Christ initially only consisted of his humanity, which in itself has three components: spirit, soul and body. Only later was the divine component added through the decent of the Spirit of God in form of a dove. During his earthly life, therefore, Christ suffered in soul and body; the spiritual and the divine components left him shortly before Pilate condemned him, so that his spiritual and divine constituents did not undergo suffering.[36] This view attains its clearest Docetist tendency in the thoughts of Stornil, when he claims, not only that the Saviour was unbegotten and incorporeal, but also that he did not suffer.[37] Thus, although the Valentinians consider Jesus Christ to be passible and impassible at the same time[38] - as standing essentially above his pathos[39] - they do not admit the possibility of divine pathos.

Basilides, who represents the other groups of Gnostics, says much the same thing as the Valentinians, albeit from a different starting-point. While the Valentinians make the humanity of Christ their starting-point, Basilides takes off from the divinity of Christ and contends accordingly, that God and the pre-existent Logos are pure spiritual beings, who have neither passions, nor the need for anything.[40] Making incorporeality the basis of his arguments, therefore, he claims - as is characteristic of all Gnostics - that although the pre-existent Logos assumed a body through the incarnation, he remained separated from the flesh throughout the earthly life of Jesus Christ. By virtue of this separation the divine component could always jump out before suffering.[41] Even when it does not seem proper to

---

35   Cf. H. Frohnhofen, *op. cit.*, pp. 158-172.

36   Much of this information is given by Irenaeus in his criticism of the Gnostic heresies. Cf. *Adv. haer.* I 7,2; I 8,2 and IV Praef. 2; See also Clem. Alex., *Exc. Theod.* 61,4.

37   Cf. P. Weigandt, *Der Doketismus im Urchristentum*, I 16 f. & 64 f.; H. Frohnhofen, *op. cit.*, p. 170.

38   Cf. Tertullian, *Adv. Val.* 27,2.

39   Cf. H. Frohnhofen, *op. cit.* p. 171.

40   Cf. Hippolytus, *Refutatio omnium haeresium* VII 21,1.; Irenaeus of L., *Adv. Haer.* I 24,2 f.; see also. H. Frohnhofen, *op. cit.*, p.

41   Cf. Irenaeus of L., *Adv. Haer.* I 24,4. According to Irenaeus' account, Basilides claims for instance that - in order to avoid attributing suffering to the divinity of Jesus Christ - it was Simon of Cyrene who was mistakenly crucified, because before the crucifixion, Christ exchanged bodies with him. He could change himself, Basilides maintains, because he is the incorporeal power. It is interesting to note here, that, in order to uphold Christ's im-

say that the divinity escapes before suffering, Basilides insists that suffering or passion can not be said to have touched the divinity of Christ: the suffering of Jesus only touched the human body. It is in this connection, that Irenaeus accuses the Gnostics of assuming two persons in one Jesus Christ: the one who suffered and the one who did not suffer.[42]

In summary therefore, it could be said that the Gnostics propagate a type of division between the divinity and humanity of Christ, so as not to attribute suffering or pathos to the former. By so doing however they weakened the tension of the Christological dilemma and thus left it unsolved. Besides, it is doubtful, from the point of view of their system, whether the Logos could be said to have *really* taken flesh. Nevertheless, prominent in their predication of apatheia to God is the attempt to safe-guide the transcendence of God.

2.2.3   Irenaeus of Lyon

Irenaeus of Lyon (+ 202), the great critic of the Gnostic heresy, upholds and applies the axiom of divine apatheia to his Logos-Christology in a manner different from the way the Apologists and Gnostics use it. Holding tight to the unity of the divinity and humanity in Christ, Irenaeus emphasises - in direct opposition to the Docetist tendencies in Gnosticism - the reality of the incarnation: Jesus Christ was invisible, incomprehensible and apathetic, while he was with his father, but after he had taken flesh, he became visible, comprehensible and passible.[43]

With his exceptional "power of synthesis",[44] Irenaeus evolves a paradoxical approach to the Christological dilemma, which helps him firstly defend the unity of Jesus Christ against the Gnostics, and then, his divinity against the Ebionites. In his attack on heresies, which looks like the work of an umpire guiding the game of theology to avoid extremes, Irenaeus maintains a consistent paradoxical

---

passibility, Basilides is ready to attribute mutability to him, a venture, which reveals that he places more importance on impassibility than on immutability.

[42] Cf. Irenaeus, *Adv. Haer.* III 16,9. This is perhaps a better description of Basilides' heresy than the accusation of Docetism. As Frohnhofen rightly argues, it is difficult to accuse Basilides of Docetism, because, though he claims that the spiritual one was a stranger in the body, he does not assert that the humanity of Jesus was feigned. Thus, his theory of separation differs from the docetist denial of the reality of the body of Christ.

[43] Irenaeus, *Adv. Haer.* III 16,6: "He (i.e. Christ) took up man into Himself, the invisible becoming visible, the incomprehensible being made comprehensible, the impassible becoming capable of suffering, and the Word being made man; thus summing up all things in Himself" (trans. by Pollard). Cf. also *Adv. haer.* III,18,1f. & 18.6; *Apost.* 1,6. See also H. Frohnhofen, *op. cit.* p. 176. Irenaeus' formulation of this paradox predicts the kenotic solution that will follow later.

[44] J. K. Mozley, *op. cit.*, p. 24.

view of divine attributes after the fashion of St. Ignatius.[45] As a result, he speaks freely, in the style of the Old Testament, about the "wrath of God" (*Apost.* I 17).

All in all, therefore, Irenaeus makes two significant contributions to our topic: Firstly, with a seasoned flexibility of mind, he restores the theological tension of divine impassibility and passibility, lost in the thought of the Gnostics. Secondly, he maintains the unity of Jesus Christ, that is to say, the unity of his humanity and divinity. Even without specifying the exact nature of the unity of the two natures, he has set the framework for the Christological discourse for the later centuries.

2.3   *Divine Impassibility in the Third Century Theologies*

Very significant theological developments took place in the third century, which have their origin in the late part of the second century. Schools of thought - orthodox and heretical, Latin and Greek - were sprouting like mushrooms from the ground of Christological and Trinitarian controversies. These schools primarily preoccupied themselves with the issue of the unity of the human and divine components of the God-man. Fundamentally, however, their main concern was how to safe-guide the unity and singularity of God himself, in the face of the biblical talk about the Father, the Son and the Holy Spirit. At that time, the dilemma of the divine impassibility (a basic assumption) and the suffering of Jesus Christ particularly constituted the major huddle on the way to an effective formulation of divine unity. Nothing was more decisive for the formation of the different schools of thought than the approach to this issue.

Three solutions to the dilemma of divine impassibility, or passibility characterise the theologies of that century: a) a total adoption of divine apatheia and Philo's style of reinterpretation of the biblical anthropopathetic expressions (e.g. Clement of Alexandria, and to some extent, Tertullian); b) a paradoxical predication of impassibility and passibility to God (e.g. Origen and Gregorios Thaumaturgos); c) unreserved predication of passibility to God (e.g. the Modalists and Lactantius). Thus, despite the fact that the predication of apatheia to God reached its highest point in the third century, a few bold attempts were made then to attribute suffering to God both in Christological and Trinitarian discourses.

---

[45]   Irenaeus was, according to Mozley, "the true successor to the passionate declarations of Ignatius". cf. Ibid., p. 21. And in the view of Pollard, Irenaeus Christology is "a God-man Christology in which the fullness of divinity and fullness of humanity are equally emphasised as both necessary for the reality and efficacy of revelation and redemption".

2.3.1 The Modalists and the Heresy of Patripassianism

The Modalists, like the Docetists, have basically the same concern, namely, that of establishing the unity of the Godhead and of guaranteeing the full divinity of Jesus Christ. But while it is characteristic of the latter to achieve this aim by claiming that Jesus' humanity was feigned, the Modalists try to attain their goal by ignoring the difference between the Father and the Son and by recognising only a nominal difference between the Father and the Son.[46] Thus, for the Modalists, the earthly life of Jesus is seen as an "existence form" (modus) of the Father. It amounts to, as Hans Küng rightly puts it, "a transitory theophany of divinity in which the Father himself appears in the figure of the Son".[47]

Noetus, the greatest proponent of Modalistic Monarchianism, is reported to have said that "the Father and the Son so-called are one and the same" and that "the Father was born and suffered".[48] This aspect of his thought is echoed further by his contemporary *Praxea*, of whom Tertullian says that he "crucified the Father",[49] and for whom he coined the term "Patripassianism". The heresy of Patripassianism (the suffering of the Father on the cross) thus represents the earliest and most crude form of Modalism, which of it self does not make any philosophical claims. The Praxean Modalism is known to have been conceived in terms of the history of salvation rather than in terms of any philosophical requirement.[50] Modalism however assumes a philosophical image in Sabellianism, as Sabellius employs philosophical arguments to assert that the same God reveals Himself in different masks (*prósopa*): the Father suffered in the mask of the Son.[51]

The belief that God can enter into the finite order and freely subject Himself to the norms of this order for the purpose of salvation is nonetheless characteristic of all forms of Modalisms.[52] It is claimed generally that God can suffer, but only out of His own initiative; He retains His sovereignty over pathos. This fact is evident in the thought of Noetus as Hippolytus reports:

---

46 Cf. W. Beinert, *Dogmatik Studieren*, pp. 62-65.

47 H. Küng, *The Incarnation of God*, p. 512.

48 Hippolytus, *Philosoph.* IX. 10. cited in: J. K. Mozley, *op. cit.*, p. 29.

49 Cf. Tertullian, *Adv. Prax.* I. According to Tertullian, the Modalists must have been influenced in this point by the Valentinian school, which, as we saw above, propagates the other extreme, namely that the pre-existing Logos was not the same as the incarnate Jesus.

50 Harnack, *Hist. Dogm.* III, p. 64. See also J. K. Mozley, *op. cit.*, p. 29.

51 Cf. W. Breuning, *Trinitarische Irrlehren*, p. 523. W. Kasper, *Jesus der Christus*, p. 208

52 J. K. Mozley, *op. cit.*, pp. 30-36.

The Father and God of the universals is passionless and immortal when He does not suffer and die, but when (the) Passion comes, He suffers and dies. (He) died and did not die.[53]

Apparently, this passage suggests a paradoxical approach of a Modalist toward the issue of divine passibility and impassibility. It is however not likely that Noetus seriously pursues the attainment of a synthesis between the two attributes in his theology. For, given the Modalistic doctrine of "a transitory theophany of divinity" in Jesus Christ, one rather gets the impression that God only passed by in the finite and retired once more to His impassive divinity. Thus while the divine impassibility is a matter of fact, it is doubtful whether suffering touched the depth of the divinity during His transitory theophany. Similarly, the transitoriness of God's involvement in the world, makes the Modalist belief in the Incarnation of God seem real.[54]

2.3.2   The Latin Fathers: Tertullian and Lactantius

Tertullian and Lactantius represent the two different approaches of the Latin Fathers to the dilemma of divine attributes. For *Tertullian*, God is intrinsically immutable[55] and impassible. To that effect, he argues that the biblical assertions of the repentance, anger and compassion of God should not be taken at their face values.[56] If at all God can be angry, His anger cannot be said to affect Him, His intrinsic immutability would not allow it constitute a danger for Him.[57] In this way Tertullian pushes the claim to divine apatheia to a level unknown to his predecessors; for not only does he consider all negative feelings unworthy of God, he also refuses - like nobody before him - to attribute sympathy or compassion to God. Rejecting the Patripassianism of the Modalist Monarchianism - i.e. the claim that the Father suffered with the Son *in sympathy* (*compassio*) - Tertullian contends:

The Father did not suffer with the Son. ... if He can suffer with another, then He is passible. ... But the Father is as unable to suffer with another as the Son is unable

---

53   Hippolytus, *Philosoph*, X, 27.

54   *H. Küng, The Incarnation of God*, p. 513. The absolutely transcendent God of the Modalists "is capable only of a purely external incident of 'appearing', which in any case does not mean that God really *became* man".

55   Tertullian, *Adv. Herm.* 39,1; *Adv. Prax.*, 27,6.

56   Tertullian, *Adv. Prax.*, 16,4. See also H. Frohnhofen, *op. cit.*, p. 224

57   Tertullian, *Adv. Marc.*, 16,7.

to suffer in virtue of His divinity....He (God) does not suffer but gives the power to suffer.[58]

Thus for Tertullian, neither the Father nor the divine nature in Jesus Christ suffered; only the human nature suffered in Christ.[59]

Standing firm in the Stoic tradition and conceiving apatheia basically as lack of suffering or passionlessness, Tertullian sees apathy as being characteristic of divine nature. Surprisingly, he uses Jesus' cry of abandonment on the Cross (Mt. 27:46) to illustrate the claim for divine apathy: God did not heed Jesus' cry, he maintains, so as to demonstrate his apatheia.[60] Similarly, he sees apatheia also as an ideal for human beings, which awaits them after the resurrection, when they must have been permeated by God.[61]

It should be noted however, that Tertullian's claims were motivated basically by the need to safe-guide divine transcendence against the Modalist tendency to reduce God to the level of the Homeric gods. Be that as it may, it has the weakness of making God's contact with the world seem unreal. However, confronting Marcion,[62] who claimed that the good God could not act as judge, it became necessary for Tertullian, to assert the reality of God's contact with the world: if God judges, His contact with the world must be presupposed. Thus in his dispute against Marcion, he tries to guarantee a natural divine tendency to care for the world, without negating divine impassibility. He admits here that feeling is possible in God and accepts by that means what he rejects in his controversy with the Modalists.[63] This should however be seen as a sign of inconsistency rather than as an acceptance of a paradoxical synthesis in the nature of God.

Writing much later than Tertullian, *Lactantius* approaches our topic of discussion differently. Like the latter, though much more in tune with his teacher Arnobius, he emphasises God's impassibility, transcendence, and freedom from external constraint. But unlike Tertullian, he strictly rejects the Platonic-Stoic conception of God, whereby immutability meant passionlessness. The true God, he contends, is not the immutable being of the philosophers.[64] For Lactantius, passions

---

58 Tertullian, *Adv. Prax.*, 29, 5.

59 Tertullian, *Adv. Marc.*, II,16

60 Tertullian, *Adv. Prax.*, 30, 2.

61 Cf. Tertullian, res. mort., 57,13 cited in H. Frohnhofen, *op. cit.* p. 224.

62 Tertullian, *Adv. Marc.*, II 16.

63 J. K. Mozley, *op. cit.*, p. 36 f.: According to Mozley, Tertullian's own "Trinitarian doctrine allows, as the Modalist doctrine did not, for the introduction of a certain natural orientation towards finitude and passibility into the Godhead".

64 Lactantius, *De ira Dei*, 2. Cf. Kuitert, *op. cit.*, p. 77.

and feelings are not incompatible with the perfection of God. He tries accordingly in the *De Ira Dei*,[65] (to an extent unknown to his predecessors), to give emotion a place in the nature of God.[66]

He distinguishes in the first place between just and unjust anger: Anger is justified when it is directed against moral misconduct. In terms of this classification, God's anger is just, and worthy of Him, since it is "the movement" of His mind "as it rises up to check sins".[67] Divine anger does not however interfere with God's freedom, "He is not ruled by it, but Himself restrains it just as He pleases".[68] This view of divine anger definitely tends to strike a balance between divine perfection and emotion. It constitutes a radically new approach to the problem, which anticipates the interpretation of divine anger as an expression of love. In this way, Lactantius tries to preserve the biblical paradoxical view of divine attributes, notwithstanding his Greek influence.

2.3.3 The Alexandrian Theologians: Clement, Origen and Gregorios Thaumaturgos

In the Alexandrian theologies, the concept of apatheia is highly internalised in the Christian doctrine of God. The use of the term "apatheia" is a abundant as the Greek thought-pattern is dominant. Yet, with more or less varied points of departure,[69] the Alexandrians arrive at different conclusions with regard to the issue of divine impassibility. While Clement denies the possibility of divine suffering, Origen speaks paradoxically about God's suffering love. With his unconventional formulation of the "suffering of love", Origen provides the ambient for a systematic discussion of this paradox. Influenced by Origen therefore, Gregorios Thaumaturgos wrote the first monograph on the paradox of divine passibility and impassibility. In general terms, however, all the Alexandrian theologians work toward the harmonisation of the philosophical and scriptural truths about God: with more or less success, this aim is pursued both in their apologies to the pagans and in their biblical expositions for the Christians.[70]

---

65 This is the first monograph we know on the issue of divine anger

66 If we should see this as a surprising departure from the Greek tradition, one is reminded by Pohlenz that Lactantius' primary sources were not the Greek philosophers and theologians, but Cicero, Seneca and Lucrez. Cf. *Vom Zorne Gottes*, p. 50

67 Lactantius, *De ira Dei*, 17.

68 *Ibid.*, p. 21.

69 Cf. H. Frohnhofen, *op. cit.*, p. 179. Clement made more use of the Stoic ethical conception of apatheia than Origen.

70 Cf. J. Pelikan, *The Christian Tradition*, p.55.

For *Clement of Alexandria*, divine impassibility denotes the freedom of God from all emotions and the denial of God's relationship with the world except "one of transcendent causality".[71] Valuing the Stoic notion of apatheia much more than any theologian before him, Clement gives it a prominent place in his theology,[72] especially in his doctrine of God.[73] And because he conceives impassibility as being identical to perfection, he contends that human beings, who are by nature imperfect, cannot be impassible; thus, "it is impossible and impracticable that anyone should be as perfect as God."[74]

For Clement, God's absolute apatheia[75] is as obvious as the difference between the divine and human modes of perfection. Consequently, he opts for the use of Philo's allegorical method of interpretation in purging the Bible of all the anthropopathetic expressions.[76] Clement's God is "without passion, without anger, without desire";[77] the only emotion He could logically have is compassion (sympathy or mercy).[78] Even Jesus Christ, the Son of God, is believed to not have really suffered any emotion, not even hunger. Naturally, one would have expected that by becoming flesh, the Logos also made Himself subject to passion. However, according to Clement, He never suffered, because He trained the flesh "to habitual impassibility".[79] Despite Clement's attack on Docetism, therefore, his views are ironically Docetist: For although he speaks of Christ who suffered for us,[80] he does not believe that Christ suffered in reality. His views on the notion of divine impassibility are undoubtedly inconsistent.[81]

---

71 Cf. *J. K. Mozley, op. cit.*, p.53.

72 H. Frohnhofen, *op. cit.*, p. 180.

73 Clement of Alexandria, *Stromateis*, vii, 67, 8. Unlike the Stoics, he pays more attention to the divine than to human apatheia.

74 *Ibid.*, vii, 88, 5-6

75 Cf. R. M. Grant, *The Early Christian Doctrine of God*, p.113.

76 Clement of Alexandria, *Stromateis*, v.

77 *Ibid.*, iv, 23

78 *Ibid.*, II 72,1,2,3,4. His departure from the Stoic concept of pathos is evident here. See also, H. Frohnhofen, *op. cit.*, p. 187.

79 *Ibid.*, vii, 7, 2. Here, one cannot avoid getting the impression, that Clement doubts the humanity of Jesus Christ. On this see also H. Frohnhofen, *op. cit.*, p. 191.

80 Stromateis, vi, 8.; cf. Mozley, *op. cit.*, p. 58;

81 Cf. Clement, *Paedagogus*, 1.8.62f. (GCS 1,126f.); 2.3.38 1 (GCS 1, 179); and *Protrepticus*, 4.53; 10.84. These passages contain contradictory views on divine passibility and impassibility. On Clement's inconsistencies see E. F. Osborn, *The Philosophy of Clement of*

Origen, like Clement his teacher, makes the axiom of divine apatheia the background of his doctrine of God. More than the latter, however, he pays special attention to the Bible, which he seeks to interpret with the aid of the language and principles of philosophy. Hence, adopting Philo's allegorical method,[82] he contends that the biblical accounts of God's anger, repentance and jealousy are to be judged like other utterances about His sleep and bodily activities: they should not be understood literally,[83] but "in a way that is worthy of God";[84] God's anger does not constitute "an emotional reaction", he uses it consciously only for pedagogical purposes.[85] "God does not suffer, He is immutable."[86]

Such unequivocal statements about divine impassibility are not characteristic of all his writings. In his later writings, especially in his homilies, Origen changed his mind and speaks about divine suffering,[87] affirming, not only that the Logos suffered in Jesus Christ,[88] but also that the Father suffered with the Son:

> He descended to earth in pity for the human race, He suffered our sufferings, before He suffered the Cross and thought it right to take upon Him our flesh. For if He had not suffered, He would not have come to take part in human life. First did He suffer, then He descended and was seen. What is that passion which He suffered for us? Love is passion. The Father Himself, the God of all things, (who is) long-suffering and very pitiful and compassionate, does not He in some way suffer? Can you be ignorant of this, that when He deals with human things He suffers a human passion? 'For the Lord thy God endured thy ways as if a man should endure his son.' Therefore God endures our ways inasmuch as the Son of God bears our sufferings. The Father Himself is not impassible. If He is besought, He is pitiful and compassionate, He suffers something of love, and in those things in which, because

---

Alexandria, p. 8; J. Hallman, Divine Suffering and Change in Origen and Ad Theopompum, p. 87.

[82] Cf. Kuitert, *Op. cit.* p. 61f.

[83] Origen, *Contra Celsum*, vi, 61ff.

[84] Origen, *De Principiis*, 2.4.4 (5,132)

[85] Origen, *Contra Celsum*, iv, 72.

[86] Origen, *Frag.* in Joh. 51 (4,526)

[87] For a detailed discussion see Mozley, op. cit., pp. 60-61; J. Hallman, Divine Suffering and Change, pp. 91-94; R. M. Grant, *The Early Doctrine of God*, pp. 30-31; H. Frohnhofen, *op. cit.*, pp. 192-212.

[88] Origen, *Contra Celsum*, ii, 24: "just as he (the Logos) *intentionally* assumed a body whose nature was not at all different from human flesh, so he assumed with the body also its pains and griefs". (trans. by Chadwick 407)

of the greatness of His nature, He cannot subsist He shares, and because of us He endures human sufferings. [89]

It is hard to reconcile Origen's Hellenistic philosophical way of thinking with his extreme view on divine suffering, which does not only negate his own claim that God is impassible and immutable, but also justifies the heresy of Patripassianism. How can one understand Origen's contradictory passages? Is it an irony or a shift toward a paradoxical way of thinking?

Theologians have interpreted Origen's double-talk about the passibility and impassibility of God differently. According to Pohlenz, the reference to divine suffering here should be interpreted after the manner in which Origen interprets the anthropomorphic languages in the Bible, that is to say, allegorically: In this sense, Origen's affirmation of divine suffering is believed to denote a sort of device for effective proclamation.[90] While this view could be sufficiently supported with Origen's own differentiation between pedagogical language and language of fact,[91] it is scarcely plausible that his talk about the suffering of the Father and the "suffering of love" are not meant to be taken literally.

In contrast, Robert Grant, argues that we are confronted here with Origen's change of mind about the impassibility of God. Believing that Origen speaks only about divine suffering in his later writings, and about divine apatheia in his earlier work, Grant contends that Origen changed his mind about the Greek concept of apatheia after coming into contact with the writings of Ignatius, who, as we had shown above, makes frequent references to the "passion of God".[92] Grant's suggestion has however been proved false by the fact that some of Origen's texts speaking about divine suffering are actually of later origin: there is indeed no chronological order in the way he uses the respective predications.

A third explanation seems to be more tenable today, namely, that Origen is conscious of the paradox of divine attributes. Arguing in this line, Henri Crouzel insists that Origen is already aware of the "mysterious" paradox of passibility and impassibility in God.[93] And according to Frohnhofen, Origen's unconventional talk about the "suffering of love" indicates an attempt to formulate the paradox of

---

89 Origen, *Homily on Ezechiel*, vi, 6. There are of course other examples. See also J. Hallman, *ibid.*

90 Pohlenz, *Vom Zorne*, p. 36

91 Cf. Origen, *Homily on Jer.* 16,6; *Contra Cels.* IV 71; *Commentary on Mt.* 17, 6.

92 R. Grant, *The Early Christian Doctrine of God*, p.31; See also *W. Maas, Unveränderlichkeit Gottes*, p. 138.

93 Henri Crouzel, Origène et la "connaissance mystique", p. 261.

divine nature, which he however leaves unexplained.[94] Similarly, J. Hallman maintains that Origen is working toward a paradoxical synthesis of divine nature, which, though he could not achieve, is passed on to his pupil, Gregorios Thaumaturgos, whose thought marks the climax of "the Greek patristic theology of God".[95]

The earliest and most solid document dealing solely with the issue of divine passibility and impassibility - in the Alexandrian theology of the third century[96] - was written, apparently, by *Gregorios Thaumaturgos*.[97] and addressed to a certain Theopompus. Right from the beginning of the document,[98] Gregorios' arguments are conditioned by three basic assumptions: a) that God is impassible (immutable); b) that his freedom is non-negotiable and c) that He became man in Jesus Christ.

The novelty in Gregorios' philosophical dialogue on the issue of divine impassibility is his emphasis on divine freedom. Like no theologian before him, he recognises the difficulty involved in reconciling divine impassibility and freedom. Gregorios lets Theopompus express the dilemma this way: if by nature God is impassible, it would imply that He is *not free* to suffer (chap. 1). If He is not free to suffer, when He wills so, it would then mean that His will is subjected to His nature (chap. 2). Not willing to compromise God's freedom and will in any way, Gregorios admits (in chaps. 2-4) that God's freedom and will are sovereign to His nature. With the same strength, however, he denies that God's nature could be at variance with His will. For it is precisely the unity of divine essence and will that constitutes the point of difference between God and humankind.

---

94 H. Frohnhofen, *Apatheia tou theou*, pp. 205-206.

95 J. Hallman, Divine Suffering and Change, p.94.

96 The original Greek text of this monograph got lost before it caught the attention of theologians. The Syriac translation, the oldest text, is still available. See G. Thaumaturgos, Ad Theopompum, De passibili et impassibli in Deo, in: J. B. Pitra, *Analecta Sacra Patrum Antenicaenorum* IV (Paris 1883) pp. 363-376 for the Latin translation, and pp. 103-120, for the Syriac translation. See also the German version in: V. Ryssel, *Gregorius Thaumaturgus*, pp. 46-99.

97 His authorship is a matter of conjecture. While theologians - like V. Ryssel, *ibid.*, pp. 118-124; H. Crouzel, La Passion de L'Impassible, pp. 269-279 - credit the document to Gregory, Origen's pupil, others - like L. Abramowski, Die Schrift Gregor des Lehrers, pp. 277-290 and A. Grillmeier, *Jesus der Christus im Glauben der Kirche*, Bd.1, p. 299, Anm. 46 - vehemently deny Gregory's authorship.

98 Written in form of a dialogue between Gregorios and Theopompum, the text moves from simple assumptions to very complex and systematic arguments designed to unravel the philosophical problems surrounding the axiom of divine impassibility.

Whereas human will and nature conflict whenever their needs vary, the will of God is ever united with His nature (Chap. 4).

Accordingly, God's nature does not hinder His will, neither does His freedom of will lead Him to activities that are at variance with His nature. Applying this view to the divine event in Jesus Christ, Gregorios claims, that God can get involved in suffering without really suffering - He suffers impassibly and triumphantly. In making this point, he does not intend to imply any mystification of the paradox; he makes his claim based on a reinterpreted concept of "suffering": suffering is no longer every negative feeling that affects the inner disposition of the personal agent, but only such feelings that are purposeless and against the will of the suffering subject. If and when the subject wills it for some higher purpose, it cannot be called suffering.

> Suffering then is truly suffering when God plans anything useless and of no advantage to Himself. But when the divine will is aroused with a view to the healing of the wicked thoughts of men, then we do not think of suffering as involved for God in the fact that of His supreme humility and kindness He becomes the servant of men... In God those are not to be accounted as sufferings which of His own will were borne by Him for the common good of the human race, with no resistance from His most blessed and impassible nature. For in His suffering He shows His impassibility. For he who suffers, suffers, when the violence of suffering brings pressure to bear on him who suffers contrary to his will. But of him who, while his nature remains impassible, is of his own will immersed in sufferings that he may overcome them, we do not say that he becomes subject to suffering, even though, of his own will, he has shared in sufferings.[99]

Hence holding firm to the axiom of divine impassibility, Gregorios contends that God participates in suffering but suffering does not affect Him. In this manner, God frustrates suffering and causes it to suffer. Gregorios thus calls divine impassibility the "suffering of the sufferings" (Chap. 10) and the "death of death" (Chap. 8). In an analogy of fire and diamond, he describes the relation of divine suffering to eternal impassibility this way: Just as the substance of fire remains the same when cut by a sword (Chap. 15), and the value of diamond is not reduced when cut to pieces (Chap. 8), so does the impassibility of God remain constant when he goes through suffering.

In these series of arguments, one can see Gregorios' effort to account for the paradox of divine passibility. His arduous attempt fails, nevertheless, at least by implication, to take the suffering of God seriously. His arguments are weak.[100] But by introducing such topics like divine will, freedom and self-limitation into

---

[99] Gregorius Thaumaturgus, *Ad Theopompum*, 6-7

[100] Despite some traces of docetist tendencies, he has tried to hold together the humanity and divinity of Christ. Cf. H. Frohnhofen, *op. cit.* pp. 219-220.

our topic of discussion,[101] and by differentiating between divine and human suffering, Gregorios contributes immensely toward a fruitful analysis of the paradox of divine nature.[102]

2.4   Divine Impassibility in the Fourth and Fifth Centuries

The issue of determining the union of the divine and human natures in Christ dominates the Christological controversies of the fourth and fifth centuries. Most Christological solutions of that time tend toward one extreme or the other, creating what one might call the right and left wing theologies. While the former overemphasises the divinity of Christ, to the extent of denying his humanity, the latter carries the defence of the real humanity of Christ too far, to the extent that the divine relevance of his activities becomes uncertain.[103] Between the two heretic wings of theology, is the orthodoxy, seeking, from council to council, for precise descriptions of the paradoxical mystery of the human and the divine natures in Christ.

In the theologies of this period, the mystery of the unity of the divine and human natures in Christ is defined in the context of the Logos Christology,[104] and indeed in two forms: *Logos-sarx* and *Logos-anthropos* Christologies. The Logos-sarx Christology constitutes the attempt made in both the heretic and orthodox Christologies to conceive the divine-human unity in Christ in the form of the Logos

---

[101] The emphasis laid on divine freedom is particularly fruitful. According to J. K. Mozley, "Gregory makes what is, in effect, the valuable suggestion that we must not sacrifice the idea of God's moral action and of the love from which His energy proceeds to a supposed necessity for maintaining a metaphysical conception of the quiescence of the divine life." *op. cit.* p. 71.

[102] Cf. J. Hallman, Divine Suffering and Change, p. 97: "The importance of Gregory's treatise does not lie in the success of its argumentation but in the direction which it suggests".

[103] The right wing Christologies would include Apollinarism (the claim that the Logos assumed merely the body and the soul of a man, but without the main human factor - the spirit) and Monophysitism (the claim that the divine nature absorbs the human nature in Christ, thereby recognising only one nature - the divine). Both theologies follow the foot steps of Docetism and Modalism. The left wing theologies are Arianism (the claim that the Logos was created by the Father) and Nestorianism (which denies the unity of the two natures and assumes two separate subjects in Jesus Christ). Both theologies have affinity to Ebionitism (which recognises Jesus only as a Messiah, but not as God) and adoptionism.

[104] Influenced by Philo's doctrine of the Logos - which was indeed a blending of the Old Testament, Middle-Platonic and Stoic ideas - some Church fathers, particularly, Irenaeus, Clement of Alexandria and Origen propose a type of Logos Christology. Its implication became evident only later during the Arian controversy. Cf. L. J. Richard, *A kenotic Christology*, p. 136 ff.

getting united only to the flesh, but not to the whole individual. The Logos practically replaces the human spirit-soul in Jesus Christ. This approach characterises the Christology of the Alexandrian school, but it equally forms the background of Arianism and Apollinarism. It is expressed differently, depending on the understanding of the term sarx (flesh).[105] One extreme form of Logos-sarx Christology limits the divinity of the Logos and makes it replace the human soul in Jesus Christ (Arius); another extreme makes the humanity of Christ incomplete in the attempt to secure his divinity. Athanasius and Cyril of Alexandria, who maintain the consubstantiality of the Logos, tend toward a more workable unity, that fully recognises the divinity and humanity of Christ. In all, however, the Logos-sarx Christology is invariably exposed to the danger of the Docetist tendency.

On the other hand, the Logos-anthropos Christology emerged later to correct the fractionalism of the Logos-sarx Christology. According to this Christology, the Logos got united with the whole of a human being with body and soul. The problem with this Christology is that it fails to arrive at a convincing conception of the unity of the two Natures. This is the case with the Antiochian Christology.

For all schools and Christologies of this time, however, the impassibility of God is a basic assumption. Not even the left wing "heretics", who tend to overemphasise the humanity of Christ, doubt the validity of divine impassibility.[106] In fact, if the left and right wing theologians have anything in common with their opponents on the side of orthodoxy, it is the assumption that the Godhead cannot suffer. The passibility of God is practically and almost unanimously denied both by the heretics and orthodox theologians in the fourth and fifth centuries. Whether one turns to the Christology of the Antiochian school - with emphasis on the distinction between the divinity and humanity in Christ - or to the Christology of the Alexandrian school - with emphasis on the union of the two natures (e.g. the hypostatic union of Cyril of Alexandria) - the tendency to defend the impassibility of God is evident.[107]

---

[105] Cf. W. Kasper, *Jesus der Christus*, pp. 247-250. According to Kasper, the basis for the various forms of the Logos-sarx-pattern is to be found in the difference between the biblical and Hellenistic understanding of the term. While for the biblical writers, sarx (flesh) stands for the whole corporal individual, for the Greeks it stands only for the body as differentiated from the soul and spirit (248). Therefore, those who use it in the Hellenistic sense are prone to conceiving the unity of Christ mechanically.

[106] This fact becomes more evident, when one bears in mind that the implicit or explicit denial of Incarnation is characteristic of both right and left wing heretics. Cf. H. Küng, *The Incarnation of God*, pp. 512-515.

[107] In both cases passibility is invariably confined to the human nature of Christ. According to Küng, theologians inclined towards the Alexandrian course "toned down the suffering of body and soul in Christ to such an extent that it could no longer 'endanger' the divinity and impassibility of the Logos". Cf. *Ibid.*, p. 521. And as F. Young writes, the emphasis the

Generally speaking, therefore, despite serious attempts, especially on the part of orthodoxy to maintain the paradoxical tension of the God-man union in Christ, one-sided solutions are predominant in the theologies of this period. In fact, R. S. Franks identifies "an incorrigible tendency to Docetism", not only among heretics but also within the rank and file of orthodox writers.[108] And it must be noted that Docetist tendencies are mostly unintended; when they occur, they invariably represent the attempt to preserve the axiom of divine impassibility. This fact can be largely observed in the letters of Cyril of Alexandria and in the work of the Latin theologian, Hillary of Poitiers.[109]

2.4.1 The Arian Controversy and the Issue of Divine Impassibility

The main thesis of *Arianism* - as is presented by Arius (260-336) - is that the Logos was created. God, he argues, cannot become flesh; and since the Logos became flesh, he cannot be consubstantial with the Father. It is Arius' belief in the absolute uniqueness and transcendence of God that leads him to deny the equality of the Logos with God the Father. The dilemma of the Arians, as Eunomius, their most literal representative, puts it, is how to insist that the Son was created or generated without suggesting that God possesses passion. Eunomius himself recognises this problem,[110] but nevertheless he affirms the passionlessness of God.

Despite the tendency to deny the divinity of the Logos, the Arians do not, at least not intentionally, compromise the axiom of divine impassibility; for in their attribution of passibility and mutability to the "created" Logos, they refer only to the human, but not to the divine nature of Christ. Yet, it is in opposition to Arianism that subsequent Christologies - especially that of Athanasius and the three Cappadocians - get to emphasise the impassibility of God.

2.4.1.1 The Alexandrian Theologians and the Impassibility of God

This is particularly true of *Athanasius*, who, in opposition to Arius affirms, not only the consubstantiality of the Logos with the eternal Father, but also the immu-

---

Antiochian theologians laid on Christ's full humanity "was a device to protect his full, changeless and passionless divinity". See F. Young, Antiochian Theology, p. 28.

[108] R. S. Franks, Passibility and Impassibility, p. 659.

[109] Hillary of Poitiers, *De Trinitate*, x, 23.

[110] Greg. of Nyssa, *Adv. Eunom*, iv, 4. (Engl. transl. in: Nicene and Post-Nicene Fathers,. vol. v, Gregory of Nyssa). In actual fact, the "created" Son could not be said to be impassible. Cf. J. K. Mozley, *op. cit.* p. 77 ff; Eunomius, Arius' Letter to Alexander, in: *The Trinitarian Controversy*, ed. and trans. by William G. Rusch (Philadelphia: Fortress Press, 1980) p. 31.

tability of the Logos.[111] The Son is also immutable, he argues, since he is of the same substance as the Father. But much as he criticises the Arian denial of the divinity of Christ, Athanasius continues to think the unity of the Natures in Christ in terms of the Logos-sarx-model, according to which the Logos became flesh merely as a "garment" and remained untouched by the exigencies of the body.[112] Hence his argument that although the Logos put on human flesh, the affections of the body "did not touch Him according to His Godhead".[113] Accordingly, the human nature of Christ suffered, but his divine nature remained impassible.

Likewise, the Cappadocian theologians attack Arianism vehemently, and argue much, though differently, for a type of unity in Christ, which does not dilute the fullness of his divinity. The type of unity which they envisage in Christ is however mechanical, that is to say, understood as the mixture of two entities, which lack mutual penetration;[114] the divine nature is made in that case to seem detachable from the human nature. Accordingly, *Gregory of Nazianzus* (329/30-390), contends that Christ is "passible in His flesh, impassible in His Godhead".[115] For *Gregory of Nyssa* (334-394), the Son, in his nature, is "certainly impassible and incapable of corruption: and whatever suffering is asserted concerning Him in the Gospel, He assuredly wrought by means of His human nature which admitted of such suffering".[116] *St. Basil* (330-379) argues likewise, that there is no suffering in the Godhead itself; the subject of the *pathe* is either the flesh or just the soul.[117] Thus, despite their numerous references to the suffering of the Logos and to *communicatio idiomatum* (communion of properties), the Cappadocians do not subscribe to the suffering of God; only the human nature of Christ is believed to have suffered.

Apollinaris of Laodicea (+ 385), using the Logos-sarx model, arrives at yet another view as extreme as Arius'. Whereas Arius denies the full divinity of the Logos, Appolinaris doubts the full humanity of Jesus Christ. Concerned as others with the issue of the unity of natures in Jesus Christ, he seeks to interpret the unification of the Logos with the flesh, not by stripping Jesus of his divinity as Arius

---

111 Athanasius, *Discourse against the Arians*, III, 4 taken from Lucien J. Richard, *A kenotic Christology*. p. 139.

112 Cf. W. Pannenberg, *Jesus - God and Man*, p. 289.

113 Athanasius, *Discourse against the Arians*, III, 32. See also *De Incarnatione*.

114 Cf. A. Grillmeier, *Christ in Christian Tradition*, , p. 280. Their conception of the unity of Christ is believed to have been influenced by the philosophy of the Stoics.

115 cited in J. K. Mozley, *op. cit.*, p. 87.

116 Gregory of Nyssa, adv. Eunom, iv, 1.

117 Cf. A. Grillmeier, *Christ in Christian Tradition*, p. 280

does, but by deifying the sarx.[118] He does this by assuming that in Jesus Christ the divine Logos replaced the human mind.[119]

The implication of his thought is the denial of the full humanity of Jesus Christ. It is definitely his concern to secure the impassibility of the Logos that makes him think that the Logos did not assume the body, but merely displaced the soul. In his *Contra Diodorum*, Apollinaris tries to use the principle of *kenosis* for the interpretation of the unity of the Logos with flesh. Incarnation, he argues, "is self-emptying", which occurred "by way of limitation, not change".[120] However, in the context of his fractional anthropology and mechanical Christology, which complicate rather than explicate the matter, his application of kenosis fails to achieve the desired paradoxical unity in Christ. Apollinarism was consequently rejected in the subsequent synods and councils.[121]

Neither the Arian nor the Apollinarian Logos-sarx-model succeeds in forging an acceptable unity of God and humankind in Jesus Christ. Consequently, *Cyril of Alexandria* (c. 380-440) picks up the Logos-sarx-model once more to develop it further, following the foot-steps of Athanasius. Getting beyond Athanasius and distancing himself from Apollinarist's conclusions, however he avoids a direct connection of the Logos with sarx, and instead initiates the method of looking "for the unity and the distinction in Christ on different levels, the unity on the level of the prosopon and the distinction on the level of the natures".[122]

Cyril, particularly the "later" Cyril, locates the source of the *natural* life of the incarnate Christ, not in the Logos *qua* Logos, but in the soul.[123] In this way, he can afford to argue in the context of an updated Logos-sarx Christology that "God the Logos did not come into a man, but he 'truly' became man, while remaining God".[124] Accordingly, the Logos inhered in Jesus as the supernatural entity, who remained untouched by the neediness of the soul or body. For,

---

[118] W. Pannenberg, *Jesus - God and Man*, p. 288.

[119] G. Newlands, Christology, p. 103.

[120] Cited in C. E. Raven, Apollinarism,, p. 203. See also D. G. Dawe, *The Form Of A Servant*, p. 60.

[121] In the Synod of Alexandria under the leadership of Athanasius (362), in the First General Council of Constantinople (381) and in the Council of Rome (382). Cf. DS 159 or J. Neuner and J. Dupuis, (eds.) *The Christian Faith in the Doctrinal Documents of the Catholic Church*, Nr 603/7. (This shall be designated as ND in subsequent quotations); W. Kasper, *op. cit.* p. 249.

[122] A. Grillmeier, *Christ in Christian Tradition*, p.364.

[123] *Ibid.*, p.404.

[124] Cyril of Alexandria, *Or. ad Dominas* 31, cited in *ibid.*, p.405

...when we say he suffered and rose again", we do not mean, "that God the Word suffered blows, nail-piercings or other wounds in his own nature (the divine is impassible because it is incorporeal) but what is said is that since his own created body suffered these things he himself 'suffered' for our sake, the point being that within the suffering body was the Impassible".[125]

It is thus obvious from this passage that Cyril does not admit the suffering of the Logos and that his version of the Logos-sarx Christology does not get very far beyond the contribution of Athanasius. Despite its reinterpretation, his Logos-sarx Christology does not maintain the Christological paradox. This is further demonstrated in the last of his twelve Anathamatismen against Nestorius (DS 263).[126]

2.4.1.2   The Antiochian Theologians and the Impassibility of God

The Antiochian Christology is basically composed in opposition to the one-sided interpretation of the Person of Christ in the Alexandrian Logos-sarx Christology. Against Arianism and Apollinarism, as well as against Athanasius, *Theodor of Mopsuestia* and his pupil *Nestorius* (ob. c. 450) argue that the unity of Christ was not merely the unity of Logos-*sarx* but Logos-*anthropos*. According to this Logos-anthropos Christology, the Logos was united an entire human being with body and soul.[127]

At the initial stage, the Logos-man formula of two complete natures seems to triumph over the fractional and Docetist tendency of the Logos-sarx Christology. But although this Antiochian Christology recognises the full divinity and humanity of Christ, it does not present a convincing argument as to what the unity of God and man in the person of Christ looks like.[128] The affirmation of the fullness of the two natures in Christ is pressed to a point where two subjects, each exercising a different power, are conceived in Christ. The logical consequence of this model, especially as it occurs in Nestorianism, is the affirmation of two persons in Christ, and the visualisation of an accidental union between persons.

---

[125] Cyril of Alexandria's second letter to Nestorius, in: *Cyril of Alexandria, Select Letters*, ed. and transl. by Lionel R. Wickham, Oxford, 1983, p. 7.

[126] "If anyone does not confess that the Word of God suffered in the flesh and was crucified in the flesh and tasted death in the flesh..." let him be anathema (DS, 263: ND 606/12). His Logos-sarx-formula is evident here through the emphasis on flesh.

[127] Theodore Mopsuestia, *Homil. catech.* V, 11: "Thus Christ must assume not only a body, but a soul as well; the soul had to be assumed first, and then for its sake the body." Taken from Grillmeier, *Chalcedon, vol. 1*, p. 147.

[128] Cf. W. Pannenberg, *Jesus - God And Man*, p. 289: "The Antiochian Theologians left unexplained how man and God could be united in the one person of Jesus".

Although, a proper union of the divinity and humanity of Jesus Christ does not seem attainable in the context of a Logos-anthropos,[129] it does indeed formulate the paradox of divine suffering in Jesus Christ. Nestorius declares accordingly, that "the son of God suffered and suffered not... He suffered all human things in the humanity and all divine things in the Divinity" (Liber Heraclidis).[130] In its own terms, this passage suggests that Nestorius has a vision of the paradox of divine nature. But it is difficult to see how such a paradox can be achieved from the perspective of the Antiochian position, which maintains that the Logos assumed a complete individual person. The absence of a paradoxical unity becomes obvious as one looks at Nestorius' claim that Mary should be known as "Christotokos, mother of God, not as Theotokos, mother of God".[131] His objection to "God-bearer" is perhaps motivated by an implicit attempt to avoid attributing passibility to the Logos. Thus even in Nestorius' heretic views, the impassibility of God remained a matter of fact.

Consequently, neither the Logos-anthropos-model of the Antiochians nor the Logos-sarx-model of the Alexandrians could satisfactorily explain the paradoxical unity of two natures in Christ. For while the Alexandrians tend toward a fractional unity, the Antiochians are prone to achieving a disjunctive unity. And since they have not arrived at an integrative unity of the natures, the basis for arguing the reality of the paradox of divine suffering bequeathed to the church eludes them.

2.4.2   St. Augustine of Hippo

St *Augustine of Hippo* (354-430), who is by far the most influential Trinitarian theologian of the West, approaches the problem of divine impassibility a little bit different from his contemporaries. His approach is defined by his whole life career, which can be seen as one "long and circuitous"[132] search for the immutable truth. [133] In search of the ultimate truth, Augustine first took to Manichaeism, which he later renounced to embrace Neoplatonism, from where he could not get

---

[129] Unlike the best of Logos-sarx-model, which presumes that the Logos assumed the human nature, the Logos-anthropos-model of Th. Mopsuestia and Nestorius maintains that the Logos assumed an individual man. By implication each of the natures has its own *prosopon* and needed a third to unite them. There was no way this could lead to a proper unity of the natures. Cf. W. Pannenberg, *Jesus - God And Man*, p. 290 f.

[130] Cited in A. Grillmeier, *Christ in Christian Tradition*, p.434.

[131] W. Pannenberg, *Jesus - God And Man*, p. 291.

[132] Cf. S. Grabowski, *The All-Present God*, p. 60.

[133] Cf. F. Copleston, *A History of Philosophy*. vol. 2, part I, p. 86.

more than a faint idea of the truth. Only as he renounced his libertine lifestyle and became a Christian, did he come to perceive God as the immutable truth, who is immanent, not just in the world, but eminently in his own soul.[134] The manner in which Augustine came to the knowledge of God, plays an important role in his theology of God: to him, the knowledge of God occurs then partly through the conscious search of the soul and partly through God's own self-revelation.[135] It is this insight that definitely prepared his mind for the task of differentiating and reconciling the philosophical with the biblical conceptions of emotions and of God.

In his *City of God*, St. Augustine rejects the Greek-Stoic understanding of *pathos*. In contrast to the Stoics, who conceive passions negatively, St Augustine sees them as neutral and characteristic features of every contingent being. Conceiving them broadly as the "movement of the mind contrary to reason",[136] he does of course see them as constituting a hindrance to the functions of reason, but he does not think that they are for that reason bad in themselves; only the will, which directs emotions, can be good or bad.[137]

As a matter of fact, Augustine considers emotions (love, fear and joy) to be indispensable for the God-human relationship. Hence his rejection of the Stoic tendency to advocating the human apatheia. Apatheia, he argues, cannot lead to blessedness in this life.[138] If apatheia is understood as the freedom of reason from emotions, it might be desirable for the life beyond death, but not in this life. Passionlessness, Augustine seems to say, is no longer possible for the human life on Earth, precisely because the will has been subjected to emotions since the fall

---

[134] Augustinus, *Confessiones*, III, 6,11: "Tu autem eras interior intimo meo et superior summo meo". This text has become a classic expression of the paradoxical tension between divine transcendence and immanence. God is accordingly, the immanent transcendence. Accordingly, St Augustine conceives God as "the most distant and nearest, the most hidden and present" being. Cf. *ibid.*, VI 3,4.; I 4,4: "Tu autem, altissime et promime, secretissime et praesentissime ..." On this paradoxical (dialectical, dialogical) unity, see Joachim Ringleben, *Interior intimo meo*, pp. 18-24.

[135] F. Copleston, *op. cit.* p. 86.

[136] *De Civ. Dei*, viii,17.

[137] *De Civ. Dei*, xiv, 6-7.

[138] *De Civ. Dei*, xiv, 9. For "if *apatheia* means a condition where no fear terrifies and pain does not vex us, it is to be avoided in this life if we wish to live rightly, that is according to God; but in that blessed life which is promised as eternal it is clearly to be the object of our hope" (transl. Mozley). Augustine rejects thus human apatheia, which he says is "worse than all vices". For just as it is inconceivable to think that the life beyond can be without love and joy, it would also be unimaginable to practise religion in this life without fear and pain.

of Adam.[139] Even the Son of God, Jesus Christ, who lived a sinless life here on Earth, left room for emotions in his life (xiv, 9), which he assumed by subjecting himself to the limitations of the human nature.

Strictly speaking therefore, apatheia (impassibilitas) can only be characteristic of God, who, by virtue of his simplicity, perfection, self-sufficiency, absolute transcendence and perfection is immutable. There is a sense nonetheless in which emotions can be attributed to God: when it does not entail disturbance, passivity or the state of being acted upon.[140] Confronted with the biblical accounts of divine repentance, anger, compassion and patience, St. Augustine makes optimal effort to show that God's emotions do not interfere with His immutability.[141] He does this employing Philo's allegorical method.[142] God, he argues, can love and be angry; He has emotions, but unlike human beings, He cannot be subject to His feelings; He is in perfect control of His emotions.[143]

St. Augustine's approach to the description of God is double-pronged: from the philosophical and from the biblical conceptions. This reflects his view that there is a sort of tension between being able to know and yet unable to understand divine nature: for, God, according to him, partly conceals and partly reveals Himself. Despite the human attempt to conceive God, He remains an incomprehensible being. Hence, irrespective of the value he places on the Plotinian conception of God as "the One" and "the Good", which he perceives as the philosophical image of God par excellence, Augustine is convinced that - in the light of the biblical revelation of God - limit is set to our philosophical knowledge.[144]

Out of this background, he considers the talk about divine emotions compatible with the axiom of divine impassibility or immutability. God is immutable, no doubt, but His immutability is conceived in terms of the steadfastness of His voli-

---

[139] *De Civ. Dei*, xiv, 10-13.

[140] *De Div. Nat.* p. 516, sec. 71 B; p. 519, sec. 74.

[141] Cf. *Cont. adv. leg. et prophet.* I, 40: "God does not repent as does a man, but as God; just as He is not angry after the manner of men, nor is pitiful, nor is jealous, but all He is He is as God. God's repentance does not follow as error, the anger of God carries with it no trace of a disturbed mind, nor His pity the wretched heart of a fellow-sufferer,...nor His jealousy any envy of mind ... (Therefore) when God repents He is not changed and He brings about change; when He is angry He is not moved and He avenges; when He pities He does not grieve and He liberates; when He is jealous He is not pained and He causes pain". See also J. K. Mozley, *op. cit.*, pp. 104-111.

[142] W.H.C. Frend, Augustinianism, p. 55.

[143] Cf. *De Patientia*, I.; *De div. quaest. ad Simpl.* II, 2.

[144] Cf. B. Studer, Credo in Deum Patrem omnipotentem, pp. 169-188.

tion, that is to say, of His will to justice and love.[145] Much depends on God's will: His transcendence, omnipotence and immutability, all depend on His volition. For it is precisely God's steadfastness to His will to justice and fulfilment of His promise for salvation, St. Augustine contends, that led His Son to the cross. Consequently, for the sake of upholding His will and love, he is ready to allow *demonstratio amoris* take the form of *demonstratio humilitas* on the cross.[146]

By implication, therefore, divine passibility can be seen as the logical consequence of God's immutable will:[147] for in order to uphold His will to justice and love, God is ready to participate even in suffering, that is to say, in that which is not of His nature. Here, not in the apatheia, lies His power.[148] St. Augustine thus, on the one hand, holds firmly to the axiom of divine impassibility, and on the other hand, practically leaves room for the possibility of divine suffering. This is most evident in his doctrine of the Trinity, for which he is most known. Making relation the constitutive element of the Trinitarian persons, he goes on to argue for the inseparability of the works of the Trinity *ad extra*. The logical conclusion of the doctrine of the unitary activity of the persons is, as he himself admits, the affirmation of Patripassianism. He does not however defend Patripassianism, neither does he make any effort to resolve the dilemma involved therein; he leaves it unexplained as a mystery of faith.[149]

2.4.3 The Councils and the Divine Impassibility (From the Fourth to the Seventh Century)

Even as the proper interpretation of the paradoxical unity of the divine and human natures in Jesus Christ eludes most theologies of the fourth and fifth centuries, the Church, in its conciliar decisions, opts for the adoption of a paradoxical tension in the issue of the divine-human unity. The search for a balance is pursued in the *First General Council of Nicaea* (325 AD). In opposition to Arius and in close affinity to Athanasius, the Nicaea Fathers confess that Jesus, as the Second

---

[145] Cf. Pérez-Paoli, Die Menschwerdung Gottes, vi; See also B. Studer, *op. cit.*, p. 176.

[146] Cf. B. Studer, Zum Gottesbegrifff des Heiligen Augustinus, p. 176 f.

[147] This view reminds one of the biblical view of immutability discussed in Chapter 1.

[148] Cf. Pérez-Paoli, *op. cit.*, vi. According to Pérez-Paoli, emotions are for Augustine, neither bad nor good as such, they derive their value from the will; what is bad is the *mala voluntas*.

[149] *Sermo*, 52, 6. On this see E. Dassmann, *Augustinus*, p. 115 f. According to Dassmann, Augustine escaped the danger of tritheism through his relational interpretation of the life and activities of the Trinitarian persons both *ad intra* and *ad extra*, but he is not free from the error of Modalism.

Person of the Trinity, is co-equal and consubstantial with the Father.[150] On the one hand, it is declared that the consubstantial Logos suffered (DS 125), on the other hand, it is argued that he could not be said to be "subject to change and alteration" (DS 126). Thus while the reality of the suffering of the Logos is somehow confirmed, the possibility of the divinity as such is practically denied.

In *the Council of Rome* (382), most of the previous errors in faith are reviewed in the attempt to maintain the balance of faith. Beside the rejection of Apollinarism, Patripassianism is also condemned anew (DS 166: ND 603/14). God's presence in Christ is then expressed with the kenotic motif (Phil. 2:7).

The *General Council of Ephesus* (431) did not come up with any new Christological framework. Rejecting Nestorianism, and its assumption of two persons in Christ, this Council reaffirms the consubstantiality of Christ with the Father, initiated by the Creed of Nicene. In the Second Letter of Cyril of Alexandria to Nestorius - which the Fathers adopt officially - the unity and distinction of natures in Christ are affirmed as a mysterious and ineffable phenomenon (DS 250). The Title of Mary as the "Mother of God" is also confirmed (DS 251). Cyril's "Twelve Anathematisms" (DS nn. 252-263) - which were read in the Council - are not adopted as definitions of faith,[151] perhaps because of the strong Logos-sarx-formula contained therein, according to which Christ suffered only in the flesh. Be that as it may, the fact remains that the Council of Ephesus has misgivings about Cyril's formulation of the Christological union of natures, which is mainly ambiguous.

An attempt toward a precise formulation of the paradox of the union of natures in Christ is made by Leo the Great in his *Letter to Flavian of Constantinople* (449),[152] where he, not only attacks Monophysitism, but also sets the framework for the emergence of the Chalcedonian formula. Using the kenotic motif, Leo argues that "He who is truly God is the same who is also truly man", the Son of God, in whom the "lowliness of man and the divine majesty coincide"; the impassible God makes Himself "subject to suffering," remains nonetheless "untouched by concupiscence" and "suffers no change because of His condescension" DS 294: ND 612).

---

[150] Rejecting Arius's thesis that the Logos was created, the Council Fathers confess faith in Jesus Christ as "the Son of God ...from the being (*ousia*) of the Father, God from God .... true God from true God, begotten not made, one in being (*homoousios*) with the Father ..... [It is he who] came down, and became flesh, was made man, suffered, and arose again on the third day." (DS 125: ND 7). Parallel to this, they condemn those who claim that the Logos was "created (*kristos*) or subject to change and alteration" (DS. 126: ND 8).

[151] Cf. J. Neuner and J. Dupuis, (eds.) *The Christian Faith*, p. 148.

[152] *Ibid.*, p. 152. This letter attains the standard of a definition of faith.

Taking a cue from Leo's letter,[153] *the General Council of Chalcedon* (451) synthesises the contributions of the Alexandrian and Antiochian schools, incorporates the Nicene decisions and rejects Monophysite tendencies. Among other things, this Council solemnly confesses that Jesus Christ is "the same perfect in divinity and perfect in humanity, the same truly God and truly man" (DS 301), and that he "must be acknowledged in two natures, without confusion or change, without division or separation...the character proper to each of the two natures was preserved as they came together in one person" (DS 302).

For Chalcedon, if each of the two natures retains its character despite unity, it then implicitly means that the divine nature of Christ must not be affected by the exigencies of the human nature. It is on this score, that Chalcedon condemns all those who declare that the divinity could be "subject to suffering" (DS 300). Thus, the paradoxical statements of Chalcedon on the unity of natures notwithstanding,[154] the suffering of God is not envisaged; God remains the Impassible par excellence. It is argued however, that the Council's adoption of the *theotokos* formula could be seen as an implicit admission of divine suffering.[155] There is definitely no precise affirmation about divine suffering in the Chalcedon formula, but it establishes the Christological equilibrium necessary for the future understanding of the dialectics of divine attributes.

However, making a clearer assertion was left to the post-Chalcedon definitions of the sixth and seventh centuries. *The Second Ecumenical Council of Constantinople* (553) approves accordingly the much disputed formula that one of the Trinity suffered (DS 532), giving the impression that God actually suffered. Similarly, it affirms that the one who suffered is the one who performed miracles (DS 523): this is an implicit recognition of the communication of properties between the two natures. Yet in reality the Council does not subscribe to divine suffering; it merely admits the suffering of Christ in flesh. Judging from the definitions of these two Councils, therefore, it is evident that - despite the Christological equation constructed in Chalcedon - Chalcedon and post-Chalcedon theologies continue to avoid direct attribution of suffering to the divine subject. This tendency seems to be perfected later in *the third Council of Constantinople* (680-681), where it is again emphasised that "both the miracles and the sufferings be-

---

153 *Ibid.*, p. 154.

154 *Ibid.*, p. 483

155 According to H. Küng, "since human birth involves suffering, the Council of Chalcedon also attribute suffering implicitly to the divine subject". Cf. H. Küng, *The Incarnation of God*, p. 523. Küng refers to *W. Elert, Der Ausgang der altkirchlichen Christologie*, p. 93. According to Elert, for the Antiochians, "das menschliche Geborenwerden ist ein Erleiden". That is why Nestorius and his followers deny the theotokos formula.

long to one and the same, according to the different natures of which He consists and which He has His being" (DS 557: ND 636). In order to avoid attributing the same action to God and creatures, the Council endeavours to improve the imprecise definition of the previous Council (DS 423) by adding the phrase "according to different natures" (DS 557). This makes it clear that suffering can only apply to the human nature.

Generally speaking, therefore, despite the attempts made in the Councils to maintain the paradoxical tension in the definition of the unity of two natures in one person, the impassibility of God remains a matter of fact. And as is most evident in the definitions of the third General Council of Constantinople, the influence of the Alexandrian Logos-sarx-formula on the Councils is more pronounced than that of the Antiochian Logos-anthropos-model. In all however, the Church decisions avoid the extreme positions of either of the schools on the issue of the hypostatic union.

2.5 Divine Impassibility in the Medieval Theologies

Just as Platonism and Stoicism form the philosophical background of the Patristic theologies, Aristotelianism constitutes the pillar of the philosophy and logic of the Medieval theologies. With the power of logic and precision in language, the Medieval-Scholasticism now makes the attempt to resolve the puzzles raised in the Patristic period. Consequently, a depth of analysis characterises the approach to the issue of divine impassibility in the Medieval theologies.

John Scotus (c. 800-877), of the early Scholastic period, uses arguments reminiscent of Aristotelians to defend the immutability of God. He goes even beyond Aristotle as he contends that "God neither acts nor is acted upon, neither moves nor is moved, neither loves nor is loved".[156] By claiming that God cannot be loved, Scotus does not deny love as such in God; what he intends to deny is a type of love that connotes passivity. It is debatable whether such a love can be conceivable. The point, however, is that he is ready to deny love in God in order to prove that God alone is the Impassible.[157]

Anselm (1033-1109), likewise upholding the axiom of divine impassibility, seeks to formulate the paradox of divine attribute in terms of God's sympathy. He admits that the impassible God is compassionate, but he insists that this does not entail suffering on God's part: God pities the sufferer however without being

---

[156] John Scotus, *De Div. Nat.* p. 504, sec. 62 B.

[157] *Ibid.*, p. 519, sec. 74: God is loved by all things, but "not because He, who alone is impassible, becomes, in respect of them, the subject of any kind of passivity, but because all things seek Him and His beauty draws all things to Himself."

touched by the wretchedness of the latter.[158] Consequently, he contends that Christ suffered only in his human nature.[159]

Thomas Aquinas (1226/27-1274), the major figure in the high Scholastic period, brings Aristotelians to bear on his conceptions of divine immutability and impassibility.[160] Aquinas' view on our topic of discussion is guided by two basic assumptions: a) that God is a pure actuality without any potentiality and b) that He is incorporeal.

Moving from a state of potentiality to actuality, Aquinas argues, is a sign of imperfection.[161] Immutability is perfection par excellence. This applies to both God and creatures. Insofar as creatures do not only consist of potentiality, but also of actuality, they can be said to be immutable to a certain extent.[162] But insofar as they possess potentiality, they are imperfect. However, beyond the imperfect beings, there must be "some incorporeal, immovable, and completely perfect being, and this is God".[163] The simplicity, incorporeality and perfection of God demand that He cannot be movable. In substantiating his point on the immutability of God, Aquinas uses philosophical,[164] patristic[165] and Scriptural[166] arguments.

---

158 Anselm, *Proslogion*, 8: "Thou art pitiful, because Thou savest the wretched, and sparest the sinners who belong to Thee; and Thou art not pitiful, because Thou art touched by no fellow-suffering in that wretchedness".

159 Anselm, *Cur Deus Homo*, 1,8: "Wherefore when we say that God suffers anything lowly or weak, we do not understand this in respect of the height of the impassible nature, but in respect of the weakness of the human substance which He wore."

160 W. Hankey, Aquinas and the Passion of God, pp. 318-333, esp. p. 324 argues a case for the Platonic influence of Aquinas, which according to him is virtually suppressed or overlooked in contemporary Thomistic theology. See also the same author, Theology as System and as Science, pp. 83-93.

161 Thomas Aquinas, *Summa Theologica*, I,9.1: God is "pure action without the admixture of any potentiality, because potentiality itself is later than action. Now everything which in any way is changed is in some way in a state of potentiality, whence it is obvious that God cannot in any way be changed."

162 On Aquinas' conception of human immutability, see M. J. Dodds, *The Unchanging God of Love*, pp. 1-38.

163 Aquinas, *Commentary on the Sentences of Peter Lombard*, I, 8,3,1; see also, M. J. Dodds, *op. cit.* pp. 67-153 for more references to Aquinas' use of the motif of divine immutability.

164 On this point he is most influenced by Aristole's view of immutability as perfection. Cf. J. M. Dodds, *op. cit.*, pp. 177-191.

The argument Aquinas presents in favour of divine impassibility is taken from his idea of divine immutability: *passio*, he contends, suggests change, which neither God's knowledge[167] nor His will[168] can allow. God, as "pure action", who is perfectly simple, cannot be passible. However, Aquinas differentiates two types of *potentia*, active and passive. Whereas active potentia, which he understands as the principle of action, can be found in God, the passive potentia (a state of deficiency) has no place in Him.[169]

Besides, in the face of divine incorporeality, Aquinas sees divine passibility as a logical impossibility. He believes that the possession of emotions is so closely connected with corporeality that passibility cannot be attributed to an incorporeal being.[170] God is incorporeal; that means that He cannot have emotions. If one understands joy and love as emotions, one might immediately object to this claim. Aquinas believes nonetheless that love and joy can eminently be attributed to God as is suggested in the Bible. By that fact, he is presented with a dilemma, which he himself thus formulates: "the denial of emotion in God seems to go against the witness of Scripture", but "the affirmation of emotion in God seems to be incompatible with the divine incorporeality".[171] He tries to reconcile this apparent contradiction by way of classification.

First, he distinguishes between *passio animalis* (passion of the soul) and *passio corporalis* (bodily passion).[172] While bodily passions characteristically entail motion and alteration, reception and loss of qualities,[173] the passion of the soul - since the soul is an incorporeal entity - does not imply any alteration; the soul can be said to suffer, nonetheless, but only "... in the sense that its operation can be hampered" by the body. As a matter of fact, the soul suffers both differently and indirectly;[174] it suffers only insofar as it is connected to the body. Hence, the

---

165 The most quoted Church Fathers are Dionysius and St. Augustine. The difference between Augustine and Thomas on this point is the latter's explication of divine immutability with the Aristoelian theory of act and potency. J. M. Dodds, *op. cit.*, pp. 167-174.

166 *Summa contra Gentiles*, I, c. 14; c.15, nr. 7, just to give a few references. For a fuller reference see J. M. Dodds, *op. cit.*, p. 364, notes 134-136.

167 *Ibid.*, I,14.15.

168 *Ibid.*, I,19,7.

169 Cf. *Ibid.*, I,25,1

170 Cf. M. Sarot, God, Emotions and Corporeality, pp. 1-27.

171 *Ibid.*, p. 15.

172 *Summa contra Gentiles*, I 89-91

173 Cf. *Sent.* II 19,1,3; *STh* I-II 22,2 ad 1; 22,1 c.; See also M. Sarot, *op. cit.* pp. 4-8.

174 *De Veritate* 26,2 c.

"passion of the soul is properly found only in the sensitive appetite".[175] In view of the incorporeality of the soul, therefore, one can only attribute passion to the soul in a "transferred sense",[176] because its passion properly belongs to the body.

Secondly, Aquinas also differentiates between the "intellective appetite" and the "sensitive appetite".[177] In terms of origin and location, the intellective and *sensitive* appetites belong each to different faculties - to reason and senses respectively. They differ basically from each other however in terms of their objects: For, while the object of sensitive appetites are sensible objects, which characteristically arouse bodily change, the objects of the intellective appetite are more universal, they are objects of the will, which are not accompanied by bodily changes. Since anger, fear, love, and in fact, all emotions, arouse bodily changes, Aquinas classifies them as sensitive appetites. They are then, properly speaking, passions. There is a sense in which these emotions can connote acts of intellective desire: when they are acts of the will, and do not arise from the senses. Hence, although an emotion like love is a sensitive appetite, it can also be seen as an act of the intellective appetite, when it implies the execution of God's will toward an object of spiritual affection.[178]

Basically, Aquinas would believe that God is immutable and impassible, but only on the condition that the emotions implied are compatible with divine immutability. Love, for instance, can only be attributed to God, when it signifies "activities of the intellective appetite".[179] Human love, according to him, involves both motion and immutability, motion, because it arises through a change in the will, and immutability, because it is the source and principle of all movements. God's love has however only the character of immutability.[180]

Consequently, God is compassionate, but He does not suffer. His compassion, unlike the human type, does not arise out of passion, but out of the effect, it has on the sufferer. In other words, God is compassionate, not because He is subject to suffering, but because He overcomes it.[181] This does not entail indifference on

---

[175] *De Veritate* 26,3 c.: "et sic in appetitiva sensitiva sola, animalis passio proprie invenitur".

[176] Cf. M. Sarot, *op. cit.* pp. 6.

[177] *De Veritate* 25,3, *STh* I 20,1; *Sent.* III 15,2,2b c.; See also M. Sarot, *op. cit.* p. 13 f.

[178] *De Veritate* 25,3 c.; *Summa contra Gentiles*, I 90,2. See also M. Sarot, *op. cit.* p. 14.

[179] *STh* I 20,1; I-II 22,3 ad 3; *De Veritate* 25,3; 26,9 ad 5; *Sent.* IV 15,2,1a ad 4.

[180] *STh* I-II, 113,2, c.; See also M. J. Dodds, *The Unchanging God of Love*, pp. 279-281.

[181] *STh* I, 21,3.; II-II, 30,4, c.; *SCG* I, c. 91, nr. 16 (§766); *Sent.* IV, 46,2,1 Qc. 1, c. Aquinas' conception of divine compassion or love as excluding passibility is supported, according to Dodds, by the argument that it is not suffering as such that we admire in a compas-

God's part; it rather means that God, in a manner beyond our knowledge, triumphs over suffering without being affected by it Himself. In view of this fact, Aquinas considers the biblical anthropopathetic expressions and images as metaphors, which, without being mere literal descriptions, are but inadequate human attempts to describe love-like, compassion-like qualities in God, which surpass our human knowledge.[182]

All that notwithstanding, Aquinas insists that although Christ really suffered on the cross, it was not the divine but his human nature that suffered.[183] Thus, Christ is God, but we cannot say that in his suffering God suffered. Christ's suffering does not reveal divine suffering; rather it manifests divine love.[184] Aquinas' argument is definitely logical, though it does not seem to have solved the problem.

His major contribution lies, however, in his analysis of love and emotions. His views do raise two significant questions for the theology of divine suffering: Can there be a sort of love that cannot principally entail suffering? And can there be emotions without corporeality?[185] These two questions would need the attention of all theologians of divine suffering.

2.6 Divine Impassibility in the Reformation Period

With the exception of Luther, whose Christology enunciates the doctrine of *communicatio idiomatum*,[186] the rest of the Reformation theologians freely accept the axiom of divine impassibility as normative.

In line with a majority of the Church Fathers, *Melanchthon*, for instance, contends "that human feelings and experiences cannot be directly ascribed to God".[187]

Calvin, who makes the recognition of the incomprehensibility of God the starting point of his doctrine of God, claims likewise that the biblical predication

---

sionate person, but the "magnitude of love that is manifested in that suffering. See M. J. Dodds, *The Unchanging God of Love*, pp. 294-312.

[182] *STh* I 20,1 ad 2; *Sent.* II, 11, 1,5 c., ad.1

[183] *STh* III, 46,12, c. ad 2; *SCG* IV, c. 55, nr. 17 (§3947); *Sent.* III, 6,2,1,ad 5.

[184] *STh* III, 46, 3; c.; III, 1,2, c.

[185] M. Sarot, *op. cit.*, p. 20 f. has already made this point. According to him, the contemporary psychological definitions of emotion agree with Thomas's view that emotions necessarily presuppose corporeality (p. 23) He concludes that most passibilist theologians attribute emotions to God in a manner that it connotes corporeality and bodily changes. .

[186] Cf. Mozley, *op. cit.* p. 121.

[187] *Ibid.*, p. 120.

of human corporeality, emotions and feelings to God should not be taken literally;[188] they must be understood figuratively.[189] Divine repentance is particularly singled out as a predication which is incompatible with the divine omniscience.[190] God has a foreknowledge of every event, Calvin argues, and cannot be said to repent.[191] He thus uses the allegorical method to explain the reality of the biblical anthropomorphism.[192] But as has been observed, he could not do that without becoming ambivalent.[193]

The doctrine of divine impassibility remains likewise a tacit assumption in *Martin Luther's theology*, despite his opposition to the speculative doctrine of God in the scholastic theology. This assumption is however greatly suppressed by his theology of the Cross and Christology, which show features of belief in the passion of God. The theology of the cross, conceived in opposition to the prevailing theology of glory[194], abound in "theological paradoxes" such as the idea of the "hidden" and "revealed" God. "The hidden God and the revealed God are completely identical".[195]

If W. von Loewenich interprets Luther rightly, the hiddenness of God "means indirect knowledge of God; the hidden God is the God whose nature and word can only be recognised under the opposite form'"[196] Luther appeals for an indirect knowledge of the revealed God on the cross, in the suffering, and in the human weakness of Jesus Christ. Accordingly, the concealment of God is precisely the revelation of God "as the crucified"[197].

---

188 Calvin, *Institutes*, I,13,1.c

189 Calvin renews the Alexandrian allegorical interpretation.

190 Calvin, *Commentaries on Genesis* vi, 6

191 Cf. H. M. Kuitert *op. cit.* pp. 77-81. Here Kuitert gives a detailed account of Calvin's view on divine impassibility and immutability. He observes how Calvin draws his argument from the platonic Church Fathers. According to his study, Calvin's denial of divine repentance on the basis of divine omniscience only echoes the teachings of Philo and Origen. See p. 79 n. 121; p. 80 n. 129 & 130.

192 *Commentary on Isaiah* Lxiii, 9: "the Prophet testifies that God, in order to alleviate the distresses and afflictions of His people, Himself bore their burdens; not that He can in any way endure anguish, but by a very customary figure of speech, He assumes and applies to Himself human passions".

193 Cf. H. M. Kuitert, *op. cit.* p. 78.

194 Also the then dominant theology of the Church.

195 W. von Loewenich, *Luther's Theology of the Cross*, p. 37.

196 *Ibid.*, p. 29 f.

197 Cf. *ibid.*, p. 30

Whereas there can definitely be other valid interpretations of Luther's doctrine of the hidden God, we can reasonably believe that this doctrine affirms the suffering of God, in a very radical manner. We can get an even clearer picture, if we put the following statements from Luther together: "...he who does not know Christ does not know God hidden in suffering",[198] therefore "we should know that God hides Himself under the form of the worst devil",[199] and "...that God can be found only in Cross and suffering".[200] The fact remains however that, despite such theopaschite expressions, Luther does not approve the "heresy" of Patripassianism.[201] It is, therefore, apparent that he invariably limited the application of the theopaschite formula solely to the person of Christ, without extending it to the whole Godhead.

It is however most probable that Luther's condemnation of Patripassianism represents merely an unconscious act of solidarity with the tradition, which has no place in his theology. His theology tends rather toward the opposite direction, namely, that what happened to the Son also affected the Father. This fact is further affirmed in his interpretation of the classical doctrine of the *communicatio idiomatum*. This means, for him, a total reciprocity of the two natures: The "two natures join their characteristics, and the divine nature gives to the human its characteristics, and, conversely, the manhood gives its to the divine nature".[202]

In his *Table-Talk*, Luther offers a vivid affirmation of the suffering of God and His active involvement in the suffering of Christ. Suffering and death could be seen as contingent experiences outside the sphere of the Deity, but by allowing Himself to be born as man, God also allows that the two natures are united in Christ, sharing with one another "their *idiomata* and characteristics". It is also on the basis of the *communicatio idiomatum* that Luther accepts Mary's title: theotokos - "true Mother of God". In general, therefore, Luther maintains that God is impassible per se, but He makes Himself passible through the incarnation.

2.7   Summary

In summary, we dare to reiterate the major features of the issue of divine impassibility in the tradition and theologies from the onset of Christianity to the

---

[198] Cf. *Weimar Edition of Luther's Works* Vol. I, p. 362, line 23, quotation taken from W. von Loewenich, *op. cit.*, p. 30

[199] *Weimar Edition of Luther's Works*, Vol. XLIV, 429, 24 ff, quoted in *ibid.*, p. 40.

[200] *Weimar Edition of Luther's Works*, vol. I, 262, 28f in *ibid.*, p.112.

[201] Cf. W. Elert, Die Theopaschite Formel, p. 203.

[202] Erlangen edition, vol. XLVII, p. 175 ff; Also cited in Mozley, *op. cit.* p. 122.

Reformation period. The trend towards avoiding the use of negatively judged emotions in the predication of God, as our sketch shows, characterises the New Testament approach to the issue of divine emotions. Yet there is no definite denial of divine emotions. In fact, not only positive, but also negative emotions are attributable to God. Both types of emotions are attributable to God as long as the ability to initiate such occurrences is reserved Him, that is to say, as long as His sovereignty in either case is not endangered. This fact is best exemplified in their understanding of the divine wrath as a reality with kenotic and eschatological dimensions. For if it is true that God adjourns the expression of His anger by means of a kenotic self-restraint, it then follows that He is still in control of the situation even when He suffers. Suffering does not befall Him. Rather He retains the freedom and the initiative to take up suffering on Himself. Thus, while His sovereignty over suffering is emphasised in the biblical writings the affirmation of divine passibility is implicit.

The paradoxical approach, which forms the background of this biblical view of emotions, is continued in the theologies of the Apostolic Fathers, especially by St. Ignatius, who, despite his exposure to the Hellenistic thought, affirms both the passibility and impassibility of God. Similarly, the Apologists also settle, at least theoretically for a paradoxical expression of the divine nature. But, since they see impassibility and immutability as that which constitutes the difference between the Christian God and the mythological gods, they tend to characterise God more in terms of His impassibility, thereby distancing themselves practically from the Semitic and paradoxical approach.

This tendency is fully realised in the Gnostic thought, where an outright denial of the divine passibility takes the place of a paradoxical approach. Perceiving impassibility as a distinguishing characteristic of the divine nature, just like the Apologists, the Christian Gnostics go yet further to see it as that which differentiates the humanity of Christ from his divinity. To them, therefore, apatheia becomes the principle for the affirmation of divine transcendence.

The paradoxical approach regains its popularity in the theology of Irenaeus. Generally, however, the paradoxical assertion of divine impassibility in the third century theologies is mostly sporadic. While in some theologies of the time, a univocal affirmation of divine impassibility obtains, in the others an outright denial of divine suffering is usual. Even in the Modalist Christology, where the heresy of Patripassianism is committed, a one-sided affirmation of the impassibility of God is surprisingly implicit, just as the initial attempt of Noetus to adopt a paradoxical approach[203] ends in an illusion. However, Origen and Gregorios Thaumaturgos make serious attempts at conceiving the passibility and impassibil-

---

[203] See the passage quoted in section 2.3.1. of this chapter.

ity of God paradoxically. In the context of their Alexandrian theology, both authors make significant contributions toward the development of divine suffering: Origen does that by interpreting divine possibility from the point of view of divine love, and Thaumaturgos, by pointing out the significance of the issues of divine will, freedom, and self-limitation for a theology of divine suffering. Their contemporaries - Clement of Alexandria and to some extent the Latin theologian Tertullian - deny the possibility of divine suffering. Such a denial is, of course, not typical of the Latin theologians, because Lactantius, writing much later than Tertullian, preserves, in contrast the biblical paradoxical approach in his description of divine anger and emotions.

In the fourth and fifth century Christologies the axiom of divine impassibility is a basic assumption, to an extent that, all theologies, orthodox and the heretic, produced during the Christological controversies, unanimously refuse the predication of possibility to God. Thus, while discussing the issue of the hypostatic union, the Arians and the Apollinarists, the Alexandrian and the Antiochian schools, the Cappadocian theologians, and practically all theologies of the time make a univocal affirmation of the impassibility of God, rather than maintaining the paradoxical tension. It must also be observed that there is no clear-cut assertion of divine suffering the decisions of the Councils (from the fourth to the seventh century). However, the effort of the Council Fathers to avoid a one-dimensional affirmation of either of the natures of Christ while settling the issue of the hypostatic union in this period signals a cordial disposition for a paradoxical approach to the God-question.

A relatively different approach to the problem, which secures the paradoxical tension, is adopted by St. Augustine. Unlike the rest of the patristic approaches, his proposal makes the passibility or impassibility of God depend on divine volition. Besides, his conception of the "relationality" of the Trinitarian Persons opens a new and fruitful dimension for the theology of divine suffering.

In the Medieval-Scholastic approach, especially in that of St. Thomas Aquinas, the topic in question receives an in-depth analysis, but not necessarily a new vision. Holding firmly to the impassibility of God, Thomas maintains that an incorporeal being cannot suffer, but that he can love conceptually. He makes significant contributions, nonetheless, as he raises the questions, whether there can be love without suffering, and whether there can be emotions without corporeality.

For the Reformers, divine impassibility is a basic assumption, but whereas Calvin denies divine suffering absolutely, Luther tends to relate it to the axiom of divine impassibility by means of his interpretation of the *communicatio idiomatum* and his theory of *Deus absconditus* and *Deus revelatus*.

Thus, in general, it can be observed that, although the affirmation of divine impassibility predominates in the Church theologies and tradition, the effort to predicate suffering and emotion to God as a mysterious and paradoxical possibility has not been totally absent. The major issue has been how to think this paradox through successfully.

3. DIVINE IMPASSIBILITY AND THE KENOTIC MOTIF (FROM THE SEVENTEENTH TO THE TWENTIETH CENTURY)

If a philosophical approach to the paradox of divine nature characterises the Medieval Christologies, the Reformation and post-Reformation theologies distinguish themselves by their attempt to illumine the dialectics of divine nature in the light of the Bible. In this endeavour, the kenotic motif plays a significant role,[1] a role which consists mainly in providing the platform on which reflections are made concerning the paradox of divine mutability and immutability, of possibility and impassibility and of the divine love. The kenotic motif itself is a paradoxical principle,[2] which could be used both for establishing the authenticity of divine impassibility[3] and arguing about the possibility of divine suffering.[4]

---

[1] The passage of the Christological hymn in Phil. 2: 5-11 reads: although Christ was in the "form of God" (*morphe theou*), he "emptied himself" (*eauton ekenosen*), and having taken the "form of a slave" (*morphen doulou*) he became like humankind. For the reason of his condescension, he was exalted and glorified, being given a name which is above every other name. As a term *kenosis* has its *locus classicus* in Phil 2:5-11, though as an idea it is believed to be equally expressed in all other places in the New Testament, where the notions of divine self-limitation, self-renunciation and self-giving are implied (cf. 2 Cor. 8: 9; Jn. 3: 13; 16: 28; 17: 5; Mk. 10: 45; Rom. 15: 3; & Heb. 5: 7 ff.). In referring to the message in the kenotic passage, which seems to summarise the whole Christ-event, it has become appropriate to speak of the "kenotic motif". For details about the role of this motif in the theology of divine suffering see D. G. Dawe, *The Form Of A Servant*, p. 19 f.; J. A. T. Robinson, *The Human Face of God*, p. 206; L. J. Richard, *A kenotic Christology*, p. 160. And on its general relevance for the whole Christ-event see E. Käsemann, A critical Analysis of Philippians 2: 5-11, pp. 45-88.

[2] Its ambiguity is not unconnected with the duality of the Christological context in which it is set. For as studies reveal, the kenotic passage could be the product of one or both of the two typical New Testament Christological presuppositions - the adoption theory (Rom. 1: 4; Acts 2: 22) and the pre-existence theory. In the light of both Christological theories, which are juxtaposed to one another, *kenosis* could be a case for the pre-existence of Christ or for the adoption of the man Jesus. The earliest exegetes had problems trying to determine which theory is being confirmed in the kenotic hymn. Cf. J. D. G. Dunn, *Unity and Diversity in the New Testament*. The two-fold meanings of the kenotic motif could be observed in different theological positions taken during the Arian controversy. While the Arians interpret the form of God as implying merely "likeness" and not "equality" (adoption and subordination) of the Son to the Father, Victorinus and Athanasius see this passage as a sure proof of the consubstantiality of the Son and the Father (pre-existence theory). Cf. M. D. Hooker, Philippians 2: 2-11, p. 162.

[3] This is typical of the patristic theologies where the kenotic motif (i.e. the kenosis and exaltation put together) is mostly interpreted in the light of the theory of the pre-existence of the Logos. Concerning the patristic use of kenotic motif in defence of divine immutability see D. G. Dawe, *The Form Of A Servant*, pp. 36-45.

Excursus: The Application of the Kenotic Motif before the 19th Century

In the patristic theology, where the belief in the pre-existence of the Logos is prevalent, the exaltation of Christ is not seen as the acquisition of a new status, but as a return to the primordial divine state of the Logos. This fact is invariably used in justifying the claim that the divine nature remained immutable and impassible even during the kenotic life of Jesus. According to D. G. Dawe, the interpretation of the kenotic motif in patristic theology is influenced by Greek substance-ontology, so much so that, for a majority of the Fathers, *kenosis* amounts to the veiling of the Logos with human nature, and consequently, the *exaltation* of Jesus signifies the unveiling, the return of the glorified Logos to his pre-existent status. This philosophically motivated interpretation of the kenotic motif, Dawe contends, makes any form of change in the divine nature inconceivable. Thus, the view of the New Testament adoptionist Christologies, which interprets the exaltation of Jesus as a movement from a lower to a higher and new status, does not appear in patristic theology.[5]

In contrast to the Fathers, the Medieval theologies tend to leave little or no room at all for kenotic theological reflections. They suspect that the kenotic motif has the connotation of divine suffering and mutability. But although there is a virtual absence of reflections on kenosis in the Medieval theologies, kenotic motif finds expression nonetheless in the sermons and devotional writings of the mystics in the Medieval period, a sign that it could give expression to faith, even when it apparently failed to fulfil the intellectual requirements.

Coming to the theology of the Reformers, one sees the kenotic motif becoming once more a basic theological principle. For although Luther agrees with the Fathers, (that kenosis is the veiling of the Logos with human nature, and exaltation the disclosure of Christ's "true nature"), he nonetheless adds something new to the arguments, as he differentiates between the "form of God" and the "essence of God". Thus, kenosis means for him that Christ, while putting aside the "form of God", retained the "divine essence" throughout his earthly life. The radical implication of this view of the divine kenosis is of course that the exigencies of Jesus' earthly life affected both the human and the divine natures. Luther does not however make it explicit that the divine nature suffered with the human. Instead, he sees kenosis as a continuous process, a recurrent act of self-emptying, of which the incarnate Christ was also the subject. Thus, unlike the Fathers, he does not see the pre-existent Logos as the sole subject of the kenosis, neither does he assume that kenosis is a one-time *fiat*. Rather, he recognises the fact that even the humanity of Jesus was involved in the act of self-emptying.[6]

This view is definitely not typical of the entire Reformation theologies. For in contrast to Luther, Calvin maintains that the pre-existent Logos is the sole subject

---

4   All passibilists use the kenotic motif to argue for the possibility of divine suffering. The next chapter of this study will be dedicated to a case study of the use of the kenotic motif in defence of the axiom of divine suffering as is evident in the writings of Geddes MacGregor.

5   D. G. Dawe, *The Form Of A Servant*, pp. 42-43.

6   One can say therefore that Luther combines the ontological understanding of the kenotic motive (as evidenced in the patristic theology) with its moral implication for human spiritual life (as St. Bernard understands it).

of kenosis. He contends accordingly that the divine nature did not share in the exigencies - suffering and death - of the earthly life of Jesus Christ, only the human nature did.[7] While Luther uses the kenotic motif to argue the unity of the natures, Calvin employs the same motif to prove the distinction of the natures in Christ.

In a sense, therefore, the understanding of the kenotic motif in the Reformation theologies differs from its interpretation in the patristic theologies, especially as the Reformers are inclined towards emphasising that the humanity of Christ was involved in the act of self-emptying. Common to both the Reformation and the patristic theologies is indeed the location of kenosis solely within the Christological frame-work and its confinement to the problem of the two natures.[8]

By restricting the significance of the kenotic motif within the context of the two natures, theologians, especially those of the post-Reformation period, made things difficult for themselves. They were forced to perform a theological hair-splitting, trying to determine what happened to Christ's divine attributes during his earthly life. On this issue, both Reformers bequeathed more questions than answers to their successors. For if the Logos retained his divine essence during the kenotic life of Jesus Christ on Earth, the question arose for the Lutherans as to whether the divine attributes were switched off or whether they were subjected to human limitations. Lutheran theologies of both the sixteenth and the seventeenth centuries offer two answers to this question: firstly, that Christ renounced the use of his divine qualities, secondly, that he made secret use of them.[9] The implicit conclusion of both Lutheran approaches is however that the two natures lacked a vital unity.

Ironically, what we now see as constituting the implicit conclusion of the Lutherans - the absence of an integrative unity between the two natures - is indeed the explicit starting-point of the approach of the Reformed orthodoxy, which in accordance with Calvin's "distinction" Christology, assumes the possibility of a "dual life" in Jesus: Kenosis, according to the Reformed theology, means either the withdrawal of the divine nature or its concealment during the incarnate life of Jesus Christ. Strictly speaking, therefore, it is obvious in the Reformed theology, that Jesus lacked divine omniscience, and that his divine nature was clearly separated from his human nature. While this approach preserves the significance of

---

7   Cf. Calvin, *Institutes*, II, XIV. 2; See also Dawe, *op. cit.*, p. 72.

8   As we shall show later, the kenotic motif has implications not only for Christology, but also for the doctrines of God and creation in general.

9   The attempt to answer this question split the Lutherans into two camps: one led by Johann Brenz (1499-1570) and the other by Martin Chemnitz (1522-1586). For Brenz, kenosis denotes that Jesus did not make use of his divine attributes in public (he made a secret use of them) even though he still possessed them. In contrast, kenosis implies, for Chemnitz, that Christ abstained totally from making use of his divine powers. Following the same style of argument a theological conflict developed between the theologians of the Tübingen and Gießen universities in the seventeenth century. While the former group sides with Brenz and argues that Christ declined to make a public use of his divine attributes of omnipotence, omniscience and omnipresence, the latter agrees with Chemnitz that although Christ possessed the divine attributes potentially, he did not make use of them at all. Cf. W. Pannenberg, *Jesus - God and Man*, p. 308.

the humanity of Jesus Christ, and proves that the Logos remained immutable, in the end it fails to show how the continuity between the pre-existent and the incarnate Christ could be argued.

Thus, despite the theological novelties, which the theologies of the Reformation purport to present, neither Lutheran nor Reformed theology uses the kenotic motif in a manner in which it could fit into the existing theological categories without endangering the unity of Jesus Christ. Apparently, an effective use of the kenotic motif is not possible, without a corresponding reinterpretation of either some of the theological categories or at least the motif itself. Since this was not done in their century, the kenotic motif lost its popularity as a Christological principle, and disappeared from the scene of theological discourses, except however in devotional hymns,[10] where little or no philosophical interpretation was needed.

The kenotic motif made a return to the theological discourses in the late-nineteenth century, when it was needed in the explication of the problems created by the adoption of the historical-critical method in the study of the life of Jesus. The exciting awareness of the significance of the historical Jesus, which this method brought, became a threat to the traditional belief in the Jesus of faith.[11] In the theological battle that ensued between the defenders of the Jesus of faith and the proponents of the historical Jesus, there were theologians who, realising that it was erroneous to play one image of Christ against the other, decided to mediate between the Jesus of faith and the Jesus of history. These mediating theologians, whose Christologies presuppose the affirmation of the full divinity and humanity of Christ, use kenotic motif for the purpose of relating Jesuology to Christology. They are today referred to as the late-nineteenth century kenoticists.[12] It is in

---

[10] Cf. D. G. Dawe, *op. cit.*, p. 83. Thus, despite the loss of its theological significance in the eighteenth century notwithstanding, the kenotic motif retained its relevance within the evangelical piety, as evidenced in the writings of N. L. Graf von Zinzendorf. Cf. *Vier und dreyszig Homilae über die Wunden-Litaney der Brüder*, p. 25; *Ein und zwanzig Discurse über die Augsburgische Confession*, p. 65, 5, 121 ff.; *Naturelle Reflexiones über aller-hand Materien*, p. 359, cited in Dawe, *op. cit.* p. 21. For in the evangelical piety, unlike in the Christological discourses, the kenotic motif is interpreted personalistically rather than philosophically. This fact is further evident in the following statement taken from a hymn written by Charles Wesley in the same period: "He (Christ) ... emptied himself of all but love". See Dawe, *op. cit.* p. 85.

[11] Cf., for instance, the works of D. F. Strauss (1808-1874) and F. C. Baur (1792-1860). It can be observed that this problem was already anticipated by the Reformation and post-Reformation theologies, as they encountered tremendous difficulties reconciling the pre-existent Christ with the incarnate Christ, who is supposed to not have undergone any change. This is particularly so, if we bear in mind that the age of Enlightenment and Romantic idealism, (which initiated the modern physical and historical sciences that led to the application of the historical critical method on the Scripture), is itself the logical development of the new religious and intellectual experiences made during the Reformation and Renaissance.

[12] The list would include the following: I. A. Dorner, Gottfried Thomasius, August Ebrard, Bishop Martensen and Ernst Neander in Germany and Scandinavian countries. Others were Bishop Gore, P. Fairbairn, P. T. Forsyth and H. R. Mackintosh in England.

their work that the close connection between the kenotic motif and theology of divine suffering becomes obvious.

3.1 Divine Impassibility and the Nineteenth Century Kenoticism

3.1.1 The German and English-speaking Kenoticists

The nineteenth century German kenoticism finds its most popular expression in the writings of *Thomasius of Erlangen*.[13] For him, *kenosis* constitutes neither a concealment nor a renunciation of the divine attributes, as understood by the earlier Lutherans; it denotes a real change on the part of the Logos. Making this claim, he reinterprets the notion of divine absoluteness. The absoluteness of God, he contends, does not consist in His changelessness, but in His ability for self-determination: the ability to change Himself for love's sake. God's power is the power of "self-determination". Correspondingly, he argues that "self-limitation" (kenosis) is nothing other than "self-determination"[14].

Thomasius' reinterpretation of divine absoluteness and sovereignty, has been sharply criticised, because, by implying divine mutability, it raises more questions than it answers. For as critics ask,[15] if the Logos underwent a real change, does it then mean that there was no God in Christ during his earthly life? And if Christ was totally emptied of his divinity, who was then in control of the universe during this incarnate life? Does it mean that at a time the Trinity was incomplete? To answer these questions, Thomasius argues that only one type of divine attributes was dropped during the incarnation. He does this by differentiating between what he calls the *essential attributes* (power, truth, holiness and love) and the *relational attributes* (omnipotence, omniscience and omnipresence). While the former are supposed to be intrinsic to God the latter are relevant only for God's relation to the world. By self-emptying, Thomasius argues, the Logos laid only the relational attributes aside.

What Thomasius says here is, in effect, that in the kenotic act, Christ did not do away with that which is intrinsic to his divine nature, but only with that which is dispensable for the being of God. With this argument, he hopes to guarantee the full humanity and divinity of Christ using the kenotic motif. For if the so-called relational attributes are strictly divine, their withdrawal from the earthly life

---

13 G. Thomasius, Ein Beitrag zur kirchlichen Christologie; ---, *Das Bekenntnis der evangelisch-lutherischen Kirche in der Konsequenz seines Prinzips*; ---, *Christi Person und Werk*.

14 Cited by D. G. Dawe, *op. cit.*, p. 94.

15 Cf. I. A. Dorner, Über die richtige Fassung des dogmatischen Begriffs der Unveränderlichkeit Gottes, pp. 188-377.

of Jesus would then mean that the divinity has been emptied in a way, in favour of the full realisation of the reality of Christ's humanity. Again, since they are not the constitutive attributes of divine nature, withdrawing them would not imply the loss of the divinity.

If this argument pacified his contemporaries at all, it was only for a while. It was soon discovered that it merely shifts the problem to another level, namely to the level of the God-world relationship. For if God withdrew His relational attributes during the earthly life of Jesus, what happened then to His relation to the world at this time? Was this not equal to abandoning the world?

When one bears in mind that the points being made here concern the God-man *personality* of Jesus Christ, it is not surprising that Thomasius' mathematical (the subtraction of attributes) interpretation of the kenotic motif does not achieve the desired result. Apparently, his fractional view of kenosis is not the only reason for his failure. Another reason, as the contributions of his successors suggest, is that his reinterpretation method does not go far enough to embrace the activities of the whole Trinity.

Continuing with Thomasius' reinterpretation method, the other mediating theologians extend the scope of the kenotic motif to a level, where it could be related to the inner life of the Trinity. On this, two-fold approaches are made: while theologians like *W. F. Gess* (1819-1891),[16] *A. Ebrard*,[17] *Bishop Martensen* (1808-1884)[18] and *P. T. Forsyth* (1848-1923)[19] seek to reinterpret kenosis so as to let it fit into the existing doctrine of God, other mediating theologians, influenced by Hegel, rather take to reinterpreting the doctrine of God so as to make it reflect the demands of the prevalent kenotic motif. Even as all the above men-

---

[16] Cf. W. F. Gess, *Die Lehre von der Person Christi*; ---, *Das Dogma von Christi Person und Werk*. According to Gess, when the Logos emptied himself of all divine attributes the duty of ruling the world was handed over to the Spirit by the Father till Christ's kenotic assignment on earth was over.

[17] Cf. J. H. A. Ebrard, *Das dogma von heiligen Abendmahl*, p. 790; ---, *Christliche Dogmatik*. In his view, the divine attributes were retained and adapted to the human nature of Christ, during his earthly life, but he was not conscious of them. Hence, the Logos was in control of the world, albeit unconsciously.

[18] Cf. H. Martensen, *Christian Dogmatics*. Differing slightly from the German kenoticist - especially from Thomasius' classification of the attributes of God into essential and non essential, and from Ebrard's distinction of conscious and unconscious levels of divine activities - bishop Martensen of Denmark, contends that the Logos should be seen as simultaneously existing in the finite and infinite forms during the earthly life of Jesus: in this way, Logos was in control of the world, even in his human appearance.

[19] Cf. P. T. Forsyth, *The Person and Place of Jesus Christ*. Forsyth treats the kenotic motif elaborately in this book. See also ---, The Divine Self-Emptying.

tioned authors undertake a reinterpretation of the kenotic motif, the nature of its application to the existing doctrine of God differs. For while the German kenoticists (Thomasius, Gess and Ebrard) tend to use the kenotic motif as a principle for understanding the inner Trinitarian life, the English-speaking kenoticists, typified in the person of P. T. Forsyth, avoid relating kenosis to the inner life of the Trinity. And although, Forsyth and other English-speaking kenoticists got their inspiration from the German kenoticism of the same period, they shun the ontological approach[20] which characterises the latter. Instead, they pay more attention to the study of the Bible, while settling for a limited, morally motivated and personalistic (though unsystematic) application of the kenotic motif to the problem of Jesus' consciousness.[21]

The kenotic motif receives a yet enriching dimension in the thought of Forsyth, thanks to his biblical approach, which enables him to conceive Christology in personalistic and moral terms, rather than in an abstract and ontological framework. By this method, he is able to emphasise the essential unity between *kenosis* and *plerosis* (the self-fulfilment) in the kenotic motif. Thinking together the pre-existence, the kenosis and the plerosis of Christ, Forsyth locates the event of divine self-emptying in the human and divine consciousness of Christ. Kenosis is, by that fact, not a veiling of the divine consciousness and activity, but a voluntary retraction of divine consciousness from actuality to potentiality, obligated by the need to fulfil a moral duty. Thus, even as he affirms Thomasius' thesis that "Self-emptying is Self-determination", he prefers to speak of "self-retraction" rather than "self-emptying", since the latter term could be misleading. Most importantly, Forsyth understands the kenotic motif as a divine kenosis, and plerosis as a descending and ascending movement of God to humankind and vice versa.[22] The kenotic act which constitutes the Incarnation is not a one-sided affair: it is at once the self-limitation of God and the fulfilment of humankind.

Using biblical categories to deepen the meaning of kenosis, as Forsyth does, is definitely the first step in the right direction. However, his attempt has failed to achieve the desired result, not because his interpretation of kenosis is wrong, but because he tries to fit his new vision of kenosis into the old doctrine of God without making any effort to reinterpret the latter. This is what D. G. Dawe calls

---

20 See for instance P. T. Forsyth, *The Person and Place of Jesus Christ*, pp. 294-295: "We cannot form any scientific conception of the precise process by which a complete and eternal being could enter on a process of becoming, how Godhead could accept growth, how a divine consciousness could reduce its own consciousness by volition."

21 D. G. Dawe, *op. cit.*, p. 131. This assessment applies also to Principal Fairbairn, H. R. Mackintosh, F. Weston and E. H. Gifford.

22 P. T. Forsyth, *The Person and Place of Jesus Christ*, p. 310.

pouring "new wine into old wineskins".[23] Forsyth's attempt is bound to fail, because as Dawe contends, a vision of kenosis that entails divine mutability cannot be compatible with the image of an immutable God, unless the prevalent notion of God is reformulated. [24]

The second approach of the mediating theologians in relating kenosis to the doctrine of the Trinity is strictly Hegelian.[25] The most outstanding Hegelian kenoticist of that century is Theodore Liebner (1803-1871).[26] In his fragmentary Christology, Liebner argues accordingly that the only way to make kenosis consistent is to see it as an act belonging essentially to God Himself. Before the historical kenosis of Jesus, there was already an eternal kenosis in the intra-Trinitarian life of God: the Father limited himself to make the being of the Son possible.

Following the pattern of the movement of the Absolute Spirit, Liebner conceives a gradual development of divine consciousness in Jesus Christ, whose accomplishment by the resurrection and ascension marks the full self-realisation of God. He regards the Hegelian idea of the Absolute as being identical with the doctrine of the Trinity. By doing so, however, he incurs upon his Christology the criticisms usually levelled against Hegelian philosophy of religion, namely, that God is made dependent on the world. Creation is no longer a free act of God, but

---

23 D. G. Dawe, *op. cit.*, p. 83.

24 Cf. D. G. Dawe, *op. cit.*, p. 140. The same argument in his words: "Kenosis implied changes in the divine life that could never be understood within the traditional doctrine of God. The kenotic motif could not be used to repair this or that part of the sagging house of orthodoxy. It had to become the basis of a total rebuilding job." (p. 143.)

25 For G. W. Hegel (1770-1831), the divine act of kenosis-exaltation is not a historical event, but the logical and necessary movement of the structure of reality, that is to say, of the Absolute Spirit on its way to his self-realisation through his other. Cf. W. Kern, Philosophische Pneumatologie, pp. 54-90, esp. p. 63; See also D. G. Dawe, *op. cit.*, p. 104-120. By implication, Hegel's ontology of divine nature does not represent the divine kenosis or God's entrance into finitude as a gratuitous act. Kenosis is basic for the triadic Movement of the Absolute Spirit and so is change entailed in God's nature. Cf. G. W. F. Hegel, *The Phenomenology of Mind*, p. 756; D. G. Dawe, *op. cit.*, p. 111. As a matter of fact, in conceiving reality in a triadic and dialectic pattern, Hegel is believed to have taken cue from the Christian doctrine of the Trinity (Dawe, p. 115). In any case, Hegel's claim that the triadic movement of the Absolute (of the Trinitarian God) follows a kenotic pattern brought a new dimension to the understanding of kenotic motif, which latter became a model for many theologians. Henceforth, the significance of kenosis is no longer restricted to the realm of Christology, it now becomes of a principle of interpretation for the whole reality.

26 Cf. T. A. Liebner, *Christologie oder die christologische Einheit des dogmatischen Systems*. Other contemporary left-wing theologians were A. E. Biedermann (1819-1895) and P. K. Marheineke (1780-1846).

a necessary one for His own self-completion. Secondly, the difference between God and the world becomes blurred, if not totally obliterated. The problem of using Hegelian philosophy to interpret the historical life of Jesus becomes yet more glaring in the work of David Friederich Strauss.[27] It is noted today, however, that the Hegelian conception of kenosis plays very little role in the kenotic Christologies of the nineteenth century, precisely because the Hegelian doctrine of God seems incompatible with many aspects of the Christian faith.[28]

3.1.2   S. Kierkegaard (1813-1855) and the Paradox of the Kenotic Motif

In contrast to the mediating and Hegelian theologians, Kierkegaard refuses to engage in any rigorous interpretation of the kenotic motif.[29] He is forced to adopt this position, apparently, because the attempt of his predecessors to use kenosis as a principle of intelligibility in the explication of divine nature failed. For him, kenosis is an absolute paradox of grace[30] which eludes any attempt at rationalisation.[31] That God assumed the form of a servant is a paradox of Christianity, an indisputable fact, that can only be illumined from the point of view of divine revelation. Kenosis is for him the only explanation that can be offered for the relationship between the divine and human natures in Jesus Christ. And on that score becoming man should still be considered contrary to divine nature.

Incarnation, he argues, "is the profoundest incognito, or the most impenetrable unrecognisableness that is possible; for the contradiction between being God and being an individual man is the greatest possible, the infinitely qualitative contradiction".[32] Thus, refusing to speculate on kenosis, either as a loss of divine attributes or change of consciousness, he rather prefers, to declare kenosis "a bold paradoxical assertion of God's sovereignty, which brings all speculation to an end".[33] Though Kierkegaard makes no explicit affirmation of either divine impassibility or passibility, his plea for a paradoxical approach to the interpretation of divine nature ushered in a new era of Protestant kenoticism which, without

---

27   D. F. Strauss, *Life of Jesus.*

28   Cf. Dawe, *op. cit.*, p. 126.

29   Although Kierkegaard's thought belongs to the nineteenth century in terms of origin, it is usually given a postion in the later theologies, since its relevance for Christology first came to lime light in the 20th century.

30   S. Kierkegaard, *Training in Christianity*, p. 131.

31   With Kierkegaard another era of Protestant kenoticism that is not basically Hegelian began.

32   *Ibid.*

33   Cf. D. G. Dawe, *op. cit.* p. 160.

being necessarily Hegelian, incorporates the positive qualities of the latter, namely that kenosis has something to do with the very nature of God.

3.1.3   The Russian Orthodox Theology and the Kenotic motif

The tendency to see kenosis as belonging to the very nature of God characterises the contribution of Russian Orthodox theologians. In their thought, the kenotic motif receives a much wider scope than it has in the Hegelian thought. In fact, the whole Russian secular and religious thought of that time operate with a kenotic interpretation of reality and life. What Nadejda Gorodetzky calls a "kenotic mind, or mood" indeed even dominates the Russian literature[34] of nineteenth century origin. And as this literature reveals, the Russian kenotic theme has no speculative origin, it emerges in the context of a cultural expression of a people's piety. Its use for the intelligibility of the doctrine of God is apparently of a later development, coinciding with the endeavour of such thinkers like *V. Soloviev* (1853-1900) and *S. N. Bulgakov* (1871-1948) to systematise the kenotic tradition theologically and philosophically.

In formulating their kenotic thoughts, both Soloviev and Bulgakov combine the Eastern Orthodox piety with Western philosophy (especially Hegelianism).[35] Much like Hegel, Soloviev believes that the world-process follows a kenotic pattern and that Christ's kenosis signifies a progressive divinisation of the universe.[36]

In a similar all-encompassing view of the kenotic motif, S. N. Bulgakov situates kenosis right within the Trinity,[37] and interprets the creation and Incarnation as divine acts of kenosis. Without however following the foot-steps of Hegel, he roots it in the intra-Trinitarian life. For unlike Hegel, Bulgakov understands kenosis essentially as self-giving, which he believes characterises the mutual act of love in the inner-Trinitarian life. God's kenotic relationship to the world (in the creation and in the works of salvation) is constituted by virtue of an outflow, an extension of the inner Trinitarian selfless relation of love. Creation, which is also a divine kenotic act, like the Incarnation, is grounded in and occasioned by the self-fulfilling kenotic act of the Trinitarian Persons and precisely in the nature of their self-sacrificial love, which is ever reaching for the other. In contrast to Hegel, he conceives the three Persons as becoming fulfilled in their mutual self-

---

34   See the novels of Gogol, Turgenev and Dostoevsky.

35   Cf. H. U. v. Balthasar, Mysterium Paschale, p. 152.

36   D. G. Dawe, *op. cit.*

37   S. Bulgakow, *Le Verbe Incarné: Agnus Dei*, pp. 138 ff. & 259 ff.

sacrificial love, so that God's relationship to the world does not bear any sign of dependency.[38]

Accordingly, he sees the Cross as a revelation of the inner-Trinitarian nature of love. As he writes in "The Power of the Cross", one of his festival sermons:

> The Cross is God Himself in His revelation to the world, God's power and glory. ... The Cross is the sacrificial essence of love, since love is sacrifice, self-surrender, self-abnegation, voluntary self-renunciation for the sake of the beloved. ...there is no bliss in love except in sacrificial self-surrender which is rewarded by responsive fulfilment. The Cross is the exchange of love, indeed love itself is exchange. ... The Holy Trinity is the eternal Cross as the sacrificial exchange of Three, the single life born of voluntary surrender, of a threefold self-surrender, of being dissolved in the divine ocean of sacrificial love. ... Love itself, God, in the eternal Cross surrenders Himself for the sake of His love. The three points in which the lines of the tri-cross end are images of the three divine self-subsistent Hypostases, and the point of their intersection is the co-inherence of the three, the Trinity in unity in sacrificial exchange.[39]

It is noteworthy that even as Bulgakov speaks of the Cross as the symbol of the self-sacrifice in the intra-Trinity, and pushes the view that "sacrificial exchange" characterises the very essence of God further, he nonetheless avoids a direct predication of suffering and change to the Godhead. Apparently, his argument is this: what the Son did, he did it for the whole Trinity, but it is not the Trinity who performed it.[40] One might wonder how Bulgakov could deny change and suffering in God and yet claims that an eternal sacrificial exchange takes place in the Godhead. To dispel this doubt, he goes further to distinguish, in a manner reminiscent of Luther,[41] between divine nature and divine form.

> The divine nature of the Logos as the source of life remains unchanged and undiminished in Christ. The humiliation affects not the nature (*ousia*) but the divine form or image (*morphe*) which is laid aside by Christ at His Incarnation.[42]

---

38 Cf. H. U. v. Balthasar, Mysterium Paschale, p. 153.

39 S. N. Bulgakov, The Power of the Cross, pp. 169-174, esp. 170-171; See also other essays and sermons in the same anthology, especially, "The Lamb of God" 114-118, "Divine Gladness" 178-182.

40 Cf. S. N. Bulgakov, *A Bulgakov Anthology*, p. 172: "It is the sacrifice not of the Son alone, but of the consubstantial and indivisible Trinity as a whole. The Son alone was incarnate and suffered on the Cross, but in him was manifested the sacrificial love of the Holy Trinity - of the Father who sends him, and of the Holy Spirit who rests upon him and upon his sorrowing Mother"

41 See the excursus in section 2.7.

42 See N. Gorodetzky, *The Humiliated Christ in Modern Russian Thought,*, p. 165-166, quoted in D. G. Dawe, *op. cit.*, p. 153.

Definitely, this distinction between the nature and the form of God cannot provide a plausible answer to the question, because, in effect, it raises a further question as to how the form and the nature of God can be related to one another. In any case, Bulgakov's contribution to the interpretation of the kenotic motif, and in fact that of the other Russian kenoticists, is enormous.[43] The Russian kenoticism has the value of conceiving the kenotic motif in a wider scope and also positively as a divine act of self-revelation. In this way it escapes the pitfalls of both the mediating and Hegelian kenoticisms: For, by making the kenotic motif relevant for the doctrines of God, creation and Incarnation, Bulgakov particularly avoids the Christological delimitation of the kenotic motif which characterises the Reformation and mediating theologies; and by interpreting the inner-Trinitarian kenosis as a mutual self-giving, which is complete and self-fulfilling in itself, he effectively evades the weakness of Hegelian kenoticism, namely, of making God dependent on the world process. Besides, by doing so, he leaves room for creation to remain a free act of God: and God retains His sovereignty.

However, no matter how attractive Bulgakov's conception of the intra-Trinitarian kenosis appears, it remains questionable whether kenosis can be used as a principle of intelligibility for the doctrine of God. Bulgakov is perhaps aware of this problem himself, because irrespective of his effort to illumine the inner-Trinitarian kenosis, he admits nonetheless that the kenosis in the Godhead is "divine mystery" which we dare "touch reverently" only because the Bible testifies to it.[44]

3.2 *Divine Impassibility and the Kenotic Motif in the Twentieth-century Theologies*

3.2.1 *The Protestant Approach*

The influence of Kierkegaard is very much evident in the twentieth-century Protestant theology. Already in the theologies of *Emil Brunner* and Karl Barth it can be seen that the understanding of kenosis as a paradox of divine revelation

---

43 The Russian kenotic Christology enjoys more popularity among the Roman Catholic theologians than among the Protestants. The reason for this is not far-fetched: it provides a Trinitarian interpretation of kenosis, which, despite its affirmation of the divine affecta-bility, makes God neither dependent on the world nor subject to change or suffering. With the discovery of the significance of the Russian kenoticism for the Trinitarian theology, Catholic theology, which has been conspicuously silent on the issue of kenosis from the anti-Arian controversy to the early part of this century, has began once more to fancy the kenotic Christology and doctrine of the Trinity. For the significance of the Russian Kenoticism on the doctrine of God, see H. U. v. Balthasar, Mysterium Paschale, p. 152 ff., and his other works; See also H. Küng, The Incarnation of God, p. 544.

44 S. N. Bulgakov, *A Bulgakov Anthology*, p. 117.

has become a basic presupposition. Interpreting the Incarnation as a sort of divine self-limitation, and admitting that the depth of this self-limitation is incomprehensible, Brunner for instance - in contrast to the claims of the mediating theologians - affirms that kenosis is the revelation rather than the concealment of divine presence:

> It is precisely the folly of the Cross which is the wisdom of God, it is precisely the *exinanitio*, the extreme point of the *kenosis*, which is the supreme height of the self-manifestation of God.[45]

By means of this statement Brunner makes two outstanding claims, which can be regarded as his contribution to the interpretation of kenosis: First, he rejects any attempt to interpret kenosis rationally, it is rather a given article of faith whose exact nature eludes every investigation. Secondly, he does not understand divine self-emptying as the hiddenness of God; kenosis is for him a form of divine revelation.

Karl Barth contends, similarly, that the kenotic motif can neither be expanded within the existing doctrine of God nor can it become a principle of intelligibility for intractable doctrinal problems. A reconstruction of this doctrine in the light of revelation is inevitable, he maintains. An improper starting point constitutes in his view the common error of the two preceding traditions (the patristic and mediating theologies): For instead of making the revelation of God the starting point of their theologies, they make "natural theology" and the popular philosophical notion of God their point of departure. So that, while the Greek philosophy overshadows divine revelation in the patristic doctrine of God, idealism obscures its reality in the nineteenth-century kenoticism.

Again, in opposition to the tendency in the mediating theologies, of perceiving a difference between the divine being and action, and of making divine self-limitation seem a laborious task on the part of God, which He had to accomplish in spite of Himself, Barth insists that "being" and "action" are one in God: God is nothing other than what He reveals Himself to be in history. His being is a being in action. To describe the being of God, one must take note of the unity of being and action in Him amply demonstrated in the revelation account of the Scriptures.[46] In effect, therefore, Barth sees God as a living God, capable of change and responsive relationship to the world. If God is capable of change and responsive relationship to the world, it does not immediately imply, however, that He is dependent on the world (Hegelianism). In view of this fact, Barth sees himself confronted with the problem of showing how God can have such a relation-

---

[45] E. Brunner, *The Christian Doctrine of Creation and Redemption*, p. 361.

[46] K. Barth, *Church Dogmatics*, pp. 257 ff.; See also D. G. Dawe, *op. cit.*, p. 168.

ship with the world and remain ultimately independent of it, and how He can change and yet remain constant.

To solve this problem, he points to the characteristic unity of love and freedom in God. Unlike human beings, who are obliged to love in order to grow and realise themselves, God loves freely. God is not dependent on His love for humankind; He is complete in Himself. His love towards us is an overflow of His being, which He employs to establish a creative and redemptive relationship. In this way, God remains Himself even while seeking a relationship with the world. God's (kenotic) love does not occur outside His being. "God is He who in His Son Jesus Christ loves all His children, in His children all men, and in men His whole creation."[47] God's freedom is twofold: negatively, He lacks any sort of constraint from the world, positively, He has the freedom to assume realities other than Himself, "without becoming unlike Himself".[48]

Accordingly, divine absoluteness does not consist in ontological changelessness. It consists primarily in God's unchanging will for love, and secondly in His ability to assume infinite individual variations in His relationship to the world without ceasing to be the transcendent God. Barth argues in his *Eklärung des Philipperbriefes*, 1933, that the exaltation of Christ should be understood as the disclosure of his hidden glory. In that case, kenosis does not entail any loss of divinity; it is rather the affirmation of God's lordship even when He is in the form of a servant. Jesus Christ is the Lord even in hiddenness.

> The way of the Son of God into the far country, i.e., into the lowliness of creaturely being, of being as man, into unity and solidarity with sinful and therefore perishing humanity, the way of His Incarnation is as such the activation, the demonstration, the revelation of His deity, His divine Sonship.[49]

The conception of kenosis as an affirmation of divinity rather than as a loss is certainly a way out of the problems that besieged the nineteenth-century kenoticism. How far it can go towards solving the problem is however debatable. At best, it weakens the sacrificial nature of God's kenotic act, and at worst, it tends to undermine the full humanity of Jesus Christ. For, as W. Pannenberg argues, if kenosis does not mean a radical self-giving, a sacrifice of "essential elements of the divine being" there is either a loss of Jesus' full humanity or a lack of a living unity between "divine majesty and human lowliness".[50] Besides, Barth's interpretation of kenosis as a revelation of divine nature exposes the dilemma of any ke-

---

47 *Ibid.*, p. 351.

48 *Ibid.*, , p. 165.

49 *Ibid.*, p. 211.

50 Cf. W. Pannenberg, *Jesus - God and Man*, pp. 319 & 322.

notic Christology, which on the one hand professes certain changes in God, but which on the other, insists on following the patristic "incarnational Christology constructed 'from above to below'".[51]

The trend towards seeing kenosis as a revelation of divine nature receives its climax in the war-time theology of *Dietrich Bonhoeffer*, who, conceiving the kenotic motif more radically than Barth, does not only perceive the ultimate meaning of Jesus' personality in his human self-emptying, but also contends that the presence of the divinity is best expressed to us in the absence of God, in His weakness and powerlessness:

> God would have us know that we must live as men who manage our lives without Him ... Before God and with God we live without God. God lets Himself be pushed out of the world on to the Cross. He is weak and powerless in the world, and that is precisely the way, the only way, in which He is with us and helps us. Matt. 8.17 makes it quite clear that Christ helps us, not by virtue of his omnipotence, but by virtue of his weakness and suffering... Only the suffering God can help... That is a reversal of what the religious man expects from God. Man is summoned to share in God's sufferings at the hands of godless world.[52]

In the thought of Bonhoeffer, the kenotic motif becomes very dialectical, a real paradox: God demonstrates His omnipotence in His weakness and suffering; He shows His presence in His absence. He is immanent in the world, even when He "lets Himself be pushed out of the world". And it is precisely in this self-limitation, in this immanence in the world that He clearly demonstrates His transcendence, which became yet more evident in the life of Jesus - a life lived only "for others".

> His (Jesus) 'being there for others' is the experience of transcendence. It is only this 'being there for others', maintained till death, that is the ground of his omnipotence, omniscience, and omnipresence.[53]

Hence, for Bonhoeffer kenosis is not foreign to a transcendent God. It would seem so only if we were conceiving God as an abstract, metaphysical idol, a working hypothesis posited to serve as the boundary of human knowledge. Bonhoeffer's main concern here is to correct our image of God, to show that the God of the Bible is not a mere "problem-solver", a *deus ex machina*, whose significance appears only when there is success. It amounts to power-worship when Christians seek their God only in the superlatives.[54]

---

51 *Ibid.*, p. 313. For details see pp. 312 - 322.

52 D. Bonhoeffer, *Letters & Papers from Prison,*, p. 360 f.

53 *Ibid.*, p. 381. See also R. G. Smith, *Secular Christianity*, p. 122.

54 See a similar argument from MacGregor in the next chapter.

Our relation to God is not a 'religious' relationship to the highest, most powerful, and best Being imaginable - that is not authentic transcendence - but our relation to God is a new life in 'existence for others', through participation in the being of Jesus. The transcendental is not infinite and unattainable tasks, but the neighbour who is within reach in any given situation. God in human form - not, as in oriental religions, in animal form, monstrous, chaotic, remote, and terrifying, nor in the conceptual forms of the absolute, metaphysical, infinite, etc., nor yet in the Greek divine-human form of 'man in himself', and therefore the Crucified, the man who lives out of the transcendent.[55]

The Protestant use of the kenotic motif becomes yet most radical in the *"Death of God" theology*,[56] where of course *the death of a particular image of God* and not the *death of God* is declared.[57] The "death of God" motif represents a radical form of kenotic Christology in most cases.[58] Indeed, to say that "God is dead" amounts to saying that the incarnate Word "empties itself of Spirit so as to appear and exist as flesh";[59] it is an indirect claim that "God is love".[60]

In his attempt to deepen the idea of divine *kenosis* using Hegel's thought, T. *Altizer*, a major proponent of the "death of God" theology, talks of a "kenotic metamorphosis" in God.[61] His representation of this view smacks of letting God disappear in a continuous self-sacrifice:[62] God annihilates Himself in the process and metamorphoses completely to the finite. On this point, Altizer fails to bring out the very best contribution of Bonhoeffer, namely, to see the absence of God, His "death" in the world as a mode of His presence, which in turn could have justified the talk about the suffering of God. The main weakness of the kenotic

---

55 *Ibid.*, p. 381-2.

56 It is true that the theme of the death of God began in the 19th century with Hegel (1820) and J. P. F. Richter (1825), and was used by Nietzsche and Feuerbach to further their anthropological interests, but the immediate impulse to this movement was given in the 60s by Barth's attack on "natural theology" and by Bonhoeffer's dictum that "God is weak and powerless" in a secular world. And just as Barth and Bonhoeffer were using their theologies to appeal to a revealed and biblical image of God in order to break the dominance of a metaphysical notion of God in Christian theology, the death of God theology influenced by their thought was meant to achieve the same aim.

57 See P. S. Fiddes, *op. cit.*, the chapter on "the death of God" pp. 175-206. There is no doubt that for some radical theologians, influenced by Nietzsche and Feuerbach, the motif of the death of God might denote the absence and non-existence of God; for such theologians the issue of divine suffering is definitely not a topic for discussion.

58 T. Altizer & W. Hamilton, *Radical Theology and the Death of God*, p. 135.

59 *Ibid.*, p. 154.

60 T. Altizer, *The Gospel of Christian Atheism*, p. 67.

61 *Ibid.*, p. 92.

62 See P. S. Fiddes, *op. cit.*, pp. 243-249.

motif in the Altizer's death of God theology can be seen however as his rejection of the concept of the Trinity.[63] This fact makes his theology lack the basis for maintaining the dialectical tension between divine transcendence and immanence.

This deficiency has been taken care of by *Jürgen Moltmann* in his Trinitarian conception of the kenotic motif. Explaining how God can suffer death, he prefers to speak of death in God as opposed to the "death of God"[64] He argues that the attribution of the direct experience of dying to God (the Father) is to be avoided, and prefers to say that the death of Jesus occurs *in* God. This view has two weaknesses: firstly, it gives the impression that Moltmann, neither takes the divinity of Jesus, nor the perichoretic unity of the Persons of the Trinity seriously; secondly, it does not show the exact consequence of dying for God. Regrettably, it lacks the dialectics of a God who can die and yet is not dead.

A clearer understanding and more precise articulation of the metaphor of divine death is to be found in the work of his counterpart, *E. Jüngel*.[65] The talk about the death of God, Jüngel contends, should be understood factually and not "only metaphorically".[66] It has a theological meaning and implies "that God is the one who involves Himself in nothingness".[67] By involving Himself in nothingness, and particularly by identifying Himself with the death of the man Jesus Christ, God locates nothingness "*within* the divine life";[68] He does not leave nothingness to itself, He conquers it:

> God is that one who can bear and does bear, can suffer and does suffer, in His being the annihilating power of nothingness, even the negation of death, without being annihilated by it.[69]

The act of localising nothingness within divine being has the double effect of determining being and non-being. Left to itself, nothingness is "chaotic" and "undefined", but once taken into divine life, it "receives its own *determination* and thus loses its abstract emptiness and its phantomly attraction".[70] This is how *creatio et nihilo* became a reality. The same act is an act of divine self-

---

63 *Ibid.*, p. 249; See T. Altizer, *The new Apocalypse*, p. 105-6. See also the critique on radical kenotic Christologies by C. Duquoc, Christologie, L'Homme Jesus, pp. 329-336.

64 J. Moltmann, *The Crucified God*, p. 207. We defer a detailed analysis of Moltmann's position to the fourth chapter of this study.

65 E. Jüngel, *God as the mystery of the world*, esp. pp. 184-224.

66 *Ibid.*, p. 217.

67 *Ibid.*, p. 218.

68 *Ibid.*, p. 219.

69 *Ibid.*

70 *Ibid.*

determination; then, by subjecting Himself to nothingness, God determines Himself as the self-giving one, as the *"one who exists for others"*. He defines and determines Himself, by the same token, as the "one who suffers endlessly ... for the sake of others" in a "peculiar dialectic of being and non-being, of life and death ... which as pacified dialectic is called love".[71] God is then the "overflowing being", whose sovereignty or abundance is defined, first and foremost, not in *self-possession*, but only in His *overflowing* nature. He constitutes Himself in "Existence", in "Going-Out-Of-Himself into nothingness" and in "Self-communication". In other words, "His 'inner being' is itself a turning toward what is 'outside'", which occurs "without *inner* necessity, but with the innermost involvement", in the "freedom of love".[72] Divine love and freedom are thus co-inclusive.

As a matter of fact, Jüngel's account of God's "struggle" with nothingness and of its location "within divine life" can stretch one's comprehension beyond limits. It does nonetheless seem to provide immense possibilities for further development of the theology of divine suffering, especially if it implies, as we suppose, that God's involvement in the finite is an expression of His freedom. For if God does not stand outside of nothingness but goes "eternally and inexhaustibly"[73] out of Himself into nothingness, into its most familiar and extreme form - death - and instead of loosing His divinity defines and determines it, then the fulfilling aspect of kenotic motif, its paradoxical and dialectical significance for the conception of God begins to appear, and the talk about divine suffering receives a more serious note.

In the realm of a Christology "from blow" and in the context of his universal historical approach to the issue of salvation, *W. Pannenberg* pays more attention to the eschatological significance of the kenotic motif than to its pre-existent root. Accordingly, he declines to conceive the unity of God and Jesus as an *a priori* phenomenon. The unity of God and the man Jesus, he contends, must be conceived "only retroactively from the perspective of Jesus' resurrection".[74] This does not imply that there was no unity between the Father and the pre-existent Christ before the Easter event; it does however denote that such a unity was hidden, not only to his contemporaries, but also to Jesus himself.[75] This latent unity was made manifest through the resurrection, which in itself consummates the

71 *Ibid.*, pp. 219-220.

72 *Ibid.*, p. 220

73 *Ibid.*, p. 224.

74 W. Pannenberg, *Jesus - God and Man*, p. 321.

75 *Ibid.*

mutual dedication of the Son to the Father and of the Father to the Son.[76] Thus, for the purpose of the Incarnation, Pannenberg argues, there was merely an intentional unity *a priori* between the pre-existent Christ and the Jesus of history; the actual personal unity is an *a posteriori* reality that emerged after the resurrection and exaltation.

In this way, Pannenberg seeks to ground the unity of God and man in Jesus using the kenotic motif. By that measure, kenosis leads to the realisation, rather than to the diminution of the divinity of Christ. For the more he lived according to the will of his Father, that is to say, the more he surrendered himself to him, the more his personal unity with the Father was attaining its consummation.[77] When considered from a historical perspective, therefore, kenosis reveals, and in fact constitutes rather than conceals the divinity of Jesus Christ.[78] This *a posteriori* unity between the Father and the Son, according to Pannenberg, presupposes a Christology "from below", which possesses the extra credit of retaining the "element of newness" of the resurrection-exaltation.[79] The exaltation of Jesus Christ does not denote a return to, but the attainment of, the divine status, which was made possible through a kenotic life.

From the point of view of such a kenotic unity, Pannenberg feels that it is possible to conceive

...a God who is alive in Himself, who can become something and precisely in so doing remain true to Himself and the same. ... God's becoming and His sameness must be considered more exactly in their relatedness.[80]

Similarly, in his book *Systematische Theologie* published in 1988, he argues that the passion of Jesus Christ is an event, which does not leave the eternal calm of the Trinitarian life of God untouched. Even as he says that, Pannenberg disapproves of any direct talk about the death of God in the Hegelian sense. Thus af-

---

76 *Ibid.*, p. 336.

77 *Ibid.*: "Through his dedication to the Father Jesus shows himself identical with the pre-existent Son already implied in the pre-Easter talk of the Father." To justify his use of "dedication" for the establishment of a historical and personal divine-human unity in Christ, Pannenberg quotes the following sentence from Hegel. "In friendship and love I give up my abstract personality and win thereby concrete personality. The truth of personality is just this, to win it through this submerging, being submerged in the other." (G. W. F. Hegel, *Lectures on the Philosophy of Religion*, Vol. III, pp. 24 f.

78 W. Pannenberg, *Jesus - God and Man*, p. 336: "The mutual dedication of Father and Son to one another, which constitutes the Trinitarian unity of God, also establishes thereby first of all the true divinity of the Son."

79 *Ibid.*, p. 321.

80 *Ibid.*, p. 320. The influence of Karl Rahner is evident here, although he criticised the latter's view on divine immutability.

firming the authenticity of the traditional thesis that the Son of God suffered only in his human nature, he contends that any direct talk about the death of God would amount to a reverse Monophysitism; this should be avoided because, in his view, the distinction of the two natures must be strictly maintained. Yet in contrast to this view, Pannenberg also claims that if God is love, we can justifiably believe and say that the Father is equally touched by the suffering of the Son.[81] This looks like a contradiction. In any case, critics observe that Pannenberg's eschatological view of the relationship of the Son with the Father does not support the idea that God is touched by the events in Jesus Christ. For, if God is conceived as the power of the future and the realisation of the divinity is made a matter of eschatology, as Pannenberg does, it would seem that God skips the hard realities of suffering in history and thus abandons the sufferer to his fate.[82]

The Hegelian conception of reality as history, which characterises most of the Protestant approach, is reformulated outstandingly in the American *process theology*. Taking its cue from the process philosophy of *Alfred Whitehead* and *Charles Hartshorne*, and departing from the dialectic and kenotic approaches of other Protestant theologies, process theologians attempt to crack the hard nut of the paradox of divine nature through a "dipolar" conception of God, which uses both empirical and a priori philosophical methods. While, from the perspective of an empirical methodology, Whitehead suggests that a dipolar distinction must be made between the primordial and the consequent natures of God, Hartshorne proposes a dipolar distinction between the necessary existence and contingent actuality of God. Despite these variations in the formulation of the divine nature,

---

81 Cf. *Systematische Theologie* 1, pp. 341-342.

82 Cf. J. Sobrino, *Christology at the Crossroads*, p. 78 n. 28. Pannenberg's excessive emphasis on eschatology has been variously criticised. Firstly, his views about the events of the resurrection and God as power of the future make the idea of divine intervention in death and resurrection of Jesus seem impossible. (Cf. J. C. DeYoung, Event and Interpretation of the Resurrection, p. 140). Secondly, his view about the retroactive significance of the resurrection, makes the claim that God was present in Jesus during his earthly life seem fake, just as it smacks of adoptionism (Cf. B. McDermott, The Personal Unity of Jesus and God, 292-294; R. E. Olson, The Human Self-Realization of God, 207-223. For more criticisms on this see S. J. Grenz, The Appraisal of Pannenberg, pp. 36-45.

all process theologies[83] proceed from a common understanding of reality as consisting essentially of processes and becoming.[84]

For process theology, therefore, God is not only the ground, but also part of the processes of reality. In what is generally called a cosmological understanding of God, Whitehead contends that "God is not to be treated as an exception to all metaphysical principles" but rather as "their exemplification ".[85] Reality follows the same order which God embodies in His nature. In His "primordial nature", God is the eternal and absolute potential of all that exists, but by virtue of His "consequent nature", He is receptive to all actualisation. His dipolar nature has two major implications with regard to His relation to the world: Firstly, He directs the world not coercively but persuasively.[86] Secondly, God affects and is also affected by everything that happens - He is "the great companion - the fellow sufferer who understands".[87] Similarly, Hartshorne, interpreting divine perfection in the light of His dipolar nature, argues for the assumption of a dual transcendence in God: God, who transcends all realities, is Himself surpassable by His own future.[88] In other words, God is absolute in His existence, but determined, partly by His own choice and partly by the state of affairs in His creation. Together with his conception of a "dual transcendence" for God, Hartshorne employs his dipolar panentheistic concept of God in the revisions of divine attributes - eternity, omniscience, omnipotence and impassibility. In that sense, God is believed to be, not outside of, but eminently within time; He knows all knowable, but not unknowable things; His power is persuasive rather than coercive. Consequently, He is ultimately passible as much as He is active, sharing the joys, pains and sufferings of His creatures in the world.

---

83 There are a whole lot of significant proponents of process thought, whose work we cannot consider in this study. It suffices here perhaps to only make reference to them. See for instance, J. B. Cobb, Jr., *A Christian Natural Theology*; J. B. Cobb and D. R. Griffin, *Process Theology*; S. M. Ogden, *The Reality of God*; D. D. Williams, *The Spirit and the Forms of Love*.

84 Cf. D. A. Pailin, *God and the Processes of Reality*, pp. 42, 466 ff.; ---, Process Theology, pp. 467-470.

85 A. N. Whitehead, *Process and Reality*, p. 343.

86 *Ibid.*, p. 215.

87 *Ibid.*, p.

88 Cf. C. Hartshorne, *Creative Synthesis and Philosophic Method*, p. 243: "The transcendent is eternally, independently, and maximally good and aware of whatever is true, but the concrete beauty, the intensity, harmony and richness, of the divine life can reach no final maximum . . . God is absolute and immutable ethically but open to increase aesthetically". See also the same author, *A Natural Theology for Our Time*, pp. 17 ff, 71 ff.; ----, *The Logic of Perfection*, pp. 40-44

All these are seen as part of God's creative activity. And it is precisely this aspect of divine creativity that seems to undermine the process conception of God. In fact, process theology, especially in the Whiteheadian approach, gives the over-all impression that God rather than creating is being created Himself.[89] Another serious objection which bedevils the process approach, despite its useful insights into the paradox of divine suffering, is the general disregard for the significance of the kenotic motif. And this no doubt separates their approach very strongly from other Protestant and Hegelian theologies of divine suffering.

In summary, it can be observed that a strong Hegelian influence is characteristic of the Protestant kenotic tradition, which, despite varied dialectical and paradoxical approaches, is prone to making much more univocal affirmations of the divine suffering.[90] Though as Pannenberg's contribution shows, Hegelian influence must not necessarily lead to a clear assertion of the passibility of God. In any case, it is the strong Hegelian influence that differentiates the Protestant from the Catholic approach. As we shall see below, the Catholic approach is much more reserved about affirming divine suffering, and characteristically seeks the middle position between Hegel and tradition on this issue.[91]

3.2.2   The Roman Catholic Approach

From the last years of the Middle Ages down to the mid-twentieth century the Roman Catholic theologies, in contrast to the Protestant theologies, were silent on the issue of divine suffering. They were also reluctant to address the issue of kenosis especially where it was evident that it connotes mutability on the part of the deity. For that reason, the kenotic motif remained unpopular in the Catholic theological circles from the counter-Reformation until recently, after it had become customary to apply it to the Trinitarian Godhead and to interpret it in a manner worthy of expressing the fullness of the divinity. Since its rediscovery however, the kenotic motif has also become the main favourite principle for addressing the issue of divine suffering in the Catholic theology. To substantiate this

---

89 Cf. D. Pailin, *The Anthropological Character of Theology*, p. 59. Pailin contends, however, that Whitehead does not in actual fact mean, as is implied, that creativity produces God, though, God is not presented as being the author of creativity either.

90 This is typical, not only of the European, but also of the Asian Protestant theologies of suffering. Cf. K. Kitamori, *Theology of the Pain of God*; J. Y. Lee, *God Suffers for Us*.

91 Cf. T. R. Krenski, *Passio Caritatis*, pp. 25 f. & 362 ff.

claim, we shall sketch the contributions of four Catholic theologians to our problem in the light of the kenotic motif.[92]

In his interpretation of the mystery of Incarnation, *Karl Rahner*, one of the best known Catholic theologians of this century, adopts an approach that draws significantly from the kenotic motif. Kenosis is seen at once as that which constitutes the human essence - "man is in so far as he gives up himself"[93] - and also as that act by which God *became man*. For this reason, Rahner dares to approach Christology, not "from above" as is characteristic of tradition, but "from below", right from the horizon of anthropology, and precisely from the fact of human transcendence. The human transcendence, which Rahner conceives as almost identical with the human kenotic act of self-surrender, "brings our existence and God's existence together"[94] in a very mysterious way. Human nature is endowed with the immeasurable openness towards the mysterious reality of God and constitutes itself in its ability to give itself to God; in fact, human nature is itself, the more it reaches out to God and surrenders itself to Him. Consequently, humanity is indefinable and incomprehensible, except in reference to God.[95]

If the essence of the human nature is thus constituted, according to Rahner, it all means that God, by becoming man, i.e. by assuming human nature, brings the constitutive endeavour of humankind to a fulfilment, so that, this occurrence can be termed "the unique, *supreme*, case of the total actualisation of human reality".[96] Therefore, by virtue of its "inmost essence and constitution", i.e. of its kenosis or transcendence, human nature is endowed "with the possibility of being assumed, of becoming... the paradigm (*Grammar*) of a possible utterance" of God Himself.[97] This explains precisely why the Word of God took human form and

---

92   On the theology of divine suffering in general, there are other significant systematic and exegetical contributions, which we cannot consider in this connection: On the German side see, K. Lehmann, God im Leiden, pp. 24-48; W. Kasper, The God of Jesus Christ, pp. 189-197; H. Riedlinger, *Vom Schmerz Gottes*; J. B. Brantschen, *Gott is größer als unser Herz*; G. Greschake, Leiden und Gottesfrage; ----, *Der Preis der Liebe*; P. Koslowski, Der leidende Gott, pp. 5622-565; A. Bodem, Leiden Gottes, pp. 586-611); H. Vorgrimler, Leiden Gottes", pp. 20-26. On the French side, the following works deserve attention: J. Galot, *Dieu-souffre-t-il?*; ---, Le Dieu trinitaire et la Passion du Christ, 70-87; F. Varillon, *La Souffrance de Dieu*; J. Kamp, *Souffrance de Dieu*.

93   K. Rahner, On the Theology of the Incarnation.

94   *Ibid.*, p. 108.

95   *Ibid.*, p. 109: "The indefinable nature, whose limits - 'definition' - are the unlimited reference to the infinite fullness of the mystery, has, when assumed by God as *his* reality, simply arrived at the point to which it always strives by virtue of its essence."

96   *Ibid.*, p. 110.

97   *Ibid.*, p. 115.

not any other form of being. If God took *human form*, it does not mean, however, that He took up an already existent human being: Incarnation is neither an admixture of divinity and humanity, nor a coating of human form with divine form. "It is something that comes to be and is constituted in essence and existence when and in so far as the Logos empties itself".[98] Thus the basic occurrence of the mystery of Incarnation can not be explained with the concept of assumption, but with .

> the self-emptying, the coming to be, the kenosis and *genesis* of God Himself, who can come to be by *becoming* another thing, derivative, in the act of constituting it, without having to change in His own proper reality which is the unoriginated origin.[99]

Thus, for Rahner, neither the Incarnation nor the creation can be adequately explained without the concept of kenosis. For "In the Incarnation, the Logos creates by taking on, and takes on by emptying himself".[100] God calls creation into existence out of nothingness, but in the Incarnation He takes on the human reality by emptying Himself - in a creative act of self-emptying. By so doing, He not only gives the finite "an infinite depth" in Jesus Christ, but also opens in him "a passage into the infinite for all the finite".

Seen from this point of view, self-emptying belongs to the very nature of God and it is identical with the divine self-communication. As a mode of divine self-communication, kenosis is not an "extraordinary" act for God: His inner-Trinitarian mutual self-giving is presupposed in His kenotic relationship toward the world in Jesus Christ. The kenotic act of Jesus is therefore the continuation of that eternal process in God which constitutes His inner-Trinitarian relatedness and distinctions. [101]Consequently, only Jesus Christ, the immanent *Word* of God - not any other Person of the Trinity nor any other human being - could have become the self-utterance of God in the world. This also explains the singularity of

---

[98] *Ibid.*, p. 116.

[99] *Ibid.*, p. 114-5: "By the fact that he remains in his infinite fullness while he empties himself ... the ensuing other is his own proper reality. He brings about that which is distinct from himself, in the act of retaining it as his own, and vice versa, because he truly wills to retain the other as his own, he constitutes it in its genuine reality. God himself goes out of himself, God in his quality of the fullness which gives away itself. He can do this. Indeed, his power of subjecting himself to history is primary among his free possibilities ... And for this reason, Scripture defines him as love - whose prodigal freedom is the indefinable itself."

[100] *Ibid.*, p. 117.

[101] *Ibid.*, p. 115: "The immanent self-utterance of God in his eternal fullness is the condition of the self-utterance of God outside himself".

the Incarnation in Jesus Christ, who is by that means "the self-utterance of God in its self-emptying, because God expresses *Himself* when He empties Himself".[102]

In view of the event of the Incarnation it is evident for Karl Rahner that the divine kenosis entails change. Yet he is of the opinion that the axiom of divine immutability, which he considers a postulate of philosophy, must be retained as an ontological principle because of its methodological significance.[103] Although, Rahner would accept the axiom of divine immutability on philosophical grounds, he is reluctant to affirm it on the ground of faith.[104] In his attempt to combine his philosophical conviction with his vision of faith, he declares: "God can become something, He who is unchangeable in Himself can Himself become subject to change *in something else*".[105] He seeks here to account for the paradox of divine nature by admitting on the one hand that the inner nature of God can have an experience of suffering and change, but denying on the other that God changes in His inner nature. On account of what he believes to be a dialectical approach, he maintains that God really suffered on the Cross and that the death of Jesus Christ could also be understood as the death of God.[106]

Rahner's dialectical interpretation of the doctrine of divine immutability in Trinitarian terms is fascinating. However, its appeal not withstanding, his conclusion is ambiguous, at least in terms of the following passages:

> ... since God is unchangeable, we must say that God who is unchangeable in Himself can change *in* another (can in fact become man). But this 'changing in another' must neither be taken as denying the immutability of God in Himself nor simply be reduced to a changement *of* the other.[107]

If God's "changing *in* another" does not imply "a changement *of* the other", what else can it mean except that God Himself underwent the change in Himself? This is exactly what Rahner would not want to admit. And if, as he writes in another

---

102 *Ibid.*, p. 116.

103 *Ibid.*, p. 114.

104 *Ibid.*, p. 113 n. 3: Here, he gives priority to faith, as he says, philosophy must "orientate itself according to the message of faith and not try to lecture it".

105 *Ibid.*, p. 113.

106 K. Rahner, *Sacramentum Mundi* II (London, 1969) p. 207: "The immutable God in himself of course has no destiny and therefore no death. But he himself (and not just what is other than he) has a destiny, through the Incarnation in what is other than himself... In that case, however, this death of God in his being and becoming in what is other than himself, in the world, must clearly belong to the law of the history of the new and eternal covenant in which we have to live."

107 K. Rahner, On the Theology of the Incarnation, p. 113 n.3.

connection, "The 'economic' Trinity is the 'immanent' Trinity and vice versa",[108] it becomes difficult to understand why he makes the distinction between God's change in Himself and His change in another. Despite Rahner's effort to interpret the doctrine of divine immutability anew, from the point of view of a transcendental Christology, his conclusion does not seem to go beyond that of the High Scholasticism as presented in the theology of St. Thomas Aquinas. Is the idea of an "unchangeable God who changes in another not identical with Aquinas concept of *relatio rationis*[109] - of a conceptual relationship?

Karl Rahner would certainly not accept this comparison. However, Küng's criticism of Aquinas' concept of *relatio rationis* can justifiably be extended to Rahner's view: namely, that "although this theory is able to explain that the Word of God in becoming man remained completely what it was - that is, God - it cannot show convincingly that the Word *itself* became man. For it is not flesh that became the Logos, but the Logos that became flesh. It is a question of the *self-emptying of the Logos*".[110]

There is no doubt, that by courageously speaking of God's changeability (albeit in another), Karl Rahner has opened a new avenue[111] for contemporary Catholic theology in its struggle to reinterpret the doctrine of God satisfactorily. As a matter of fact, Karl Rahner's formula sets the framework within which every serious

---

[108] *Ibid.*, p. 89.

[109] Cf. Aquinas, *Summa contra Gentiles* II.12; *Summa Theologica* I. q.13 a.7; also A. Krempel, *Doctrine de la relation chez St. Thomas*, 563, 570 and Küng, *op. cit.*, 531. Aquinas uses this concept to describe the relationship of the divine Logos to human nature, according to which the divine Logos is said to have remained unchanged in the Incarnation while the human nature alone changed. Explaining what the conceptual relationship means, Aquinas gives an example of a situation where someone is sitting beside me. Assuming this person was sitting at my left and I on his right, if he changes to my right, I would automatically be sitting on his right, without having changed my position. Since it is the other who made the move, I have not "really" changed my position, I have merely acquired a new "conceptual relationship. In a similar manner, the Incarnation brought change to human nature but not to divine nature.

[110] H. Küng, *The Incarnation of God*, p. 532; H. U. v. Balthasar has also criticised Rahner's reinterpretation of divine immutability as insufficient, because it tends to depict the inner-Trinitarian life as unaffected by the event in the world (Cf. Balthasar, *TD II/2*, 466, 479; *TD III*, 300). Similarly, W. Pannenberg criticises Rahner's idea of kenosis on the same ground that it denies the "radicality of self-relinquishment". "It will hardly suffice to speak only of a becoming 'in the other' as if an inner being of God were to be distinguished that remains completely untouched by such becoming." (W. Pannenberg, *Jesus - God and Man*, p. 320.) These are all theologians who want to see kenosis having relevance in the inner Being of God.

[111] See P. Schoonenberg, *Auf Gott hin denken*, p. 69.

Catholic solution must be presented. For it takes the middle course between two extreme positions of tradition and modernism respectively. By maintaining that "God is unchangeable in Himself", Rahner declines to follow the extremes of Hegelianism and process thought which tend to allow the being of God to disappear in the fluidity of continuous process.[112] By adding that God changes in another, he has on the other hand taken a bold step to improve on the classical doctrine of divine immutability, without departing from the track set by the tradition.

However, *P. Schoonenberg*, who like Rahner makes a Christology "from below" his starting point, formulates a much more radical theory of the kenotic motif. The latter's concept of kenosis is perhaps the most radical within Catholic theology. Being reluctant to apply kenosis to any event in the celestial sphere, due to epistemological reasons, he restricts the significance of kenosis to the earthly life of Jesus Christ.[113] Contending that the pre-existent Word, the pre-existent Christ should not be made the immediate object of our reflection,[114] he declines to use the kenotic motif in the interpretation of the Incarnation.

For him, kenosis is not a divine occurrence that concerns the vertical relationship between heaven and earth, nor that between the pre-existent Christ and the historical Jesus, but rather a horizontal act, which occurred only in the earthly life of Jesus Christ, in his choice and decision to renounce his heavenly glory. What Jesus emptied was not his divinity, he merely renounced the people's misconceived notion of the Messiah: publicity, throne, kingship, political power and self-regard. Since Schoonenberg only recognises the human kenosis, the Incarnation does not of course involve change on the side of the Logos.

This view is hardly acceptable, for if kenosis is reduced in this sense to the level of being the mere renunciation of "misconceptions", it is doubtful whether Christ *actually* emptied himself. Is kenosis for that reason not bereft of its theological meaning and significance?

In an article written after the death of Karl Rahner,[115] Schoonenberg tries to further develop Karl Rahner's thesis that the unchangeable God does not change in Himself but *"in* another", in the human nature of Christ. Although in the be-

---

112 However, as Küng has shown, Rahnerism also has traces of Hegel's influence which he combines with the influence of Heidegger. H. Küng, *op. cit.*, p. 539; See also, K. Rahner, On the Theology of the Incarnation, p. 113 n.3. According to Küng, even Balthasar, despite his consciousness of tradition, made more use of Hegel than he acknowledges in his work. See op. cit., p. 544.

113 P. Schoonenberg, Kenosis, p. 25.

114 *Ibid.*, p. 28 ff.

115 P. Schoonenberg, Gott ändert sich am andern, pp. 323-332. Or in his book, *Auf Gott hin denken*, pp. 69-81.

ginning of his article he sets out to justify Rahner's claim, he ends his reflection affirming the dialectical truth that "the immutability and mutability, being and becoming of God all obtain in the same Being".[116] Of course, we cannot assess his views here in terms of this last statement, which seems to be out of the way, but rather in terms of his presuppositions. In that sense, the criticisms of Rahner's view apply equally to him.

Hans Urs von Balthasar, who, perhaps like no other Catholic theologian in recent times, makes use of the kenotic motif to develop and interpret the doctrine of God, goes beyond Rahner without, however, leaving the framework set by the latter. Combining his profound knowledge of the Catholic tradition with a deep insight into the Scriptures, Balthasar makes kenosis the basis of a theology of the Cross. And following the example of the Russian theologian, Bulgakov, who applies kenosis not only to the event of the Cross, but also to creation and to the understanding of the doctrine of the Trinity, Balthasar sees the earthly kenosis of Christ presupposed by a primordial kenosis (*Urkenose*) in the Godhead, which he interprets as the mutual "selflessness" of the divine Persons.

Balthasar's contribution is very significant for our study because he uses the concept of kenosis in a manner that allows discussions on the very important aspects of a theology of divine suffering: the issues of a dialectical understanding of divine immutability, of the Trinitarian dimension, and of divine omnipotence and freedom feature prominently. Above all, he tries to reflect on this problem taking a midway position between two extremes of immutability and mutability in God and, while illuminating the paradox of the divine nature, seeks to maintain the tension between divine passibility and impassibility.[117] Balthasar's contribution will be treated separately in the sixth chapter.

Another significant contribution towards the application of the kenotic motif to the doctrine of God in contemporary Catholic theology is provided by *Heribert Mühlen*. In his short, but very provocative, article,[118] he proposes a reinterpretation of the old Christological dogma in the light of a Trinitarian theology of the Cross.[119] The cross-event reveals uniquely, he contends, both the unity and the difference of divine persons, and is, for that reason, the beginning, the middle and the end, not only of Christology but also of all theology.[120]

---

[116] P. Schoonenberg, *Auf Gott hin denken*, p. 74.

[117] We shall dedicate chapter six of this study to an analysis of Balthasar's kenotic Christology and passiology.

[118] H. Mühlen, *Die Veränderlichkeit Gottes*.

[119] *Ibid.*, p. 33.

[120] *Ibid.*, pp. 33 & 37.

Mühlen argues that a new hermeneutic method is required because, in his view, it is impossible to do a theology of the Cross today from the background of a static "substance-ontology". In place of the prevalent substance-ontology, therefore, he proposes the use of personal categories for the reinterpretation of the old dogmatic statements. This, he believes, is in line with the biblical hermeneutic.[121] Consequently, he suggests that the Nicene formula of Homousia (one in being) with the Father should no longer be understood in its substance-ontological terms (as a spatial, object-like (*dinghafte*) unity, not as a unity of indivisible and simple substance),[122] but rather in terms of a personal unity (the unimaginable immediacy and directness of the presence of the Father in the Son),[123] occurring in the "horizon of a personal dialectic".[124]

Thus mediating with the aid of personalism, between tradition and the Scriptures, Mühlen comes to the following conclusion:

> The Father and the incarnate Son are co-existential (*gleichseiendlich*) in so far as they are a "We-community", absolutely exclusive but historically and economically (*heilsgeschichtlich*) effective.[125]

The Father is for that reason, the "I", the Son the "Thou", the Holy Spirit, the "We" of the relationship between the I and the Thou.

The personal unity of the Trinitarian persons is not of a later development; it is a constitutive unity, which obtains a priori as *perichoresis*, as a prehistoric mutual interpenetration of the divine persons.[126] The "We-ness" of the divine being should therefore be seen as intrinsic and original to the Trinity.[127] This perichoretic unity does not however obscure the individuality of the persons, the Father and the Son perpetually subsist in the mutuality of I and Thou. The dialectic of divine love is such that, at the point of their most radical contrast (the Cross) the depth of the nearness and unity of persons appears, and inversely, the identity of

---

[121] Arguing that the bible is composed in terms of personological categories, Mühlen insists for instance that the self-introduction of God as "I am who am" (Ex. 3,14) should not be understood as in terms of "being" in the abstract-ontological sense, but primarily as "being" in the sense of "being-with" (*Mitsein*), as being in relation, as being a person (*Ibid.*, p. 21). Similarly, the Johannine passages speaking of Jesus' "oneness" with his Father (Jn 10: 15,30,38; 14: 11; 17: 11,21,22), would be best understood if explained on personal terms.

[122] *Ibid.*, p. 22.

[123] *Ibid.*, p. 13.

[124] *Ibid.*, pp. 13 & 28.

[125] *Ibid.*, pp. 22 & 23.

[126] *Ibid.*, pp. 24 & 33.

[127] *Ibid.*, p. 25.

their personal unity is only a proof of their differentiation.[128] Mühlen sees this differentiation in the Trinity as the only explanation for Jesus' cry of dereliction on the Cross.[129]

Although the personal and perichoretic unity of the Trinitarian persons is an a priori reality, our knowledge of it, Mühlen adds, comes a posteriori through the revelation; accordingly, no assumptions should be made about the inner nature of God, which he believes lies beyond the reach of our intellectual endeavour.[130] The revelation of God, especially His revelation on the Cross, should be the starting point of theology, though reference could be made to the prehistoric Christ to illuminate what happened on the Cross. Focusing on the activities of the economic Trinity in history, we learn therefore that the essence of God consists in His self-giving, in His kenosis.[131]

The Father gives himself away by giving away the Son, that which is strictly his own; and the Son gives himself away by his surrendering (Kph. 5: 2,25) and emptying himself (Phil. 2: 7). Besides revealing the "sameness" of identity of the Father and the Son, this double kenosis, according to Mühlen, shows the essence of the divine being (*das Wesen seines Wesens*) as self-giving (*Weggabe des Eigensten*).[132]

The fact that God is essentially self-giving and that He demonstrates this to us through the giving away of His Son does not imply, however, that the Cross is a part of divine nature. In order to retain the specific Christian significance of the Cross, we must see the Cross as a scandal and as a painful occurrence for God.[133] In other words, the Cross is not a part of God's course for salvation, but it had to be, by virtue of God's fidelity to His plan and covenant. In this sense, the event of the Cross occurred in the spirit of "being for us" of both the Father and the Son.

This further demonstrates the procession of the Holy spirit and for that reason also the Trinitarian structure of this event.[134] Thus pneumatologically speaking, the event of the Cross is the real temporal (*Zeitwerdung*) epiphany of the proces-

---

[128] *Ibid.*, pp. 32-33.

[129] *Ibid.*, p. 32.

[130] *Ibid.*, p. 37.

[131] *Ibid.*, pp. 30-33.

[132] *Ibid.*, pp. 30-1.

[133] In the same score, he rejects Hegel's "speculative Friday", which suggests that the Cross is a process of God's self-realisation or self-development. Cf. *Ibid.*, p. 30.

[134] *Ibid.*, pp. 33-4.

sion of divine love consummated in the strong identity of the Father and the Son. It is, as such, the divine mode of existence - that process, in which the *a priori* divine unity becomes concretised in the third mode of existence. Hence, while the Incarnation is the temporal concretisation of the divine Thou, the event of the Cross is the temporal epiphany of the divine "We".

At this point, Mühlen's argument seems to become ambiguous, and more so when he insists that the Trinitarian activity (*die geschichtliche Selbstdurchsetzung des trinitarischen Wir-Aktes*) on the Cross should neither imply that the Father and the Son offered themselves together nor that the Father himself suffered.[135] In any case, his effort to remain within the tradition of modern Catholic theology is evident, namely, that of seeking a midway between tradition and Hegel: Unlike the tradition, he wants to maintain that the Cross affects God in the most intimate and unpleasant way.[136] But unlike Hegel he does not allow the Cross to become intrinsic to divine nature.

Concretely therefore, he reinterprets rather than rejects the axiom of divine immutability. According to Mühlen, divine immutability is not to be conceived however as an ontological component of God, as a static self-identity on His part, but rather as God's consistent fidelity to His promises,[137] which derives from the stability of His moral attitude.[138] Mühlen's reinterpretation, however, leaves the unfortunate impression that personalism is a direct opposite of ontology. This view is highly questionable.

Mühlen's attitude to Hegelianism is similar. For although he is convinced that Hegel's understanding of God as spirit is right, he rejects the latter's thesis that the spirit comes to be through the negation of negation. This process is unacceptable because it leaves no room for the reality of a "Thou". And it is precisely the lack of "Thou" in Hegel's understanding of the movement of the spirit that explains the circular movement of the spirit in his thought. In contrast, following the personal

---

135 *Ibid.*, p. 33.

136 *Ibid.*, p. 30 f.

137 *Ibid.*, p. 29.

138 H. Küng also readily appeals to the biblical understanding of divine immutability as divine resolute fidelity (Küng, op. cit., pp. 538) It is, however, doubtful, as F. Meessen (*Unveränderlichkeit*, p. 336 f.) rightly points out, whether the biblical understanding of divine immutability does not actually denote more than immutable fidelity. The reduction of divine immutability to a mere moral stability and fidelity in history would certainly not do. A stable morality must necessarily presuppose a steady ontic nature. Galot and Balthasar have rightly insisted that the ontological understanding of divine immutability is inevitable. (See Galot, *Dieu souffre-t-il?*, p. 156 f.; see also Balthasar, *Theodramatik IV*, p. 200)

principle, Mühlen sees the procession of the Spirit manifested in the events of the Cross and the resurrection: The reality of the Spirit emerges in the mutuality of the "I" of the Father and the "Thou" of the Son, and not through the spirits negation of its own negation.[139] In this way, he evades the Hegelian inclination to see the event of the Cross as part of the divine nature or to explain it away as a process of "becoming" or of spiritualisation. On this score, he also rejects Hegel's dialectic of love, which he considers to be at best pre-personal and at worst non-personal, that is to say, a mere epistemological dialectic. Thus, Mühlen's personalist dialectic of love differs greatly from that of Hegel.

3.3 Summary

From the seventeenth to the twentieth century, the debate on the issue of divine suffering has been carried on mostly in the realm of a kenotic theology. In both theologies of the Cross and of the Trinity, the kenotic motif becomes the basic category for the expression of the paradox of divine nature. The fascinating thing about this category, and that is perhaps the reason for its importance, is its double connotation in the theology of divine suffering. For while kenosis denotes the impassibility of God in some theologies, it implies divine passibility in others. It is also significant, in that it is a principle commonly employed both in some non-Hellenistic, philosophical conceptions of reality (e.g. Hegelian and Russian) and in the biblical and Christian visions of God. It is noteworthy, that its renewed application in theologies of this era corresponds to a new consciousness among theologians of thinking divine sovereignty and transcendence, not only in the superlative but also in the conventionally negative experiences, i.e. in weakness and suffering.

As is evident in this sketch, two systems of thought prove very fundamental for the development of the kenotic theology of suffering: Hegel's and Kierkegaard's philosophies. Hegel's influence is prominent in the nineteenth century kenoticism and mediating theologies and continues to be predominant down to the twentieth century theologies of divine suffering, especially in the Protestant approach. In fact, it is the combination of Kierkegaard's notion of paradox with certain Hegelian components that forms the basic characteristic of the Protestant approach to the problem: the attempt to see kenosis as God's self-manifestation. The "Death of God" theology is, to some extent, the only exception to this rule; for its radical conception of kenosis tends to prove God's absence more than His presence. The Hegelian influence in the Catholic kenotic theology of divine suffering is also obvious, especially in the Trinitarian and Incarnation theologies of Karl

---

[139] *Ibid.*, pp. 34-35.

Rahner and Urs von Balthasar. That fact notwithstanding, the attempt to take the middle course between Hegel and the tradition characterises the Catholic theology of divine suffering.

SECTION TWO:

THE KENOTIC AND TRINITARIAN MODELS OF DISCOURSE IN THE MODERN-WESTERN THEOLOGIES OF DIVINE (IM)PASSIBILITY

... Chapters Four, Five and Six ...

4. THE IMPASSIBILITY OF GOD IN A KENOTIC THEOLOGY ACCORDING TO GEDDES MACGREGOR

4.1 Kenoticism Reconsidered

While accounting for the failure of the nineteenth century kenoticism, J. A. T. Robinson rightly argues that the principle of *kenosis* could become "a fruitless expenditure of theological ingenuity" or "a marvellously rich vein for theological exploration".[1] All depends however on how it is interpreted and employed in the explication of the divine nature. The kenotic theology of Geddes MacGregor,[2] an American philosopher of religion, seems to be such "a marvellously rich vein for theological exploration". His approach is bold, provocative and fascinating. Without taking to Hegelianism, he makes the radically philosophical affirmation that "God is kenotic", an affirmation he sees as confirming the biblical statement that "God is love".

In his essays, MacGregor foregoes an elaborate exegesis of the kenosis-hymn in Philippians 2. Subjecting the earlier kenoticisms to a critical evaluation nonetheless, he undertakes a religious and philosophical restatement of the kenotic motif. He does this with the conviction that a kenotic theory, if revitalised, offers a valuable concept for exploring the nature of God, in a manner that is both biblically and philosophically accountable to a modern world.

He identifies three factors that are responsible for the failure of the kenotic theories of the earlier centuries. These are factors, which, as he observes, must definitely be overcome before an attempt should be made to revitalise this motif. The first factor borders on the restriction of kenoticism to Christological discussions of the Incarnation. A larger theological context for the application of the kenotic motif, he contends, is indispensable.

> For if the kenotic theory ought to be applied to philosophical understanding of the nature of divine Being, the restriction of it to a narrow and dogmatic Christological rescue operation would be more likely to distort than to express it.[3]

Hence it is more appropriate to speak of a kenotic theology than of a kenotic Christology, because, as a matter of fact, kenosis is basic to Being itself.

---

1   Cf. J. A. T. Robinson, *The Human Face of God*, pp. 207-208.

2   G. MacGregor, *He Who Lets Us Be*. His kenoticism is most explicit in this book, but there are traces of this idea in his other books: *Introduction to Religious Philosophy*, pp. 252-88; *Philosophical Issues in Religious Thought*. For our purpose his other books on Gnosis, Karma, Immortality and Reincarnation lie outside our scope.

3   G. MacGregor, *He Who Lets Us Be*, p. 73.

Another problem as MacGregor sees it is the wrong dogmatic context - immutability tradition - in which earlier kenoticism was invariably developed. The dominance of this axiom crippled its progress. The problem of nineteenth-century kenoticism, therefore, lies in the adherence of its proponents "to an unexamined understanding of immutability".[4] For fear of a possible confrontation with such an axiom considered as "given", theologians were forced to express kenosis in the most impossible way.

Thirdly, earlier kenoticists erred by conceiving kenosis as the self-abandonment of divine attributes. This notion clouded the kenotic theory even for the most sympathetic observers. For if the self-emptying were to mean self-abandonment, the doctrine of the Trinity would be disfigured. MacGregor argues instead that God retains all His attributes even at the time of His self-emptying; He merely restrains Himself. Kenosis, he seems to argue, consists in self-restraint, and not in the loss of self-identity. In his words:

> If these attributes were absent or even in any way quiescent, God would be undependable ... One could not usefully pray, for instance, to a divine Being whose omnipotence was in any way capable of being abandoned, for to the extent that he abandoned it he might not be able to help; nor could one confidently pray to a God who could in any way set aside his omniscience, for he might lack knowledge at the very point at which he needed it to help; and least of all would one be content with a God who could be occasionally bereft of his omnipresence, for then, when most needed, he might not be there. We might well ask also: if one set of attributes can be laid aside, why not another?[5]

4.2   God is Love

MacGregor calls his kenotic theology a theology of love. By so doing, he makes an analysis of love the starting point of his reflections, and thus lets his version of kenoticism reflect the Johannine affirmation that "God is love". That God is love should be seen as the centre of the Christian faith, he contends, because, although the affirmation "God is love" is stated categorically only in the first letter of John, the nature of God as love is symbolised in many sections of the Bible. God as a faithful husband (Hosea), God as shepherd (Psalmists), and God as Father (Evangelists) are all images the Scripture uses to communicate this fact. Apart from this biblical testimony, there is also a simple philosophical proof for God's love: our "bare existence".[6] God is love simply by the mere fact that He lets us be. The God of love is the God who lets us be. Letting us be is a sign of

---

4   *Ibid.*, p. 91.

5   *Ibid.*, pp. 87-88.

6   *Ibid.*, p. .17.

His love, and for that purpose, it is irrelevant whether we are blessed with good living or not. The mere fact that we have been called into existence is "the *summum bonum*, the greatest possible good".[7]

MacGregor observes that this affirmation "God is love" has very rarely been explored by learned Christians. It is regrettable, he laments, that even when it at all received an attention, it had been invariably treated like "alleluias and other shouts of praise that are conspicuous for their exuberance rather than for their logical explorability".[8] That God is love is for MacGregor an ontological fact; it is no mere emotional expression, but a fact that is both philosophically and theologically explorable. Though he admits that the nature of love as emotion makes it difficult to be grasped, he however suspects other reasons for the rare inquiry into the affirmation "God is love". Hence, he attributes three factors to the lack of a sound theology of divine love in the history of theology. These are a) idolatry of power, b) the axioms of immutability and impassibility, c) the ambiguity of the doctrine of the Trinity. MacGregor not only aims at overcoming these problems through the use of the kenotic motif, he also proposes to give a kenotic interpretation to the dogmas they are meant to protect. Thus, without renouncing the significance of the classical formulas, he goes on to reinterpret them in the light of the divine love.[9]

The first obstacle on the way to a proper conception of God as love is the exaggeration of His power and omnipotence in Christian theology and practice. MacGregor sees this as the direct influence of the dynamolatory, power-worship, of the ancient religions, which especially characterised the mytho-poetic and philosophical conception of the deity in the Greek culture.[10] Undue preoccupation with the power and omnipotence of God has been obscuring the "specifically Christian notion of Agape".[11] This seemed unavoidable as long as God was conceived as a king whose omnipotence meant not only "the ability to do anything" but also the "unrestricted use of that ability".[12] In contrast, MacGregor proposes the interpretation of God's omnipotence in the light of His love. "To say that God is omnipotent can only mean that nothing diminishes his love."[13]

---

7   *Ibid.*

8   G. MacGregor, *He Who Lets Us Be*, p. 3.

9   Cf. *ibid.*, p. 4 ff.

10 Cf. *ibid.*, p. 27 f.

11 *Ibid.*, p. 174.

12 *Ibid.*, p. 72.

13 *Ibid.*, p. 128. To illustrate this point he refers to W. D. Hudson, *Philosophy*, pp. 24-25.

If we can subdue "the old models of power-worship", MacGregor argues, we can revolutionise our notion of God and allow "a radically new vision of God" to emerge.[14] His argument here is made on kenotic-anthropological terms: human experience shows that it is easier to do what one can, than to restrain oneself from doing that; it is empirically observable that in some situations human beings find self-limitation more difficult than self-assertion. Similarly, it should be all the more difficult for a powerful Being like God to limit Himself and to make Himself powerless for love's sake. His power is "the power of sacrificial love".[15] It is a kenotic power, a power that is derived from infinite self-emptying without being exhausted. God is infinitely creative and infinitely self-sacrificial. His almightiness is to be derived from His everlasting love. In this case, one can see that God's power is His love, and His love is His power.[16] Consequently, in God "love and power might be shown to be identical".[17] Divine omnipotence should not for that reason be understood as the "ability to do everything or to control everything". It should rather be conceived as

> ... the infinite power that springs from creative love. That is the power that is infinite, being infinitely creative and therefore infinitely sacrificial.[18]

For MacGregor, it would amount to making God a monster, if we were to ascribe unlimited power to Him. Divine power must be seen as conditioned by God's love; God does not exercise power "except in support of love".[19] MacGregor does accept St. Thomas' dictum that God cannot do anything contrary to His nature. But explaining this on kenotic terms, he goes beyond Thomas to maintain that "God cannot do anything contrary to his nature of letting-be".[20] In fact, it is part of the paradox of divine omnipotence and almightiness that the God of love, who, for love's sake, became the "all-powerless God", is actually and for that reason the "all-powerful God".

---

[14] G. MacGregor, *He Who Lets Us Be*, p. 168.

[15] *Ibid.*, p. 15.

[16] Cf. *ibid.*, p. 75. To substantiate this point, MacGregor cites Simone Weil, *First and Last Notebooks*, p. 297: "If God had not been humiliated, in the person of Christ, he would be inferior to us." The view that divine humiliation reveals God's omnipotence has also been defended by H. Fries, *Fundamentaltheologie*, p. 269; and W. Kasper, *Der Gott Jesu Christi*, p. 242.

[17] G. MacGregor, *He Who Lets Us Be*, p. 75.

[18] *Ibid.*, p. 15.

[19] *Ibid.*, p. 120.

[20] *Ibid.*, p. 133.

MacGregor also sees the classical conception of the axiom of divine immutability and passibility as "a logical consequence of power-worship".[21] The formulation of the doctrine of divine immutability in the context of Greek cultural thought presupposes a conception of power as the highest attribute for a being. To the Greeks, gods were to be differentiated from mortals by the degree of power they possessed. In comparison to mortals gods had more power: in contrast to mortals Zeus accomplished things with less vigour (Homer & Hesiod); by mere thinking Zeus accomplished things (Xenophanes). Continuing on the same belief, their philosophers argued that perfect being should have no movement (Parmenides) and that gods must suffer no change (Plato). This conception of power gave rise, MacGregor contends, to the doctrine of immutability, which in turn raised the question of how a Being who suffers no change could move things.

For MacGregor, it is clear that Aristotle had this power-worship in his mind as he writes that God "moves by being loved".[22] The "Absolute Being" has become an "unmoved mover", who in Himself remains unmoved but moves other beings by virtue of His "magnetic" love. Such is Aristotle's conception of power that "Absolute Deity " dare not move for the sake of love. So, not only can the God of Aristotle not be moved by His creatures, He also cannot move His creatures directly; for it is not the divine love that moves mortals, but rather the love of these mortals for the Absolute Being that sets them in motion.

In the light of the Aristotelian doctrine of God, MacGregor continues, there can be no logical connection between divine immutability and divine love. And regrettably this practice of setting a division between divine love and immutability continued to be propagated in the Christian theology even after Augustine had recognised love as the essence of God's nature, and tried, with the aid of the doctrine of the Trinity, to relate divine love to the "vital" doctrine of the immutability and impassibility of God.[23]

In contrast, MacGregor tries to conceive love and immutability together, not in the sense of fitting the Greek notion of immutability into the pure love of God, as had apparently been the case, but rather by thinking divine immutability in terms of His love:

> ... the immutability of God must so far surpass any immutability we know in man or Nature as to encompass the divine love, and the divine love must so excel even the most sacrificial human love as to embrace what has been called the immutability of God. The immutability is the love, the love the immutability. So also with the omnipotence, omniscience, and omnipresence of God: they are not at all to be ac-

---

21 *Ibid.*, p. 31.

22 *Symposium* 207, cited in G. MacGregor, *He Who Lets Us Be*, p. 37.

23 Cf. MacGregor, *He Who Lets Us Be*, p. 41.

counted an infinite degree of human power and wisdom and presence. If God is as worshipful as Christians have always claimed, these attributes must be so far beyond their human analogues as to be fused together ... with all possible divine attributes in the Being of God, which as classical Christian thought has perceived must be perfectly 'simple'. The simplicity need not consist, however, in the impassibility of divine Being. It might consist in the simplicity of love, which is simple in needing no attributes other than itself.[24]

In effect, MacGregor does not condemn the immutability of God, he only says that it consists in love. With Mackintosh, he concludes therefore, that "what is immutable in God is the holy love that constitutes his essence".[25] God can only be said to be impassible, he argues, "if by impassibility we mean that God's love cannot be undermined by anything outside itself".[26]

The third factor that has been hindering the explorability of the Johannine affirmation "God is love" is, according to MacGregor, the classical doctrine of the Trinity. Recognising the fact that the formulation of this doctrine was itself motivated by the need to reconcile two apparently contradicting attributes of God, love and immutability, MacGregor's viewpoint is that the doctrine of the Trinity obscured that which it was meant to expose. St. Augustine had hoped to use the doctrine of the Trinity to provide "a theological solution to the paradox that God is both immutable and impassible on the one hand, on the other, pure love".[27] This venture failed, however, because the Trinitarian formula could not perform the miraculous "binding" of the two attributes. The philosophical idea of immutability was thus left to predominate. In fact, it is the bringing together of the Greek notion of divine immutability and the biblical proclamation of God as pure love, that perpetuates subordinationism in the classical Trinitarian formula. For one "hearing that God the Father is the remote but necessary ground of all Being, while God the Son is the One who is accessible and susceptible to encounter, would hardly avoid the conclusion that the Son is, after all, somewhat less than the Father, though the denunciation of such subordinationism was, at least in part, what the Trinitarian formula had been designed to accomplish".[28]

However, insurmountable subordinationism, MacGregor argues, is not the only weakness that the idea of immutability has implanted in the classical Trinitarian formula. In addition, the view that only the Father is the ground of being and the other *personae* are merely the Relatedness, which the classical Trinitarian for-

---

24 *Ibid.*, p. 92.

25 *Ibid.*

26 G. MacGregor, *He Who Lets Us Be*, p. 184.

27 *Ibid.*, pp. 41-42.

28 *Ibid.*, p. 46.

mula connotes,[29] makes the attribution of the work of the Trinity *ad extra* to the whole persons of the Trinity very difficult. It is for the same reason that tradition has failed to explore John Damascene's theory of "perichoresis" - the doctrine of the interpenetration of the persons of the Trinity - thereby missing the sole chance to show the unity of God in all divine activities in Trinitarian terms. MacGregor, on his part, wants to take perichoretic unity seriously, so that "what is predicated of one *persona*, one *hypostasis*, must surely be predicated of all"; this would imply that "the whole Trinity was incarnate".[30] The cardinal difficulty of the doctrine of the Trinity is the "traditional notion that suffering is incompatible with the First Person of the Trinity".[31] This has also led to the misrepresentation of the "father-symbol" of the biblical literature. Rather than fall prey to this error, MacGregor takes upon himself the charge of being a Patripassionist.[32] The Father's suffering for love's sake can be represented, however, only in kenotic terms. He therefore concludes that the valuable aspects of the doctrine of the Trinity should be restated within a kenotic framework.[33]

4.3   God's Love is Creative - "God as Creator is Kenotic Being"[34]

Love is basically self-giving. For MacGregor, this means that God's love has a self-sacrificial character, and is thus only explorable in kenotic terms.[35] The kenotic nature of divine love is first and foremost, and perhaps most eminently revealed in the act of creation, which, according to MacGregor, is primarily the product of a divine act of self-limitation or self-giving love. In fact, "The kenosis, traditionally understood as an interpretation of the incarnational mystery that appears at the heart of Christian dogma, may be considered in the larger context of divine creation."[36]

Enunciating the process of divine creativity, MacGregor therefore goes on to unfold the core of his kenoticism and also the true nature of kenotic love: letting

---

29 Cf. *ibid.*, p. 48.

30 *Ibid.*, p. 51.

31 *Ibid.*

32 Cf. *ibid.*, pp. 4 & 51.

33 This is in effect what the Russian kenoticists and contemporary Catholic theologians of divine suffering do, as they locate kenosis in the inner life of the Trinitarian Godhead. See chapter 3 of this study.

34 *Ibid.*, p. 104.

35 Cf. *ibid.*, p. 9.

36 G. MacGregor, *He Who Lets Us Be*, p. 107.

creatures be. Creation, he argues, "... is a voluntary self-diminution, a metaphysical kenosis",[37] an act of restraint and renunciation for God, who, despite His superiority allows lesser, inferior beings to exist beside Him.[38] He elaborates this kenotic understanding of divine creativity using both philosophical and theological arguments drawn mainly from other thinkers.

His conception of kenosis as belonging to the inner nature of God is definitely influenced by S. Bulgakov and S. Weil,[39] but it is F. H. Brabant's interpretation of *creatio ex nihilo*, that is most decisive for his views on the kenotic import of the divine creativity. For Brabant, if God creates *ex nihilo*, 'out of nothing', the nothingness out of which He creates "can only mean 'nothing other than Himself'".[40] MacGregor goes on to specify, accordingly, that creation "out of nothing" means that God creates "out of God himself" - He creates by giving Himself out. Love is His nature and the nature of His love is self-giving, self-limitation or kenosis. It is therefore logical for MacGregor that God cannot give Himself out by expanding Himself. He does that through self-limitation. Hence:

> To say that the biblical God is love is to say that his creation is an act, not of self-expansion but of self-limitation. For the biblical God, being ontologically perfect himself as well as sovereign over and independent of his creatures, could have nowhere to go by way of expansion. He could have no ambitions to fulfil or goals to attain or projects to promote either for his aggrandisement or for his betterment. The only way he could go in his creative act would be a way of self-limitation, self-emptying, self-abnegation. That is what *agape* would entail.[41]

Since God, by virtue of His perfection, has no other possibility at His disposal than to engage in self-renunciation in order to let creatures be, His kenotic creativity is a continuous process. Here, MacGregor sees creation, with Origen, as an ongoing process: There was no time when God was not creating; He never began to create, He has always been creating. His argument seems to be that since the

---

37 *Ibid.*, p. 104.

38 Cf. *ibid.*, p. 73.

39 Cf. *ibid.*, pp. 70 f., 73 ff.

40 F. H. Brabant, God and Time, p. 353, cited in MacGregor, *He Who Lets Us Be*, p. 105. See the preceding chapter for E. Jüngel's similar view.

41 *Ibid.*, p. 19. He repeats this same proposition while enunciating the nature of divine omnipotence: "I am proposing that by 'God' we cannot mean Being that exercises omnipotence as an act of self-expansion, because ... there would be nowhere into which an infinitely powerful Being could expand. Having nowhere to go by way of self-expansion he would still have infinitely available to him the way of self-limitation, self-abnegation" (*Ibid.*, p. 107). The same argument is used to explain God's attitude to suffering in the world. See *Ibid.*, p. 98. By simply including the idea of expansion in his argument, MacGregor shows his version of kenosis to be too literal, too spatial, in fact non-personal.

essential nature of God is self-giving, there was no time in which God was not giving and limiting Himself to allow the existence of lower creatures.[42]

Through this exploration of the nature of divine creativity, MacGregor comes to the core of his thesis: Kenosis is in the very nature or being of God, who for love's sake, and for the sake of His creation, has to limit Himself eternally. Creation implies that God is love, and that His love is kenotic. God however is not kenotic just because He creates, He would also be kenotic even without the creation, MacGregor seems to argue. Creativity is but a product of His self-sacrificial love. At the root of creativity itself and at the source of existence lies kenosis. Thus, going beyond creation as the implicate of love, he locates kenosis at the very heart of Being:

> I wish to consider kenosis as the root principle of Being. To call God kenotic Being is to specify what we mean by saying 'God is love'.[43]

In this way, he sees kenosis not only as that which joins the world to God, but also as the very means of existence, "a law of life".[44] Making use of S. Weil's theology of creativity, MacGregor also sees true human life as kenotic. Kenosis performs two roles for us: firstly, it makes us yield ourselves to God, and, secondly, it makes us co-creators with God. In fact, to be, in the real sense of the word, is to be kenotic. The kenotic nature of being human is "the secret behind the Gospel paradox that I must give up my life to gain it".[45]

4.4   *Divine Permissiveness, Human Freedom and Suffering*

MacGregor's particular and peculiar way of describing God's kenotic relationship to the world is expressed succinctly in the term "letting-be". God lets us be, not only in the sense of granting us existence, but also in the sense of allowing creation to develop through an evolutionary process. God lets us be and allows the necessity in nature to have its unrestrained course. Thus, God's relationship to the world is characterised by permissiveness and providence. Divine permissiveness, as MacGregor conceives it, has both negative and positive implications. While in positive terms, divine permissiveness makes human freedom possible, in negative terms, it allows not only moral evil to arise, but also the blind necessity in nature, which is responsible for all the natural catastrophes (dysteleological evil). However, God shows us, by virtue of His providence, ways to escape the

---

42 Cf. *ibid.*, p. 182.

43 G. MacGregor, *He Who Lets Us Be*, p. 107.

44 *Ibid.*, p. 183.

45 *Ibid.*

grip of destiny. It is apparent, therefore, that for MacGregor providence is a corrective principle that must accompany the necessity in nature.

At this point, MacGregor's intention becomes clear. Neither does he want to explain evil without God, nor does he see the need to attribute it to Him. In this connection, he objects to the conception of God as the first Cause, because conceiving of Him as such would mean that He is the direct cause of evil.[46] He rejects the idea of predestination apparently for the same reason. It is his firm conviction, that no matter to what extent theologians twist the idea of predestination, it always conjures up the image of predetermination, the view that God had programmed everything right from the beginning. Hence his view that the notion of causation is incompatible with the fact of human freedom.[47]

As at many other points he calls attention to Simone Weil's conception of God, who, though accepting that God is the cause of all that exists, insists that He "consents not to command it".[48] This abdication, this permissiveness, is the root of human freedom and the blind necessity of nature. God does not administer the world in terms of causation but in terms of freedom. He abdicates His power of control to two forces: to the "blind necessity" of matter and to the autonomy of thinking persons.[49] The course which the development of the world takes could then be attributed to these two forces. The world of nature is moving irrevocably in accordance with its God-ordained laws and God does not interfere, even when its ways cross human situations. Such a necessity accorded to nature is blind to morality, so that for example petrol, when set on fire, burns, not caring whether a child happens to be sleeping nearby; and water necessarily runs down slopes, even when 20 bags of salt meant for refugees were to stand in its way. Thus natural catastrophes and earthquakes could be seen as expressions of this necessity.

But if the blind necessity of nature is so arbitrary, why does a God of love give control to it? MacGregor's explanation for this is surprising: "... without a world of blind necessity we could not know 'how to be free'".[50] He sees 'necessity' as a prerequisite for the realisation of freedom. What a paradox !

---

[46] MacGregor is apparently unaware of St. Augustine's conception of evil as the privation of good. If that fact is taken care of, thinking of God as the first Cause would then not necessarily imply making Him the author of evil.

[47] Cf. *ibid.*, p. 115: "divine causation and human freedom do not sit well together at any point".

[48] *Ibid.*, p. 134.

[49] Cf. *ibid.*, p. 121-124.

[50] *Ibid.*, p. 121.

Necessity and freedom are correlative terms. Such is freedom that it is meaningless apart from the necessity within which it is exercised. We can neither choose any course of conduct nor do any action except within a framework that presents us with obstacles ... Necessity, then, far from being a hindrance, is the indispensable condition for the development of freedom.[51]

Necessity does not hinder freedom, it makes its development possible. For this reason, it would be wrong to consider nature a human enemy. Necessity does not hinder human freedom; the God who lets us be does not hinder it either. In fact, necessity is advantageous in two ways: first, it makes freedom possible; secondly, it makes science possible.[52] If nature were to be so unstable, so that fire would only burn if it were not destructive, science would not have been possible. And if there is no necessity and no confrontation in the world, human freedom could not have been realisable. In other words, necessity must exist as a correlative of freedom because the former makes the latter possible. The only force that can hinder human freedom is man's insufficient kenotic act.[53] As a principle of Being, kenosis is a way to freedom. Its contradiction, i.e. the lack of a kenotic lifestyle, causes grief for humanity.[54]

MacGregor subscribes to an evolutionary understanding of the universe. He sees it also as implied by God's unconditional bestowal of freedom on His creatures. For him the implication of divine permissiveness and its resulting creaturely freedom "is that creation *must* be evolutionary in the sense that everything that Being creates must struggle to enter into the fullness of its potentialities, presumably over the course of trillions of years as measured in our temporal reckoning".[55] Struggle and accidentality belong to this ongoing creation, they are implied in the process of world development.

To this extent MacGregor concludes that "what we call evil is an integral part of a cosmic process". Suffering, inflicted on us by nature and free agents, is the price for the gift of human freedom and God's love for us. God in His everlasting love gives us freedom and permits the unrestricted use of that freedom. Thus, while moral evil results from the misuse of human freedom, natural evil occurs

---

51 G. MacGregor, *He Who Lets Us Be*, p. 125.

52 Cf. *ibid.*, pp. 111-128.

53 Cf. *ibid.*

54 Cf. *ibid.*, p. 127.

55 G. MacGregor, *Issues*, p. 455.

because God restrains Himself from interfering in nature.[56] Suffering could for that reason be termed the price of our freedom.[57]

4.5   Divine Passibility and Theodicy

With his theory of divine permissiveness, MacGregor accounts for the origin of evil. But the question why a God of love should allow nature or misused human freedom to oppress innocent human beings remains unanswered in his model. Why should so much suffering be entailed in such a cosmic process? The creative and evolutionary processes seem highly extravagant. Why must accidentality be so arbitrary? What does it bring a sufferer when God adamantly refuses to interfere in his destiny? MacGregor has no answer to these problems of theodicy. He points however to another aspect of divine relationship to the world, which might prove useful in our search for an answer. He points to God's own suffering and providence. That God neither interferes nor interrupts the free running of His creation does not mean that He abandons His creatures; He always provides for them in a special way. He is providentially concerned about human suffering because He suffers with us in our predicament. God suffers "in the sense of enduring the consequences of his own self-renunciation and self-sacrifice"[58].

Providence, as MacGregor understands it, is neither an occasional alteration of human predicament nor God's whimsical change of natural happenings. God does not change what we call predicaments because such occurrences themselves "belong" to the cosmic process, which the kenotic God allows to be. Providence should rather be understood as God's readiness to make us aware of better possibilities that could make us escape certain accidentalities. "When we ask Providence 'to come to our aid', then, we dare ask for help in directing us to opportunities we have overlooked".[59] We know very little possibilities, but God knows all. And He shows us these other possibilities, when, and only when we ask for it in prayer.[60]   That is to say, providence comes on invitation - through prayer. Providence so understood is not incompatible with human freedom. For God's

---

56   Cf. *ibid.*, p. 141

57   In a sense, it is also the price for God's kenotic love, since freedom and necessity in nature result from self-limitation. See a similar view in G. Greshake, *Der Preis der Liebe*.

58   G. MacGregor, Issues, p. 168.

59   *Ibid.*, p. 158.

60   Cf. *ibid.*, p. 156.

intervention, not interference, comes only on invitation.[61] God does not alter the natural order. Instead He suffers with us.

From his theology of creativity, MacGregor again comes to the conviction that creation has a self-sacrificial nature[62] and that self-sacrificial love is an "inalienable character of Being". He sees self-sacrifice and agony as common features of creativity, both divine and human. With reference to the human experience of self-sacrifice in creativity, MacGregor argues that God's creativity must likewise entail "an intrinsic sadness",[63] because "in conferring existence on creatures, God must somehow endue that existence with some reflection of, or some potentiality for, his own self-limiting creativity, with all the anguish inherent in it".[64]

The nature of love is moreover such that it must entail suffering. In fact, "to say that love is essential to the Being of God is to say in one way or another suffering is essential to his nature".[65] The experience of genuine human love shows us that to love is to suffer. Hence MacGregor's question: "If... we take seriously the affirmation 'God is love' how can we avoid the entailment that suffering is essential to the divine Being?".[66] God suffers the consequences of His love, of His permissiveness, of His determination not to exercise His power absolutely. For love's sake and in order to accord freedom to His creatures, God refrains from interfering in the affairs of the world.[67] The God of love suffers when His beloved creatures fail to return His love, and when they turn away from Him.

> For a creature to withdraw from God as we creatures do must surely be infinite agony for him who is the God of love ... if God is indeed as we have depicted him, he too must know the pain of seeing the millions of creatures who absent themselves from *him*. The profound truth of this is dramatically presented in the Catholic devotion to the Sacred Heart.[68]

MacGregor would want to go beyond the devotional creed of the Sacred Heart of Jesus, by "putting the Heart not in the breast of Jesus but at the deep core of him who has been traditionally designated the triune God".[69] Suffering is at the

---

[61] Cf. *ibid.*, p. 162.

[62] Cf. *ibid.*, p. 19.

[63] *Ibid.*, p. 98.

[64] *Ibid.*, p. 19.

[65] G. MacGregor, *He Who Lets Us Be*, p. 4.

[66] *Ibid.*, p. 4.

[67] This view is decisive for MacGregor's version of theodicy. We shall expatiate on this later.

[68] *Ibid.*, p. 149.

[69] *Ibid.*, p. 188.

heart of God. The logic of MacGregor's argument is this: God created the world and left it to develop on its own without interfering with its laws; He lets it be. But wherever creation is in pain (Rom. 8:22), God nonetheless enters and "endures that pain".[70] Our God is "a God of anguish because (He is) a God of love".[71] This does not make Him face "conditions not of his own making"; He merely takes suffering upon Himself in accordance with His love.[72] It is absolutely true that God "cannot suffer in the sense of being acted upon by another agent", but He can "suffer in the sense of enduring the consequences of his own self-renunciation and self-sacrifice".[73] Logically, God suffers freely, but He remains ever-joyous even when He is in anguish, precisely because of His freedom. Naturally, creativity entails anguish, but it also brings joy. "We may say, therefore, that God as Being is also ever-joyous in his self-emptying".[74]

Closely connected to his theology of divine suffering is theodicy, which he formulates guided by three basic principles or assumptions:

a) God's love knows no jealousy, since He has no ontic rivals.[75] For this reason, God can afford to give His creatures unlimited room for growth and development. Not even the intransigence of the creatures can make Him change His plan or interfere at all in creation. He simply lets all creatures be. Human limitations and encounter with nature should not be seen, therefore, as God's interference in nature; they are simply results of accidentality that is inevitably involved in a process, where every creature has the 'freedom' to move in its own course, where even germs are granted unrestricted development in the human body.

b) Every creature, not just man, is "imago Dei".[76] Every creature reflects the proper image of God, each in its due measure. MacGregor does not however say what this image consists of. It appears to have something to do with man's common nature of creatureliness with all created beings. Consequently, MacGregor believes that human beings should have no preference or special treatment from God; God's love, which lets every creature be, also allows man's struggle with nature, even when such a struggle disfavours human beings. MacGregor takes

---

70 *Ibid.*, p. 155.

71 *Ibid.*, p. 5.

72 Cf. *ibid.*, p. 99.

73 MacGregor, *Issues*, p. 168.

74 G. MacGregor, *He Who Lets Us Be*, p. 187.

75 Cf. *ibid.*, p. 140.

76 *Ibid.*, p. 142.

this to be the only way one can account for man's place in the evolutionary process and for the origin of natural evil.

c) The third principle of MacGregor's solution to the problem of theodicy specifies that all divine attributes should be reinterpreted on the basis of God's divine love.[77] This is meant to explain the fact that God is necessarily kenotic, and that it is for love's sake that He "bestows on every creature an unlimited potentiality for development". MacGregor believes that "when we take these three points into account, the evil in the universe is seen in a light that makes the standard critical objections irrelevant".[78]

According to his model of theodicy, God cannot be held directly responsible for evil in the world, since His relation to the world is not deterministic; He is nonetheless the initiator of those conditions of freedom and necessity responsible for moral and natural evil. In other words, man is partly responsible for his suffering, and God is remotely responsible for the evil in the world, which results from the nature of freedom and necessity. The only difference between their authorship is that while man's misuse of his freedom and the eventual moral evil stem from his greed, the natural evil occurs by virtue of God's love, which takes the form of letting creatures take their natural course unhindered.

This explanation is definitely provocative, but it does not answer the main intractable question of theodicy, namely, why the nature of divine love must be such, and His creation so structured, that the suffering of the innocents cannot be avoided?

4.6   Evaluation

MacGregor rightly identifies the problem of the earlier kenoticism as the undue confinement of the doctrine of kenosis to Incarnation and Christology and the conception of kenosis as the loss or abandonment of some divine attributes. In his attempt to evade these shortcomings, he interprets kenosis as an act that not only characterises God's creativity, but also His very nature; that is to say, he conceives divine action and being in kenotic terms. All these do not constitute new ideas,[79] except of course his understanding of God as being essentially kenotic, and kenosis as the main characteristic of love.[80] It is also novel that he expounds

---

[77] Cf. *ibid.*, p. 143.

[78] *Ibid.*

[79] We have already met similar views especially among the Russian Orthodox theologies.

[80] Cf. *ibid.*, p. 107: "To call God kenotic Being is to specify what we mean by saying 'God is love' ".

a kenotic image of God, not from a theological, but from a pure (non-Hegelian) philosophical perspective.

The problem of his contribution however lies exactly at this point, namely at his non-theological approach to kenosis, which makes his view about God's essential kenosis susceptible to the very problems the Hegelian proposal faces: making God dependent. Although MacGregor does not give a detailed explanation why the affirmation "God is love" should be identical with the expression "God is a kenotic Being", it is implicit in his thought that "letting-be" and "self-limitation" mean the same thing as "self-giving". It is on this score that he makes the affirmation "God is love" identical with his philosophical assertion that "God is kenotic". Whereas his assumption can be seen as being logical, there seems to be a substantial difficulty latent in the view that God is essentially kenotic. That God is *essentially* self-giving would mean that He must always be giving Himself out in order to be and that His being is dependent on giving. Does such a view not enslave God? Does it not make Him dependent on His creation?

There is unfortunately nothing in MacGregor's philosophical approach to correct this impression. He would definitely have been able to avoid the problem of making God a "slave" to His nature of self-giving, if only he were ready to expound his kenotic theory in the context of a Trinitarian theology. To the extent that he disparages and avoids the doctrine of the Trinity, MacGregor misses the basis on which kenosis can be seen as constituting the being of God without putting Him under compulsion.[81] His kenotic God is thus compelled to always be emptying Himself in order to remain God. We must, for this reason, consider the lack of a Trinitarian theology the basic weakness of MacGregor's model of kenotic theology. The doctrine of the Trinity cannot be replaced by a mere philosophical theory of kenosis without making self-giving seem a constraint on God's part. If the claim that God is kenotic should have any justification at all, it must necessarily be developed in the context of a Trinitarian theology, because self-giving can only be eternal for God if it has been occurring in His inner-Trinitarian life, before ever the world was made. Of course, MacGregor mentions the doctrine of *perichoresis* favourably, but he fails to incorporate it into his kenotic vision of God.

Another major weakness of MacGregor's kenoticism, as far as we can see, has to do with his very "spatial" conception of kenosis. He conceives the divine self-emptying in the same material categories with which one would describe the emptying of a container. His concept of kenosis is so literally conceived that it is

---

[81] In this connection, Bulgakov, Lossky and Balthasar make a better claim, since they see the place of kenosis in the Godhead only on the basis of the Trinity. Cf. H. U. v. Balthasar, Mysterium Paschale, pp. 149-153.

non-personal and non-dialectical. This weakness shows itself more in his interpretation of the divine act of creation and human freedom, especially at the point where he tries to show that God is a kenotic creator (Being). On this he argues that God (even though He creates *ex nihilo*) does not create by expansion, because as a perfect Being, nothing can be added to His Being: there is no plus side to perfection. "Having nowhere to go by way of self-expansion he (God) would still have infinitely available to him the way of self-limitation, self-abnegation".[82] The mere fact that MacGregor had to negate self-expansion, shows that he conceives kenosis materially and spatially - as the emptying of material entities in a given space. MacGregor certainly does not intend this, but his conception of kenosis nonetheless conjures up the image of a God who must withdraw in order to make room for man. Such a notion of kenosis or self-emptying so physically conceived gives the impression that God and man are vying for space.

MacGregor's theory of divine permissiveness, his understanding of the divine relationship and his notion of divine freedom are all logical consequences of his non-personalistic conception of kenosis. In his view, God must limit His freedom in other to allow the freedom of His creatures. This view immediately leads one to ask how MacGregor relates human freedom to divine sovereignty? Is a creature free only to the extent to which it is independent of God? Do the scriptures not show the opposite, namely that a creature is only free to the extent to which it depends on God. In other words, is human freedom directly or inversely proportional to divine freedom?

MacGregor's conception of divine kenosis and freedom in terms of divine permissiveness and self-withdrawal from creation does not represent the biblical concept of freedom. We dare not conceive divine self-renunciation as the limitation of divine freedom. Nor should divine permissiveness mean withdrawal from creation, to the extent that the question of "re-entering" should arise at all. Is it not possible to visualise God's relationship to the world in a manner that sees Him as always being present in His creation to the extent that the need to enter anew does not arise?

If divine self-emptying is to be correctly understood, it should not involve God's withdrawal from His creation; it should rather mean that God can be there even in the most wretched state of His creatures without in any way sacrificing His sovereignty. God is not in a competitive relationship with His creatures. For as Rahner rightly observes, "being at God's disposal and being autonomous, do not vary for creatures in inverse, but rather in direct proportion".[83]

---

82 *Ibid.*, p. 107.

83 K. Rahner, *Foundations of Christian Faith*, p. 222.

Thus while we agree with MacGregor that God is a kenotic Being, we insist that kenosis does not consist in permissiveness or in self-withdrawal. Kenosis does not entail a minimised immanence, but a total immanence in transcendence. MacGregor's theory of divine non-interference therefore tends to deny God's continuous presence in the world, and is for that reason not convincing. God does not hinder evolution, but He can be seen as being present in evolution, without Himself being evolutive.

The third major problem of MacGregor's conception of kenosis is its lack of a Christological background. His attempt to take kenosis beyond the realm of Christology, right in the heart of God is laudable, though he exaggerates it. For by that means, he overlooks the significance of Christology for the kenotic motif. The price for this negligence is paid with a one-sided view of kenosis. He sees the sacrificial aspect of kenosis, but fails to represent the fulfilling aspect of it, which the idea of exaltation stands for. In other words, he fails to realise that *kenosis* and *plerosis* - self-emptying and self-fulfilment - are complementary. By this very fact, MacGregor's view makes kenosis loose its fulfilling aspect, and thus sacrifices the transparency of the paradox of divine self-emptying (i.e. self-fulfilment through self-emptying) to the gods. Thus, his conception of kenosis misses the newness, the fulfilment, which kenosis should entail if it is to be seen as a "law of life".

The lack of a kenotic Christology is indeed the Achilles' heel of MacGregor's kenotic theology. He makes very little reference to the event of Christ, and when he does at all, he invariably propagates a Christology 'from above'. MacGregor rarely uses his very penetrating insight on human kenosis[84] to illuminate the nature of divine kenosis. The historical personality of Jesus Christ thus plays little or no role at all in his thought. L. Richard rightly points out that in order for a kenotic theology to be worth its salt, it has to begin as a Christology "from below", taking its point of departure from a humanity in which God is already present. Only by making Christology its point of departure can a kenotic theology avoid working either with an *a priori* understanding of man or an *a priori* understanding of God. Both extremes would definitely merit Karl Barth's criticisms against "natural theology", against the absence of a revelation theology. This means that philosophical kenosis can hardly do if it is not rooted in Christology, i.e. in revelation.

His kenotic theology has yet other problems, precisely at the point where his contribution is expected to be most significant, namely, in his solution to the problem of theodicy. With the image of God as a kenotic Being, a Being who

---

[84] His positive contribution lies more in his understanding of human kenosis as the law of life. This will be shown later.

suffers because of His love, MacGregor certainly formulates one of the most exciting and inspiring theodicies in contemporary theology. His explanation for the origin of evil in the world is certainly satisfactory. Yet his theodicy has the weakness of making God indifferent to the problem of the sufferer. The thesis that God does not interfere can hardly provide solace to a sufferer. Besides, it rather gives the impression that the individual human beings are insignificant and that they are victims of the struggle in the evolutionary process.

He does of course argue that God suffers Himself, but he fails to conceive divine suffering in a manner that it can contribute towards alleviating human suffering. There is no indication that God suffers with the sufferer; rather, he alludes invariably to the suffering of God in Himself. God suffers for having to limit Himself, on the one side, to allow existence, and on the other, to let the order in the world run its course. Although MacGregor mentions that God enters to endure our pain only on invitation,[85] he does not allow this thought to lead to an elaborate view of God's co-suffering with the (innocent) sufferer. MacGregor's God suffers, but He suffers more from His own problem of creativity than from a concern for His creatures. As W. McWilliams aptly observes, "MacGregor is so concerned to keep God from disrupting nature and infringing on creaturely freedom that he borders on totally detaching God from the course of history".[86] For this reason, MacGregor's theology of divine suffering fails to show the aspect of divine empathy, which other theologians of this motif have always fruitfully employed in defence of theodicy.[87] That he misses this point certainly has something to do with the absence of a theology of Christ's passion in his model. If he did evolve a Christology, his theory of divine non-interference would have looked different.

Similarly, if MacGregor had taken the event of Christ seriously, he would not have called God "a laissez-faire God",[88] who, without leaving His creatures "utterly alone ... nevertheless leaves them perfectly free, so that they may work out their own salvation".[89] The God who reveals Himself on the Cross of Christ, who gave away His own Son for our sake, can certainly not be called a laissez-faire God. The theology of the Cross shows that the God in Jesus Christ is a God who gets involved, a God who does not abandon human beings to "work out their own salvation" as MacGregor would want us believe. In fact, rather than distance

---

[85] Cf. *ibid.*, p. 155.

[86] W. McWilliams, *The passion of God*, p. 92.

[87] Cf. C. Y. Lee, *God Suffers for Us.*

[88] G. MacGregor, *Issues*, p. 140.

[89] *Ibid.*

Himself from His creatures, He gets involved in their predicaments all the more. This is another proof of MacGregor's misconception of divine kenosis. Kenosis conceived as self-limitation does not necessarily have to imply withdrawal, it can only mean that God is present in the lowliness of the world, without in any way tarnishing His transcendence. That is the paradox of kenosis. God can be kenotic (self-emptying), He can still be seen as restraining Himself, but this should not warrant our conceiving Him as a laissez-affaire Being. God's kenosis does not put a division between Him and His creatures; it is rather the bond that connects Him to His creation. This point seems to have escaped MacGregor's very penetrating insight.

Moreover, he also neglects the significance of eschatology for the problem of theodicy. It is certainly right not to defer every solution to theodicy to the eschaton as in John Hick's soul-making theodicy,[90] but it is also wrong to ignore the eschatological dimension of theodicy. As W. McWilliams likewise observes, MacGregor could significantly improve his theodicy, if only he could relate his eschatology, which he develops amply in other connections,[91] to the problem of suffering.

Besides, if God does not interfere and prefers to suffer His non-interference, for the simple reason that He values human freedom, and if for that reason, human suffering could be seen as the price for human freedom, the question arises whether human freedom is worth all the suffering in the world, which God could have been able to forestall through the slightest use of His omnipotence. This problem, however, does not only arise for MacGregor's model, but for all models that see suffering as the price of divine love or human freedom.[92]

MacGregor's kenotic theology might not offer a satisfactory theodicy, but it does provide a fruitful basis on which the relation between theodicy and anthropodicy becomes visible. His kenotic theodicy does not satisfactorily justify God in the face of suffering, but it does appeal to human kenosis as a theodicy in praxis. His understanding of kenosis as "the law of life"[93] could be seen as a plea for the integration of anthropodicy to theodicy. What improvement could the motif of a suffering God bring to theodicy, if it did not imply an incentive for humankind to modulate its way of life so that moral evil could be reduced? If the

---

90   Cf. J. Hick, *Evil and the God of Love.*

91   Cf. W. McWilliams, *The passion of God*, p. 94. See also G. MacGregor, *Issues*, pp. 289-309; ---, (editor) *Immortality and Human Destiny*, esp. pp. 72-84

92   Cf. G. Greschake, *Der Preis der Liebe.*

93   G. MacGregor, *Issues*, p. 183.

suffering of God with the sufferer does not generate a sense of corrective activity in the believer, it would be good for nothing except for arousing self-pity.

His conception of the human kenosis as the way of life could be seen as a possible answer to the issue of theodicy. This would mean that God justifies Himself, not only by suffering with us, but also by showing humankind how to overcome suffering through a kenotic life-style. This view is also implied in the philosophical theology of Simone Weil, the Jewish lady, whose work constitutes MacGregor's source of inspiration in this regard.

> God denied himself for our sakes in order to give us the possibility of denying ourselves for him. This response, this echo, which it is in our power to refuse, is the only possible justification for the folly of love of creative act.[94]

Even though MacGregor does not emphasise the significance of the Cross for theodicy, on the basis of his idea of human kenosis, one can argue that by virtue of the event on the Cross, God reveals to us how we overcome suffering by emptying ourselves for love's sake. That is perhaps the only way we can justify God, who, by emptying Himself for our sake, calls us to do the same for ourselves and neighbours, for kenosis is the only means of salvation and self-redemption. Only by justifying ourselves in the kenotic act, can we justify God, who justifies Himself by getting involved in our suffering. This is the implication of MacGregor's conception of kenosis as "the law of life",[95] the law of existence and the principle of being.

True, MacGregor's kenotic theology does not offer a definite solution to the problem of theodicy, nevertheless his kenotic anthropology points to a genuine road in the exploration of the mystery of God and human suffering.

4.7   Summary

The first thing MacGregor undertakes while evolving his kenotic theology is a courteous examination of the errors of the earlier kenoticisms. Building on his findings, therefore, he makes three significant corrections to revitalise this motif: firstly, he extends the scope of kenosis beyond the realm of Christology, secondly, he reinterprets it to imply, the self-restraint of God and no longer the reduction or elimination of the divine attributes, and thirdly, he explicates divine immutability in terms of love. And making the Johannine affirmation that "God is love" his main point of departure, MacGregor goes on to demand a reinterpretation both of the omnipotence and of the Trinity itself in terms of love; that means, in terms of kenosis.

---

94 S. Weil, *Waiting on God*, p. 102.

95 G. MacGregor, *Issues*, p. 183.

Kenosis, which he perceives mainly as divine permissiveness or self-restraint is considered to be characteristic of divine being and activities. In line with His nature, therefore, God permits human freedom and the blind necessity of nature to take their full course in the world. The evil in the world, both moral and natural, arise, MacGregor maintains, when human freedom and necessity collide in the open space of their own non-limitation. To that effect, he maintains that God is not the cause of evil and suffering. Suffering is the price of freedom. Due to His permissiveness, God does not interfere to redress the harm caused by the blind necessity of nature or unrestricted freedom of personal agents.

And since God obliges Himself not to interfere, MacGregor contends, God suffers: He suffers precisely " in the sense of enduring the consequences of his own self-renunciation and self-sacrifice".[96] In that case, His suffering is not imposed on Him, He suffers freely. His suffering arises out of His kenotic nature. God is essentially kenotic, and therefore, He suffers essentially. Kenosis is also creative, for it is the principle with which God grants existence to beings.

MacGregor's kenotic theology of divine suffering definitely makes some significant contributions, by understanding kenosis as a principle of life and interpreting it in terms of love. However, some conceptual problems arise out of the fact that it is conceived almost exclusively in a philosophical context, outside the realm of a Trinitarian theology, and bereft of a Christological basis. This leads to his additional error of conceiving kenosis spatial and non-personalistic, in a manner in which even divine suffering loses its empathic dimension. Consequently, God suffers, but He does not suffer with the sufferers. Besides, since he sees kenosis as God's withdrawal, the paradox of a God who can be immanent and yet transcendent is lost.

---

[96] MacGregor, *Issues*, p. 168.

5. DIVINE IMPASSIBILITY IN A TRINITARIAN THEOLOGY OF THE CROSS ACCORDING TO JÜRGEN MOLTMANN

5.1 Trinitarian Hermeneutics

Moltmann develops his theology in two phases. The first phase consists of his first three major works[1] dedicated to the issues of eschatology, crucifixion and pneumatology. Each of these themes which he took from the history of salvation[2] is elaborately and separately discussed in a monograph. The three monographs however form a unit and could rightly be called a trilogy. They are united both in style and purpose: they are outstandingly set within a Trinitarian framework and designed to illustrate the significance of these subjects for our understanding of God. Moreover, Moltmann contends that each of these themes can be a sufficient starting point for a genuine Christian theology.[3]

The second phase of his theological construction, which began with the publication of *The Trinity and the Kingdom of God*[4] in 1980, shows a different methodology. Whereas he earlier tried to discuss concepts and doctrines in isolation, he now seeks to illustrate them in a broader systematic sequence.[5] Besides, at this stage, as the title of the above mentioned book suggests, he goes further to construct and consolidate his Trinitarian approach which was initiated in the first phase. So he argues accordingly that only a Trinitarian conception of God, that is to say, Trinitarian hermeneutics,[6] can be made the starting point of theology. In his view, one cannot perceive the context and correlation of concepts without such hermeneutics.[7] Neither can we make dialectical judgements,[8] get into

---

1 J. Moltmann, *Theology of Hope*; -----, *The Crucified God*; and -----, *The Church in the Power of the Spirit*.

2 J. Moltmann, *The Trinity and the Kingdom of God*, p. XI.

3 In the process however he unconsciously outlines a one-sided theology, which has been massively criticised. Cf. Michael Welker (Hrsg.), *Diskussion über Jürgen Moltmanns Buch "Der gekreuzigte Gott"*. In his answer to his critics, Moltmann says he would no longer continue the method he employed in the trilogy, not so much because of the criticisms as for the fact that the earlier method has served its purpose. It was merely meant to prepare the ground for a wider theological system, which begins hereafter. Cf. J. Moltmann, Antwort auf die Kritik an 'Der gekreuzigte Gott', pp. 165 ff.

4 J. Moltmann, *The Trinity and the Kingdom of God*.

5 *Ibid.*, preface.

6 *Ibid.*, p. 19.

7 Cf. *ibid.*, p. xi.

8 Cf. J. Moltmann, *The Crucified God*, pp. 25-27.

"dialogue in history"[9] and represent God and the Trinitarian history of God as proclaimed in the Bible if a Trinitarian framework is lacking.

For Moltmann, the doctrine of the Trinity should be seen, therefore, as the authentic representation of the biblical image of God,[10] irrespective of the fact that as a doctrine, its formulation has a philosophical origin.[11] He distances himself accordingly from the claims made by some liberal Protestant theologians[12] that the doctrine of the Trinity is a mere philosophical speculation devoid of authenticity. In contrast, he argues in defence of the authenticity of the doctrine of the Trinity and for the adoption of the "Trinitarian thinking".[13] He goes on to contend, not only that the stories of the New Testament are told in Trinitarian terms, but also that the biblical history itself has a Trinitarian origin.[14]

In this connection, Moltmann perceives a dialectical relationship between the doctrine of the Trinity and Christology. For in a sense, the doctrine of the Trinity has "*Christology* as its premise",[15] and in another sense, it is itself "the theological premise for Christology and soteriology".[16] In accordance with the perceptible interconnection between the doctrine of the Trinity and Christology, he contends that every aspect of the Christ-event has a corresponding resonance in the inner-Trinitarian life, and that the history of salvation is a display of the inner-Trinitarian relationship. Strictly speaking, therefore, a genuine Christian theology is for him a Trinitarian theology.

5.2 Divine Unity and Self-differentiation

Moltmann observes that the issue of the unity of God, which characterised the Christological controversies of the third century still constitutes a problem for to-

---

9   J. Moltmann, *The Trinity and the Kingdom of God*, p. xiii.

10   Cf. *ibid.*, p. 62.

11   Cf. *ibid.*, pp. 61-96.

12   Perceiving a visible "hermeneutic difference" between the patristic dogmatisation of the Trinity and the New Testament proclamation of God, these theologians, in the manner of Kant and Schleiermacher, declare that the Trinity is unbiblical. *Ibid.*, p. 61.

13   *Ibid.*, p. 20.

14   Cf. *ibid.*, p. 64.

15   *Ibid.*, p. 97.

16   *Ibid.*, p. 129. Concretely, Moltmann gives his dialectical judgement of the relationship between Christology and Trinity thus: Christology makes the theology of the Trinity necessary, but it is only in the context of a theology of the Trinity that Christology gains it eschatological significance - its openness towards the transfiguration of the world.

day's theology and that the modalistic thinking, which lead to the failure of the Arian subordinationism and the Sabellian modalism still lurks behind even the most meaningful Trinitarian theology Today.[17] This means that the doctrine of the Trinity has not yet solved the problem which led to its formulation, namely the problem of the Arian subordinationism and the Sabellian modalism.[18] The characteristic problem of the theologies that make modalistic thinking their starting point is the inability to account for the unity and self-differentiation of God. This problem is aggravated by the fact that they take the unity of God as given, instead of allowing it to develop in the history of the Trinity and the world.

In fact, the earlier attempts to account for the unity and multiplicity in God invariably led to modalistic conclusions, because, as Moltmann sees it, where philosophical starting points were adopted, the unity of God was taken as given, and the task was to merely account for their differentiation. In the light of the biblical history, however, the direction should be reversed: Theology should first affirm the differentiation of the Father, the Son and the Spirit in their activities in the world, before the task of searching for the unity of God can even begin. The unity of God should be posed as an "eschatological question" awaiting an answer that is to come at the consummation of the Trinitarian history of God, when the unity of the three Persons is being expected and hoped for.[19]

If the unity of God should at all be presupposed, it must be conceived as an eschatological unity open to the world and to the future, a unity that is inviting, inclusive and capable of integration.[20] This is different from the traditional notion of the divine unity, which, by adopting the concept of one substance and identical subject, remains an exclusively closed unity leading constantly to a monadic

---

17 Moltmann argues that idealistic modalism is veiled in modern terminologies in the Trinitarian theology of Karl Barth and Karl Rahner (See *Ibid.*, pp. 139- 148). Following the example of German Idealists, Barth rightly replaces supreme substance with absolute Subject (139), but by making divine Lordship his starting point and putting it before the Trinity he could not avoid the monotheistic conclusion "that all activity proceeds from the Father, both within the Trinity and in history"(143). The origin of Rahner's own error, he claims, has to do with the use of a concept of person which conveys a form of "extreme individualism"(145). Rahner adopts this form of "personalism" because he is not keen to allow three different "centres of activities" or "subjectivities" in the Trinity. And in order to attribute only a single consciousness to the Trinity, Rahner denies the possibility of "mutual Thou" and interpersonal relations of the triune God. See *Ibid.*, p. 156), and K. Rahner, Der dreifaltige Gott als transzendenter Ursprung der Heilsgeschichte", p. 366, esp. footnote 29.

18 J. Moltmann, *The Trinity and the Kingdom of God*, pp. 129-136.

19 *Ibid.*, p. 149.

20 Cf. *ibid.*

premise. In contrast, an eschatological unity does not express a condition but a relation, a "unitedness",[21] a fellowship which presupposes the self-differentiation of the divine persons.

At this point, Moltmann emphasises that the unity of God can neither be conceived as the homogeneity of divine substance nor as the identity of an absolute subject; neither should the Father, the Son and the Spirit be *distinguished* from one another merely by their character as Persons. The three Persons should rather be thought of being "as much united with one another and in one another".[22] "The Trinitarian Persons *subsist* in the common divine nature; they *exist* in their relations to one another".[23] Indeed, in this connection, he claims that the unity of God "must be perceived in the *perichoresis* of the divine Persons".[24] An eschatological unity is therefore a "*perichoretic* unity",[25] a social unity which enables the Persons to constitute themselves in an eternal mutual interrelation and interpenetration, "without reducing the threeness to the unity, or dissolving the unity in the threeness".[26] The eternal perichoresis excludes subordinationism and modalism.

This has consequences for the traditional distinction between the economic and immanent Trinity, between the triune God in the works of salvation and for the differentiation among the Persons themselves. Such a distinction inevitably leads to a contradiction in God,[27] as it introduces a polarity between a self-sufficient God and a God who gets involved. *God in Himself* cannot be different from *God for us*, since His works reveal precisely His goodness.[28] With regard to this, Moltmann agrees with Rahner that "the economic Trinity is the immanent Trinity", especially as it helps to remove the impression that there is an "inwardness" and "outwardness" in the triune God.[29] The economic Trinity must be under-

---

21 It has been observed that Moltmann replaces "unity" (*Einheit*) with "unitedness" (*Einigkeit*) to show that divine unity is eschatological and open to the world and community. Cf. F. Meessen, *Unveränderlichkeit*, p. 345.

22 J. Moltmann, *The Trinity and the Kingdom of God*, p. 151.

23 *Ibid.*, p. 173.

24 *Ibid.*, p. 150.

25 Moltmann borrows this idea from John Damascene. The concept of *perichoresis* understands the Persons as existing in their relations to each other. That which divides them holds them together - their relation.

26 *Ibid.*, p. 178.

27 Cf. *ibid.*, p. 158.

28 Cf. *ibid.*, p. 151.

29 Cf. *ibid.*, p. 161.

stood for this reason as the pure revelation of the immanent Trinity, even though we, for lingual convenience, dare to continue qualifying them with different terms. However, what needs to be noted is that the "outward" activities of the Trinity must then have a retroactive effect on the inner-Trinitarian process itself. In that case, the retroactive effect of the *opera trinitatis ad extra* on the triune God should be termed the *opera trinitatis ad intra*.

Based on this assumption, Moltmann argues in favour of the suffering of God: "the *opera trinitatis ad extra* thus corresponds to the *passiones trinitatis ad intra*".[30] For this reason, the Cross of the Son and the history of the Spirit are believed to have their impact on the inner-Trinitarian life.[31] If it is accepted that the *actio* of God has a corresponding *passio* in Him, Moltmann says, we can go further to give two classifications of the *opera trinitatis ad extra*: firstly, as the opera dei ad extra interna, and secondly, as the *opera dei ad extra externa*.[32]

5.3   God-world Relationship

With the above reclassification of the works of the Trinity ad extra, Moltmann intends to show that there was a continuity of the inner-Trinitarian life, even during the earthly life of Jesus. God's relationship to Himself is different from His relationship to the world; but this difference cannot be conceived in such a way that the latter has no significance for the former. The immanent Trinity must be seen as "part of eschatology as well", awaiting its consummation at the end of time when everything will be in God and God will be in everything.[33] In this capacity, God is not the sole actor in His relationship to the world: between Him

---

30 *Ibid.*, p. 160.

31 Cf. *ibid.*, p. 161. Moltmann's main concern here is to see that the different Persons of the Trinity are recognised as independent subjects, initiating actions relevant to the inner-Trinitarian life. If that is achieved, the fact that God directs His action not only outwards but also inwards would be evident. The Son reveals the triune God concretely (*Ibid.*, p. 61 ff.), the Spirit is the subject, who unifies and glorifies the Godhead (*Ibid.*, p. 125; J. Moltmann, *The Church in the Power of the Spirit*, p. 57 f.) God varies the pattern of His relationship to the world, therefore, depending on which Person of the Trinity initiates a particular Trinitarian action in the world. (J. Moltmann, *The Trinity and the Kingdom of God*, p. 95, 127).

32 Here Moltmann follows K. Barth and E. Jüngel, who according to him also took over this expression from the early Protestant orthodoxy. (Cf. J. Moltmann, *The Trinity and the Kingdom of God*, footnote 2, p. 99).

33 Cf. J. Moltmann, *The Trinity and the Kingdom of God*, p. 161.

and the world *actio* and *passio* are reciprocal. The God-world relationship is a living one; it must be *reciprocal*;[34] it cannot be one-dimensional.[35]

> Just as God goes out of himself through what he does, giving his world his own impress, so his world puts its impress on God too, through its reactions, its aberrations and its own initiatives. It certainly does not do so in the same way; but that it does so in its *own* way there can be no doubt at all. If God is love, then he does not merely emanate, flow out of himself; he also expects and needs love: his world is intended to be his home.[36]

By insisting that God's relationship to the world is retroactive and reciprocal, Moltmann aims is to think of the world process and the inner-Trinitarian process as one, without mixing them up. It should be possible, he contends, to see "*God in the world* and *the world in God*"[37] and yet be able to avoid the extreme positions of the *Christian theism*[38] and *panentheism*.[39] In fact, "in order to understand the history of mankind as a history in God, the distinction between the world process and the inner-Trinitarian process must be maintained and emphasised".[40]

There is thus a continuity in the *presence* of the triune God in the world, just as the history of the world is part of the Trinitarian history of God: the Father is particularly present in the creation, the Son in the Incarnation and the Spirit in the *indwelling*. Renewing the doctrine of creation, Incarnation and eschatology in the

---

34 *Ibid.*, p. 98.

35 *Ibid.*, p. 160.

36 *Ibid.*, p. 99.

37 *Ibid.*, p. 105. Here Moltmann tries to borrow from the Jewish theology of Shekinah and the panentheistic ideas of the process theologians.

38 According to Moltmann, Christian theism depicts the world in such a way that it has no significance for God. For this tradition, creation is merely the work of God's free will; God abides in His self-sufficiency, exercising absolute liberty and unlimited power - His action is arbitrary and His image despotic. This is the view that makes the world appear merely circumstantial and the following questions inevitable: "Is the question of the creation of the world necessary for God Himself, or is it merely fortuitous? Does it proceed from God's nature, or from His will? Is it eternal, or temporal?" See J. Moltmann, *The Trinity and the Kingdom of God*, p. 105.

39 "Panentheism understands itself as a form of theism, but it criticises traditional theism for depicting the world as external to God." See J. Cobb, Panentheism. Process theologians are the main advocates of this tradition in the twentieth-century. For seeing the world in God, this tradition also appeals to Moltmann, but he condemns its unrestrained "will towards synthesis" which weakens its capacity to make distinctions.

40 *Ibid.*, p. 107.

perspective of a Trinitarian history, Moltmann therefore speaks of a "Trinitarian creation",[41] a "Trinitarian Incarnation",[42] and a "Trinitarian glorification".[43]

Moltmann understands creation as an open system,[44] an uncompleted process[45] awaiting a messianic future.[46] Through the mediation of Christ and the glorification of the world in the Spirit,[47] the consummation of the Trinitarian process of creation will follow at the end of time, when God will be "all in all" (I Cor. 15:28). Until the alienated world is united with God, creation remains incomplete. Moltmann's main concern here is to maintain that creation is a Trinitarian act involving all the Persons of the Trinity. All the activities of the different persons of the Trinity are unified by a common eschatological purpose. Consequently, all the events of the salvation history could be subsumed under the one continuous creative process running from the initial to the new creation. Creation and redemption are for that reason not isolated divine activities in the history of God with the world.[48]

This obliges Moltmann to not only account for the relation between the creation and Incarnation, but also for the implication of the two for the concept of God. Historically, i.e. from the point of view of the history of salvation, the creation is prior to the Incarnation, but intentionally, i.e. as far as the pre-existent Logos is concerned, "the Incarnation precedes the creation of the world".[49]

The creation and the Incarnation are thus dialectically inter-connected works of the Trinity, which deeply affects the inner relationships of the triune God. If both works are so much rooted in the inner-Trinitarian process, the questions must arise as to how significant they are for our conception of God. Are they necessary for God Himself or are they merely fortuitous? How can such temporal

---

41 *Ibid.*, p. 111.

42 *Ibid.*, p. 121.

43 *Ibid.*, p. 126.

44 Cf. *ibid.*, p. 115 ff.

45 Cf. J. Moltmann, *The Future of Creation*, p. 119.

46 Cf. J. Moltmann, *The Trinity and the Kingdom of God*, p.102.

47 Cf. *ibid.*, p. 104 ff.

48 Moltmann supports this point with the "soteriological understanding of creation" from the Old Testament theology, which shows how Israel's historical experience of divine liberation led to their belief in creation. The eschatological and soteriological understanding of creation implies that theology must conceive the creation of the world, as having a beginning, a history and an end. J. Moltmann, *The Future of Creation*, p. 118 ff.; See also G von Rad, *Old Testament Theology I*, p. 136 ff; L. Köhler, *Old Testament Theology*, p. 88.

49 J. Moltmann, *The Trinity and the Kingdom of God*, p. 11.

events be located in the eternity of God? In other words, are they necessary products emanating from His nature, or are they the results of an extraordinary divine decision? Moltmann attempts an answer to these questions in his analysis of divine love and freedom.

5.4   Divine Love and Freedom

While discussing the suffering of God, Moltmann pays special attention to the implications of divine love and freedom for the Christian conception of God.[50] The Johannine statement that 'God is love' (I Jn. 4:8) is for him a basic assumption, which he goes on to interpret ontologically and functionally. The triune God is basically love, because the three persons are constituted ontologically in their inner-Trinitarian relations. The three persons constitute their beings in the love which they have for themselves. This is its ontological component. Besides, it belongs to the nature of this love, which he qualifies in the Platonic terminology as the *love of like for like*, to communicate itself to the other, so that "it is no longer addressed to the Other in the like, but to the like in the Other".[51] It would be a contradiction and insufficiency for the divine love to remain a love of like for like,[52] because love is the good that needs to be communicated. Love, as "the self-communication of the good",[53] is thus necessarily creative, and remains incomplete if it does not communicate itself creatively. This is its functional component.

As an expression of divine love, creation therefore owes its existence to this self-communicating aspect of divine love and for that reason cannot be fortuitous.[54] It is eternally presupposed by God's eternal love.

> From eternity God has desired not only himself but the world too, for he did not merely want to communicate himself to himself; he wanted to communicate himself to the one who is other than himself as well. That is why the idea of the world is al-

---

[50]   Cf. *ibid.*, p. 52 ff., 57 ff.

[51]   *Ibid.*, p. 59.

[52]   Frank Meessen considers this one of the three most important thoughts of Moltmann, namely that there was insufficiency on the part of the immanent Trinity, before it expressed its creative love in the creation. Cf. F. Meessen, *Unveränderlichkeit*, p. 342.

[53]   J. Moltmann, *The Trinity and the Kingdom of God*, p. 57.

[54]   Moltmann takes this idea from I. A. Dorner: 'The world is a goodly purpose, in correspondence with God's love, not a fortuitous one'. See J. Moltmann, *The Trinity and the Kingdom of God*, p. 107, footnote 20; see also I. A. Dorner, *System der christlichen Glaubenslehre II, I*, p. 358.

ready inherent in the Father's love for the Son. The eternal Son of God is closely related to God's idea of the world.[55]

With his understanding of love as the self-communication of the good,[56] Moltmann explains the significance of the Incarnation for the conception of God even further. The Incarnation is part of God's eternal communication of His love;[57] it is as such not necessitated by human sins,[58] but by 'God's own nature. It must be admitted however, that whereas the *reason* for the Incarnation is to be sought in the nature of divine love, its concrete occurrence was *occasioned* by the human conditions.[59] In other words, although the Incarnation was intended eternally, the concrete form it took in history is an emergency measure. In this way, Moltmann tries to steer the middle course between the extremes positions of the "functional" and the "intention" Christologies. Hence, his paradoxical statement: "The Incarnation of the Son is neither a matter of indifference for God nor is it necessary for his divinity".[60]

If the creation of the world and the Incarnation of the Son are expressions of the divine love as such, according to Moltmann, it then follows that God is touched intimately by the events in this world, and that He cannot be indifferent to the problems and suffering of His creatures.

The creation of the world and the Incarnation of the Son out of love further prove that God's love is kenotic. The divine works *ad extra* and *divine presence in the world* are characterised by divine self-limitation. For if there should be no

---

55 J. Moltmann, *The Trinity and the Kingdom of God*, p. 108.

56 Cf. *ibid.*, p. 57 ff.

57 Cf. *ibid.*, p. 114. This view is also influenced by I. A. Dorner, *System der christlichen Glaubenslehre II, I*, pp. 422 f. According to this notion the incarnation of the Son was intended by God from eternity. His intention is formed together with the idea of the world. For this reason Moltmann considers the fundamental theological question whether the Son of God would have become man if the human race had remained free of sin, irrelevant.

58 Moltmann rejects the claim of "functional Christology" that incarnation is merely an 'emergency measure' on God's part, taken in order to counter the emergency of sin in the world" (J. Moltmann, *The Trinity and the Kingdom of God*, p. 114). This soteriological approach makes the human sin its starting point. Consequently incarnation is itself a means to an end and looses its significance as soon as the end - redemption - is attained. This view leads to the unavoidable, and certainly unacceptable, conclusion that the person of the incarnate Son of God would be superfluous once the world is reconciled with God. Moltmann criticises the Christology of Calvin, A. von Ruler and D. Sölle precisely on this point. Cf. J. Moltmann, *The Crucified God*, pp. 256-266.

59 Cf. J. Moltmann, *The Trinity and the Kingdom of God*, p. 116.

60 *Ibid.*, p. 117.

reality outside God, we must assume that He relates to the world kenotically. Moltmann finds the kenotic motif particularly relevant to the interpretation of the omnipresence and omnipotence of God in a manner that does not suggest a partition of God into outward and inward sectors. Affirming the panentheistic and dialectic view that *the world is in God*, Moltmann therefore contends that God created the world "'in himself', giving it time in his eternity, finitude in his infinity, space in his omnipresence and freedom in his selfless love".[61] In a manner reminiscent of MacGregor's kenotic theology, he maintains that creation is a work of God's withdrawal; God withdraws into Himself to let other realities be.[62] The Incarnation thus followed a kenotic law:[63] "The *outward Incarnation* presupposes *inward self-humiliation*".[64] Consequently, creation is not so much an *actio* as it is a passio Dei. That is how the Incarnation of the Son affects the inner relations of the Trinity.

The kenosis does not, however, constitute weakness on the part of God, it rather shows the strength of God's love. "God is nowhere greater than in his humiliation. God is nowhere more glorious than in his impotence. God is no where more divine than when he becomes man".[65] By arguing that God is truly God, when He becomes the "*human God*" and that "The divine kenosis which begins with the creation of the world reaches its perfected and completed form in the Incarnation of the Son",[66] Moltmann formulates his central idea of the paradox of the divine kenosis.

Yet, his claim that the divine love is necessarily self-communicating, logically creative and kenotic, does suggest that he places God under a compulsion: God is compelled to perpetual self-limitation. In his view, this danger does not arise, because "if God's nature is goodness, then the freedom of his will lies in his will to goodness", to an extent that one can say that "in God *necessity and freedom* co-

---

61 *Ibid.*, p. 109.

62 However, he borrows this idea of God's Self-limitation in the creation process from the Jewish kabbalistic tradition, to be precise, from Luria's doctrine of *Zimsum*. He believes that a reformed version of this doctrine would offer us "the chance to think of *the world in God* without falling victims to pantheism, and to see the history of the divine self-humiliation and the history of human freedom in a continual relationship of reciprocity". *Ibid.*, p. 110.

63 Cf. *ibid.*, p. 118 ff. Moltmann favours kenoticism as a better way of conceiving God's relation to the world, but he is not willing to develop it in the framework of the Christology of the two-natures. J. Moltmann, *The Crucified God*, p. 205-206.

64 J. Moltmann, *The Trinity and the Kingdom of God*, p. 119.

65 *Ibid.*

66 *Ibid.*, p. 118.

incide".[67] At this point, Moltmann tries to relate divine love to His freedom, by harmonising His nature and will. Hence, God's love is God's freedom, "the self communication of the good".[68] Freedom is not the Lordship of one and the servitude of the other.[69] God does not make "the choice between being love and not being love";[70] He has not got a "torment of choice".[71] Through His self-limiting love, He gives freedom to His creatures. His consistency in love assures His own freedom. "Through his freedom he keeps man, his image, and his world, creation, free - keeps them free and pays the price of their freedom".[72]

Consequently, divine suffering is the price God pays for letting human beings be free. This does not imply a restriction of His own freedom; His suffering is an expression of His own freedom based on "friendship", "mutual and common participation in life".[73] Moltmann thus concludes, that only a passionate God, who suffers by virtue of His passion for people, can indeed be the foundation of the human freedom, in a manner that no immovable and apathetic God can be.

5.5   The Trinitarian Suffering of God

5.5.1   The Cross as a Trinitarian Event

Having established the unity of the triune God to be eschatological and perichoretic and understood God, out of His self-communicating love, to have allowed the state of the world to have a retroactive and kenotic effect on Him, Moltmann sees his road to a Trinitarian theology of the Cross adequately prepared. The Cross must be interpreted in Trinitarian terms " as an event concerned with a relationship between persons in which these persons constitute themselves in their relationship with each other".[74] On the basis of this relationship, what

---

67   *Ibid.*, p. 107.

68   *Ibid.*, p. 55.

69   Moltmann vehemently rejects the nominalist concept of freedom, which understands freedom merely as freedom to choose and possess power. He criticises Barth's interpretation of God's freedom for adopting this nominalistic and formalistic notion of freedom; it led the latter to the attribution of absolute power on the "God the Lord". J. Moltmann, *The Trinity and the Kingdom of God*, p. 54 f.

70   *Ibid.*, p.54.

71   Here, Moltmann refers to the German proverb: "wer die Wahl hat, hat die Qual" - the person who chooses has the torment of choice.

72   J. Moltmann, *The Trinity and the Kingdom of God*, p. 56.

73   *Ibid.*

74   J. Moltmann, *The Crucified God*, p. 245.

happened to Christ is believed to have happened to God; his suffering is the suffering of a "crucified God".[75]

In the light of the above, it is also impossible to develop a Christian concept of God, Moltmann contends, without incorporating the theology of the Cross,[76] just as there can be no reasonable theology of the Cross outside the context of a Trinitarian theology.

> That is why we must say: the material principle of the doctrine of the Trinity is the Cross of Christ; the formal principle of the theology of the Cross as theology is the doctrine of the Trinity.[77]

By perceiving a close relationship between the doctrine of the Trinity and the theology of the Cross, Moltmann improves on the *theologia crucis* from Luther, his mentor, whose theology, he says, regrettably lacks "a developed Christological doctrine of the Trinity".[78] A theology of the Cross must primarily understand the event of the Cross as the self-revelation of God, because, in his view, Christ's entire experience on the Cross is more "a statement about God" than it is "an assurance of salvation".[79]

In this light, he sees the "God-forsakenness" experienced by Christ on the Cross, as God's special revelation. The cry of Jesus - "My God, why hast Thou forsaken me?" - therefore reveals "a dichotomy in God".[80] He sees this view endorsed by the earlier claims that the Cross was an event "between God and God" (Luther), that "God himself is forsaken by God, God himself rejects himself"

---

75 *Ibid.*, pp. 200-290.

76 Moltmann accuses the Christian tradition of having compromised the position of Christ's passion in our doctrine of God in favour of a metaphysical tradition of Greek philosophy. Consequently, he wonders whether Christian theology has not, for that reason, inevitably "failed to develop a consistent Christian concept of God". Cf. J. Moltmann, *The Future of Creation*, p. 59.

77 *Ibid.*, p. 74.

78 J. Moltmann, *The Crucified God*, p. 235. The reason why Luther could not develop a Trinitarian theology of the cross is, according to Moltmann, that his Christology was developed within the context of the doctrine of two natures, a doctrine that makes the thinking of the cross as an event relevant to God Himself impossible. For as long as the division between the human and divine natures are invariably maintained, the cross can not be conceived as touching the being of God, who is supposed to have been living self-sufficiently "untouched by evil and death". This is the main criticism Moltmann levels against Rahner's and Barth's theology of the cross. Cf. J. Moltmann, *The Future of Creation*, p. 62 f.

79 Moltmann distances himself from the claims of the early Protestant theology that the suffering of Christ on the cross has a solely salvific role to play.

80 J. Moltmann, *The Crucified God*, p. 151.

(Helmut Gollwitzer) and that no one is against God except God Himself - "*Nemo contra Deum nisi Deus ipse*" - (Goethe).[81] For Moltmann, the paradox of the theology of the Cross consists in conceiving the "God in God-forsakenness" of Jesus as an event of love. This, he believes, is "a revolution in the concept of God",[82] which cannot be achieved through an analogical principle of knowledge of like by like, but only through a dialectical principle of the knowledge of God "in his opposite".[83]

The claim that God reveals Himself in the God-forsakenness of Jesus could be termed the central theme of Moltmann's Trinitarian theology of the Cross. It is the climax of the paradox of divine revelation, and cannot be excluded in the search for a true Christian concept of God. For the Cross, according to him, is the sole source of the Christian identity,[84] which itself consists in the "act of identification with the crucified Christ".[85] The failure of theology to understand the Cross of Christ as the unique revelation of God inevitably leads the Church to "a double crisis" which he identifies as "the crisis of identity and the crisis of relevance".[86] In the face of this danger, the God-forsaken death of Jesus is for us "either the end of every theology, or else the beginning of a theology that is specifically Christian".[87]

5.5.2   The Nature of the Trinitarian Suffering

Out of this background, Moltmann goes on to affirm that both the Father and the Son suffered the God-forsakenness, albeit differently, for both were involved in the act of surrender - in the *paradidonai* - in the "delivering up" (Rom. 8:32; Gal. 2:20). "The Son endures the being forsaken by the Father...the Father endures the being forsaken by the Son whom he chose and loved".[88] The claim that the Father and the Son had the same experience of self-surrender is significant for

---

81   See J. Moltmann, *The Future of Creation*, p. 65.

82   *Ibid.*, p. 75.

83   *Ibid.*, p. 78. Moltmann is however quick to add that "the dialectical principle of revelation in the opposite" does not substitute "the analogical principle of knowledge of what is similar", just as *theologia crucis* should not replace *theologia gloriae*. Both should supplement each other.(J. Moltmann, *The Future of Creation*, p. 79; J. Moltmann, *The Crucified God*, p. 27.

84   Cf. J. Moltmann, *The Crucified God*, p. 24.

85   *Ibid.*, p. 19.

86   *Ibid.*, p. 7.

87   J. Moltmann, *The Future of Creation*, p. 60.

88   *Ibid.*, p. 73.

Moltmann's theology; he employs it not only for asserting the suffering of God, but also for the interpretation of the *Filioque*. For as he writes: "The forsaking God and the forsaken God are one in the Spirit of surrender. The Spirit proceeds from the Father and the Son, for it has its source in the *derelictio Jesu*".[89] There is a uniformity of Will and Spirit among the Father and the Son, Moltmann concludes, because in the same Spirit the Father willed to deliver up his Son, and the Son willed to deliver up himself. Thus, whereas there is a uniformity of Will and Spirit among them, there is also a difference in the type of suffering each experienced. In other words, the Father and the Son suffered together, but differently.

At this point, one sees Moltmann struggling to avoid the heresy of Patripassianism, thereby suggesting that Patripassianism can be avoided even as one asserts divine suffering in a Trinitarian framework. He prefers to speak of "Patricompassianism"[90] in this regard: "The Son suffers and dies on the Cross. The Father suffers with him, but not in the same way".[91] He therefore rejects the claim of the 'God-is-dead' theologies in which the death of Christ means "the death of God", and rather maintains that the death of Christ is a "death *in* God, but not "the death of God".[92] For while "The Son suffers dying, the Father suffers the death of the Son".[93]

In the light of this Trinitarian theology of the Cross, Moltmann feels justified to say that a form of divine suffering necessarily belongs to a Christian concept of God.[94] This, he continues, would further imply that we should consider the tendency to regard impassibility or apathy as the essence of God in some theologies as unchristian. For, not only does such a claim disregard the Christian proclamation and devotion of the crucified Christ as God, it also fails to recognise the 'dialectic'(the logic) of divine nature. The traditional argument for divine apathy,[95] he says, has the inherent tendency to behold only a "single alternative": either God is *essentially* impassible or he is *fatefully* passible. For Moltmann, however, God is neither essentially impassible nor helplessly passible. The logic of

---

89 *Ibid.*, p. 73 f.; cf. also J. Moltmann, *The Trinity and the Kingdom of God*, p. 178 ff.

90 J. Moltmann, *The Future of Creation,*, p. 73.

91 J. Moltmann, *The Crucified God*, p. 203.

92 *Ibid.*, p. 207.

93 *Ibid.*, p. 243.

94 Cf. J. Moltmann, *The Trinity and the Kingdom of God*, p. 23.

95 According to Moltmann the patristic claim for the axiom of divine impassibility was motivated by the need to differentiate God's essence from that of the word, and also to show that eternal life is different from earthly life. For him these concerns could still be taken care of within the context of a dialectical understanding of the Trinity.

divine nature accommodates what he calls "active suffering - the voluntary laying oneself open to another and allowing oneself to be intimately affected by him; that is to say, the suffering of passionate love".[96] God who suffers voluntarily and actively, suffers out of love.

In accordance with this line of argument, it would be right to say, that Moltmann is not so much rejecting as reinterpreting the axiom of the divine impassibility. He is rather of the opinion that, if this axiom is properly understood, it should be seen, not as an attribute of God but as a *statement of comparison*, merely stating that God does not suffer the same way as transient creatures. Consequently, God, whose essence is love, is for Moltmann both pathetic and apathetic:

> God does not suffer out of deficiency of being, like created beings. To this extent he is 'apathetic'. But he suffers from the love which is the superabundance and overflowing of his being. In so far he is 'pathetic'. [97]

5.5.3   Sources of Inspiration for Moltmann's Theology of Divine Suffering

The development of Moltmann's theology of divine suffering and of the Cross were influenced by some primary sources, which need to be mentioned here for better perception of his own contribution.

Hegel occupies the first position of importance. From his *Philosophy of Religion*, Moltmann learnt not only the use of dialectics to understand the Trinitarian implication of the Cross, but also its application to the history of God.[98] His thesis that the eschatological consummation of the Trinitarian relations will only follow when the redemption of the world is completed at the end of time[99] is directly derived from Hegel's philosophy of history. However, in locating the Cross within the Trinity Moltmann is under the influence of Schelling and Kant.[100]

Besides, he also pays homage to Origen, who, so unusual for his time, was able to recognise Christ's suffering as divine suffering, and divine suffering as the suffering of love.[101] Origen's Trinitarian approach is for him a testimony that "we

---

96   *Ibid.*, p. 23.

97   *Ibid.*

98   Cf. J. Moltmann, *The Crucified God*, pp. 253-254

99   Cf. J. Moltmann, *The Trinity and the Kingdom of God*, p. 74 f. According to Frank Meessen this should be termed one of Moltmann's most important thoughts. Cf. F. Meessen, *Unveränderlichkeit.* p. 345.

100   Cf. J. Moltmann, *The Future of Creation*, p. 74 f.

101   Cf. J. Moltmann, *The Trinity and the Kingdom of God*, p. 24.

can only talk about God's suffering in Trinitarian terms".[102] Similarly, in conceiving of the unity of God, Moltmann makes elaborate use of Luther's doctrine of *communicatio idiomatum* and John Damascene's doctrine of *Perichoresis*.

The Johannine theology of love and Pauline kenotic theology are also significant. His analysis of John's "God-is-love" motif leads Moltmann to the conclusion that only a suffering God can love. He also uses a lot of Paul's kenotic theme in Philippians 2, without however absorbing the weakness of earlier kenoticists, who remained within the framework of the doctrine of two natures. In fact, he goes beyond this doctrine to locate Kenosis in the Trinity and in the whole creation.[103]

Moltmann cherishes the contributions of the Jewish tradition towards a theology of divine suffering. He is most indebted to Abraham Heschel's theology of the "pathos of God",[104] whose interpretation of the covenant relation between God and Israel satisfactorily accounts for the connection between divine freedom and passion.[105] By freely committing Himself to a covenant, God is disposed to suffer with His partners. Moltmann sees Heschel's covenant theology perfected in the early rabbinical theology of divine self-humiliation and the kabbalistic doctrine of the Shekinah.[106] God lives with Israel in His Shekinah, goes to exile with her and consequently suffers hard times together with her.

Adopting this view, Moltmann supplements it with eschatology,[107] and therefore insists that the Shekinah should be understood here not only as God's *in-*

---

[102] *Ibid.*, p. 25.

[103] Cf. J. Moltmann, *The Crucified God*, pp. 205-206.

[104] Cf. A. Heschel, *The Prophets*.

[105] Cf. J. Moltmann, *The Trinity and the Kingdom of God*, p. 27; ----, *The Future of Creation*, p. 70. Heschel's dipolar theology makes God's *pathos* (concern) and human *sympathy* interdependent. His theology of covenant shows that God, out of concern (pathos) for human beings, freely enters a covenant with Israel, taking upon Himself her suffering.

[106] Cf. J. Moltmann, *The Trinity and the Kingdom of God*, p. 27; see also: P. Kuhn, *Gottes Selbsterniedrigung in der Theologie der Rabbinen*, Munich 1968; A. M. Goldberg, *Untersuchungen über die Vorstellung von der Shekinah in der frühen rabbinischen Literatur*; G. Scholem, *Von der mystischen Gestalt der Gottheit*, pp. 135 ff. On Moltmann's use of these ideas see J. Niewiadomski, *Die Zweideutigkeit von Gott und Welt in J. Moltmanns Theologien*.

[107] We have to be suspicious of the use of Shekinah here as a justification for an eschatological understanding of the Trinitarian history of God, because it is doubtful whether rabbinical understanding of Shekinah involves the eschatological aspect Moltmann wants. The texts he refers to in P. Kuhn's book do not make such a suggestion. The text merely shows that through the Shekinah Israel is assured of God's presence in hard as well as in good times. Cf. P. Kuhn, *op. cit.*, pp. 82 - 92.

dwelling in Israel, or as "the *condescension* of the Eternal One", but most importantly as the "*anticipations*" (living in hope) of the universal indwelling of God's eternal glory.[108] Developing his own idea of the eschatological unity of God, Moltmann keenly refers to a passage in the work of Gershom Scholem, where it is said, that according to the Kabbalistic conception of "the exile of the Shekinah", God will "be one and his name one" only after the restoration of the original harmony in the act of redemption.[109] Even for his theory of "God against God", Moltmann finds a corollary in the Jewish mysticism, especially at the point where Franz Rosenzweig speaks of the descent and indwelling of God among human beings (Shekinah) as "a divorce which takes place in God himself".[110] All in all, Moltmann adopts many ideas from the wealth of Jewish tradition and supplements them with his eschatological and Trinitarian thinking.[111]

He also cherishes the Anglican theologies of divine suffering from the nineteenth and twentieth centuries, which understand the Eucharist sacrifice as a 'self-sacrifice of love' and the Cross as a revelation of God's eternal nature. The most impressive contribution to this theology was made by C. E. Rolt,[112] who, according to Moltmann, developed a doctrine of the Trinity open to the world,[113] and a dialectical theory which enables us to understand "that God's eternal bliss is not bliss based on the absence of *suffering*". On the contrary, pain is not avoided in the eternal joy of the Trinity but "accepted and transmuted into glory."[114] Rolt's view became something of political importance in the practical work of G. A. Suddert Kennedy,[115] whose attempt to connect theopathy and political theology inspired Moltmann in the development of his own theology of the Cross.

Another interesting contribution comes from a Spanish writer and philosopher, Miguel de Unamuno, who developed a theology of God's universal *sorrow*.[116] Unamuno follows a particular dialectic which Moltmann identifies as "the contra-

---

[108] Cf. J. Moltmann, *The Trinity and the Kingdom of God*, p. 28.

[109] Cf. *ibid.*, p. 29; see also G. Scholem, *Die jüdische Mystik in ihren Hauptströmmungen*, p. 253.

[110] F. Rosenzweig, *Der Stern der Erlösung III*, pp. 192 ff.

[111] Cf. J. Moltmann, *The Crucified God*, p. 275.

[112] Cf. C. E. Rolt, *The World's Redemption*.

[113] Cf. J. Moltmann, *The Trinity and the Kingdom of God*, p. 33.

[114] *Ibid.*, p.34.

[115] Cf. G. A. Studdert Kennedy, *The Hardest Part*.

[116] Cf. M. de Unamuno, *The Tragic Sense of Life in Men and Nations*.

diction in the correspondence and the correspondence in the contradiction".[117] This dialectic says more or less that if one is aware of what one is or does, one is also aware of its contradiction. If God loves, He suffers too, and when He suffers, He suffers for us, and if He suffers for us, He is a God of sorrow. Though Moltmann appreciates this dialectic, he criticises it for its lack of eschatological dimension. It fails, he argues, to mirror the *joy of God*[118] which should overcome His *sorrow*.[119]

Again, the influence of the Russian-Orthodox philosophy of religion on Moltmann is obvious. He particularly appreciates Berdyaev's philosophy of history[120] especially as it is able to think the theology of history and the theology of freedom together.[121] Berdyaev speaks of the tragedy in God based on two assumptions: *God longs for* man as His *"Other"* to whom He can express His love; secondly He *desires* the *freedom* of His "Other" so that the latter can return His love.[122] Berdyaev's positive thoughts were unfortunately overshadowed by Moltmann's conception of dichotomy in God.

5.6   Evaluation

Two points are emphasised   in Moltmann's Trinitarian conception of God: firstly, that God constitutes Himself in the "social" or relational life of the Trinity, and secondly, that it is intrinsic to this Trinitarian social life to be open both to the world and its future and to the eschatological fulfilment or unity of God Himself. Apart from being an alternative rather than a modalistic thought pattern, these views have the merit of thinking about the God-world relationship (in the creation, Incarnation, redemption etc.) in terms of its relevance to both God and hu-

---

[117] J. Moltmann, *The Trinity and the Kingdom of God*, p. 37.

[118] This shows that Moltmann is not opting for a solely sorrowful image of God as his critics argue. The complaint from R. D. Zimany, that Moltmann does not incorporate joy in his concept of God is not completely true. Cf. "Moltmann's crucified God" in: *Dialog* 16 (1977) p. 56.

[119] Cf. J. Moltmann, *The Trinity and the Kingdom of God*, p. 42.

[120] Cf. N. Berdyaev, *The Meaning of History*, ET Geoffrey Bles and Scribner's 1939.; also ----, *Spirit and Reality*, ET Bles and Scribner's 1939 and 1946.

[121] Cf. J. Moltmann, *The Trinity and the Kingdom of God*, p. 47.

[122] Cf. N. Berdyaev, *The Meaning of History*, p. 57; ----, *The Spirit and Reality*, p. 98. According to Berdyaev, if the mystery of the human freedom is to be located in God, we must also assume a movement, a passion in God Himself. God preserves human freedom through the suffering of His love. Movement belongs to God's *triune nature*. God's longing for the Other is therefore no sign of deficiency, but rather an expression of the superabundance of His creative fullness. Cf. ----, *The Meaning of History*, p. 51.

mankind.[123] To this effect, Moltmann has undoubtedly formulated a praxis-oriented doctrine of God. However, there are some conceptual problems concerning his notion of God and God-world relationship, which tend to diminish the merit of his theology.

a) "God against God": a problem of double identity.

In his interpretation of the event on the Cross, especially the God-forsakenness of Jesus, Moltmann gives the impression that there is a tension, a dichotomy between God and God, that God the Father forsakes God the Son, and that God is against God. This view is problematic, especially as he does not see the tension of God-forsakenness as an event that took place once and for all on the Cross of Jesus, but as a permanent event in the very heart of the Trinity.[124] By locating a permanent tension in God, Moltmann conceives God as divided and contradictory, a God of double identity, who is both the executioner and the victim at the same time. By implication, God is the source of good and evil. As a matter of fact, Moltmann feels too good for the world and too bad for God, that, instead of seeing the world as the battleground of good and evil, he transfers the battle ground into God. Such a God, as Niewiadomski rightly observes, is a "tragic God".[125]

If this should mean Moltmann's conception of the dialectics of the divine nature, then it is wrongly conceived, because, as Walter Kasper observes, the dialectic which Moltmann employed for the conception of God has in the end turned out to be God's own identity.[126] Placing contradiction in God Himself is definitely a misuse of dialectics, which has no precedence, not even in Hegelianism. Indeed, dialectic in the Hegelian sense does not make God incorporate His con-

---

123 This aspect of his view has been widely acclaimed for its pastoral relevance. According to Douglas Meek assessment, Moltmann's conception of God is praxis-oriented and provides a means for reconciling "theology and church practice". Cf. D. Meeks, Moltmann's contribution to Practical Theology, pp. 58 & 63. See also Yannaras, Rez. J. Moltmann, Der gekreuzigte Gott, p. 374; G. O'Collins, Rez. J. Moltmann, Der gekreuzigte Gott, p. 160. On the same acclamation from the point of view of his theology of the cross see R. J. Hunter, Moltmann's theology of the cross and the dilemma of contemporary pastoral care, p. 75 f; J. M. Lochmann / H. Dembowski, Gottes Sein ist im Leiden, p. 31; D. L. Migliore, Der gekreuzigte Gott, p. 41 f; R. Bauckham, Moltmanns Eschatologie des Kreuzes, p. 53; H. H. Miskotte, Das Leiden ist in Gott, p. 90; A. Blancy, 'Der gekreuzigte Gott' von Jürgen Moltmann, p. 124; M. Barth, Aus einem Brief an Jürgen Moltmann, p. 162.

124 Cf. H. H. Miskotte, Das Leiden ist in Gott, p. 89.

125 "Der Gott Jürgen Moltmanns ist ein zerrissener, widersprüchlicher und somit auch ein tragischer Gott". J. Niewiadomski, *op. cit.*, p.144.

126 Cf. W. Kasper, Revolution im Gottesverständnis?, p.144.

tradiction, it rather states that God comes "in the fullness of self-identity in the overcoming of the contradiction between himself and the world".[127]

Besides, Moltmann's theory of dichotomy in God practically contradicts the kenotic motif, which he theoretically adopts.[128] It is difficult to see how his avowed "Trinitarian understanding of kenosis"[129] could have led him to profess the theory of "God against God". In line with his Trinitarian notion of kenosis, one would have expected him to understand the issue of God-forsakenness as a sign of divine self-withdrawal, rather than as a dichotomy in God. It would definitely have made more sense if Moltmann believed that in the God-forsakenness, Jesus is allowed to kenotically experience the worst thing that could happen to human beings, namely, abandoned to be abandonment by God. In that case, one would have had the courage to argue that by the God-forsakenness, Jesus descended into hell, a descent that meant liberation for the Godless.

b) God's need for redemption and the impossibility of theodicy.

Moltmann proposes his theory of divine suffering as a practical solution to the problem of theodicy. In his view, the faith in a suffering God should lead a Christian to a better life, based on sympathy and compassion, because just as the faith in God's suffering "preserved Israel against desperate self-destruction and self-surrender" in exile, "we cannot become apathetic" if we affirm the suffering of God.[130] There is no doubt that on pastoral level the belief in God's suffering can influence Christian life positively, since it gives the assurance that God cares for us and that what we do affects God in a certain way. However, since Moltmann does not stop at saying that "suffering affects God externally",[131] but rather claims in addition that suffering - "the negative element" - is in God,[132] his divine-passibility theodicy has conceptual problems also.

Even if God can be justified before the suffering in the world, for being a "co-sufferer" the claim that suffering is in Him raises doubt as to whether He can save the sufferer at all. In this case one would agree with K. Rahner and A. Jäger that a God who has suffering engrafted in His being cannot save, because He is Him-

---

[127] Cf. D. Turner, Dialectic.

[128] Cf. J. Moltmann, *The Crucified God*, p. 204 f.

[129] *Ibid.*, p. 205. Moltmann is even recognised as a kenotic theologian. Cf. L. Richard, Kenotic Christology in a New Perspective, p. 14 f.

[130] Cf. J. Moltmann, *The Passion for life*, p. 23.

[131] Cf. J. Moltmann, *The Crucified God*, p. 274.

[132] Cf. *ibid.*, p. 277.

self helpless and in need of salvation.[133] Moltmann does not even deny that God Himself is in need of redemption.[134] If God Himself can be in need of redemption, how can He still be a redeemer? Does this not mean an implicit rejection of the traditional theory of redemption?[135] Does it not mean compromising the omnipotence of God, without due effort to reinterpret it? If Moltmann wants to tackle the problem of theodicy with the affirmation of divine suffering, he has to reinterpret the concept of divine power and other divine attributes.[136] Besides, he has to go into dialogue with the tradition to re-examine some basic doctrines, namely the doctrine of providence[137] and the doctrine of atonement.[138] Until he does that, it seems to us, that his theory of divine suffering, in spite of its laudable practical solutions, fails to formulate an acceptable theodicy.

c) The common history of God and the world: God's dependency.

For Moltmann, the history of the world is engrafted in the history of God, to such an extent that the Trinitarian life cannot come to its fulfilment and self-realisation without the world. By that means the destiny of the world is conceived as forming a part of the triune God. This would not only mean that God suffers with the world essentially by the simple fact that the world is a part of Him, but also that He does not suffer freely. This view is problematic. For if God suffers necessarily and not out of His free decision, that is to say, as a logical consequence of His nature, of what merit is His suffering to humankind? This is only but one implication of Moltmann's conception of the God-world relationship.

Basically, the problem with his notion of the God-world relationship borders on an insufficient differentiation between God and the world.[139] Moltmann's God is so much part of the world and entangled in its weaknesses that He cannot transcend this world. This does not mean that he has no idea of divine transcendence. He attributes transcendence to God, but only as an eschatological reality:[140] God

---

[133] Cf. K. Rahner, Probleme der Christologie von heute, pp. 169-222 bes. p. 199; A. Jäger, *Gott. 10 Thesen*, p. 150 f.

[134] He quotes the thesis of the kabbalistic doctrine of Shekinah approvingly, which argues that if God suffered with Israel in exile, the deliverance of Israel also meant His own deliverance J. Moltmann, *The Trinity and the Kingdom of God*, p. 28 f.

[135] Cf. J. Niewiadomski, *op. cit.*, p. 147 f.

[136] Cf. W. McWilliams, *The Passion of God*, p. 48

[137] Cf. *ibid.*, p. 49.

[138] Cf. C. E. Braaten, *op. cit.*, p. 114.

[139] Cf. F. Meessen, p. 363; M. Barth, Aus einem Brief an Jürgen Moltmann, in: M. Welker (editor), *Diskussion*, p. 161.

[140] Cf. J. Moltmann, *The Future of Creation*, p. 1-7.

is seen as temporally loosing His transcendence, so as to regain it at the end of time, when He might have realised Himself. Apart from the impression such a historical and eschatological conception of divine transcendence creates, namely that God was not fully transcendent at a given time - a problem that ruined the kenoticism of the mediating theologians[141] - it is hardly conceivable that there can be an historical transcendence for God, if there were no prior ontological transcendence for Him. Judging from this point, therefore, it is evident that despite his dialectical method, Moltmann does not succeed in representing the dialectic relationship between divine transcendence and immanence; for, the more he emphasises the immanence of God, the more he looses sight of the divine transcendence.

This problem also amounts to an implicit denial of the divine freedom.[142] By identifying the history of the triune God with the history of the world and by coupling the "self-realisation" of the triune God to the events in the world, Moltmann makes the inner-Trinitarian reality dependent on the historical process of the world. His aim to conceive a reciprocal relationship between God and the world finally turns out to be an ontological interdependence, which essentially affects God. Consequently, God no longer directs history, the history of the world directs Him and conditions His inner-Trinitarian reality. By this fact, God's aseity and freedom, as well as His power over creation is lost.[143] Of course Moltmann tries to conceive divine freedom in personal terms, not as if God has limitless power to perform.[144] Divine freedom is for him rather a sort of liberty which emerges in the context of an inter-personal relationship, in friendship, where mutual acceptance enables self-communication.[145] While freedom can undoubtedly be conceived in this way, it must be observed that it represents only a type,[146] which can only occur between God and personal agents. In the God-world relationship however, where the relation of God to personal and non-personal creatures is concerned, another type of freedom, which might be called ontological, must be conceivable in God. And it is precisely because Moltmann's system has no place for such a notion of freedom, that it lacks a proper differentiation between the divine and the world processes.

---

[141] Cf. 3.1.1. of this study.

[142] Cf. also F. Meessen, *Unveränderlichkeit*, p. 364.

[143] Cf. Meessen, *op. cit.* p. 355; see also J. Niewiadomski, *op. cit.*, p. 145

[144] Cf. J. Moltmann, *The Trinity and the Kingdom of God*, p. 55.

[145] Cf. J. Moltmann, Antwort.

[146] Cf. F. Meessen, *Unveränderlichkeit*, p.359.

Again, Moltmann conceives the self-communicating love of God in a sense that implies the denial of the divine freedom. By insisting that God is necessitated to create because self-communication is intrinsic to His nature, Moltmann gives the impression that creativity is a compulsory act for God, indispensable for the fulfilment of His inner-Trinitarian life. God is accordingly put under a creative compulsion, as His love is made to function as a "self-communicating automatic", to use the words of Meessen.[147] By this means, the significance of grace in God's creative activity is apparently lost.[148]

Besides, by interpreting the being of God eschatologically, Moltmann implies that God is ontologically dependent on the development of the world. This claim has two negative consequences for his notion of God. First, it means, as we had seen in another connection, that the triune God is insufficient in Himself and awaits an eschatological fulfilment. Secondly, an eschatological concept of God suggests that God Himself needs salvation, and cannot save Himself either. His salvation comes through the redemption of the world, whose lot He shares. This view of God, which Moltmann made up through his interpretation of the Jewish notion of Shekinah, conjures up a miserable image of God. This is definitely the price his theology pays for insisting that the God-world relationship is reciprocal.

d) Methodological Inconsistency

Moltmann's language and method have been observed as being inconsistent[149] and ambiguous.[150] This is to a great extent attributable to the difficult task he sets for himself - wanting on the one hand to do a practical-narrative theology and on the other to construct a metaphysically well-argued theology.[151] This is evident in his analysis of divine love. For, whereas he assigns an ontological role to divine love while discussing the unity of God,[152] he speaks of divine love in other cases as if it were merely a good passion to be differentiated from other

---

[147] Cf. *ibid.*, p. 360.

[148] Cf. *ibid.*, p. 358; J. Galot, Le Dieu Trinitaire et la passion du Christ, p. 86.

[149] C. E. Braaten, A Trinitarian Theology of the Cross, p. 117: Despite his condemnation of Modalistic tendencies in the concept of God Moltmann "reverts time and time again to simple concept of God, where God as such is the subject of the sentence without any Trinitarian differentiation". For similar criticisms see F. Meessen, *Unveränderlichkeit*, p. 349.; Roland D. Zimany, Moltmann's crucified God, p. 53 f.

[150] Cf. J. Niewiadomski, *Die Zweideutigkeit von Gott und Welt in J. Moltmanns Theologien.*

[151] Cf. F. Meessen, *op. cit.*, p. 350. This dilemma characterises his whole theological work, according the judgement of Niewiadomski (*op. cit.* 136 f.).

[152] Cf. J. Moltmann, *The Trinity and the Kingdom of God*, p. 148 ff.

"destructive passions".[153] His attempt not to commit the heresy of Patripassianism and yet affirm "Patricompassianism goes in the same direction.[154] His inconsequential avoidance of Patripassianism raises further doubts as to how real he considers the divine nature of the Son.[155] This suspicion becomes obvious in his distinction between "the death of God" and "death in God".[156] He is ready to admit that Jesus died in God, but not that God died on the Cross. Does the distinction between "the death of God" and "dying in God" actually make a difference for a Trinitarian theology, which conceives of perichorese and communicatio idiomatum in the triune God?

5.7   Summary

Moltmann begins his Trinitarian theology of the Cross with the basic assumption that every Christian theology should be modelled according to a Trinitarian framework, that is to say, defined in terms of the Trinitarian history of God. With such Trinitarian hermeneutics, he elaborates on three biblical themes - eschatology, crucifixion and pneumatology - which, as he contends, had hitherto received little attention in theology. In this framework, he brings these themes to bear on the classical issue of God's unity and differentiation, and on His relationship to the world.

He notes that despite the attention given to the doctrine of the Trinity in the tradition, theologies had often tended towards modalistic conclusions and subordinationism. This, he argues, follows from the habit of making philosophy, rather than the biblical proclamation, the starting point of theology. Such conclusions are the inevitable results of the theologies that assume the unity of God *a priori*, that is to say, ahistorically. To evade such conclusions, Moltmann - just like Pannenberg, as discussed in the third chapter above - adopts the stance of a Christology from below and proposes the conception of the divine unity in terms of eschatology. By that means the unity of God is not given, but attained eschatologically through the perichoretic social life of the Trinity, which encompasses all the divine activities in the world.

---

153 *Ibid.*, p. 54.

154 Cf. C. E. Braaten expresses surprise at Moltmann's view on this issue as he asks: "Why be afraid of Patripassianism? Why not meet it head-on if one seriously hopes to challenge the old Greek philosophical concept of God that placed restrictions on the more passionate language of God in the Bible?". *Op. cit.*, p.118.

155 See also P. S. Fiddes, *The Creative suffering of God*, p. 196.

156 J. Moltmann, *The Crucified God*, p. 207.

Reminiscent of Barth's thesis that God is no other than who He has revealed Himself to be in history, Moltmann also echoes Rahner's dictum that the economic Trinity reveals the immanent Trinity perfectly, to an extent that the works of the Trinity *ad extra* correspond to its work *ad intra*. Although the Persons of the Trinity perform different works, they are unified in all of them through a common eschatological purpose of consummating the Trinitarian processes of creation and redemption at the end of time. The Trinitarian love, Moltmann emphasises, is essentially self-communicative. By its very nature, it cannot be exhausted within the inner-Trinitarian relations; it has to be expressed "outside" the Trinitarian sphere. This is how creation and Incarnation came to be. Creation, Incarnation and the works of redemption are for that reason expressions of divine love and freedom. Moltmann emphasises this point as he tries to show that God did not become man for the purpose of redemption, but because of the nature of His love to communicate itself.

Therefore, the reason for the creation and Incarnation must be traced back to the nature of divine love as self-communication. However, this is also the root of the divine suffering. While God's love is kenotic and self-less, He grants both existence and freedom. Out of His love, He grants freedom to humankind, and suffers the consequence of this freedom. Like MacGregor, Moltmann argues that God suffers His kenotic nature, but unlike the former, who maintains that God suffers His withdrawal, Moltmann contends that God takes up the suffering upon Himself. This is the basis on which the Cross affects God.

In their mutual self-surrender, both the Son and the Father suffer the Cross and the God-forsakenness: the Father suffers the loss of the Son and vice versa. In that way God reveals Himself in the contradiction of the Cross. With this point, Moltmann also illustrates his claim that all the persons of the Trinity suffer with one another, albeit differently. By this means, he tries to avoid the heresy of Patripassianism and rather speaks of Patricompassianism. In contrast to common opinion, Moltmann maintains that God is both passible and impassible. If passibility means a state whereby God is acted upon, he agrees that God is impassible, but if it means the ability to take up suffering on oneself and suffer voluntarily, he contends that God is passible. God, he agues further, suffers actively. He neither suffers passively, nor out of insufficiency. But much as Moltmann would believe that God suffers actively, he is careful not to make God seem subject to suffering. He rather makes the much disputed claim that God inflicts suffering on Himself. This is entailed in his thesis of "God against God".

Moltmann has definitely made a significant contribution towards the development of a divine suffering with his Trinitarian hermeneutics, which has the credit of illustrating the inner Trinitarian life and the relation of God to the world. On this point, his theology supersedes that of MacGregor. However, his inclination to perpetuate dichotomy and weakness in the Godhead, and to make God's self-realisation dependent on the world-process must be registered as the major weak points of his Trinitarian theology of the Cross. In the next chapter, we shall see how Balthasar, who uses more or less the same Trinitarian and kenotic principles, overcomes the pitfalls of Moltmann's approach.

6. DIVINE IMPASSIBILITY IN A TRINITARIAN AND ANALOGI-CAL CONCEPTION OF GOD ACCORDING TO HANS URS VON BALTHASAR

6.1 The "Christological Analogy of Being" as a Theological Method

Balthasar's basic theological assumption, as the titles of his monumental trilogy[1] demonstrate, could be stated as follows: the logic of the triune God (*Theologik*) is revealed primarily in the glory (*Herrlichkeit*) of the creation[2] and ultimately in the divine drama (*Theodramatik*) of Christ's person and work on earth.[3] For him, this means in effect that the divine revelation (divine logic) must be seen as the material principle and reason (human logic) as the formal principle of theology. With this conviction, he tries to avert the dichotomy, which most theologians of the Cross put between revelation and "natural theology",[4] between faith and reason (metaphysics). Believing though that it is not epistemologically impossible for the human intellect to grasp the genuine reality of God - since the creation radiates the glory of God[5] - Balthasar sees in Jesus Christ the highest and most exact vision of God. St. John testifies to this point as he calls Jesus the "way" and "truth" of God (Jn. 14: 6). So, although the human intellect is intrinsically open towards the reality of God, it cannot, for the above reason, discover God, except when the latter reveals Himself to humankind.[6] For Balthasar, phi-

---

1 H. U. von Balthasar, *Herrlichkeit: Eine theologische Ästhetik*, Einsiedeln/Trier: *Herrlichkeit* I (1960); *Herrlichkeit* II/1 (1965); *Herrlichkeit* III/2 (1966); *Herrlichkeit* III/2,2 (1969). ---, *Theodramatik*, 4 Bände, Einsiedeln/Trier: *Theodramatik* I (1973); *Theodramatik* II/1 (1975); *Theodramatik* II/2 (1978); *Theodramatik* III (1980); *Theodramatik* IV (1983). ---, *Theologik*, 3 Bände, Einsiedeln/Trier: *Theologik* I (1985); *Theologik* II (1985); *Theologik* III (1987).

2 When Balthasar speaks of creation he mostly refers to that of humankind in the "image and likeness of God" (Gen. 1:26).

3 Here, the Johannine theology of Logos is the main source of reference.

4 He distances himself significantly from Barth's denial of "natural theology". And this confrontation, to a great extent, determines his understanding of "being". Cf. L. Roberts, *The theological Aesthetics*, pp. 42 & 43; see also, W. Löser, *Im Geiste des Origenes*, p. 29. He seeks to integrate the methods of philosophy and theology in the search for a genuine Christian image of God (*Theologik* I, xv). Only an integrated method co-ordinating all philosophical systems, even to the extent of uniting "empiricism and rationalism, idealism and realism, objectivism and existentialism" (xiv) - can be a real "theo-logic", i.e. "the logic of the world" that respects the analogy and the revelation of being in nature. A sense for synthesis runs through his whole academic works. See also a similar assessment in the article by Meinrad Walter, Die Fülle des Glaubens geistlich verstehen, pp. 127 f., esp. 133.

5 *Theologik* I, p. xi

6 *Theologik* II, p. 286.

losophy and metaphysics must be put at the service of divine revelation, so as to open up reason to faith, and human logic to divine truth.[7] His whole theological career is indeed one consistent attempt to explore the logic behind divine revelation, the logic which is believed to be lying behind the history of salvation.[8] Thus, with the conviction that God allows the "totality" of reality become expressible even in "fragments"[9] - as the revelation of the triune God in creation and the history of salvation and Incarnation suggest[10] - Balthasar adopts a theological hermeneutics, which seeks to make a double movement from God to the world, and from the world back to God.[11] This double movement, or "epistemological circle",[12] is inseparable and inevitable for our theological inquiry, because, as Balthasar contends, the first movement, which begins with God's own act of descending from above (*Katabasis*) through a process of self-disclosure (*kenosis*), especially in the Incarnation of His Son Jesus Christ, is indeed the "ontic presupposition" of the second movement (of theology) upwards (*Anabasis*), from the concrete, historical Jesus to the Christ of faith in the sphere of the immanent Trinity.

Consequently, Balthasar obliges his theology to an upward and downward (circular) movement between economic and immanent Trinity, between the Jesus of history and the Christ of faith, between Christology "from above" and "from below". Concretely, this would mean supplementing the "analogical"[13] with the "katalogical"[14] routes of the knowledge in Christology, so that the ontic presup-

---

7   This must be done, he contends, so that theology can avoid narrow and erroneous anthropomorphism. *Theodramatik* II/1, p. 173.

8   *Theologik* II, pp. 27-113.

9   One of Balthasar's work bears this as its title: *Das Ganze im Fragment. Aspekte der Geschichtstheologie.* In this book, however, Balthasar warns against greed for synthesis and against the claim to know the totality of the Absolute through our fragmentary history. We can neither reconstruct the future nor know the exact nature of God merely through human reason (a critique of Hegel's philosophy of history). See especially p. 13.

10 *Theologik* II, p. 155.

11 *Theologik* I, p. xviii; *Theologik* II, pp. 155 & 171.

12 Cf. T. R. Krenski, *Passio Caritatis*, p. 122 ff.

13 Taken alone, this method, which Balthasar considers typical of natural theology of religion, can only lead to a faint knowledge of God, when it does not give room to divine revelation. Thus "analogical" thinking must be supplemented and perfected by "katalogical".

14 See esp. *Theologik* II, p. 159 ff. Even the reality of the world can only be properly understood in the light of God's explicit revelation.

position of theology revealed in Jesus Christ becomes obvious.[15] Jesus Christ is in that sense the meeting point of divine self-disclosure and human inquiry. This in turn proves that Christology is the authentic starting-point of theology.[16]

If God has opened the curtain to His inner-Trinitarian mystery in Jesus Christ,[17] it then means for Balthasar that the theological method must be modelled according to God's own self-revelation in Jesus Christ.[18] He perceives the God-man personality of Jesus, not only as an expression of the inner-Trinitarian relationship, but also as a model of God's relationship to humankind,[19] that is to say, as the right "*proportio*" between God and His creation.[20] As a matter of fact, Christ proved himself to be the proto-humankind, the human nature as God wants it, by living the truth of God in human nature. Thus, in thinking the paradoxical unity of Jesus Christ, Balthasar, unlike Moltmann, does not hesitate to follow the doctrine of the two natures. He rather tries to deepen its meaning. For although he would accept that the Chalcedonian formula[21] expresses the paradoxical personality of Jesus Christ adequately, he would nevertheless want to get beyond Chalcedon by locating the paradox of the hypostatic union in God himself, whose Trinitarian nature, as he believes, is constituted in a unity-in-difference.

Just as there can be no mixture in the Persons of the Trinity despite their unity, the paradoxical personality of Jesus Christ must be thought of as a unity-in-difference, neither confused nor separated (DS 302). Thus, according to Balthasar, the popular practice of using the idea of *communicatio idiomatum*[22] to argue the unity of Persons should not lead to the error of forgetting that there is always a persistent difference between the created human and the uncreated divine nature in Christ, between God and the world.[23] Expressing the paradox involved in the personality of Jesus, who proportionately synchronises the divine and human na-

---

15 Cf. T. R. Krenski, *Passio Caritatis*, p. 125.

16 *Theologik* I, p. xvii.

17 *Theologik* II, p. 117 f.

18 Cf. A. Schilson / W. Kasper, *Christologie im Präsens*, pp. 62-70, esp. p. 69.

19 *Theodramatik* II/2, p. 206.

20 *Theologik* II, p. 288.

21 For Balthasar's view on Chalcedonian formula see *Theodramatik* II/2, pp. 191-202, and also H. Heinz, *Der Gott des Je-Mehr*, 1975, pp. 261-262.

22 *Theodramatik* II/2, p. 203. The doctrine of *Communicatio Idiomatum*, according to Balthasar, can not express the paradoxical personality of Jesus adequately, because it tends to explain away the insurmountable difference between divine and created natures.

23 Balthasar emphasises this point against Moltmann's denial of the distinction between the two natures.

ture, without mixing or separating them, Balthasar therefore speaks of unity-in-difference, of a great likeness within a greater unlikeness.[24] This relation of unity-in-difference between the two natures in Christ is for him an "analogy", a model of the God-world relationship, made possible by a permanent analogous unity-in-difference in the Trinitarian nature.

He sees this analogy, which he terms a "Christological analogy of being"[25], as a modification of the classical concept of *analogia entis*,[26] classically used in expressing the peculiar relation of similarity-in-difference between the absolute and contingent beings. The *analogia entis*, he contends, must be understood theologically as a double concept, which, on the one hand, demonstrates the unparalleled uniqueness (*Unvergleichbarkeit*) of God in relation to His creatures,[27] and on the other hand, expresses the fundamental and indestructible "image-character" (*Bildcharakter*) of man's spiritual nature, whose reason (*Vernunft*) and freedom find their archetype in God.[28] Getting beyond its classical application, therefore, Balthasar sees Jesus Christ himself as this "analogia entis",[29] the measure of being,[30] who manifests that analogy between God and His creation; he thus becomes the "analogy of all analogies".[31]

The point of emphasis in this reinterpreted scholastic concept of analogia entis lies in the fact that in spite of the great similarity between God and creatures - created after His image and likeness - a permanent, prehistoric and infinite distance between God and His creatures remains.[32] This primordial distance forbids the attribution of any univocal concept to God.[33] In summary, Balthasar contends, that since the Christological analogy unveils to us both the God-world relationship and the inner nature of the Triune God, we must allow our God-talk to be regulated by the event of Jesus Christ, so as to not end up in the impasse of empty and abstract statements.

---

24 Cf. G. F. O'Hanlon, *The immutability of God*, p. 44; J. Saward, *op. cit.* p. 18.

25 *Theodramatik* II/2, pp. 202-210; *Theologik* II, pp. 284-288.

26 The Munich philosopher, Erich Przywara, influenced Balthasar on this point. See *Theodramatik II*, p. 202.

27 *Theodramatik* II/2, p. 204.

28 *Ibid.*, p. 205.

29 *Ibid.*, p. 203.

30 *Theologik* I, p. 35.

31 *Ibid.*, p. 263.

32 *Theologik* II, p. 288.

33 *Theologik* I, p. 263 f.

6.2 God-world Relationship

Balthasar sees creation as a forum for divine revelation.[34] The God who created creatures, especially humankind, in His "image and likeness"(Gen. 1:26) also made human beings serve as gongs (*Klangkörper*) to resound His glory.[35] By that fact alone, any type of negative theology which conceives the God-world relationship solely through the principle of infinite negation is disqualified.[36] The world is not the negation of God, he argues, neither does nature constitute the absence of the supernatural. The sphere of the supernatural interpenetrates the world of nature, so much, that there is no "neutral ground" without divine imprint.[37] This should not imply however that God is part of the world process: God, who is at once partly veiled and partly unveiled,[38] remains a mystery[39] beyond the confines of the world. We meet in God the obscurity of the revealed (*die Verborgenheit des Geöffneten*),[40] for just as an image differs from and yet at the same time resembles its archetype, the world stands in a primordial relation and distance to God.[41] The relation of the world to God cannot be thought of without the corresponding distance to Him.

Balthasar likens the relationship between God and His creatures to that between an Archetype and its copy. However, the former differs from the latter in that it is not rigid and stereotype. The God-world relationship is rather a free and lively relationship, corresponding to the all-embracing nature of divine Being, who is able to encompass all contingent beings, even at the point of their greatest distance. It belongs to the nature of a divine Being to encompass finite beings: secular time in the eternal movement of divine eternity, secular space in God's unending space, secular Becoming (*weltliches Werden*) not in a motionless divine Being, but in God's eternally eventful life.[42] This means for Balthasar, as O'Hanlon rightly comments, that "the decision to create is not taken in time, and the

---

34 For details see *ibid.*, pp. 257-278.

35 *Theologik* II, p. 76.

36 *Ibid.*, p. 91.

37 *Theologik* I, p. xi.

38 This mysterious aspect of divine revelation applies equally to truth; the mystery of truth as transcendental, consists in its simultaneous unveiling (*Enthüllung*) and veiling (*Verhüllung*) of reality (*Theologik* II, 233 f.).

39 *Theologik* I, p. xxii.

40 *Theologik* II, p. 109.

41 *Ibid.*, p. 80.

42 *Ibid.*, p. 78; *Theodramatik* IV, pp. 87-102.

space occupied by creation is not outside God but is rather within the divine, eternal life".[43] This fact does not entail any sort of compulsion on God's part, because, for Balthasar, creation is itself an out-flow of the divine love.[44]

The emphasis Balthasar places on the "image-character" (*Abbildlichkeit*) of creation is purposeful. It enables him to establish that the contingent and finite beings are created as "self-transcending immanence", ever reaching out for God.[45] Creation is thus seen as a "copy" (*Abbild*) which points to God as its "original". Again, it provides the means for explaining how the divine-triune logic can find its adequate expression in the world through the incarnating Logos.[46] And because the Incarnation of the Son presupposes the "image-character" of the creation, Balthasar, in contrast to Karl Barth, maintains that the incarnate Word, by the Incarnation, did not go into a foreign land (*in die Fremde*), but into a land whose "language" he understands, for the logic of God is not foreign to the human logic.[47] Balthasar bases this claim on the simple assumption that "images" cannot be the direct opposite of their "original".[48] This means that if creatures are made according to the image and likeness of God, they cannot be the contrast of God; there must be something in them which reflects the nature of God.

Making this point, Balthasar does not stop at making a simple assumption about a possible Trinitarian analogy in the world. He goes further to show that the world has a triadic structure reflecting the Trinitarian Being of God.[49] This, he believes, had been sensed by some thinkers like Augustine, Hegel and the philosophers of dialogism, who have tried, consciously or unconsciously, to reconstruct this *imago Trinitatis* in the created reality.[50] Their attempts remained unsuccessful, however, because they lacked the vision of the creative aspect of a

---

43 G. F. O'Hanlon, *The immutability of God*, p. 51; See also *Theodramatik* III, p. 304; *Theodramatik* II/1, pp. 233, 236, 238.

44 Balthasar maintains this fact with maximum care, avoiding the approval of the emanation theory and shunning the Hegelian idealism at the same time.

45 *Theologik* II, p. 76 f.

46 *Ibid.*, p. 155.

47 *Ibid.*, p. 78.

48 *Theodramatik* IV, p. 99.

49 *Theologik* II, pp. 35-40.

50 For Balthasar, Augustine was trying to depict the imago Trinitatis on the structure of the world in his "De Trinitate"; Hegel was doing the same thing in his account of triadic movement of all beings, and also the philosophers of dialogism - Rosenzweig, Buber and Ebner - in their "I-Thou" pattern of thought, which always presuppose a third, the eternal Thou. But it was impossible for them to reach the totality of reality through their triadic patterns. Cf. *Theologik* II, pp. 35-56.

triadic structure.[51] For a structure to bear the imago Trinitatis and be able to assure the place of the Spirit, it has to portray the procreative aspect of nature. Apparently, Balthasar sees the Hegelian synthesis as lacking the creative newness that the objective third of a triadic structure should entail. Dialogism was near to getting this structure, he admits, but it failed to see "fruitfulness" as the "objective third" part of the Triad of an inter-personal relationship. It therefore got no further than being a "double monologue" of "I-Thou", and thereby failed to provide the basis on which the Spirit can be presented in the world. The image of God in the world must be able to portray the dynamism of the Spirit, which drives the "I" to the "Thou" and enhances the "fruit of every encounter.

For Balthasar, the woman-man-relationship in marriage (including its possible procreative component) is the best natural analogy to the Trinitarian God. The natural *imago Trinitatis* in humankind does not mean however similarity with God, it merely shows that humanity has the potential to receive the "primordial image" of God (*das göttliche Urbild*). With the possession of the "*imago*", humanity is prepared to attain the "similitudo" with God, but not through the dialects of its own development, but through grace, which makes us "children of God". Through grace, we participate as finite beings in divine nature, so that the created *imago* can be raised to *similitudo*.[52]

6.3   The Economic and the Immanent Trinity

Balthasar closely follows the Christian tradition while developing his own doctrine of the Trinity.[53] However, his mediation between immanent and economic Trinity is anything but conventional. This is largely due to his manner of perceiving the hypostatic union - the relation of similarity in dissimilarity of the two natures in Christ - as a model for the relation between the immanent and the economic Trinity.[54] In this light, the immanent and the economic Trinity should neither be separated nor confused.[55] On this, Balthasar is particularly critical of the theologians who confuse the economic and immanent Trinity,[56] because, as

---

51   *Ibid.*, pp. 54-57.

52   *Theodramatik* II/2, p. 482.

53   For details see, *Ibid.*, pp. 141-145, 207-208, 463-486; *Theologik* II, pp. 117-170; G. F. O'Hanlon, *The Immutability of God*, p. 110-144.

54   *Theodramatik* II/2, pp. 141-145 & 466-467.

55   *Theodramatik* III, p. 298.

56   *Theodramatik* II/2, p. 466; *Theodramatik* III, pp. 298-302. He considers Rahner's popular thesis - "The economic Trinity *is* the immanent Trinity, and *vice versa*" (*MysteriumSalutis II*, pp. 328,336) - misleading. With this axiom, Rahner perhaps wanted to show nothing

he contends, if the distinction is blurred, the door is opened wide for an unrestricted and univocal attribution of suffering to God.

Going against the popular tendency in the contemporary theologies, Balthasar insists that God *in himself* must not be confused with God *for us*. God's transcendence must be related to His immanence in the world, in such a way that we can say, God is "*above*" and "*beyond*" (*über*) the drama of the world. He is not entangled in it, but He is in it, because He is wholly engaged in the world,[57] directing its drama, which is definitely not His own. God is not part of the world process.[58] For Balthasar, we can not identify the inner-divine process with the process of the salvation history since this would God drown in the happenings of the world; it would make him appear as a "tragic and mythological god".[59]

There must be a way, he insists, of interpreting the immanent Trinity so that it can always stand as the ground of all processes in the world (including even the event of the Cross), without either appearing as a mere "formal process of divine self-communication" (Rahner) or as hopelessly "entangled in the world process" (Moltmann). Such a model must be able to show how the triune God remains ontologically the same in himself, without loosing His "liveliness". So that, it could be made evident that God neither needs the world process nor the Cross in order to become or to communicate himself: God's free self-giving to the world is an act of love, not a necessary development.[60] "God is love" already in himself, the Father and the Son loving one another in the Spirit, before, "above and beyond" the world.[61] In this context, one could see the economic Trinity as an extension of the immanent Trinity. The former is certainly not identical to the latter, but there is no cessation between them.

In arguing for the continuity between the immanent and the economic Trinity, Balthasar settles for the single identity of the pre-existent Christ and the Jesus of history, which he sees rooted in the *processio* and *missio* in the Trinity. Using the

---

more than how difficult the differentiation can be (*op. cit.* 329) given the fact that through the principle of appropriation all the Persons are affected by the activities of each single Person of the Trinity. But his concept of "divine self-communication" gives more importance to the economic Trinity, says Balthasar (*Theodramatik* III, p. 300). The confusion however becomes glaring in Moltmann, who, arguing under the umbrella of Hegel and the "Process Theology", totally reduces the immanent Trinity to the economic Trinity. See also J. Saward, *The Mysteries*, p. 10.

57 *Theodramatik* II/2, p. 471.

58 *Ibid.*, p. 484.

59 *Theodramatik* III, p. 300.

60 *Ibid.*

61 *Theodramatik* II/2, p. 466; See J. Saward, *The Mysteries*, p. 11.

doctrine of kenosis,[62] he contends that the generation and sending of the Son from the Father constitute one single act of self-emptying, so that, there is in fact a "paradoxical identity of person and mission";[63] the Person of Jesus in the inner-Trinitarian life is one with his Person on mission.[64] This explains why Jesus identified himself with his mission.[65] Even though, Balthasar differentiates between the Person of the Son in the immanent Trinity and the historical Jesus - the former he calls "supra-personal" (*überpersonal*)[66] - he warns against the danger of splitting the personality of Jesus into two, differentiating between the one on mission, who suffers, the other, who, is immutable and pre-existent, as if there were double consciousness and identity in Jesus Christ. The one sent is the eternal One, who operates in time. So, if we are at all justified to refer to them differently, we must do that in terms of the "difference-in-identity" between the eternal One, who proceeds (*processio*) from the Father, and the One, who, by virtue of the procession, is sent (*missio*) into the world.[67] In that case, we must not fail to see the mission/sending as an "extension" of the generation/procession of the Son from the Father.[68]

Balthasar, for this reason, maintains that the participation of the economic Trinity in the world drama neither constitutes a "qualitative rise" (*Überstieg*), nor a new beginning of the divine activity in the future; it is not a "successive" revelation of the activities of the Persons in time. Rather, the Trinitarian economy in Jesus life should be seen as an "ongoing revelation of the Trinity" in the world, which continues even after the resurrection, as the "eternal aspect" of the mission". It is necessary to note, Balthasar argues, that there is nothing like "reversal" or "inversion" in the activity of the Trinity even when, through the resurrection, the economic Trinity had to be taken into the immanent Trinity. By that measure the "temporal" activities of the Trinity regain their "eternal" significance without of course being suspended.[69] The distance between heaven and earth remains secondary (economic), but it is now preserved in the primary (immanent) distance between Father, Son and the Spirit.[70] Thus, given the activities of the

---

62 *Ibid.*, p. 209.

63 *Ibid.*, pp. 143, 144.

64 *Ibid.*, p. 468

65 *Ibid.*, p. 208.

66 *Ibid.*, p. 468.

67 *Ibid.*, p. 211 f.

68 *Theodramatik* III, p. 304.

69 *Theodramatik* II/2, p. 479.

70 *Ibid.*, p. 484.

Spirit in the world, who sustains the post-Easter activities of the economic Trinity concretely in the world,[71] the mission of Jesus could definitely be considered consummated in time, but nonetheless, the content and implications of this mission obtain infinitely.[72]

Balthasar's claim here that the Son's *missio* is a modality of his *processio* from the Father is significant for his doctrine of divine "passibility". On the basis of this fact, he goes on to argue that divine suffering is not something foreign to God, but something that is intimately connected to inner-Trinitarian nature.[73]

6.4 The Paradox of Identity-in-difference as the Constitutive Principle of the Trinitarian Love and Nature

As should have become evident in the foregoing, Balthasar emphasises the issue of unity and difference in God,[74] as that paradox which Jesus Christ embodies in his Personality and which he discloses to us.[75] In his earthly life Jesus Christ revealed his relation to the Father as consisting of a real distinction between him and his Father and also of a prehistoric identity with him. He identifies this inner-Trinitarian relationship of identity-in-difference as the logic of love itself. Love, as constituted in unity and differentiation, is the ontological explanation for the relation of the Persons to themselves. Balthasar then argues accordingly, that the Persons are constituted in the relationship of identity and difference to one another: there has never been a divine substance, he argues, without the "Fatherhood, Sonhood and Spirithood" of God.[76]

The coexistence of unity and difference in God is a mystery, but we dare to interpret it since the Persons are always revealed to us in the modality of this identity-in-difference.[77] And it is precisely in the attempt to understand this mystery as the essence of the Trinitarian love, that Balthasar comes to recognise it as a pointer to the very nature of every love: love, whether divine or human, is only

---

71 *Ibid.*, p. 364.

72 *Ibid.*, pp. 469-471. Note: "Die missio ist nunmehr zeitlos in die processio des Sohnes aufgenommen, und vom Sohn her gilt das Analoge für den Heiligen Geist" (*ibid.*, p. 471).

73 *Ibid.*, p. 208.

74 *Theologik* II, pp. 117-170.

75 *Ibid.*, pp. 119-138.

76 *Ibid.*, pp. 126-128; *Theodramatik* III, p. 304. The Trinitarian drama has an eternal duration.

77 With Barth he counts it as an error on the path of the earlier Christian tradition that the essence of God was always being considered first and in isolation from the inter-personal relationship of the Persons (*Dreieinigkeit*). Cf. *Theologik* II, p. 129.

possible in the paradoxical relation of identity and differentiation. It is however so typical of the Trinitarian life as the love in perfection, that it defines its ontology and attributes. To bring out the full significance of this paradox for the Trinitarian being, Balthasar calls it the "event in God",[78] and goes on to trace the paradoxical divine attributes - like transcendence and immanence, omnipotence and receptivity, freedom and relationality - back to it.

6.4.1   Kenosis in the Triune God

For Balthasar, kenosis represents the core of this inner-Trinitarian event. It is in the kenotic motif that the mystery of the divine identity-in-difference opens itself to us theologically. He thus conceives "a real kenosis" in the inner-Trinitarian nature of God,[79] as that event which intrinsically belongs to God's inter-personal nature. Apart from noting the exegetical and dogmatic difficulties associated with the kenotic motif,[80] Balthasar, just like MacGregor and Moltmann, tries to identify the problems that led to the theological debacle suffered by the 19th century kenoticisms. Like others, he also believes that the confinement of this motif to the Christological context is one of the major problems of the earlier kenoticists.[81] Another serious problem was the kenoticists' tendency to forget that the pre-existent and the incarnate Christ are of one identity, an error, which in his view, invariably led to the suppression of the Trinitarian dimension latent in their Christological theory of kenosis.[82] For Balthasar, however, a fully developed doctrine of kenosis must entail a Trinitarian dimension, within which the thinking of the paradox of the divine nature - the processions, relations and missions of the Persons of the Trinity[83] - becomes possible.

Thus employing the kenoticism of Bulgakov - which as we saw earlier interprets creation and the inner-Trinitarian life kenotically - Balthasar goes further to interpret the generation of the Son as a primordial kenosis (*Ur-kenose*) on the part of the Father, who selflessly gives himself to the Son, making him consubstantial with him.[84] The Son on his part reciprocates this donation of divine nature with an eternal *eucharistia*, an eternal "thankfulness" which takes the form of

---

[78] H. U. von Balthasar, Mysterium Paschale, p. 144.

[79] *Ibid.*, pp. 143-154.

[80] *Ibid.*, p.143.

[81] *Ibid.*, pp. 143-147; See also G. MacGregor, *He Who Lets Us Be.*

[82] H. U. von Balthasar, Mysterium Paschale, p. 147 f.

[83] *Ibid.*, p.147.

[84] *Ibid.*, pp. 152-153.

an eternal obedience to the Father, as selfless as the Father's primordial self-giving to the Son.[85]

Since the Son obediently and thankfully returns the donation as selflessly as the Father's primordial kenosis, Balthasar contends that the self-renunciation of the Son is identical with that of the Father who begets him. In the same way, the Spirit shares in this "Ur-kenose" (primordial kenosis), inasmuch as he does not want to be anything for himself other than the "We" that personally confirms the self-renunciation of the Father and the Son, nothing other than being the proclamation and donation (*Verschenkung*) of that love between the Father and the Son.[86] Balthasar thus sees the primordial kenosis, the "supra-kenose", as an act that does not belong to the Father alone, but as an event of the whole Trinity. The root of this fundamental Trinitarian kenosis lies in the "selflessness" of the Persons who are pure relations in the inner-Trinitarian life of love.[87]

The "primordial Kenosis" in the immanent Trinity gives rise to three other kinds of Trinitarian kenosis evident in the economic Trinity, that is to say, in the activities of the Triune God to the world. The triune God exercises "self-restriction", first, in the process of *creating free beings*, next, in the institution of His *covenant* with the world (of humankind), then, in the *Incarnation* of the Son and in all the Christ-events (from the conception to resurrection). In this connection, Balthasar makes it clear that the Christ-events should not be seen as having only a Christological relevance; they belong fundamentally to the Trinitarian economy.[88]

Balthasar interprets the primordial kenosis as a self-restriction of the divinity:[89] In his love for the Son, the Father absolutely forgoes to be God alone, a divine "Godlessness" (of love) which, though it differs from the inner-worldly "Godlessness", overtakes the latter and makes it possible. The divine act of self-giving in the generation of the Son has yet another implication: it is at the same time a "separation" of the Father from the Son; by generating the Other, the Father was at the same time positing an "infinite difference" between him and his Son.[90]

---

[85] *Theodramatik* III, pp. 301, 303, 307.

[86] *Ibid.*, p. 308.

[87] H. U. von Balthasar, Mysterium Paschale, p. 153.

[88] *Theodramatik* III, p. 308.

[89] H. U. von Balthasar, Mysterium Paschale, p. 151; *Theodramatik* III, p. 301.

[90] *Theodramatik* III, p. 301. Here Balthasar is struggling, as usual, to make sure that there is no reality outside of God. But at the same time he wants to maintain the aseity of God.

Balthasar sees this primordial separation, difference and distance between the Father and the Son as an essential part of the act of love. Influenced by the dialogism of Martin Buber, he sees love as consisting of primordial distance and relation. God's love consists infinitely of this primordial distance and relation, and it is in this capacity that God accommodates every relation and every distance, including sin. In this connection, he describes the kenotic generation of the Son, whereby God (the Father) gives His divinity consubstantially (*gleichwesentlich*) to God (the Son) as an "incomprehensible and unsurpassable separation of God from himself", within which every possible separation, even the darkest and most bitter of all separations (hell), can occur; generation is, by that, no less a self-communication of absolute love as it is the institution of a creative differentiation.[91]

The nature of God is such that, it presupposes and surpasses every separation, pain and alienation in the world, as well as every self-giving of love, every fruitful encounter and holiness. In other words, the presupposition of every relation and division is in God's own triune nature. This does not mean, however, that God is divided or that He is awaiting an eschatological unity as Hegel and Moltmann would like us to believe.[92] The inner-Trinitarian division already persists in an accomplished unity,[93] which is wrought in the unifying Person of the Spirit: The Spirit proceeds from both the Father and the Son, as their subsistent "We" and keeps his seal on the infinite difference between them as the Spirit that unites both.[94]

All said, one must always bear in mind, that even though the Father expresses and surrenders himself without retaining any thing for himself, since the whole essence of God is in the self-giving, He does not loose Himself in the process either, His inner-divine kenosis consists of infinite power and powerlessness, that run simultaneously.[95] One must also note that the eternal separation in God is neither "tragic"[96] nor is its reconciliation through the Spirit a "comedy".[97] Ac-

---

91 *Ibid.*, p. 302.

92 Balthasar vehemently distances himself here from the Hegelian "process theology". Whereas God realises himself in history in the Hegelian dialectic, the whole history presupposes the (kenotic) self-giving of God himself.

93 Even the worst of all separation - hell - owes its ontic possibility to the absolute and real separation between the Father and the Son. Cf. *Ibid.*, p. 303.

94 *Ibid.*, p. 301. The unity of Persons in their separation could be seen here as the essence of love. We shall see more of that later.

95 *Ibid.*, p. 303.

96 At first sight it seems as if Balthasar's theory of separation in God resembles Moltmann's theory of dichotomy in God, as discussed above. Both believe that there is a perpetual

cording to Balthasar's theology, the "Trinitarian drama" of the divine powerlessness, is not that God needs to go through the contradiction of the world in order to realise Himself. The contradiction of the world is itself made possible by the paradox of His own nature.[98]

In exploring the paradox of the divine kenosis, therefore, Balthasar carefully avoids being driven to extremes. He thus approaches the Trinitarian mystery from two sides: on the one side, he adheres to a negative theology that excludes every mythological involvement of God in the world process, on the other, he conceives a world drama, which must have God as the reason (*Bedingung*) for its existence (*Möglichkeit*).[99] In this way, it is possible for him to argue that God does not "risk" anything by allowing His Son to take up the Cross upon himself, precisely because the "powerless power" of the divine self-giving already encompasses every "risk" that God can take.[100] This means, in effect, that while one cannot say that suffering contradicts divine nature, it must be admitted that suffering is possible only when and if God allows it in the wider context of His eternal self-giving.

But unlike other modern kenoticists, Balthasar is against the identification of divine substance with kenosis. That the origin of kenosis should be traced back to the nature of God Himself, as its "ontic possibility"[101] does not mean that the

---

separation in God, which makes the self-differentiation of the Persons possible. But while Moltmann sees this separation as an act of "God against God", as a tragic event, Balthasar sees the separation as that prime distance that belongs to the act of give and take in love and relationship. Such a notion of separation in God can not be conceived outside of love, it is a kenotic component, not a competitive event. In other words, whereas separation or differentiation is creative and enriches the being of God in Balthasar, in Moltmann, it detracts from God's image, because it makes God seem like an aggressor, and at worst a sadist, entangled in a tragic situation.

97   As we shall see, the kenotic act that institutes human freedom affects God seriously, especially when the creaturely freedom leads to sin. This is perhaps the source of "pain" in God.

98   It is noteworthy, that Balthasar only uses "paradox" to designate the divine logic. He does not see it as implying contradiction, but as a mystery, as a secret, partly revealed in the structure of creation. Divine logic is mysterious, but it is not contradictory to the human logic; that is why a faint notion of it can be read in the structure of the world. For Balthasar, mystery, divine logic and paradox signify the same thing. Cf. H. U. von Balthasar, *Man in History*, p. 210.

99   *Theodramatik* III, p. 304.

100 *Ibid.*, p. 305. Far from being a risk, the steadfast suffering of the Son in the world of sin, lent credence to the everlasting thankfulness of the Son to the Father for the consubstantial generation.

101 H. U. von Balthasar, Mysterium Paschale, p. 147.

198

substance of God is univocally kenotic.[102] Balthasar considers this the error of modern kenoticism.

6.4.2 Divine and Human Freedom
in a Relation of Inclusiveness-in-opposition

Balthasar also sees the nature of divine freedom defined by the mystery of divine identity-and-differentiation. In the second volume of his *Theodramatik*, where he extensively discusses the relation between infinite and finite freedom,[103] he makes it clear that the triune God exercises "self-restriction" in order to let created freedom have its full realisation. This "self-restriction" does not, however, entail any constraint on God or any restriction of His own freedom and "sovereignty". There is a paradoxical relationship between the divine and finite freedom, which is untypical of both mythological and philosophical conceptions of freedom.[104] In contrast, Christianity sees the compatibility of finite and infinite freedom, without denying that there is an "opposition" between them. Though there is a real opposition between them, they do not relate exclusively to one another.[105] From the perspective of the "philosophy of revelation",[106] human freedom is only possible within the divine freedom. This is a "double and irrevocable postulate" of Christian theology: that the "Absolute" can contain the freedom of the finite beings, without being hampered nor reduced to human level.

This inclusiveness-in-opposition is for Balthasar a modality of the inner-Trinitarian difference (a Christological opposition) between the Father and the Son which is not exclusive but inclusive.[107] He therefore maintains that this

---

[102] *Ibid.*, p. 148.

[103] *Theodramatik* II/1, pp. 170-288.

[104] According to Balthasar the mythological and philosophical approaches to the reality of God are unaware of the paradox of divine freedom: Whereas the issue of divine freedom was suppressed and at worst denied in the pre-philosophic era due to incessant conflict between the gods and other powers, in the philosophic era (from Socrates till neo-Platonism) the freedom of the individual was at stake because it was seen as contradicting the freedom of God as the unapproachable "One". In both cases divine and human freedom are conceived as incompatible realities. See *ibid.*, pp. 170-170.

[105] The relation between divine and finite freedom must be thus conceived, "*so, daß unbeschadet der Unendlichkeit der Freiheit Gottes eine echte Opposition der Freiheiten entsteht*". See *ibid.*, p. 171.

[106] H. U. von Balthasar, *Man in History*, p. 69.

[107] Employing the motif of a Christological analogy, Balthasar reiterates that even though Jesus lived the will of his heavenly Father harmoniously on earth, he never blurred the dif-

"Christological opposition" simultaneously expresses two dimensions of freedom: on the one hand, it reflects the type of freedom prevalent between God and the fallen will of sinners, and on the other, it stands for the type that marks the inner-Trinitarian, the inner-unending difference of the divine mode of being.[108] Hence, it is a biblical paradox that God can be free without depriving humankind of its real freedom, it is equally an expression of divine omnipotence that God can communicate genuine freedom to His creatures.[109]

The implication of the paradox of divine freedom, which philosophy perhaps fails to see is this: Humankind and its freedom can no longer be interpreted within the area of its own mystery, but "within the space prepared by God's love".[110] It has to be interpreted in the light of the inner nature of God. In this connection, Balthasar does not see the rationality behind calling God the "total other".[111] He rather acclaims the perception of Nicholas of kues, who calls God "Non-aliud", the "non-other". Yes, God is such a pure unity, that He cannot have finite beings as His "other", as that which is His opposite. The fact that God encompasses us to this extent obliges us to engage ourselves in a double-talk: whereas we must call ourselves the "others" before God, by virtue of our finite freedom, we dare not conclude that we are for that reason "others" to God.[112] We are "others in non-others".[113] This must be understood, he repeats, in terms of the Trinitarian opposition.

Balthasar goes to this extent in order to maintain the full sovereignty of God's will while making human freedom a reality. This is particularly necessary for his theology of sin. But above all, his notion of divine freedom helps to strengthen his theology of covenant. By entering a covenant with man, God suffers a "self-restriction" which does not detract from His sovereignty. His partner to the covenant, humankind, affects Him essentially, but only in a manner presupposed in his being, that means, in a manner that He Himself dictates. In all, the "reciprocity" of the covenant, which guarantees the identity of free creatures, whose will can-

---

ference between his "will" and that of his Father (Lk. 22:42), he rather made the difference sharper at every stage of his life. *Theodramatik* II/1, p. 172.

[108] *Ibid.*, p. 172.

[109] *Ibid.*, p. 173.

[110] H. U. von Balthasar, *Man in History.* p. 69.

[111] *Theodramatik* II/1, p. 174.

[112] *Ibid.*

[113] *Ibid.*, p. 175.

not be merged in the absolute will of God, is a Trinitarian mystery, and can only be expatiated within a Trinitarian framework.[114]

6.4.3   Omnipotence as the Power of Divine Love and Self-limitation

Balthasar develops his views on divine omnipotence based on the biblical, especially Pauline, understanding of power as an expression of love and kenosis. From this perspective the omnipotence of God appears in its proportionality towards human power: "His omnipotent power neither overwhelms nor crushes the little power of the creature";[115] the absoluteness of the divine power is believed to enhance rather than diminish the human power. Balthasar sees this fact testified to particularly in Jesus words: "Apart from me you can do nothing" (John 15:5) and in Paul's statement: "I can do all things in him who strengthens me" (Phil. 4:13). The intricacy of the relation between the divine and human power, Balthasar contends, can only be understood in the context of divine love, which shows itself kenotically in God's covenant relationship to His creatures.

> However immeasurably the power of God is above all creaturely power in its sovereign independence, God still seeks to preserve in the working of his grace the covenant mystery of mutualness, as he laid down in his creation and he reveals as his inner Trinitarian secret.[116]

In line with His covenant commitment, therefore, God chooses not to exercise His power absolutely. This "*self-restriction* of His absolute power", which is evidently an expression of love, is in itself, a *demonstration of divine power*.[117] While interpreting St. Paul's conception of power in weakness, Balthasar says:

> Since "in this self-limitation of divine power in love there lies the absolute removal of limits and, thus the revelation of the divine omnipotence before the world (Eph. 1:19) ... one must say that the self-limitation of the *potentia absoluta* of God for love is therefore itself omnipotence, because it is compelled by nothing outside God ... his absolute power is pure inner self-determination and, therefore corresponding to the divine inner being, proves to be absolute freedom of self-giving, humility, and loving selflessness. Hence, the mystery of the weakness of God, that

---

[114] H. U. von Balthasar, *Man in History*. p. 204.

[115] *Ibid.*, p. 201.

[116] *Ibid.*, p. 204.

[117] Balthasar makes ample reference to the expressions of the mystery of the power of divine weakness in the New Testament: John speaks antithetically of Jesus' "power of laying down" his life and "of taking it up again" (Jn. 10,18); similarly, Paul writes that "... God's weakness is stronger than human strength" and that "God chose what is weak in the world to shame the strong" (1 Cor. 1:25,27), and that the power of God "is made perfect in weakness" (2 Cor. 12:9). Cf. H. U. von Balthasar, *Man in History*. pp. 210- 211.

> appears in the life and suffering of Jesus ... is actually the mystery of his manifested omnipotence.[118]

Thus on the one hand, the limitation of the divine power is necessitated by God's covenant commitment, and on the other hand, it is determined by the paradoxical and mysterious nature of divine nature of expressing power in its opposite (weakness or powerlessness). In other words the divine self-limitation is itself an expression of immense power of divine love, which can transcend all bounds, finding expression both in power and powerlessness.

In thinking about the omnipotence of God, therefore, Balthasar appeals to the nature of the inner-Trinitarian love and kenosis. Accordingly, the divine "power" is so constituted that it makes provision for such limitless "self-emptying" as in the Incarnation and on the Cross, without implying any contradiction on God's part.[119] Kenosis is essentially the revelation of the Trinitarian God,[120] who is not primarily "absolute power" but "absolute love". His sovereignty does not consist of absolute "self-possession", but is revealed in that limitless "self-giving" beyond all inner-worldly power and powerlessness.[121] Thus the divine power as it is revealed in the Bible and as it appeared in Christ is the "power of love".[122]

Accordingly, the power of God is best demonstrated among human beings, especially at the point of their weakness and humility, at the point where "the weak man offers less resistance to the power of God's love".[123] For Balthasar, this explains St. Paul's dictum: "when I am weak, then I am strong" (2 Cor. 12:10). This is a summary of what is already obvious in the entire Bible.

> The 'poor and little ones' of the Old Testament are those who are called blessed in the first beatitude of the Sermon on the Mount, because they offer empty room for the Holy Spirit, just as Mary, who was empty for God, praises in her song of praise the 'lowly ones' whom God raised, while he put down the mighty from their seats.

This view further implies that human beings must meet God's self-limitation equally with a kenotic life-style, so that the power of God can shine. God manifests His presence in this dual kenosis, as God encounters humankind in His Spirit.

> The creature is no longer just a vessel for the presence of divine power, nor is he now only the occasion for the epiphany of the sovereign majesty of God, but is

---

[118] *Ibid.*, pp. 209-210.

[119] *Ibid.*, p. 209 f.

[120] *Ibid.*, p. 149.

[121] *Ibid.*, p. 147.

[122] *Ibid.*, p. 205,208.

[123] *Ibid.*, p. 211.

united directly in his impotent self-giving with the absolute self-giving of the triune, absolute ground of all being.[124]

6.4.4   The Logic of the Cross - the Logic of Love.

In accordance with his understanding of the divine omnipotence as the power of love, Balthasar goes on to interpret the Son's weakness on the Cross as the "self-presentation of the innermost secret of the Trinity".[125] He sees this point already presupposed in some earlier interpretations of the weakness of the Son on the Cross: according to him, St Francis and Tauler speak of the "poverty of Christ" which manifests the "poverty of God" and Catherine of Sienna says the weakness of Christ on the Cross gave expression to the very heart of God. Even Origen, the Platonic thinker, Balthasar says, sees it as an indication that "the Father (as the 'supreme God') is perhaps not free of suffering". The same thing could be said of the whole Godhead, he claims, if one accepts that St. Paul's idea of the kenosis of the Son of God gives an "adequate expression of his divine attitude of love, and, hence of divine being itself". Illustrating this point, he goes on to write:

> In the weakness of the poverty of the Cross (in all its forms), there appears finally the Spirit of God, as the original in the copy; the Spirit of absolute love, which in its freest self-limitation exists beyond strength and weakness, dominion and humility ... Accordingly, the Holy Spirit...is weakened together with the weak, limited together with the finite spirits caught in their clouded subjectivity, frightened and lashing out around them. It flows together with the whole process of the world which struggles for the manifestation of its Sonship of God.[126]

For Balthasar, the above clearly shows that the Cross has a Trinitarian significance. It touches a mystery, which cannot be explored philosophically. That is why philosophy says either "too much or too little" about the significance of the Cross.[127] The application of philosophy on the theology of the Cross, be it dia-

---

[124] *Ibid.*, p. 213.

[125] Cf. *ibid.*, p. 212.

[126] *Ibid.*, p. 212.

[127] Cf. H. U. von Balthasar, Mysterium Paschale, p. 170. He sees unsuccessful attempts made to philosophise the Cross in (a) the Neo-Platonic oriented theology of the Cross (in the Apocryphal acts of the Apostle), *Ibid.*, p. 164, (b) where the Cross is made a general symbolic idea (R. Guénon, C. E. Raven and Teilhard de Chardin), (c) where the Cross is understood as a mere contradiction, a paradox without logic (Luther), or as a "world order" (Hegel), *Ibid.*, p. 168, and (d) where the Cross is seen to be intrinsic to divine nature (Moltmann), *Ibid.*, p. 169.

lectical or non-dialectical, is bound to lead to a misconception,[128] except of course philosophy is made to "empty itself" (*ihrer selbst entäußern*) of preconceived ideas, and to dedicate itself wholly to the crucified Christ, so that it can get to the depth of the hidden wisdom of God, set out before all times for our salvation.[129] The full significance of the Cross opens itself, according to Balthasar, only to a theologian of faith, who, by confessing the mystery of the Cross, can discern its logic.[130] But even a man of faith misses the point if he conceives it as an illogical occurrence, as a contradiction *per se*. For although, the Cross is a scandal, it is neither illogical nor contradictory to the logic of God.[131] There is a theo-logic of the event on the Cross.

The Cross conquers the only true contra-diction, which is "sin".[132] And if the flesh of humankind has become an enemy of God (Rom. 8:7), it is not because it is primarily opposed to God, but because, its tendency to self-seeking continuously brings it into opposition to God. Not the flesh is contradictory, but its rebellion. Thus by taking flesh (Verbum-Caro), the incarnate Son experiences the rebellion of the flesh from within, and by freely enduring this experience till death

---

128 *Ibid.*, p. 184. It is for this reason that Balthasar distances himself from Luther's dialectical theology of the Cross, which by insisting on its thesis of *sub contrario* allows its pure "dialectical Christology" turn to a mere "philosophical dialectics". Cf. *Ibid.*, p. 16 ff.; *Theologik* II, p. 305 ff.

129 H. U. von Balthasar, Mysterium Paschale, p. 171.

130 *Ibid.*, p. 182.

131 This is his main criticism of Luther's "theology of contradiction", which by denying the place of the principle of non-contradiction (*des Nichtwiderspruchssatzes*) in the God-talk installs contradiction between God and the world, between human spirit and flesh, and consequently introduces it into Christology and into the doctrine of God. For that reason, Luther gives metaphysics, analogy and the logic of God little or no place at all. In contrast, Balthasar sees nothing in creation (not even the flesh), except sin, as being opposed to God. Cf. *Theologik* II, p. 305 ff.

132 *Ibid.*, p. 310. For Balthasar, sin is the only true contradiction that exists, the only reality that is opposed to God. What is contradiction except the conscious (*widersprechen*) denial that Jesus Christ is the true image of God? Another term for the sort of contradiction in question is "dialectics": dialectics etymologically comes from "*dia-legein*" - to contradict. Hence, Balthasar claims that dialectics, in Johannine theology, can only be used to denote the denial of the single truth: that God is that boundless love, which he shows in the self-giving of the Son (*Ibid.*, p. 289). According to this view dialectics can also mean falsehood or pure lie, the diabolical negation of the witness of Christ (*Ibid.*, pp. 289-294). He differentiates the theological dialectics however from the philosophical dialectics like that of Hegel, because that the latter does not connote the idea of sin. But in spite of that, he maintains that philosophical dialectics was derived from theological dialectics.

on the Cross, he counters the disobedience (rebellion) of the flesh through his own obedience to the Father.[133]

Hence, for Balthasar, what took place on the Cross is not illogical; it is merely an incomprehensible Trinitarian logic, a Trinitarian mystery, which for lack of adequate expression could be termed the "dialectics" of all dialectics, the "contradiction" of all contradictions, because through a sort of "dialectics" (an apparent contradiction) every dia-lectic (contra-diction) is conquered. This divine measure of countering the disobedience of the flesh with the ever-persisting obedience of the Son, is for Balthasar an inalienable part of the Verbum-Caro and theo-logy.

He terms this divine economy the only acceptable theological "dialectics"[134], the only possible "negative theology" in Christian sense. "Negative Theology" does not therefore signify the incomparability of divine majesty, but that act of God on the Cross, by which the Logos took the contradiction of sin (all its false-hood and illogicality) into the logic of the triune love, not to preserve it, but to damn it in the flesh of the Son.[135] This is possible only through the consistent obedience of the Logos to the Father, which runs through his whole "sending" or mission, (from the Incarnation, through death on the Cross till his descent into hell), infiltrating the rebellion of Adam to the point of overcoming "the contradic-tion between God and sinners".[136] This consistent obedience is Christ's perfect identity in all contradictions, which also leads to the conquest of the last of all contradictions - the hell.[137]

With A. v. Speyr, Balthasar argues that through the obedience of the Logos to descend into hell, hell itself has become a Trinitarian event.[138] Interpreting Jesus' cry of dereliction on the Cross in the line of this logic, Balthasar sees the experi-ence of divine absence as part of the Son's sending: the Father withdraws so that the Son can experience the last of the contradictions - hell - as the absence of God. Abandonment here becomes a way of the Trinity to demonstrate that near-ness and distance, that mobility, that incomprehensible mutability in the immuta-bility of the Triune God.[139] Hence, the presence of God is no where better shown

---

133 *Ibid.*, p. 295 ff.

134 *Ibid.*, p. 298.

135 *Ibid.*, p. 297.

136 *Ibid.*, p. 314.

137 *Ibid.*, p. 323.

138 *Ibid.*, p. 321.

139 *Ibid.* See the two quotations he takes from Adrienne von Speyr in the same page: "Der Vater is niemals gegenwärtiger als in dieser Abwesenheit am Kreuz." "Im Herzen der Un-

than in this abandonment, which has been used to shatter the prison (yard) of every abandonment, so that the Son - together with the liberated world - enters the heaven of the Father.[140] In this manner theo-logic shows the conquest of the inner-worldly contradiction through the Trinitarian logic.[141]

In conclusion, Balthasar affirms that what seems like an illogical contradiction, in the short-sightedness of the worldly logic, is actually the logic of love, which guarantees the adequate manifestation of the Triune God and proper exposition of the sinful world in the unity of Cross and hell.[142] What seems to be the foolishness of God, that the Father delivered up his Son to the anti-divine power of contradiction, is, in effect, the revelation of God, as the Trinitarian love, in the simplicity of the Son's obedience. In this manner, the Cross and the Trinity give mutual prove of each other.[143]

He enunciates the logic of the Cross further with the aid of the doctrine of Kenosis. Karl Barth's understanding of divine kenosis is for him a special source of inspiration for the development of a *theologia crucis*.[144] For Karl Barth, the exaltation and the self-renunciation of Christ should not be seen as two successive status, two different lives, one divine and the other bereft of divinity, as earlier Kenoticists were prone to think. They are rather two forms of a single divine act in Jesus Christ, corresponding to his double *Gestalt*. There was never a time when Jesus was not the exalted *and* the humiliated - already in his self-renunciation he is the exalted, and in his exaltation the self-renunciating one.[145] In his conviction that the exaltation and the self-renunciation can only be explained with reference to each other, Barth concludes that there is "no paradox, no antinomy, no dichotomy" in divine nature: that God can become man without

---

veränderlichkeit hat unbegreiflicherweise die Veränderung einen Platz ... Man müßte sagen: jeder Veränderlichkeit der Schöpfung gegenüber gibt es in Gott von jeher eine Über-Veränderlickeit". In this connection, Balthasar speaks of a mobility (without potentiality), a "supra-mutability" in God, which is always presupposed by God's paradoxical behaviours like the abandonment of his Son on the Cross.

[140] *Theologik* II, p. 322.

[141] *Ibid.*, p. 323.

[142] *Ibid.*, p. 330.

[143] *Ibid.*, p. 331.

[144] H. U. von Balthasar, Mysterium Paschale, p. 182 f.

[145] Cf. K. Barth, *Die Kirchliche Dogmatik* IV/1, pp. 145-147. For more details see also pp. 196-199. 205 ff.

ceasing to be God, means that the ability to perform this singular act is part of His *nature*.[146]

Leaning on this Barthian notion of kenosis, Balthasar sees the ability of God to give up Himself even to the point of self abandonment on the Cross without loosing himself as a sign that God is both immanent and transcendent to the world, thanks to His inner Trinitarian love.[147] Thus, for Balthasar, the theology of the Cross can only be understood with reference to the theology of glory and vice versa.[148]

6.5 Impassibility and Immutability of God

So far, we have tried to outline aspects of Balthasar's theology with direct bearings on our topic. His views on the doctrine of divine impassibility and immutability must have emerged out of his understanding of revelation, analogy (the paradoxical unity-in-difference), the God-world relationship, the Trinitarian and the Christ events (especially the primordial kenosis and the Cross) as sketched above. Yet, for the sake of clarity, we need to streamline the points constituting his theology of the divine suffering.

Balthasar does not dedicate any book to the axiom of divine impassibility. Yet this issue seems to lie at the background of all his major theological discussions. His approach is evidently skilful and tactful. He characteristically seeks the middle course between the classical axiom of divine impassibility and modern univocal attribution of suffering to God.[149] On the one hand, he admits that there is "an event in God" Himself, which not only presupposes "the possibility and the permissiveness of all pains in the world", but also occasions "the participation of God" in all suffering (to the point of "effectively" and "vicariously" taking "Godlessness" on to Himself).[150] On the other hand, he avoids all fashionable and unqualified talks about the "pain of God". He likens his approach to this paradox with the dance of an acrobat on a tightrope, or his walk on "knife's edge",[151] which is characterised by optimal balancing, fully aware of the fact that any excessive inclination on either side is bound to mar the undertaking.

---

[146] Cf. *Ibid.*, pp. 202-204.

[147] H. U. von Balthasar, Mysterium Paschale, p.183.

[148] *Ibid.*, p. 184.

[149] *Theodramatik* III, p. 304.

[150] *Ibid.*, p. 302.

[151] *Ibid.*

We must assume, he maintains, that the Absolute can be free from all inner-worldly feeling and suffering and yet be the sole precondition of any possible feeling and suffering. That is the mystery, "the mystery of all mysteries", and "the unfathomable ground of the history of salvation", which can neither be approached by negating the world, nor by identifying it with God. The faith in the *Oikonomia* in Christ, in his kenosis, urges us to go beyond both methods.[152] In that sense, he agrees with the Patristics and the Scholastics, that we cannot attribute suffering and change to God univocally. He goes beyond them however to affirm an analogous suffering in God. By this means, he reinterprets the axiom of divine impassibility so as to make provision for the divine eternal "vitality", that is to say, for the possibility of the divine sovereignty even in suffering.

He accordingly advocates the Patristic axiom of divine *apatheia*, which, if broadly conceived as in the case of Origen, would entail the attribution of *pathos* to God in a certain way.[153] In the Patristic tradition, pathos could be attributed to God if and when it does not imply an influence from an external agent, that is to say, when the affectivity implied could be seen as an outgrowth of a preceding (absolute) act of divine will. In other words, divine *apatheia* means, in the mainstream of Patristic tradition, that God is denied *pathos*, only if this would entail an involuntary and an externally influenced determination of His being.[154] The Fathers, Balthasar says, make qualified use of the terms apatheia and pathos, more than some modern proponents of divine suffering have been able to acknowledge.[155] That an impassible God can have the emotions of "pity", "wrath"

---

[152] *Ibid.*

[153] See 2.3.3. of this study.

[154] *Theodramatik* IV, p. 201: The same points about the positive contributions of the Fathers to this issue in Balthasar's words: "Nicht zu überholen sind folgende Stellungnahmen: *Pathos* kann in Gott nicht sein, sofern dieses ein ungewolltes Bestimmtwerden von außen her besagt. Oder positiv gewendet: Gott (und auch der Menschgewordene) kann passiv nur betroffen werden, sofern dies einem vorausgehenden aktiven freien Willensentschluß entspricht. Ferner können, ja müssen Formen der ewigen göttlichen Lebendigkeit (wie Erbarmen, Geduld usf.) in Analogie zu menschlichen Affekten verstanden werden, ohne daß dadurch 'Veränderlichkeit' in Gott einzuzeichnen wäre."

[155] On this point, Balthasar is particularly critical of H. Mühlen, W. Maas and J. Moltmann, who, according to him, distance themselves from the Patristic doctrine of divine *apatheia*, without having taken note of the fact that the Fathers while affirming divine impassibility accommodate a certain form of the predication of *pathos* to God. Cf. *Ibid.*, p. 199 f., note 33.

and "concern" as the scripture testifies is amply demonstrated in the thoughts of Lactantius and Gregory Thaumaturgos.[156]

Similarly, Balthasar contends that one can conceive God as impassible and yet maintain that He can go into suffering *freely*. It has been an error on the part of the post-Patristic era, he argues, to conceive divine impassibility so narrowly, that it had to exclude God's real relation to His creatures.[157] He is particularly critical of St. Thomas' thesis, that while we can speak of a "real relation" from creatures to God, we can only assume a *"relatio rationis"* from God to creatures.[158] This view, he argues, implicitly reduces the biblical account of God's "reactions" to the human conduct to the level of mere anthropomorphism. This would amount to making the divine activities in the history of salvation seem unreal.[159] Balthasar also criticises some modern theologians like H. Küng,[160] who tend to understand divine immutability merely morally and historically, i.e. only on the basis of God's faithfulness and steadfastness in His commitment to the covenant promises.[161] He rather prefers to go beyond its moral implication, for the simple reason that faithfulness to the covenant is itself only a modality of God's unchanging and ontological nature. The Bible testifies to the immutability of God's inner being, and even when it "glimpses *through* his economic attitude" it definitely goes to focus on "an attribute of the Divinity in itself".[162]

Thus, Balthasar reinterprets the axiom of divine impassibility and immutability by broadening its scope. For, whereas he would not speak of divine "passibility" and "mutability" in the human sense, he insists that the "vitality" in God (His pity and patience etc.) is "analogous" (like and unlike) to human emotions.[163]

---

[156] As we indicated above in section 2.3.2., Lactantius gives emotion a place in the nature of God. See his *De ira Dei*, 17. On his part, Gregorios Thaumaturgos, argues that the attribution of suffering is only negative if it is of no advantage to God himself. But since God suffers to overcome suffering, it cannot be negative. See 2.3.3. above, and his *Ad Theopompum*, 6-7.

[157] *Ibid.*, p. 200.

[158] See *Ibid.* and Thomas Aquinas, *De Pot.* 7,8-11; 1a 13,7.

[159] *Theodramatik* IV, p. 200 f.

[160] "When Scripture speaks of God's immutability, this is not to be understood in a metaphysical sense of a world-cause rigidly immobile by its very nature, but in the historical sense of his essential fidelity to himself and to his promises, guaranteeing permanence and continuity in his action." H. Küng, "Immutability of God?" in: *The Incarnation of God*, p. 533.

[161] *Theodramatik* IV, p. 200.

[162] *Ibid.*

[163] *Ibid.*

Besides, he rejects every form of "process theology", which, in the tradition of Hegel, "identifies the cosmic process (together with God's involvement in it, including the Cross) with the eternal and timeless 'process' of the hypostasis in God".[164] He finds the transposition of finitude (negation and contradiction) into God's very essence unfortunate.[165] This trend began with Hegel's honest but problematic attempt to mediate between what E. Jüngel calls "atheistic modern feeling and the Christian truth of the death of God".[166] According to Balthasar, Hegel's claim that moments of finitude like "pain" and "death" are, on the one hand, real in God, and on the other hand, simultaneously overcome in God, did not meet up to his expectation. His proclamation of the "death of God" as "the negation of negation" does not effectively destroy atheism. It rather leads to the introduction of *ambiguity* in the Christian concept of God as is characteristic of Hegel's whole theological method.[167]

All later "pain-of-God" theologians, who, in the tradition of Hegel, see the essence of God as part of the world process, inherited this ambiguity. This is Balthasar's main criticism of Moltmann,[168] Gerhard Koch[169] and also of Kitamori, who posit a conflict between divine love and wrath.[170] For Balthasar, divine freedom is at stake in every method, where an inner contradiction is read into the essence of God.[171] Even the non-Hegelian approach of the Scottish

---

[164] *Theodramatik* III, p. 301.

[165] *Theodramatik* IV, pp. 202-204.

[166] E. Jüngel, *God as the mystery of the world*, pp. 63 ff. It is interesting to note that, unlike Balthasar, Jüngel considers this mediation, not only positive, but also as "Hegel's most significant achievement for theology" (*ibid.*, p. 97).

[167] *Theodramatik* IV, p. 203. By this, Balthasar shares Feuerbach's criticisms of Hegel's connection of Christianity to atheism, but only in this regard. In his "Principles of the Future" (1843), Feuerbach argues that Hegel's grand attempt to mediate between "belief and unbelief, theology and philosophy, religion and atheism, Christianity and paganism" by philosophising on the "death of God", conceals an inherent contradiction, which "escapes the eye and is obfuscated in Hegel only through the fact that the negation of God, or atheism, is turned by him into an objective determination of God; God is determined as a *process*, and atheism as a moment within this process". Cf. L. Feuerbach, Principles of the Future, pp. 205 f.

[168] *Ibid.*, p. 205

[169] *Ibid.*, p. 208.

[170] *Ibid.*, p. 214.

[171] *Ibid.*, p. 211.

Episcopalian theologian Bertrand Brasnett merits rejection due to its consequent conclusion that suffering belongs to an inner moment of divine nature.[172]

Balthasar sees a promising approach to our problem in K. Barth's Christology and the theology of covenant, especially where the latter tries to conceive the "passion of God" in a manner that avoids conjuring up any sort of inner-contradiction in God (unlike Moltmann) and excludes any form of external constraint for Him even from human freedom.[173] He finds it disappointing, however, that Barth, in addition to his inability to account for the soteriological significance of the suffering of Christ on the Cross, could not go further to explore the significance of the inner-Trinitarian processions for divine passibility.[174] In effect, the weakness of Barth's approach, as Balthasar sees it, has to do with the failure to illustrate the Trinitarian dimension of his passiology.

Balthasar finds the Trinitarian and kenotic implications of the New Covenant, which he judges missing in Barth's exposition, well worked out by Jean Galot in his book, *Dieu souffre-t-il?*.[175] He is particularly fascinated by the following three aspects of Galot's attempt to give an answer to the issue of divine "affectivity" and "receptivity". Firstly, the fact that Galot holds firm to the axiom of divine immutability without denying that suffering can affect God in a certain way. Secondly, his insistence on the existence of a genuine analogy between divine and human suffering, which is real and not merely linguistically classical. Thirdly, Galot's assumption that there must be something like an "ontological" basis in the immanent Trinity for the bond between love and pain. Balthasar subscribes to all the above views and believes that Galot is moving in the right direction. Nevertheless, Galot's distinction between the untouchable inner life of the Trinity and the "affectively" touchable relation of the latter to the world seems exaggerated in Balthasar's view.[176]

Drawing from the reflections of Maritain, who is also Galot's source of inspiration, Balthasar goes further to relate the "intuition" of this philosopher to the Trinitarian vitality, so that the aforementioned "ontological foundation" in the

---

172 *Ibid.*, pp. 211-213.

173 Cf. K. Barth, *Die Kirchliche Dogmatik* IV/1, pp. 202 f., 209: The impact of the freedom of sinful humankind does not constitute any sort of constraint on him, for it is already engulfed in his eternal plan; hence, God acts, even when he allows himself to be acted upon.

174 *Theodramatik* IV, p. 213-6.

175 Lethielleux, Paris 1976. See also Balthasar, *Theodramatik* IV, 216-8; *Theodramatik* III, pp. 291, 300.

176 *Theodramatik* IV, p. 218

immanent Trinity could be concretised.[177] In his philosophical reflections, Maritain assumes the existence of an essential attribute in God, that can both justify (*begründen*) and form an analogy with worldly pains, but, unlike our sufferings and sorrows, excludes any sort of imperfection.[178] Tradition has no name for this essential attribute but it could be described as a "victorious adoption" (*Ergreifen*) - "acceptance" or "overcoming" of pains.

Similarly, Balthasar argues that there is a type of receptivity in God, which could best be termed "supra-suffering" or "supra-mutability.[179] It occurs primarily in the framework of the give and take of the Trinitarian love. To him, this divine phenomenon justifies the assumption that our actions can have a "painful" effect on God.

> Within God himself there is the original of that of which man's relationship to God is a copy: (there is) room for love between Father and Son - for God in the mode of created receiving and giving back in full measure - in the unity of the Spirit of love which alone emerges from the double fount of love and, as the eternal fruit of love, unites and distinguishes the Father and the Son.[180]

This receptivity in God however differs from the creaturely receptivity in that it is an aspect of divine perfection.[181] His receptivity does not presuppose any sort of deficiency, it is a self-fulfilling type of receptivity, which makes love possible, and which empowers, activates and perfects an I-Thou relationship. Balthasar substantiates his points with the inner-Trinitarian processions. It is in the interpersonal relation of the Trinity that we see divine love revealed as consisting of receptivity and self-giving. In the absolute relation of the Trinitarian life, receptivity is as positive as the creative "differences" of the hypostasis[182] and like the latter, it makes "the mutual interaction and exchange " in the Trinitarian love possible. The Trinitarian receptivity could be seen as the Archetype of the human self-fulfilling receptivity found in the realm of human inter-personal,[183] and "subject-

---

177 *Ibid.*, p. 219.

178 *Ibid.*, p. 218.

179 *Ibid.*, pp. 191-192.

180 H. U. von Balthasar, *Man in History.* p. 69.

181 See G. F. O'Hanlon, *The Immutability of God*, pp. 121-124.

182 *Theologik* II, p. 169.

183 On this see *Theodramatik* II/1, pp. 231-243; *Theodramatik* IV, pp. 74-86; *Theologik* II, pp. 77-79, 321, note 57. Cf. also G. F. O'Hanlon, *The Immutability of God*, p. 120. Balthasar uses human sexuality to illustrate the nature of divine receptive, not implying however that there is a sexuality in God. (p. 122)

object" relationships.[184] This also points to the positive aspect of passivity in love.[185]

Again, Balthasar sees the divine receptivity different from the human receptivity. As *Actus Purus* God lives His passivity within His activity.[186] In the inner-Trinitarian life, receptivity is an ongoing process and as such excludes potency. It is part of the continuous giving and receiving of love among the Persons of the Trinity. In this sense, the divine receptivity is an active receptivity, and is thus taken beyond the classical categories of potency and act, as it becomes one single flow of passivity and activity.[187]

Hence, even if we must agree with the Fathers that there is no mythological change or suffering in God, and that there is no external determination for God, we must not fail to see that there is something in God which is analogous to worldly suffering, something that makes God freely allow sin to affect Him in such a way that we can justifiably speak of the soteriological significance of the Cross of Jesus Christ.

The basis for attributing receptivity to God is His Trinitarian life of self-giving.[188] Both the Father and the Son are receptive: the Son owes his "Sonship" to the Father and the Father owes his "Fatherhood" to the Son.[189] This is not metaphorical in the sense of Hegel; it belongs to the nature of divine love that the hypostasis donate themselves selflessly to each other. In fact, such a mutual interaction within the Trinity presupposes the free decision of each of the hypostasis to be receptive and affective. It is on this basis that Balthasar sees Karl Rahner's thesis that God "who is unchangeable in *himself* can himself become subject to

---

184 *Theologik* I, pp. 36-57, 80-107, 113-28; G. F. O'Hanlon, *The Immutability of God*, pp. 122-123.

185 *Theodramatik* IV, pp. 74-80, 472-3, 82-6, 106-7; *Theodramatik* II/1, pp. 242-3.

186 *Theodramatik* IV, p. 74 f.

187 Balthasar explains the perfection of the divine receptivity with the Trinitarian processions. O'Hanlon summarises this point as he writes: "This means that the Son and Holy Spirit in particular receive their being: and yet because they are both God it also means, very significantly, that within this reality of love to receive is just as divine as to give." In his view, Balthasar's attribution of receptivity (as a perfect potency) to God constitutes perhaps his most striking departure from tradition, because traditionally it was not possible to attribute a passive potency to God, since it connotes the imperfection of a creature. Cf. G. F. O'Hanlon, *The Immutability of God*, p. 121.

188 Balthasar cites F. Varillon, Martelet, H. Schürmann and N. Hoffmann to support his view that divine suffering can only be meaningfully discussed in the framework of a Trinitarian theology.

189 *Theodramatik* IV, p. 221.

change *in something else*[190] to be insufficient. It is clear for Balthasar that in the Incarnation,

> God in himself does not change himself; the immutable God rather goes into a relationship (*Beziehung*) with his creatures, (and this God-world relationship) gives his inner-Trinitarian "relations" (*relationen*) a new look, certainly not in a superficial sense, as if this relationship directed outside does not involve him really, but so, that the new relationship with the world of nature, which is hypostatically united in the Son, brings one of the infinite possibilities that lie dormant in God's eternal life to the lime light.[191]

This is one of the few texts in which Balthasar formulates his notion of a modified axiom of divine immutability. This seems to fare no better than Karl Rahner's solution. Either he is imprecise or he contradicts himself. On the one hand, he confesses ontological and ethical immutability, on the other hand, he talks of an adjustment in the inner-Trinitarian life, due to the Incarnation. If there is any justification in asking Rahner, where the difference lies that God changes Himself outside Himself but not in Himself, it is all the more justifiable to ask Balthasar, how he can still hold to the axiom of immutability, while admitting that the relationship of the world to God affects the inner-Trinitarian relations.

Balthasar would however answer that even the new adjustments in the inner-Trinitarian life do not constitute change in the divine nature, they are merely the realisation of some of the infinite possibilities in the divine dynamism. The dynamism in divine nature, he argues, is so immense that it encompasses the infinite distance both between the Persons of the Trinity and between God and the world. To that effect, every event that takes place in the finite domain can only happen *within* the divine dynamism, which encompasses it.[192] In other words, the triune God engulfs the world, so to say, but only within the framework of the inner-Trinitarian dynamism, which, by virtue of the infinite difference and distance between the Persons, makes the accommodation of the tragedy of the world in God possible, without God loosing His eternal bliss (*Seligkeit*).[193]

Although Balthasar claims that there is affectivity and receptivity in God (albeit in a positive and perfect sense), he detests and there cautions theologians against the fashionable talk about the "suffering of God".[194] All that the reality of the inner-Trinitarian receptivity and paradoxical unity-in-distinction[195] allows us to

---

[190] K. Rahner, *Theological Investigations IV*, p. 113.

[191] *Theodramatik* II/2, p. 479 (my translation).

[192] *Theodramatik* IV, p. 221.

[193] *Ibid.*, p. 222.

[194] *Ibid.*, p. 192.

[195] *Ibid.*, p. 221.

say, Balthasar insists, is that there is a possible suffering in God; he declines however to explicitly affirm that God suffers. For whereas he follows the Fathers to condemn "Patripassianism", he admits that "only a hairsbreadth separates the real suffering of the God-Man and the non-suffering of God".[196] So, in spite of his emphasis on the *circumincessio* of the inner-Trinitarian life, Balthasar insists that the real suffering of Christ on the Cross can only affect the God-head analogously. Hence, he reiterates: the infinite distance between the Father and the Son makes it impossible for the Father and the Son to suffer in the same way on the Cross.

In the face of this fact, one wonders if Balthasar has gone beyond the attribution of suffering only to the human nature of Christ, despite all the talk about the dynamism and receptivity in God. Apparently, his answer to the question whether God can suffer is yes and no. If asked whether God suffers, he would say:

> in God is the starting-point of that, what can become suffering when the risk (*Vorsichtlosigkeit*) with which the Father gives away himself (and *all* that is his) ... meets a freedom, which rather than respond to this risk, constitutes itself as that precaution (*Vorsicht*) that is part of the wish-to-begin-with-oneself.[197]

Being able to identify nothing more than the foundation, the starting-point of every mutability and possibility in God, Balthasar forces himself to the conclusion, that though there is something like an "anonymous attribute" (in the sense of Maritain), which explains the liveliness in God, we must affirm that "the God of *Theodramatik*", the God of revelation, who, by creating finite free beings commits Himself to their destiny, "is neither mythologically mutable (passible) nor philosophically immutable (impassible)".[198] Balthasar's God is, as the title of H. Heinz' book suggests,[199] a God proportionately "ever-more", whose nature is beyond what human language can describe. How the nature of God can be de-

---

196 *Theodramatik* II/1, p. 45; See also J. Saward, *The Mysteries*, p. 12.

197 *Theodramatik* III, p. 305. This is my translation of the original: "in Gott ist der Ansatzpunkt für das, was Leiden werden kann, wenn die Vorsichtlosigkeit, mit der der Vater sich (und alles Seinige) weggibt ... auf eine Freiheit stößt, die diese Vorsichlosigkeit nicht beantwortet, sondern in die Vorsicht des Bei-sich-selber-beginnen-Wollens verwandelt." Balthasar's use of *Vorsichtlosigkeit* has no precise theological equivalent in English. For want of better alternatives, we prefer the term "risk", because it brings out its theological import better than other possible equivalents like "carefree", "recklessness", "nonchalance", "extravagance", lack of precautions etc. *Vorsichtlosigkeit* denotes God's readiness to relate to humankind without reckoning His own gain and not minding his "honour".

198 *Theodramatik* II/1, p. 9.

199 Cf. H. Heinz, *Der Gott des Je-Mehr*, (Bern/Frankfurt, 1975). See H. U. von Balthasar, *Man in History*. p. 200.

scribed beyond all extremes of classical axioms and fashionable (mythological) claims of modern theology is the puzzle Balthasar has been seeking to solve.

6.6 Assessment of Balthasar's passiology

Even though Balthasar does not undertake a thematic discussion of divine suffering, he seeks however to supply a hermeneutic basis or presupposition with which one can justifiably say that "God suffers" without undermining the reality of divine freedom and transcendence.[200] He believes to have found that in the modality of the inner-Trinitarian life, especially in processions and in the mode of the Trinitarian mission in the world. With that, he sets already the context within which divine suffering can be gainfully discussed as well as the scope within which his contribution to the theology of divine impassibility can be assessed.

It cannot be gainsaid that Trinitarian theology offers a better structure than the "dipolar" model of the process theology,[201] when it comes to maintaining the truism of both the transcendence and immanence of God simultaneously, and when we, due to the paradox of divine impassibility, intend to be as close as possible to the proclamation of God in the Bible. So, like Moltmann, it is to his credit that this problem is being expounded wholly in a Trinitarian framework. However, we need to specify his contribution within the Trinitarian theology by setting his model over and against other Trinitarian approaches in order to evaluate the significance of his contribution.

Trinitarian theologians differ as to how to express the relationship between the immanent and the economic Trinity. And it is evident that the extent to which they can mediate successfully between God's immanence (which in itself knows no pain) and God's economy (which experiences the pain of unreciprocated love from the world) determines the weight of their contributions to the issue of divine impassibility. It is certainly no exaggeration, when Thomas R. Krenski claims that the consistency of every theological passiology can best be assessed when we judge its "exact determination of the relationship between immanent and economic Trinity".[202] Thus in order to assess Balthasar's contribution towards formulating an acceptable theology of divine impassibility, we need to assess his art of mediating between the immanent and economic Trinity, which definitely fits

---

[200] Cf. *Theodramatik* III, p. 302.

[201] Cf. P. Fiddes, *The Creative Suffering of God*. See especially pp. 123-135.

[202] T. R. Krenski, *Passio Caritatis*, p. 346.

into one of the known possible hermeneutic models: the models of "equivocation", of "univocation" and of "analogy".[203]

First, there is the model of equivocation, which seems best propounded in the theology of Gregorios Palamas, whose refusal to see a correspondence between divine being and divine activities in the world has also been interpreted to mean a denial of any connection between the immanent and the economic Trinity.[204] According to D. Wendebourg, Palamas does not believe that there can be any knowledge of God's inner nature through inference from His activities in the world.[205] With due appreciation of the intention of the model of equivocation, which certainly aims at preserving the divine transcendence and freedom, one wonders whether the denial of an ontological connection between God's economy and His inner nature does not constitute a "qualitative jump", which could ultimately make divine acts of salvation (Incarnation, Cross etc.) lack any basis in God Himself.

There is perhaps no explicit equivocation model in the sense of palamite standard in modern doctrine of the Trinity. There are suspicions however, that there are traces of such models (i.e. of the denial of an ontological connection between the being of God and His economy in the world) in modern theology.[206] There can be no meaningful discussion of the passibility/impassibility of God, where such a model prevails, because would be lack the *immanent-Trinitarian basis*,[207] which is the guarantor for God's participation in the affairs of the world,. In other words, even though the model of equivocation can account for the freedom of God, it fails to qualify as a genuine hermeneutic method for passiology since it is not able to posit an event in God, that can justify His involvement in the drama of the world.[208]

In the model of univocation, the distinction between the immanent and the economic Trinity is denied, so that the one becomes tautologically identical with the

---

203 This classification is taken from T. R. Krenski, *Passio Caritatis*. For much of what follows on this point, we are indebted to his very constructive views on H. U. von Balthasar especially pp. 345-370 of his book.

204 Cf. See G. Mantzaridis' view in: G. Mantzaridis / G.Galitis / P.Wiertz, *Glauben aus dem Herzen*, p. 88. For more references see T. R. Krenski, *Passio Caritatis*, p. 356, note 39; J. Kuhlmann, *Die Taten des einfachen Gottes*; H.-G., Beck, Die byzantinische Kirche: Das Zeitalter des Palamismus, pp. 589-624.

205 D. Wendebourg, *Geist oder Energie*, p. 161.

206 Cf. T. R. Krenski, *Passio Caritatis*, p. 358-359.

207 Cf. *Theodramatik* IV, p. 218: "Immanent-Trinitarische Grundlegung".

208 For Balthasar's rejection of this model and the Palamite doctrine see *Theodramatik* IV, pp. 218, 373; *Theologik* II, p. 373.

other. The God *in Himself* then becomes strictly identical with the God *for us*. In other words, God is the same in Himself as He is in history. The concern of the univocal model, not to posit a contradiction between the immanent and the economic Trinity is certainly genuine.[209] However, by failing to maintain the distinction between the immanent and the economic Trinity, this model is also unable to provide a genuine hermeneutic basis for a theory of God's paradoxical nature. Balthasar is particularly critical of this model, not only because its exponents like Moltmann read insufficiency into the very nature of God, but more because it compromises divine freedom and transcendence.

It is therefore evident that both models - equivocation and univocation - lead to impossible conclusions, which bring the theology of divine suffering to a blind alley. With his theory of (Christological) analogy, Balthasar tries now to dodge this dead-end. He proposes a third model, which we can refer to as the model of analogy. The principle of analogy is certainly not new to theology, and in fact, one can say that it characterises all specific Catholic solutions to theological problems, yet it is to Balthasar's credit that he calls our attention anew to the significance of analogy in determining the relation between the immanent and the economic Trinity.

By using his revised version of the principle of analogy, not only in describing the relation between God and the world, but also the relations within the inner-Trinitarian life, Balthasar is able to speak of distinction and inter-connection between the immanent and the economic Trinity at the same time. Consequently, he could afford to claim on the one hand, that divine freedom is real and on the other hand, that there is an *"immanent-Trinitarian basis"* in God, which not only serves as the presupposing principle of every possible suffering in the world, but also justifies the assumption of an ontological divine involvement in the events of the world.[210]

The strength of Balthasar's version of analogy seems to lie in its integration of a widely conceived theory of kenosis that can be used to describe the inner-Trinitarian life pattern. By understanding the inner-Trinitarian processions as "primordial kenosis" (*Urkenose*)[211] and the divine economy in creation (covenant, Incarnation and on the Cross) as extensions of the same divine kenosis, Balthasar seeks to strike a balance between two extreme positions. In contrast to the thesis of the equivocation model, he does not see the broad spectrum

---

209 This also corresponds to Balthasar's thesis that the Son is the adequate expression of God as he is in himself. See T. R. Krenski, *Passio Caritatis*, p. 353.

210 Cf. *Theodramatik* III, p. 302.

211 Cf. *ibid.*, p. 300; *Theodramatik* IV, p. 74; H. U. von Balthasar, "Mysterium Paschale", p. 148.

of divine economy in the world as something foreign to divine nature. And unlike the proponents of the univocal model, he refuses to accept the view that the economic activity of the Trinity constitutes the very nature of God. In his view, the activities of the Trinity *ad extra* can only be analogous and not identical to the inner-Trinitarian events. This means in effect that divine economy and its implied affectivity can have an "immanent-Trinitarian basis" without entailing the projection of what is worldly into the very being of God. In this way, Balthasar believes to have made sufficient provision for the freedom and sovereignty of God. In fact, in accounting for the relation of the immanent and the economic Trinity Balthasar is primarily concerned with the thought of how to affirm God's immanence in the world without denying or destroying His divine transcendence.[212] He therefore prefers to speak of transcendence in immanence.[213]

It is certainly right to describe Balthasar's model of analogy in the mediation between the immanent and the economic Trinity as *analogia exinanitionis*,[214] for the fact that he himself sees the Son's state of self-renunciation (*status exinanitionis*) as analogous to the "selflessness" that constitutes the "primordial kenosis" of the inner-Trinitarian life. Again, when one considers the fact that kenosis is itself an expression of love, which God is, and that the *dissimilitudo in similitudine*, which Balthasar attributes to the relations of the Persons, does not belong to kenosis as such, but to love, it then becomes evident that his version of analogy could also be called *Analogia Caritatis*.[215] The analogy of love says more than the analogy of kenosis. The former encompasses more than the latter. For while love constitutes God's being (1 Jn. 4:8), *kenosis* does not. Christ's *status exinanitionis*, i.e. his unrelenting obedience till death on the Cross, is indeed only but one expression of that love which constitutes the being of God.

Yet we are of the opinion, that Balthasar's method and ontology of being could best be termed an *analogia relationis*, because as indicated above, Balthasar sees the paradox of the unity-in-difference, of similarity-in-dissimilarity, of *dissimilitudo in similitudine*, as intrinsic not only to love but also to all forms of inter-

---

212 Cf. G. O'Hanlon, *Does God change?*, p. 161-162.

213 H. U. von Balthasar, Mysterium Paschale, p. 151.

214 Cf. T. R. Krenski, *Passio Caritatis*, p. 347.

215 Cf. M. Lochbrunner, *Analogia Caritatis*. See especially pp. 281-304. The author interprets Balthasar's whole theology from the point of view of an "Analogia Caritatis", which he sees both as the formal as well as the material principle, the method and content of Balthasar's theology (p. 311).

personal relationships.[216] He uses the analogy of relation however much more fundamentally in interpenetrating the relationships between the Persons of the Trinity without making them loose their specific identity. By seeing the hypostatic union as a form of *maior dissimilitudo in similitudine*, Balthasar thus understands the God-world relationship as a modality, and also as an analogy of the inner-Trinitarian relations. He feels justified in this context to speak of an analogous suffering in God, of a "supra-suffering" which is in a certain way like but also very much unlike the human suffering.

The awareness that God is transcendent and at the same time immanent in the world obliges theology to think of His being as a paradox. A God, who is merely passible cannot be said to be transcendent, just as a God, who is *absolutely* impassible can hardly be proved totally immanent. Hence the importance of maintaining the dialectical tension between the divine immanence and transcendence, a fact that some theologians have been justifiably emphasising.[217] For being able to incorporate the positive aspects of dialectics and dialogism in analogy of being as love,[218] Balthasar's modified notion of analogy, has an advantage over a univocation or an equivocation model in expressing the tension between the one and the many (differentiation), between transcendence and immanence, between nearness and distance, between freedom and necessity, between mutability and immutability, between possibility and impassibility in God. In this sense, his theology of divine suffering offers a working model, a hypothesis for an acceptable theology of divine impassibility; and it is above all able to institute a dialogue between tradition and modern theology.

But despite the many useful insights that could be gained for our topic from Balthasar's analogy and ontology of love, and despite the fact that he provides us with a way of speaking about God that leaves ample room for His transcendence and immanence, his solution is full of imprecision.[219] This has not only to do with his non-thematic approach to the problem, which often makes him render an account of the view of the Fathers without saying his own, thus repeatedly leaving the reader in the dark as to what he actually means. It has more to do with his

---

216 At this point, the influence of Martin Buber on him is evident. For Balthasar, the analogia relationis applies to being itself, so that one could also see that as the basis of a relational ontology.

217 Cf. W. Kern, Philosophische Pneumatologie, p. 87; L. Oeing-Hanhoff, Die Krise des Gottesbegriffs, p. 300 f.; J. Macquarrie, *In Search of Deity*, pp. 171-184; F. Meessen, *Unveränderlichkeit*, p. 437 f.; T. R. Krenski, *Passio Caritatis*, p. 369.

218 Cf. *Theologik* II, pp. 98-113.

219 See also G. F. O'Hanlon, *The Immutability of God*, p. 171.

use of the scripture,[220] which does not seem always to take account of the standpoint of current exegesis. Moreover, his failure to discuss the views of modern thinkers elaborately, even where he disagrees with them, and his almost too cheap resort to the big "MYSTERY" add to this imprecision.

Any attempt to follow his foot steps must necessarily involve an elaborate comparison with other theologians. Such a comparison would show for instance how his view agrees with that of St. Thomas on certain issues about the axiom of impassibility, even though he does reject the view of the angelic Doctor.[221] The issue of perfection is certainly decisive for Balthasar, when it comes to determining whether impassibility or passibility is a worthy attribute for God. In effect, God can be seen as passible or impassible provided that such an attribution indicates the perfection of divine love. Similarly, for St. Thomas, mutability or immutability could be attributed to God, if only it is a sign of perfection.[222] Even impassibility is unworthy of God if it connotes imperfection. Consequently, Balthasar's main contribution has to do with the understanding of divine receptivity and affectivity (supra-suffering) as an aspect of the perfection of divine love, which he elaborates with the aid of an *Analogia Relationis*.

6.7   Summary

Without disregarding the significance of a philosophical inquiry, Balthasar is determined to make revelation the starting point of his reflection. He does this out of two basic convictions: firstly, that human reason can explore the logic of the divine revelation, and secondly, that the human logic, despite its limitations, is neither contradictory nor juxtaposed to the divine logic. An analogous relationship is believed to be obtained between the divine and the human modes of being. By implication, therefore, Balthasar finds the popular question of whether to begin theological reflections "from above" or "from below" irrelevant. He rather adopts what seems to be a circular (up and down) approach to the reality of God. This sort of approach makes neither reason nor faith its exclusive point of departure, but by combining both, seeks to discern the similarity and difference between the divine and the human realities.

---

[220] Unfortunately, we cannot go into the analysis of his use of the Bible, which would certainly add to a better assessment of his passiology.

[221] J. Saward, *The Mysteries*, p. 16. It seems however that J. Saward makes an erroneous citation here. The book on Thomas that inspired his point is not written by a certain Mr. M. Woods, it is rather written by Michael J. Dodds, O. P. Unless of course the same author bears both same names. See the next note below.

[222] Cf. M. J. Dodds, O. P., *The Unchanging God of Love*, pp. 215 ff, esp. p. 219.

In Jesus Christ, he finds the meeting-point of the divine self-disclosure and human inquiry. He argues that in the God-man personality of Jesus - which is characterised as a unity-in-different of natures - God displays the model of reality. The Christological unity-in-difference is for Balthasar a "Christological analogy of being". In a double sense, this is the measure of being: for not only does this principle of analogy correspond to the inner-Trinitarian relationship, it is also a model for the God-world relationship. Using this principle therefore Balthasar describes the inner-Trinitarian love as consisting of a unity-in-difference and the world as the copy of a reality whose original is in God. Creation is an out-flow of the divine love.

For Balthasar the kenosis is the most appropriate theological motif with which we can represent the Trinitarian love in its constitutive form of unity-in-difference. Kenosis is thus the single act that describes the ontology of love and the Trinitarian events, in their immanent and economic dimensions. In this connection, Balthasar speaks of a primordial kenosis - a primordial selflessness - in the immanent Trinity, through which the Persons are united and differentiated at the same time. The relationship between the immanent and economic Trinity is also seen in the light of this principle of unity-in-difference. So that, while the immanent Trinitarian events could be said to find their continuation in the economic Trinity - in the creation, covenant and Incarnation - a certain discontinuity between them must be conceived. Unlike Hegel and Moltmann, therefore, he sees the unity of God fulfilled and realised in the immanent Trinity, prior to the world processes.

God is therefore free from and independent of the world, at least for the fact that His relationship to the world is that of similarity and difference, of continuity and discontinuity. For this reason, God cannot have the same destiny as the world, though by virtue of His kenotic love, He is receptive of the events of the world. Balthasar discusses the divine receptivity in the same connection with the divine omnipotence, which, as he contends, is the omnipotence of love. Conditioned by His love and commitment to the covenant, God declines to exercise His absolute power, and thus allows the Cross to affect Him. In the light of the divine receptivity, Balthasar rejects the views (Moltmann, Luther) which tend to explain the Cross as a contradiction.

For him the Cross is neither a contradiction nor an illogicality. It is a Trinitarian logic, a Trinitarian mystery, the mystery of God's ways of conquering the only contradiction - sin. In the same light, instead of understanding the God-forsakenness of Jesus on the Cross as a divine intrigue, he sees it as God's way of letting the Son descend into hell - God-forsakenness - so as to also conquer this last of all contradictions. Besides, the God-forsakenness demonstrates also the paradox of that nearness and distance which characterises the divine kenotic self-differentiation and love.

As much as Balthasar emphasises the divine receptivity, little does he speak directly of suffering in God. However, given this receptivity in God, it would be wrong to assume, he contends, that the affirmation of divine suffering is merely metaphorical; in God we find the ontological presupposition of suffering and pain in the form of receptivity. For this reason Balthasar prefers to speak of an analogous suffering in God, thereby insisting that God has emotions analogous to human emotions. Divine suffering is a "supra suffering", which is like but very much unlike the human suffering.

Significant about Balthasar's passiology is its setting in a Trinitarian framework and most importantly his application of analogy to the understanding of the Trinitarian suffering. In this way, he could avoid the pitfalls of Moltmann's Trinitarian theology of the Cross, which mainly makes God divided in Himself and dependent on the world. The use of Christological analogy, therefore makes it possible for the paradox of the passibility and impassibility of the triune God to be affirmed. However, despite the merits of Balthasar's analogical theology of the divine suffering, his approach is full of imprecision, especially with regard to the evaluation of other theological contributions and his negligence of modern exegesis.

SECTION THREE:

THE (IM)PASSIBILITY OF GOD IN THE LIBERATION THE-
OLOGIES OF THE OPPRESSED AND THE THIRD WORLD

... Chapters Seven, Eight and Nine ...

7.   DIVINE SUFFERING IN THE LATIN AMERICAN LIBERATION THEOLOGY

7.1   The Background of the Liberation Theology in Latin America

The Latin American liberation theology can only be understood from the perspective of the social and historical context of the poor people in Latin America.[1] The yearning of the oppressed peasant majority for liberation out of the injustice perpetrated on them by the rich minority in their midst gave rise to this theology. Perceiving clearly that the cause of their immeasurable suffering is not destiny, but human injustice - engraved in an unjust structure and marginalisation - they became inclined to the belief and hope that their liberation would be effected by God. Despite the hopelessness of their situation and the apparent indifference of their God to the societal status quo, their faith in God as a liberator remains unruffled, especially as they learn to perceive a similarity between their situation and that of the suffering people of God in the Old Testament period, whom God liberated from oppression in the land of Egypt.

This amounts to a rediscovery of the liberating dimension of the biblical God, and to a belief in a God who opts for the poor and the oppressed. It is noteworthy that the poor did not arrive at this conviction so much through reflection as through experience. To a large extent, this experience remained unarticulated, until two conferences of the Latin American bishops in Medelin (1968) and in Puebla (1979) encouraged theologians to make further theological reflections based on this religious conviction of the poor. Thus, what might be called the academic theology of liberation began after these conferences.

As a matter of fact, it is precisely the oppressed peasant's experience of God, and the close identification of their situation with that of the Old Israelites that inspires both the spirituality and theology of liberation. Their unarticulated experience and belief have been aptly described as the "first act" while the decisions of the various Latin American bishop's conferences as well as the reflections of the individual theologians are termed the "second act" in the overall development of the theology of liberation in Latin America.[2] In this light, the liberation theology appears more as a documentation and articulation of the people's experience of God in a state of suffering than as a corpus of solid theological and philosophical systems. It is as such rightly referred to as the product of a "co-operative endeav-

---

1   For the historical development of this theology see G. Gutiérrez, *A Theology of Liberation.*

2   G. Gutiérrez, *On Job*, p. xiii.

our",[3] of theologians and the poor. It is not an academic enterprise of any individual theologian, but a community theology, done and sustained in a continuous dialogue between theologians and the poor.[4]

This fact is believed to preclude any danger of abstract thinking sponsored by any particular ideology. However, due to the emphasis liberation theologians place on the social and political context of the poor, they have often been accused of being Marxist in orientation. Though they cherish Marx' philosophical appeal for the transformation rather than interpretation of the society, and some aspects of his social analysis, most liberation theologians, with few exceptions,[5] strictly deny the adoption of Marxist ideologies.

In any case, liberation theology does not purport to be introducing new doctrines to replace the old. It is, as Gutiérrez says, "simultaneously traditional and new".[6] Reflecting on the old themes in a new way, it sees the contextualisation of theology as its main objective. This consists in making theology become sensitive to concrete human problems to an extent that it can liberate people from oppression and also transform those structures of the world which breed evil and injustice. In other words, it marks the way, but does not determine the content of theology. This explains why the academic liberation theology pays more attention to the methodology and preconditions of doing theology than to single dogmatic themes. Before we then proceed to consider the concept of God and divine suffering in liberation theology, we need to sketch the many hermeneutic principles,[7] which form the basic structures of this theological understanding.

7.2   The Hermeneutic Principles of Liberation Theology

Basically, liberation theology seeks to redefine the starting point and the epistemology of theological understanding. For the purpose of accomplishing this task, it identifies and employs the following six major groups of principles: the

---

3   A. Rossa (Editor), *The Theology of Liberation*, p. 4.

4   In view of the communal and co-operative nature of this theology, we shall adopt an integrative method in this chapter. The views of three celebrated liberation theologians, Gustavo Gutiérrez, Leonardo Boff and Jon Sobrino on the issue of God and divine suffering should all be considered at the same time. However, the purpose of this method is not to compare the authors, but to allow them to supplement one another in a non-repetitive manner.

5   Cf. J. P. Miranda, *Marx and the Bible*.

6   G. Gutiérrez, *A Theology of Liberation*, p. xiv.

7   See J. Sobrino, *The True Church and the Poor*, and ---, *Christology at the Crossroads*, chapters 1 & 2.

principles relating to historicity, relationality, hope, dialectics, praxis and poverty. These principles are considered to be indispensable for an effective interpretation of the phenomenon of faith. As presuppositions and requirements of faith, they could be rightly termed the hermeneutics of liberation theology. Even though they seem to embrace many aspects of non-theological epistemology, they are not endlessly universal in relevance.[8] Each of them is a pure hermeneutics of faith eminently presupposed in the biblical revelation.

Faith, as understood in liberation theology, is not chiefly "believing in a message, but believing in someone".[9] By implication, therefore, the relationship between the believer and the person of Christ first receives attention, followed by the interpretation of texts and articles of faith. For Leonardo Boff, it means that one should first seek to define one's life and religious situation before trying to objectify the truth of faith.[10] In this sense, faith becomes a "precomprehension" and not a preconception. The difference between the two is that while the latter tends to overlook the situation of the believer, the former establishes an existential relationship between the believer and the person of Christ.[11] This does not of course entail an excessive emphasis on the subjectivity of the believer or interpreter, as is the case with Bultmann.[12] All that is sought for is the assertion of the authenticity of every religious experience and the justification of the believers to "reread" the Bible from the point of view of Latin America's poor and oppressed.[13] In effect, the liberation hermeneutics makes room for a pluralistic interpretation of the biblical texts, and keeps the door open for non-religious inter-

---

[8] C. Boff, *Theologie und Praxis*, pp. 222-223.

[9] G. Gutiérrez, *The Power of the Poor in History*, p. 209.

[10] L. Boff, *Jesus Christ Liberator*, p. 47. In his view, "we ought to speak of Jesus Christ, not with a view to defining him but rather ourselves, not the mystery but our position when confronted with the mystery".

[11] *Ibid.*, p. 38: "Comprehension...like the word *com-prendre*, suggests a knowledge that is *com* (with) a subject and that shackles itself to that subject. In order to comprehend a person, there must be some vital relationship with that person. If not, then we objectify the person and make the person an object of science."

[12] The hermeneutics discussed here is believed to occupy the middle position between a positivistic and an existential hermeneutics. Cf. J. Sobrino, *Christology at the Crossroads*, pp. 249-250. Marxen's practical hermeneutics, which reduces the reality of the Jesus-event, especially that of resurrection, to the bare fact of the disciple's personal faith and witness, is also disqualified. Marxen's, like Bultmann's subjectivity trivialises the significance of history. (See *ibid.*, pp. 237-238).

[13] G. Gutiérrez, *The Power of the Poor in History*, p. 18. This is corollary to the call to read history from the point of view of the "Underside of History". Cf. *ibid.*, p. 21.

pretations, which, according to Boff, could "enrich our comprehension of God's revelation in the world".[14]

For a better understanding of their concept of God, let us now sketch the basic facts about the six outstanding hermeneutic principles in the Latin American liberation theology.

7.2.1   The Principles of Historicity

Liberation theology has the basic assumption that theological understanding is essentially historical. This fact is reflected in two of their theological claims: firstly, that history is the locus of divine revelation, and secondly, that the historical Jesus is the authentic starting point of every theological inquiry. Both claims are usually made in the conviction, not only that God reveals Himself in His actions in the world, but also that the revelation of God is ongoing in the history of the world. So that, in order to interpret His actions correctly, we need to interpret them historically.[15]

7.2.1.1   History as the Horizon of Divine Revelation

Since the interest in critical reason and historical studies was awakened in the Enlightenment of the eighteenth and nineteenth centuries, the significance of historicity in the issue of theological understanding has become obvious. In the contemporary time, the historical critical method, Bultmann's existential interpretation and Pannenberg's universal conception of history have immensely popularised the use of historical studies in theology. Liberation theologians give credit to them all, but they are quick to point out the weak points of these studies.

The historical critical method is criticised, firstly, because it tends to treat the Gospel as a biography of Jesus, instead of seeing it as accounts of "witness of faith" arising out of earlier theological interpretation,[16] secondly, because it objectifies historical issues, thereby ignoring the place of faith in a theological interpretation and replacing God with humankind as the "carrier" of history,[17] and thirdly, because its positivistic conception of history lacks an eschatological dimension. Without an eschatological vision, it can neither perceive the dialectical relation between the past and the future, and between the positive and negative

---

14   L. Boff, *Jesus Christ Liberator*, p. 42.

15   *Ibid.*, pp. 128,133; J. Sobrino, *Christology at the Crossroads*, p. 246 ff.

16   L. Boff, *Jesus Christ Liberator*, p. 3.

17   Cf. J. Sobrino, *Christology at the Crossroads*, pp. 247-9.

sides of history nor recognise the divine action in history.[18] The universal and the existential interpretations are also criticised for misrepresenting the stages of history. Bultmann's existential interpretation, which interprets the past and the future solely from the perspective of the present, is accused of making the status quo (this "unredeemed world") the measure of the future. According to such views, the future does not bring any change, because it is already defined and determined.[19] Similarly, Pannenberg's universal approach also rejected for various reasons as Sobrino contends: firstly, it sees the future already determined, secondly, it interprets history solely from the positive side (resurrection), thirdly, it ignores "the *negative* side of history", and fourthly, it fails, for that reason, to incorporate a dialectical knowledge of history.[20]

In contrast to all these three conceptions of history, liberation theology conceives history as a process whose full reality can only be perceived dialectically and eschatologically. History can only be understood in terms of the future, and not future as a mere addition to an incomplete present, but future as a promise, opposed to the present and past experiences,[21] as a promise God made in the past and whose fulfilment is dependent on the transformation of the present through our mission. There is the "negative side of history" in the present - oppression and misery - which must be overcome so that a radically new future can be ushered in.

This transformation of the present, which makes the future of history possible, and lets the plan of God come to fulfilment, occurs through the conjoint actions of God and humankind. Humankind is not the carrier of history, but it is actively involved in the process that leads to its fulfilment. In this sense, tension, but not division, is perceived between the history of the world and the history of salvation; there is a dialectical relationship between the objective and subjective components of history.[22] Leonardo Boff characterises it as that persistent "dialectic

---

18 *Ibid.*, pp. 249, 251.

19 *Ibid.*, pp. 249, 250.

20 *Ibid.*, p. 251. For liberation theology, the future is essentially open. "It is only through the concrete overcoming of some concrete negative aspect that history is opened up further, though we cannot decide in advance what the full result of such opening up might be. History cannot be comprehended as a whole so long as suffering, misery, and injustice exist."

21 At this point, Sobrino leans very much on Moltmann. Cf. J. Sobrino, *Christology at the Crossroads*, p. 251.

22 There is a general inclination among the liberation theologians to conceive history in biblical terms as salvation-history. The Bible, as L. Boff sees it, interprets history in terms of God's promise, a promise (*pro-missio*) that always evokes a mission (*missio*). Cf. L. Boff,

between the salvific proposal of God and the human response, between the concreteness of reality and the transcendence of human liberty."[23] Every historical model must uphold and mediate rather than resolve the tension between God's proposal and human response, for it is precisely this proposal-response dialectic that continually defines the future anew. Similarly, Gutiérrez talks of a certain dialectic of memory and liberty in the faith of the Israelites. According to him, the memory of their past liberation by God has always evoked a sense of "freedom: openness to the future" for the Israelites. It was this same dialectic of memory and freedom, of past and future that provided the framework within which the revelation of God in Christ was to be understood.[24]

7.2.1.2   The Historical Jesus as the Starting Point of Theological Inquiry

The implication of conceiving history as open, is that "we can never grasp the totality of reality as such" except of course God reveals it to us.[25] This is what has occurred in Jesus Christ. In him, God has revealed Himself and reality, and he is for that reason the principle of interpreting history and reality, the perfect meeting point of God and man. In Jesus Christ, God opens the window to Himself, giving us a foretaste of the end of history in a most radical way and thus completing in him, as   Gutiérrez says, "the basic circle of all hermeneutics", which runs "from human being to God and from God to the human being".[26]

Although the revelation of God in history has been consistent, the reality of Jesus has brought it to its climax even before the end of history. And as L. Boff writes:

> In Jesus Christ there occurred a qualitative jump within the history of salvation: For the first time, divine proposal and human response, word and reality, promises and realisation, arrived at a perfect accommodation. In him, therefore, salvation was given in an absolute and eschatological form. In him the dynamism and latent possibilities of all creation became concrete and achieved full clarification. In him we catch a glimpse of the future of the world and the radical meaning of the human person and the cosmos. In this way Christ is constituted as the meeting point of religious hermeneutics, of the history of the world and human beings.[27]

Jesus Christ Liberator, p. 262 and J. Sobrino, *Christology at the Crossroads*, p. 253: "Grasping a historical fact or event means realising the mission that it sets in motion".

23   L. Boff, *Jesus Christ Liberator*, pp. 41-2. See also J. Sobrino, *Christology at the Crossroads*, p. 275.

24   G. Gutiérrez, *The Power of the Poor in History*, p. 12.

25   L. Boff, *Jesus Christ Liberator*, p. 42.

26   G. Gutiérrez, *The Power of the Poor in History*, p.15.

27   L. Boff, *Jesus Christ Liberator*, pp. 42-3.

In the light of such thoughts as these, liberation theologians, without failing to recognise the significance of the Christ of faith, see the historical Jesus as the legitimate theological point of departure.[28] This, according to them, is the only way of taking care of the concrete life-situation of Jesus and the believer, so as not to overlook the specific revelation of God in the history of Jesus.[29] For, if the historical Jesus is the "way" to the Father, as St. John narrates,[30] there can be no prior conception of Christ more authentic than the one revealed in his historical life, no matter how sketchy it appears in the Gospels.

A Christology "from below" is for this reason considered inadequate even for the interpretation of the doctrine of incarnation. Interpreting the incarnation from the perspective of the pre-existent Christ is a kind of fallacy of begging the question (*petitio principii*), for by that means theology makes its conclusions its starting point.[31] Granted, the affirmation that the Son of God *became* man is the central truth of the incarnation, it would be presumptuous to think that we can understand that affirmation without first ascertaining the true "natures" of God

---

28 L. Boff, *Jesus Christ Liberator*, p. 10 ff.; J. Sobrino, *Christology at the Crossroads*, Chapters 1 & 9. Sobrino makes it abundantly clear that making the historical Jesus their point of departure entails going out from the *totality* of Jesus' life - including all his positive and negative life experience. The tendency to atomise the life of Jesus, in the sense of singling out either the aspect of his titles or the Kerygma (M. Kähler) etc. would not do. The historical Jesus signifies the totality of Jesus' life. Cf. J. Sobrino, *Christology at the Crossroads*, pp 5-9.

29 J. Sobrino, *Christology at the Crossroads*, Chapters 1 & 11; L. Boff, *Jesus Christ Liberator*, Chapter 2. For both authors, our starting point must be such that the earthly life of Jesus, the history of the dogmas and the peculiar historical situation of the interpreter or theologian are adequately taken note of.

30 J. Sobrino, *Christology at the Crossroads*, pp. 271, 338.

31 As L. Boff puts it: "...the Incarnation should not be one's starting point, but one's destination". See L. Boff, *Jesus Christ Liberator*, p. 188. In making this point, Boff especially attributes the failure of the Nestorian and monophysite Christologies to the fact that they made Incarnation their point of departure, and thought in terms of a static ontology rather than in terms of the historical features of God's revelation in the man Jesus. Similarly, J. Sobrino maintains that "... the Incarnation cannot serve as the *starting point* for theological reflection on Jesus; both logically and chronologically it is the *culmination* of such reflection". See J. Sobrino, *Christology at the Crossroads*, p. 268. In another connection, Sobrino follows D. Wiederkehr to refer to dogmatic definitions as "limit-concepts", i.e. concepts brought in to limit Christological speculations. Such formulations are not proportional to the whole content of faith, they naturally say less than the Scriptures, they presuppose earlier reflections, and cannot as such constitute the starting point.

and man respectively.[32] According to liberation theology, the true concept of God and man which we need in order to understand the meaning of the incarnation can only be learnt by examining the concrete life of the historical Jesus. Any reflection on the unity of the divine and human nature in Jesus Christ that fails to be informed about the historical life of Jesus himself nurtures abstract and ideological images of Jesus Christ.[33] It is for these reasons, that the liberation theology declines to make the Chalcedonian formula the starting point of Christology.[34]

It is indeed believed that a historical approach to Christology would aid the conception of God and man from the point of view of Jesus' own faith and hope, which in effect emerged out of the vicissitudes of his life.[35] Thus, differentiating the historical approach of the liberation theologians from the classical dogmatic approach, Boff writes:

> We will try the inverse route: we will attempt to understand the human being and God with Jesus himself as our starting point. Humanity in its greatest radicality was revealed in Jesus and this also revealed the human God. Hence it is not by means of an abstract analysis of humanity and divinity that one can clarify the mystery of Je-

---

[32] "We may use 'divinity' and 'humanity' as nominal definitions to somehow break the hermeneutic circle, but we cannot use them as real definitions." See J. Sobrino, *Christology at the Crossroads*, p. 82.

[33] Such reflections naturally mistake natural theology and philosophical anthropology for Christian theology and end up making "Christian faith take on a religious structure in the pejorative sense" (Barth and Bonhoeffer). See J. Sobrino, *Christology at the Crossroads*, pp. 277, 305.

[34] J. Sobrino, *Christology at the Crossroads*, pp. 3-5. The truth of the *intention* of Chalcedon - to affirm that the Jesus Christ is "true God and true man" - is not disputed. Boff is even accused of being too uncritical of that formula. See J. Macquarrie, *Jesus Christ in Modern Thought*, p. 317. What liberation theology claims is that theology should first seek to understand the concepts of "man" and "God" in the light of the historical Jesus, before coming to the Chalcedonian affirmation. Besides, the categories of "person", "nature", "hypostatic union" as they were used in the fifth century should first be "reread" in today's language, so that we can grasp its meaning (L. Boff, *op. cit.* p. 194). For Sobrino, this means using categories that have concreteness, historicity and relationality. Cf. J. Sobrino, *op. cit.* pp. 328-335.

[35] Another reason for the adoption of the historical Jesus as the starting point of theological reflection in liberation theology seems to be the perceivable similarity between the situation of oppression during the time Jesus grew up in and the current situation of oppression in Latin American society. Cf. J. Sobrino, *Christology*, pp 9-14; H. Assmann, *Theology for a Nomad Church*, p. 103; L. Boff, *Jesus Christ Liberator*, Chap. 1 and Epilogue, esp. pp. 279 - 280; I. Ellacuria, *Freedom Made Flesh*, chap. 1, 15 - 26.

sus of Nazareth, who so fascinated the apostles that they called him God. Anthropology ought to be elaborated with Christology as its point of departure.[36]

7.2.2   The Principle of Relationality

After closely observing the life style of the historical Jesus - his life of faith, his intimacy with the Father, his dedication to the service of God's kingdom - liberation theology affirms that the personality of Jesus is "essentially relational, not absolute in itself".[37] Jesus never expressed himself in isolation, but always in relationship with his Father and in connection with his "being" for the kingdom of God. Consequently, it is his being-for-the-Other, "his *relationship* to the Father that constitutes the essence of his person".[38]

According to Sobrino, who makes the most use of this principle, the importance of the category of relationship is most evident in Jesus' own mode of preaching. Jesus, he contends, proclaimed God in terms of his relationship all the time: he "did not preach about himself, or even simply about God, but rather about the kingdom of God",[39] that is to say, about God's activity and involvement in the world. Jesus thought of himself ultimately in relation to his Father.[40] According to Sobrino, no clue to Jesus' self-awareness is given in the New Testament.

> All we can get at is his *relational* self-awareness: i.e., what he thought about himself in relation to the kingdom, and the decisive importance of his own person in its arrival.[41]

This means by implication that we must seek to understand God from Jesus' own conception of God, and not through any sort of preconceptions. Sobrino accordingly shows the significance of the principle of relationality for theological

---

36   L. Boff, *Jesus Christ Liberator*, p. 195.

37   J. Sobrino, *Christology at the Crossroads*, p. 50. This fact further proves the historicity of Christology, because, strictly speaking, relationality can only be expressed in the context of history. Cf. p. xxii.

38   *Ibid.*, p. 104.

39   *Ibid.*, pp. 41-45, 60-61. "Formally speaking, his relational nature is seen in the fact that he himself is not the central focus of his preaching or his activity. The central focus is the coming kingdom of God, Jesus' unreserved confidence in the Father, and his work for the realisation of the kingdom." See *ibid.*, p. xxii.

40   *Ibid.*, pp. 67 & 72. Liberation theology denies that Jesus could have had any apriori knowledge of his divinity, and claims that his self-awareness grew in history.

41   *Ibid.*, p. 70.

understanding while discussing Jesus' faith and prayer-life,[42] which in his view provide the most reliable source of information about Jesus' notion of God.[43] In contrast to Thomas Aquinas, who vehemently argues that Jesus could not have had faith (ST. iii, q. 7, a 3), Sobrino sees in Jesus' faith a paradigm for an authentic conception of God. For Sobrino, faith primarily connotes relationship and not ignorance. Besides, Jesus ignorance of the day of Yahweh, for instance, "is not an imperfection at all", but rather "the historical condition that makes real his trusting surrender to the Father and his solidarity with humankind".[44] In other words, the ignorance of the historical Jesus is kenotic, it is an expression of a noncompetitive relationship with the Father, the willingness to "let the Father be the Father - i.e., the absolute mystery of history".[45]

According to this view, the human attributes of Jesus are not at variance with his divinity; it is precisely his exemplary humanity that demonstrates his divinity. In fact, what is most human in Jesus - his relationships, the fact that he lived his faith "in all its pristine fullness" till the end - confirm his participation in the divinity.[46] Again, in line with Boff, and in the light of the above view, Sobrino pro-

---

42 He observes that though H. U. v. Balthasar and W. Thüsing had earlier called attention to the significance of Jesus' faith for Christology, they only saw the relational faith of Jesus in the Father, but not his faith in the realisation of the kingdom of God. The contribution of liberation theology is seen here in the fact, that it calls attention to the relational aspect of Jesus faith in the arrival of the kingdom of God. See *ibid.*, pp. 85-87.

43 See J. Sobrino, *Christology at the Crossroads*, Chapter 4. Jesus inherited the faith of the Jewish orthodoxy, but faced with the hazards of temptation and ignorance of the future, and of abandonment on the Cross, he had to adjust his faith, and change his notion of God. He always retained his confidence in the Father. "Viewed theologically, Jesus' life is the shift from his initial faith to his final, definitive faith." (*Ibid.*, p. 103) In that sense, he demonstrated that "faith does not signify possession of God and his kingdom but rather an ongoing search for them".(*Ibid.*, p. 95).

44 To buttress his point, Sobrino cites the following passage from Pannenberg. "The limitation on Jesus' knowledge, even where his own relationship to God is concerned...belongs rather to the perfect completion and fulfilment of his personal surrender to God's future." See *Ibid.*, p. 102.

45 *Ibid.* It is surprising that Sobrino does not make any direct reference to the theory of kenosis in this connection. But it is implicit in the view that Jesus lets God be God - that means that he lived a life of conscious self-limitation and of a kenotic relation to the Father.

46 L. Boff, *Jesus Christ Liberator*, Chapter 10; J. Sobrino, *Christology at the Crossroads*, pp. 105-107. Sobrino makes it clear (p. 81) "that divinity and faith do not rule each other out at all. Indeed it is the faith of Jesus that provides us the key to understanding what constitutes his divinity in the concrete." In fact, ""The divinity of Jesus consists in his concrete relationship to the Father. This unique, peculiar, and unrepeatable way of being in

poses "a relational conception of Christ's divinity", and attempts to "reformulate in relational categories what Chalcedon affirmed in ontic categories".[47] Both theologians see this point testified to by the abundance of relational categories in the Bible and by the current departure of modern thought from substance ontology to relational ontology. Both authors illustrate the second point with the modern concept of person, which traces its origin back to the views of St. Augustine and Richard of St. Victor.

The essence of personhood, they contend, does not consist in "self-possession" but in "self-surrender", in "self-openness" and in "relationality".[48] So, while for the Fathers the terms "nature" and "person" signified substance-ontological realities, for modern thought and for the liberation theologians, these terms are essentially dynamic concepts, indicating that human nature and person presuppose a long process of evolutionary (biological, environmental, cultural and educational) development. If personhood in the biblical and social thoughts are today expressed in relational terms, Christology, in Sobrino's view, must seek access to the nature of Christ using relational and not ontic categories.[49] Relationality is the hermeneutic locale for understanding his divine and human nature, and for understanding being in general.

7.2.3 . The Principles of Hope and Eschatology

Since Albert Schweitzer's important study on the historical Jesus,[50] the close connection between the principle of historicity and the principle of eschatology have become obvious. And, thanks to exegetical studies, it is also evident today that both the Old Testament account of the salvation-history and Jesus proclamation of the kingdom of God (*parousia*) can best be understood in the context of

---

relationship with the Father is what constitutes his concrete way of participating in divinity." (105)

47 J. Sobrino, *Christology at the Crossroads*, Chapters 3, 4 & 5, especially pp. 60, 73 & 105-106. "Instead of using ontic categories, we here choose to use relational ones. They include the *personal* category of a person's submission to God and the practical category of obedience to a mission." (p. 106). See also L. Boff, *Jesus Christ Liberator*, pp. 191-192.

48 J. Sobrino, *Christology at the Crossroads*, p. 73.

49 In what seems to be an implicit kenotic conception of personhood, J. Sobrino summarises the point in question as follows: "In the New Testament it is the relationship of Jesus to the Father in trust and obedience that typifies his person. It is also far more in accord with the present-day conception of the person insofar as its use for systematic theology is concerned. For today we see "person" more in terms of surrender or dedication to another." See J. Sobrino, *Christology at the Crossroads*, p. 74.

50 Cf. A. Schweitzer, *The Quest of the historical Jesus*.

the eschatological expectation which they embody. God's promise and covenant, as Sobrino observes himself, had always evoked expectation and "hope in the future of history".[51]

For the liberation theology, this principle is much more significant because it helps to illuminate the different interpretations of history. Sobrino and Boff, for instance, interpret resurrection in terms of the eschatology, that is in terms of the hope it raises, but their conceptions of hope vary.[52] While Boff indefatigably points to the anthropological dimension of hope, Sobrino would go beyond that to emphasise its theological significance, making the realisation of hope dependent on the victory over the negative side of history. Boff sees the resurrection of Jesus Christ, for instance, as an event signifying "a total realisation of the capacities God placed within existence": what used to be *utopia* (seemingly impossible) has become *topia* (seemingly possible), so much, that in effect, human hope "is already being realised in each person"[53] since after the resurrection. While agreeing with Boff that the resurrection of Jesus Christ offers a justification for our hope, Sobrino rejects Boff's view that this hope is already being realised in this world. Christian hope as Sobrino sees it, is a "qualified hope": it has its justification from the resurrection of Jesus, but it remains unrealised insofar as the negative side of history still persists; it is "hoping against hope".[54]

For Sobrino, Christian hope presupposes the apocalypticism of the scriptural literature. That implies that the current Christian hope is to be understood in the light of the earlier apocalypticism. The Old Testament apocalypticism, as Sobrino sees it, was not merely looking forward to the end of history, but specifically to the "vindication of God's justice" at the end of history.[55] Christian hope must necessarily be interpreted in this line, as the hope for the triumph of God's justice. In fact, there is a continuity between apocalypticism and Christian hope in that

---

51 J. Sobrino, *Christology at the Crossroads*, p. 242.

52 *Ibid.*, pp. 236-271, esp. pp. 241-246. See also L. Boff, *Jesus Christ Liberator*, Chapter 7. There seems to be a consensus among the liberation theologians that the resurrection opens up a hopeful future for humankind. In the resurrection, God allows us to perceive what the future of humankind would look like. This is however nothing more than a faint idea of the future of humanity. Following the view of the New Testament evangelists, Sobrino explicitly states that the resurrection "is an eschatological event in which the final reality of history makes its appearance in the midst of history - whatever that final reality may be understood to be". *Ibid.* p. 236.

53 L. Boff, *Jesus Christ Liberator*, p. 135.

54 J. Sobrino, *Christology at the Crossroads*, p. 244. Sobrino seems to have adopted the notion of "hope against hope" from Moltmann.

55 *Ibid.*, p. 243.

both are concerned with the justice of God. Thus for Sobrino the ultimate significance of the event of resurrection is God Himself and the triumph of His justice.[56] Christian hope is a hope for justice, and it obliges Christians to seek justice themselves. If so, it calls for praxis.[57] Only when we have pulled down the structures of the evil of oppression and injustice in this world through a liberative praxis, can we talk of a realised hope. Till then it is "hope against hope".[58]

No matter what the different conceptions of hope in the liberation theology may be, there is a common belief in the significance of eschatology, not only in the interpretation of the Christ-event but also in giving meaning to the future of the oppressed people.

7.2.4   The Principle of Dialectics

Given the negativity of the event of the Cross, and the peculiar situation of oppression and injustice in which most of the believers find themselves, liberation theology sees dialectical thinking as an indispensable route to understanding God and reality. Moreover, for liberation theology, dialectical thinking seems to provide the most suitable means for making faith in eschatology assume the form of a concrete hope for the change of an oppressive situation of the wretched of the earth. It should therefore be expected that,

> In a continent where beauty, love, reconciliation, and justice are in short supply and the plight of the masses is catastrophic, theological discourse is much more dialectical than analogical, more practical than analytical. Wretched conditions and a situation of sin and oppression prove paradoxically to be the locus of encounter with God. God must then be thought of ... as the contradiction of the wretched conditions of real life.[59]

The liberation theologians trace the root of dialectical thinking back to the scripture, especially to the apocalyptic and eschatological expectations. The eschatological dimension of the person and message of Jesus Christ, Sobrino observes, has not only shown the "element of *kairos* and the future, but also of an-

---

56   *Ibid.*, p. 240.

57   *Ibid.*, p. 253.

58   Sobrino and Gutiérrez see praxis as the natural implication of a theology of hope. Sobrino talks of "praxis as a hermeneutic principle for understanding the resurrection" (*Ibid.*, p. 253). For him, the ultimate hermeneutic for understanding the resurrection is "apostolate itself ... the determined effort to carry on the hope that appeared in Jesus' resurrection that the very same hope becomes comprehensible to us" (*Ibid.*, p. 254). Gutiérrez on his part, claims that " the rediscovery of the eschatological dimension in theology has also led us to consider the central role of historical praxis". Cf. G. Gutiérrez, *A Theology of Liberation*, p. 8.

59   J. Sobrino, *The True Church and the Poor*, p. 27.

other essential element: *krisis* (crisis, judgement)."[60] The way from the present world to the reign of God does not always run in a lineal manner, neither does it follow the laws of logical thinking. God as the ultimate reality is not readily accessible to natural human existence. Consequently, the ways of the world cannot also conform to the way to God.

Theology must therefore embark on an "epistemological break", after the example of the scripture, which not only makes theological understanding *distinct* from natural understanding, but also affirms "the transcendence of a crucified God" as "*contrary* to natural understanding".[61] For liberation theology the "epistemological break" must mean not just "*going beyond*, but *going against* natural knowledge; it must be a total break that incorporates the elements of crisis. Sobrino accuses the European theology of rarely recognising this fact.[62] This is the point at which European theological method differs from the Latin American liberation hermeneutics: Whereas the former conceives the epistemological break by way of reflection, the latter affirms it out of experience.[63] This is to be expected, Sobrino insists, because, whereas for the European (Greek) thought it is a certain sense of "wonder" or "admiration" that stimulates reflection on God, for the liberation theology, it is suffering, the cry of the oppressed that motivates the knowledge of God, who is known to be engaged in the act of liberation.

> In Latin America, the suffering of the present, no wonder, plays the active role in the process of understanding. ...this suffering provides the authentic analogy for understanding God: the recognition that the present history of the world is the ongoing history of the suffering God.

From this perspective the epistemological break entails a practical dialectics, a change of heart (*metanoia*),[64] that has practical implication for theodicy. Theodicy would then turn to be anthropodicy. It would turn from the theoretical question of how to justify God to the practical question of how the human being is to be justified before God. For, if God justifies Himself by entering history to recre-

---

60 *Ibid.*, p. 26.

61 *Ibid.*, p. 24 ff.

62 Sobrino argues that whereas the Catholic tradition had always overlooked this aspect of crisis, and thus hardly arrived at conceiving dialectics as a complete contrast of natural thought pattern, the Protestant theology apparently shows more readiness to incorporate the elements of crisis in its theological understanding. Barth, Bultmann, Bonhoeffer and Moltmann are given as the theologians who have rightly observed Paul's thesis, that the break should be seen as a scandal and as a form of madness. CF J. Sobrino, *The True Church and the Poor*, pp. 25-28.

63 J. Sobrino, *The True Church and the Poor*, p. 27.

64 *Ibid.*, p. 25.

ate humankind,[65] as the Bible suggests, it all means then that humankind has to justify itself in the face of evil by getting involved in the praxis of liberation. Epistemological break, in the sense in which liberation theology uses it, is, strictly speaking, an epistemology of praxis. This means that God can only be known in a liberating action. G. Gutiérrez radicalises this point by saying that "to know God is to do justice".[66] Thus rather than making the "death of God" an issue as does the Western theology, liberation theology prefers to consider the death of the oppressed human beings as the crisis of meaning par excellence.[67]

In effect, therefore, liberation theology wants to approach the crisis of reality head-on, not in the sphere of thought, but in the world of experience. The dialectics takes place in the life of the oppressed and not merely in our thought. The concrete mediation of God of Jesus occurs in a life with the oppressed, not in mere reflective thought, but in emulation of God Himself, who readily immersed Himself in history in order to liberate human beings.[68]

> In the oppressed the Other is discovered dialectically and through a sharing of suffering ... The break therefore takes place not at the level of self-understanding or feeling but at the level of reality.[69]

According to Sobrino, theological knowledge first begins to grow at the point where an *aporia* (a quandary, a paradox) of two seemingly contradictory realities shows up.[70] The effort to solve them always leads to a new conception of God.[71] For liberation theology, aporia comes up at the point of the "powerlessness of love against injustice." It is at this point that epistemological break occurs i.e., the awareness that theological understanding has reached a dead-lock on speculative sphere, and that only practice can unlock this way.[72]

---

65 *Ibid.*, p. 30.

66 G. Gutiérrez, *The Power of the Poor in History*, pp. xii, 7 f. See also J. Sobrino, *The True Church and the Poor*, p. 55 f.

67 "If the death of God is the expression of a crisis of meaning, human death is the expression of a crisis in reality ... For this reason the epistemological break is formulated not so much on the basis of the death of God as on that of the death of the oppressed." See J. Sobrino, *The True Church and the Poor*, p. 32.

68 *Ibid.*, p. 30.

69 *Ibid.*, p. 33.

70 J. Sobrino, *Christology at the Crossroads*, p. 21 ff. Such theological aporia are many and varied: they include the problems of one and many, transcendence and immanence, subject and object etc. See J. Sobrino, *The True Church and the Poor*, p. 35.

71 J. Sobrino, *The True Church and the Poor*, p. 34

72 *Ibid.*, p. 35. Basically, the main criticism, liberation theology brings up against European theology is that the latter tries to resolve dualism in the world almost exclusively at the

7.2.5   The Principle of Praxis

There is an unanimous view in liberation theology that correct action, done after the mind of Christ, should precede correct thought about Jesus and his person. The primacy of orthopraxis over orthodoxy is a basic assumption.[73]

In emphasising the priority of practice,

> The intention, however, is not to deny the meaning of *orthodoxy*, understood as a proclamation of and reflection on statements considered to be true. Rather, the goal is to balance and even to reject the primacy and almost exclusiveness which doctrine has enjoyed in Christian life and above all to modify the emphasis, often obsessive, upon the attainment of an orthodoxy which is often nothing more than fidelity to an obsolete tradition or a debatable interpretation. In a more positive vein, the intention is to recognise the work and importance of concrete behaviour, of deeds of action, of praxis in the Christian life.[74]

Liberation theology acknowledges that the classical theology had also given attention to the issue of praxis, but it notes, however, that the issue of correct action had been placed on the periphery of theological reflection; it had at best been relegated to the area of spiritual and moral theologies.[75] In contrast, liberation theology wants the doctrines in the realm of systematic theology to be illumined by the principle of action, so that orthodoxy would become less abstract. Again, Sobrino tries to differentiate the European from the Latin American hermeneutics of theology: Whereas the European theology makes the "history of ideas" its basis for authentic theological interpretation, liberation theology sees "concrete action" as the basis of a legitimate theological interpretation of doctrines.[76]

---

level of thought. In contrast, liberation theology, at least as Sobrino sees it, prefers to overcome such theological dualism as "that of believing subject and history, of theory and practice" not at the level of thought, but in the real world, in praxis. Cf. *Ibid.*, p. 38.

[73]   L. Boff, *Jesus Christ Liberator*, p. 46. See also J. Sobrino, *Christology at the Crossroads*, p. 45; ---, *The True Church and the Poor*, pp. 21 ff.; G. Gutiérrez, *On Job*, p. xiii.

[74]   G. Gutiérrez, *A Theology of Liberation*. p. 8.

[75]   *Ibid.*, p. 6:   Even later, in this century, as *charity* was reinstated at "the centre of the Christian life", the shift from abstract theory to practice-borne theologies in the West took place in the area of spirituality and moral, but not in systematic theology.

[76]   J. Sobrino, *The True Church and the Poor*, pp. 23-24. "For example, an understanding of what the "divinity" of Christ means in the Chalcedonian formula requires one to know the historical development of an *idea* that began in the New Testament and that led to Chalcedon via the Apologists and the Fathers." That is the case within the European theology. In liberation theology the approach differs. "The confession of the "divinity" of Christ is not reached through an understanding of the history of ideas such as person, personal union, and divine nature. The truth stated generally by Chalcedon is clarified through concrete praxis."

242

In advancing this point the liberation theology sees itself inspired, not only by the historical Jesus, but also by the theories of action in modern philosophy. An appeal is made to the primacy of action using the philosophies of Maurice Blondel and Karl Marx. Blondel's philosophy of action is hailed, for instance, by G. Gutiérrez, mainly because it tries to work out the internal logic of action and does in fact root philosophical speculations on action.[77] Karl Marx's theory of praxis is most valued both for showing the primacy of action and additionally affirming that action must be transformational.[78] Transforming the world is another way of liberating the world. At this point, liberation theologians credit the liberation of the mind and the individual (at the level of explanation - *Aufklärung*) to the Enlightenment, but contend, that Marx effected a second stage of the Enlightenment as he made the transformation of the society the main issue.[79] Even as it makes a selective use of Marx's social, religious and political analysis, liberation theology denies being "Marxist". It does admit however making use of the hermeneutics of praxis from Marxist' thought.[80]

Although Marxist thought has relevance for political actions, the liberation theologians do not take Marx, but Jesus as the model of their political theology. The relationship between faith and action, between eschatology and politics is central, not that between philosophy and politics. Political actions are mainly actions in favour of justice in the society and directed against unjust and alienating social order. Such political actions are known to have been performed by Jesus himself, and they inevitably led to his death at the hands of the political authori-

---

[77] See G. Gutiérrez, *A Theology of Liberation.* p. 7. He makes reference to Maurice Blondel, *L' Action*, Paris 1893, and lists related literature on Blondel in note 30, p. 180.

[78] This view is best summarised in the following popular statement from Karl Marx: "The philosophers have only *interpreted* the world, in various ways; the point, however, is to *change* it" ("Theses on Feuerbach", no. 11), in Karl Marx and Friedrich Engels, *On Religion*, New York 1964, p. 72.

[79] J. Sobrino, *Christology at the Crossroads*, pp. 34; G. Gutiérrez, *The Power of the Poor in History*, p. 181f. Liberation theology, Sobrino claims, distinguishes two phases of Enlightenment. The first phase, which Kant stands for, was a rational affair, meant to liberate humanity from mental "infantilism" and dogmatism. The second stage, ushered in by Karl Marx, was intended to liberate humankind from the "wretched conditions of the real world", not merely at the level of thought, but at the level of action. European theology has been responding mainly to the challenges of the first phase, which takes the form of the liberation of faith from myth. In contrast, Liberation theology professes to respond to the challenges of the second stage, by seeking transformation and not rationality. See p. 10f.

[80] Cf. J. Sobrino, *Christology at the Crossroads*, p. 35: "We come to know reality really only insofar as we come to realise the necessity of transforming it."

ties.[81] Consequently, actions in question have eschatological dimensions. Hence, given the eschatological dimension of Jesus' actions and the message of the Gospel, liberation theology sees it as a part of the task of Christian life to initiate political actions that would transform the world, liberate and direct it towards the future, so as to attain the transcending meaning of history.[82]

Thus the foremost concern of liberation theology is to answer the challenges of practice. In this connection, Gutiérrez sees points of convergence and divergence between Latin American liberation theologies and European political theologies (Metz's political theology and Moltmann's political theology of hope).[83] Liberation and political theologies are poised to come to terms with the challenges of modernity: how to think God as love in the structure of modern society, where the growth and freedom of democratic nations mean a simultaneous "exploitation of the very poorest" - of the wretched of the earth in other parts of the world.[84] There is however an evidence of limitations in European theologies with regard to achieving this aim. They are incapable of making their reflections from the point of view of the poor, Gutiérrez contends. It is at this point that liberation theology sees itself going beyond the scope of political theology of the West. Apparently, Bonhoeffer's theology is an exception, it provides the most acceptable answer to the challenge of modernity.[85] In contrast to Metz and Moltmann, Bonhoeffer is believed to have made his reflections on the problem of God and modern world

---

81 G. Gutiérrez, *A Theology of Liberation*. pp. 131-133.

82 In illustrating the relationship between eschatology and politics, Gutiérrez makes use of the concept of *utopia*. Utopia, according to Gutiérrez, does not signify illusion, if rightly understood; it is rather characterised by its *relationship to the present historical reality*. This is evident in Freire's understanding of utopia, as a concept signifying "denunciation and annunciation" of current disorder and future order respectively. See Freire, "Education as Cultural Action: An Introduction," in Louis M. Colonnese, ed., Conscientisation for liberation, Washington D. C., p. 119, cited by G. Gutiérrez, *A Theology of Liberation*. pp. i36 & 241.

83 G. Gutiérrez, *The Power of the Poor in History*, p. 185.

84 *Ibid.*, p. 186.

85 To answer the challenge of modernity, therefore, Bonhoeffer asks Christians to believe "irreligiously". Since the notion of God always connotes power in religion, believing "irreligiously" implies "to believe in the weak and suffering God of the Bible". See G. Gutiérrez, *The Power of the Poor in History*, p. 180. Hence, from Gutiérrez point of view, "No one else, perhaps, has appreciated the challenge of modernity as profoundly as Bonhoeffer. The very depth of his posing the question grasps the thinking of modernity by its stalk and its roots start cracking." Ibid., p. 186.

from the point of view of the poor, the oppressed, the despised, the suffering people of this world.[86]

7.2.6   Poverty as a Hermeneutic Principle

The issue of poverty occupies a central position in the liberation theology, so much that it understands itself as a theology from the perspective of the poor. In this, it sees itself confronted with the task of working out the theological meaning of the poor. As Gutiérrez observes, the biblical meaning of "poverty" is unfortunately anything but easy to determine, because of its paradoxical usage: in some cases the Bible speaks of "poverty as a scandalous condition" to be overcome, and in another it advocates the adoption of "poverty as spiritual childhood".[87] The classical classification of material and spiritual poverty, he contends, can hardly represent this paradox. It misrepresents it indeed, not only by the fact that it creates an illusory division between material[88] and spiritual poverty, but also because by the interpretation of the Biblical texts, one is almost always left to guess, what the authors of the Bible have in mind when they speak of poverty: whether, they mean material or spiritual poverty. The aftermath of this classification, he goes on to say, is for instance the popular "spiritualistic" interpretation of the phrase "the poor in spirit" in Matthew's version of the Beatitudes, which gives the erroneous impression that a mere interior detachment without a corresponding action against poverty would do.

In contrast, liberation theology contends that there can be no proper spiritual poverty, if there is no corresponding external act that protests against poverty.[89] Any interpretation which is lacking that, amounts to "spiritualising" poverty, and making "comforting and tranquillising conclusions" that are grossly illusory.[90] In the liberation theology the attitude of the prophets and Jesus to poverty are seen as models: Jesus and the prophets did not stop at denouncing poverty, but fought

---

[86]   Gutiérrez refers to Bonhoeffer's article titled "apprenticeship" as a proof to this point. See Bonhoeffer, *Gesamelte Schriften*, Munich: Kaiser, 1965, vol. 2, p. 441. See also G. Gutiérrez, *The Power of the Poor in History*, p. 231.

[87]   Gustavo Gutiérrez, *A Theology of Liberation*. p. 165 ff. See the whole of Chapter thirteen of his book for more details on the notion of poverty in the liberation theology.

[88]   From the mere anthropological perspective, the issue of material poverty can no longer be thought in terms of the lack of material goods, without also including the lack of "cultural, social and political values", which are neither purely spiritual nor material. Cf. *ibid.*, p. 163.

[89]   *Ibid.*, p. 164.

[90]   *Ibid.*

against it, and in the process lived poverty.[91] In their preaching and life-style they demonstrated the paradox of poverty: protesting against poverty as something scandalous (by way of intervention), and encouraging poverty as spiritual childhood (by being basically open and available to God).[92] Accordingly, the liberation theology does not see spiritual poverty so much "as an interior detachment from the goods of this world", but primarily as "a spiritual attitude which becomes authentic by incarnating itself in material poverty".[93] Spiritual poverty does not designate a mere passive acceptance, but "an ability to receive", an attitude that "defines the total posture of human existence before God, persons and things".[94] As such, poverty defines itself in relation, and not in detachment.

Understanding poverty as something that simultaneously encompasses the fight against material poverty as a scandalous condition, and the attitude of openness to God (spiritual poverty), in the language of liberation theology, means viewing "poverty as a commitment of solidarity and protest".[95] Thus:

> Christian poverty, an expression of love, is solidarity *with the poor* and is a protest *against poverty.* ... It is a poverty lived not for its own sake, but rather as an authentic imitation of Christ; it is a poverty which means taking on the sinful human condition to liberate humankind from sin and all its consequences.[96]

Liberation theology therefore sees the Church obliged to live a life of poverty in solidarity with the poor.[97] In addition to guaranteeing the authenticity of Church's mission, poverty which is understood as solidarity and protest serves a

---

91 *Ibid.*, p. 165 f. There are three reasons for that: 1) In the light of Mosaic tradition, to "accept poverty and injustice is to fall back into the conditions of servitude which existed before the liberation from Egypt" (*Ibid.*, p. 167); 2) For the prophets poverty is not neutral, it is a product of oppression and injustice. And seen from the light of the mandate of Genesis (a creature in the "image and likeness of God"), poverty dehumanises humankind; 3) As the image of God, humankind is *the sacrament of God.* Corollarily, "to oppress the poor is to offend God; to know God is to work justice". (*Ibid.*, p. 168)

92 This is most evident in the kenotic life of the historical Jesus. Christ emptied himself (Phil. 2,6) and became poor for our sake (Cor. 8,9). This sort of poverty characterised his whole life: his attitude to his Father and his commitment to the realisation of the kingdom. See J. Sobrino, *The True Church and the Poor*, p. 137; G. Gutiérrez, *A Theology of Liberation.* p. 172.

93 G. Gutiérrez, *A Theology of Liberation.* p. 171.

94 *Ibid.*

95 *Ibid.*

96 *Ibid.*, p. 172.

97 Only by rejecting poverty and by making itself poor in order to protest against it can the Church preach something that is uniquely its own: "spiritual poverty," that is, the openness of humankind and history to the future promised by God. *Ibid.*, p. 173.

hermeneutic function in liberation theology;[98] it helps to make theological discourse more authentic. For it is no accident that the poor are designated to be the privileged recipients of God's message (cf. Isaiah 25 & 61). God is the God of the poor and He reveals Himself eminently to them. That has been so right from the beginning, as can be seen in the Old Testament.[99]

Apparently, the argument can be presented this way: If God directs His "good news" to the poor, it follows that He makes poverty, in the sense we explained above, the privileged situation for His revelation. And if that is true, then we not only need spiritual poverty as a proof for the authenticity of our discipleship,[100] but primarily, as a hermeneutic principle for gaining access to God. This seems to be the implicit argument of liberation theologians as they make poverty a hermeneutic principle.

7.3   The God of the Poor

7.3.1   The Mystery of God

From the above, it is clear that all the basic structures of the liberation theology could be classified as hermeneutic principles. This is a further indication that it does not claim to be presenting a new doctrine, but a new way of doing theology. Its methodology nonetheless signals a departure from the classical conception of God: for an attempt is made to conceive God from the perspective of the poor. The converging point of all the hermeneutic principles is accordingly God's partiality for the poor. God is believed to have always been on the side of the poor and the oppressed, i.e., for the losers of history.

Liberation theology gains this conviction not so much through reflection as through the analysis of the revelation of God in the Old Testament Exodus experience and in the Christ-event. The Exodus experience demonstrates, that God goes through misery with His suffering people, and thereby reveals Himself as their liberator. God's self-revelation to the poor is believed to be a mystery. It is a mystery why He identifies Himself with the poor, and not with the rich, why He chooses to reveal Himself to the ignorant, and not to the wise (Mt. 11:25-26). The

---

[98]   J. Sobrino, *The True Church and the Poor*, p. 137 f.

[99]   The theme of God's partiality for the poor is very central in liberation theology. In fact according to Araya, "the profession that the God who liberates is the God of the poor is its very backbone, as well as its principal point of convergence and unity. This theo-logical reflection is very emphatic on one essential point of the biblical message: the God of the Bible takes sides with the poor and oppressed, at the heart of history, with a view to their deliverance." V. Araya, *God of the poor*, p. 52.

[100]   G. Gutiérrez, *A Theology of Liberation*. p. 173.

liberation theology is particularly interested in "explicating" this mystery.[101] Thus, as Victorio Araya puts it, "the specificity of the Latin American theology of liberation consists in its elucidation and concretisation of the revelation of the mystery of God as *God of the poor*".[102]

God's option for the weak and poor of the society, as this theology fondly contends, reveals two basic facts about Him: firstly, the gratuitous nature of God's love and revelation, secondly, the dialectics of divine self-revelation in the negative side of history, i.e. the dialectics of a historical transcendence. God loves the poor, the weak and the ignorant, Gutiérrez says, not because of their moral integrity, but simply because of the gratuitous character of His love. His love is "free and unmerited".

> The ultimate basis of God's preference for the poor is to be found in God's own goodness and not in any analysis of society or in human compassion, however pertinent these reasons may be.[103]

The affirmation that God is love seems therefore to be one of the basic fundament on which the vision of God of the Latin American theology of liberation is built.

Secondly, the fact that the poor are the privileged addressees of revelation, implies that no limit can be set to the modes of God's self-revelation. God reveals Himself in contradiction and contrast, in the negativity of history - in the negativity of injustice, sin, and oppression. God reveals Himself in a manner beyond intelligibility.[104] God fights against everything that vitiates against His plan for creation. He goes into a kenotic solidarity with the sufferers, liberating them through His salvific praxis, without giving up His transcendence.

There is the strong belief that God's identification with the poor does not detract from His transcendence. As a matter of fact, He is believed to be more transcendent the more human He becomes.[105] This is the paradox of divine transcendence and immanence, Sobrino says, which Jesus demonstrated in his own kenotic life. By "letting God be God", Jesus meditated the mystery of God, as the God who is both the "greater God" and the "lesser God", a God beyond comprehen-

---

[101] G. Gutiérrez, *On Job*, p. xi. God is a mystery, but not mystery as "something that is hidden and *must remain* hidden". The mystery of God, in the biblical sense, must be expressed, not concealed; communicated, not kept to itself". Consequently, if the revelation of God as God of the poor is a mystery, it is a mystery that must be proclaimed.

[102] V. Araya, *God of the poor*, p. 129. For more information about the conception of God in Latin American liberation theology, see also J. L. Segundo, *Our Idea of God*, and R. Pablo, *The Idols of Death and the God of life*.

[103] G. Gutiérrez, *On Job*, xiii.

[104] V. Araya, *God of the poor*, p. 126.

[105] L. Boff, *Jesus Christ Liberator*, p. 218.

sion, and yet partial to the poor, a God who opts for those who have nobody on their side, a God, who despite His transcendence is completely immanent through His kenotic solidarity with the poor.[106]

The significant point liberation theology makes in this connection is that it is precisely in the simplicity and down-to-earth life-style of Jesus, that God's transcendence is optimally proclaimed. According to Sobrino, Jesus revealed God as the "greater" God in the vertical and horizontal dimensions of his simple life. On the horizontal level, he shows that God does not so much abide in the Temple and cultic worship as in the poor and oppressed people. On the vertical significance, God does not mediate His greatness through the administration of justice, but through His grace. God draws near to the people because of His grace and not because of their merits. The God of Jesus is a mystery, since He is "a God of surprises", a God beyond our preconceptions, and more than what our good works can merit.[107]

If we put these mysterious and paradoxical aspects of the God of the poor together with the implicit views about Him in the aforementioned hermeneutic principles, we get a working notion of God in the liberation theology: The God of liberation theology, is a God who mediates Himself in history, whose essence and ways cannot be known apriori, a God, who defines Himself in relationship, and not in aseity, a God, whose future is open; He is a God, who reveals Himself even in His contradiction, a God beyond intelligibility. He is a God, who cannot be experienced in a state of indifference and cold detachment; He encounters people mainly in the work of justice and in the practice of love. He is a God who gets involved, a God who opts for the oppressed, He is a God of the poor, the oppressed and the "non-persons" of history. He is the liberating God.

7.3.2   God as Love and Transcendent: a Historical Fact

The claim that the essence of God is love is common to all current theologies emphasising the paradigm shift from the more philosophical to the more biblical conception of God. The Latin American liberation theology concurs also to the truth of this affirmation, but its approach differs. Whereas many contemporary theologies characteristically make the Johanine affirmation that God is love their point of departure, liberation theology, in its radical dedication to the issue of the historical Jesus, makes the totality of Jesus' life - his life of faith and prayer - the main starting point. In that case, the Johanine dictum that God is essentially love

---

[106] Cf. J. Sobrino, *The True Church and the Poor*, pp. 144-151.

[107] J. Sobrino, *Christology at the Crossroads*, p. 208.

is not a point of departure, but rather a conclusion that is to be arrived at through a thorough investigation of the life of Jesus Christ.

This explains why, Sobrino, rather than to philosophise on love as the essence of God, prefers to base the authenticity of this affirmation on Jesus' own notion of God. Jesus' prayer-life, he contends, reveals much about his conception of God: The mere fact that he prayed at all, signals a belief in a God who is transcendent, and in a God whose reality is love.[108] Besides, the content of his prayers reveal that there were changes and stages in his conception of God,[109] and that his ultimate and unique notion of God crystallised first toward the end of his historical life.

Jesus' notion of God, Sobrino observes, is an original synthesis of the various traditions he inherited. He did not just hold tenaciously to a particular conception. Neither a prophetic, an apocalyptic, nor a sapiential notion constituted Jesus' ultimate idea of God.

> In his concrete history he gradually wove together strands from the various traditions about God in order to form his own fabric. The originality of Jesus lies precisely in the concrete synthesis that he was fashioning his whole life long.[110]

This claim is based on the assumption that Jesus' self-awareness and knowledge of God grew with time. The ultimate notion of God that Jesus gained after synthesising the different concepts of God, according to Sobrino, is a notion of God that is full of tension. Then as he maintains: "Toward the end of Jesus' life, God seems to be both a presence and an absence, both power and importance".[111] Despite this apparent tension, the historical synthesis in Jesus' notion of God points to two basic conclusions: "that God ever remains greater than hu-

---

[108] *Ibid.*, p. 159.

[109] In the conflict-ridden situation of his life, his notion of God was changing but his faith remained unswerving. His experiences, his crisis in Galilee, and the loss of hope in the "imminent arrival of the kingdom of God", must have made him realise that God, does not so much demonstrate his love with power as with triumph in failure. Hence Sobrino's observation: "Jesus' prayer in the garden of Gethsemane does not presuppose the same conception of God that Jesus had at the start of his life." *Ibid.*, p. 94. Cf. pp. 90-95.

[110] According to Sobrino, Jesus was definitely aware of the *prophetic* tradition, with its emphasis on the partiality of God in defence of the oppressed. He was acquainted with the *apocalyptic* tradition, stressing the plan of God to renew reality at the end of time. He was familiar with the *sapiential* tradition, preaching a providential God, who gratuitously allows the existence of both the just and unjust, awaiting his justice at the end of time. In addition, he experienced God on the Cross, in a dimension, which, though imagined (in the "Psalms, in the book of Lamentations, and in the book of Ecclesiastes") remained unimaginable to a majority of the Jews. He lived God in his seeming absence and silence. *Ibid.*, pp. 160-161.

[111] *Ibid.*, p. 161.

man beings, and that his innermost reality is love".[112] This means in effect that Jesus revealed a paradoxical image of God in his own religious life.

Jesus, he goes on to say, neither conceived nor made use of divine transcendence in abstract terms. He lived it historically and concretely in different forms of his life. Jesus' view about the sovereignty of God however came up mostly when he was showing how incomprehensible and unimaginable God's grace and gratuitousness was. In his parables, especially in the one about a good father (Lk. 11:11-13) and that about the prodigal son, (Lk. 11:11-24), Jesus depicts the sovereignty of God in terms of His love that goes beyond the limits of human possibilities. When Jesus was asked whether God could do "impossible" things such as save the rich, he replied: "For mortals it is impossible, but not for God; for God all things are possible" (Mk 10:27). Thus, Sobrino concludes:

> Realisation of the impossible, then, is an expression of the transcendence of God ...
> This realisation of the impossible by grace is the way that God's transcendence is
> mediated in the eyes of Jesus.[113]

The notion of God's transcendence that Jesus had was "that God ever remains greater than human beings" in question of love. It means also that God ever remains greater than human conception. In his life, especially in times of hardship, Jesus realised that his God transcends all single notions of God that occur in Jewish tradition, and that God was more than he himself could have imagined at the start of his public life.[114]

Thus, the awareness of God as a God whose nature and ways transcend human imagination and conception is evident in the life of Jesus. His attitude to life generally and to his future was definitely influenced by the conviction that the future belongs to God, and that at the end, God conquers everything vitiating against His Kingdom. In Sobrino's view, it is this awareness of the sovereignty of God over every historical situation at the end of history, that sustained Jesus' trust and confidence in his Father and made him surrender himself to God's will even in his times of crisis.[115] Divine transcendence, so conceived, is not abstract, it is historical and concrete. To all intents and purposes, Jesus testified to this fact: He

---

[112] *Ibid.*, p. 162.

[113] *Ibid.*, p. 164. In this connection, Sobrino quotes approvingly the following passage from Braun. "Here the impossible is not depicted as supernatural events coming from a world beyond and producing weird consequences in this world. Instead it appears in the fact that the poor, the impious, and the wicked can unexpectedly go back to calling themselves human beings once again." See Braun, *Jesus*, p. 167.

[114] *Ibid.*, pp. 164-165.

[115] *Ibid.*, p. 165.

was ever discovering new dimensions of God throughout his life, and at the end, he was sure that nothing and nobody could put limits on God.[116]

According to Sobrino, not any philosophical proposition, but the entire length of Jesus' own life should be the basis for investigating into the nature of God. Therefore, in the name of liberation theology, he identifies at least three features of Jesus' life that authenticate the affirmation that God's essence is love: his calling God "Father", his option for the poor and his attitude to cultic worship.[117]

Evidently, Jesus did not call God "Lord" or "King"; he chose to call him "Father" - *Abba*. There is no historical or logical reason, Sobrino maintains, why Jesus favoured this expression, except that it was basic to his understanding of God. This expression stands for a relationship of love, trust and confidence, which existed between him and God.

> Hence the term 'Father' addressed to God by Jesus tells us right away how he pictured the ultimate ground of reality. It was not to be viewed in terms of beauty or power but in terms of love. That is why he chose to address God as 'Father'.[118]

Secondly, Jesus' option for the poor (Lk. 6:20-22) is also motivated by his conception of God as love. His attack on the powerful oppressors of the poor, and his condemnation of injustice, should not, in Sobrino's view, be judged solely from a moral perspective, but primarily from the standpoint of Jesus' own conception of God as love. "Because God is love he cannot tolerate the oppression of the lowly."[119] Thus, love is so much the essence of God, that in defence and expression of it, He sides with the lowly. Apparently, this is the explanation for the partisanship of God's love. Moreover, Jesus' own basic option for human beings also demonstrates, that love is the essential nature of God. His entire life was an expression of God's option for humankind, and it thus defined God as love.[120]

Thirdly, Jesus, in a very radical manner, made humanity the basis for evaluating the authenticity of cultic worship (Mt. 9:13) and Sabbath observance (Mk 2:27). By making humankind the privileged sphere for divine encounter, Jesus equates the praxis of love to neighbour with love for God (Mk 12:28-34; Mt.

---

[116] Cf. *ibid.*, p. 174: "At no point in his history can Jesus get a 'fix' on God once and for all."

[117] *Ibid.*, pp. 165-172.

[118] *Ibid.*, p. 166.

[119] *Ibid.*, p. 166.

[120] *Ibid.*, p. 169: "His God is not an egocentric being. He is a being for others, not a being for himself alone."

22:34-40; Lk. 10:25-27).[121] This ultimately means that God is to be encountered in the praxis of love, and precisely as the One who transcends in love. In encountering the God who loves unconditionally, we come to gain insight into His greatness, His sovereignty and profundity. At this point Sobrino perceives a dialectical relationship between the praxis of love and divine transcendence. For,

> If there is any historical reality at all that can mediate the transcendence of the Christian God, it is the historical reality of love. On the one hand love is the reality that brings out most clearly the extra something, the "more" of reality and meaningfulness. On the other hand the historical praxis of love is the place where one experiences the fundamental quandary of existence. The person who loves truly is persecuted. Those who set their feet on the pathway of love feel all the weight of sin upon themselves. It is here that we encounter the formal Christian structure of transcendence as a vis- -vis, as one thing over "against" another. Christian acceptance of transcendence is not any naive identification with the existence of some Absolute; it entails corresponding to some Absolute *in spite of the fact* that the latter is called into question by history ...it means hoping against hope.[122]

Judging from the above quotation, one can rightly say, that for Sobrino, divine transcendence must not be conceived metaphysically in abstraction, nor vertically in spatial terms, but concretely horizontal in history. Divine transcendence is seen as a historical reality, as that "beyond" of every dead-end in history. It is that "more" and the unending resilience of God's love, which Jesus lived himself. Jesus lived the transcendence of love, for neither conflict, nor failure, nor rejection, nor death was able to set a limit to God's option for humankind. He showed it in his resolute hope, trust and confidence in God.

7.4. *A Historical Theology of the Cross and Resurrection*

7.4.1 *The Cross: a Scandal*

In agreement with other contemporary theologies of the Cross, liberation theology sees the revelation of "a new and revolutionary concept of God" in the suffering and death of Jesus Christ on the Cross.[123] God reveals Himself in the negativity of the Cross. This is the dialectical truth, which must be noted, because the

---

121 *Ibid.*, p. 172: "The praxis of love constitutes one unique experience. Materially it is love of neighbour. Formally, when that love is given without reservations, it is also an experience of God and hence can be formulated as love for God."

122 *Ibid.*, pp. 172-173. Sobrino's points in this lengthy quotation bear some resemblance with Martin Buber's view that we encounter the "eternal Thou" (God) in the "I- Thou" relationship. Secondly, by saying that the "person who loves truly is persecuted", Sobrino makes an implicit reference to the issue of divine suffering on the basis of love. See M. Buber, *I and Thou*, p. 75 ff.

123 Cf. J. Sobrino, *Christology at the Crossroads*, chapter 6, especially p. 179. See also L. Boff, *Passion of Christ, Passion of the World*, especially Chapter 8.

more the Cross is understood as something negative, as something scandalous, the more we recognise the face of God on the Cross of Jesus Christ. Liberation theology finds the classical theology of the Cross wanting in this regard, for it claims, that the tradition hardly went beyond pious adoration and idealistic interpretation of the Cross. It is believed that a mystification of and the habit of playing down the scandal of the Cross were common in the past, a trend that invariably not only led to an erroneous interpretation of both the resurrection and redemption, but also to their blindness to the dialectical revelation of the specifically Christian image of God on the Cross.

As Sobrino sees it, the trend towards displacing the element of scandal in the interpretation of the Cross can be traced back to the New Testament writers themselves. Perceiving the Cross primarily in terms of its soteriological and salvific implications for human beings, the earliest Christians found it hard "to preserve the scandal of the Cross".[124] Since they were more preoccupied with the issue of redemption than with gaining a vision of God, they tended to approach the Cross with an existent conception of God, searching for its implication for their own salvation, than its relationship to God. With the exception of Paul, the New Testament writers were writing for an audience whose concern had more to do with the issue of redemption than with that of the notion of God. By that fact, the true message of the Cross was blurred.

For Sobrino the primary message of the Cross is not salvation, but what sort of God is on our side. The revolutionary image of God on the Cross can only be perceived, if we see the Cross as it is - a scandal - and try to understand it without any preconception. Liberation theologians claim, therefore, that in order to recognise the presence of God on the Cross, we must break with our traditional way of conceiving God, because, as Boff writes, the Cross is "the death of all systems".[125] Sobrino is likewise definitive in his warning:

> We must break with every logical schema we had entertained previously insofar as knowing God is concerned. We cannot explain the Cross *logically* by appealing to God, who supposedly is known already, because the first thing the Cross does here

---

[124] Cf. J. Sobrino, *Christology at the Crossroads*, pp. 184-6. "This is evident in the fact that the very death of Jesus as one abandoned by God is mollified. It is also evident in the fact that the title 'Servant of Yahweh' is soon dropped as a title embracing the overall figure of Jesus." (184) Paul is perhaps the only NT writer, who did not evade the element of scandal (1 Cor. 1,23; Heb. 5,7).

[125] L. Boff, *Passion of Christ, Passion of the World*, p. 115. Boff rejects Moltmann's and von Balthasar's attempt to work out a logic of the Cross. In his view: "The Cross cannot be posited as the generating principle of a system of intellection ... The Cross is the death of all systems ... The Cross has no intelligibility, and therefore can never function as a link in a logical, cohesive system ... It tears every system to shreds ... The Cross is not there to be understood."

is raise questions about God himself and the authentic reality of the deity. The first thing the Cross unmasks is people's selfish interest in seeking to know God.[126]

The trend towards disregarding the scandal of the Cross continued far into the patristic and medieval periods. But unlike the New Testament writers, who adopted this attitude almost exclusively for soteriological reasons, the Fathers and the medieval theologians weakened the harsh realities of the Cross, mainly because of the influence of the Greek conception of *apatheia*. For fear of implying divine weakness, the theologies of the time were neither ready to accept that Jesus Christ, the Son of God died in disaster, nor to admit that God *really* abandoned him. They could not entertain the thought that the almighty God could be absent or passive on the Cross of Jesus Christ. Since, for them, viewing the Cross from its scandalous perspective would have amounted to declaring God a failure, they tended to glorify and see the Cross as God's plan.

Sobrino interprets Anselm's theory of vicarious satisfaction in the same line. Anselm's theory according to which the Cross should be seen as Father's arbitrary choice for the reparation of sins, is, in Sobrino's view, a perfect example of the tendency to disregard the harsh realities of the Cross.[127] Furthermore, the effort that was made in the first centuries to understand the Eucharist in terms of sacrifice - not in terms of a pagan sacrificial cult, but as "the unbloody repetition of Jesus sacrifice" - increased the tendency to overlook the "irrepeatable and scandalous uniqueness".[128] In this sense the Cross was "de-historicised".

Regardless of the reasons of the early Christians for explaining the scandal of the Cross away, this tendency led to a twofold forgetfulness in the theology of the Cross: the forgetfulness that it was the Son of God who died on the Cross, and that the Cross affected God Himself. For Sobrino, the main cause of this development is to be sought in the adoption of the Greek pattern of thought in theology. Greek thought, he argues, is notably unable to think of being and perfection historically. For this reason it is unable to "contemplate the negative pole of real-

---

[126] J. Sobrino, *Christology at the Crossroads*, p. 188. Selfish concern for salvation, Sobrino argues, makes believers conceive God in the way they want to and not in the way God wants them to see Him. Sobrino insists that openness in the conception of God, i.e., "letting God be God", is one of the major lessons we must gain from Jesus' own notion of God. G. Gutiérrez makes the same point based on his analysis of the Book of Job. The major theme of the Book of Job is not suffering but the question of disinterested faith in God, in a state of suffering. "In the Book of Job, to be a believer means sharing human suffering, especially that of the most destitute, enduring a spiritual struggle, and finally accepting the fact that God cannot be pigeonholed in human categories". See G. Gutiérrez, *On Job*, pp. 15-16.

[127] J. Sobrino, *Christology at the Crossroads*, pp. 191-193.

[128] *Ibid.*, p. 194.

ity".[129] It is an ahistorical pattern of thought, conceiving perfection in terms of immutability and impassibility. Logically, such a pattern of thought renders a genuine theology of the Cross impossible, because it is unable to see God's voluntary acceptance of suffering as a perfection of His "being as love".[130]

If the message of the Cross is to be understood, Sobrino concludes,

> ...we must get beyond the older view of God's immutability and apathy and move closer to the concrete reality of history. We must consider the possible revelation of God in the Cross of Jesus.[131]

To perceive the presence of God in the midst of His absence on the Cross of Jesus, the customary principle of analogy prevalent in Greek thought would not do; we must incorporate dialectical thinking, in order to get to the mode of divine being on the Cross, where He appears *sub specie contarii*. Before the Cross of Jesus, before the litany of crosses of the poor, a believer is overwhelmed by a sense of sorrow, not wonder. We come to know the God on the Cross, not by mystifying the Cross, but by seeing the Cross as a scandal which arouses sorrow. For, faced with the harsh realities of the Cross of Jesus,

> ...we get a sym-pathy and a con-natural knowledge that enables us to grasp some sort of divine presence on the Cross of Jesus and in the overall suffering of the oppressed.[132]

7.4.2   The Cross of Jesus: no Accident, no Design of God: the Consequence of a Life's Option

> Our theology of the Cross must be historical. Rather than viewing the Cross as some arbitrary design on God's part, we must see it as the outcome of God's primordial option: the incarnation. The Cross is the outcome of an incarnation situated in a world of sin that is revealed to be a power working against the God of Jesus.[133]

With the above thesis Sobrino summarises both his views and that of other liberation theologians on the issue of the Cross. They generally detest any theological discourse which gives the impression that the Cross is God's design for salvation (Anselm). It is believed that such a view usually arises out of the failure to see the Cross as a scandal. By that means God is made to seem arbitrary and sadistic and as an accomplice of the oppressors. To present God in this light, would

---

129 *Ibid.*, p. 195.

130 *Ibid.*, p. 195.

131 *Ibid.*, p. 198.

132 *Ibid.*, p. 199. For more details about the illustration of divine suffering based on a concept of sympathy, see the work of the North Korean theologian, C. Y. Lee, *God suffers for us.*

133 J. Sobrino, *Christology at the Crossroads*, p. 201.

amount to a denial of God's basic option for humankind, signified by the incarnation.

The Cross, Sobrino contends, is not God's design for salvation, neither is it an accidental occurrence. It is the consequence of his life option for the poor and of his notion of God, which contradicted that of the political and religious leaders of his time. To get an authentic knowledge of the Cross, therefore, one must trace the route that led Jesus to the Cross.[134] God's primordial option for humankind runs through the whole life of the historical Jesus, who lived and preached this God as the love, that offers and effects liberation. His preaching and especially his conception of God, exposed him to the aggression of the powers that be in his contemporary Jewish community.[135]

In the quest for the cause for the Cross, Sobrino identifies the issue of the conception of God (Mk 2:23-28) as the main bone of contention between Jesus and his Jewish opponents. Jesus was accused of blasphemy and condemned mainly because of his conception of God.[136] He proclaimed a God who does not correspond to the existing religious values: a God who is more available in human life than in the temple or in cultic worship, a God who is not so much present with the pious as with the poor, a God who places priority on the protest against religious and political oppression than interiorised devotion. For both the religious and political leaders these facts embodied an attack against their own habitual views of God and society. Given this situation, it should not be surprising, therefore, that they did not hesitate to crucify him.

> We do much better to say that Jesus died because he chose to bear faithful witness to God right to the end in a situation where people really wanted a very different type of God ... Jesus' Cross is no accident. It flows directly from the self-justifying efforts of the 'religious' person who tries to manipulate God rather than letting God remain a mystery.[137]

Besides his conception of God, Jesus' wish and work toward the realisation of the kingdom which got him involved in the socio-political sphere, equally pulled down the contempt of the political authorities on him. It is no accident, Sobrino says, that Jesus got the punishment of a political agitator (crucifixion) and not that of a religious blasphemer (stoning).[138] The reason for this apparently lies in the

---

134 *Ibid.*, p. 202: "If God did become incarnate in history and accepted its mechanisms, ambiguities, and contradictions, then the Cross reveals God not just in himself but in conjunction with historical path that leads Jesus to the Cross."

135 *Ibid.*, p. 203.

136 *Ibid.*, pp. 204-206.

137 *Ibid.*, pp. 208-209.

138 *Ibid.*, p. 211.

fact, that Jesus' conception of God as love urged him to actions that had political implications and repercussions - it forced him to the Cross. In his actions however he was mediating the image of a God who gets involved in the affairs of the world. And on the Cross, he stood to the consequences of his religious and political actions. This fact, and not the need for the reparation of sin, led him to the Cross.

> The Cross is not the result of some divine decision independent of history; it is the
> outcome of the basic option for incarnation in a given situation.[139]

The belief in the liberation theology is that, by understanding the Cross as a consequence of Jesus' own life, not as a Stoic acceptance of pain, sorrow and resignation, a Christian definition of a positive suffering would emerge. Suffering is not desirable for its own sake, not even when it is conceived as a means for perfection, except when it arises out of the commitment to do good. Thus, for the Christian, suffering could only be positive when it is the logical consequence of a life lived in the spirit of Christ.[140] Suffering only then becomes a Christian Cross, when it arises out of the fight against suffering. Christian spirituality, does not consist in the "mystique of the Cross", but in following the path of Jesus. This type of spirituality, Sobrino observes, is embodied in the political theology of liberation. The true nature of God and the power that mediates him can best be tested in political actions directed toward the realisation of God's kingdom on earth.[141]

7.4.3   The Suffering of God the Liberator

For Leonardo Boff and Jon Sobrino, the logical conclusion of a liberation theology of the Cross is that "God can suffer".[142] God lets Himself be affected by all that is negative (all sorts of suffering including divine abandonment and death). Then, right from the onset of the incarnation, God concretely identified Himself with the human situation. He has pledged His love to humankind and remained faithful to it, in spite of the disappointing responses of humankind to this love. He suffers the sin of the world and the unreciprocated response to His love. Together with the poor He suffers the oppression and injustice perpetrated against them. Essentially, God suffers His love, but concretely, He suffered it on the Cross of

---

[139] *Ibid.*, p. 214.

[140] Cf. *Ibid.*, pp. 215-217.

[141] *Ibid.*, p. 216 "Insofar as it is *theo-logy*, then, political theology seeks to clarify the essence of power and to unmask all forms of power that seek to pass themselves off as God."

[142] L. Boff, *Passion of Christ, Passion of the World*, pp. 102-116, 134; J. Sobrino, *Christology at the Crossroads*, p. 217 ff.

Jesus and suffers it today in other Crosses of this world. Both authors see the Cross as the symbol of divine love, and believe that God's presence on the Cross authenticates the affirmation that "God is love.[143] As Sobrino puts it, the biblical affirmation that God is love can best be substantiated in the light of the Cross, because as we probe into the reality of God on the Cross, we discover that suffering is a mode of divine being.

According to the liberation theologians, the divine abandonment of Jesus on the Cross reveals something about the nature of God. However, in order to perceive this abandonment properly, it must not be seen as an event limited to the Cross, but as a kenotic act evident in Jesus' relationship to his Father throughout his life. It is observed that Jesus lived his life in accordance with the will of God and made repeated references to his intimacy with his Father and to his confidence and trust in him. In the light of such a relationship to his Father, the ultimate question about God was posed on the Cross, not so much by the fact that Jesus had to suffer, as by the fact that God abandoned him, leaving him to his fate and consequently to die. The abandonment of Jesus on the Cross is, for that reason, the height of the scandal of the Cross. It shatters our notion of God more than any other fact. How could God abandon His Son, who had trusted him so much that he called him "Father"? What does this episode have in common with the whole life of Jesus? What theological lessons can be drawn from this occurrence? Or is the issue of divine abandonment on the Cross so much out of place that theology should relegate it to the background?

In answering these questions, Sobrino certainly speaks for other liberation theologians, when he maintains that the abandonment of Jesus on the Cross is very central to the Christian conception of God despite the fact that it is a scandal. In his view,

> What typifies the death of Jesus, and what differentiates it from the death of other religious and political martyrs, is that Jesus dies in complete rupture with his cause. Jesus feels abandoned by the very God whose approach in grace he had been preaching.[144]

This means, Sobrino goes on, that God's abandonment of Jesus on the Cross made his death unique, and different from that of the other prophets, for it gives the impression that God Himself sanctioned the death of his Son.

If God sanctioned the suffering and death of Jesus on the Cross through his abandonment, and if Jesus is (the Son of) God, was God an agent of his own persecution or the victim of his own situation? This seems to be the basic question

---

[143] J. Sobrino, *Christology at the Crossroads*, pp. 217 & 225; L. Boff, *Passion of Christ, Passion of the World*, pp. 110 & 134.

[144] J. Sobrino, *Christology at the Crossroads*, p. 217.

on the lips of liberation theologians. Their answers vary: Whereas Sobrino and Gutiérrez share similar views on the issue of divine abandonment, Boff's approach to it differs.

7.4.4.1 God as both the Agent and Victim of the Cross

Sobrino follows Moltmann very closely in his interpretation of Jesus' dereliction.[145] Like Moltmann, he interprets God's abandonment to mean that "God himself is against God". God abandons His Son to the power of sin. "God 'bifurcates' Himself on the Cross, so that transcendence (the Father) is in conflict with history (the son)".[146] God's abandonment of His Son should be seen as a double expression: a criticism of the world and an expression of His ultimate solidarity with it. The Father rejects the Son carrying the sin of the world, but in the Son He identifies himself with the world. Thus God's abandonment designates His activity and His passivity at the same time. By letting Himself be affected by injustice and death, God is involved in passivity, and by that he actively protests against and criticises the world. Divine abandonment concretises the dialectics of divine presence and absence.

> On the Cross of Jesus God was present (2 Cor. 5:19 f.) and at the same time absent (Mk. 15:34). Absent to the Son, he was present for human beings. And this dialectics of presence and absence is the way to express in human language the fact that God is love. ...In the Son's passion the Father suffers the pain of abandonment. In the Son's death, death affects God himself - not because God dies but because he suffers the death of the son. Yet God suffers so that we might live, and that is the most complete expression of love.[147]

Divine abandonment then is an expression of love. For the sake of love, God Himself experiences the worst thing that can happen to human beings: divine abandonment. This paradoxical form of divine abandonment manifests the "internal structure of God himself", Trinitarian love historicised. This is one of the ways the Trinitarian God takes all history into Himself, by incorporating the negative side of history in Himself in order to overcome it.[148]

In a sense, divine abandonment designates God's way through the negative to the positive elements. This point becomes clear if we see it in the light of the dialectics of the Cross and the resurrection. Then we see divine abandonment and the Cross as part of the process of incorporating history into God. Looking at the

---

[145] *Ibid.*, pp. 217-219.

[146] *Ibid.*, p. 225.

[147] *Ibid.*, p. 226.

[148] *Ibid.*

dialectics of the Cross and resurrection, of failure and triumph, we get the assurance that,

> God's active presence in the resurrection should be viewed in connection with his
> absence from the Son on the Cross.[149]

In yet another sense, the dialectics of God's presence and absence on the Cross of Jesus signifies the relation between transcendence and immanence. Sobrino does not see God's abandonment of Jesus on the Cross as a withdrawal from the harsh realities of human beings; rather it means that God allows Himself to experience the pinch of divine abandonment through Jesus. By abandoning His Son on the Cross, God has not become an accomplice to the evils that nailed Jesus to the Cross; He was not exercising a sinister sort of power. His action merely indicates that God does not intend to overcome the power of the negative from outside but from inside.

> On the Cross God does not show up as one who wields power over the negative
> from *outside*; on the Cross we see God submerged *within* the negative. The pos-
> sibility of overcoming the negative is realised by submersion within the mechanisms
> and processes of the negative. The new relationship between God and history,
> between transcendence and immanence, is formulated in a definitive and totally un-
> suspected way.[150]

Thus for Sobrino it is obvious that suffering and immersion into the realm of the negative is "a mode of being for God".[151] God is passible.

Gustavo Gutiérrez' conception of divine suffering slightly resembles that of Sobrino. Though he analyses the "cross" of Job (not that of Jesus) and has Bonhoeffer as his mentor (not Moltmann) he practically arrives at the same view that God can be against God. He experiences his suffering as an abandonment by God,[152] and thus curses the day of his birth. Even though he does not curse God, he complains to "God against God". This is in effect a dialectical appeal to God.

> It might almost be said that Job, as it were, splits God in two and produces a God
> who is judge and a God who will defend him at that supreme moment; a God
> whom he experiences as almost an enemy but whom he knows at the same time to
> be truly a friend ... This painful, dialectical approach to God is one of the most
> profound messages of the Book of Job.[153]

This should however be seen from the standpoint of the main theme of the Book of Job, which according to Gutiérrez, "is not precisely suffering ... but

---

[149] *Ibid.*, p. 231.

[150] *Ibid.*, p. 220-221.

[151] *Ibid.*, p. 217.

[152] G. Gutiérrez, *On Job*, pp. 6-8.

[153] *Ibid.*, p. 65.

rather how to speak of God in the midst of suffering".[154] But it becomes even more significant for our reflection, when we agree to Gutiérrez' view that the concept of God that emerges in a situation of suffering is always truer to the notion of the God of the Bible.[155] To have experienced God as defender and as judge means that God identifies Himself with the lot of the sufferer. "God uses different modes of self-manifestation, and suffering can be one of them..."[156]

Experience has taught Job, Gutiérrez contends, that gratuitous love and freedom, not power, are central to God. In God's speech to him, and in his despair, Job learnt that God is not so much a judge as He is a defender, that gratuitousness of divine love, and not retribution, is "the hinge on which the world turns", and that free love, and not justice, dictates the action of God.[157] In the speeches of God, Job is also taught the true nature of divine freedom and the relation between divine and human freedom. When the reign of justice is rejected in the world, God does not impose His will on the world, rather He imposes limitations to His power.

> God's power is limited by human freedom; for without freedom God's justice would not be present within history... In other words, the all-powerful God is also a 'weak' God. The mystery of divine freedom leads to the mystery of human freedom and to respect for it.[158]

Thus after the fashion of Bonhoeffer, Gutiérrez sees God as both mighty and weak. The mighty God is responsible for marvels done in the world (Job 42:3), but He imposes limitations on Himself out of respect for human freedom and thus becomes "the 'weak' God who is heedful of human freedom and its historical rhythm".[159] Consequently, for Gutiérrez, the correct way of talking about God, emerges, as soon as we realise with Job, that there is a paradoxical relationship between divine justice and gratuitousness, between divine power and weakness, between His freedom and human freedom. In the light of the Pauline theology, Gutiérrez concludes that God must be seen from the point of view of the paradox

---

154 *Ibid.*, p. 13.

155 *Ibid.*, p. 14.

156 *Ibid.*, p. 46.

157 *Ibid.*, p. 72.

158 *Ibid.*, p. 77-78. Gutiérrez makes explicit reference to the significance of divine love. By that he gains an edge over Sobrino, who hardly makes any explicit interpretation of the issue of freedom. His idea of letting God be God and appeal to the incomprehensibility of God certainly mean the same thing. But given the centrality of divine freedom to the notion of God, one would have expected an explicit treatment of the concept.

159 *Ibid.*, p. 79.

of His power on the Cross;[160] this in effect means believing "in the weak and suffering God of the Bible",[161] like Bonhoeffer did.

7.4.4.2   God as the Victim of the Cross

Leonardo Boff shows more originality than Sobrino and Gutiérrez on the issue of divine passibility. He opts for a more precise interpretation of divine suffering, so as to avoid any irrational conception of God and a glorification of suffering. In view of the suffering and oppression in the world and our faith in God's act of liberation, we are bound indeed, he says, "to move away from the notion of a static, a-pathetic (nonsuffering) God to that of a living God, a 'pathetic' God (one with pathos, one who can suffer)".[162]

It is also true, Boff argues further, that we cannot conceive God's liberative act and His loving care without affirming that He suffers (Bonhoefer), at least in solidarity with the oppressed people of the world. In expressing God's suffering or the death of God, theologians must avoid simplistic deductive arguments bereft of any idea of theological symbolism. The description of divine suffering, he emphasises, requires a precise usage of theological language. Unfortunately, most theological discourses exhibit "a *profound* lack of theological rigor".[163]

Like many theologians of the Cross, Boff sees the Cross of Jesus as a scandal, and understands divine abandonment as its highest expression, but unlike Sobrino, Gutiérrez and Moltmann, he does not see divine abandonment on the Cross as a struggle between God (the Father) and God (the Son). God cannot be made the subject of suffering and pain, he objects. Nor can we say that God wilfully crucified His Son on the Cross, or that "he effectuated the sacrifice of His Son on the Cross".[164]

Such a view of divine absence or silence on the Cross is absurd and irrational. For one, it presents an ambiguous image of God, of a God who is both object and subject of the suffering and violent death of Jesus on the Cross. Secondly, it eternalises and justifies suffering by projecting evil into the being of God. By making

---

160 *Ibid.*, p. 100.

161 G. Gutiérrez, *The Power of the Poor in History*, pp. 181, 222-228.

162 L. Boff, *Passion of Christ, Passion of the World*, p. 111.

163 *Ibid.*

164 *Ibid.*, p. 112. Boff criticises Moltmann and von Balthasar at precisely this point, accusing them of making an absurd proposition that God the Father murdered his Son. This problematic proposition bears semblance with Freudian theory of Oedipus complex, except that ironically it is not the son but the Father that kills his son. This amounts to an irrational conclusion about God.

God the Father the single cause of Jesus' historic death, this view exonerates Jesus' adversaries and underrates the wickedness that led Jesus to the Cross.

For Boff, therefore, any interpretation of Jesus' dereliction on the Cross that projects suffering and conflict onto the very Being of God is not Christian. Of course, it is still in order to say that God (the Son) suffered divine abandonment on the Cross, but we dare not see such an abandonment as God's design to inflict pain on Himself. God is not a masochist. Divine abandonment has no part in God's plan to demonstrate the sacrifice of His Son for our own redemption. God's silence on the Cross is not wilful; it does not indicate a revolt in the Godhead either.

> The real reason God is silent in the face of suffering is that God is suffering. God takes up the cause of the martyred, of the suffering (cf. Mt. 25:31). God is acquainted with suffering. But God has not undertaken to eternalise it and deprive us of all hope. On the contrary, God assumed it because God means to put an end to all the crosses of history.[165]

Unlike his colleagues, Boff exercises "utmost caution" in the interpretation of God's role on the Cross of Jesus. His argument mainly goes as follows: The Cross, suffering and death are not essential parts of divine plan for salvation. The Cross is doubtlessly a scandal and must be interpreted as such. Nonetheless, we cannot preserve the scandalous character of the Cross, by conceiving it as a God-ordained instrument of divine salvation, nor can we achieve our aim by making God Himself a perpetrator of Jesus' crucifixion.

The Cross is a scandal, because it is an evil, which God Himself overcomes by going through it. To say that God took part in the crucifixion of His Son, amounts to saying that he does evil. God Himself was a victim on the Cross. God's role on the Cross can not be dual. He does not demonstrate His active role by standing up against His Son. His steadfastness, which made him to accept suffering as the logical consequence of His love, is a sufficient expression of His activity. We cannot therefore give meaning to the Cross by viewing it as an apriori plan of divine solidarity.

> In a word, we may not force God and the Cross into a bond that would be intrinsic to the divine identity. ... If suffering is an expression of God's very essence, if God hates, if God crucifies, then there is no salvation for us. God would be simultaneously good and evil, and we would be the hapless flotsam of the eternal alternation of that good and that evil. How would we speak of a redemption that comes from God, *were God also in need of redemption?*[166]

---

[165] *Ibid.*, p. 114.

[166] *Ibid.*, p. 115.

How then does the Cross affect God? What is God's relation to the Cross. The Cross, Boff maintains, must be interpreted in the light of human freedom. This is a fact that most theologians of the Cross grossly overlook.[167] The Cross springs out of the misuse of human freedom, out of the human freedom to "reject God and create hell". The Cross is a sin and as such has no intelligibility. It is absurd. And yet God assumes it, not to link it to Himself, but to overcome it with His love. The Cross is therefore neither love nor the fruit of love. It is the place where the power of love is shown. As such it lacks intelligibility, and evades any attempt to systematise it, that is to say, to bring it a cohesive system of thought. It remains an absurdity, but it does not however obstruct God's plan, which he executes in spite of the Cross.[168]

For Boff, it is a forgone conclusion that God suffers. So that, the question is not "Does God suffer?" but rather "How does God suffer?":

> To say that God is love is to say that God is vulnerable. In other words, God loves, and we can accept or reject this God who loves. ... Salvation history shows the human capacity for rejecting love. God is not indifferent to this rejection. God suffers from it. Love, however, does not desire suffering. Love desires felicity. And because it is so supremely desirous of the felicity of the other, it continues to love that other even in the face of that other's rejection. Now love takes up the other's pain, because it loves that other and wishes to share that other's pain. This is the manner of God's suffering: to suffer as the fruit of love and of the infinite capacity of love for solidarity.[169]

7.5   Summary and Conclusion

Emerging out of the background of a people's experience of God in a state of suffering, the Latin American liberation theology does not intend to introduce a doctrinal, but a methodological novelty. It's objective as such is the redefinition of the theological method from the perspective of the poor, which, in effect, reflects the biblical viewpoint. Although liberation is the grand motif of this theology, it employs about six major hermeneutic principles considered indispensable for every theological understanding: historicity, relationality, eschatological hope, dialectics, praxis and poverty.

The importance of historicity for a theological understanding is indicated by two points: firstly, in the perception of history as the locus for the divine revelation, and secondly, in the institution of the historical Jesus as the authentic starting point of every theological inquiry that is Christian. History, consisting mainly

---

[167] *Ibid.*, pp. 115-116.

[168] *Ibid.*, p. 116.

[169] *Ibid.*, p. 114.

of God's proposal and human response, is seen as a process with an open future, which is essentially unknown. God has revealed it to us in the historical Jesus; hence the claim that Jesus is the measure of our knowledge of God and humankind. As a matter of fact, historicity is the principle on which all other principles are based.

Closely related to the principle of historicity therefore is the principle of eschatological hope. The interpretation of the resurrection in eschatological terms is common in the Liberation theology, because it makes the hope for liberation meaningful. For some theologians, this eschatological hope is already paradoxically realised through the event of the resurrection of Christ (Boff), for others its realisation awaits the end of all injustice in the world (Sobrino). In which ever way, however, whether immediate or protracted, the prospect for the realisation of the eschatological hope is indispensable for a theology of liberation.

Liberation theology likewise sees relationality as a basic category for the interpretation of God and humankind: God's self-introduction in the Old Testament, especially in the Book of Exodus, and Jesus' self-awareness are all relational by nature. Concretely, Jesus defined God and himself in terms of his relationship to the Father. For liberation theology, this means that we can only understand God in relational categories.

Parallel to this, it is believed that theological knowledge begins to grow at the point of apparent contradictions. This makes dialectical thinking inevitable. Dialectics, understood as an epistemological break, unlocks the dead-end of speculative inquiry. It is brought in at the point, where every logic and every system seems to come to an end - like on the Cross.

Closely related to this is the principle of praxis, which denotes the priority of orthopraxis over orthodoxy. Since the triumph over injustice in the world is the grand motif of this theology, that is to say, since the transformation of the society is its basic hope, actions that are liberating and transformational take precedence over abstract reflection. Liberating action is believed to be a locus for divine revelation.

Poverty is also believed to have a hermeneutic function for the revelation of God. According to the biblical testimony, God makes the poor the privileged locale for His self-revelation. In this context, special attention is paid to the paradoxical meaning of poverty in the Bible, as solidarity in protest.

All these principles lead to the knowledge of God as "God of the poor", whose partiality for the poor is a mystery. In His unconditional option for the poor, God reveals Himself as the gratuitous love. Apparently, the poor receive His attention, not because of merit, but because of His own goodness, and abhorrence of injustice. Yet, that He should favour the poor and not the rich is believed to be a part of His mysterious and paradoxical nature, which becomes evident in Jesus' own notion of God. The image of God, as Jesus lived Him, is full of tension: the tension of absence and presence. For this reason Jesus was always discovering new dimensions of God till the end of his life. Through him, it has become evident that God is beyond human imagination, that no limit is set to God's unconditional love. It is God's triumph over every dead-end in history, and the incalculable possibility of His unconditional love that proves His transcendence. The mystery of God consists therefore in His being a God of surprises, a God who is ever-greater in His love.

This fact makes it possible for Him to reveal Himself on the Cross, in His very opposite, in the contradiction of life, in a scandal. For the Liberation theology, the Cross is neither a divine plan for the reparation of sins, nor is it an accident. The Cross is a scandal, the consequence of God's option for humankind, and the dedication of His Son to live this option till the end. Rejecting the classical tendency to interpret the Cross from the perspective of redemption, therefore, liberation theology insists that the primary function of the Cross is the revelation of God, as the God who allows the Cross to affect Him. This conclusion is believed to be inevitable, if the scandalousness of the Cross were recognised and if the principle of dialectics were applied.

The logical consequence of God's resolute option for the poor is that He suffers their lot with them. God allows Himself to be affected by the negativity of suffering, death and even divine abandonment. The event of the divine abandonment of Jesus on the Cross is seen as the most significant point in the theology of divine suffering. There are varied approaches to this occurrence. On the one hand, Sobrino and Gutiérrez interpret it like Moltmann, as a situation where God is against God. For them God is not only a victim but also an accomplice in the suffering of His Son on the Cross. In their attempt to think the paradox of God, a sort of dichotomy is envisaged in Him, as He who takes initiative even in the crucifixion of His Son. On the other hand, Boff criticises the above view for projecting evil into the heart of God; God is not a masochist, he says, that He should inflict pain on Himself. His silence on the Cross, Boff insists, should not be seen as God's wilful design to demonstrate His self-sacrifice, but rather as the very proof that God suffers. God did not respond to the call of His Son because, He Himself was suffering. This is a much more original approach to the issue than that adopted by Sobrino and Gutiérrez, though, like the other view, it is problematic.

In general terms, the attempt the Latin American liberation theology makes toward the redefinition of the theological method from the perspective of the poor and the Bible is very significant for the development of the theology of divine suffering. Of course, very little is new in its claims. The importance of historicity, dialectics and eschatological hope for instance had been amply emphasised by other theologies. The influence of the Western theology especially that of Moltmann is very obvious in this connection. However, the emphasis it places on the use of relational categories, on the recognition of the primacy of praxis over theory, and on the need to do theology from the perspective of the poor is of special importance.

Although the emphasis laid on praxis is laudable, it is highly disputable whether praxis has primacy over theory. Definitely, there is a sort of reciprocity between thinking and doing, between faith and action, between orthopraxis and orthodoxy, which tradition had not always taken care of. It is nevertheless erroneous to mistake this reciprocity for the primacy of one over the other. This tendency in the liberation theology, as has been rightly observed, smacks of antiintellectualism.[170]

Again, while it is rightly shown that the issue of divine suffering is a matter of fact for any theology of the oppressed, the emphasis that liberation theology places on divine passibility excluding any sort of impassibility is problematic. By doing so, the tension which the paradoxical nature of God denotes is lost. This is most evident in their various interpretation of the divine abandonment of Jesus Christ on the Cross. By adopting Moltmann's thesis of God against God, of a dichotomy in God, liberation theology incurs the criticisms levelled against Moltmann's theology of divine suffering on itself.[171] Fortunately, however, Boff has rightly criticised this aspect of liberation theology. Nevertheless, his correction does not solve the problem. For, by claiming that God's silence was caused by His suffering, he does give the impression that God was helpless. In either case, therefore, liberation theology gives the impression that God was in need of redemption on the Cross. Their theory of divine suffering is one-dimensional.

---

[170] Cf. J. Macquarrie, *Jesus Christ In Modern Thought*, pp. 318-319.

[171] See 5. 6. of this study.

8. DIVINE SUFFERING IN THE NORTH AMERICAN BLACK THEOLOGY OF LIBERATION

8.1 The Emergence of Black Theology

Christianity occupies a very significant position in the history of Black suffering and struggle for liberation in the United States of America. As is the case in other similar histories of the Black man's burden, the role of Christianity has been at best mysterious and at worst ambiguous. On the one hand, Christianity was used implicitly and explicitly in defence of slave trade, and on the other hand, it provided the slaves with the only forum for a sort of relief from their daily burden.[1] Definitely, one can only understand the notion of God in the Black theology, if it is considered from the background of the ambiguous role of Christianity in the history of Black people's suffering.

Having been uprooted from their families and clans, cut off from their pasts, stripped of their human dignity and denied the right to practise their religions,[2] the Black slaves in North America, who were by nature religious, adopted Christianity as a substitute for their lost religions. Christianity for them became a wel-

---

1   Christianity implicitly endorsed slavery in two ways: (a) through "permissive silence" on the issue of slavery and racism, and (b) because the slave traders and slave-holders were Christians - Catholic traders from Portugal and Spain, Protestant businessmen from England were selling to Christian slave-masters in the United States, citizens of an avowed Christian country. As if that was not bad enough, the Church leaders repeatedly gave explicit blessings and biblical justifications for the enslavement of Africans. For the Catholics, it was better to bound the body of a "heathen" (African) and save his soul than to leave him free but damned. For the Protestants, the enslavement of the Black people was God's will, because since they are the supposed "descendants of Ham", Blacks were condemned to eternal slavery. Hence, while in the Catholic Church for instance, Popes Alexander III and Paul II are said to have given their blessings to slavery with the condition that the slaves be baptised and never sold to non-Christians, less they be damned twice, the Protestants, who justified slavery with the Bible, were reluctant to evangelise to the Black people, whom they believed were not "capable of being made whole through the saving ministry of Jesus". The approach of the Catholic countries therefore differed from that of the Protestants, especially the Calvinists. For while the Calvinists discouraged the evangalisation of the Black people for fear they would realise the nature of their bondage, the Catholics were zealous to Christianise them for the simple purpose of universalising the church. Cf. C. E. Lincoln, The Development of Black Religion in America, pp. 5-20, esp. pp. 9-10. See also J. Ki-Zerbo, Die Geschichte Schwarzafrikas, 228. This difference in approach was however short-lived. As soon as it was realised that the slaves became "more tractable and less troublesome" when they were Christianised, all the denominations began to encourage the evangalisation of the Black people. By that means Christianity became an opiate for the Black people. Cf. C. E. Lincoln, op. cit. , pp. 12-13.

2   R. Bennett, Biblical Theology and Black Theology, p. 10. C. W. Cone, The Identity Crisis in Black Theology, p. 33.

come medium for the expression of their religious needs. It is in this capacity that Christianity played a positive role in the lives of the Black people, at a time when some oppressors were still using it as an instrument of oppression. At this stage the Churches were the only places where the slaves could partly realise their dignity as human beings and develop strategies (like the use of spirituals and story-telling) for motivating the struggle for freedom.

As would be expected, personal experience with the God of Jesus Christ constituted the main source of energy for the struggle for survival in the absurdities of slave existence. While, at that time, slavery and racism were ironically still being defended in the name of the "Christian God", the slaves had already begun to experience this same God (of Jesus) as their most intimate companion in the situation of oppression.

It must be observed, that the Black slaves readily adopted Christianity, not only because it was the only religion they were allowed to practise, but because they perceived a certain parallel between their slave situation and that of the Israelites in Egypt. Besides, they also noticed a conceptual affinity between the Black people's notion of God and the Old Testament image of God,[3] between their religious heritage and the biblical *Weltanschaung*.[4] These last two factors explain why the Black slaves cherished the Bible and appropriated it to an extent that "they were able to derive meanings from it that were hidden to their oppressors".[5]

Their religious experience helped to whet their desire for freedom. For shortly after internalising Christianity, it became obvious for the Black people that their "religious sensibilities" could not be adequately contained and expressed within the Euro-American Church structures: The dissimilarities between Black people and White people in the perception of religious values and in the manner of religious expressions, especially in the manner of worship became conspicuous. From that moment onwards the hunger for religious and cultural freedom grew in proportion to their desire for immanent personal freedom. Even as personal freedom

---

[3] C. W. Cone, *op. cit.* , p. 36.

[4] The Scriptures are records of long oral traditions handed over to later generations. Accordingly, literary forms such as myths, proverbs, poetry, parables, prophesies, and stories were elaborately used. These are forms familiar to Africans with a culture mediated in oral tradition. Thus, as people of African heritage, whose tradition is passed down orally, the Black slaves found the style of the biblical writings very familiar, and made more spiritual and personal use of the Bible than their oppressors. For more details see the works of some Black biblical scholars: C. H. Marbury, An Excursus on the Biblical and Theological Rhetoric of Martin Luther King, pp. 14-28; ---, Myth, Oral Tradition and Continuity, pp. 19-22. See also, Robert Bennett, *op. cit.*

[5] J. D. Roberts, *Black Theology Today*, p. 9.

became possible for some Black people in the Northern states of America, between 1777 and 1818, most Black people intensified their search for religious freedom.[6] And once in search of the freedom to worship according to their temperament, the Black people did not stop at vying for positions in the "biracial" churches; they went further to found Independent African Churches.[7] No matter what could be taken as the remote and immediate factors leading to the establishment of Afro-American Independent Churches, the desire to be Christians without losing their own identity as Black people was paramount.

As a matter of fact, the establishment of the African Independent Churches prepared the ground for the emergence of Black theology. The seed for Black theology was sown as early as the 1740's during the establishment of the Independent Churches. It germinated however only later in the 1960s, during the Civil Rights and Black Power Movements. This is true, not only because "the term 'Black theology' was not coined until the end of the 1960s",[8] but largely because most of the religious leaders in the independent Churches continued with the theology they inherited from the White Churches,[9] which could mostly not be reconciled with the Black experience and identity.

The contribution of Martin L. King, the Black Civil Right activist, to the founding of Black theology was singular. He was the first preacher to relate the Christian gospel to the Black struggle for justice. His religious and charismatic leadership found positive echo in the Civil Rights Movement of the 1960's, which he initiated "with the Montgomery bus boycott in 1955".[10] His interpretation of the Black struggle for freedom in the light of the Bible was popular, but his emphasis on non-violence as a means of achieving liberation aroused scepticism among his followers. For most Black people the theory of non-violence was unrealistic in the face of an upsurge of White brutality against the Black people.

---

6   See W. B. Gravely, The Rise of African Churches in America (1786-1822), pp. 301-317, esp. 312.

7   There are three main causes for this search for religious independence among Black people: White racism, the moral failure of American Churches to confront oppression, and the need to uphold Black culture in the Churches. In addition to these three major factors, Gravely points to power struggle as the more immediate cause: the conscious exclusion of Black members from "positions of power" were perennial in the biracial Churches. Cf. *Ibid.*, p. 302.

8   J. Cone, *For My People*, p. 19.

9   Commenting on how the conservative Black ministers had internalised slave mentality, James Cone writes, that "many had worn masks so long that they had forgotten their true identity". *Ibid.*, p. 17.

10   *Ibid.*, p. 7.

Distrust and opposition developed within the members of the Civil Rights Movement as series of peaceful demonstrations failed to yield positive results. Rather than bringing success, the non-violent demonstrations brought more jail sentences for Black radicals. In contrast to King's approach, Stokely Carmichael, another Black leader, proclaimed "Black Power", calling for the affirmation of Blackness and Black consciousness, and for the pursuit of the liberation of the Black people "by any means necessary".[11]

This led to the development of two camps in the Civil Rights Movement: the adherents of King's non-violence and the advocates of Black Power. With his model, King was able to expose the evil of racism in the light of the gospel, but his approach lacked the radicality needed to effect total liberation. This situation provided an opportunity for the nationalist philosophy of Malcolm X to thrive. Malcolm X, whose main goal was to unite the Black people in the fight against racism and to liberate them from their "inferiority complex", was of the opinion that Christianity is irredeemably White and racist, and that its doctrine of love and non-violence (as King emphasised) was nothing short of the conspiracy of the White Churches to make Black people docile and tractable. Malcolm therefore opted for the replacement of Christianity with Islam. In response to his call, most promoters of Black Power went on to replace Christianity with African religions.

This meant an "existential dilemma"[12] for young radical Black preachers, who, on the one side, were convinced that Christianity is essentially a religion of liberation (evident in the lives of the slave Christians), and on the other hand, were aware of the weakness of Christianity as preached by the White Churches. Although they valued Martin King's adaptation of the gospel to the Black struggle, they disfavoured his politics of non-violence at all cost. The thesis of the Black Power Movement, that Blackness must be affirmed, was attractive to Black radical preachers, but they did not see it as a substitute for Christianity.

In such a situation, it was clear to some Black radical preachers, that the only way to maintain the relevance of Christianity to many Black people was to reconcile the claims of Martin L. King and Malcolm X, i.e. to harmonise Christianity and the Black Power Movement. The response to this challenge gave birth to Black theology. It was in this context of a struggle for the restoration of Black identity and for the accommodation of Christianity as a Black religion, that James Cone hurriedly wrote his *Black Theology and Black Power* (1969), the first book on Black theology.[13] To get a clearer view of the notion of God in the Black

---

11 J. Cone, Black Theology as Liberation Theology, p. 181.

12 *Ibid.*

13 In his *Black Theology and Black Power* (1969), Cone tries to relate the Christian message to the identity of the Black people. He does this by identifying "liberation as the heart of

theology, we shall where necessary also consider the views of other Black theologians in this study.[14]

8.2. The Hermeneutics and Sources of Black Theology

Black theology is an attempt to reflect on the reality of God from the perspective of the oppressed Black people. It is a God-talk that "seeks to be a Black-talk"[15] at the same time: on the one hand, it attempts to effect the self-understanding and self-affirmation of the Black people in the light of the God of the Bible, and on the other hand, to conceive Him in terms of His involvement in the situation of the oppressed.[16]

8.2.1 The Liberation of the Oppressed as a Motif

For James Cone, a theology that seeks to accomplish this task, i.e. to be a Black theology, must have an anthropocentric point of departure.[17] It has to be contextual, in the sense of making the social context of the believers its passionate concern.[18] This means talking about God from the standpoint of the history,

---

the Christian gospel and Blackness as the primary Mode of God's presence" (Preface to 1989 Edition). Two years later, he wrote his *A Black Theology of Liberation* (1970), a systematised work, meant to confirm liberation as the central concern of Black theology. The style of these two earlier works have been noted as aggressive, immature and dependent on Barthian theology. In response to his critics, Cone wrote *The Spirituals and the Blues* (1975), which could be seen as an attempt to make Black experience the primary starting point of Black theology. A more mature work in this new corrective style, *God of the Oppressed* (1975), followed soon. But if this brought a change to his language, it did little to dispel the fear that his theology has been dangerously exclusive for Black Americans. Now in his two later works, *For My People*, (1984) and *My Soul Looks Back* (1986), Cone takes the problems of other oppressed people in the Third World seriously - sexism, classism and colonialism.

14 James Cone can be seen as the most popular pioneer writer of Black theology, but his views are by no means representative of the Black theological approach. There are other approaches, which we meet in the theologies of Joseph Washington, Albert Cleage, Major Jones, William Jones and James Deotis Roberts. We shall allow these approaches to supplement each other.

15 J. Cone, *A Black Theology of Liberation*, p. 38.

16 If Black theology had, at its earliest stage, made revelation its starting point, it has now, in its mature phase, begun to emphasise the Black religious experience as its prime point of departure. Then as James Cone later realised, through the criticisms from his colleagues, there is "no 'abstract' revelation, independent of human experiences ... God encounters us in the human condition". Cf. *ibid.*, (Preface to the 1986 Edition), p. xxi.

17 *Ibid.*, p. 18.

18 James Cone, *God of the Oppressed*, pp. 39-52.

experience, social and political situations, goals and aspirations of the Black people.

Emphasising the significance of the social context for Black theology, therefore, James Cone attempts to dispel the myth about universalism and abstract philosophical conception of God. We cannot move, he contends, from the universal to the particular while conceiving God, because He is not to be encountered in the abstract, but in the concrete human situation of a particular people.[19] The problems and the particular experience of a people are indeed the only authentic points of departure.[20] Hence for Cone, there is nothing like objectivity in the theological language; theology "is subjective speech about God"[21] in the social conditioning of a people. By emphasising the relativity of theological language, he is bent on dismissing the claim that a theological tradition can have a universal validity. By doing so, he also appeals for the recognition of theologies from the perspective of the oppressed.

He justifies his point with the Old and New Testaments accounts, which show that God invariably reveals Himself in a particular social context, the social context of the poor and the oppressed.[22] God tends to reveal Himself at a point where social justice is being restored to the poor and the oppressed.[23] That is why divine revelation in the Old Testament is "inseparable from the social and political affairs of Israel"[24] and also "identical with their liberation from bondage".[25] Liberation is considered as God's major project in the Old Testament. The same is true of the New Testament,[26] except that here God's involvement in the struggle for liberation of the oppressed takes a new and higher dimension: He

---

[19] *Ibid.*, p. 39. On this point, Cone takes his inspiration especially from H. R. Niebuhr, Feuerbach, Marx.

[20] *Ibid.*, p. 137.

[21] *Ibid.*, p. 41.

[22] *Ibid.*, pp. 62-78.

[23] *Ibid.*, pp. 63-72. Hence: "To think biblically is to think in the light of the liberating interest of the oppressed. Any other starting point is a contradiction of the social a priori of the Scripture." See *ibid.*, p. 97.

[24] *Ibid.*, p. 62.

[25] *Ibid.*, p. 70.

[26] *Ibid.*, pp. 79-80.

Himself, in the person and work of Jesus Christ,[27] enters the social context of the poor, and effects liberation as one of the oppressed.[28]

If we believe, Cone goes on to say, that Jesus Christ through his life and work in the social context of the weak and the oppressed, is "the special revelation" of God,[29] and that the content of his message for the oppressed is liberation, liberation must then be made the grand hermeneutic principle for exegesis and theology.[30] Liberation, Cone argues, must be the "hermeneutic principle of the exegesis of the Scriptures",[31] because we come to know the God of the Bible in the light of His activities to liberate the oppressed. Liberation therefore becomes both the measure of a theological truth that is not ideological,[32] and also the only locale for divine revelation.[33] It is the basis on which theological ethics must rest.[34]

---

[27] *Ibid.*, pp. 72-81.

[28] "The Jesus story is the poor person's story, because God in Christ becomes poor and weak in order that the oppressed might become liberated from poverty and powerlessness. God becomes the victim in their place and thus transforms the condition of slavery into the battleground for the struggle of freedom." *Ibid.*, p. 80 & p. 98. The Cross-resurrection event introduces a new style of God's defence of the oppressed unparalleled by any event in the Old Testament. Through the presence of God in the battleground for freedom, freedom is no longer mere freedom *from* socio-political limitations (as in the Old Testament), it is now a freedom *"for* struggle, for battle in the pursuit of humanity", encouraged by God's own participation (*ibid.*, 80-81). It is however noteworthy that divine freedom is not merely spiritual, it builds on historical freedom and transcends it, it goes from the particular freedom to the universal.

[29] J. Cone, *A Black Theology of Liberation*, p. 51-52.

[30] "For if the essence of the gospel *is* the liberation of the oppressed from socio-political humiliation for a new freedom in Christ Jesus...and if Christian theology is an explication of the meaning of that gospel for our time, must not theology itself have liberation as its starting point or run the risk of being at best idle talk and at worst blasphemy?" J. Cone, *God of the Oppressed*, pp. 50-51.

[31] J. Cone, *God of the Oppressed*, p. 77.

[32] For James Cone, there is no abstract criterion for truth or for the reality of God. "In the struggle for truth in a revolutionary age, there can be no principles of truth, no absolutes, not even God. For we realise that...we cannot speak of God at the expense of the oppressed." James Cone, *A Black Theology of Liberation*, p. 18 ff. Even in his later works, the relativity of truth is still being emphasised. See J. Cone, *God of the Oppressed*, pp. 16-13, 102. In another work, he insists that truth and logic in Black theology must be defined from the perspective of the oppressed. Cf. J. Cone, *Speaking the Truth* p. 14 ff.

[33] J. Cone, *A Black Theology of Liberation*, p. 42 ff.

[34] Black theology emphasises that liberation must be presupposed before discussions on morality and reconciliation can be meaningful. Cone accuses White people of defining morality from the perspective of the oppressors, who, ignoring the violence of racism and slavery, call on the oppressed Black people to practise non-violence. That is an ill-defined

For Cone, a theology that does not emerge from the perspective of the poor or from the consciousness of the oppressed for liberation is nothing short of an ideology.[35]

While most Black theologians would accept Cone's emphasis on the significance of the social context of the poor and of the need to develop theology on the line of liberation, not very many would want to equate liberation with revelation, nor base the whole of theology on the liberation-oppression formula.[36] James Cone makes revelation and liberation categorically identical: "God's revelation means liberation - nothing more, nothing less"[37]. "There is no revelation of God without a condition of oppression which develops into a situation of liberation".[38] By implication Cone makes liberation dependent on oppression. This view is certainly questionable. Can God not reveal Himself independent of a situation of oppression and sin? Cone does not seem to have an answer to this question.

8.2.2   "Blackness" as a Theological Symbol

The main programme of the Black Power Movement which inspired Black theology was the promotion of "Black consciousness". Black people were to be reminded of their worth and of the beauty of their Blackness. After centuries of slavery and humiliation Black people were developing inferiority feelings, losing their human dignity and values and tending towards self-abnegation. It was obvious to Black leaders that the ultimate liberation of Black people would be wrought only when Black people began to regain their self-determination and self-affirmation. The prevalent prejudice toward the black colour was believed to be one of the factors breeding an inferiority complex.

---

ethics. The measure of Christian ethics is consistency with the struggle for liberation, he insists. Cf. J. Cone, *God of the Oppressed*, pp. 195-246. If violence is necessary for self-defence and for the purpose of liberation, Cone considers it morally justifiable. Cf. *ibid.*, pp. 219-224; J. Cone, *A Black Theology of Liberation*, pp. 22, 138-152. J. D. Roberts has however criticised Cone's "situation ethics", which he fears endangers the idea of reconciliation. Because, for him, while all Black people should insist that equality and liberation precede reconciliation, the means for liberation must not be such that it makes reconciliation impossible. Roberts is more careful than Cone not to sanction violence or "any means possible" as a means for achieving liberation. Cf. J. D. Roberts, *Liberation and Reconciliation*; ---, *Black Theology Today*, pp. 102-104, 115-122.

[35] J. Cone, *God of the Oppressed*, pp. 89-106.

[36] J. D. Roberts has criticised Cone's liberation-oppression formula as being too narrow a basis for "unlocking the biblical understanding which flows from the Black Christian experience". See ---, *Black Theology Today.*, p. 10

[37] J. Cone, *A Black Theology of Liberation*, p. 46.

[38] *Ibid.*, p. 45.

Excursus: The Origin of the Pejorative Use of Black Colour

The tendency to perceive Blackness negatively has a distant history; it can definitely be dated earlier than the slave period. While some researchers of antiquity, contend that it goes back into the early Christian era, especially in the medieval period, when Christians began to equate white with goodness and paint demons with black,[39] some others trace its root farther back to ancient philosophy. The proponents of the first view claim - with varying or similar emphasis - that this early colour symbolism in Christianity helped in initiating the tendency of the whites to look down on Black and dark-skinned people with an air of superiority. (Today's economic and technological dominance of White people is but the reinforcement and not the cause.) This Christian colour symbolism, as Eulalio Balthazar rightly argues, was in turn influenced by the philosophical development of the preceding centuries.

According to E. Balthazar, the colour symbolism of "darkness" and "light" were used in describing the state of the soul in the time of Plato and Aristotle. It was not used then for the evaluation of the body. This would have been senseless in view of the fact that for the Greeks the body was essentially depraved. However, in the subsequent philosophies of the medieval period (Augustinian and Thomist), a "metaphysical shift" occurred in the colour symbolism. "The color symbolism which was previously applied to the condition of man's soul now came to be applied to man's skin..."[40] This metaphysical shift was consistently pursued in what Balthazar calls the "aryanization of Christ" - the attempt to paint Jesus' dark hairs light and his dark eyes blue so as to improve on the colour symbolism of his Jewish body.[41]

In order to boost Black people's self-esteem that was damaged through negative colour symbolism, and also to correct the pejorative understanding of Blackness, Black leaders began to affirm "Blackness". This meant in effect reasserting that on the basis of which injustice is perpetrated, so as to let its beauty come to the limelight.

Taking a cue from the Black Power Movement, Black theology adopted "Blackness" as a theological symbol, not only to promote "Black consciousness", but largely to qualify that which is specific about Black experience. In its theological usage, it could be literal or symbolic: In a sense, Blackness stands for the ethnicity or race of a people, of the dark-skinned people of African origin. In an-

---

39 R. Bastide, Color, Racism, and Christianity, pp. 312-327; F. M. Snowden Jr., *Blacks in Antiquity - Ethiopians in the Greco-Roman Experience*, pp. 196-215; and, *Before Color Prejudice*, (Cambridge: Harvard, 1983); Peter Frost, Attitudes toward Blacks in the Early Christian Era, pp. 1-11.

40 E. Balthazar, *The Dark Centre: A Process Theology of Blackness*, p. 29. Also cited in J. D. Roberts, *Black Theology Today.*, p. 12.

41 E. P. Balthazar, *The Dark Centre*, p. 32.

other sense, it is an "ontological symbol"[42] for all oppressed people in the whole world. For James Cone claims, Blackness "symbolises oppression and liberation in any society".[43]

Consequently, he says that Jesus Christ, who is the oppressed One par excellence is symbolically Black.[44] To say that Jesus is Black means that he has taken upon himself the reason for the oppression of the Black people. God, who is believed to have become the oppressed One in Jesus Christ, is also Black.[45] This is the one way in which Cone tries to affirm Blackness in the light of the Bible, and in the light of the negative experiences of the Black race.[46]

For most other Black theologians, however, Blackness primarily signifies the uniqueness of Black experience, history and culture. The affirmation of Blackness then is a call on all Black people to go back to their African roots, so as to discover the indestructible "soul" of Blackness,[47] which centuries of humiliation and slavery have not been able to destroy.

Some of these indestructible elements of Blackness, which Black theology must elevate, were acquired through the experience of suffering. In James Cone's theology, they are identified as the Black people's will for life: the will to survive and to be human in spite of a social and political set-up that defines a Black person as "non-being" or as "nobody".[48]

Today, Blackness has also come to stand for that intrinsic "rest" from the African heritage, which survived years of slave existence and alienation. Apparently, there is now a consensus among the Black theologians to make the unique aspects of Blackness, embodied in the African heritage, the foundation of Black theology. Going back to the African roots is now seen as a necessary measure to be taken

---

[42] J. Cone, *A Black Theology of Liberation*, p. 7.

[43] *Ibid.*, p. viii (Preface, 1970 Edition).

[44] James Cone, *Black Theology and Black Power*, p. 68 f.; and, *A Black Theology of Liberation*, pp. 119-128.

[45] J. Cone, *A Black Theology of Liberation*, pp. 63-66.

[46] J. Cone does not enjoy the support of other Black theologians on this point. He has been vehemently criticised for making Blackness synonymous with oppression. J. D. Roberts accuses him of "provincialism", an uncritical reduction of the immense oppression in the world to Black experience. See J. D. Roberts, *Black Theology Today*, p. 39.

[47] "*Soul* sums up the Black experience, whether religious or secular, better than any other term." J. D. Roberts, *Liberation and Reconciliation*, p. 9.

[48] J. Cone, *A Black Theology of Liberation*, pp. 11, 25; and --, *My Soul Looks Back*, p. 23.

in order to gain self-knowledge and overcome identity crisis.[49] As the works of Gayraud S. Wilmore,[50] Cecil W. Cone,[51] J. Deotis Roberts,[52] and, only recently, those of James Cone,[53] demonstrate, the tendency to look back to the African Traditional Religions as the roots of Black theology is very much in vogue. As they do that, it is being discovered that Black people have a "characteristic mode of perceiving, experiencing, and orienting reality", which centuries of slavery and humiliation could not destroy.[54]

Excursus: The Intrinsic Aspects of "Blackness"

American Black theologians hold to at least four basic characteristics of the African thought, which they consider to be intrinsic to the symbol of "Blackness".[55]

(1) It is characteristic of an African religious world-view to perceive and conceive reality in its wholeness or totality. Black people naturally have a holistic vision of reality that engulfs ones entire being, including the profane and the sacred. In an African life the "secular and the sacred, the rational and the mystical, the individual and the social interact and are held in a dynamic tension in one continuum of experience."[56] To a great extent, this sense of wholeness in the African pattern of thought accounts for the uniqueness of the Black religious experience in America during and after the slave period.

(2) A high sense of spirituality and reverence to the "Almighty and Sovereign" God. The idea of God which the slaves brought from Africa helped them understand the Old Testament conception of the "Almighty Sovereign God".[57]

---

49 Cf. J. Cone, *My Soul Looks Back*, p. 28: "without self-knowledge others can make you become what they desire".

50 As a theologian and historian, Wilmore did much to encourage Black theologians to study African religions. See his *Black Religion and Black Radicalism*, first published 1973. The same concern continued to influence the choice of texts for his anthologies: G. Wilmore & J. Cone, (ed.). *Black Theology: A Documentary History, 1966-1976*; G. Wilmore, (ed.), *African American Religious Studies*.

51 Cf. C. W. Cone, *The Identity Crisis in Black Theology*.

52 J. D. Roberts, *Black Theology Today*; and ---, *Black Theology in Dialogue*, p. 20f.

53 J. Cone, *For My People*, chapter 3; and ---, Black Theology as Liberation Theology, pp. 183-185.

54 C. W. Cone, *The Identity Crisis in Black Theology*, pp. 31-32.

55 For details about these and other aspects of Black cultural heritage, see chapter nine of this study and also B. Bujo, *African Theology in its Social Context*, pp. 17-33; A. Shorter, *African Christian Theology*, pp. 34-36.

56 J. D. Roberts, *Black Theology Today*, pp. 28-29.

57 C. W. Cone, *The Identity Crisis in Black Theology*, p. 36. Cecil Cone, like most Black theologians, takes his information about African traditional religions exclusively from the works of J. S. Mbiti, especially from his *Concepts of God in Africa*, and ---, *African Re-*

(3) A strong sense of communal life (*sensus communis*) and an understanding of human community as embracing the "living" and the "living dead" and the "yet-to-be born" is prevalent. It is also apparent that the belief in the presence of the dead ancestors in the African community, helped the Afro-American slaves to read the Bible as a "living Book", as a book, whose stories, though of the past, exercise such catching effects in the present, that it begins to dawn on the African reader or listener that the dust of past years cannot cover the route to the "living dead". As James Cone's interpretation of the Spirituals demonstrate, the sense for community was present in the slaves conception of heaven: Heaven was for the slaves primarily the place where they would reunite with their families. The concern of the slaves to join their fathers, mothers, sisters, after this life, was so much that the fear of missing that community was more tormenting than the acute physical pain inflicted by the inhumanity of slavery.[58]

(4) Closely related to the *sensus communis* is the African understanding of personhood. In most African communities, being a person is not based on "thinking" (Descartes) or on "self-subsistence" (Boethius-Scholastic tradition), but on belonging to a family or community.[59] The understanding of person in most African cultures is thus relational. That is why any normal African does all he can to be at peace with his community.

8.2.3   The Sources of Black Theology

From the above, the following could stand for the hermeneutic principles of Black theology: the motif of liberation, the social context of the oppressed as the starting point of theological reflection, the exploration of the Black religious thought and culture using the category of Blackness. In the light of these principles, Black theology considers four major sources as vital for its development.[60]

---

ligions and Philosophy. This is a risky venture. Because, despite Mbiti's laudable attempt to present a common view of African religions, it has been observed that given the size of Africa his comparative interpretations end up as conclusions too generalised to be truly representative of the whole African religious tradition. For criticism on this point see Kwame Gyekye's review of Mbiti's *African Religions and Philosophy*, pp. 86-94; J. O. Awolalu, Sin and Its Removal in African Traditional Religion, pp. 275-287. Thus, while we hold the return to the African roots in high esteem, Black theologians are better advised to diversify their sources of information. Mbiti is not the sole spokesman for African traditional religion.

[58] J. Cone, *The Spirituals and the Blues*, chapter iv.

[59] J. S. Pobee, *Toward an African Theology*, p. 49.

[60] In 1970 James Cone named six sources of Black theology: Black experience, Black history, Black culture, revelation, scripture and tradition. Cf. J. Cone, *A Black Theology of Liberation*, pp. 21-35. We can however bring all his sources under the first three in our list. As His more recent works suggest, Cone has also realised the need to recognise the Third World theologies as sources, because Black theology does not only inspire them but is itself inspired by the other Third World Theologies. Cf. J. Cone, *For My People*, pp. 140-156; ---, *My Soul Looks Back*, p. 93-113. His brother Cecil W. Cone recognises the three but one source, that being Third World Theologies. Cf. C. W. Cone, *The Identity*

(a) *The African Roots*. This would include, the African Traditional Religions, the true history of the Black race before slavery, especially with regard to the contribution of Black Africans to the Egyptian Civilisation.[61]

(b) *The Black Experience*. This embraces the various experiences of suffering and humiliation of the Black people in the Diaspora (in the United States, in Latin America, in the Caribbean Islands), and on the African main land. In the Diaspora it was gained through the encounter with slavery and racism; in the African continent through the confrontation with racism (South Africa), colonialism, poverty and corruption.

(c) *The Bible*. The Black people's attachment to the Bible has been peculiar. Although we have noted that the affinity of Black spirituality and conception of God to the Jewish tradition made the slaves cherish the Bible as a book of spirituality and prophecy, it must equally be borne in mind, that the Bible influenced the Black spirituality, the experience of God and methods of worship in the States. The Black Churches make the Bible their primary document - a book of consolation in suffering and a book of liberation in struggle. Since Black theology purports to be a "Church theology", it follows the example of the Black slaves and Churches to make the Bible its primary document, so as to be true to the Black experience of God as Christians. In addition to the Bible, the Spirituals, Blues and folklore are considered as sources. Tradition could be consulted, but only the portions that speak the language of liberation.[62] Every aspect of the Black Churches that mediates the people's experience with the story of Jesus could serve as sources of Black theology.

(d) *Other Third World theologies*. According to Maulana Karenga, "Black Liberation Theology helped inspire and was in turn inspired by Third World the-

---

Crisis in Black Theology, pp. 73-144. J. Deotis Roberts equally acknowledges the above listed sources. Above all, he emphasises that in drawing from its sources, Black theology should have a universal and ecumenical vision. Cf. J. D. Roberts, *Black Theology Today*, pp. 25 ff.; and ---, *Black Theology in Dialogue*, pp. 11-19. It is in this connection that he criticises Cone's Christology as being too Barthian, and implicitly exclusive of non-Christological sources of divine revelation.

61 Cf. M. Karenga, Black Religion, pp. 271-300.

62 J. Cone, *A Black Theology of Liberation*, p. 35; J. D. Roberts, *Black Theology in Dialogue*, p. 37. Although the Black theologians do no say much about their influence from the Euro-American theology, it is evident that much of Black theology is shaped either in accordance with or in opposition to the Western theology. The influence of the theologies of Karl Barth and R. Niebuhr are evident. And even as they are critical of the process theologians they make use of process thought nonetheless. Cf. E. Balthazar, *The Dark Centre: A Process Theology of Blackness*.

ology".[63] Despite the initial tendency of Black theology to be restrictive, especially in Cone's version of it, it had always seen the Latin American Liberation theology as a partner in the same cause for the oppressed people in the world. While it is apparent that Black theology propagated liberation theology before Latin American theology,[64] the former got the impulse towards a systematisation of liberation theology from the Latin Americans. Today, with the realisation on the part of the Black theologians that apart from racism, there are other forms of institutionalised oppression in the world, like classism, sexism, imperialism, neo-colonialism, the urge to identify with the liberation theologies all over the world has become paramount. Black theologians, like their counterparts the world over, have become aware of the fact that not only are "commonalities and divergences" among Third World theologies, but that a "cross-fertilisation" of ideas is taking place today.[65]

8.3. The Doctrine of God in Black Theology

8.3.1 The Reality of God and His Liberating Activities

The reality of God is an unquestionable presupposition in Black Theology. Of course, faced with the absurdities of slavery and racism, and embarrassed by the seemingly unending suffering of the innocent slaves, questions about God's role in the lives of African Americans were definitely posed, just as doubts whether God was not Himself a racist were occasionally expressed. Yet, there were virtually no doubts about God's existence in the history of the oppressed Black people. The questions about God's activity rather than his reality formed the common feature of Black existence. Consequently, cases of atheism among the African Americans are very rare today, and in fact virtually non-existent in the history of the slave period. Like Black people in other parts of the world, they have been said to "live in a pool of divinity"[66]

Subsequently, the Black slaves posed questions of "why?" and "how long?" with bitterness, but they were ever resolved in their conviction that God was against racism and that He would liberate them in the future. The assurance that

---

63 M. Karenga, op. cit. , p. 290.

64 James Cone published His first two books on liberation theology in 1969 and 1970 respectively; three years later in 1973 Gustavo Gutiérrez wrote his celebrated pioneering work on Latin American liberation theology.

65 K. C. Abraham (ed.), Third World Theologies: Commonalities and Divergences.

66 Cf. J. D. Roberts, Black Theology in Dialogue, pp. 38 & 35. This vision of God, which also characterises Black people elsewhere is believed to be another proof of the "African presence" in the Black theology.

God detests slavery was gained however from the biblical story of His liberation of the oppressed Israelites. With this vision of the biblical God, it was clear to the slaves that God could not sanction slavery, and that "...the God of the Exodus was the Black man's God."[67] Strictly, speaking, the Black slaves drew two lessons from the Exodus. First, that God reveals Himself in the act of liberation. Secondly, that in this process God defines Himself as a God of and for the oppressed. Significantly, this inference, which the slaves made without any biblical training, has turned out to be the foundation on which the academic Black theology builds its doctrine of God. For Black theology, the idea of the biblical God and the phenomenon of liberation should then be the basis and starting point of the Christian doctrine of God.[68]

Liberation is, for that reason, the measure of the authenticity of a conception of God that claims to be Christian. God acts against the oppressors and in favour of the oppressed to effect their liberation. This divine partiality was evident in the Exodus and in the life of Jesus. Thus any conception of the divinity that does not present God as a liberator of the oppressed is believed to be false and idolatrous. For "God-talk is not Christian-talk unless it is directly related to the liberation of the oppressed."[69]

8.3.2   The Visions of God and God-talk

At the end of his book, "*Is God a White Racist?*",[70] William Jones testifies to the fact "that the Black theologians are torn by conflicting theological agendas". On the one hand, they wish to conceive Black theology as a theology that grows out of the experience of Black churches: as such it would embrace all theologies evolved by the African Americans. On the other hand, they would want to understand it as a liberation theology, whose central motif and content is the issue of liberation. Given the fact, however, that not all Black churches have humanising and liberating ideas of God, Black theologians are often caught in a dilemma of insisting that liberation is the main content of the Black theology and also wanting to understand Black theology as a theology of all the Black churches. In what seems to be an attempt to resolve this dilemma, Cecil Cone writes, "Black Theology must come to terms not with Black people as such, but with the God of Black

---

67   J. D. Roberts, *Liberation and Reconciliation*, p. 99.

68   J. Cone, *A Black Theology of Liberation*, p. 60: "The point of departure of Black theology", James Cone insists, "is the biblical God as related to the Black liberation struggle". See also J. D. Roberts, *Liberation and Reconciliation*, p. 83, for a similar affirmation.

69   J. Cone, *Ibid.*

70   W. R. Jones, *Is God A White Racist?*, p. 202.

people."[71] What the true nature of the God of Black people should be in this context is anything but definite.

The only definite thing seems to be that the conception of God in Black theology presents itself in the background of a whole net of tensions.[72] Hope and faith in a God who is good and liberates conflict invariably with the awareness of a persistent suffering and of obvious absence of a definitive liberation of Black people from racism and underprivileged existence. Without any clear sign of a privileged liberation of the Black people, the God of the Black people is, in spite of all odds, believed to be a liberator God.

Beyond and behind the issue of liberation however lies the problem of theodicy, which, by all intents and purposes, seems to constitute the invisible anvil on which the Black concept of God is forged. Whether it is admitted or not, the intractable problem of theodicy is inseparable from the conception of God in Black theology. This is true whether Black theology is conceived primarily as a response to the crisis of Black suffering, or largely in terms of a liberation-oppression / liberation-reconciliation formula.

The background function of theodicy for the Black God-talk becomes yet more evident when one considers what some Black theologians term the central question of their theological investigations. According to James Cone, the central question for Black theology is this: "How do we dare speak of God in a suffering world, a world in which Black people are humiliated because they are Black?".[73]

J. D. Roberts holds a similar view as he writes,

> I am taking the position that the problem of God presents itself to Blacks in terms, not of the existence of God, but rather in terms of the moral attributes of God. ... The Christian understanding of God must develop out of the Black experience of oppression endured for almost four centuries.[74]

Thus, it is the task of Black theology to work out "a Biblical basis for absorbing the experience of suffering into a faith in a God who is Creator, Redeemer, and Judge". (98)

Similarly, but more poignantly, William Jones argues for the "priority" of theodicy in God-talk. Theodicy, he claims, is "the controlling category for Black

---

71 C. W. Cone, *The Identity Crisis in Black Theology*, p. 144.

72 There are tensions between the African roots of Black religion and Euro-American influence on the Christian theology, between Black faith in liberation and persistent suffering, between the struggle for liberation and the need for reconciliation. Details of such tensions can be taken from the works of Cecil Cone and J. D. Roberts.

73 *Ibid.*

74 J. Deotis Roberts, *Liberation and Reconciliation*, p. 83.

theology".[75]   Other Black critics have warned Jones against reducing the whole of Black theology to the theodicy issue. Roberts, for instance, even objects to making theodicy the starting point of theology.[76]

Despite such explicit objections to the reduction of the whole of Black theology to theodicy, one cannot avoid getting the impression that theodicy, as Jones argues, is the controlling category for Black God-talk. Then, confronted with the unfair distribution of suffering in this world - the unproportionality of Black suffering - Black theology is necessarily conditioned by the problem of theodicy. Theodicy haunts all God-talk in Black theology. The reason for this phenomenon is not far-fetched: Since Black people take the reality of God for granted, theologians are ever obliged to reconcile the goodness and power of God in the face of suffering. In that case the question of God, whether one likes it or not, begins with an inquiry into God's role in suffering.

There are varied and conflicting accounts about God's role in the suffering of the oppressed in Black theology. While for some theologians like James Cone, God is absolutely on the side of the poor and must for that reason be conceived in terms of His partiality for the poor, for others, God is neutral. God's neutrality is invariably conceived in two senses: in the sense that He does not interfere in human affairs (William Jones) and in the sense that He cares equally for the oppressed and the oppressors (Major J. Jones and James Deotis Roberts).

8.3.2.1   God's Partiality for the Poor (James Cone)

The controlling idea of James Cones' theology is liberation. The conviction that God intervenes to liberate the oppressed thus forms the basis for his conception of God. God, he contends, breaks the chains of slavery, not from without but from within the struggle for liberation. He joins the oppressed in the struggle for liberation, taking side with them to such an extent that He makes their liberation His cause of action.[77] For Cone, God's identification with the oppressed Black people is so boundless and His immersion in the situation of their oppression so

---

75   William Jones, *Is God A White Racist?*, p. xix.

76   J. Deotis Roberts, *Black Theology Today*, p. 37.

77   J. Cone, *A Black Theology of Liberation*, p. 56: "It is God's cause because God has chosen the Blacks as God's own people. And God has chosen them not for redemptive suffering but for freedom. Blacks are not elected to be Yahweh's suffering people. Rather we are elected because we are oppressed against our will and God's, and God has decided to make our liberation God's own undertaking."

total that one could speak of the Blackness of God. "The Blackness of God means that God has made the oppressed condition God's own condition."[78]

Cone does not however see God's assumption of the condition of the poor as an extraordinary act: God takes sides with the oppressed, not out of pity, but because the liberation of the oppressed is "part of the innermost nature of God" and "the essence of divine activity".[79] He goes on to contend that God's election of the Israelites and in His Incarnation in Christ should be understood in this term, i.e. as events neither motivated by pity nor by merit, but dictated by God's own nature and disposition to take side with the oppressed. The conviction that God is Black, that is, that He is essentially on the side of the oppressed liberating them from oppression has two implications for Cone's conception of God.

First, it means, according to James Cone, that God is partial. For him there can neither be a "God of all peoples" nor a "colourless God". In other words, he contends that God cannot be for the oppressed and the oppressors at the same time.

Either God is identified with the oppressed to the point that their experience becomes God's experience, or God is a God of racism.[80]

The second implication is epistemological. "Knowing God means being on the side of the oppressed, becoming one with them, and participating in the goal of liberation. We must become Black with God."[81] The knowledge of God is practical, excluding every sort of quietism in the face of oppression. God must be known in the context of the human condition. That means that there can be no knowledge of God "as God is *in se*",[82] except as He reveals Himself in the work of liberation.

Using God's partiality for the oppressed as a theological motif, James Cone undertakes a reinterpretation of the Trinity[83] and a review of some divine attributes.

a) *Divine Love and Wrath*. Black theology, Cone argues, agrees with other modern theologies that love is the essence of God. But it distances itself from the view that tends to deny the reality of the wrath of God. Justice and love of God

---

78 J. Cone, *A Black Theology of Liberation*, p. 63.

79 *Ibid.*, p. 64.

80 *Ibid.*, p. 63.

81 *Ibid.*, p. 65.

82 *Ibid.*, p. 71.

83 *Ibid.*, p. 64: "Taking seriously the Trinitarian view of the Godhead, Black theology says that as Creator, God identified with oppressed Israel, participating in the bringing into being of this people; as Redeemer, God became the Oppressed One in order that all may be free from oppression; as Holy Spirit, God continues the work of liberation."

are not mutually exclusive, they supplement each other in God.[84] In contrast to those who feel that divine love excludes divine wrath, Black theology insists that wrath - just like love - belongs to the nature of God. His wrath emerges out of His nature as liberator.

> A God without wrath does not plan to do too much liberating, for the two concepts belong together. A God minus wrath seems to be a God who is basically not against anything.

In Cone's opinion, God must be against oppressors, if His activities of liberation should have any meaning at all. Wrath is part of divine nature, because it is part of love that liberates.

> ...then wrath is an indispensable element for describing the scope and meaning of God's liberation of the oppressed. The wrath of God is the love of God in regard to the forces opposed to liberation of the oppressed. Love without righteousness is unacceptable to Blacks: this view of God is a product of the minds of enslavers.[85]

b) *God's Creatorship.* James Cone observes that the priestly account of creation was written in exile. If in the situation of captivity, the oppressors and the oppressed were prone to forgetting the proper order of creation, it was necessary for the Israelites to remind themselves that God, and not the oppressors, is the sole author of creation. Thus, strictly speaking, "the biblical view of God as creator is not a paleontological statement about the nature and origin of the universe, but a theological assertion about God and God's relationship to the oppressed of the land".[86]

Creation and God's authorship can only be properly understood from the perspective of the oppressed. From this point of view, creation out of nothing (*ex nihilo*) does not merely emphasise God's aseity as classical theology teaches. Rather, it primarily means that our "being finds its source in God. I am Black because God is Black!"[87] God is the sole author and purpose of creation. Accordingly, the main message of the doctrine of creation is the equality of all humanity. And in actual fact, the struggle for liberation is equally at the service of creation,

---

84 J. Cone expressed the relationship between divine love and justice more precisely in his first work, *Black Theology and Black Power*, p. 51. "Love prevents righteousness from being legalistic, and righteousness keeps love from being sentimental. Both express God's desire to be for man when man will not be for himself. Love means that God rights the wrongs of humanity because they are inconsistent with his purpose for man. Righteousness means that God cannot turn his back on evil, that he cannot pretend that wrong is right."

85 James Cone, *A Black Theology of Liberation*, p. 71.

86 *Ibid.*, p. 75.

87 *Ibid.*

because it aims at returning the Lordship of creation, usurped by the oppressors, back to God, the real Lord of creation.

c) *Divine Immanence and Transcendence*. In Black theology, the immanence and transcendence of God are conceived as inclusive terms. For as much as the divine involvement in the "human now-experiences" is emphasised, the view that "God is always more than our experience of God" is very much held.[88] Thinking the relationship of inclusiveness between God's transcendence and immanence seems easy for Cone, perhaps because immanence and transcendence are for him no spatial concepts; they should be seen as relational terms expressing God's relationship to finite human beings, especially to the oppressed, so that He can be one with them and yet transcend them.

d) *Divine Providence and Power*. In the light of evil in the world, James Cone finds it obligatory for Black theology to reinterpret the doctrine of providence. The popular view of divine providence, typified in the thought of Emil Brunner, according to which all that happens is taken to be in accordance with the divine plan must be rejected. Such a view would lead to the logical conclusion, that God is responsible for all that happens, including evil. Black theology "cannot accept any view of God that even indirectly places divine approval on human suffering".[89]

The major content of divine providence, as Cone sees it, is freedom. God provides ways that now make the realisation of freedom possible. Providence is neither a statement about the future nor about God's power to do everything. "Providence is a statement about present reality". And it is apparent that the freedom to struggle for liberation is the only present reality.

As a corollary, God's omnipotence does not consist in making all things work out well in this world for those who love Him. It is implied in the human freedom to struggle for liberation.[90]

8.3.2.2   God's Neutrality and Non-interference (William Jones)

In the view of William Jones, it is presumptuous and in fact nonsensical to speak of God's privileged partiality for the oppressed. Normally, every Black theology begins its reflection with the presupposition that God is intrinsically good, and that he is on the side of the oppressed. But looking at the long history

---

88   *Ibid.*, p. 77.

89   *Ibid.*, p. 78.

90   *Ibid.*, p. 81.

288

of Black suffering and at its proportional increase in the present time, Jones feels that the goodness of God cannot be assumed, it has to be proved.

In his opinion, it is illegitimate to claim the goodness of God by just looking at the biblical account of His liberative activities. What God does for the Black people at present must be taken note of. It is evident, no doubt, that "the biblical writers establish Who God is by reference to what He has done or is doing".[91] This suggests that the nature of God must be established in view of His actions, both past and present. It also means that Black theology must conceive God today in the light of what God does for the Black people, not in the light of what He did for the Israelites.

> When one makes conclusions about *Who God* is on the basis of *what He has done* for Black people, when one accents what is central to the Black past - oppression and slavery - as the primary materials for reaching conclusions about the divine attributes...it is not difficult to see the category of divine racism surfacing.

The sum of God's activities in the long history of Black oppression and slavery, is anything but encouraging. Then, even if there were enough cases of God's liberating activities in the Black experience, the question would still remain why a particular race must suffer more than others. Why ethnic suffering?

Is God a racist? This is a question which every Black theology must have occasion to answer. Judging from the available evidence of God's activities in the Black experience, the probability of divine racism is as tenable as the claim of His goodness. According to William Jones, therefore, divine racism must be rebutted if the claim that God is good and a liberator should have any credibility at all. Jones observes that all the major Black theologians work with a theological framework unsuitable for the rebuttal of divine racism.[92]

All Black theologies of liberation are built on the assumption that God disapproves slavery and that He acts on behalf of the oppressed. This assumption cannot be justified on the basis of Black experience, Jones maintains. Black theologians make constant reference to the biblical experience of the Israelites, when they intend to show that God is good and that He is a liberator. But as W. Jones sees it, till now, there is no basis in Black history for projecting the view that God is a liberator. The liberation of the Black people is not yet definite, given the enormity of the ongoing sufferings of the Black race.

As long as we cannot demonstrate the nature of God based on His actions in the history of the Black people, the claim that He is intrinsically good and that He is a liberator remains theoretical and unsubstantiated. And as the liberating ac-

---

91 W. Jones, *Is God a White Racist?*, p. 13.

92 *Ibid.*, p. 23. See also pp. 71-166 for details about his critiques on Joseph Washington, James Cone, Albert Cleage, Major Jones, and J. Deotis Roberts.

tivities of God are not so visible in the Black experience, William Jones thus maintains that the emphasis Black theology places on liberation is illegitimate. He seems to argue that God is to be charged with racism, if He is a liberator and has not yet liberated the Black people.

He therefore contends, "that the liberation of non-Blacks, e.g. the Jews in the Exodus account, can never count decisively against the charge that God is a White racist".[93] The reasons for divine attributes must be evident in the Black experience.

In search of the meaning for Black suffering, Black theologians are always prone to affirming that Blacks are the "chosen people" of God, His suffering servants. This "favourite motif of Black theology", according to William Jones, is absurd and unjustifiable. It is too early to make that conclusion about Black suffering. Because, given the ambiguity of the biblical view of suffering - in some cases, suffering can be a punishment, i.e. a sign of God's disfavour; in other cases, it can be a mark of the selection of an individual or a people - it is not yet evident whether Black suffering is a punishment or an evidence of God's choice of Black people to be His suffering people. Suffering is "multi-evidential".[94]

In fact, even in terms of the Bible there can be no justification yet for seeing Black suffering as a sign of God's favour. For, it is evident, Jones argues that suffering can only be vindicated or shown to be God's instrument of election, if there is liberation or the "*exaltation event*" at the end. In all cases in the Bible, where the claim of suffering servant could be made, exaltation or liberation serves as criterion. The Exodus event for instance gave the sure sign that the Israelites were the suffering servants of God. Similarly, Job's suffering was vindicated by a happy end. And most evidently the resurrection of Jesus Christ supplies the necessary confirmation that the crucified Christ was the suffering servant of God. All these facts therefore imply that the claim of being the suffering servant of God, can only be made at the end of suffering, not while it persists.[95] Since there is no such confirmation in the history of the Black people yet, the model of suffering-servant in Black theology has no justification. William Jones makes this point abundantly clear in these rhetorical questions:

> Is it possible to declare that Jesus is Lord if we affirm only the Cross and omit the Resurrection? Can we declare that Blacks are the suffering servant if the only evidence is the fact of their suffering?.[96]

---

93 William Jones, *Is God a White Racist?*, p. 78. See also all of Chapter of v.

94 *Ibid.*, p. 6 ff.

95 *Ibid.*, pp. 17-20.

96 *Ibid.*, p. 16.

He therefore contends that the belief "that Blacks are God's chosen people must be abandoned",[97] because in the absence of liberation-exaltation in the lives of Black people today, such a model raises rather than resolves the issue of divine racism.

With the same strength, he rejects an eschatological option as an answer to divine racism. The persistence of Black suffering puts a question mark on all eschatological options that are not based on the concrete experience of Black people. "On what grounds can the Black theologian affirm that God's activity will be different in the future - i.e., effecting the liberation of Blacks - when the present and past history of Blacks is oppression?"[98]

How can we defend the probable charge of divine racism? This is William Jones' main question. And his conviction is that no theological model working with the proposition of divine partiality can answer the charge of divine racism. Contrary to the views of his critics,[99] the intention of William Jones here "is not to demonstrate that God is a White racist or an anti-Semite. Rather, it is to question the theological frameworks within which these charges legitimately surface".[100]

William Jones believes that it is the duty of every Christian theologian to uphold the intrinsic goodness of God, but he contends that in the face of the persistent and excessive Black sufferings, Black theology has the extra burden of demonstrating the truth of divine goodness. References to non-Black experiences cannot suffice; divine goodness must be inferred from the Black existence, otherwise it is question-begging. It is apparent however for William Jones that any theological model that admits God's interference in history cannot justify God in the face of ethnic suffering.

He therefore suggests that the only way to answer the charge of divine racism in Black theology is to maintain the neutrality of God in history. He advances this view in the context of his *"humanocentric theism"*, a model which he finds eminently substantiated in the existentialist and personalistic thoughts of Martin Buber, Harvey Cox and Howard Burkle.[101] According to Jones, the basic characteristic of humanocentric theism is the advocacy of the *"functional ultimacy of man"*.

---

[97] *Ibid.*, p. xxii.

[98] *Ibid.*, p. 12.

[99] J. D. Roberts, *Black Theology Today*, p. 37.

[100] W. Jones, *Is God a White Racist?*, p. 23.

[101] *Ibid.*, pp. 186-194.

Man must act as *if* he were the ultimate valuator or the ultimate agent in human history or both. Thus God's responsibility for the crimes and errors of human history is reduced if not effectively eliminated.[102]

Humanocentric theism emphasises human freedom and suggests the self-limitation of divine power. According to this view, God endows man with "controlling and overruling sovereignty over the essential aspects of the human situation". God does not intend to rule the world alone.[103] In accordance with God's mandate in creation (Buber) and as a consequence of the covenant commitment (Cox), God assigns *"codetermining power"* to human beings, and thus imposes a self-limitation of His sovereignty on Himself.

By virtue of the human status as co-creator, and of his endowment with freedom of choice and activity, human beings therefore have the whole responsibility for the human predicament. God does not interfere, He merely persuades. Racism must thus be seen as the "consequence of human activities alone", the consequence of human misuse of power.[104] For William Jones, a theory of divine non-interference is the only logical pattern of thought "to account for the maldistribution of Black suffering";[105] it is the only appropriate model that can eliminate the charge of divine racism.

Consequently, the God of William Jones creates and abandons His creatures to their predicament and possibilities. God gives human beings the freedom to be co-creators in His creation, but He withdraws out of respect for human freedom. Although Jones' idea of God's non-interference entails God relating to the world persuasively, it undoubtedly implies that God does not care. This view is in sharp contrast to what a majority of Black theologians and believers think. As J. Deotis Roberts rightly points out, no theist or believer can accept this view without renouncing his faith.[106] If anything, the history of Black religious experience in America suggests that even at the worst point of slave existence, the Black slaves shared the conviction that God was with them.[107]

---

[102] *Ibid.*, p. xxii.

[103] This view bears a semblance of MacGregor's kenotic model discussed earlier.

[104] W. Jones, *Is God a White Racist?*, p. 195.

[105] *Ibid.*, p. 201.

[106] J. D. Roberts, *Black Theology Today*, p. 37.

[107] Major Jones, another pioneering Black theologian points out lamentingly, that the number of Black people who share William Jones's view are however on the increase today, especially since the first phase of the Civil Rights Movement failed to achieve the complete victory desired by Black people. Many Black people with a "non-religious mood" do no longer believe that God can work their liberation. They rather tend to believe in their own ability to effect liberation, as few victories in the past have revealed. Because of their

8.3.2.3 God's Neutrality and Care for All (Major J. Jones and James D. Roberts)

Another direction in the conceptualisation of God in Black theology is evident in the thought of Major J. Jones. He neither agrees with James Cone's extreme form of God's partiality nor with William Jones' idea of God's neutrality that boils down to God's indifference. For Major Jones, God is a caring God; He is not against anybody. He is only against evil and suffering.

Major Jones appreciates William Jones' reasons for proposing the idea of God's neutrality. He does not however fully accept the views of the latter, especially those ones that seem to conjure up an idea of God's absence in the Black liberation. For while it is true that a kind of restlessness and protest had always accompanied the hope and faith of Black people in God due to seemingly unending suffering, such misgivings were not able to suppress their assurance that God is on their side fighting against evil and suffering.[108]

In contrast to William Jones, therefore, Major Jones recognises the indispensability of a view of God's involvement in the affairs of mankind in the Black conception of God. Agnostic and impersonal conceptions of God have no place in a Black religious consciousness. Neither was the idea of a hidden God commonplace.

> God for us has never been a reality totally removed from the world or uninvolved in the historical process. For the Black person of faith, God is, and always has been, Almighty both Transcendence and Immanence on the march and sitting-in.[109]

As Major J. Jones further observes, the belief in "a caring God" is common both to African and Afro-American religious experiences. There are certainly differences between the African and Afro-American "God-consciousness" based on varied effects of colonisation and slavery, but the personal encounter of individual Black people with God - whether they were dispossessed by colonisation or uprooted and made homeless by slavery - reveal the image of a caring God.[110]

Although Major Jones sees the image of a caring God imbedded in the Black religious experiences during and after the absurd colonised and enslaved exis-

---

conviction that it is better to rely on themselves than wait for God, "God's reality has been played down to the point that many feel no need for a living God's role in human affairs". See M. J. Jones, *The Color of God*, pp. 24-25.

[108] M. J. Jones, *The Color of God*, p. 36.

[109] *Ibid.*, p. 43.

[110] *Ibid.*, p. 31.

tence, his proposal of the image of a caring God is not made primarily for the sake of maintaining a continuity in Black tradition. He knows too well that continuity alone would not suffice, because as William Jones, his counterpart, rightly contends, the "humanising and liberating quality" of a concept, not its continuity, should be the measure of a valid Black theological statement about God.[111]

Major Jones is also aware of the fact that the Afro-American God-concept, far from being concluded, is still evolving. He suggests nonetheless that our groping for a "usable" concept of God must be done "in terms of understanding what 'God' means personally" for Black believers.[112] Thus, while admitting that as of yet there is no fixed Black God-concept valid at all times - Black people are still in search of a usable concept of God[113] - Major Jones contends nonetheless that the chief particularity of the Black God-concept is the affirmation that He is a personal and caring God.[114]

The grand hermeneutic task of Black theology is to affirm that God is a personal being. God relates to persons in terms of their natures - colour and sex. God can become "everything in everyone".[115] Major Jones sees this fact as a justification for the "God is Black" talk in Black theology. But even though "this tendency to color God black", as Jones observes, "is characteristic of the tendency to interpret God and religion from too narrow a frame of reference", he still argues in favour of God's Blackness. Thus, despite the limitations or reductionism apparent in the theme of God's colour, Jones considers it a necessary and unavoidable anthropomorphism that helps to illustrate the primacy of God's personal encounter with individuals or groups.[116] Here, particularity seems to have primacy over universality; the latter must grow out of the former, if our God-concept must not be abstract.

One might ask, as William Jones does above, from where Black people get their assurance that God cares, when the peculiar suffering of the Black people still persists in this world. Major Jones would answer that the conviction that God is a personal being who cares and responds does not depend on empirical experi-

---

[111] W. Jones, *Is God a White Racist?*, p. 202. In the same connection, William Jones makes known his suspicion, namely, "that perhaps some of the cherished beliefs of Black people are in fact part and parcel of their oppression".

[112] M. J. Jones, *The Color of God.*, p. 46.

[113] *Ibid.*, p. 37.

[114] *Ibid.*, pp. 31 ff.

[115] *Ibid.*, p. 33.

[116] *Ibid.*, pp. 41 ff.

ence alone, but mainly on what he calls "faith-knowledge".[117] Faith-knowledge is a knowledge of God in terms of faith. Because God is an absolute mystery, whose nature and ways are beyond our comprehension we can only make assumptions about Him based on the biblical revelation and on our own nature. Since the future remains unknown to us, we cannot say that God does not liberate totally.

Moreover, we meet ample evidence about God's care for human affairs in the Scriptures especially in songs and prayers. God cares because He is a personal being. That God is a personal being cannot be reasonably doubted; our own self-knowledge as personal beings gives us the assurance that God Himself is a personal being. It is hardly conceivable that an "impersonal source" could be the source of the self-conscious human beings" we are.[118] Rather than believe in an impersonal God, Black people prefer to affirm that God's ways are strange.

For Major Jones, God's personal and caring nature dictates all that can be said about Him. Like J. Deotis Roberts, he describes God's attributes in terms of divine morality.[119] God's nature, he claims, must be described in terms of God's personal and moral perfection. What makes God unique is His perfection, His holiness. Accordingly, Jones sees all the major divine attributes summarised as follows: "God is a personal being of perfect holiness". From Jones one gets the impression that emphasis on God's holiness or spirituality is very vital from the Black theological perspective. Because as he writes:

> To say that God is holy is to assert that God is outside all evil and to affirm that God's ethical perfection excludes from the divine personality all tendencies toward or any delight in evil. ... Positively stated, this means that God delights only in good, that God is devoted solely to goodness, and that in God's personal holiness the concept of moral perfection is wholly realised.[120]

Because God is a holy being, He is by nature against evil and for good. And because He is holy He is love par excellence. The sum of God's love and justice is His holiness, that is, His definitive "no" to evil. For Major Jones, as for James Cone, God's wrath is part and parcel of His love. But in contrast to Cone, Jones does not believe that God's wrath is directed against evildoers, but against evil itself. It is at this point that he distances himself from Cone's claim that God is

[117] *Ibid.*, p. 27.

[118] M. J. Jones, *The Color of God.*, p. 50. Moreover, "Black people of faith prefer a God who cares - with all the theological problems that it entails - to a world of blind forces that do not care". p. 68.

[119] M. J. Jones, *The Color of God.*, pp. 51 ff. Cf. J. D. Roberts, *Liberation and Reconciliation*, pp. 83 & 88.

[120] M. J. Jones, *The Color of God.*, p. 53.

partial. Not even Cone's addendum that God loves those against whom His wrath is directed, justifies the view, that God can be against His creatures.

> God is not on anyone's side, right or wrong. He is against any wrong actions and for anything perfective of his creation. God takes all sides and applies his love or his wrath in balance as needed. Contrary to the usual human sense, God transcends all sides.[121]

Major Jones, and in fact all Black theologians with few exceptions, emphasise that Black ethnic suffering is no sign of God's punishment, and that it has no redemptive purpose either. Black people are not to be viewed as the elected suffering servants of Yahweh, neither should their suffering and oppression be identified with redemption. Jones nonetheless sees the Black situation or Blackness as "a profound and mysterious assignment from God by which Black people have been called to bear witness to the message of his judgement and his grace to all nations".[122]

Does the claim that Blackness is a mysterious assignment not imply that Black people are chosen as a special people? Is the God of Jones not as partial as that of James Cone? How can God be Black and yet not partial to the Black people? Major Jones seems to be in a dilemma here. However, he is less emphatic on the issue of divine election of the Black people than James Cone. Rejecting the image of a partial God He emphasises that of a God who cares for everybody, who can become everything to everyone and yet cares deeply for the Black people. Thus, unlike Cone, Jones contends that God can take any colour.

> God's Blackness does not negate his Whiteness or his Brownness. In African myth, the divine is sometimes referred to as the chameleon. God has taken on oppression in all the colours of human skin.[123]

That God can enter any condition, no matter how depraved is the work of His grace. God is a God of grace, whose mercy is unfathomable. He hates evil, but He allows sinners to live. There is something like a tension between God's mercy which accords creatures every freedom and His wrathful justice, which is committed to redressing evil. God overcomes this tension through His "omnipotent redemption", which, as is exemplified on the Cross, consists in His suffering love.

> Through God's suffering on the Cross, inflicted upon him by human beings, God's grace hopes to win over the hearts of people in spite of themselves.[124]

---

121 *Ibid.*, p. 55.

122 *Ibid.*, p. 98.

123 *Ibid.*, p. 99.

124 *Ibid.*, p. 57.

In accordance with God's perfect holiness, Major Jones, like J. Deotis Roberts, insists that God's all-goodness and omnipotence must be maintained. This is not an easy claim to make in the face of persistent evil in the world, especially as it is presupposed that God cares (Jones) for Black people and that He is present (Roberts) in their condition. Admitting that the issue of evil poses a serious problem to the attribution of absolute goodness and power to God, Roberts suggests that Black theology "must hold to the all-goodness and all-power of God...out of sheer necessity".[125]

Moreover, Major Jones claims on the one hand that God has an absolute power, but on the other hand he speaks of self-restraint in God's exercise of power. God's respect for human freedom makes Him restrain Himself.

> Though God's power is absolute, God mercifully restrains himself when dealing with human beings. Through the loving self-restraint of God's power, we experience the grace and mercy of divine persuasion at its supremely mature level. This is a God who is all-powerful, restraining himself to deal with powerless creatures by means of love's power of persuasion only.[126]

8.3.3   The Suffering of God in Black Theology

The belief in God's care, in His involvement and presence in the history of human beings are the central claims of the Black theology of liberation. When these claims are made from the perspective of the oppressed people, they lead naturally to the affirmation of God's suffering. If one overlooks William Jones' humanocentric theism, with all its doubts about a God who liberates, it can thus be said of all Black theologies of liberation, that divine passibility is the last resort for an acceptable approach to theodicy. It is the logical consequence of the belief in a God, who, by becoming human, assumes the lot of human existence.

Black people are less interested in a God, whose perfection consists in His non-interference in history. Theirs is a God who feels what they feel, who suffers what they suffer, because His presence in the human condition is His priority. Faced with the inexplicable Black ethnic suffering, therefore, all Black philosophers and theologians would honestly want to exonerate God from the responsibility for evil in the world. None would like to blame God as such, not even William Jones, who asks if God is not after all a White racist. He avoids this conclusion himself, as he proposes that God does not interfere.

With this view, Jones sacrificed what is most central in Black faith, namely, that God is present in the situation of the oppressed. He could do that perhaps be-

---

[125] J. D. Roberts, *Liberation and Reconciliation*, p. 93.

[126] M. J. Jones, *The Color of God.*, p. 57. Williams substantiates the kenotic power of God with views from the Russian theologian Nikolai Berdyaev. See 3.1.3. of this study.

cause, although he is Black, he leans more on philosophical principles than on the Black experience and biblical accounts. Other Black people with more theological inclinations find it however more representative of the Black and biblical faith if the idea of God's suffering is used to argue for God's innocence in the face of persistent Black suffering. For the majority of Black thinkers, who realise the centrality of the belief in God's experiential presence in Black religious consciousness, the affirmation of divine passibility is imperative. God cannot be held responsible for evil if He is Himself really present in human conditions.

It can be observed that the theme of divine suffering has not been developed systematically in Black theology as Jürgen Moltmann does for instance in the Western theology. Nonetheless, the idea of a suffering God is perhaps more central in Black theology than in any other theology. The symbolism of God's Blackness, the awareness of His presence in the worst period of slave existence, which are recurrent themes in all Black theologies of liberation, are all clear indications of God's boundless identification with the human situation of the oppressed. To get a clearer idea of how this theme is developed in Black theology, I shall sketch the views of James Cone and Major Jones.[127]

James Cone, as has been observed,[128] does not develop the theme of divine suffering systematically, but there is hardly any of his theological statements that does not suggest God's real experience of suffering. He speaks of God's active involvement in the struggle for the liberation of the oppressed, in a style that knows no restraint in the use of anthropomorphism.[129] God's identification is total, in action and colour - God is Black.

The idea of a suffering God emerges first in Cones' thought as he traces the rejection of a retribution dogma in the Old Testament. In his view, the prophet Isaiah introduced the idea of the Suffering Servant to correct the impression that suffering is always retributive. With reference to ethnic suffering therefore, Israel, like Job, suffers, not just because of her sins, but because God has chosen her to be His Suffering Servant. God's election of Israel "is not a privileged status that is given to favourite people. It is a call to serve, to suffer with God in the divine

---

[127] J. D. Roberts also treats this theme approvingly, see *A Black Political Theology*, (Philadelphia: Westminster, 1974), 95-116; ---, *Black Theology in Dialogue*, p. 39.

[128] W. McWilliams, *The Passion of God*, p. 66.

[129] Cf. J. Cone, *My Soul Looks Back*, p. 105. As Cone puts it, the "apparently crude, anthropomorphic way of speaking of God is the Third World theologians way of concretising Paul's saying that 'God chose what is foolish in the world to shame the wise, God chose what is weak in the world to shame the strong, God chose what is low and despised in the world, even the things that are not, to bring to nothing the things that are' (1 Cor. 1: 27-28 RSV)".

realisation of justice in the world."[130] This interpretation of the popular Protestant theme of divine Election here, presupposes a strong belief in the suffering of God for justice. For Cone, divine suffering is a proof that the law of retribution cannot explain the reality of suffering.

This becomes however concrete in the New Testament, as Jesus assumes the role of the Suffering Servant. If the theme of the Suffering Servant in Isaiah helped to demonstrate that suffering can be vicarious and redemptive, and that the innocent can suffer purposefully for the guilty, its application to Jesus' life in the New Testament introduces a new and deeper dimension: it now shows that "God became the Suffering Servant in Israel's place, and thus took upon divine-self human pain".[131]

James Cone sees Christology as the favourite locale for developing the doctrine of divine suffering. The whole life of Jesus testifies to the fact that God's response to evil is not speculative, but practical. God does not merely sympathise with the sufferers, He gets involved to such an extent that He becomes one with them.[132]

> This is what the Incarnation means. God in Christ comes to the weak and the helpless, and becomes one with them, taking their condition of oppression as his own and thus transforming their slave-existence into a liberated existence.[133]

In Black theology, the true divinity and true humanity of Jesus are established facts. Without any rigorous theological speculation, Black people accept the divinity of Jesus and the inner Trinitarian relationship as given. In Black tradition, the distinction between the sacred and the secular is not forcibly made. This could account for the ease with which Black people accept the Chalcedonian formula without being aware of all the sophisticated theological reflections leading to it. The feeling that Jesus is their friend, and that his presence in their lives continues as a divine reality in the form of the Holy Spirit is common.

Divine involvement and participation in the human predicament reaches its climax on the Cross of Jesus Christ. With the divinity of Jesus Christ in view, Cone sees the Cross-resurrection events as the very work of God to liberate the oppressed. Besides, the Cross-resurrection events introduce a new style of God's defence of the oppressed unparalleled by the events of the Old Testament: God experiences oppression Himself and emerges victorious. That God was involved personally on the Cross of Jesus, and that He still suffers with the oppressed

---

130 J. Cone, *God of the Oppressed*, p. 172.

131 *Ibid.*, p. 174.

132 *Ibid.*, p. 174-175.

133 *Ibid.*, p. 77.

when they are persecuted is the basic truth that Black theology tries to establish, when it says that God is Black and that Jesus is Black. "Jesus' Cross is God's election of the poor by taking their pain and suffering upon the divine person."[134] The divine participation in suffering on the Cross of Jesus "counts decisively against any suggestion that God is indifferent to human pain".[135]

The event of the resurrection helps to underline this fact.

> The Cross-resurrection events mean that we now know that Jesus' ministry with the poor and the wretched was God himself effecting his will to liberate the oppressed. ...God in Christ becomes poor and weak in order that the oppressed might become liberated from poverty and powerlessness. God becomes the victim in their place and thus transforms the condition of slavery into the battleground for the struggle of freedom.[136]

So much as Black theology emphasises the suffering of God, it does not admit that God is weak.[137] God suffers not out of weakness but out of the boundlessness of His being. Divine suffering is an affirmation of divine freedom and transcendence. In Cone's view, divine freedom means divine self-affirmation and transcendence over creaturely existence. That God is free means that He is "free to be for us", He is free to enter into the wretchedness of human existence. This is in fact, the basic meaning of the Exodus, the Incarnation and the Cross of Jesus Christ. If God goes to such an extent to affirm His freedom and to effect the freedom of the oppressed, it means therefore, Cone maintains, that the Black people are encouraged to struggle for freedom at all costs.[138]

God's involvement in the human condition is no doubt impressive. Yet it remains a mystery why God should choose to suffer and not effect freedom through other means. Granted that God suffers, and that He is not for that reason a weak God, must James Cone not explain why there should be divine suffering at all? Unfortunately, he does not indicate why God must suffer. His main concern is to maintain that God suffers out of solidarity with the oppressed. He is well aware of the fact that the affirmation of divine suffering does not adequately supply the reason for the ethnic sufferings of Black people, but prefers to see it as a mystery.

> The meaning of Black suffering remains a part of the mystery of God's will. But the presence of Jesus in their social existence did reveal that God was at work liberating them from bondage.

---

[134] *Ibid.*, p. 105.

[135] *Ibid.*, p. 176.

[136] J. Cone, *God of the Oppressed*, pp. 80-81; and, ---, *Speaking the Truth*, p. 5.

[137] Cf. E. P. Wimberly, The Suffering God, pp. 61-62, referred to by J. Deotis Roberts, *Black Theology Today*, p. 196.

[138] J. Cone, *God of the Oppressed*, p. 139.

One might perhaps turn to other sources in search of the reasons why God makes the singular choice to suffer, i.e., if we want to maintain, as is common in Black theology, that God does not suffer out of weakness.

Apparently, *Major J. Jones* provides a better account of divine suffering than James Cone. He develops the doctrine of divine passibility in a Trinitarian context, giving due attention to the relevance of Christology and Pneumatology, to an extent yet unknown perhaps among other Black theologians. God suffers and subjects Himself to changes because He is personal, relational and responsive.

Traditionally, Black people believe in a God who is personal, caring and all-powerful. Every Black theology, Jones insists, must uphold these vital divine attributes evident in Black belief. This, of course, confounds the problem of theodicy for Black theology, because it is left to explain how a good and powerful God could allow the unproportional Black ethnic suffering. But that notwithstanding, Black theology is more interested in fashioning an "intelligible concept of God" out of the background of Black experience than it is in providing a satisfactory answer for theodicy. Faced with the problem of theodicy, it does not primarily seek to know how to justify God, but rather to find out "what God is doing in evil times".[139]

In the view of Major Jones, "To understand God and evil in the world more fully, one must look at evil in terms of how it touches God personally".[140] The most popular classical Christian answers to theodicy fail to satisfy the religious experience and expectation of Black people,[141] precisely because they work with impersonal concepts of God that are alien to the Black God-concept. They tend to compromise what is most precious for Black faith, namely, the absolute goodness and power of God, and the assurance of His personal care. An impersonal concept of God is not attractive to Black people, even when it makes room for all the important attributes of God. Process theology is an example of such beautiful speculations about God, which Black theology cannot accept for the mere fact that it is conceived impersonally.

> ... the identification of God with the creative processes render Process theology unattractive to Black thinkers. Process thought is dressed in the right symbols, but the meanings are alien. Black people have lived too close to evil and suffering in 'the process' to accept the impersonal God of Process thought, who, although he suffers lovingly the evil of the process, seems impotent to change the anti-Black process.[142]

---

[139] M. J. Jones, *The Color of God.*, p. 61 ff.

[140] *Ibid.*, p. 68.

[141] *Ibid.*, p. 63 ff.

[142] *Ibid.*, p. 71.

As oppressed people, Blacks cannot accept the notion of a God limited in goodness and power. This is the paradox of the faith of the oppressed people. God must be powerful, but He must as well be able to experience weakness.

> There must be no doubt about his caring or his victory. And oppressed people must have complete assurance of the ultimate victory of the good God. Oppressed people necessarily reject the concept of a weak God, whether in muscle-power or in morals.[143]

Moreover, evil can only be properly assessed, especially as it affects God and the oppressed, if it is interpreted in the light of a personal conception of God. An impersonal conception of God can easily lead to ignorance or denial of the reality of evil as it affects the oppressed. Then, the reality of evil is no where better confirmed than in the context of a personal relationship, in a situation where personal beings are involved. When a theology that works with an impersonal conception of God reflects on evil, "one senses a tendency to play verbal games with the real and unpleasant realities of evil, a tendency that extends to calling evil the mere absence of good, when in reality malevolence is much more than merely the absence of benevolence".[144]

In a true Black Christology, the affirmation of the personal unity of the Father and the Son is fundamental. Although classical Christologies had ever recognised that God was in Jesus Christ, God's presence was not always interpreted to mean a personal unity with Jesus Christ. It was more of a rational unity, not personal. Beyond the usual rational conception, Black theology sees God's presence in Jesus Christ or Jesus relationship with God as a full personal unity, a mutual unity with personal and "relational effects on God himself".[145]

In the light of the mutual and personal relationship between Jesus and God, Black theology concludes that God was in Christ personally experiencing all that Jesus experienced. His experience of our human condition has consequences even in His inner-Trinitarian nature.

> To assert that God himself is capable of human experience...is to say that something took place radically, in the very root of the personhood of God, when God expressed himself in the person and work of Jesus Christ. ... How could God have undergone a birth like ours, the divine coming forth of a human being, and still remained the same? Nevertheless, when we say that he truly became a human person by the assumption of human mind and soul, flesh and blood, we also believe that

---

143 *Ibid.*, pp. 66-67.

144 *Ibid.*, p. 73.

145 *Ibid.*, p. 77.

> God still remained truly God in nature and person. To say that God remained God, however, is not to say that God did not change.[146]

In this passage, Major Jones asserts on the one hand that God cannot be changed by external forces, but on the other, he maintains that God has the freedom to change Himself, without loosing His identity. In the Incarnation, in "God's act of becoming human, something happened to him and something also happened to his creation".[147] Major Jones would accept that God is immutable and impassible, but only if by that we mean that God is not subject to any external determination. God is however mutable and passible, in as much as He has the freedom to subject Himself to change and suffering in response to the demand of His personal and relational nature.

The mystery of Incarnation is the height of God's personal relationship with human beings. Approaching this mystery from the background of Black personalism, Black theology tries to establish that God had a personal experience, in Jesus Christ, of what it looks like to be human in an absurd human situation in which Black people find themselves. Prior to the event of Incarnation, God had only a "theoretical" knowledge of human suffering, but now in the person of Christ He has acquired a personal experience of divine abandonment, of the endurance of injustice and suffering.[148]

From the perspective of Afro-Americans, God's human experience in Jesus Christ gives one the assurance that God has a personal experience of suffering. It is a thing of relief for believers to know that the God whom they are going to meet and who is going to judge them is "a God who has actually experienced and now knows, at the lowest human level, what it means to be human".[149]

In this way, Major Jones undertakes a reinterpretation of divine omniscience. There can be a limitation of knowledge in the realm of personal relationship that does not entail imperfection. By virtue of the freedom that God bestows on human beings, He can be ignorant of the outcome of future events related to the exercise of their freedom.

> We believe human actions to be truly free, such that whereas God's knowledge of the past is total and absolute, God's knowledge of future events is not yet complete, particularly so far as acts of human freedom are concerned. The perfection of divine omniscience, then, must be construed to be God's always perfectly increasing knowledge taking in, with the passage of time, all knowable reality as it expands. Not to know as real and sure what is, as yet, neither sure nor real, is not

---

[146] *Ibid.*, p. 99.

[147] M. J. Jones, *The Color of God*, p. 94.

[148] *Ibid.*, p. 96.

[149] *Ibid.*, p. 93.

imperfection; to know the unreal and the unsure as uncertain and still forming is to know perfectly whatever is to be known. God could, of course, preclude uncertainty by determining beforehand what is to be and what all are to become; the high price he would pay for this, however, would be the freedom of his creatures to develop and grow.[150]

The limitation of divine omniscience is here part of divine strategy to make human freedom possible. For if human freedom is to be real, and not pre-programmed by God, it means that God has to impose a limitation on His own knowledge of the products of free agents. God's omniscience consists in knowing what is the case, and not what is unreal. But is this not a dangerous conclusion? Does it not mean that God is Himself not sure of the outcome of His creation? Does it not imply that God is not in any way in control of the end result of His creation? If that is the case, how then can God be sure of His victory over evil at the end of time, which forms the main content of Black hope, as oppressed people?

Major Jones would certainly find it difficult to answer these questions. Except perhaps he sees such limitations as God's kenotic act. Even though he does not explicitly speak of God's kenosis, it can be inferred from His line of thought, that God's self-limitations in knowledge and in the exercise of His power is kenotic. God limits Himself to authenticate human freedom, the first of God's priorities in His plan for creation. Incarnation is, therefore, a pure kenotic act, "the final and complete self-humiliation". By this kenotic act, i.e., by becoming human, "God accepts every condition of humanness and embraces the whole of human existence within his own being". He makes Himself "subject to all human limitations and to all inhuman treatments".[151] This means in effect that God carries this limitation and suffering into His own being. Both human and divine nature are thus affected, when God assumes the human condition. But because, God imposes these limitations and changes on Himself, because it is a "self-change", Black theology insists nonetheless, that "within the inner-personal unity of the Trinity of divine beings (God *ad intra*), the responsive relationship" of the three divine Persons "was not subject to changes wrought upon God by external events", but dependent on "self-change".[152]

God's suffering care is not only Christocentric, it is also Pneumatological. God's presence is not seen as limited to the period of Jesus' earthly life. His presence continues today in the Person of the Holy Spirit. For Black people, the Holy Spirit is God's continuing personal responsive Being with us since the resurrec-

---

[150] *Ibid.*, p. 95.

[151] *Ibid.*, p. 99.

[152] *Ibid.*, p. 95.

tion of Christ.[153] Just as the awareness of God's presence in Jesus Christ gives Black people the assurance that God knows the depth of their suffering personally, the awareness of the presence of the Holy Spirit in their lives makes it evident that God continues to feel their suffering at each moment.

The reality of the Holy Spirit is central in Black faith. For Black people the proclamation in Jesus that "God is with us" receives its concretion in the role of the Holy Spirit as abiding agent of God in Black lives. The feeling of God's presence and nearness highly cherished in Black faith is no where better expressed as in the personal experience of the Holy Spirit. Not just now in the current religious, charismatic and Pentecostal movements of this century, but also earlier during the slave period did belief in the nearness of God in the Holy Spirit add "a needed dimension" to Black spirituality.[154]

Although in Jones view, the Black people's personal familiarity with the Holy Spirit is strongly influenced by their African religious heritage, especially by the African belief in spirits or in the "Spirit of God" common to African religions,[155] he insists that the Afro-American concept of the Holy Spirit "has its historical roots in more explicitly Trinitarian and traditional Christian thought".[156] As the union of God and Jesus Christ, sent to inhere in the world, the Third Person is experienced as the abiding, personal and relational presence of God.

In the Person of the Holy Spirit it becomes yet more evident that it is God who is experiencing what the oppressed suffers. The Holy Spirit enables and perfects the personal relationship between God and human beings. Traditionally, the Father is related to the Son through the Holy Spirit.

> God becomes a subjective living reality within the lives of human beings. ... The Holy Spirit is that subjective reality who relates God personally to the inner core of human existence. In the person of the Holy Spirit, God is present and active with and within us, a God-awareness continuously present in every moment of human history (Matt. 28: 20; John 14: 16).[157]

Major Jones sees this indwelling of the divine subjectivity of the Holy Spirit as "the deeps of God confronting the deeps of human subjectivity". This is the height of divine-human personal relation, which continues even today. By implication, it emphasises that God becomes one with the human beings, in their lives' struggle, in their pains and suffering.

---

153 Major J. Jones, *The Color of God.*, p. 101.

154 *Ibid.*, p. 102.

155 *Ibid.*, p. 106.

156 *Ibid.*, p. 102.

157 *Ibid.*, p. 103.

The Holy Spirit is God at work in the human condition. And as in Jesus Christ, it is a work that can entail change and suffering.

> Wherever God is at work, he works in and through Jesus Christ and the Holy Spirit. In Jesus Christ, God communicated his Word, the substance of his personal being, and committed thus himself in a relationship to humanity that led him to the Cross . ... In the Holy Spirit, it is the same God doing the same work, working the same deeds of sacrifice and liberation, divine love in the current struggle to set all God's oppressed people free from every form of evil.[158]

8.4   Summary and Conclusion

With time, as Black people were gradually regaining their personal freedom, they began also to entertain the desire for a religious freedom. They started to establish separate Black churches among the Black slave communities in the United States of America. Through the constitution of such independent churches, the Black people hoped to effect their freedom even in the religious domain. But as it soon became evident, separate churches did not bring the desired religious freedom immediately, because the established forms of worship and interpretations of doctrines were still too alien to the Black mentality to such an extent that they hindered free expressions of Black spirituality. The necessity for a theology that took note of the Black religious experience was perceived. It was therefore the attempt to reconcile Christianity with Black identity and goal that gave birth to the development of the Black theology of the African Americans.

The major desire of Black people was freedom. Accordingly, liberation became the motif and in fact the principal hermeneutic principle for Black theology. The use of the motif of liberation differs however, for, while some Black theologians perceive liberation merely as an important theological category, others, like James Cone, see it as being identical with revelation and thus constituting the main content of theology. In the background of Black theology lies the motivation to promote that which is essentially characteristic of Black people. It is in this sense that "Blackness" is made a theological symbol. "Blackness" is however a symbol with double significance. For some Black theologians, it symbolises suffering and could thus be applied to all who suffer the same fate as Black people. For others it is a category for the description of that essence or "soul" of Black people, which years of slavery and alienation could not destroy. In other words, it constitutes for the latter the indestructible identity of Black people in the world. In developing Black theology from this background, the following are considered the most dominant sources: the African roots, Black experience in the history of slavery and racism, the Bible and the other Third World theologies.

---

[158] *Ibid.*, p. 119.

The God-talk of Black people takes the reality of God as given, so that instead of posing the question whether God exists, Black theology occupies itself primarily with the issue of His role in the lives of Black people. Its God-talk is for that reason conditioned to a great extent by the problem of theodicy. It conceives God in terms of defining what God does in the face of the Black predicament. Basically, therefore, Black theology is as sure of God's involvement in the human conditions as it is of the reality of God. Three different accounts of God's relationship to His creatures are evident: while two of them propagate the idea of divine involvement in the human affairs, one argues for God's neutrality and non-interference.

James Cone's theology represents one account of God's involvement in the world made in terms of His partiality for the poor: In his view, God is by nature against the oppressors and for the oppressed. As a result, His taking side with the poor is no sign of pity, but an act that arises out of His being (of love and justice), which of its nature includes wrath. Using his idea of divine partiality, Cone reviews divine transcendence and immanence and sees them as interdependent attributes. Similarly, he reinterprets providence to mean that God makes freedom from oppression possible.

The most important criticisms that could be brought against Cone's views were formulated by William Jones while proposing his own thesis for divine non-interference. Jones considers some aspects of Cone's theology inadequate: his idea of divine partiality for the oppressed Black people, his conception of Black suffering as a sign of divine election of Black people to the status of suffering servants, and also the use of an eschatological theodicy in defence of the charge of divine racism. Jones is rather of the opinion that the only effective theodicy is a theory of divine non-interference, a theory that makes humankind responsible for all that happens in this world (anthropodicy). This view which he propounds as a "humano-centric theism" leaves much to be desired however, because it makes God among other things impersonal.

This is the main criticism Major Jones brings against him. For Major Jones, God is a personal and relational being, and is by that fact involved in human affairs. He shares this view with Cone; but unlike the latter, Jones declines to accept the claim that God is partial to the poor. God, he argues, is on the side of the poor, without, however, being against anybody; He is only against evil. He is Black, but He can also take any other colour. Major Jones also criticises William Jones' point that since Black people have not yet experienced total liberation there is no basis for the claim that God is a liberator. This would have been the case, Major Jones contends, if our knowledge of God were solely experiential. Our knowledge of God as the liberator is however a "faith-knowledge". This, he maintains, justifies the claims about God's nature as a liberator.

With the exception of William Jones' theory of divine neutrality, all the other conceptions of God in Black theology that propose the reality of divine intervention accept ultimately that God can suffer. For Cone, God suffers to effect justice in the world, and elects the oppressed Black people to suffer with Him.[159] It is also clear to him that God suffered with Christ on the Cross. But while affirming divine suffering, Cone is however careful not to suggest that divine passibility implies weakness on the part of God. Asked why God has no alternative means for the realisation of justice than suffering Himself, Cone says that it is a mystery. Cone's theology of divine suffering lacks, for that reason, a strong base; a recourse to mystery is definitely too easy.

For a better developed theology of divine suffering one must turn to Major Jones, who conceives it in a Trinitarian context. The inner-Trinitarian relationship, and particularly the person and work of the Holy Spirit in the world, makes the possibility of divine suffering implicit. Rather than posit mystery as the explanation for divine suffering, Major Jones attributes it to God's nature as a personal and relational being. There exists a personal unity between the Father and the Son, he contends, so that what happened to Jesus in his earthly life touched God. In fact, since God is also in relation with His creatures, what touches them touches Him also. For Major Jones, this must not imply an external influence on God. God is Himself engaged in a "self-change"; He can subject Himself to change, but He is not under any external influence. Thus, God is, in one sense mutable, in another, immutable.

Significant of Black theology is that it is critical of itself. One can hardly single out a weak point which had not been criticised within its own circle of theologians. The most one can do is to point at the most criticised views: The reduction of revelation to liberation, and theology to the oppression-liberation parameter; the use of Blackness as a symbol of the oppressed are just a few cases of delimitation and reductionism, which must be overcome, if views of Black theology should have any global theological relevance. James Cone's emphasis on the relativity of truth and theological language is an example of such erroneous conclusions. The contextualisation of theology must not, in our view, entail the relativity of truth. Relevance could be contextual, but not the truth as such. Cone's understanding of transcendence and immanence as non-spatial concepts as well as Major Jones' emphasis on the relational interpretation of divine nature could be seen, however, as positive contributions toward the development of the theology of divine suffering. However, despite the use of some paradoxical notions of concepts from the African notion of God, Black theology tends towards a one-dimensional conception of God. The paradoxical tension between divine passibil-

---

159 J. Cone, *God of the Oppressed*, p. 172.

ity and impassibility typical of many contributions from the Fathers are virtually non-existent here. Thus, while William Jones' theory of divine non-interference represents an extreme form of divine impassibility, Cones and Major Jones' thesis of divine intervention are capable only of presenting the reality of divine passibility, but incapable of conceiving God as a being in whose nature passibility and impassibility are compatible.

9. DIVINE SUFFERING IN THE AFRICAN CHRISTIAN THEOLOGIES

9.1   The Background and the Factors of Contextual Theology in Africa

The history of Christianity in Africa has been extremely intermittent. In the third century, in the Patristic era, it flourished in North Africa, Nubia and Ethiopia but later declined.[1] And weakened by the Islamic presence, it could not make its impact felt in other parts of Africa until 15th century, in the medieval period, when it arrived at the Atlantic coasts of Africa through the Portuguese missionary activity. Although this was Africa's second encounter with Christianity,[2] it did not last longer than two centuries and vanished from the face of the Sub-Saharan Africa in the 17th century. It returned much later at the end of the eighteenth century. This was the third encounter between Black Africa and Christianity.[3]

Since then the history of the Christian presence in Black Africa has been unbroken. Christian Churches have also consistently grown both in number and importance. This is definitely the result of decades of intensive Protestant and Catholic missionary activities. Now, one can even count the achievements of Christianity in Africa with some feelings of satisfaction and of assurance that it has come to stay. In fact, series of celebrations being organised across the western coast of the continent in this decade, especially among the Catholics, to mark the inception and progress of Christianity in the Sub-Saharan Africa deliver this impression.[4] But much as such celebrations are justified, people can hardly forget that Christianity in Africa has still unresolved problems.

Despite its partial success, it has not yet got beyond the stage of a foreign religion. It has not yet outgrown its infantile stage after more than a century of consistent growth. It is neither rooted nor assimilated in the lives of most African Christians. Apparently, one of the most obvious signs of the African Christianity today is its continuous dependence on the Western world in theology, finance and administration. The popular assumption is of course that the dependence of the African Church on external sources is part of growth. This is however scarcely convincing, especially in a situation, where such reliance is increasing rather than decreasing. It has become probable to see it as a structural problem rather than as

---

1   See S. Neill, *A History of Christian Missions*, pp. 37 ff; For more details see C. P. Groves, *The Planting of Christianity in Africa*.

2   See J. Baur, *2000 Years of Christianity in Africa*, pp. 43-99, esp. p. 45.

3   *Ibid.*, p. 103 ff.

4   See for example, Celestine A. Obi and co. (eds.), *A hundred Years of the Catholic Church in Eastern Nigeria 1885-1985*.

a process of growth. Even a sympathiser of African Christianity might be moved to ask critical questions: Is the Church in Africa condemned to be a perpetual suckling, feeding from the finished products of the Western Christianity? Is a century perhaps too short for maturity or was the African Christianity programmed to lack identity right from the onset? In other words, how long would it take the Church in Africa to be self-reliant in finance and theology?

These are all questions bordering on the future of the Church in Africa. Earlier and recent reflections in this direction, invariably lead to one conclusion: Christianity in Africa must be contextualised, if its relevance, self-subsistence and future is to be guaranteed. It is not surprising therefore, that in the last couple of decades, the contextualisation of Christianity at all levels - in liturgy and theology - has become a major ecclesiological and theological orientation among Christians in Africa.

It should be noted however that the quest for authenticity is not new in the African Church. The first faint outcry for the contextualisation of Christianity was made earlier in the nineteenth century by such pioneer African missionaries like Samuel Ajayi Crowther, the first African to be consecrated a bishop (1864) in Nigeria. As early as that time bishop Crowther, together with his counterpart, James Johnson from Sierra Leone, pledged for an indigenous expression of the Christian faith.[5]

However, concrete steps towards the contextualisation of Christianity in Africa were not taken until 1945 when Placide Tempels, a Belgian Franciscan missionary, worked out the ontology of the "Bantu philosophy". The dominant aim of this pioneering work, and in fact of all his philosophical and other theological writings, was to replace Greek categories with African concepts, derived from the African thought pattern.[6] In 1956, a decade before the second Vatican Council, a group of French-speaking catholic priests published the papers presented in a Symposium with the title: *Des Prêtres Noirs s' interrogent*.[7] In terms of content, this collection should be seen as one forceful pledge for an African theology.

Although similar attempts to relate Christianity to African culture were made a year earlier in Ghana among the Protestant West Africans,[8] West Africa was to

---

5 Cf. J. A. Ajayi, *Christian Missions in Nigeria 1841-1891*, pp. 224 & 235.

6 P. Tempels, *Bantu Philosophy*. See also his *Notre Rencontre*. His books had a tremendous influence on many later catholic theologians like Alex Kagame, *La Philosophie Bantu-Rwandaise*, and V. Mulago, Nécessité de l' adaptation missionaire chez les Bantu du Congo.

7 Paris: Presence Africain, 1940.

8 C. G. Baeta, *Christianity and African Culture*.

wait for about a decade before initiatives with far-reaching consequences for the project of contextualisation began to appear. The first of such noble conferences, with later influence on the direction of African theology, was held 1965 in Ibadan (Nigeria).[9] That conference, organised under the sponsorship of the "All African Council of Churches", was a landmark in many ways: for the first time, Protestant and Catholic, French- and English speaking, West and East (Central) Africans came together (in a pan-African and ecumenical forum) to discuss the prospect of African theology. Its major importance lay in confirming earlier efforts and encouraging further attempts towards an African theology done in the light of the Biblical revelation.

The deliberations of this conference seem to have ushered in a new era of productivity, evident in the number of publications - in the 1960s - urging for contextualisation.[10] Such publications have helped immensely to make the project of doing African theology soar from the level of mere desire to its current stage as a normal theological programme in Africa. For while it used to be an issue in the 1960s, whether there could be anything like an African theology,[11] it has become an accepted project with immense support today. In fact, since John Paul II used the term "African theology" in his speech to Bishops in Zaire, in 1983,[12] even sceptics have come to the realisation, that doing African theology is no longer a mere desire, that seeks justification, but a Church mandate for the interest of a new and contextualised evangelisation for the third Millennium.

If doing theology in Africa is now equivalent to doing "African theology", it is only because the latter has assumed broader dimensions. In the past, African theologies were prone to using the outmoded strategy of *négritude*, focusing almost

---

9   It was later published in English (and French) as *Biblical Revelation and African Beliefs*, ed. by K. Dickson / P. Ellingworth. Similar Conferences were organised in the subsequent years as follows: In 1971 a conference was held in Dar es Saalam (Tanzania) dedicated to the issue of Black identity and solidarity. In 1972, another one followed at Makerere University (Uganda) to define and affirm African theology. The first conference of Third World Theologians in Dar es Saalam (Tanzania) in 1976 also helped define African Christian Theology. Another mile stone in the constitution of African Christian Theology was laid by the Accra (Ghana) conference of 1977 organised by the Pan-African Conference of Third World Theologians. The papers from this conference were later published as *African Theology en Route*, ed. by Kofi Appiah-Kubi and Sergio Torres.

10   See, for instance, B. Idowu, *Towards an Indigenous Church*; H. Sawyerr, *Creative Evangelism*; J. S. Mbiti, *New Testament Eschatology in an African Background*.

11   See the popular theological debate between Tharcisse Tschibangu and Alfred Vanneste in a seminar held on 29th January organised by the academic staff of the Catholic Faculty of theology in Kinshasa (Zaire), published in as "Débat sur la 'theologie africaine'", in: *Revue du Clergé Africaine* 15 (1960) 333-352.

12   Cf. *AFER*, Oct. 1983, pp. 313-319.

exclusively on the past cultural alienation of the Black people, sometimes in utter disregard for the current problems in the society. Now, however, efforts are being made in contemporary African theologies to synthesise the different approaches to cultural revival and socio-political liberation.[13] Today, to say the least, a Christian theology that is truly African responds to the past and present socio-political challenges, and is, for that reason, both an inculturation and liberation theology - a contextual theology, in every respect, sensitive to the peculiar life situations or contexts of the "hearers of the Word".

The fire of contextualisation has been inflamed at different times in the history of Christianity in Africa by some religio-cultural, historical, theological and socio-political factors. We shall sketch these factors here so as to get a clearer view of the tensions in the conception of God in the African Christian theology.

a) *Religio-cultural factors*. According to data from sociologists, our century has witnessed a shift from monolithic to pluralistic concepts of culture: cultures are no longer evaluated in terms of an idealistic model of one particular culture, but more in their own terms. This shift has helped Africans to come to the realisation that certain aspects of their culture had suffered undue rejection in the hands of the European missionaries. The missionaries were only able to assess the African culture in the light of their own culture. In all good faith, they only selected familiar cultural elements and suppressed the others. In this way, a partial integration of Christianity and African culture was achieved, but the inhibition of some cultural values could not be avoided. The conscious or unconscious efforts on the part of Africans to retain such values and still practise Christianity was bound to create a sort of "cultural tension",[14] a situation whereby the attempt to be a good Christian meant alienation from one's culture. Becoming a convert was then for many a mixed blessing,[15] because they were caught between the joy of a new religion, which enjoyed the status of being the religion of the colonial masters, and the sadness of parting from their cherished ways of life and African identity. Caught in this tension, most African Christians have been living a life full of *syncretism* and religious alienation. Archbishop Desmond Tutu aptly calls this "a religious or spiritual schizophrenia".[16]

---

[13] B. Bujo, *African theology in its Social Context*, p. 66. This book was originally published in German: *Afrikanische Theologie in ihrem gesellschaftlichen Kontext*, Düsseldorf 1986.

[14] J. S. Ukpon, The Emergence of African Theologies, p. 503.

[15] Cf. G. v. Paczensky, *Teurer Segen. Christliche Mission and Kolonialismus*. Reviewing the role of the Christian missions in the colonised Africa, the author considers missionary activities to be a mixed blessing.

[16] Desmond M. Tutu, Black Theology and African Theology - Soulmates or Antagonists? p. 47. Syncretistic beliefs and practices in Africa, it must be noted, are partly subtle and

Opinions differ as to how best to evaluate the phenomenon of syncretism in Africa. For some theologians it is a negative development,[17] for others it is positive.[18] But to our knowledge, it is indicative of an unfinished process of integration; it is at best a yearning for proper contextualisation and, at worst, a symptom of an ill-digested faith. In other words, syncretism is a sort of religious "barometer" showing the different levels of religio-cultural integration just attained, indeed, a reminder for theologians, that Christianity is not yet properly incarnated, and above all, that proper inculturation is indispensable and urgent for an effective evangelisation.[19] Viewed thus, as an honest quest on the part of African Christians to be "Christian" and "African" at the same time, syncretism be-

---

partly crude, and could be found not only among the illiterates but also in the rank and file of the educated elites. See K. Dickson, *Theology in Africa*, p. 10. It is not uncommon to see a baptised Christian, honestly dedicated to Christian principles, avail himself of the services of the traditional religion - the religion of his ancestors. This subtle form of syncretism is often accompanied by guilty conscience. Crude forms of syncretism are also found especially among the members of the African Independent Churches. These Churches make no secretes of the fact that they perform an uncritical alignment of the spiritual elements of both the African traditional and the Euro-christian religions.

[17] For Aylward Shorter, syncretism is a negative phenomenon. It essentially entails a lack of proper integration of two juxtaposed elements of spirituality; it is an indication of the absence of a dialogue between two religions, and indeed, a sign of unresolved duality, whereby a weaker religious tradition gets fixed in terms of the other. Shorter fears that the adaptation approach to African theology might be perpetrating this sort of syncretism. A Shorter, *African Christian Theology*, pp. 2, 14 & 18.

[18] According to Leonardo Boff, syncretism should be valued positively as a normal process in the development of a religion in cross-cultural milieu. Cf. L. Boff, *Church: Charism and Power, Liberation Theology and Institutional Church*, pp. 89-107. In his view, Christianity is "One Huge Syncretism", integrating elements of Jewish, Egyptian, Greek, and European cultures into its characteristic features. Syncretism thus belongs to the universal character of the Church. For Boff, "The question is not whether or not there is syncretism in the Church. The Problem is in the type of syncretism that exists at present and which one should be sought." (99) Despite his understanding of syncretism as a positive phenomenon - as an essential expression of the Church's thrust for relevance in every culture - he admits nonetheless, that syncretism can be negative. It becomes negative, indeed, if, in the process of cultural alignment, the identity of Christianity gets lost. He sees the Christian identity as that experience that joins us together with the experience of Jesus Christ himself. False syncretism occurs then, when this experience is sacrificed for another religious tradition. This is what Boff believes to be the case in the Yoruba religion in Brazil, which he terms a perfect example of a false syncretism. Here the identity of Christianity is lost to that of the voodoo religion. Boff's view, as we see it, can only have relevance in a Christian circle.

[19] P. Schineller comes close to our view of syncretism. See his article Inculturation and Syncretism: What is the Real Issue? Syncretism, according to him, should stand for inadequate inculturation.

comes a challenge *par excellence* for an urgent contextualisation of theology and can no longer be considered as a diabolic work in the lives of undecided Christians.

In the same connection, the rapid growth of the *Independent African Churches* in the continent could be seen as another factor that moves the established Churches to contextualisation. In the African society today, there is a phenomenal drift of the members of the established Churches to the Independent Churches and sects.[20] Threatened by the massive loss of their members to these other Churches, the established Churches are increasingly coming to the realisation that the contextualisation of Christianity could offer the necessary solution to their problems. Apparently, the success of the Independent Churches could be credited to their radical tolerance and encouragement of syncretistic practices[21] - they lure members away from the established Churches into their fold, because they are believed to be pacesetters in the Africanisation of Christianity. In fact, according to the ex-members of the established Churches, the drift to the Independent Churches is motivated by the desire to worship in accordance with the African mentality, i.e. by the quest for an authentic African spirituality.[22]

The current programme of contextualisation in the established African Christian Churches is dictated by the need, not only to stop the loss of members to the Independent Churches, but largely to satisfy the religious yearnings of the African Christians.

b) *Historical factors*. It is still puzzles to many African thinkers and theologians, that the Churches of North Africa could just disappear, after about four centuries of fertile existence, during which the Church produced such great theologians like Tertullian, Cyprain, Augustine, Origen, Cyril, Clement of Alexandria and Athanasius. It is even all the more perplexing to note that only the Coptic and

---

[20] In some cases the drift to these Churches is gradual, taking merely the form of an occasional participation. See K. Dickson, *Theology in Africa*, p.10.

[21] Heinrich Loth, an East German researcher, makes the extreme claim that the power-house of the authentic African Christianity is only to be found among the Independent Churches. Cf. his book, *Vom Schlangenkult zur Christuskirche - Religion und Messianismus in Afrika*, pp. 256 ff. His claim is highly disputable, because the crude form of syncretism among these Churches can clearly give Christianity a pseudo-orientation. Their style of Africanisation is very uncritical. The danger of Christianity loosing its identity in the process, as Boff notes above, is evident.

[22] K. Dickson, *Theology in Africa*, p. 114. As Dickson rightly observes, the "Independent Churches are seekers, as much as the historic Churches, after ways to satisfy their people's spiritual longings".

Ethiopian Churches survived the Arab-Islamic onslaught.[23] Today, the African Church keenly wants to learn from the fateful, instructive history of the latinised Christianity in North Africa and Nubia (today's Sudan).

The main reasons for the disappearance of the Church in North Africa is very easy to identify. Both in theological and official Church documents, inadequate contextualisation or lack of inculturation have been noted,[24] among others,[25] as a major reason for the demise of the Latin Church in North Africa. Already, the inadequate contextualisation or lack of inculturation is believed to have been one of the chief causes for the disappearance of Christianity in North Africa. The Roman Church in Egypt was Latin, and it was chiefly conceived for the upper class. Neither the Bible nor the liturgy was translated into the native Berber language. Consequently, the Church in North Africa, despite its high standard in theology,

---

[23] The ambivalence embodied in the history of these Churches is a lesson for the contemporary Church. For on the one hand, the North African Churches had immense influence on the Western Christianity, especially as the flag bearer of monasticism. Cf. Jedin, H. and Dolan, J., Eds., *History of the Church*, p. 337. On the other hand, the same Churches are known to have produced most of the heresies in the history of the Church. Cf. J. Parratt, *Theologiegeschichte der Dritten Welt: Afrika*, p. 23. This paradoxical history might begin to be logical if we see it a natural feature of an ill-adapted Church. Were the heresies not symptomatic of cultural indigestion? Were they not perhaps the consequences of deficiencies in the integration of Christianity in the North African milieu? How far did the suppression of heresies also mean the rejection of inculturation? In terms of the views in D. Baker, (ed.), *Heresy and Schism as Social and National Movements: Studies in Church History*, it might not be totally out of order, to agree with Zablon Nthamburi - see his article, The Relevance of Donatism for the Church in Africa Today - that the suppression of the Donatist schism amounted to silencing the cry for social and economic justice, made on behalf of peasants, oppressed in the name of religion. (p. 217) Consequently, it "meant the destruction of a golden opportunity for Christianity in North Africa" to be truly African (p. 219).

[24] See *The Church in Africa and her Evangelising Mission towards the Year 2000, "You shall be my witnesses" (Acts 1:8) - LINEAMENTA for the Synod of Bishops, Special Assembly for Africa 1994* (Kenya, Nairobi: St. Paul Publications), pp. 2-6. According to the authors of this document, inculturation is being looked upon today as a necessary process towards the consolidation of the place of Christianity in Africa. For more information about the fruits of this synod see: Synodus Episcoporum, Coetus specialis pro Africa, *Nuntius*, E. Civitate Vaticana; A. G. Nnamani, The African Synod and the Model of Church-as-Family, in: Bulletin of Ecumenical Theology, vol. 6/2 1994.

[25] The adverse effect of the theological disputes between the Donatist and the Rome oriented theologians on the Churches of North Africa is another well known reason for the extinction of these Churches. Cf. L. R. Holme, *The extinction of the Christian Church in North Africa*; Z. Nthamburi, *Op. cit.*, pp. 215-220.

did not have roots in the native population. Naturally, it was too weak to resist the Arab-Islamic incursion.[26]

Both the inculturation and liberation theologies in Africa have much to learn from the fateful history of the North African Churches. For if these ancient Churches disappeared largely because they were neither inculturated nor contextualized, the African Church of today is challenged to intensify the project of inculturation. Again, if the peasants abandoned the Latin Church in North Africa specifically because it was not sensitive to their social problems, the Church is advised to confront the structural injustice in the world today head-on. In order words, if the fate of the Church in North Africa should not repeat itself, i.e. if the future of Christianity in Africa is to be guaranteed, the programme of liberation theology must be encouraged, inasmuch as it works towards effecting structural changes that would end the fast perennial African problems of poverty, oppression and discrimination.

c) *The theological factors*.[27] Here, the *theological renaissance* initiated by the period of Enlightenment must be mentioned, especially with regard to the introduction of the scientific historical method in the study of the Bible. This prepared the way for the second theological factor, the *theological pluralism*, ratified by the theology of the Second Vatican Council. With its special emphasis on the adaptation of the Christian values to the world (*Aggiornamento*), the Second Vatican Council stimulated the urge for inculturation, the erection of a "world Church" and the positive evaluation of the African Traditional Religions.[28]

d) *The socio-political factors*. Political movements of the pre-independent and post-independent Africa played significant roles in calling the attention of the African Christians to the formulation of a Christianity with an African face. Great African leaders such as Léopold Senghor, the proponent of *négritude*, Kwame Nkrumah, the prince of Pan-Africanism, Kenneth Kaunda of Zambia, the cham-

---

26 The role that the inadequacy of contextualisation played in the disappearance of the Latin Church in North Africa becomes yet more evident, when it is observed that, in contrast, the Orthodox Coptic and Ethiopian Churches have survived till today. Their survival is apparently due to the fact that they were better inculturated and adapted to the needs of the people. See M. Ghebremedhin, The Survival of Christianity in Ethiopia, pp. 3-32. In fact, both the Bible and the liturgy were, for instance, translated into the Coptic and the Ethiopian languages. Today, these Orthodox Churches standing as oasis in a desert of Islamic influence. They serve as the legacy of a well inculturated African Christianity from the distant past. Their survival speaks volumes in favour of the contextualisation of theology in Africa South of the Sahara.

27 For details see, J. S. Ukpon, The Emergence of African Theologies, pp. 502-509.

28 Cf. Vatican II, *Lumen gentium*, 9-14, 22, 26, 27; *Christus Dominus*, 4-6, 11; *Nostra aetate* 2.

pion of African Humanism, Julius Nyerere, the apostle of African socialism, made implicit and explicit appeals to the African Churches to evolve a Christianity for Africa, a Christianity free from the cloak of neo-colonialism and imperialism.[29]

The influence of socio-political factors on the formulation of theology is even more evident in the South African version of liberation theology. The primary aim of this theology is to liberate the oppressed Black Africans from the web of political oppression and racial discrimination using biblical materials. For, the struggle against racial discrimination and political oppression takes its inspiration from the Black nationalism in the United States.[30]

A great many Africans have realised that the attainment of political and economic Independence, initiated during the political upheavals of the 1960s, is becoming an illusion. Instead, neo-colonialism and imperialism are getting more and more engraved in the oppressive and unjust structures of the world's political and economic order. The main causes of the African problems of underdevelopment and hardship could be attributed to these latent means of oppression. In secular and religious circles the opinion is gaining ground, therefore, that an African spirituality can help reverse the downward trend of Africa's development.[31] This awareness provides the major motivation for the emergence of various forms of liberation theologies, which make the liberation of Africans from the problems of hunger, oppression, debt and corruption a theological priority.

9.2   *The Hermeneutics of African Christian Theology*

A wide margin of the hermeneutics of African Christian theology would out of necessity embrace the questions about its sources and methodologies. Before we

---

[29]   Cf. L. S. Senghor, *Prose and Poetry*; K. Nkrumah, *Neo-Colonialism: The Last Stage of Imperialism*; K. Kaunda, *Letter to My Children*, especially the Essay, Faith and Values; J. Nyerere, The Churches Role in Society, pp. 117-128.

[30]   Black Nationalist Movement in the United States is believed to have had an enormous influence, not only on the South African "Black Theology" via the African American Black Theology, but also on the "African theology" via the Pan-Africanist Movement. Cf. G. H. Muzorewa, *The Origins and Development of African Theology*, pp. 46-56. Contrary to common knowledge, Muzorewa sees a closer connection between the aims of Black Theology and African Inculturation Theology based on their common sources of political inspiration. Black Nationalists influenced the authors (Nkrumah) of Pan-Africanism while they were studying abroad. The latter in turn inspired the inception of African theology in Africa. Hence Muzorewa's assumption, that "the spirit of African theology is influenced by Black nationalism as well as African nationalism" (54). The spirit is the same for African and Black theology, namely, "restoring the proper image of Black humanity, an image that had been grossly distorted by Europeans and white Americans" (55).

[31]   Cf. M. Sebahire, Saving the Earth to save life: An African point of view, pp. 42-45.

delve into these questions, we are required to streamline the scope of this theology. The term "African Christian theology" is reserved for a cluster of theologies reflecting both Christian and African realities. This means that the African Moslem theologies and the theologies of the African Traditional Religions would be outside our focus, since they are not Christian. Likewise, Christian theologies in African soil which are "closed to the realities of the African presence"[32] - like the white South African Christian theologies of the Dutch, British and German origins - are not, as J. Mbiti rightly observes, within the orbit of our discussion.

Openness to the Christian and African realities are therefore the two essential characteristics of African contextual theology. Special emphasis is usually laid on the African realities, either of past cultural heritage or of the current existential situations. The earlier writers of African theology had tended to believe that a theology is legitimately African only if it makes the cultural aspects its concern. This is definitely the assumption that lies at the background of Mbiti's much criticised claim that the South African "Black Theology" is not a legitimate "African Theology". His reluctance to include "Black Theology" in the fold of African Christian theology generated many reactions in defence of the legitimacy and relevance of "Black Theology" in Africa.[33] It must be observed that such theological disputes characterised the reductionist and apologetic approaches of the earliest stages of the African Christian theologies. Recent studies tend to opt rather for a more integrative, "problem-solving"[34] and "multidimensional"[35] approach. And it is in this sense, that we must see the theologies of inculturation and the "South African Black Theology" as models of the one African Christian theology.

Similarly, it is no longer an issue whether this theology has external or internal influences, but whether it makes its reflections on the Gospel of Christ from the perspective of the African Christians, and whether it is sensitive to the cultural and concrete realities of the African milieu. It is not particularly relevant, whether the writers are expatriates or Africans. What matters, in effect, is incorporating

---

[32] J. S. Mbiti, *Bible and Theology in African Christianity*, p. 17. In pp. 14-20 the author distinguishes four strands of Christianity in Africa: a) the Coptic and Ethiopian Orthodox Churches of North and Horn of Africa, b) the mission Christian Churches, c) the African Independent Christian Churches, and d) the Churches of the white South Africans.

[33] Cf. D. M. Tutu, Black Theology and African Theology, pp. 46-57; M. Buthelezi, Black Theology or Black Theology?, pp. 29-35. For the broad scope of this debate see the Black American perspective: J. U. Young, *Black and African Theologies*. Among the Black theologians, there were also views that tended to see Black theology as the only authentic theology for South Africa.

[34] G. H. Muzorewa, *The Origins and Development of African Theology*, p. 15.

[35] A. Shorter, *African Christian Theology*, p. 58.

the African history, ideas, feelings, categories and contexts into the interpretation of the Christian message. The single criterion for judging the Africanness of a theology is contextualisation.

There are ramifications in the cultural and socio-political life situations in different parts of Africa. In view of this fact the urge for contextualisation would inevitably lead to the multiplication of theologies. But irrespective of possible divergence, it is common to collectively refer to all such theologies as the "African Christian theology". This collective name is preferred in order to differentiate the African contextual theologies from the Western and other Third World theologies. But when we speak of "African theologies" in the plural, we do that to characterise the different trends of theological reflections in Africa.[36] In that sense, inculturation and liberation theologies are but distinctive forms of the one African Christian Theology.

9.2.1   The Sources of African Christian Theology

The African Christian theology takes its materials for reflection from two main sources: from the *African situation*, (i.e. from the African Traditional Religions and cultural life), and from the general *Christian sources* (the Bible and the Church tradition).[37]

The principal elements of the heritage of the *African Traditional Religions and Culture* would include a) the concept of a Supreme God, whose immanence and transcendence are equally emphasised, b) the veneration of the ancestors as the "living-dead", whose spiritual presence permeates the domain of the living, forming part of the community but sometimes acting as the agents of God, c) the concept of good and evil, d) the concept of life as related to ethics and ecology, e) the concept of being and humanity, which is basically relational and communal, f) African spirituality: sense of the sacred, rituals, rites of passage and initiation, f) the African cosmology and holistic thought-pattern. These and many other values could be termed the material principles of African Christian Theology.

When the African Christian theologians make use of these sources, they do that in the belief that divine revelation is possible in their culture. This is an implicit rejection of Karl Barth's theology, which denies any sort of revelation in natural religions.[38] In contrast, revelation is perceived here as an ongoing phenomenon, that is possible in every culture. Hence, African Tradition is seen as a sort of *Pra-*

---

36   Cf. *Ibid.*, pp. 13-17.

37   C. Nyamiti, My Approach to African theology, p. 39.

38   G. H. Muzorewa, *The Origins and Development of African Theology*, p. 114, note 4.

eparatio Evangelica, "a prerequisite for African Theology".[39] In this sense, it is not only believed that the African conception of the Supreme God finds its continuity in the Christian image of God (B. Idowu and J. Kibicho), but also that the conception of God in the traditional religion is even qualitatively better than most of what goes for the Christian view of God (G. Setiloane).[40]

Similarly, the *Bible* plays a tremendous role in the African Christianity. It is central, even among the members of the Independent Churches, where the adoption of the African traditional heritage seems unrestricted. Reading the Bible is so much part of these people's lives that in Ghana "they have been nicknamed 'the people with the dirty Bible'".[41] The use of the Bible is however not limited to its "literalistic interpretation" in the hands of these Churches. In the mission-founded Churches, effort is being made, especially in the Protestant Churches, to ground the African Christianity on the Bible, which Pobee calls "the foundation document of the church".[42]

The Christian Tradition. Despite the programme of "Africanisation", the African Church does not and cannot cut itself off from the long history of Christian tradition. The link with the tradition of the Church might be faint among the Independent Churches, and less emphasised among the Protestants than the Catholics, but the Christian theological heritage, fashioned in the Western culture, remains an indispensable source of African theology.

The approach of the African Christian theologies to tradition differs remarkably from that of the Western theologies, and in fact, in two ways. While on the one side, an effort is being made to retain only that, which is not peculiarly Western, on the other hand, African theologians are being called upon to adopt an ecumenical approach to the wealth of Christian tradition. Calling on the Churches to practise "co-operation and sharing of resources" among themselves, John Pobee appeals to African Christian theologians to avoid "factionalism and be ecumenical".[43] This should make it possible for the established Churches to borrow useful ideas from the sects. Muzorewa even thinks that the African Independent Churches should be seen as a legitimate source of African Christian theology.[44]

---

[39] E. I. Metuh, Contextualization, p. 149.

[40] Cf. J. Parratt, *Theologiegeschichte der Dritten Welt: Afrika*, p. 110. The implication of this view, Parratt insists, is the denial of the absolute revelation in Jesus Christ and the singularity of Christianity.

[41] K. Appiah-Kubi, *Man Cures, God Heals.*

[42] J. S. Pobee, *Toward an African Theology*, p. 20.

[43] *Ibid.*

[44] G. H. Muzorewa, *The Origins and Development of African Theology*, pp. 92 f.

Similarly, J. S. Mbiti concludes his book with the appeal for a "theological and ecclesiastical contact between" the new Christian Africa and "ancient and well-established Christianity of Egypt and Ethiopia", because, it is his conviction that "The Orthodox Church in these two countries can certainly contribute a great deal to the church elsewhere in Africa".[45]

9.2.2   Methodologies and Models of African Christian Theology

The aforementioned factors and sources dictate the development of the African Christian theology as it embarks on its programme of contextualisation. In general terms, it can be observed that the process of contextualisation in Africa runs on two major paths - the paths of inculturation and liberation.[46] An African Christian theology today invariably takes one or both of these paths. Both themes make up the contents of theological reflections in Africa. Hence, following the sense in which inculturation or liberation is approached, various models of African theology can be identified.

The theological reflections that emphasise culture are known as the *African inculturation theologies*. It is a model that champions the course for the restoration of the African cultural identity, which years of colonialism of the pre-independent and neo-colonialism of the post-independent Africa have terribly damaged. It also seeks to incarnate the Christian values in the African cultural context by identifying and correcting the shortcomings in the encounter between the Western form of Christianity - passed on through the missionary activities - and African religion (and culture). For this theological trend, contextualisation means inculturation. In its earliest form, to be found among the pioneering works in African theology, the significance of liberation is either unknown or denied.

The South African Black theology constitutes the second model. It is characterised by its emphasis on liberation. Here cultural revival receives little or no attention. This model arose out of the struggle against racial discrimination and the allied socio-political oppression in South Africa. Contextualisation then consists in the liberation of Africans from oppressive racial powers and inferiority complex, which years of Apartheid regime have injected into their individual and collective feelings.

Most people are aware of only these two models. However, it has become common to see the emergent *"African liberation theologies"*, which emphasise

---

45   J. S. Mbiti, *Bible and Theology in African Christianity*, p. 229.

46   One can also speak of two schools of African theology. See C. Nyamiti, *African Christologies Today*, p. 3.

inculturation and liberation alike, as a third model.[47] Those theological reflections, which by equally focusing on both socio-cultural and politico-economic problems, i.e. on both past and present issues, tend to overcome the exclusive tendencies of the earlier trends belong to this model. It addresses the issue of poverty and underdevelopment in Africa caused by oppressive structures and systems. Like Black theology, it makes liberation a major issue. However, liberation is more broadly conceived here, as liberation from cultural alienation, poverty, exploitation and corruption. Liberation means cultural freedom, and inculturation implies liberation from cultural alienation. In effect, contextualisation must address the issues of culture and existential necessities.

Furthermore, there are differences in the methodological approaches based on confessional inclinations. Within the African inculturation theologies alone, for instance, there are marked variations in the Catholic and Protestant contributions. Among the Catholic theologians, the theological methods are much more formal, speculative and philosophical. The works of Placide Tempels, Mulago, Tschibangu and Nyamiti demonstrate a great deal of the Catholic methodologies. In their theologies the encounter is more between the African culture and the classical Church theologies. Geographically, this approach is more prevalent in the Eastern and Central part of Black Africa. For their Protestant counterparts, the main concern is to relate the Bible to the African culture. The search for an African philosophy or for usable philosophical categories is not as common as the search for forms of revelation in African Traditional Religions equivalent to the Christian revelations in the Biblical literature. The works of E. B. Idowu, K. Dickson, J. S. Mbiti, and to a lesser extent J. Pobee, exemplify the Protestant methodological inclinations. This methodology is more common in West Africa.

There are also methodological differences arising from the manner in which theologians view both the local African and external Christian sources of theology. For some African theologians, the external sources are seen as finished products of Christianity, which in effect, only need to be internalised and absorbed without any virtual attempt at structural changes. This is the way of the so called "adaptation", "adoption" and "accommodation" approaches. This is also known as the "moderate approach", because it seeks to translate the message of Christianity into the lingual and cultural African ways of expression, with little or no analysis of the assumptions of the received Biblical and classical theologies.

---

[47] J. S. Ukpon, The Emergence of African Theologies, pp. 501-536; see also his book, African Theologies Now - A Profile. The author bases his classification on the dominant problem, each of the trends offer solutions for - cultural alienation, racial/colour discrimination and poverty. For other attempts at a classification of African Christian theology see also E-J. Pénoukou, The Churches of Africa, pp. 121-122; E. I. Metuh, Contextualization.

This approach tends to scrutinise the local tradition more than the received theological models.

The more "radical approach" - to be found among Protestants and Catholics alike - seeks to effect structural changes in the process of contextualising Christianity. Here earlier theologies and Biblical interpretations are received critically. The local sources are more or less exposed to scrutiny, but they are valued to be very potent for the enrichment of Christianity itself. This approach makes much more frequent use of such terms like the "indigenisation", "Africanisation", "inculturation", "interinculturation", and "incarnation" of theology. Here the basic assumption is that in the encounter of local and external sources, something new can result. For this radical approach, the classical theologies and Biblical literature are not expected to provide finished answers, but guiding principles toward the contextualisation of Christianity.

From the historical point of view, therefore, the "moderate adaptation approach" characterised more by the earliest stages of African Christian theology, while the "radical incarnational approach" is typical of the more recent stages of the inculturation theologies.

9.3   God in the African Traditional Religions

As the above discussions sufficiently suggest, the African Christian theology can only be illuminated in the light of the African Traditional Religions and Culture. It is common for an African Christian to perceive God in terms of certain assumptions he inherited from his traditional religious views. This fact obliges us to outline the basic features of the notion of God in the African Traditional Religions, before examining the peculiarities of the African Christian God-Talk. The reality of God is a basic assumption in an average African society. All things speak of the reality of God.[48] And accordingly, an all-pervading consciousness of the divine presence is also factually affirmed in every cultural expression - in languages, names, songs, proverbs and in behavioural patterns. Even if there is no certainty as to whether a "scientific" knowledge of God was prevalent in Africa before the influence of foreign cultures, it is obvious that Africans have always had what Idowu calls a "saving knowledge of God"[49] - a knowledge of God's nature and attributes. For although the nature of God is mostly undefined, it is always implied in the huge collection of the African religious and cultural expressions.

---

[48]   O. Bimwenyi-Kweshi testifies to the truth of this fact in the German title of his book, *Alle Dinge erzählen von Gott. Grundlegung afrikanischer Theologie.*

[49]   E. Bolaji Idowu, God, p. 21.

In this connection, a noble attempt to classify the obvious nature and attributes of God in the African religious views has been made by a Kenyan theologian, J. S. Mbiti. In a comparative research based on at least 300 different religious groups in Africa, he catalogues the divine attributes into four major groups: the intrinsic, the eternal, the moral and practical attributes of God.[50] Africans generally believe, he maintains, that God has intrinsic attributes - omnipotence, omnipresence, omniscience, transcendence and immanence.[51] According to him, there is also a common belief among Africans in the eternal attributes of God, namely, that God is an immutable, invisible, incomprehensible, infinite, mysterious, self-subsistent and pre-eminent spirit, who is essentially one in a multiplicity of mediator deities. And while mercy, love, justice, anger, goodness and faithfulness are supposed to be His major moral attributes, creatorship, providence, sustenance and governance of the world are His practical attributes.

Strictly speaking, all the above mentioned attributes are conventional and to be found in all the world religions. They are by no means peculiar to African religious views. Neither have we affirmed them here in order to demonstrate that Africans, contrary to popular assumptions, have an acceptable concept of God.[52] The repetition is rather in keeping with the African context, where the real belief is often cloaked in a cloud of apparent contradictions. In such a context, even obvious attributes need to be reaffirmed. Hence irrespective of the fact that the reality of God is a basic assumption in Black Africa, a knowledge of His true nature is not less difficult to come by. Our effort below shall therefore be directed towards illuminating those ambiguous features of the traditional African views, which complicate the African Christian image of God.

9.3.1 One God and Many Deities

Most Africans believe in the existence of One Supreme God and many minor deities and spirit forces - human and non-human - who occupy various positions in the ontological hierarchy of being. This is a vision of God that often leaves for-

---

[50] J. S. Mbiti, *Concepts of God in Africa*, pp. 3-41.

[51] However, it should be noted that this thesis has already been vehemently criticised by Okot P'Bitek,. In his book, *African Religions in Western Scholarship*, pp.80-89, he argues that the predication of such attributes to God as well as the claim that there is a monotheistic vision of Him in African religion are signs of an undue hellenization of the African religious thought. Similar objections have also been made by a few other African intellectuals. See for instance, Donatus I. Nwoga, *The Supreme God as Strager in Igbo Religious Thought*.

[52] It is probable that Mbiti's research was motivated by the need to affirm that Africans share similar notions of God with the rest of the world religions. Our purpose is different.

eigners and shallow observers to wonder, whether African religionists are theists or deists, monotheists or polytheists. The confusion is further provoked by the fact, that while one can find shrines for the worship of various deities, benevolent and malevolent spirits, ancestors, and witches conspicuously positioned in homes, village squares, and at revered corners, temples dedicated to God are rare.[53]

Hence the popular impression, that Africans make flagrant veneration and sacrifices to small divinities, but none to the Supreme God. In some circles, it has been argued, that Africans do not worship a Supreme God, but a litany of deities. This perception is certainly false. In reality, the belief in One Supreme God is the central idea of African Traditional Religions.[54] The Supreme God is worshipped, albeit indirectly.

Among the Igbos of Nigeria, for instance, the Supreme God is supposed to be behind everything. He is known to be the "Creator of everything including deities".[55] In the Igbo world-view, there are two classes of spiritual beings: the first class - non-human - comprising of *Chukwu* (the Supreme God), *Muo* (the deities) and *Arusi* (spiritual forces) and the other - human - the *Ndichie* (ancestors). Although *Chukwu* is Himself one of the spiritual beings, He is the author of all beings. He occupies the highest position in the hierarchy of spiritual beings. The deities, who are themselves creatures of God, have power and influence over human beings. Each of them is designated to monitor a particular domain of creation and aspects of human affairs.

The spiritual beings - the deities and the ancestral spirits - are in a sense functionaries of God; and according to S. N. Ezeanya,

> God created these spirits and assigned them their special responsibilities and areas of jurisdiction. They have resources and have full powers to act without consulting God or asking for his permission. They, unlike the Supreme God, can sometimes disappoint man; this is why success and failures are attributed to them. ... They can

---

[53] There are exceptions, no doubt. In Igboland, for instance, it has been observed that shrines for *Chukwu*, "the Great Spirit or Providence", or for *Ezechiteoke Abiama*, "the King, Providence and Creator of the universe" still exit in Ihembosi and in Nsukka areas of the Northern Igbos, where direct worship of the Supreme God are practised. See Emefie Ikenga Metuh, *God and Man in African Religion*. In his own findings, Parrinder also claims that a visible temple and direct worship to God are common only among the Ashanti of Ghana and the Kikuyu of Kenya. Otherwise, direct and conventional worship of the Supreme God is a rare phenomenon in tropical Africa. Cf. B. G. Parrinder, *West African Religion* (1969), pp. 15 ff.

[54] J. S. Mbiti, *Concepts of God in Africa*, p. viii; -----, *African Religions and Philosophy*, p. 29.

[55] E. I.-Metuh, *God and Man*, p. 11..

be hungry, angry, jealous and revengeful. In view of this, man must always seek to be on the best of terms with them.[56]

They are therefore justified, as intermediaries of God, to receive sacrifices, for themselves and on God's behalf.

Usually, more direct sacrifices and worships are made to these intermediaries - the deities and ancestors - than to God Himself. In all devotions, however, an implicit homage is always paid to the Supreme God. In some cases, the deities are explicitly asked to convey the prayers to God[57]. In principle, therefore, God is the ultimate recipient of devotions, even when in practice, the deities are the immediate addressees. Admittedly, cases abound, where worshippers are so much preoccupied with the deities, that they lose sight of the significance of the Supreme God. He is sometimes pushed to the background and practically forgotten. These are nevertheless exceptions - deviations - rather than the rule.

The deities are, for that reason, no rivals to the God of the African Traditional Religions. They administer their assignments with a great deal of sovereignty and independence, but the "ultimate power and authority rest with God".[58] In that sense, His omnipotence is not threatened; neither does the existence of the deities challenge His sovereignty and unity. The deities merely have powers delegated to them and they mediate between God and man.

This illustration notwithstanding, doubts might still remain as to how the omnipotence of God could harmonise with the relative sovereignty of the deities and how the paradox of one God and a multiple divinities could be defended. According to Metuh, this puzzle could be best explained in the light of the African conception of royalty and nobility: "...the number and power of the subordinate deities enhance the importance and supremacy of Chukwu, just as the prestige of a king is sometimes measured by the number and power of his subordinate chiefs."[59] Rather than constituting a challenge to the Supreme God, therefore, the existence and power of the minor deities are themselves manifestations of His power and magnanimity.

Thus the God of the African Traditional Religions could be called the "one God who is served by many divine beings". This characterisation of God certainly springs the bounds of polytheism and monotheism. It is neither one nor the other.

---

56 S. N. Ezeanya, God, Spirits and the Spirit World, p. 42.

57 Ibid., p. 102.

58 Ibid., p. 62.

59 Ibid., 62.

Hence the suggestion of E. Bolaji Idowu that the notion of God in the African Traditional Religions should be termed "diffused monotheism".[60]

The fact that neither polytheism nor monotheism can express the African notion of God adequately, proves, beyond doubt, that Africans conceive God in a manner untypical of the Western thought pattern. In effect, then, what mostly seem like discrepancy between the worship of multiple deities and ancestors on the one hand, and the belief in One Supreme God on the other, might after all be part of the peculiar African thought pattern. Africans are keen on holding to a sophisticated tension between two apparently opposing concepts. G. M. Setiloane considers this tendency a special prerogative of the African world-view.[61] Setiloane's view certainly smacks of an exaggeration, but we cannot deny the fact that most African religious phenomena only become intelligible, when they are seen in the lime light of a spirally circular and holistic thought-pattern.[62]

This fact partly explains why there is no rigid separation of the spiritual from the mundane life in an average African world view - no sterile detachment of the divine from the secular, and of the dead (the living-dead) from the living. Dualistic thinking is not a common feature of the African mode of thought. Like the Igbos, most Africans have a holistic view of reality, entertaining no dichotomy between the spiritual and the material world. There is no isolated being, *Ens a se*, existing in a world of its own. There is rather a "vital relationship between beings", so that practically, "what happens to any part affects the other".[63] This view also defines the African sense of morality. [64]

---

60   E. B. Idowu, *Olódùmarè, God in Yoruba Belief,* p. 204; ---- *African Traditional Religion: A definition,* p. 135.

61   G. M. Setiloane, *African Theology,* p. 39.

62   The importance of this thought pattern for theological reflection cannot be neglected, because as an American theologian recently pointed out, Africa's contribution to the world might be "to help us see life as a single reality in which both material and spiritual dimensions have place". W. A. Dryness, *Learning about Theology from the Third World.*

63   E. I. Metuh, *God and man,* p. 58.

64   Morality and immorality are defined according to how far the ontological harmony of being is preserved or disrupted. God is believed to have arranged the order of being, and any interference with this order is an offence against Him. The major preoccupation of an Igbo - and that is also the case among many Africans - is to preserve the ontological order of being. It has been noted, in fact, that the highest percentage of sacrificial offerings are made in order to restore the disrupted ontological order. *Ibid.,* p. 135.

9.3.2 God as the Immanent Transcendence

In an average African religious-view, God the creator is not supposed to be anywhere outside His creation. He is immanent in the world, but He keeps His distance. The intermediaries are supposed to be nearer to human beings, and, they are for that reason, the immediate partners in communication.[65] This does not mean however that God is remote. In reality, an African feels God's presence and active role in his life. The consciousness of God's all-engulfing presence and nearness accompanies him all through life. God is not believed to be distant from the human sphere. He is invisible like all spirits, but His domain and the invisible zones of the spiritual beings are all located in this world.

According to G. M. Setiloane, divinity is never located "outside" nature in an ideal African view: there is a continuous feeling of the active presence (immanence) of God in the totality of life; His transcendence is but "another part of this reality".[66] In the Igbo world-view, for instance, there is a diffusing presence of the spiritual domain within our world. It is perhaps for this reason, that unlike for the Christians, the Igbos have no clear concept of Heaven, as a domain opposed to the world. The ancestors are not rewarded by joining God in a different world, but by being sent back to join their relations and kindred in a better and more blessed life on earth. In the light of the Igbo view of life-after death, life is conceived as one continuous cyclic process of living and dying.

> After a brief stay in the spirit-land one is allowed by God to reincarnate to continue the joyous cycle of life. The wicked are deprived of the joy of reincarnating.[67]

There is a continuous movement from immanent to transcendent life, a continuity in being. Life and death are versions of one single existence. The dead do not cease to exist, they continue their existence in an invisible state as the "living-dead" (Mbiti). In this connection, Shelton observes that for the Nsukka Igbos of Nigeria, "'man' and 'ancestors' are not terms which one can easily separate, for the living man is a reincarnated ancestor and, when he dies, will become a spiritualised ancestor".[68] Similarly, divine transcendence is thought of in connection with His immanence; transcendence does not place God outside His creation, but in a special position within it. For the Igbos God is the *Eze bi n' elu, ogodo ya n' akpu n' ala* - "the king living up in the sky, whose robe touches the ground." This view of God reveals a keenness towards achieving a balance between divine transcen-

---

65 E. I. Metuh, *God and Man*, p. 134.

66 G. S. Setiloane, *op. cit.*

67 E. I. Metuh, *God and man*, p. 150.

68 A. J. Shelton, *The Igbo-Igala Borderland*, p. 82.

dence and immanence.[69] That God can be transcendent and immanent simultaneously is a view held, not only by the Igbos, but, as Mbiti says, by most African Traditional Religions.[70] Africans make a vast use of anthropomorphism in the qualification of divine attributes, but their notion of God nevertheless displays a depth of paradoxical thinking - a tenuous blend of the nearness and remoteness of God is typical of this thought pattern. Thus a typical African thinks neither linearly nor dualistically, but paradoxically and holistically.

The failure to perceive this African view of reality has led some experts to gross misrepresentation of the notion of God in the African Traditional Religions.[71] D. Westermann is one among many such experts, who have unwittingly distorted the African notion of God. As he could not find conspicuous shrines and elaborate rituals reserved for the worship of the Supreme God, Westermann hurriedly concluded that the African God is a *Deus otiosus* (an inactive God), a *Deus absconditus* (a hidden and withdrawn God), and *Deus remotus* (a God remote to worshippers).[72] His misconception was perhaps further aided by the availability of myths which tell the stories of God's withdrawal from humanity.[73] But as E. I. Metuh rightly contends, it would be a hurried conclusion to claim that such stories - though illustrative of some elements of the African notion of God - necessarily suggest the remoteness of God.

In fact, the myths about God's withdrawal tend to say more about His nearness than about His remoteness. Such myths as told in the Igbo and Ashanti traditions, begin usually with a picture of God's immanence, and end up with His eventual withdrawal. As is told in some African myths, God was initially very close to human beings, but as people would not allow Him rest, he had to withdraw. There are apparently two reasons for God's withdrawal. For one thing, God's supposed withdrawal underlines His willingness to afford human beings unrestricted freedom of movement (Ashanti), and secondly, it is God's way of letting

---

69 E. I. Metuh, *God and Man*, pp. 14-17.

70 J. S. Mbiti, *African Religions and Philosophy*, p. 29.

71 J. S. Mbiti, *Concepts of God in Africa*, p. 12.

72 D. Westerman, *Africa and Christianity*, p. 74.

73 Among the Igbos of South Eastern Nigeria, for instance, there is a myth about the withdrawal of God. God used to be very close to people, but He was incessantly disturbed with major and minor complaints. The disturbance was too much for Him so that He had to withdraw into the Heavens. Human beings can still relate to Him, but only through the mediation of the deities and the ancestors, whose help they must solicit for through the performance of certain rites and rituals. Similar stories about the withdrawal of God abound in other ethnic groups in West Africa - among the Akans, Yorubas and the Mende of Sierra Leone. See H. Sawyer, *God: Ancestor or Creator*, p. 105.

His creatures become relatively independent in their attempt to solve life's problems.[74] The myths about God's withdrawal are, mainly, attempts "to explain the universal human experience of divine transcendence",[75] and, we might add, attempts to convey human freedom. It is therefore implicit in the setting of these stories themselves, that detachment is not an essential part of God's nature. His immanence was expressed before His transcendence. Besides, there are other myths and sayings that make exclusive reference to the immanence of God. Consequently, the proper nature of God in the African Traditional Religions, cannot be inferred from only one myth, but through a synthesis of all the attributes hinted at in the various myths about the divinity.

9.3.3   God as the Great Ancestor

In the African world-view, the ancestors occupy a special position in the order of beings - they have natural and supernatural status. Through death, which, in the strict sense, is understood as a passage into a new life, the dead relatives, who lived morally well, acquire a singular status that places them in an unbroken relationship with the living, and also in a spiritual and invisible state with God. There are of course some other requirements other than death and probity of life, which make a dead individual qualify as an ancestor. He must be male and have died in an adult age. While some people might see sex and age as limitations placed on the qualification for the status of an ancestor, all would agree that uprightness of character essentially belongs to the image of an ancestor. Ancestors are therefore primarily venerated as models of behaviour for the living, and thus as mediators in the relationship between God and the living. Even though the veneration of ancestors differs from culture to culture in Africa,[76] it is no exaggeration to claim that a deep insight into the African understanding of life, death, being and God-human-world relationship cannot be gained without explicating the cult of ancestors. In fact, the cult of ancestors belongs to the African doctrine of God, because, God as father, is sometimes referred to as an ancestor.

How can God be an ancestor? In the African world-view, life is a participation in the source of being, a sharing in the life-giving principle. The principle of being, or life-giving force, which sustains all that have life, is not conceived as a

---

[74] Cf. the stories respectively in: E. Rubingh, *The African Shape of the Gospel*, p. 3, and E. I. Metuh, *God and Man*, p. 13.

[75] E. I. Metuh, *God and Man*, p. 14.

[76] The Masai of Eastern Africa for example have no ancestral veneration. And even in those cultures where it is a common practice, the degree of veneration differs. Cf. C. Nyamiti, *Christ as Our Ancestor*, p. 15.

philosophical abstraction, but concretely, as that which vitalises. According to E. B. Idowu God is for the Africans the "Immense, overflowing Source of Being",[77] the source and giver of life. God transmits life through the parents, and through blood-relationships. In that capacity He is an ancestor.

Being in relationship with the parents, whether living or dead (ancestors), amounts to being in relation with the source of life. God transmits life through the parents corporeally and mystically. This explains why for some Africans, especially the Akans of Ghana, blood symbolises this life principle from God. Blood establishes the corporeal link between parents and descendants, the same link continues even after death, albeit in a mystical form, and must be maintained through the performance of certain rituals. Such ritual relationships, besides refreshing the mind of the living about the dead relatives, have the additional function of holding the channel to the source of life open. This makes good relationship with parent-ancestors compulsory. For the abandonment of this relationship would amount to breaking with the channel of life. Implicitly, therefore, life without relationship, in the African world-view, means non-existence. What J. S. Pobee writes in this connection about the Akan ontology definitely applies to all Africans.

> Whereas Descartes spoke for Western man when he said *cogito ergo sum* - I think, therefore I exist - Akan man's ontology is *cognatus ergo sum* - I am related by blood, therefore I exist, or I exist because I belong to a family. And a family, which is the basic unit, consists of the living, the dead, and the yet-to-be-born. The family relationships determine the view of man.[78]

If in the African world-view, death does not destroy the parental link, the ancestors are still the channel through which the Source of being communicates life to the living relatives.[79] Logically, the "participation in the life coming from the

---

77 E. B. Idowu, God, pp. 25-26. He arrives at this conclusion through the analysis of two African names for God: *Orise* from the Owo people of Yorubaland and *Chukwu* from the Igbo people of Nigeria. God's name *Orise* is a compound word consisting of a noun *Ori* (the essence of being) and a verb se (to originate). God's name Orise could therefore be translated as "the very source of being". *Chukwu* the Igbo name for God has the same connotation. It is composed of two words, *Chi* and *Ukwu*. Chi could mean spirit, providence, but also Source of being. Ukwu means great or immense. As *Chi-Ukwu*, God is the main-source of Being. The two words *ori* and *chi*, which form part of the divine names are also, as Idowu rightly observes, the very the terms used to qualify the essence or destiny of human beings. Each person has his chi or ori, " a semi-split entity which assumes the role of man's guardian-angel".

78 J. S. Pobee, *Toward an African Theology*, p. 49.

79 As the grand-parents of the living, it is believed that they care for their living descendants. They are expected to protect their kins from sickness and calamity. If the Ancestors are offended, for instance, by lack of proper burial, they might cause suffering and hardship for the living. So, Africans do all they can to maintain a good relationship with the ances-

ancestors is the only way the individual shares the life of the community. Cut off from this source he ceases to exist."[80] Hence, participating in the life of the community guarantees both life and contact with God. To live is to participate in the life-principle, which God transmits through the ancestors.

It is obvious from the above that the transmission of life is the main characteristic of parenthood. Since God Himself is the ultimate source of life, He must also be the Great Parent, the Ultimate Ancestor. This is the logic of those Africans who attribute parenthood to God. It must be noted however that this view does not find a general acceptance among all Africans. For although all African cultures know God as father, and some even call Him mother, only few of them freely attribute parenthood to Him. When fatherhood is used it is most probably meant to be metaphorical.

Similarly, opinions differ in the African circle as to whether the fatherhood of God should also imply His ancestorship. While the Igbos, for instance, believe that God is the Source of life, and could, for that reason, be called father, they do not conceive Him as an ancestor, because, as Metuh contends, there is no family relation between God and the first parents in the Igbo world-view. For them, "God is not an ancestor but creator of the first ancestors."[81] In contrast, the Akans of Ghana believe that God is the Great Ancestor. This forms the main thesis of J. B. Danquah in *The Akan Doctrine of God*. Other Ghanaian theologians like P. Sarpong and H. Sawyer confirm Danquah's claim.[82] Sawyer goes even further to affirm that the same belief is held by the Yorubas and the Mende people of Sierra Leone.

Is God a creator or an ancestor, or is He both? Danquah and Sawyerr would affirm that God is both creator and ancestor. God is the Great Ancestor because all life comes from Him. He is as such the Chief, the King, and Creator of the world. This view is most vivid among the Akans, perhaps because they arrive at the Ancestorship of God through a matrilineal and royal system.[83] Despite the

---

tors. Where favour cannot be obtained through the ancestors, direct appeal to God is the last resort. It is in this sense that prayers are made both to God and the ancestors. In many cases, prayers to the ancestors do not differ greatly from those made to God, but the "tone of submission and supplication which appears in prayers to God and the deities is significantly absent" Cf. E. I. Metuh, *God and man*, p. 94

80 E. Uzukwu, The God of our ancestors and African unity, p. 347.

81 *Ibid.*, p. 12.

82 P. Sarpong, *Ghana in Retrospect*.

83 "Among the Akan...the concept of God as the Great Ancestor can be traced back, first, to the *kra*, that spark of fire that comes from *Nyame*; every one receives this spark at birth

disagreement on the issue of divine ancestorship, it has begun to play a significant role in the fashioning of the African Christian Christology and the doctrine of God, as we shall soon see.

9.4   God in the African Christian Theology

When a theologian attempts to define the notion of God that is peculiar to the African Christianity, he is inevitably confronted with clarifying questions as follows. Where are the points of continuity and discontinuity between Traditional Religion and Christianity? Are there positive views about God in the African Traditional Religions worthy of emulation? How does the African Christian conception of God integrate such elements of belief?

To begin with the first question, there is a basic assumption among African Christians, that Christianity has not introduced a new God to the Africans, but indeed the same God their ancestors had always worshipped. Accordingly, the experience of God is not new to an African. What is new is the experience of God in Jesus Christ. Actually, if an African of the pre-Christian era worshipped God through his natural ancestors, an African Christian would do the same thing today, however through Jesus Christ, from whom he expects the "ultimate answer to his religious questions".[84] With a sense of assurance that there is a continuity in revelation and in the experience of God, African Christians feel themselves justified to echo the writer of the Letter to the Hebrews: "Long ago God spoke to our ancestors in many and various ways...but in these last days he has spoken to us by a Son" (cf. Heb. 1:1-2.).

This awareness of a continuity in religious experience is today equally accompanied by the consciousness for the relevance of tradition in the religious expressions. If the earliest African Christians were initially persuaded by the missionaries to abandon their tradition in order to encounter God in Jesus Christ, African Christian theology makes it a task today to affirm the contrary, namely, that one can hear God's speech in Jesus Christ without having to break with tradition. This claim is made in the conviction, that what Jesus said to the Jews applies to Africans also: I have not come to abolish your (legal and ancestral) tradition but to fulfil it (Mat. 5:17). Preparing the tradition as a vehicle for conveying the message of God in Jesus Christ is today, among other things, the major assignment African Christian theology sets for itself.

---

through his mother; second, to the collective *kra* of the Royal ancestors which kings receive at their coronation." H. Sawyerr, *op. cit.* p. 96.

[84]   M. Ntetem, Initiation, Traditional and Christian, p. 107.

Strictly speaking, Jesus Christ is the novelty in the religious experience of an African Christian. This implies, in effect, that the Christ-event must be the criteria and the ultimate basis for differentiating the African Christian image of God from the traditional African notion of God. Christology, in the African Christian theology, is then not only central in the conception of God but also the common starting-point for a Trinitarian doctrine of God. Only through Christology can we identify what is new about the conception of God in an African Christian theology.

9.4.1 The African Ancestral Christologies

Names and titles are significant in the African tradition. They are generally self-explanatory, saying something about the bearer. An inexplicable name looses its meaning, because it can no longer establish a link between the owner and the community. Where a name or title ceases to be intelligible to a people, alternative names are introduced. This seems to have also been the case in the biblical and patristic tradition. Christ was initially introduced as the "Messiah". But as the meaning of this title became less intelligible to the Hellenised Christians, both the biblical writers and the Fathers of the Church began to replace it with such titles of Jesus like *Logos* (Word), *Kyrios* (Lord) or even "the new Orpheus".[85] These later titles were supposed to be more familiar to the Hellenised audience. Similarly, African theologians now say that the time has come for theologians to find alternative titles that would communicate the person and messiahship of Jesus Christ to the African Christians better than the terms *Logos* and *Kyrios* have done hitherto.

Already, series of Christological titles borne out of an African experience are emerging. Jesus has been called the "master of initiation",[86] "healer",[87] "elder-brother",[88] "ancestor par excellence".[89] Among all his titles, those expressing his ancestral figure are most popular, perhaps because all the other titles are believed to be implied in the ancestor-tradition. The image of an ancestor has thus become something like a paradigm for African Christian theology, a key theme on which theologians can fruitfully discuss the person of Christ and the nature of God, as well as other issues like salvation, death and life.

---

[85] E. Schillebeeckx, *Jesus, and experiment in Christology*, p. 22.

[86] A. T. Sanon, Jesus, Master of Initiation; see also M. Ntetem, Initiation, Traditional and Christian, *op. cit.*

[87] C. Kolié, Jesus as Healer? pp. 128.

[88] F. Kabasélé, Christ as Ancestor and Elder Brother, pp. 116.

[89] See B. Bujo and Charles Nyamiti, *passim.*

In recent times a number of theologians have made ancestral tradition their starting point. Bénézet Bujo and Charles Nyamiti are the most distinguished proponents of this tradition. Although both have the same point of departure, their approaches differ. While Bujo aims at incarnating Christianity on the ancestral tradition, especially emphasising the natural connection between ancestral Christology and Ecclesiology, between ancestry and liberation, Nyamiti seeks to adapt elements of ancestral tradition to classical (Thomistic) tradition, and thus sees the doctrine of the Trinity as the natural implication of an ancestral Christology. Favouring a Christology "from below" Bujo tends to base the ancestorship of Jesus on ethical grounds. In contrast, Nyamiti heavily leans on a Christology "from above", and does not hesitate to use ontological categories to account for Jesus' ancestorship. For our purpose, we shall discuss the views of these two authors, who, in our opinion, embody the two major trends in the African ancestral theology.

9.4.1.1 Jesus as the Proto-Ancestor (Bénézet Bujo)

Bujo begins his ancestral Christology with the basic assumption that ancestors are models of behaviour. This is in line with his understanding of ancestorship. Ancestors are those who lived morally well and died in a state of friendship with God, he says. They can, for that reason, mediate between God and man, care for and maintain a good relationship with their descendants. They are remembered mostly because of their good deeds. In fact, the reality of the cult of ancestors takes its origin from the commemoration of the good deeds and last words of the ancestors.

The commemoration of the deeds and words of the dead normally begin out of the need to keep contact with the cherished dead relatives, to honour and to emulate them. With time, however, such commemorations become normative codes of conduct for the living, which must be observed as a "memorial narrative act of salvation".[90] Through such commemorations, known as the ancestral cult, a permanent contact, and indeed a vital union between the ancestors and the community of the living are instituted and maintained. This communion brings life,[91] be-

---

90 B. Bujo, *African Theology in its Social Context*, p. 78.

91 *Ibid.*, pp. 75-79. This vital union with the ancestors is situated in the general context of the African understanding of the community, as encompassing the living and the dead. Other theologians also plead for the integration of the African ancestral tradition into the Christian doctrines of the community of the faithful and of the communion of the saints, *communio sanctorum*. The African understanding of community includes the Church militant on earth and the triumphant in heaven. See Fasholé-Luke, Ancestor Veneration and the Community of Saints, pp. 209-221.

cause ancestors, as intermediaries between God and the living, are believed to communicate life mystically to those who maintain a relationship with them. In other words, the ancestors are mediators, intermediaries, sources of life, and guarantors of unity in the community.

This ancestral tradition, Bujo contends, finds its continuation and fulfilment in the events of Jesus Christ. Historically, the ancestors are the "forerunners" of Jesus in the works of salvation.[92] But in terms of universality and efficacy, the salvific work of Jesus surpasses the mediation of our natural ancestors. In contrast to our human ancestors, who mediate exclusively for their own relatives and friends, Jesus extends his mediation to the whole human race. He universalises the significance of the works of salvation and transcends the aspirations of the ancestors. It is in this way that Bujo sees Jesus as the one who corrects and completes the traditional morality of Africa.[93]

Jesus is an ancestor with a difference. As "the ultimate embodiment of all the virtues of the ancestors, the realisation of the salvation for which they yearned", Jesus is not merely an ancestor. He is "the Proto-Ancestor, the Proto-Life-Force, bearer in a transcendent form of the primitive 'vital union' and 'vital force'".[94] He is the "Proto-Ancestor" because of the quality and uniqueness of his ancestorship. Unlike the ancestorship of the dead relatives, the ancestorship of Christ is not particularly biological, neither does it follow consanguinity. It is analogical and supernatural, and thus "begets in us a mystical and supernatural life".[95]

Since Jesus is not our ancestor by blood (his ancestorship is merely analogical), it would be necessary to know when this ancestorship began in the life of Christ. From the standpoint of Bujo's model, the ancestorship of Jesus Christ did not begin earlier than when he commenced his earthly work of salvation; it began precisely with his pre-Easter activities and was fulfilled in the post-Easter experience. By implication, one cannot speak of an earlier ancestral relation between God and man prior to the paschal mysteries. It is only through the passion, death and resurrection of Christ, that a new ancestral and mystical relationship was opened up between Jesus and his descendants.[96]

---

92 Bujo, *op. cit.*, p. 83.

93 *Ibid.*, p. 88.

94 *Ibid.*, p. 81.

95 *Ibid.*, p. 94.

96 *Ibid.*, p. 81. See similar ideas in J. Mutiso-Mubinda, *Anthropology and the Paschal Mystery*, 1979), p. 52. Mutiso-Mubinda, unlike Bujo, does not explain Christ's Ancestorship solely with the event of the paschal mystery, he makes the biblical teaching that Christ is the "first-born of all Creation" his starting-point.

In a sense, Jesus is our ancestor by merit - through his special mediation. In another sense, it appears as if he is our ancestor only by the grace of God - through a mystical relationship. The precise point at which the ancestorship of Christ began is not very clear in this model. At some points in his book, Bujo makes a few allusions to the Incarnation as an event with an ancestral significance. Theoretically, this would imply that the Incarnation plays a role in determining the ancestorship of Christ. In practical terms, however, it is derived from the soteriological and eschatological dimensions of the Christ-event, i.e. from the realities surrounding his salvific acts and paschal mysteries. The Incarnation plays little or no role in Bujo's justification of the ancestorship of Jesus.

Apparently, Bujo does not want to trace the ancestorship of Christ from any pre-existent, apriori, inner-Trinitarian relationship. For him, the mystical ancestorship of Jesus cannot be inferred from the reality of the pre-existent Christ. It has to emerge out of the realities of the historical Jesus. This does not mean however that he denies the significance of the Christ of faith in the formulation of an ancestral Christology. But to all intents and purposes, Bujo does not allow the Christ of faith to feature as the pre-existent Christ, but rather as the glorified Christ. The glorified Christ is the Proto-ancestor *par excellence*, the one, who by passing through death to life has been initiated as an ancestor. Thus in his system, the paschal mystery does determine Christ's ancestorship more than the Incarnation.

Folowing the evaluation this model made above, it would not be wrong to say that Bujo overemphasises eschatology at the expense of the Incarnation. And although he is determined "to keep the earthly Jesus and the Christ of faith in a kind of dynamic tension",[97] it is doubtful whether that tension was successfully maintained all through his work. Neither could he balance the tension between a "descending" and "ascending" Christology as he theoretically recommends.[98] By de-emphasising the incarnational event, his model is bound to end up as a one-dimensional account of Jesus' ancestorship. There is no doubt that the paschal events play a significant role in making Jesus the "vehicle of life-energy",[99] "the life-giving grace which flows into all his descendants, the true 'life-source' which Africa has been seeking", "the unique source of life".[100] But by failing to recognise the place of the Adamite origin in the Jesus' ancestorship, Bujo owes us an

---

[97] *Ibid.*, p.

[98] *Ibid.*, p. 81.

[99] *Ibid.*, p. 87.

[100] *Ibid.*, p. 94.

explanation of how the relationship between Jesus - the mystical, spiritual Proto-Ancestor - and our biological ancestors can be possible.

If the ancestorship of Jesus Christ is not based on a descending ancestral link, on a phylogenetic relationship with us, how can Bujo still affirm the biblical fact that Jesus is the first born of all creation? In other words, if the "Proto-Ancestor" is merely a "Model-Ancestor" and not also the "Prime-Ancestor", how can one reasonably establish an ancestral link between Jesus Christ and our biological ancestors who died before the earthly life of Jesus? Is there no link between the natural life principle from God and the mystical life source of the Post-Easter event?[101] If the divinity of Jesus Christ is not a factor in his ancestorship, how can we still see his life as a kenotic existence? As far as we can see, there would be no adequate basis for suggesting Jesus' ancestorship, if his relationship to us were merely spiritual and analogical, and not also human and natural.

This brings us to the major shortcoming in Bujo's model, namely, the failure to apply his model convincingly to the doctrine of God. In our opinion, an ancestral Christology must have serious implications for the Trinitarian doctrine of God. Bujo blocks this possibility. His objection to the idea that God could be called an Ancestor made other alternatives seem remote. The absence of an incarnational theology in his system made the matter worse, because, by that fact alone, he missed the chance to trace the source of life in God. How else, then, could he have forgotten the Johannine message that Jesus was the source of life even before his death-resurrection events.

> He was in the beginning with God. All things came into being through him, and without him not one thing came into being. What has come into being in him was life, and the life was the light of all people.(Jn. 1:1-4)

As this passage shows, Jesus Christ was the author of being right from the beginning, even before the events of the paschal mystery. Does this fact not make him

---

[101] On this point see J. Parratt, *Theologiegeschichte der Dritten Welt: Afrika*, p. 190. Parratt goes on to criticise Bujo for idealising the African past, as if everything had been perfect before colonialism. It is certainly not wrong to liken Jesus to only those ancestors who were good and God-fearing, but it would be wrong to say, as Bujo does, that only the good ones are ancestors. This is a delimitation of the ancestor tradition, which many Africans would find difficult to accept, because, not only is ancestorship essentially based on the blood relationship, it would also be impossible to have a clear-cut separation of the good from the bad ancestors. In many African traditions, a father does not cease to be a father after death, simply because he lived badly. He might not be revered, but only placated to avoid calamity, but he remains a father. However, the so called negative sides of the ancestors as Parratt calls the power of the ancestors to inflict evil on their communities, should not be exaggerated. Unlike the evil spirits, the ancestors only cause evil to call the attention of the descendants to a broken relationship or harmony in the order of being (Igbo).

our common ancestor, even as pre-existent Christ? At some points in his work, Bujo was able to work out the ancestral relation in the inner-Trinity, especially since it concerns the "vital union" among the Persons of the Trinity,[102] but he failed, nevertheless, to integrate such reflections into the mainstream of his model. To assess the Trinitarian implication of the ancestral Christology we must turn to the views of other authors,[103] typified in the personalistic and ancestral theology of Charles Nyamiti.

9.4.1.2 Jesus as Brother-Ancestor (Charles Nyamiti)

Charles Nyamiti approaches the Ancestorship of Jesus Christ differently. In line with his understanding of the African ancestorship, he contends that every ancestorship, including that of Christ, must be based, a) on *natural relationship* - through parenthood or brotherhood, b) on *supernatural* or *sacred status* - acquired through the events of death.[104] While one is protological the other is eschatological. Ancestorship is confirmed after death (eschatologically), but it takes its origin in the prime (protological) relationships at the inception of life.

The eschatological dimensions of the ancestorship must therefore presuppose the protological levels, which could be spiritual or corporeal. Nyamiti thus traces the origin of Christ's ancestral relationship back to two facts - Christ's common

---

[102] While discussing Sanon's view of initiation, Bujo made some remarkable points which he did not pursue further. Consider for instance the following: "The Father has the fullness of eternal life and begets the Son. They live for each other in a total and vital union, mutually reinforcing their common life. The vital power goes out from the Father to beget the Son and finally returns to the Father. In terms of the vital union of traditional Africa, there is a mutually-reinforcing stream of energy which results in the building-up of community. This vital union which produces the interaction between Father and Son, and which constitutes the bond between them, is nothing else than that divine power which, being within the Godhead, takes actual form and is identified as the Holy Spirit." B. Bujo, *African theology*, p. 86. On the issue of Incarnation and divine immutability, Bujo once again adopts Karl Rahner's view, that through the Incarnation the human is taken into the mystery of God, but he does not go further to reflect on the implications of this statement for the ancestorship, or fatherhood of God. See p. 82.

[103] See for instance Pénoukou's ancestral Christology. Applying his Ewe-Mina (Togo) conception of life and death to the Christ-Event, Pénoukou calls Christ the Jete-Ancestor, i.e. the ancestor who is the source of life. In this tradition, death is seen as a passage into life, a completion or fulfilment of the ontological relationship between God and man, because, being human consists in being in relation with God and it is not completed till one goes back to life through death. With the Ewe-Mina concept of death and ancestorship, Pénoukou explains the Trinity in terms of a relational ontology. Cf. E. J. Pénoukou, Christology in the Village, pp. 24-51.

[104] C. Nyamiti, *Christ As Our Ancestor*, p. 15.

Adamite origin with us and Incarnation. As true man, the God-*man* shares the same Adamite origin with us - in assuming our humanity he also assumed the Adamite origin; this makes him consanguineously related to us as our natural brother-ancestor. Both the Scripture and Church Tradition, Nyamiti contends, attest to the truth of our having corporeal and consanguineous ties with Jesus Christ, not merely because of our common Adamite origin, but also for the extra reason that, "by eating His body and drinking His blood in the Eucharist, we likewise obtain mystically true consanguineous ties with Him and through Him, with one another".[105]

Secondly, he is our *brother*-ancestor through adoption. Although Christ is the only rightful Son of his Father, he has made us share in his divine Sonship as the adopted and privileged children of God. Through this adoption we have become descendants of God and Christ has become our brother-ancestor, "both in His divinity and his humanity".[106] As the natural Son and Descendant of the Father, the Logos was in an ancestral relationship within the Trinity, prior to this adoption. And it is precisely because he is truly man, that our relationship with him is natural. Evidently, therefore, his ancestorship "is rooted not only in consanguineous ties but in the mystery of the Trinity itself".[107] Indeed, for Nyamiti, Christ's "divine-human structure" (the Incarnation) is more important a factor in determining his brother-ancestor than his common Adamite origin with us.[108]

And since Christ's ancestorship is derived from his divine-human structure, it is obviously protological; this means that his ancestorship was a reality right from the beginning. Prior to his death and resurrection, Jesus became our ancestor by the Incarnation - at the moment of his conception. His ancestorship, however, was to attain its fullness only through his death and the consequent resurrection and exaltation. Nyamiti sees the events of the paschal mystery as a sort of initiation rite that brought Christ's ancestorship to its plenitude. As *man*, Jesus is our natural brother in Adam. But as God-*man*, he is also our incarnate brother, the source and fountain of our supernatural life.

Having noted the Adamite origin and Incarnation as the two points of departure of Christ's ancestral relationship to us, Nyamiti goes further to identify the paschal mystery as the point of its factualisation. The Incarnation itself is incomplete

[105] C. Nyamiti, The Incarnation viewed from the African understanding of person, in: *African Christian Studies* vol. 8, June 1992, p. 11. Nyamiti rightly criticises Bujo for denying this fact.

[106] Charles Nyamiti, *Christ As Our Ancestor*, p. 25.

[107] *Ibid.*, p. 21.

[108] *Ibid.*, pp. 27-28.

without its fulfilment in the eschatological events. Strictly speaking, therefore, it is in the mysteries of Incarnation and paschal events that both Christ's filial ancestorship and our adoption to divine Sonship is shaped and realised.[109] According to Nyamiti, Christ's ancestorship is dynamic and nascent. For although it principally began with the Incarnation, it only got factualised later through the redeeming activities of the paschal mystery - passion, death and resurrection.[110]

Like Bujo, Nyamiti believes in the superiority of Christ's ancestorship to that of our African ancestors. But unlike the former, he accounts for this superiority with a more intrinsic reason. As we saw earlier, Bujo justifies the superiority of Christ's ancestorship with two extrinsic reasons - the supremacy of Jesus' own conduct and the universality of his mediation. For Nyamiti, the reason is more intrinsic: it is to be found in the mystery of Incarnation, in the reality of the hypostatic union. Thanks to the divine-human structure, which the person of Jesus Christ embodies, he is immeasurably closer to God, the main source of life. He is by that fact the pre-eminent giver of life, the *inner* source and *vital* principle of the life of his descendants. Without him his descendants can do nothing (Jn. 15:5). No human ancestor is as near to God as the God-man. For Nyamiti, it is this fact, more than any other, that places Jesus Christ above every human ancestor.

The centrality of the Incarnation in Nyamiti's ancestral theology is outstanding. Not just because he dedicates a series of magazine articles to the issue of "incarnation as viewed from the African understanding of person",[111] but because, in his view, all events in the life of Jesus - birth, life, passion, death, resurrection and glorification - are simply stages of an ongoing Incarnation.[112] In the light of an African notion of person, there is growth in the Incarnation, which only came to its fullness through the acquisition of human ancestral status initiated through death. The notion of person in an African context, as Nyamiti sees it, in-

---

109 *Ibid.*, p. 30.

110 *Ibid.*, p. 36. Christ's ancestorship therefore reached its fullest maturity at the eschatological fulfilment. "It is important to note", Nyamiti reminds his readers, "that like His Incarnation Christ's Ancestorship gradually grew and reached its highest maturity after His glorification. Such growth must have been proportionate to the growth of the Incarnation. As Christ grew in humanity so also did His Incarnation grow, in the sense that Christ became existentially more perfect as a human being and, hence, more perfect as incarnate and Ancestor. "

111 See Charles Nyamiti, The Incarnation viewed from the African understanding of person, in: *African Christian Studies* (= *ACS*), Nairobi, vol. 6, March 1990, pp. 3-27. Continued with the same title in *ACS*, June 1990, 23-76; *ACS*, vol. 7, March 1991, pp. 29-52; *ACS*, June 1991, pp. 41-68; *ACS*, vol. 8, June 1992, pp. 1-28.

112 C. Nyamiti, The Incarnation, in: *ACS*, vol. 8, June 1991, 42.

cludes, among other things, the *fullness of life, ancestral wisdom, fulfilled relationality* to other personal beings both living and dead, mystical vital power and sacredness.[113] If one were to observe that such a concept of person is so lofty and virtually unattainable, Nyamiti would not deny it. Indeed, he states categorically that "for the African the fullness of life or personality is an ideal which can never be perfectly realised here below, because the potentialities of the personal elements are indefinitely open to fulfilment".[114] By that standard, death is a necessary experience that contributes to the fulfilment of life - i.e. to being human.

Consequently, the death of Christ was, for Nyamiti, not only a necessary initiation into the status of an ancestor, it was also a vital part of the Logos "becoming man". This means that Christ would not have become fully a human person, in an African context, if he did not taste death. In this connection, Nyamiti's view is very similar to that of the Togolese theologian, Efoé Julien Pénoukou, who holds that, in Ewe-Mina ontology, "the human being is completed only in passing from life to death, for a better life".[115] Nyamiti likewise contends that without death Christ's ancestorship would not have been fulfilled. And neither would he have got the *mystical vital power*, which naturally belongs to those who have passed through death to new life. It is death, after all, that ushers in the period of ancestorship. According to this view, the resurrection was particularly necessary for Jesus Christ, because, without that event, the kenotic human condition, which the Logos assumed by the Incarnation, would have prevailed. The resurrection put an end to the kenotic condition and the God-man was exalted and restored to his throne.[116]

---

113 C. Nyamiti, The Incarnation, in: *ACS*, March 1990, 23-25.

114 C. Nyamiti, The Incarnation, in: *ACS*, June 1992, 15. Nyamiti perceives a certain parallelism between this African notion of person and those of some classical writers: "Thou hast made us for thyself, O Lord, and our heart is restless until it rest in thee " (St. Augustine); "man has a natural desire to see God" (St. Thomas); "man is transcendentally open to the Absolute [God]" (K. Rahner).

115 E. J. Pénoukou, Christology in the Village, p. 31.

116 It should be noted that for Nyamiti, Christ's kenotic condition began with the Incarnation. That view is not new. But he seems to be introducing something new, namely, what he calls the African interpretation of kenosis. According to this view "kenosis in the God-man involves different stages: it was deeper at His babyhood...but it became less at His adult age". (C. Nyamiti, The Incarnation, in: *ACS*, vol. 7, June 1991, 57). Here, kenosis means lack of an "accomplished personal adulthood". (C. Nyamiti, The Incarnation, in: *ACS*, vol. 6, June 1990, 70). This view suggests that the kenotic life of Christ was being reduced towards the end of his life. In addition, it makes childhood seem inferior to adulthood. Is that true?. Does Christ's call on Christians to become childlike not say the contrary? We think that Nyamiti's understanding of kenosis is erroneous. If kenosis means self-giving, as we believe, how can he justify his view that Christ was more kenotic as a

Christ's Cross and resurrection are seen here as the climax of his ancestral activity,[117] and, of course, the fulfilment of his personhood. Although his resurrection is, from the human point of view, a unique and new phenomenon, it is nonetheless, Nyamiti says, "the fullest accomplishment of the African ideals of personality". Fortunately, this same event "reveals God's ultimate purpose for our personality". What is God's ultimate purpose for our personality, which he so discloses to us in the Christ-event? By implication, Nyamiti believes that liberation is that ultimate purpose.

> By raising Him from the dead, God has officially acknowledged Him as our unsurpassable eldest Brother - as the absolutely mature man with the highest possible human rank and dignity, and has thereby accomplished in His being the unique principle of our total *liberation* from spiritual and material ignorance, poverty, disease, and all forms of oppression or servitude.[118]

It is therefore apparent, in Nyamiti's ancestral theology, that redemption is the main reason for Incarnation. For "it was precisely in order to show concretely how we, as human beings, could fulfil God's command and acquire our true personality that the Logos became man, and used His humanity to achieve that goal".[119] That the Logos became man is for Nyamiti the height of *kenosis*; the act of Incarnation implies more humility, more self-sacrifice than Christ's passion and death.[120] Thus, by the Incarnation, the work of redemption was already initiated, the paschal mysteries merely brought it to its climax. Nyamiti is indeed convinced that there is an "intrinsic link between the Incarnation and Christ's paschal mystery" - "an intimate link" between Incarnation, ancestorship and the redeeming activities of Christ - which necessitates that "Christology and Soteriology cannot be treated separately".[121] The ancestorship of Christ is practically soteriological, precisely because it bridges the gap (between humankind and God) created by our sins.[122]

Christ's ancestorship features in a double relationship.[123] Besides, his ancestral relationship to us with all its soteriological significance, Christ has an ancestral

---

child than as an adult? His idea of kenosis is too biologically conceived to be theologically relevant.

117 Charles Nyamiti, *Christ As Our Ancestor*, pp. 42 ff.

118 C. Nyamiti, The Incarnation, in: *ACS*, vol. 7, March 1991, 47.

119 C. Nyamiti, The Incarnation, in: *ACS*, vol. 8, June 1992,15.

120 *Ibid.*, p. 4.

121 Cf. *ibid.*, p. 9 and c. Nyamiti, *Christ As Our Ancestor*, p. 50

122 C. Nyamiti, *Christ As Our Ancestor*, p. 35. African soteriology, according to Nyamiti, consists in bridging the gap between God and humankind.

123 *Ibid.*, pp. 31-33.

relationship within the Trinity, which is in itself ontological. According to Nyamiti, Christ has an ancestral relationship with his Father in the immanent Trinity. An eternal descendency and ancestorship obtains in this inner-Trinitarian relationship. The Father and the Son relate to each other in a "mutual giving of the divine Spirit", who is a token of the love between them.[124] The Holy Spirit is love, but he is also life. The act of giving (life) to the other is a basic characteristic of African ancestorship. Implicitly, therefore, the relationship of the Son to the Father, whereby the former gives the divine Spirit to the latter, is ancestral. Hence Nyamiti's claim that in their mutual self-donation, the Father and the Son are Descendant and Ancestor to each other, and, that accordingly the Son has the status of an ancestor in the immanent Trinity, even before he extended it to us through adoption. The ancestorship of Christ is further confirmed by the fact that the Holy Spirit proceeds from the Father and the Son (*filioque*) alike.

Thanks to divine grace, both Father and Son extend the ancestral relationship in their inner-Trinitarian life to us *ad extra*. They jointly send us the Holy Spirit as gift of their love. The Spirit in us makes us cry "Abba, Father" (Gal. 4:6) and thus not only confirms our privileged participation in the eternal Sonship of Christ but also our right to call God our Ancestor. For, by just being united with the Son and his Father in Spirit, we are made descendants of both the Logos (as our Brother-ancestor), and the Father (as our Parent-ancestor).

9.4.2   The Triune God of the African Christian: an Ancestor and Liberator

From the preceding presentation of two model African ancestral Christologies, we can go on to sketch the significance of the ancestral tradition for the African understanding of the Christian God. We have shown, that while both models give sufficient indication of the Christocentricism of ancestral theology, only that of Nyamiti provides us with the suitable basis for reflections on the Trinitarian implications of the category of ancestorship. His model will once again serve as an example of an ancestral conception of the Christian God.

9.4.2.1   The Ancestorship of a Triune God

In his book, *African Tradition and the Christian God*, Nyamiti proposes an analogical application of ancestorship to God.[125] Just as God is similar and dis-

---

[124] *Ibid.*, pp. 58-59.

[125] Cf. C. Nyamiti, *African Tradition and the Christian God*, pp. 45-52. He sees the adoption of the principle of analogy as the surest way to escape the pitfalls of excessive anthropomorphism in the African thinking. (p. 61).

similar to man, divine ancestorship is like and unlike the human ancestorship. The differences obviously outweigh the similarities, but one can, nevertheless, find sufficient parallels between the human and Trinitarian relationships, which could warrant the use of a single category (ancestor) to qualify the nature of these relationships. Nyamiti also, among other things, observes that we, as human beings, cannot claim to have consanguineous ties with God; neither can the best of human (ancestral) relationship measure favourably with the perfect and most fruitful relationships of the inner-Trinitarian life. For although "ancestorship", in its true African sense, is a term applied only to the well-behaved dead relatives, human ancestry entails certain imperfections and limitations (including death), which cannot be thought of God.

In what sense then does Nyamiti hope to apply this term to God without implying the imperfection which it connotes in human sphere? He attempts that by locating the foundation of ancestorship in God Himself. God is an ancestor in a "formal and proper sense", not in a figurative or metaphorical, but in the true sense of the word. The term "ancestor" does not connote any sort of imperfection; it is not unworthy of the divine nature either, because God is Himself the true ancestor. "Human ancestorship is but a faint and imperfect replica of divine ancestorship. The Trinity is the exemplar of all human ancestorship."[126] By applying it to God, therefore, we are reminded that the divine ancestorship is a model for human ancestry and not vice versa.

Nyamiti sets out to justify the authenticity of divine ancestorship at two levels - first, in the inner-Trinitarian interaction, and secondly at the God-world relationship. God is truly an ancestor, primarily, in relation to Himself, in His triune life. The inner-Trinitarian events of generation and procession together with the fact of the Son's likeness (being a real image) of the Father are the proofs for divine ancestorship. God the Father gives life to the Son, and the Son becomes "the perfect image of the Father", "his archetype and norm",[127]and the Holy Spirit proceeds from both Persons as the bond of love. There has been a true ancestorship-descendancy in God, even before His providential creation and incarnation. But beside this inner-Trinitarian occurrence of *generation*, which, of itself, would suffice to establish the divine ancestorship, our author sees yet another reason in the Person of Christ - he is, as the revelation of God, the perfect image of his Father. Nyamiti contends, therefore, that if there is truth in the ancestorship of Christ, as was shown above, the same ancestorship due to Jesus Christ the Son of God should also be applicable to God the Father, inasmuch as the Son is the perfect image of the Father.

---

126 *Ibid.*, p. 48.

127 *Ibid.*, p. 47.

God is Ancestor because he not only generates the Son but is also the Prototype of the Son and because there exists between him and the Son an intimate relationship of sacred communication of nature and love through the Holy Spirit. [128]

Secondly, the origin of the extra-Trinitarian relationships with the cosmic and human beings should be seen as denoting the origin of divine ancestorship to us also. Here Nyamiti refers to the Incarnation and not to the creation. For, in his view, it is by virtue of the mystery of Incarnation of the Logos in Jesus Christ, that God took into Himself, what is human to protect and preserve. In the process, Christ did not only divinise human ancestorship, he also humanised the Trinitarian ancestorship. For irrespective of the supernatural qualities he acquired after his death and resurrection, he did not cease to be human.[129] Strictly speaking, therefore, he carried the virtues of human ancestry into God, and maintains a mediation superior to that of the ancestors. In other words, Christ had earlier incorporated the human ancestors into his Mystical Body to be perfected. For that reason, Nyamiti dares to say that

God has become - like human ancestors - an Ancestor through man (Jesus). Just as human ancestors can operate mystically only after death, so also can God's ancestorship bear its fruits for us only after the death and resurrection of Jesus Christ, through the communication of the Holy Spirit.[130]

In a word, the categories of ancestorship and descendancy as applied to the Trinity are terms used to express the parenthood of God - the Fatherhood and Sonship in God - to which we are acquainted from the biblical tradition. If one were to wonder why Nyamiti should prefer the categories of ancestorship and descendancy to the classical Father and Son images, he would contend that, the former present the nature of the Trinity better than the latter. For while the Father-Son category tends to eclipse the Holy Spirit and make Him a "stranger", the Ancestor-Descendant category perfectly embraces the three Persons and even defines the role of the Holy spirit more vividly in the works of the Trinity *ad extra*.

According to the African conception of ancestry, an ancestor is *essentially*, entitled to the sacred communication with his descendant. Since in God, this sacred communication can only be made through the Holy Spirit, divine ancestorship and descendancy demand by their very nature the presence of the Holy Spirit.[131]

Consequently, "Divine love based on ancestorship and descendancy appears to us deeper than that which is founded on the Father-Son relationship alone."[132]

---

128 *Ibid.*, p. 48.

129 *Ibid.*, p. 47.

130 *Ibid.*, p. 50.

131 *Ibid.*, p. 49.

132 *Ibid.*, p. 50.

9.4.2.2 The True Nature of an Ancestor-God, Who liberates

In an African context reality is usually interpreted in terms of life. Things are valued according to how they promote or diminish life. God Himself is conceived and differentiated from other realities to the degree He communicates life. In fact, to say that God is an ancestor means ultimately that He is a life-giver, a progenitor. He is the Great Ancestor because He possesses and communicates life in fullness. Strictly speaking, life is then the central idea behind any ancestorship.

Accordingly, Nyamiti makes life the controlling concept in his investigation on the nature of God who is an ancestor. While other Trinitarian and liberation theologians emphasise love as the key idea in defining the attributes of God, Nyamiti makes life the inspiration for the conception of God. "God is pure unlimited activity...because he is Life itself and the ultimate Source of life".[133] In God there is an ongoing activity, an activity of giving and receiving life.

The Trinitarian life abides in the solidarity, totality and communion of the divine Persons. God is the eternal source of life and for that reason is the "Living Power". According to African thought, life is a sign of power in solidarity and communion. In God, life, power and activity are identical, each must be thought of in terms of the other. The divine activity of giving and receiving life in solidarity is ongoing, and this makes God the eternal and supreme Source of Life. Out of the fullness of life in the Trinity, God communicates life to people through the Incarnation and grace.

Logically, since God is the sole author of life, and life is the highest form of power, He Himself is omnipotent. He can give and take back life. Nyamiti illustrates this point further using the African philosophy of solitude and community. In the African world-view, a solitary being is weak. Separation ushers in weakness, but being together - in union - gives strength. This also applies to God in His inner-Trinitarian life, says Nyamiti. For the Persons of the Trinity, strength consists in giving and receiving life. In them "power is based on the intrinsic unity and plurality of shared life".

In keeping with such a Trinitarian theology, Nyamiti further maintains, that we are obliged to define the omnipotence of God in terms of life, solidarity, totality and participation. God is almighty because He is the fullness of life. Life is the highest form of power. He who has it in fullness, ultimately possesses the fullness of power. The possession of the fullness of life only seems possible in the Godhead, where mutual giving and receiving is perfected. This means then for Nyamiti that the Trinity is the ultimate basis of divine omnipotence.

---

[133] *Ibid.*, p. 53.

In terms of the Trinity, God is omnipotent only because in him there is perfect solidarity and oneness of life, with an unbounded sharing of this life among the divine Persons.[134]

According to Nyamiti, it should be noted that the Bible speaks of the power of God only in Trinitarian terms (Lk. 1:35; 1 Cor. 1:24). And it is only in terms of Christ's solidarity and communion in the Trinity that we dare to understand the Cross as the manifestation of the power of God in weakness (1 Cor. 18-25).

Closely connected with the idea of *life* and *power* in God is *communion* and *sharing*.[135] Life and power are shared and nurtured in participation. This is the case with every existent being. For just like an African believes that his power depends on communal life, he also assumes that the cosmos derives its force through participation in a communion of being and life.[136] Beings are held in existence through their participation in God. Similarly, but surely in a higher degree, the Trinitarian life takes the form of participation. Participation (or communion and communication as Nyamiti prefers to call it) explains God's power and life. He is almighty because He shares His life totally and endlessly in an intimate solidarity, to an extent beyond the possibility of any other being. In fact,

the secret of God's power and life lies in communication and sharing: without communicating his life and power to the Son, the Father is powerless and lifeless, and without sharing in the Father's life and power, the Son and the Spirit are powerless and non-existent.[137]

In other words, Communication finds its perfection in God. His self-communication in Jesus Christ gives us that assurance, says Nyamiti. For if there were to be any doubt as to the nature of divine communication in the inner Trinity, the event of the Incarnation (the highest participation ever willed by God in His creation) sufficiently shows, that God communicates His life, power and love unreservedly. "No one else can share his being so totally with another that he becomes identical with that other without thereby losing his own identity." [138] Human life follows the same principle, albeit, as a poor replica of the communal life

---

134 *Ibid.*, p. 55.

135 *Ibid.*, pp. 58-65.

136 It is again necessary to note that participation is used here in an African sense. It is not to be understood as "pars capere", to take part of a certain whole, as its etymological meaning in Western philosophy suggests, rather it implies a communion. For as Nyamiti emphasises, "to participate", in an African sense, "is not firstly to *appropriate to oneself a part of a whole*, but rather to *belong to that whole*, to make with it a certain totality of communion". See *Ibid.*, p.60

137 *Ibid.*, p. 62.

138 *Ibid.*

in God. In the African anthropology, humanity is defined in terms of relation, and ultimately in relation to the source of life. For the African Christianity - in keeping with the African view of personality - humanity therefore consists in a person's nearness to God, in the sharing in God's life and power, says Nyamiti.[139]

Similarly, he defines divine sanctity in terms of God's creative power. God is holy because of His moral purity and opposition to evil and sin; that means, He is holy in an absolute and moral sense. His holiness first and foremost consists in His "radical difference from creatures". That God is holy because of His fundamental difference from His creatures is evident both in the biblical and African understanding of the sacred. But that this radical difference is connected with moral purity is a view held only in the biblical tradition. According to Nyamiti, an African Traditional Religion does not seem to include the moral aspect in its understanding of the sacred, because in most cases something could be evil and also sacred in an African context, especially when it concerns evil spirits.

Today, African Christian theology corrects this part of traditional belief and emphasises the role of morality as the basis for sanctity. Holiness hence means God's resolved opposition to evil and injustice. But although Nyamiti sees God's radical difference from His creatures and the purity of His morality as the two constituents of divine holiness, he emphasises the issue of difference more than morality. At this point; his approach differs from that of the liberation theologians, especially the Black theologians. For while the Black theologians of liberation see the holiness of God determined by God's strong sense for justice, Nyamiti sees it in God's uniqueness. This makes him reject any theology that implies suffering, change or evolution in the divinity. Then, in his view, the belief in divine passibility would inevitably lead to the blurring of the difference between God and man.[140]

In an article entitled "My approach to African theology", Nyamiti says that he is not a liberation theologian;[141] he is also definitive about his opposition to the approaches of liberation theology, which, in his view is unduly restricted to sociopolitical matters. He is however a strong advocate of an African liberation theology, if only it is placed within the realm of the inculturation theology, and specifically the ancestral theology. Nyamiti perceives a certain parallelism between the two theologies in their approaches to the theology of the Cross. God's triumph on the Cross over the passion and death of Christ reveals the divine power and life.

---

[139] *Ibid.*, p. 65.

[140] *Ibid.*, p. 68.

[141] C. Nyamiti, The Incarnation, in: *ACS*, vol. 7, March 1991, 35.

These two characteristic features of God are both seen as signs of divine ancestorship and liberation.

The connection Nyamiti makes between ancestorship and liberation becomes clear in the following argument:

> Since then (after the resurrection) the Cross has been the source of, the sign of, and the way to divine power. And this means that it is also the way to divine life, a life that means liberation from the powers of evil, a life that means participation in all the fullness of God. The inner liberation that comes from the Cross is the necessary requisite for all efforts at socio-political liberation. In a word: when endured in and for God, suffering and death are the gate to true African authenticity.[142]

Viewed in the light of our topic, the above passage shows how Nyamiti brings divine life, power and holiness to bear on his image of God as a liberator. He understands liberation as an essential characteristic of God and sees the history of salvation as a history of liberation. Since after the Fall, says Nyamiti, God's activity in the world has become a work of liberation, a liberation that consists in God's effort to turn humanity away from its trend towards doom, back to Him, who is the goal of humankind. According to Nyamiti all other intentions to liberate humankind from suffering, moral evils, death and corruption receive their meaning from God's salvific act as liberator.

> It is by bringing men back to their origin and goal, God, that the Christian faith attacks the very root of all oppression: human selfishness and fear. Without this return to God, the very struggle for liberation may be inspired by the desire to dominate and oppress others.[143]

In that case, liberation is primarily liberation from sin. Although this type of liberation is believed to have originated through the events of the paschal mystery - Cross and resurrection - it takes precedence over the liberation from socio-political oppression. [144]

---

[142] C. Nyamiti, *African Tradition and the Christian God*, p. 22. One might agree with Nyamiti that the Cross has a liberating dimension and that it manifests God's power in weakness. But his theology of the Cross here smacks of a glorification of suffering. He does not avoid creating the wrong impression that the Cross is desirable and that God is out to multiply the of the Cross so as to demonstrate His power over life. The criticism Heribert Rücker levels against African theologies is too generalised to be valid, but it definitely applies to Nyamiti. According to Rücker, the African theologies of the Cross misrepresent the biblical revelation when they give the impression that suffering is indispensable for salvation. Those holding such views are reminded that - *Gott will nicht das Leiden, sondern das Leben* - God does not want suffering, but life. See H. Rücker, *"Afrikanische Theologie"*, p. 212.

[143] C. Nyamiti, *African Tradition and the Christian God*, p. 41.

[144] *Ibid.*, p. 42.

9.4.3   *Impassibility and Passibility of the Ancestor-liberator God*

Earlier in this chapter, it was pointed out that, in the African Traditional Religions (ATR), God is, among other things, transcendent, immutable and impassible. His omnipotence and sovereignty are held in high esteem. His transcendence is so much emphasised that some earlier writers wrongly thought that Africans were worshipping an inactive and remote God. The theory of a withdrawn God has been refuted since the realisation that a normal African believer is always conscious of a pervading presence of God in his life. It nevertheless remains a fact, that transcendence, impassibility and immutability are essential characteristics of God in the ATR.

That God cannot suffer change or weakness is a well-established fact in the African Traditional Religions. This might seem contradictory in the face of its unrestricted use of anthropomorphism, and its relentless claim that God can be perceived and experienced in all realities. However, when it noted that there are no stories of God's direct intervention in history in ATR, the claim for divine impassibility becomes logical. The African understanding of history does not seem to encourage the conception of a God, who changes or suffers in any way, not even when the theory of a withdrawn God is accepted. Africans conceive history as a cyclic occurrence.[145] History is a life-death repetition, and humanity is fashioned in a seemingly unending process of reincarnation. God is both inside and outside of this circle that He does not need to re-enter. God's extraordinary intervention or His phenomenal revelation through a prophet is not envisaged. This partly explains why no African Traditional Religion is centred on a religious hero.[146] In this system, God is expected to reveal Himself ordinarily in nature, as is common in other natural religions.

---

[145] On this point, the African world-view, usually different from the Greek thought, bears a resemblance to the Hellenistic conception of time. The African conception of history as a cyclic phenomenon calls to mind Aristotle's conception of time as an uncreated circular motion. This, we know, lies behind his conception of the Absolute as the "unmoved mover". Paraphrasing Aristotle's view on this, Bertrand Russell lets him say that "There is one unmoved mover, which directly causes a circular motion. Circular motion is the primary kind, and the only kind which can be continuous and infinite. The first mover has no parts or magnitude and is at the circumference of the world." Russell also observes, that while the Christian followers of Aristotle rejected the latter's notion of time as uncreated - since the Bible is explicit about the beginning of the universe - there is no indication that his theory of "unmoved mover" was dropped. See B. Russell, *History of Western Philosophy*, p. 216.

[146] According to J. Parratt, *Theologiegeschichte der Dritten Welt: Afrika*, pp. 119-121, the lack of a historical figure in the African Traditional Religion constitutes one point of its discontinuity from Christianity. The African and Christian understanding of or approach to history differs.

Christianity brought a new conception of history for African believers - history as a lineal process leading to an eschatological fulfilment in God. God's intervention can be anticipated within such an eschatological history, but not within history as an eternal repetition, as a cyclic occurrence. The role of historicity in the conception of divine mobility and passibility is obvious as German idealism has shown.[147] God's special entrance in history in the person of Jesus Christ brought Him into the vagarious movement of history heading towards an open future. God is in the history of the world to direct it. In contrast, the African tradition, in its characteristic cyclic visualisation of history is prone to see perfection in the immutability and impassibility of God. Hence while the Supreme God is supposed to be perfect and almighty, immutable and impassible, His intermediaries, are known to be erratic and unpredictable in the expression of their favours and anger.[148]

Now, it is left to us to investigate the views of the African Christian theologies on the impassibility-passibility debate, bearing in mind that the African Traditional Religions, which inspire them to a great extent, profess belief in the impassibility of God. Our survey will reveal two approaches to the problem. While some would hold to the doctrine of divine impassibility, others see in the passibility of God the logical attribute of a God who, according to African realities, must be conceived in relational terms. On this issue an invisible line seems to be drawn between the pure inculturation theologies (of adaptation) and the African theologies of liberation.

(i) *Charles Nyamiti* is an exponent of the first group and an advocate of the impassibility of God in the African Christian theology. As we saw above, he explicates Christology and the doctrine of the Trinity in ancestral terms. Like no other African theologian, he works out the ancestral implication of the Cross for the Trinitarian image of God and agrees with Moltmann that the Cross should be interpreted in Trinitarian terms. But he stops short at admitting that God Himself was involved on the Cross of His Son and rejects any further implication of Moltmann's theology of the Cross leading to the "error of the Patripassianism" - that the Father himself suffers the Cross.[149]

Nyamiti also disagrees with Karl Rahner's thesis that God, who is immutable in Himself, can be mutable in another. He finds this idea very contradictory. In the same connection, he criticises the kenotic theology of Geddes MacGregor with the reason that the latter's idea of self-limitation in God contradicts divine tran-

---

[147] Cf., A. Schilson and W. Kasper, *Christologie im Präsens*, p. 18.

[148] Cf. S. N. Ezeanya, *op. cit.*, p. 42.

[149] C. Nyamiti, *Christ As Our Ancestor*, p. 44.

scendence.[150] Paradoxically, Nyamiti would accept that God the Father becomes an ancestor through the ancestorship of the Son, but he would not admit that God the Father suffers with God the Son.

At many points in his works, he warns that if the positive African elements are to be adopted into Christianity, the characteristic African sense of anthropomorphism must be pruned away from them. The African belief in God's immutability should rather be allowed to flourish. God could be called father and mother, in the African sense, provided that there is no corporeal connotation attached to it.[151] Nyamiti also believes that God reveals His power in a special manner "through the weakness of Christ's Cross",[152] and it is through his triumph on the Cross that we become partakers of the divine nature",[153] yet he insists that God the Father was not involved in the suffering of the Son.

However, as he begins to explicate the nature of God in terms of power, life and holiness, one gets the impression that his insistence on divine impassibility is no longer as definitive as the African conception of God would have impelled him to be. The logic of the Cross has brought in a new vision of divine power in weakness that seems to make the discontinuity of Christianity from traditional religious philosophy imperative. At this point a new vision seems to be operative, as he comments:

> What is new to the African is the fact that God's power is manifest in weakness: in Christ's humility, meekness, forgiving of sins, and - most astoundingly - in his suffering, his death on the Cross, and its glorious consequences in Christ himself and in the whole of creation.[154]

To all intents and purposes, what Nyamiti wants to say here is that the Cross has introduced a conception that would not have been acceptable otherwise in African philosophical and religious circle. On this point, he does not hide his indebtedness to the Scholastic philosophy and Thomistic theology, which he sees as the yard stick for measuring authentic theology. But as much as he insists on the immutability and impassibility of God, his acceptance of God's power in

---

[150] C. Nyamiti, The Incarnation, in *ACS*, vol. 7, June 1991, 45, note 15. Nyamiti's rejection of self-limitation in God is not surprising, because of his negative conception of kenosis. In his system, kenosis refers to an unaccomplished personality (see C. Nyamiti, The Incarnation, in: *ACS*, vol. 8, June 1992, 3 ff.); he could not, therefore, view self-giving or self-limitation as an enhancement of power as Geddes MacGregor does.

[151] C. Nyamiti, *African Tradition and the Christian God*, pp. 11-19; See also his article, The African sense of God's motherhood in the light of Christian faith, 269-274.

[152] C. Nyamiti, *African Tradition and the Christian God*, p. 40.

[153] *Ibid.*, p. 55.

[154] *Ibid.*, pp. 56-57.

weakness makes the issue of *Deus patiens* implicit. We would be belabouring the obvious to say that Nyamiti contradicts himself on this point, for it seems irreconcilable to admit on the one hand that God manifests His power in suffering, and on the other hand to maintain that He is impassible, especially since he rejects Rahner's view.

(ii) Just as Nyamiti was forced to minimise his insistence on the impassibility of God at the point where he began to reflect on the liberating dimension of the Cross, the opinion of African theologians of liberation on this issue is more or less tilted towards the acceptance of divine passibility. Here we would want to begin with the African liberation theologians with firm root in inculturation theology before moving to the South African Black theology of liberation.

Bénézet Bujo, who understands African inculturation theology essentially as a liberation theology, gives an implicit approval of divine mutability. Reflecting on the mystery of Incarnation in the light of his ancestral theology, he follows the foot steps of Karl Rahner and implicitly maintains, that God is changeable. God's mutability is expressed in His *kenosis*, which, in this context is understood as the taking up of what is human into the "mystery of God".[155]

In a more profound manner, *Jean-Marc Éla* evolves a theology of divine suffering based on God's involvement in history. God defines Himself through His intervention in history. To say that God is impassible in the face of the vicissitudes of history (especially of Africans) is to say that He is not involved in history.

> But in the official churches, God's divinity has been posited in a changelessness, an immutability, an impassibility such that the history of human beings is effectively abandoned to its own devices, deprived of the capacity to appear as the locus of manifestation of God's action. If the God of preaching ... is simply the God of theodicies, that is, of Greek metaphysics, then God is nothing but a supreme, eternal idea, having no connection with anything that happens on earth, where human beings live their lives. Devoid of any openness to the world, God cannot become involved in the human drama, for God cannot compromise the divine purity in any historical becoming.[156]

That is, according to Éla, the very God the missionaries introduced to the colonised Africans. The colonised people could not identify this image of an impassible God with the God of the Exodus, of whom they hear that He was bent on putting an end to oppression, servitude and colonisation among the Israelites, because He was moved by their suffering. The notion that the passibility of God is the only effective theodicy is implicit in the above passage. In the face of human

---

155 B. Bujo, *African Theology*, p. 82.

156 J.-M. Éla, *African Cry*, p. 30.

suffering, God can be "justified" for the fact that the God of the Exodus is the God, who gets involved and not the God of theodicies, Éla implies. According to him, the Exodus event does not suggest that God is impassible, it rather presents a God, who defines Himself by "intervening in peoples history". It is an event that informs us about "the living relationship between revelation and history".[157]

Again, Éla continues, it should be noted that God introduced Himself in the Exodus-event, not as a being "turned inward upon itself", but as the one "turned towards human beings". Consequently, "God is God" to the extent that He intervenes in history.[158] In addition, the Exodus event reveals that God owns the future personally; human beings are thus referred to the future of God - a future as promise and hope. Accordingly, "History is the tension between promise and fulfilment". In-between lies an indefinite reality. Even the knowledge of God is "provisional - impossible without a transformation of the world".[159]

The intervention of God in history is, for Éla, the scandal of Christian faith, which is not limited to the event of the Exodus but is most profoundly exhibited further in the mystery of the Cross. The Cross reveals that God is involved in liberation, that He is on the side of the poor and oppressed. The Cross of Jesus Christ shows that God takes the place of the helpless to effect their liberation. Like Nyamiti, Éla believes that it is on the Cross of Jesus Christ that God's omnipotence in weakness is revealed. But unlike the former, he contends that "God is not neutral".[160] He takes the side of the underside of history. It is in Christ that we discover the God "who frees and transforms life in solidarity", a "God of life" and a "God of hope".[161]

All in all, Éla is convinced that a relevant image of God can only emerge for the Africans, if due connection is made between the African cult of ancestors and the Christian faith. The significance of death, the communion between the visible living and the invisible dead must be recognised, not for the sake of rediscovering "within Christianity an African vision of humanity",[162] but most significantly to aid the "symbolic understanding of our relationship with God".[163] For the Church

---

[157] *Ibid.*, p. 31.

[158] *Ibid.*, p. 33.

[159] *Ibid.*, p. 35. At this point Éla seems to take his inspiration from Moltmann's theology of hope. His faith in eschatological dimension of history is as obvious as his departure from the African cyclic, or better said, spirally cyclic conception of history.

[160] J-M. Éla, *My Faith as an African*, pp. 102-112.

[161] See *ibid.*, pp. 99, 100, and 101 respectively.

[162] *Ibid.*, p. 25.

[163] *Ibid.*, p. 45.

in Africa to become authentic, says Éla, the ancestral tradition must be related to the Gospel, in fact, there is the "need to reread the Bible itself in the light of the African's relationship to the invisible world",[164] rather than to approach the Gospel with a borrowed personality, which the author identifies as Scholasticism. Practically, therefore, Éla advocates an "epistemological break with the Scholastic universe" and a nurturing of the African culture and symbolism, so as to avoid making an abstract image of an unconcerned God.[165]

The most radical approach to our topic comes from *Mercy Amba Oduyoye*, a native of Ghana, who is equally a convinced inculturation, liberation and feminist theologian.[166] In her view, the biblical image of God is that of a caring and compassionate God. This makes Him suffer with His people. Having due recourse to the Old Testament literature to substantiate her point, Oduyoye thus observes: "At the centre of the Hebrew story is a God of compassion who suffers with the world to keep it from falling apart." [167] The Jews understood God's liberative activity "as the outcome of the nature of God as a caring God".[168] With reference to the Genesis' account of a creation out of chaos and in view of the understanding of creation as ongoing, Oduyoye conceives God as always being at work, transforming chaos into order, redeeming by creating. She sees creation as liberation. And implicitly, this divine liberative and creative activity is painful. God is for that reason a vulnerable and a suffering God.[169]

Turning to the New Testament account, Oduyoye finds useful images about God that suggest divine passibility. Firstly, it is Luke's father image of God, and secondly the image of God as a shepherd, which, though of Old Testament origin,

---

[164] *Ibid.*, p. 141.

[165] *Ibid.*, pp. 41-42, and 142-142.

[166] M. A. Oduyoye, *Hearing and Knowing*. Oduyoye's contribution is significant in many respects. Because of her membership in the Ecumenical Association of Third World Theologians (EATWOT) and in the Ecumenical Association of African Theologians (EAAT), she is apt to hold a broad and representative view of liberation theology. Liberation theology is a Third World theology *par excellence*, she contends. However, Third World theology is not, she continues, a theology of a particular geographical location, but a theology that encompasses all theologies done from the underside of history with the noble aim to redress injustice and unrighteousness, (p. 2) to liberate the oppressed not only from the strangling grip of foreign nations but also from the oppressive traditions, from the ugly side of African tradition, for example. (p. 81) Her views on God are therefore typical of African inculturation, liberation and feminist theologies.

[167] *Ibid.*, p. 67.

[168] *Ibid.*, p. 80.

[169] *Ibid.*, p. 92. Oduyoye's view of creation as a painful act of liberation reminds one of MacGregor's account of creativity as a tedious act.

find ample use in the New Testament, especially in the expression of divine love and care. "This (father) image together with that of a caring shepherd and the lost coin presents us with a God who suffers to give us the chance of a second birth."[170] For the fact that God owns the earth and cares for His creatures, makes Him bear the burden of human irresponsibility and failures. If that is not a good enough reason for God to suffer, Oduyoye continues, He suffers out of love; "... God actually searches for us and suffers until the community is complete."[171] God's activity in this regard is ongoing in the world of today.

After all is said and done, what we need, Oduyoye goes on, is a "relational language about God".[172] The talk about God's vulnerability or His passibility is one such language. It would help us not only in the explication of an integrated community, but most importantly in the interpretation of the doctrine of the Trinity. Like most African theologians Oduyoye sees in the Trinity a model "full of vitality" that would help give "a unique meaning to our being created in the image of God".[173]

As would be expected, the theology of divine suffering is common in *South African Black theology*. On this issue, the voice of Archbishop *Desmond Tutu* is as distinct as his appeal for a biblical image of God. The Bible, especially in the Exodus account, reveals God, as a God who acts in history, God who intervenes, a God who takes side, a God of compassion, who cannot remain neutral in the face of injustice.[174] According to Tutu, divine action in history is the characteristic of Yahweh. And herein lies the kernel of the revelation of God in the Old Testament. For it is through the activities of the God of the Israelites in history, that we come to understand that "History, unlike the ancient Greek and Roman understanding, was not cyclic but moved towards an end, *Telos*, and so was lin-

---

[170] *Ibid.*, p. 95.

[171] *Ibid.*, p. 96.

[172] *Ibid.*, p. 136.

[173] *Ibid.*, p. 142. For more details about her feminist view on the totality of humankind as the authentic image of God, see also her article: M. A. Oduyoye, In the Image of God, pp. 41-53.

[174] D. Tutu, *Hope and Suffering*, pp. 38, 51, 79 & 82. Similarly, Allan Boesak endorses this vision of God when he says that "God makes himself vulnerable". See his article, Liberation Theology in South Africa, p. 174; On God's activity in history, with reference to the Ethics of Black Theology, see also A. Boesak, *Farewell To Innocence*, pp. 66 ff. In his article, A Holy Rage for Justice, pp. 44-45, Boesak admires the Kaj Munk's post-war theology of divine suffering; cf. also T. A. Mofokeng, *The Crucified among the Crossbearers*, p. 263.

ear, teleological and eschatological."[175] Even though history is neither a deterministic nor a closed system, God envisages a consummation for it; accordingly, God is not an onlooker, He is not indifferent to the affairs of this world. He is moved by the agony and suffering of His people, and He intervenes to let history have its course and attain its consummation.

For that reason, the image of the God of the Bible is authentic only if He is depicted as a God of compassion, who can be touched by the events of this world.

> Surely God can't remain aloof and untouched by our suffering as some Aristotelian unmoved mover. The Bible assures us that God is really like a nursing mother in his tender concern for his people who suffer. He longs after us, even when we are wayward, waiting for our return like the father of the prodigal waits for the return of his son. He is like a mother hen who would collect her young under the shadow of her wings, and in Jesus Christ he weeps over a beloved city. Yes God weeps with and for us, because our God suffers the exquisite pain of a dying God.[176]

Generally, Black theology demands that God be represented in relational images, as *Sabelo Ntwasa* and *Basil Moore*, have suggested in their article, The Concept of God in Black Theology.[177] These writers prefer to replace the image of God as Person or God as Love with God as freedom. To say that "God is Freedom", they contend, is the best way to conceive transcendence and immanence in relational terms. Not very many theologians would buy their idea that freedom expresses God's nature or relationality better than personhood and love. Even as they qualify God as freedom *par excellence*, they could not get beyond what personalism says about God. However, their emphasis on freedom is not irrelevant, because it helps to show that God enjoys boundless freedom, even the freedom to undertake suffering, or to make Himself vulnerable as Boesak and others say. God's possibility is often seen as a sign of His unlimited freedom.

9.5   Summary and Conclusion

The first major point which this Chapter brings to our notice is that the African vision of the Christian God can only be grasped from the perspective of Africa's quest for a contextual theology. The urgency of contextualisation, as was shown above, is dictated by various factors, which are religio-cultural, historical, theological and socio-political in nature. In view of these factors, the relevance, self-subsistence and future of the Church in Africa is believed to be certain only if a measure of contextualisation is undertaken. Contextualisation dictates the hermeneutics of African Christian theology, not just in terms of the sources (which must

---

[175] D. Tutu, *Hope and Suffering*, p. 79.

[176] D. Tutu, The Theology of Liberation in Africa, p. 167

[177] See pp. 18-28, especially pp. 26-27.

be African and Christian), but in terms of its methodologies. For, as a venture which entails interpreting the Bible and the Church tradition from the point of view of the African situation (traditional religion, life and culture), the target of contextual theology is to use categories familiar to Africans in evolving a theology sensitive to the peculiar problems of Africa, problems of past and resent origins. The nature of this programme makes the different, but inclusive approaches of inculturation and liberation theologies inevitable.

Having situated the African view of the Christian God within the overall project of contextualisation, our study went on to examine some tenuous elements of belief embodied in the notion of God in African Traditional Religions. Such paradoxical elements of belief like unity in multiplicity, transcendence in immanence and the ancestorship of God were examined by pointing out the specific African thought-pattern that lies at the background of the African notion of God. Characteristic of this thought-pattern is, as we observed, a paradoxical and holistic approach to reality, which, in its special form, shows itself as a relational thought-pattern. This view of reality influences the African notion of the Christian God greatly, especially where the category of ancestorship becomes a paradigm for discussing Christology and the doctrine of the Trinity.

For an African Christian, the person and life of Jesus Christ constitute the new content of his faith; this makes the difference between his experience of God and that of an African who is not a Christian. The Christ-event is therefore the ultimate point of differentiation between the African Christian image of God and the traditional African notion of God. The route that leads to the specifically African concept of the Christian God inevitably passes through Christology. So far, it is within the African ancestral Christologies that Africans have attempted to gain a new vision of the doctrine of the Trinity. And evidently, the significance of the ancestral tradition in the African understanding of the Christian God is enormous. In keeping with the African ancestral tradition, God could be called both an ancestor and a liberator.

God intervenes in human affairs in the person of Jesus Christ. For it is in the person, life and work of Jesus Christ that the liberating dimension of the African ancestry finds its fulfilment. However, the logic of his Cross introduces a sort of epistemological break, a break that perfects the discontinuity between the logic of a natural religion (African Traditional Religions) and a revealed religion (Christianity). The message of the Cross contradicts the religious philosophy of the traditional African. In the face of God's revelation of power in weakness on the Cross of Jesus Christ, the African theologian is indeed at pains to maintain and justify the African Traditional image of God as the transcendent, immutable and impassible One. This, however, does not imply an immediate denial of these attributes. Thanks to the African understanding of person as fullness of life in relationality, the divine omnipotence could be reinterpreted to such an extent that it can harmonise with the reality of the Cross.

However, when God's immutability and impassibility are reinterpreted in terms of relationality, they seem to loose their distinctiveness. In fact, as Africans interpret the Cross in the light of the African philosophy of relations, and from the point of view of the liberation theology, they arrive at a point where a conscious or unconscious affirmation of the divine suffering and change becomes irresistible. Confronted with the stark realities of the Cross and liberation, theologians, like Nyamiti, whose thoughts are rooted in both African and Church tradition, begin to be less categorical in their affirmation of the axiom of divine immutability and impassability. The issue of endless suffering in Africa is yet another factor. A majority of African Christian theologians have begun to see the possibility of divine passibility as possible solution to the problem of theodicy.

10. GENERAL CONCLUSION

10.1 Review

10.1.1 The Roots of the Theological Dilemma

As was shown in the first chapter, the attempt to merge the Hellenistic and the Semitic conceptions of God into one acceptable notion of God has been a basic preoccupation of theology since the onset of Christianity. It has been a challenge for theologians to harmonise these two apparently contradictory understandings of the divine reality. In practical terms, this has always meant mediating between the immutable and impassible God of the (Greek) philosophers and the dynamic and passionate God of the Semitic biblical experience. The difficulties associated with such an endeavour are all too obvious in the history of Christian theology. Of course, in view of the difference between the Semitic and the Hellenistic perception of the God-world relationship, the task of evolving a feasible mediation between their various conceptions of the divine reality is wearisome. In fact, it does at times seem impossible. Yet it is indispensable for any theological inquiry that is truly Christian.

If the significance of these various conceptions of God bequeathed to Christianity is to be perceived, they must be seen in the light of the God-world relationship, which they entail. In conceiving the God-world relationship, as this study depicts, the Hellenistic philosophers give priority to the difference between God and the world. To that effect, they make the *discontinuity* between the absolute Being and the contingent creatures their starting point. Consequently, philosophical theology tend to conceive God by negating the world. In contrast, the Jewish tradition interprets the God-world relationship primarily from the point of view of the *continuity* or similarity between God and the world. Accordingly, it conceives human beings first and foremost as the image of God (Gen. 1:27). This also explains the inclination of Semitic thought towards an anthropomorphic vision of God and a theomorphic view of humankind (the world).

The evaluation of the divine attributes to a great extent then depends on whether discontinuity or continuity is considered to be more important in the God-world relationship. The emphasis that the Hellenistic philosophers place on the impassibility (immutability) and aseity of God could be seen for instance as the logical development of a vision of reality that gives priority to differentiation over commonalities and to discontinuity over continuity in the God-world relationship. The same thing could be said of their tendency to conceive an inverse relationship between divine transcendence and immanence and of their understanding of apatheia as a measure of perfection. Their inclination to disparage emotions proves this point beyond doubt. Conversely, since the biblical writers and prophets emphasise the continuity between God and the world more than the discontinuity, they are able to conceive divine transcendence and immanence paradoxically, that is to say, in their mutual inclusiveness. The affirmation of the suffering, mutability and emotions in God seems apparent (1.4).

Based also on their varied ways of conceiving the God-world relationship, the two traditions inherited by Christianity interpret divine immutability differently. According to Greek philosophy, God is ontologically immutable in His *essence*, that is, in that which differentiates Him from His creatures. In the Semitic religious view, however, He is immutable in His *presence*, i.e. in terms of that which keeps Him in contact with His creatures.[1] The Old Testament conceives divine immutability accordingly in relational terms: God is said to be immutable in His will, precisely because He is resolute in His primary option for humankind, i.e. in His commitment to the covenant promise. Even where the Old Testament speaks about God changing His mind, it invariably implies a change undertaken to maintain the basic immutability of His relationship and option for humankind. Consequently, the biblical notion of immutability is believed to provide dynamism and flexibility on the part of God. Such is the paradox of divine attributes conceived in terms of God's relationship to humankind. Thus, while the search for God's essence and substance in the Hellenistic philosophy reflects a basic emphasis on the differentiation of God and the world, the Jewish description of God in terms of His presence and relation to His people presupposes a strong faith in the human image of God mentioned above in this book.

Christianity not only inherited varied conceptions of God from the Hellenistic Judaism, but also an allegorical method of integrating them, which Philo of Alexandria initiated. Definitely, the significance of Philo's allegorical method does not lie in its efficacy - it does not even do justice to the use of anthropomorphic metaphors in the Bible (1.5). It demonstrates however, that harmonising rather than contrasting the Hellenistic with the Semitic attributes of God was the earliest approach Hellenistic Judaism adopted toward resolving the dilemma of divine predication. In fact, Philo's method paved the way for the subsequent tendencies in the Judaeo-Christian tradition of mediating between two apparently contradictory axioms, rather than displacing one with the other. Even though this ideal could not be said to have been realised in Philo's allegorical method, it could be said nonetheless, that his approach presupposes a preference for matching the discontinuity with the continuity, the differences with the similarities between God and the world. Thus, despite his own one-sided affirmation of divine impas-

---

[1] Cf. A. J. Heschel, *The Prophets*, p. 275: The Bible does not speak "the language of *essence*", but "the language of *presence*".

sibility and excessive leaning on the Hellenistic philosophy, his allegorical method signifies an implicit rejection of a one-dimensional approach to the issue of divine reality. It indeed points to the fact that the authenticity of God-talk must be measured according to the degree of success in the endeavour to harmonise the "God in Himself" with the "God for us", i.e. in mediating between God's continuity and discontinuity with the world, between His possibility and impassibility.

The succeeding Christian theologies follow the example of the Hellenistic Judaism in seeking to mediate between the philosophical and the anthropomorphic attributes of God. However, Philo's attempt to mediate between the opposing attributes of God, by explaining away the authenticity of the anthropomorphic expressions in the Bible, does not enjoy an unanimous acceptance. Some Church Fathers, especially the Apostolic Fathers, rather prefer to adopt the New Testament tradition, which tolerates anthropomorphism insofar as God's freedom is not tampered with. In practical terms, this means that even a negatively judged emotion like suffering could be attributed to God if it proves rather than disproves God's sovereignty and His ability to take initiative.

It is in this sense that the New Testament, despite avoiding direct attribution of negatively judged emotion to God, takes up the Old Testament theme of the wrath of God and gives it a kenotic and eschatological dimension: God adjourns the expression of His anger by means of a kenotic self-restraint. (2.1.1). By that means, an implicit reference is made to His passibility, albeit in a manner that demonstrates His freedom to take up suffering. Thus, while conceiving divine suffering in terms of God's relation to humankind, the New Testament makes divine freedom and sovereignty a priority. This must be seen as a continuation of the Old Testament's trend of conceiving divine immutability, in terms of God's relation to His people and not in terms of divine aseity. The God of the Bible has a limitless freedom to undertake an action that might seem philosophically incompatible with His nature. This provides for the dynamism of God's action in history and for the paradoxical nature of His attributes. The priority the New Testament gives to God's freedom offers a reliable basis for the effective conception of the paradox of divine nature. For, in line with His freedom no limitation can be set to His mode of action. Besides, although there is no explicit reference in the New Testament to either the impassibility or passibility of God, an implicit assumption of the divine suffering can be inferred from its use of the metaphor of the relationship of a "father" to his "son" in typifying God's relationship to the world.

Therefore, whereas the Hellenistic Judaism bequeathed the idea of the harmonisation of the attributes to Christianity, the New Testament supplies the basis on which this mediation could take place. In the light of the legacy of Philo's method and the New Testament's approach to the problem, three major approaches or tendencies from the patristic to the reformation period, can be observed in the Christian theologies, in their attempt to portray the God-world relationship and to unravel the theological dilemma of a God who is both impassible and passible: a one-sided affirmation of divine impassibility, an unconditional assertion of divine passibility and the paradoxical conception of the passibility and impassibility of God. Here again all depends on the starting point, whether discontinuity or continuity of the God-world relationship is presupposed.

10.1.2   The Three Major Approaches in the Classical Theologies

10.1.2.1   A One-dimensional Affirmation of Divine Impassibility

The *Apologists* (2.2.1) are the first in this group. Using Philo's allegorical method they try to explain the authenticity of the anthropomorphic expressions away and thus ultimately deny the possibility of divine suffering. Theoretically, some of them are poised to conceive these axioms in their paradoxical tension. In practical terms, however, they take to a one-dimensional affirmation of divine impassibility. The influence of the Hellenistic philosophy is strikingly evident in their views, so much that, in their attempt to differentiate the Christian God from the mythological gods, they make divine impassibility and immutability seem identical with God's transcendence and perfection.

Similarly, the *Christian Gnostics* (2.2.2) emphasise the discontinuity between the divinity and humanity of Christ, so much that an outright denial of divine passibility becomes unavoidable. Perceiving the Greek doctrine of divine apatheia as an attestation of the divine transcendence, the denial of the possibility of divine suffering in effect becomes an attempt to preserve God's sovereignty. The Christological tension is thus totally absent. This trend continues in the third century Christologies, especially in the thoughts of *Clement of Alexandria* (2.3.3) and *Tertullian* (2.3.2). Clement rejects any possibility of divine suffering and insists that absolute apatheia constitutes the very nature of God. Conceiving apatheia as being identical with perfection, he uses it to differentiate God from His creatures. For Tertullian, therefore, neither God nor the divine nature in Jesus Christ suffered on the Cross.

Such a one-sided affirmation of divine impassibility is most evident in the Christological controversies of the fourth century. There is unanimous consent among both the orthodox and heretic theologians that passibility is unworthy of God. The *Arians* and the *Apollinarists*, the *Alexandrian* and the *Antiochian* schools, the *Cappadocians*, and in fact other theologians of this period (2.4), affirm the impassibility of God without reservation, despite their differences in approach. The axiom of divine impassibility is a basic assumption in the whole discussion concerning the hypostatic union. Even a theologian like Cyril of Alexandria, who, in the tradition of the Alexandrian Christology, emphasises the hypostatic union (the union of two natures) also makes a one-dimensional affirmation of divine impassibility. The reason for this phenomenon seems to be the general tendency towards the prevalent Docetism at this time. The docetist denial of the true humanity of Christ inevitably leads to an unreserved affirmation of divine impassibility. Hence, the paradoxical unity of Christ remained elusive for both the Antiochians and the Alexandrians. For, while the former arrived at a disjunctive unity using their Logos-anthropos-model, the latter conceived a unity of natures that is fractional employing a Logos-sarx-model which cannot conceive human nature entirely.

The unconditional affirmation of divine impassibility reaches its climax in the Medieval-Scholastic (2.5) approach to the problem. *Thomas Aquinas*, thanks to his in-depth analysis of the nature of emotions, contends, for instance, that an incorporeal Being like God cannot suffer because He lacks the organ for the experience of emotions and passibility. Though Thomas' solution is peculiarly philosophical, and consequently prone to one-dimensional affirmation of divine impassibility, his reflections on the possibility of love without suffering and of emotions without corporeality prove to be important for the development of a theology of divine suffering.

Later, among the Reformers (2.6), only Calvin unreservedly affirms divine impassibility and denies the passibility of God. For Calvin, God is basically incomprehensible and can thus only be conceived by way of negation.

10.1.2.2 An Unconditional Affirmation of Divine Passibility

This is rare in the tradition of the Church. In the period in question, only the *Modalists* (2.3.1) make an explicit and exclusive affirmation of divine passibility. Their main concern is the preservation of the unity of the Godhead, which they try to attain, not by denying the humanity of the Son (Docetists), but by recognising only a nominal difference between the divinity and humanity of Christ. By implication the Father and the Son are merged into one identity. Noetus, Praxeas and Sabellius propagate this view in various ways. However, although the Modalists are mostly remembered in this connection because of the Praxean heresy of Patripassianism, which entails the explicit claim that the Father suffered with the Son, their gravest error, in our view, is not the affirmation of divine suffering, but the tautological identity given to the Father and the Son. For, as a result, the basis for establishing the paradoxical unity of the God-man is eroded.

However, notwithstanding the explicit affirmation of the divine passibility, there are signs that the Modalists firmly held to the belief that there is an enduring impassibility of God, which survived the "transitory theophany of the divinity" during the earthly life of the Son.

10.1.2.3 A Paradoxical Approach to Divine Impassibility and Passibility

This approach, which characterises the New Testament's contribution, finds its explicit formulation in the theologies of the Apostolic Fathers, especially St. *Ignatius of Antioch*, (2.1.2) who, without any attempt at a rigorous theological reflection, affirms both the passibility and impassibility of God. He does this in the context of his Christology, making it clear, by that fact, that for the Christians this paradox is primarily a Christological dilemma, a dilemma in conceiving the unity of God and humankind (the world) in Jesus Christ. As a Christological dilemma, the axioms of divine impassibility and passibility are to be conceived together with the divinity and humanity of Christ. His paradoxical approach is therefore set in a Christological framework. Though it is not possible to evaluate his views, since he did not reflect further on this issue, his expression of these attributes in their paradoxical tension is exemplary.

Irenaeus of Lyon follows his example and evolves a paradoxical approach to the issue of the Christological dilemma (2.2.3). This is however much more developed in the third century theologies of Origen and his pupil Gregorios Thaumaturgos. *Origen* conceives the impassibility and passibility of God as both belonging to the paradox of His "suffering love". Without elaborately reflecting on this paradox, however, he immensely contributes towards the development of divine suffering. His pioneering attempt to resolve this theological dilemma by appealing to the nature of divine love, is an insight which no theology of divine suffering today can afford to ignore. Using brilliant arguments, *Gregorios Thaumaturgos* goes still deeper to account for the passibility of God without denying His impassibility. His attempt at conceiving this paradox is not so successful, but he makes significant contributions towards a better approach to it, especially since he shows the significance of the issues of divine will, freedom and self-limitation for a theology of divine suffering.

Though there is no explicit affirmation of divine suffering in the decisions of the *Councils*, from the fourth to the seventh century (2.4.3), the endeavour to avoid a one-dimensional understanding of the two natures in Christ is apparent. This paradoxical approach is thus pursued in connection with certain aspects of the Christological tension, but not necessarily as it concerns the suffering of God.

St. Augustine of Hippo perceives the paradox of divine attributes better than all theologians before him. Without doing away with philosophical conceptions of

God, yet recognising the limitations of a philosophical knowledge, he pays special attention to the biblical revelation of the nature of divine attributes. He rejects the Stoic conception of apatheia and contends that emotions can be compatible with the immutable nature of God, if God wills it. According to St. Augustine, the nature of divine attributes depend on God's will. To uphold His will for justice and love, God is ready to participate in suffering. By appealing to God's volition and to the relational constitution of the Persons of the Trinity and also by arguing that the works of the Trinity *ad extra* are inseparable, St. Augustine does not merely lay a foundation for the conception of the paradox of the divine nature; he also opens a new fruitful dimension for subsequent theologies of divine suffering. For, as we shall soon demonstrate, the conception of divine suffering outside a Trinitarian frame-work is bound to end in a one-sided solution to the theological dilemma.

10.1.2.4 Lessons from the Classical Approaches.

The various approaches to the issue of divine suffering, from the onset of Christian reflection down to the Reformation period, have some indispensable and unforgettable lessons, which later approaches cannot afford to neglect. Among them is the New Testament attempt to make the issue of divine freedom the criterion of judgement of what is worthy or unworthy of God. In all discussions about divine passibility or impassibility, the freedom of God must be secured. This point is repeated by Thaumaturgos. And once the freedom of God is respected in the project of divine suffering, the idea of divine self-limitation becomes a reality, as is evident in the theologies of the New Testament and Thaumaturgos. Thus, although the idea of divine self-limitation (kenosis) was to be employed much later, its significance for our project was discovered earlier in the search for a solution to the paradox of divine nature in the first four centuries. In the same connection, the importance St. Augustine and Thaumaturgos place on the divine will in the attempt to secure God's freedom even in suffering is a point to be noted. For, according to them, the paradox of God's dynamism and flexibility in action is entailed in the immutability of the divine will, as it appears in the Old Testament. Divine volition is thus a factor in the paradoxical tension of a God who suffers and does not suffer.

The issue of corporeality and emotions, as Thomas Aquinas formulates it, is also vital. Future theologies of divine suffering will have to state the relationship between emotions and corporeality, and indicate whether an incorporeal being can have emotions - no matter whether negative or positive. Besides, the limitations of the one-dimensional affirmation of divine impassibility show that philosophical reflection cannot provide the only answer to our theological dilemma. A combination of the pure philosophical and biblical approach is indispensable (cf. Augustine 2.4.2). The major problem with an unconditional assertion of divine suffering is definitely its excessive reliance on the philosophical reasoning, which, as we saw above, is prone to focusing on the discontinuity rather than on the continuity between God and the world. Similarly, the Modalists' error, of conceiving a tautological identity of the Father and the Son, basically has its roots in the misrepresentation of the God-world relationship. It is thus clear that a meaningful theology of the divine suffering can neither underestimate the continuity (like the philosophers) nor overlook the discontinuity (like the Modalists) between God and the world.

Hence, it would be impossible for any reasonable theology to get behind Ignatius' paradoxical approach to the issue in question. This is perhaps the only way to realise the intention of the Councils to maintain the balance between the two natures of Christ. The question arises however, as to whether there can be a meaningful affirmation of the Chalcedonian Christology of true God and true man, if there should be no way by which the passibility of God can be endorsed. Origen's idea of a "suffering love" and Augustine's pioneering attempt to situate this problem within a Trinitarian frame-work are in our view the most important contributions of this period towards a realistic representation of this paradox. For, as it later became evident, the discussion about divine passibility begins to be fruitful when it is interpreted as an element of love within the Trinitarian realities.

10.1.3   The Kenotic Motif in Classical and Contemporary Theologies

Like no other principle, the kenotic motif plays a significant role in the theological debate about the divine (im)passibility. The history of its usage has been sporadic: At one time, it served as the key principle for Christological interpretation, at another, it suffered from total rejection. Despite its fictitious origin and history, however, its value and popularity has always been on the increase. Earlier, it was only important for Christological discourses, later, it became vital in the description of the God-world relationship, but today, it has even turned to be a key category for the interpretation of the Trinitarian events.

Kenosis is an equivocal category, which has been understood in various ways. It is used in at least two major senses for the explication of the God-world relationship: as a substance-ontological or as a relational principle of intelligibility. In its history, it has always been interpreted according to the prevalent philosophical perception, so that sometimes it was employed to contend the discontinuity, and at other times to argue for the continuity between God and the world. Accordingly, whereas the substance-ontological explication of kenosis characterises the theological contributions of the period from the patristic down to the Reformation, its relational understanding is typical of the time from the seventeenth to the twentieth century.

10.1.3.1 Kenosis in the Substance-ontological Thinking

For some of the Fathers and the Reformers, who, in accordance with their Hellenistic philosophical background, emphasise the pre-existence of the Logos, kenosis means the veiling of the Logos with human nature. In that case, the Logos merely passed through life being indifferent to and untouched by the events in the earthly life of Jesus Christ. At that time He hid Himself and underwent no change. At the resurrection and exaltation of Christ, He was then unveiled. The exaltation is by that fact merely a *return* of the impassible Logos to His primordial state of aseity. Nothing seems to have made a difference between the pre-existent and the resurrected Christ, since nothing "happened" to the Logos. At the background of this conception of kenosis lies an implicit substance-ontological thinking, which sees perfection in immutability and imperfection in mutability. Besides, this pattern of thought is accompanied by a spatial conception of the relationship between God and the world, which conceives God's perfection and sovereignty by excluding the world.

The Reformers (2.6), especially Calvin and the post-Reformation theologians also basically conceive kenosis as concealment. Luther, whose theology of the Cross is well developed, does not however, strictly follow the substance-ontological interpretation. Kierkegaard's paradoxical approach (3.1.2) to kenosis apparently also belongs to this model, since kenosis is for him mainly an incognito, a hiddenness of the divine in the world. However, unlike the others, he is reluctant to affirm either the immutability or mutability of God. The reality of God's sovereignty even in His kenosis is for him a paradox, a mystery, which surpasses every human imagination.

10.1.3.2 Kenosis in the Relational Thinking

In the relational thought-pattern, kenosis signifies the relatedness of God to the world, and not His concealment. It is accordingly termed divine self-disclosure (Barth), self-determination (Thomasius) or self-realisation (Hegelians), permissiveness (MacGregor) or sacrificial love (Bulgakow). This understanding of kenosis, which is typical of the period from the seventeenth to twentieth century, is variously emphasised.

(a) *Kenosis as a divine act of self-determination or self-realisation.* This understanding is popular in the theological and philosophical kenoticism of the mediating theologians of the seventeenth century (3.1.1). Despite differences in emphasis, these theologians commonly share Thomasius' thesis that "Self-emptying is self-determination". God accordingly retains the power to determine and change Himself. By that fact, He could regulate His omnipotence and omniscience in His relation to the world. This view, which characterises the German kenoticism (Thomasius, Gess, Ebrard), has the advantage of reinterpreting some of the divine attributes in terms of God's own freedom of self-determination.

However, God's power for self-determination is mostly misrepresented. For, in line with this understanding, the Logos is believed to have dropped some of His attributes during the earthly life of Jesus. Apart from the impression this view creates, namely, that the personality of the incarnate Logos was incomplete, it also portrays the Logos as lacking a unified personal identity. Besides, the divine kenosis appears to be a half hearted act. The same applies to the English kenoticists (P. Forsyth, P. Fairbairn, H. Mackintosh, F. Westons and E. Gifford). Despite their attempts to evolve a biblical and personalistic vision of kenosis, they, in contrast to their German counterparts, equally tear apart the personality of Jesus Christ since they restrict the kenotic act to his consciousness. For them, kenosis is only concerned with the divine and human consciousness of Christ. Since this notion of kenosis presents a disjointed personality of Christ, it cannot provide a sound basis for a paradoxical affirmation of the divine impassibility and passibility.

(b) *Kenosis as self-disclosure or revelation*. Karl Barth is the most outstanding proponent of this view (3.2.1). For him, kenosis is an act of divine self-revelation: God is nothing other than what He has revealed Himself to be in history. Consequently, divine being and action are identical. This also implies that kenosis is neither a laborious nor an extraordinary act for God. It is an expression of His freedom, which does not merely imply being free from "external" constraint, but above all God's liberty to assume realities other than Himself, "without becoming unlike Himself".[2] If kenosis is a self-disclosure of God, it means that it does not entail loss on God's part.

In his view, therefore, the kenosis and the exaltation of Jesus should not be seen as two successive statuses, one lower, the other higher, or as two different lives, one human, the other divine. *Kenosis* and *plerosis* are merely two forms of the one divine act in Jesus Christ; there was never a time, Barth contends, in which Jesus was not both the humiliated and the exalted. In this, there is "no paradox, no antinomy, no dichotomy".[3] The ability to perform this act is part of the divine nature.

---

2   K. Barth, *Church Dogmatics*, vol. II, Part I, p. 351.

3   K. Barth, *KD IV/1*, 202-204.

Even though the credit of conceiving kenosis holistically could be given to Barth, in a certain sense, his view makes kenosis lose its singularity. Kenosis appears to be such a normal act for God, that one wonders whether the paradoxical tension can still be maintained. If kenosis is nothing extraordinary for God, is the Cross not stripped of its pain and scandalousness? Besides, as W. Pannenberg rightly objects, Barth robs kenosis of its radicality and self-sacrificial element,[4] such that the distinction between God and the world is blurred.

Similarly, Karl Rahner understands kenosis as a divine act of self-communication (3.2.2). God expresses Himself, when He empties Himself. For him, as for Barth, kenosis is not an extraordinary undertaking for God; it belongs necessarily to His nature. However, unlike Barth who equates divine being and action, Rahner perceives a discontinuity between the being and the action of God: God is believed to change, accordingly, not in Himself, but in another; by implication, He suffers in another, but not in Himself. In other words, whereas Rahner minimises the radicality of the kenotic act, just like Barth, unlike the latter, he does not actually perceive a correspondence between the God in Himself and the God in another, a point that definitely contradicts his dictum that the immanent Trinity is identical with the economic Trinity. In effect, the paradoxical tension of the continuity and discontinuity between God and the world, does not seem to be fully maintained.

(c) *Kenosis as a process of divine self-realisation*. This is typical of the Hegelian philosophy of kenosis, which, by conceiving God as a part of the world processes, sees kenosis as a principle of divine self-realisation. God realises Himself in the history of the world. In the thought of T. Liebner, the celebrated Hegelian kenoticists, this implies a total change for the Logos and consequently the continuity between the two natures of Christ, i.e. between the Christ of faith and the Jesus of history. Apparently, this view of kenosis guarantees the continuity between God and the world, though it is achieved at the expense of the divine sovereignty and freedom. As a result, God is made to be dependent on the world for His self-realisation. The main problem of this conception of kenosis is - this also applies to Moltmann's Trinitarian theology of the Cross - that it pins down God's self-realisation to the processes of the world, to an extent that the distinction between God and the world, i.e. His freedom and sovereignty get lost.

(d) *Kenosis as self-giving and self-sacrificial act of love*. This conception of kenosis which was first popularised by the Russian kenoticist, Bulgakow (3.1.3), envisages a sort of self-fulfilling change and passibility as exemplified in the inner-Trinitarian life. For Bulgakow, the kenotic act in the Trinity is a mutual and complete self-giving and a self-fulfilling act of love between the Persons of the

---

4   W. Pannenberg, *Jesus - God and Man*, pp. 319 & 322.

Trinity. According to this concept, God's self-realisation does not depend on the world, but on the consistency of this kenotic act in the inner-Trinitarian life. God's relation to the world, is by that fact, an extension, an outflow of the inner-Trinitarian life of mutual love. This approach is popular among the Catholic theologians, as evidenced in the thoughts of H. Mühlen and H. U. von Balthasar (3.2.2).

Strictly speaking therefore, the Russian kenoticism improves on the shortcomings of the preceding relational models of kenosis as presented by the mediating and Hegelian theologians. For the fact that it posits a radical kenosis within the inner-Trinitarian life, it is able to conceive a dynamic event in God, which is not dependent on the processes of the world for its self-fulfilment. But despite the self-reliance of the Trinity, the continuity between God and the world is intact, since the latter is conceived as an outflow of divine love.

Whether such a kenotic interpretation of the inner-Trinitarian life is justifiable is questionable. For, if this notion of kenosis entails a self-sacrificial love, it is doubtful whether there is any justification in conceiving the inner-Trinitarian love as a self-sacrifice. Whereas God's relation to His creatures could be conceived in form of a self-sacrifice, it seems inappropriate to think the same about the relationship of the Father to the Son and vice versa. Apparently, Bulgakow realises the difficulties that are entailed in positing kenosis in the Godhead, hence his later view, that kenosis is a divine mystery. We shall return to this point later when we come to the Trinitarian models. At this point, it would suffice to note that this approach succeeds in conceiving the unity and differentiation between God and the world better than the Hegelian approach.

(e) *Kenosis as "permissiveness" and self-limitation.* This is reflected in MacGregor's idea of a kenotic God, who lets creatures be (4.4). Here, kenosis consists essentially in God's self-restriction and self-renunciation. God withholds Himself to allow human freedom to have its full course. He allows the world to develop on its own terms without interference.

The problem with this approach is that it presupposes a situation where divine and human freedom are inversely related, in a way that granting human freedom would imply the restriction of the divine freedom. For the sake of the human freedom, God declines not to control the world. The idea that God does not interfere in human affairs[5] seems to acquit of the responsibility for evil in the world, but it also makes Him seem not to be in control of the world. Though MacGregor's God of love suffers the consequence of His own self-restriction, His suffering does not bring the world anything, since He dares not interfere.

---

5   William Jones makes a similar point with his theory of divine neutrality. See section 8.3 2.2 in Chapter Eight

10.1.3.3 Lessons from the Classical and Contemporary Understanding of Kenosis

From the above, it is clear that a gradual but steady shift from the substance-ontological to the relational understanding of kenosis has been taking place since the seventeenth century. It is a shift from the understanding of kenosis as concealment to its interpretation as self-disclosure. Though the shift is not yet complete, and perhaps will never be, we can say nonetheless, given the popularity of the relational interpretation in the recent time, that the substance-ontological understanding of kenosis now belongs to the past. Definitely, it proved helpful in the classical affirmation of the immutability and impassibility of God. However, when trying to make the connection between the Christ (Logos) of faith and the Jesus of history intelligible, it is found wanting. For though it secures the distinction between the humanity and the divinity of Christ (between God and the world), it invariably looses sight of their unity and relationship.

The application of such a notion of kenosis to the interpretation of the personal unity of Christ and Trinitarian realities cannot, as history shows, be very successful. To that effect, the superiority of the relational approach over the substance-ontological understanding of kenosis for our theological inquiry is indisputable. This accounts for its attractiveness in the contemporary theological discourses. Its success is, however, conditional. All depends on how personalistic kenosis is conceived. For although kenosis as a word has a spatial connotation, its meaning gets lost as soon as it is conceived physically and spatially.

If a spatial understanding of kenosis is to be avoided, it must not be interpreted literally, but in the context of its New Testament usage, as the paradox of love, which, as Jesus himself affirms, consists in self-gain by self-giving (Mk 8:34-35). Conceiving kenosis in relational terms necessarily entails seeing self-realisation in self-giving, transcendence in utter immanence, fulfilment in emptying, self-affirmation in self-renunciation; that is to say, perceiving *kenosis* and *plerosis* as one single act.[6] The best analogy for kenosis is perhaps the contemporary philosophical understanding of the human "self-transcendence", which, among other things, shows that self-giving and self-disclosure lead to self-realisation and self-determination.[7]

Again, it is evident, especially from MacGregor's approach, that a personalistic interpretation cannot be possible, if God's freedom is considered inversely pro-

---

6   Cf. C. F. D. Moule, The Manhood of Jesus in the New Testament, as cited in J. A. T. Robinson, *The Human Face of God*, p. 208; J. Macquarrie, Kenoticism Reconsidered, p. 123; L. J. Richard, *A kenotic Christology*, p. 179.

7   Cf. E. Coreth, *Was is der Mensch? Grundzüge einer philosophischen Anthropologie*, p. 136.

portional to human freedom. The notions of kenosis that propagate God's withdrawal or non-interference mostly imply that God is occupying a space, which He must vacate to make room for human beings. This is completely at variance with the New Testament conception of freedom, which envisages more freedom for human beings, the more they are in the hands of God. Rather than withdraw, God meets humankind in Jesus Christ. Consequently, the more a creature is dependent on God, the freer it can be. This is the paradox of divine freedom and omnipotence, to which Kierkegaard testifies, when he says, that only omnipotence can have the world in His hand, without hindering the independence of His free agents.[8] It is on this point that the biblical understanding of divine self-limitation differs from its philosophical conception. For whereas the Bible conceives self-limitation as God's compassionate attempt to withhold His anger, MacGregor, whose contribution typifies a philosophical interpretation, identifies self-limitation with non-interference and withdrawal.

Another advantage that a relational conception of kenosis has over a substance-ontological interpretation is that it allows an analogical explication of the God-world relationship. For, since one can speak of divine and human kenosis at the same time, it becomes possible to conceive the continuity and discontinuity between God and the world alike, using the kenotic motif. On the same score, the connection between the doctrine of the Trinity and the kenotic motif becomes vivid. It is thus not accidental that the relational understanding of kenosis is becoming much more popular today, in a time, when Trinitarian presupposition is beginning to prevail.

10.1.4   The Trinitarian Interpretation-models of Divine (Im)passibility in the Contemporary Theologies

The Trinitarian reasoning is one single phenomenon that differentiates the contemporary from the ancient approach to the issue of divine (im)passibility.[9] Whereas it was common in the ancient attempts to make philosophy and natural theology the starting point of such theological debates, it is almost imperative today that every meaningful theology of divine suffering should presuppose a Trinitarian framework. To that effect, the popularity of Trinitarian thinking today seems in fact to have a corresponding effect on the conception of divine immutability and impassibility. Though in some cases it does not bring about more than a reinterpretation of these attributes, in some others it occasions the recognition

---

8   S. Kierkegaard, *Tagebücher*, p. 216 f.

9   For a confirmation of this point see also Frank Meessen, *Unveränderlichkeit*, p. 435. According to him, the new conceptions of divine immutability are advanced solely in terms of a Trinitarian God.

of a form of mutability and passibility, which are at times accorded primacy over divine immutability and impassibility. In all cases, however, the issue at stake is how to mediate between God and the world. In other words, the question is how to relate the immanent and economic Trinity. There are three major approaches to this issue, which also characterise the various attempts in the contemporary theologies to come to terms with the paradox of divine predication - these are the equivocal, univocal and analogical models of Trinitarian interpretation.

10.1.4.1 The Equivocation Models

This model conceives of an "unbridgeable" separation between the immanent and economic Trinity, between the "God in Himself" and the "God for us". Disputing that the divine acts in the history of salvation have their basis in the immanent-Trinitarian realities, it insists, accordingly, that change and passibility, predicated to the activities of the Trinity *ad extra*, neither touch nor find a correspondence in the Trinity *ad intra*. This view could be seen as the contemporary and Trinitarian version of the classical tendency towards a one-dimensional affirmation of the axiom of divine impassibility, as discussed above. Although, this view is not held explicitly by any contemporary theologian, there is an ambiguous tendency towards it in some recent theological statements: Karl Rahner's thesis that God does not suffer in Himself but in another is only a fanciful representation of this equivocation model.

As a matter of fact, however, the same Karl Rahner, together with Barth, is the most vehement critic of this model as he argues that "The 'economic' Trinity is the 'immanent' Trinity and vice versa". This statement is more in keeping with the general trend today to perceive a continuity between the nature of God as He is in Himself and His activities in history. Karl Barth makes it clear that there can be no total discontinuity between immanent and economic Trinity, no incompatibility between the being and action of God. To this effect, no serious Trinitarian theology can afford to perceive *relatio rationis*, instead of a *relatio realis* between God in Himself and God for us; and none can dispute God's active and real involvement in history.

In fact, the problem of the equivocation model, which consists essentially in the one-sided affirmation of the discontinuity between God and the world diminishes today as we deepen our understanding of the Trinity. However, its conclusions and dangers are yet existent in those non-Trinitarian theologies where God's non-interference in human affairs is propagated, as is the case with MacGregor's (4.5) and William James' (8.3.2.2) theologies. When one bears in mind that both authors use pure philosophical arguments, with little or no Trinitarian implications, it becomes evident that the tendency to emphasise the discontinuity in the

God-world relationship is a typical problem of philosophical theology. As a corollary, it could be said that the deeper Trinitarian reflections go the more unlikely it becomes for theologians to conceive a disparity between the immanent and economic Trinity, and the more difficult it becomes to deny divine suffering. It is therefore not surprising that St. Augustine, the Trinitarian thinker par excellence, is the lone voice in the patristic and Medieval period, which decries the limitations of the philosophical knowledge, when it comes to conceiving the mystery of God (2.4.2).

10.1.4.2 The Univocal Models

The univocal model is characterised by its inability to safeguard the distinction between the immanent and economic Trinity. Its legitimate effort is to counter the extreme discontinuity the equivocation model posits between God in Himself and God in history by emphasising the continuity between God and the world. This attempt misfires however, as the perceived continuity turns to a fusion and to a tautological identity of the two. The repercussion is clear: the divine freedom is jeopardised. Like in the Hegelian philosophy, God is made part of history, a history in which He must realise Himself. Accordingly, what is predicated of the world is predicated of God unconditionally.

In this model divine suffering and mutability are taken for granted. And they are predicated univocally to God, giving the impression that God and His creatures suffer and change in the same way. The impassibility of God is either totally denied or made to appear unreal. This model finds its obvious expression in Moltmann's eschatological theology of the Cross as well as in many versions of the liberation theologies, especially among Black and Latin Americans. There is a tendency towards a univocal fusion of God and the world in Pannenberg's eschatological interpretation of the Christological unity. Here, too, much emphasis is laid on the continuity between God and the world at the expense of the distinction.

Moltmann's basic motivation is to conceive a reciprocal relationship between God and the world, on account of which God is open both to the world and to the future. For him, however, reciprocity amount to an ontological interdependence between God and His creatures. God's self-fulfilment is accordingly coupled with the history of the world, in such a way that the Trinitarian God must await His self-fulfilling unity at the end of time. God does not actually transcend the world; He depends on the world much as the world depends on Him, and He directs the world less than the world directs Him. Apart from obliterating the divine freedom, this eschatological conception of God paves the way for the projection of deficiency into the very being of God. This also applies to Pannenberg, who conceives the ultimate unity of the Trinitarian persons eschatologically (3.2.1). Even though he would not accept the implication of his eschatological conception of divine perfection, it is evident that his model fails to meet the mark as far as maintaining the paradoxical tension is concerned.

The same applies to the Latin American liberation theologians (7.0), whose thoughts are to a great extent defined by the principle of eschatological hope. Except for a few, the liberation theologians generally forfeit a rigorous philosophical assessment of the problem. An attempt is made, however, more than in the classical and in the Western theologies, to approach the problem from the biblical perspective. Hence the importance given to the Exodus experience, to historicity, relationality and eschatology. Yet little is new in their arguments: On the issue of divine abandonment Gutiérrez and Sobrino repeat Moltmann's arguments, without improving upon his shortcomings. Even Boff's own interpretation of the divine abandonment, in a much more original style, equally contains a univocal predication of suffering to both the Father and the Son. According to Boff, God was silent on the Cross because He Himself was also suffering with or in Jesus Christ. By implication, God does not abandon His Son, He is weighed down by suffering. The dangerous implication of this view is that God did not rescue His Son because He was unable to. Was He perhaps in need of redemption? This is but one example of how the liberation theologians and in fact most theologies conceived from the perspective of the poor and the oppressed tend to make an exclusive claim to the possibility of God, with little or no attempt to account for the impassibility of God.

The situation among most of the North American Black theologians of liberation (8.0), who make the problem of theodicy their basic starting points is nearly the same. The point at stake is the extent of divine involvement in the world. While James Cone conceives God's *total* identification with the world, which he dramatises by saying that God is Black, William James conceives God's non-interference to the point of denying God any responsibility for the world. For the former, God suffers univocally; for the latter, He is totally impassible; in either case an extreme position is held, which makes the process of thinking the paradox of divine nature impossible. Major Jones is perhaps the only person who predicates both passibility and impassibility to God. We shall come to him later.

The African Christian inculturation and liberation theologies equally concede to a univocal affirmation of divine suffering (9.4.3) This is of course not in line with the tenets of African Traditional Religion (ATR), where transcendence, immutability, impassibility and omnipotence are considered to be the essential attributes of God. Although Charles Nyamiti tries to hold firm to the axiom of divine impassibility, which he sees confirmed, not only in the ATR, but also in the Thomistic and Scholastic theologies, he changes his mind and affirms divine passibility, as soon as he begins to take the Trinitarian theology and the theology of the Cross seriously. He does not of course deny the immutability of God, but he fails to seek a paradoxical integration of the two opposing attributes. B. Bujo, who accepts the notion of divine mutability and passibility, also stops short of seeking to relate the two to each other. Whether his approach is equivocal or univocal is not yet clear.

The univocal affirmation is, however, most explicit in the theology of J-M. Éla, whose attempt to mediate between inculturation and liberation theology is laudable. He rejects the axiom of divine impassibility without reservation, on grounds of God's involvement in history and for reasons of theodicy problem. M. A. Oduyoye also over-emphasises divine passibility against divine impassibility. The same applies to Desmond Tutu. The univocal tendency is however carried to its highest point in the views of S. Ntwasa and B. Moore, as they allow God's personhood to disappear in a conception of freedom, which precisely means the freedom to undergo suffering. In all, however, a majority of the African contributions lies somewhere between a univocal and an equivocal affirmation of divine suffering, especially as many try to relate ATR's conception of God with the Christian Trinitarian thinking.

10.1.4.3 The Analogical Models

The analogical model[10] seeks the middle course between the extremes of equivocal and univocal models of interpretation. It endeavours to accord equal importance both to the similarity and difference in the God-world relationship and to the continuity and discontinuity between the immanent and the economic Trinity. Whereas some theologians, like H. U. v. Balthasar (see 6.0), seek to establish this fact by positing kenosis in the heart of the Trinity, others, like H. Mühlen and M. Jones, try to attain the same goal through a mere phenomenological interpretation of the reality of love or relationship. In other words, while one sees the reason for the analogical and paradoxical predication of God in the mystery of kenosis, the other perceives the basis for such a predication in the reality of love.

H. U. von Balthasar summarises his approach when he asserts that the God of revelation "is neither mythologically mutable (passible) nor philosophically immutable (impassible)".[11] Making this assertion, he seeks the middle course between

---

10 The analogical model corresponds to what F. Meessen calls "inclusions scheme"; the equivocal model is identical with the "confrontation scheme", just as the univocal encompasses what he calls the "additions" and the "subordination schemes". Cf. F. Meessen, *Unveränderlichkeit und Menschwerdung Gottes*, pp. 419-428. Our own classification here is much closer to that proposed by T. R. Krenski, *Passio Caritatis*, pp. 345-370.

11 H. U. v. Balthasar, *TD* II/I, p. 9.

the univocal and the equivocal models. His endeavour is motivated by the conviction that there is both a continuity and a discontinuity between God and the world, and that the God-world relationship is analogous to the inner-Trinitarian relationship of unity and distinction. In this light, he makes a plea for the distinction between the immanent and the economic Trinity and an appeal for their unity. However, he emphatically warns against the attempt (of the univocal model) to conceive this unity as though the two Trinitarian realities were tautologically identical, that is, as if the God-world relationship were identical with the inner-Trinitarian relationship.

For Balthasar, the continuity and discontinuity must be thought together, but only in such a way that the events affecting the economic Trinity should be seen as having their foundation in the inner-Trinitarian events. Thus, without implying a tautological identity, the suffering of the Son on the Cross could be seen as having its presupposition in a sort of receptivity in God, which Balthasar understands as the divine "supra-mutability" or "supra-passibility". The human realities of mutability, suffering, emotions and passions in the life of Jesus Christ are supposed to be analogous to these divine presuppositions. Accordingly, the kenotic act in the economic Trinity finds its presupposition in a corresponding "*Urkenose*" (primordial kenosis) in the triune God. Thus, In fact, this primordial kenosis, which took or takes place between the Trinitarian Persons is for Balthasar, the very basis of the receptivity in God, and strictly speaking the analogous presupposition of God's kenotic relationship to the world. It is noteworthy, that Balthasar does not, in his effort to bring out the analogy between the immanent and the economic Trinity,   consider the mission of the Son as the primordial kenosis. The primordial kenosis is rather the generation of the Son and the Son's eternal thankfulness. The *missio* of the Son is the second kenotic act, so to speak, while its presupposition is the generation of the Son by the Father, which together with the thankfulness of the Son are termed the primordial kenosis.

The conception of a primordial kenosis in the inner-Trinitarian relationships could be very helpful in accounting for the divine activity in history, as we saw in Bulgakow's contribution above. But to interpret the *generation* of the Son as a primordial kenosis is in our opinion not without problems. For, if kenosis as we indicated above entails self-sacrifice, it is hardly conceivable that the generation of the Son should be kenotic, that means, self-sacrificial. Yet there is no doubt that the generation of the Son is for Balthasar a self-sacrificial undertaking for the Father, who, as he claims, generated the Son because He forfeits being God alone.[12] Again, his interpretation of the act of generation as a self-sacrificial act

---

12   H. U. v. Balthasar, *TD* III, p. 301.

on the part of God lets one suspect, that for Balthasar, the generation of the Son entails the risk of an unreturned love for the Father. In this way, he parallels the act of the generation of the Son with the act of the creation of the world, so that, it appears as if the Father takes the same risk in generating the Son as He does in the creation of the world. At this point, questions cannot be withheld any longer. Must God's generation of the Son entail a risk of love? Must the Father's love for His Son entail a sacrifice on His part? We must definitely resist the temptation to assume that there can be a risk of an unreturned love in the immanent Trinity.[13]

In the same connection, Balthasar contends also that there is an "absolute and infinite distance" between the Father and the Son, within which every possible distance in the world, including sin, is entailed and encompassed.[14] The visualisation of an infinite distance between the Father and the Son appears in our view to be inappropriate,[15] in our view, even though we know that Balthasar's reason for positing the infinite distance is to make "room" for the negative elements in the world, for sin and hell. By doing so, he parallels the Trinitarian distinctions with the God-world distance. It appears that Balthasar's view here amounts to making an infinite distance out of what should be a mere distinction between the Father and the Son. Is this not another way of reading limitations into the being of God as is common in the Hegelian and univocal model? The distinction between the Father and the Son must definitely not be so extremely dramatised that a negative possibility - absolute distance - should be projected into the heart of God.

The problem with Balthasar's contribution is, we suppose, that he conceives kenosis spatially, or better still, that he uses kenosis literally as it appears in Phil. 2: 6-11. As a result, the idea of "self-emptying", "self-renunciation" (*humilitas*) dominates the idea of a relational self-giving and creative love. Apart from raising questions about Balthasar's use of metaphors, as to whether for him they are mere significations or statements of fact, his use of a spatial metaphor (selfless "self-emptying") to qualify the inner-being of God, does limit the possibility of conceiving the relational and the personal nature of God. Undoubtedly, it is his spatial conception of the divine relationships that led him to posit an "infinite dis-

---

13 Cf. *ibid.*, p. 305.

14 *Ibid.*, p. 301.

15 It is evident, that what Balthasar wants to affirm here is the distinction and difference, which must be part of every relation of love (cf. T. R. Krenski, *Passio Caritatis*, p. 205). He definitely intends to echo Martin Buber's thesis that a primordial distance and relation necessarily belong to the reality of love (M. Buber, Distance and Relation, pp. 59-71. However, if we must take Balthasar at his words, we must nonetheless ask with Cl. Kappes how he can justify the claim that there is an infinite distance in the immanent Trinity. See Cl. Kappes, *Freiheit und Erlösung*.

tance" between the Persons, a distance within which "self-emptying" can take place. As a result, the mutuality of the inner-Trinitarian self-giving is inevitably misrepresented, so that instead of visualising the inner-Trinitarian self-giving of love as a self-fulfilling affair, a self-confirming act, Balthasar repeatedly perceives the kenotic act as something presupposing a "self-loss", "self-lessness" and even "God-lessness" (TD III, 301). By that means, he gives the impression that the freedom of the Son and even that of the world must imply God making "room", cutting-in into His own freedom sacrificially. Does this view not misrepresent the nature of divine freedom? Is the kenotic representation of the inner-Trinitarian life not an over-interpretation?[16]

Heribert Mühlen, who also admits that the Cross affects God in an intimate and annoying way, seems to have taken care of Balthasar's pitfalls (cf. 3.2.2) as he uses the phenomenology of love instead of kenosis to explicate the paradoxical nature of divine realities. While contending for instance that the inner nature of God lies beyond our intellectual endeavour, he declines to see the generation of the Son as a kenotic act. Rather he sees the *missio*, the sending of the Son as having a kenotic significance for the whole "We-community" of the Trinity: the Cross could be seen as having occurred in the spirit of the "being-for-us" of the Father and the Son, in their relation to us, but not in their relation to themselves. In this way, neither negativity, nor division is read into the being of God. Without overlooking their distinction the Persons are primarily seen in their personal, relational "We". While Mühlen avoids a spatial-conception of kenosis, he could therefore speak of an unimaginable immediacy and directness of the presence of the Father in the Son. The use of relational terms is an advantage, because it removes the burden of having to talk spatially about the "intra" and the "extra" of the Trinity. Mühlen's contribution, however, gives the impression that he wants to replace ontology with personalism. We are however of the opinion that for personalism to be an adequate hermeneutical method for the conception of the biblical God, it must develop its own ontology. So that, what should be replaced is not ontology as such, but "substance-ontology", in favour of a personal and relational ontology.

Arguing in a similar line, the Black theologian *Major Jones* (8.3.3.), who conceives God essentially in His relations, contends that God on account of His relational nature is both passible and impassible: God is impassible and immutable, if by that we mean that God is not subject to any external determination; He is how-

---

16 We must agree with Jürgen Werbick that it suffices for a theology of the Trinity to note that God is that love that overflows. It is not necessary to say more than that, because any "more" might in the end prove to be fatally too "little". Cf. Jürgen Werbick, Das Leiden Gottes in sich. An sich selbst?

ever mutable and passible, in as much as He has the freedom to subject Himself to change and suffering in response to the demand of His personal and relational nature. Forfeiting a rigorous philosophical argument, and yet making the problem of theodicy his starting point, as is common in Black theology, Jones summarises the paradox of the faith of the oppressed people, as he says, God must be powerful, but He must have the experience of weakness, God remained God, but He did change by becoming man. On account of the personal unity between the Father and the Son, the Christ-event did have "relational effects on God Himself".[17] The responsive relationship of the Trinitarian Persons among themselves cannot be attributed to external agents, their responsiveness is always initiated by themselves. Jones emphasises the role of the Holy Spirit, who assures the presence and immediacy of God to the world. As the union of the Father and the Son, the Holy Spirit guarantees the abiding, personal and relational presence of God. In this way, Jones escapes the danger of the univocal model, of imply a tautological identity between God and the world. He describes the indwelling of the Spirit in the world as "the deeps of God confronting the deeps of human subjectivity". Like Mühlen, Jones does not seem to go far enough; his insight remains basically phenomenological; the relational significance of God's relation to the world, we believe, could be deepened, if it is conceived as an ontological reality.

10.1.4.4 Lessons from the Contemporary Trinitarian Theologies of Divine Suffering

It is clear from the above, that neither the equivocal nor the univocal model can properly conceive the paradox of divine nature. For, while the former conjures up an extreme difference between God and the world, so that there is no basis for assuming that what happens in the world affects God, the latter mixes up the realities of the two, so that God becomes hopelessly entangled in the world. The two models err gravely in misrepresenting divine freedom. It is self-evident that the univocal or the Hegelian approach compromises divine freedom. The same is ironically true of the equivocal model. It is true that the main concern of the proponents of the equivocation model is to defend God's ultimate transcendence and freedom. They intend to achieve this by perceiving a discontinuity, not only between God and the world, but also between the immanent and the economic Trinity. The irony is that by denying that God could be susceptibility to and affected by the events of the world, they limit His freedom and possibilities, which their approach sets out to secure. The divine freedom conceived solely as the invulnerability of God to every external reality is incomplete. For although it could be conceived primarily in terms of God's liberty *from* external constraint, it

---

17 Major Jones, *The Color of God*, p. 77.

must also imply freedom in the sense of being *free to* perform such apparently "extra-ordinary" things, like allowing the Cross to affect Him intimately. This is the aspect of freedom which the equivocation model does not envisage for God.

It is clear from the above, that the analogical method provides a better approach to the paradox of divine nature and freedom. This depends however on how the analogy is represented. The attempt to use primordial kenosis to explicate this paradox is, as we saw above, problematic, especially since it again tends to limit divine freedom by employing spatial categories of thought. Any attempt to situate the precondition of earthly realities in God must eschew positing an infinite difference between the Father and the Son. It definitely suffices if God is understood as that love that overflows in order to see in Him the basis for His suffering in His Son Jesus Christ. Kenosis is of course an expression of divine love in His economy, but it is by no means its own precondition. Just as the event of the resurrection-exaltation demonstrates, that the kenosis is not the last of God's acts, we must equally assume that it is not the first act in the inner-Trinitarian relationship. The first act is love, which, of its nature, entails kenosis and suffering. Our God is a God of relationship, and for that reason, a God who imposes limitation on Himself, a God who condescends in the history of His love, and takes upon Himself the risks of entering into a relationship with His unequal and unreliable human partners.

Accordingly, the mystery of the *caritas diffusiva sui*, of the overflowing nature of divine love, cannot be adequately described in terms of divine self-sacrifice. Thus, in conceiving the mystery of divine love, in which the paradox of divine passibility and impassibility should be presupposed, we are better advised not to conceive a self-sacrifice in God, but an unlimited creative power, which puts being into existence, including the Trinitarian beings, who are veritably constituted in their relations. If we must use kenosis, because of its conceptual advantages, as discussed earlier, it must be divulged of its spatial connotations, and be interpreted in personalistic terms, as a self-fulfilling, self-constituting self-giving.

In order to give the analogical model a proper perspective (?), its basis must therefore be sought beyond the kenotic motif. It must be understood as a reality corresponding to the mystery of love. The fact of love presupposes a necessary distinction and unity between the lovers, in such a way that, without being infinitely distant from each other partners in love are convinced of their single identity, which grows and is confirmed the more they are united in love. Phenomenologically, love makes the lovers freer, while they are still united with each other. However, in conceiving the ultimate reality, we cannot remain at the level of the phenomenology of love. Our reflection must go beyond that to encompass the ontology of a personal relation. For if the God-talk, especially the talk about the paradox of divine nature should get any further, it must, in our opinion, be supported by a relational ontology. The phenomenology of love must necessarily presuppose a relational ontology. This is the limitation of Mühlen and Jones.

In what follows, therefore, we would want to consider love as the regulative metaphor, which must be used in exploring the possibility of a relational ontology. Love not only provides the best analogy for the God-world relationship, but also the basis on which all other attributes of God can be measured.

10.2   Inferences:

10.2 1   Divine Attributes and the Problem of Religious Language

10.2.1.1   Love as the Regulative Metaphor for God-talk

St. John's statement that "God is love" (1 John 4:8) is commonly taken to be self-evident, definitely because love is believed to be a noble attribute. It is easily forgotten, however, that love essentially entails pain, something most people would find difficult to attribute to the all-powerful God. Thus, no matter how excellent love is conceived, whether as something descriptive of divine action or being, it cannot be stripped of the negative experience that accompanies it. Suffering is an inevitable possibility in a true love, especially in the type that is attributable to God. Paradoxically, this negative aspect of love does not make it inferior; it rather perfects it.

More than anything else, this fact underlines the anthropomorphic nature of divine attribution. The human language can hardly get beyond the scope of human imagination and experience. This again makes our God-language essentially metaphoric. Thus, the qualification of divine nature and action with the human category is not only anthropomorphic, but also metaphoric. In predicating love to God, therefore, we are doing nothing other than attributing the best human "experience or conception of love" to Him. Love is an ideal human experience, which we readily use for the description of the highest grade of relationship. The predication of love to God is therefore a metaphoric statement made in the light of our human experience. As such, it cannot be claimed that it offers an exhaustive description of the divine being. For, although we have enough evidence, from the revelation of God in Jesus Christ - to see him is to have seen the Father (John 14: 19 f.) - to assume that the idea of love significantly and essentially portrays His inner nature, we cannot by that means say that we have an *exact* idea of how His love operates.

In this connection, we can thus agree with Jürgen Werbick that the predication "God is love" does not transmit an absolutely closed knowledge of God. It rather raises new questions about how God is, that He should be love, and how love should be understood when it is attributed to God: Is love as conceived of God constitutive of His being or is it a mere attribute? Be that as it may, the predication "God is love" merely gives direction to our questions about God, but it is surely an indication that God must be approached analogically through the metaphor of love.[18]

Since we must seek to understand God's love from the perspective of our own experience or conception of love, we must proceed from the analysis of human love. Of its nature, the best human experience of love always entails a provision for possibility; a true lover is naturally ready to suffer with his partner, when the need arises. If love is attributed to God out of the human experience, it would be difficult to deny God's ability or readiness to suffer with his beloved ones. This again underlies the fact, that the predication of "love" to God must have a metaphorical import.

Moreover, if we believe that Jesus Christ is the adequate revelation of God, it would be difficult to deny that God suffered in him. That the activities of the Son affect the father personally is sufficiently testified to at all places in the Bible, where the real and personal unity between God and His Son Jesus Christ is indicated.

All in all, whether in its ontological or mere attributive significance, the predication of "love" to God is the conceptualisation of the mode of His encounter with human beings, which, though positive, does not exclude pain. Love is a regulative metaphor, in a sense, a conceptual predicate, with which we qualify God's experience with His people in history. It expresses itself in various way; it can be abstract. The Bible accordingly seeks to explain it further with such other metaphors as shepherd, father etc. The experiences of shepherds and fathers cannot exclude possibility. Therefore, in order to understand God as "love", we need to interpret the Johannine statement with the aid of metaphors in the Bible, which signify peculiar experience. For, as has become evident in the last thirty years, there is an intrinsic relationship between concepts and metaphors: "metaphors need conceptual interpretation while concepts need metaphorical richness".[19]

Excursus: What does a metaphor actually signify?

Since the last century, the Aristotelian understanding of metaphor as a rhetorical appliance meant only for the genius has given way to its comprehension as a basic vehicle for thoughts. Metaphor is basically understood today as a familiar word, concept or phrase used in describing an unfamiliar reality having some re-

---

18 Cf. J. Werbick, *Bilder sind Wege. Eine Gotteslehre*, p. 116.

19 S. McFague, Metaphor, p. 360. According to McFague, this development is obvious in the writings of Paul Ricoeur, Langdon Gilkey, Gordon Kaufmann, and David Tracy.

semblance with the known. It has become popular in this sense, not only in poetry, but also in atomic physics. This is largely because of its appropriateness in representing the processes which creative thoughts follow from the known to the unknown. It is perhaps becoming more important in Christian theology than in any other academic discipline, for the simple reason, that theological language is essentially metaphorical: it seeks to understand the unknown reality of God through the known human categories, symbols, images and analogies.

It is also dawning on theologians that the biblical image of God builds fundamentally on metaphors. One only needs to think about the predication of Father, Son, Holy Spirit, shepherd, lion, rock, judge, king etc. to God in order to perceive the power of metaphors in our conception of God. From this biblical perspective, it is evident that not only the anthropomorphic metaphors, but also metaphorical language, is indispensable for our God-talk. It is noteworthy, as McFague observes, that although the significance of metaphor has been very often less emphasised in the past, "the great theologians from Origen through Augustine to Thomas, Luther, Calvin and up to Barth and Tillich have known it and in one way or another have acknowledged both the inadequacy of all language about God and the need for metaphorical language to express our relationship to God".[20]

Significant about divine metaphors is that they give insight into the nature of God, without "de-fining" Him. They associate the familiar with the unfamiliar reality analogically, without claiming that they are perfect copies of the reality to be described. Those who use metaphors must always recognise the similarity and difference between the known and unknown realities and hold them in constant tension. In theological language, they need to be vigilant about maintaining this *tension* which is characteristic of metaphors, less metaphors turn into "idols and literalism".[21] For a metaphor to retain its value, this tension must be held in such a way that the two extremes which lead to idolatry can be avoided:[22] First, the danger of failing to perceive a relationship between God and the divine metaphors must be avoided. For, although metaphors do not claim to construe a tautological identity between the known and unknown reality (God), the God-metaphors always say something about the essential reality of God Himself. Secondly, the tendency of assuming a literal equivalence between God and the metaphors must also be avoided, because an element of discontinuity always exists between the God-metaphors and God Himself. Not to recognise that would amount to reducing God to human imperfection.

There is a sense in which metaphor, understood as such, appears to represent the paradox of the predication of divine reality yet better than an analogy. More than any analogous interpretation, metaphorical language tends to draw upon the historical experience of the user,[23] (cf. Jesus' "Whoever has seen me has seen the Father." Jn 14:19 f.). For that reason, metaphors work on various levels: on the levels of cognition, emotion and will.[24] And apart from allowing the ultimate

---

20 *Ibid.*

21 *Ibid.*

22 Cf. T. Fretheim, *The Suffering of God*, pp. 7-8.

23 J. Werbick, Prolegomena, p. 3.

24 T. Fretheim, *The Suffering of God*, p. 9.

reality to remain incomprehensible, since they do not attempt to describe the content of the other, metaphors have the advantage of describing a reality from different perspectives: from the symbolic (God is a "rock"), relational (God is shepherd, father and Son), conceptual (God is the truth, life, way etc.), and behavioural (God is merciful) perspectives. As a corollary, a God-metaphor does not purport to represent more than a perspective of God as the ultimate reality. Thus in line with their historical connotations, metaphors are best at representing the relativity of our perspectives and the limitations of religious language. To say that is to imply that there can be no historical, cultural or conceptual limits to the list of appropriate God-metaphors. This implies again, that the acquisition of a new God-metaphor does not necessarily lead to the displacement of the previous metaphors. Hence, recognising the metaphorical import of our God-language could help make us less rigid about the acquisition of new metaphors. For as Fretheim rightly argues, "One of the dangers for the people of God in any age is that they will be content with a rather limited fund of metaphors", we should keep on "evaluating our operative metaphors" so as to subtract or add to our list of God-metaphors in accordance with the requirements of our changing views of God. [25]

10.2.1.2 Divine Passibility and Impassibility as Metaphorical Attributes

On account of the points made above about the theological significance of metaphorical language, we believe that the axioms of divine impassibility and passibility could be better appraised in terms of their metaphorical import. To begin with, the tension which is part of metaphors, could help in conceiving the paradoxical relationship of the two attributes. For, as we believe, the point is not to replace one axiom with the other - our study reveals abundant evidence for the authenticity of both axioms - but to show the abiding significance of these axioms for our God-talk, and how they can be fruitfully employed. One basic fact is that, since we cannot know the *exact* nature of God exhaustively except as He is revealed in Jesus Christ, He remains a mystery whose profundity is not fathomable for human intelligibility: our God-talk will remain essentially metaphorical. This applies to all theological conclusions, whether they are arrived at conceptually through negative theology or experientially through an encounter with the divine reality. That we cannot know *what God is* in Himself, is one of the basic and evident truths of a negative theology. But when negative theology goes further in view of this fact to "define" *what God is not*, it is making a claim that lies beyond our human cognitive capacity. The avoidance of these extreme views which Thomas Aquinas tries to take care of in his analogous explication of divine nature, seems to us better expressible in a metaphorical language. A metaphorical language forfeits exact definitions; this, according to Werbick, makes it say more about the unknown reality than defined concepts. Again, by virtue of its nature to

---

25 Cf. *Ibid.*, pp. 8-9.

conserve tensions and make pictorial presentations of reality, a metaphor can represent a reality more authentically than an analogy and express the vital points much more reservedly than concepts.[26]

The recognition of the religious language as a metaphorical language can help in regulating the interpretation of the biblical anthropomorphic metaphors. When Philo's allegorical method, which aims at distinguishing the literal from the non-literal, is used for instance, "negative" God-metaphors end up, as we tried to show in the first chapter, in misrepresenting the basic language of the Bible. In fact, if the anthropomorphic metaphors cannot be interpreted in terms of their own value, one can only wonder with T. E. Pollard whether we are not merely left with the impossible alternative: "either to re-write the Scriptures or treat them as a collection of books embodying primitive anthropomorphic conceptions of God".[27] It must be noted however that a God-metaphor, though an "expression of the inadequacy of human talk about God", is also an "expression of the liveliness of faith in a personal God".[28]

Therefore, the question arises how we can differentiate worthy from unworthy God-metaphors. It is evident that the philosophical *via negativa* and *positiva*, which express the divine reality with the contradictions and the superlatives of the human realities, respectively, cannot exhaust the nature of the incomprehensible God. By becoming human in Jesus Christ, God allows Himself to be described in human metaphors. Every anthropomorphic metaphor can then become an authentic God-metaphor, provided that it says something about the reality of God as is revealed in the history of salvation. There is no doubt that the biblical anthropomorphic metaphors - like the repentance, wrath, sadness of God, which conjure up an image of a contingent God - say something about the reality of God, even when they cannot be taken literally. These metaphors, which suggest the suffering of God, might not correspond to God's exact nature; they are nonetheless pointers to the divine reality, which must be allowed to remain a mystery. They are not antithetical to His nature; only sin, as Balthasar rightly observes, is contradictory to God.

If we agree that the anthropomorphic metaphors suggesting divine passibility in the Bible points to the very reality of God, and that Jesus Christ reveals God absolutely, the possibility of divine suffering must be taken for granted. Our question is therefore not *whether* God suffers, but *how* He suffers. Answering this within the scope of a metaphorical language, we can only affirm with Walter

---

26 J. Werbick, Prolegomena, p. 30.

27 T. E. Pollard, The Impassibility of God, p. 360.

28 W. Post, Anthropomorphismus, p. 189.

Kasper that if God suffers, He suffers in a divine way; this means that His suffering is an expression of His freedom; for He is not just touched by suffering, He *allows* suffering, in His freedom, to touch Him. He does not suffer like creatures out of a deficiency in being, He suffers out of and in His love, which is the abundance of His being.[29] Thus, the point of discontinuity between God and humankind is not that God does not suffer, but that He suffers differently: Whereas human beings suffer out of deficiency, even when they suffer for the sake of love, God suffers freely and solely out of and in the fullness of His love.

If God suffers differently, it means that the predication of passibility to Him is metaphorical and analogical. Is that not also the case with every predication of God, including impassibility? In fact, since the immutability and impassibility are only antonyms of mutability and passibility, i.e. the negation of the human experience of the latter in nature, we cannot claim that they correspond one-to-one with the inner nature of God. For that reason they remain human (metaphorical) visions of God, which are no more pointers than passibility and mutability. To this effect, we can see the axioms of impassibility and passibility as metaphorical couples rendering a partial representation of the true nature of God.

To say this is to support the view that the axioms of immutability and mutability, impassibility and passibility when predicated to God should be perceived in their dialectical tension,[30] that is to say, as a paradox (Ignatius), which though having their roots in the divine nature, can only best be explicated in metaphorical language. In our view, this tension cannot however be understood in a substance-ontological framework which inevitably leads to the thesis that God, who is immutable in Himself is mutable in another of Himself (K. Rahner). It must be thought in the framework of a relational ontology, aided by metaphorical language, where it can become possible to affirm that God really changes in Himself by virtue of His relationality; He changes but only in His own divine way. If it is true, as John Macquarrie claims, that we human beings have "an inherent tendency to see things in a one-sided way, and perhaps we are especially prone to this error when we try to think of God",[31] we must try to overcome this tendency using relational thought.

It is hardly imaginable that a one-dimensional visualisation of God can embrace the complexity of the divine nature, which, according to the biblical revelation lies somewhere beyond the scope of formal logic. A one-dimensional hermeneutics might be defensible from the perspective of the Hellenistic philosophy,

---

29 W. Kasper, *Der Gott Jesus Christi*, Mainz 1982, p. 242.

30 Cf. W. Kern, *Philosophische Pneumatologie*, p. 87.

31 J. Macquarrie, *In Search of Deity*, p. 27.

but it fails to reflect the biblical views of a God who, for the sake of love, reveals Himself even in the contradictions of the Cross. Neither does a rigid vision of God have any chance of attaining some level of intelligibility for today's pluralistic world. If the God of the Bible is not necessarily the God of the philosophers, a different hermeneutics, which reveals the truth in apparent contradiction, is indispensable.

10.2.2 God Suffers: A Paradigm Shift in God-talk?

Divine suffering cannot be proved. Neither can it be denied. For, even though it could be deduced from the numerous anthropomorphic metaphors in the Bible, and also from the phenomenology of the human love, which is presupposed in the predication of love to God, and most importantly from the fact of the personal unity between the Father and the Son, divine passibility is *not an object of logic*, but *an item of faith*. The evidence is definitely overwhelming, and enough for faith in the suffering of God, but, given the incomprehensibility of the divine nature, which inheres in a mystery, it is too little for logical proof. The same applies to the axiom of divine impassibility.

However, if we accept that our God-talk is essentially metaphorical, and that any prevalent God-metaphor, borne out of people's encounter with the divine reality in a particular age, reflects both the religious need of people[32] and gives insight into an aspect of the divine reality, then the affirmation of divine suffering is legitimate in an age of pluralism and cultural relativity, in an age in which flexibility and passionate responsiveness to the needs of others are more highly prized than impersonal impassivity. If the prevalent God-metaphors always points to the divine reality, can we, for want of solid arguments, dismiss the axiom of divine passibility as an absurdity, when, as we know, there is both implicit and explicit recognition of it in the mainstream of contemporary theology? The frequent and almost global reference to the axiom of divine passibility in contemporary theologies, even when it is not always presented with perfect and fruitful arguments, seems to signal a shift in our modus of theological conceptualisation of God. This is the major message that the third part of this study centring on the Third World liberation theologies tries to deliver.

The appropriateness of the arguments for divine suffering might rightly be disputed, but it is impossible to overlook the fact that it is a fundamental presupposition in a majority of theological reflections today, just as the axiom of divine impassibility was a basic assumption at the background of all the theologies of the early church. It is in view of this fact that contemporary theologians talk of a

---

32 D. A. Pailin, *The Anthropological Character of Theology*, pp. 140-162.

"revolution",[33] a "metaphoric shift",[34] a "structural shift"[35] and "rise of a new orthodoxy"[36] in the Christian conception of God. The affirmation of divine passibility is certainly not new, as the first part of this study demonstrates. It has however never occupied such a central position in the theological understanding as today. In fact, from the point of view of the implications of the axiom of divine suffering in today's pluralistic theology, it is all right to speak of a paradigm shift in the theological orientation. As we have seen, the affirmation of divine suffering lies at the heart of all liberation theologies, and the same can be said of all the Third World theologies. And it is certainly no exaggeration to say that the issues of divine mutability and passibility have become the measuring-points for the departure of the new theological movements from certain ancient theological doctrines. The divine passibility talk signals a series of paradigm shifts in the search for theological solutions.

10.2.2.1   The Shift from "Transitive" to "Intransitive" Theodicy and Anthropodicy

For ages, it has been an issue for theologians to reconcile the presence of evil in the world, especially the suffering of the innocents, with the Christian belief in a good God. The usual attempt has been to justify God, to explain why God can still be good in spite of evil and suffering. From 1710, when Leibniz articulated this art of justifying God as theodicy, until today, the justification of God has always remained an intractable problem. Leibniz' significant solution to this problem was a "cosmodicy", as he declared that this world full of evil is "the best possible world". As he gave this solution, little did he suspect the 1755 earthquake, which not only destroyed a great part of Lisbon but also the whole structure of his cosmological solution to the problem of theodicy. The little that remained of his attempt and some other theistic solutions was reduced to insignificance in the period of the Enlightenment. In the emergent atheistic world-view, the question of how to justify God was giving way to that of how to vindicate humankind (anthropodicy).[37]

If the appeal made for anthropodicy then seemed like ridiculing theodicy, it soon became clear in the face of the atrocities human beings committed against

---

33   J. Moltmann, *The Crucified God*, p. 204.

34   T. Fretheim, *The Suffering of God*, p. 13 f.

35   D. D. Williams, *What Present-day Theologians Are Thinking*, p.138.

36   Cf. R. Goetz, The Suffering God. The Rise of New Orthodoxy, pp. 385-389.

37   The shift from theodicy to anthropodicy dates earlier than this. Cf. J. L. Crenshaw, The Shift from Theodicy to Anthropodicy, pp. 1-16.

their fellows in Auschwitz and Hiroshima that putting man in the dock before directing further questions to God is a serious theological insight. Developments in the field of social sciences, especially in psychology and sociology, have since then tended towards evolving series of defence mechanisms to justify human culpability by blaming the parents or society for the individual guilt. Despite such attempts by the social scientists to pass a verdict of "not guilty" on humanity, human culpability for evil in the world is all too evident. The awareness of the gross human culpability for evil and suffering in the world was so shocking that theologies after the World War II and Holocaust no longer stop at acquitting God, but go further to declare Him a victim of the human atrocities.[38] God Himself suffers with the victims. He does not atone for the sins of the world from a distance, He is there Himself suffering the plight of His people, who could be culprits and victims at the same time. To a great number of theologians the only acceptable answer to the problem of evil is the assurance that God suffers with the victims.

It is doubtful whether divine suffering can satisfactorily answer the problem of theodicy. For one thing, the question remains why God should suffer, if He has the omnipotence to overcome suffering. If God can do nothing to alleviate or stop suffering other than to suffer in *sym-pathy*, then He has not done a whole lot. If in His suffering, God can do no more than give a psychological assurance to the co-sufferers, the question of evil has not been answered, but merely moved to a different plane. Thus, divine suffering cannot offer a decisive solution to the dilemma of theodicy. Yet, in a way, it contributes immensely toward a solution of the problem of evil and suffering. For if God is said to suffer only in so far as He freely gives Himself kenotically in the act of love, the affirmation of His suffering could be seen as an indirect appeal to humanity to emulate God's kenotic involvement in the campaign against suffering. Definitely, the only suffering that can be attributed to God, even metaphorically, is the suffering that ensues from the fight against suffering (liberation theology). God's suffering is an appeal to human beings to fight evil through a kenotic life-style (cf. MacGregor). The attempt to pass a verdict of "not guilty" on God (theodicy) is as inadequate as the effort to acquit humankind of the responsibility for evil on the ground of the human frailty (anthropodicy).

To say that God suffers kenotically, that is to say, not in terms of self-withdrawal, but in terms of His commitment to liberate humankind, irrespective of disappointment, is to call on human beings to exercise restraint in their dealings with one another; it is a call to the oppressors to check their actions because

---

[38] Today God is believed to suffer with human beings when they suffer injustice; Like during the eradication of the American Indians, the Australian Aborigines, slavery etc.

God Himself is "hanging on the gallows"; it is a call on the oppressed not to give up because God Himself is spearheading the campaign to establish justice and the reign of truth as He is believed to be personally present in the battle-field of the human predicament. In this way, the job of justification becomes personalised, intransitive, i.e. no longer transitive: God justifies Himself in His kenotic suffering (graphically in the person of Jesus Christ), and humankind justifies itself as it tries to effect mutual self-giving (human kenosis). This might not mean the end of evil, but the beginning of the victory over suffering. If, in the light of the axiom of divine passibility, both theodicy and anthropodicy have become "intransitive" projects of "self-justification", we might not be wrong to maintain that the adoption of the axiom of divine suffering brings a functional, though not logical, solution to the problem of evil.

10.2.2.2 The Shift from Substance-ontology to Relational Thought-pattern

The affirmation of divine suffering has apparently ushered in a new formulation of the God-question. The characteristic God-question in today's theology is best articulated in E. Wiesel's book, *Night*, especially in the story of a youth hung by the German SS in Auschwitz. As the youth died slowly in struggle and under the pangs of death, a question came from a bystander: "Where is God?".[39] This question summarises the whole of the human God-question in our time. Where is God when such atrocities against humanity occur? The popularity of this question in contemporary theologies, especially the theologies of the oppressed, is enormous. More than any other question, it marks the direction of today's God-talk. The major question is no longer "Who is God?", but "Where is God?"[40] This means that the issues of God's presence (Where is God?) and God's action (What is God doing now?) have priority over the question of His nature and essence (Who is God?) in contemporary theology.

The contrary used to be the case in the patristic and Medieval period. At that time, philosophers and theologians were very much preoccupied with issues bordering on the *essentia* of reality. As a result, permanence, self-subsistence and immutability were seen mostly as constituting the perfection of a reality. This was reflected not only in their conception of impersonal objects but also in their perception of personal beings. Boethius's definition of *persona* as the "*rationalis naturae individua substantia*", the indivisible substance of a rational nature, testifies abundantly to the truth of this fact. It is evident that for Boethius being a

---

39 Cf. W. Wiesel, *Night*, p. 75 f.

40 Cf. C. Duquoc, "Who is God?" becomes "Where is God?" pp. 1-10; M. Deneken, God at the Heart of Hell, pp. 53-63.

person consists primarily in the indivisibility of the personal being (*individuum*) in the subsistence of the substance. Here, the significance of the relation for the person is not existent. Following this definition, Thomas also conceives personhood as consisting of self-return to oneself (subsistence).[41] Perfection consists accordingly in the immutability and impassibility of a reality. Today, in contrast, being a person amounts to being in relation, i.e. going out of oneself - *Ek-sistenz* (Heidegger). Accordingly, *praesentia* is more a priority in the evaluation of a human person than *essentia*, and the perfection of a reality tends to be measured more in terms of its relatedness, interconnection, and dynamism, than in terms of permanence and immutability. The movement away from the axiom of divine impassibility to divine passibility therefore mainly reflects a shift in the understanding of person from "being-in-itself" to "being-for-others".

The widespread affirmation of divine suffering thus seems to mirror an actual concern in our time to measure reality and perfection in terms of relationality rather than substance; it reflects the desire to disassociate power from tyranny and "non-affectability" of a being. The tendency is to define power and being in terms of love or relatedness to others. It should not be surprising therefore if the popularity of democratic aspirations[42] and high esteem for community in contemporary society reflect this shift to relational approach. Does the disdain for kingship and feudal systems prevalent today not also confirm this change in the conception of reality? Be that as it may, these are equally signs of the shift from substance-model to relational-model of thinking. The fact that this shift is contemporaneous with the renewed affirmation of divine suffering today is food for thought. Despite the differences in approach however, between the equivocal, univocal and analogical models, all the theologies of divine suffering share the common conviction, that the Hellenistic philosophy, with its strong leaning on an ontology of substance and essence, lacks the potential for conceiving the historical, emotional and dynamic realities of God's economy of salvation. The relational model of thought is therefore considered more appropriate for interpreting revelation than substance-ontological thought-pattern.

This common spirit (*Geist*) of the time has greatly influenced both the idea of perfection and the God-question, and occasioned the aforementioned shift. Certainly, if one thinks in terms of a personal relationship, it is more likely that mutability, flexibility and passionate concern would be considered more perfect than an impassive, immutable stance towards a suffering neighbour. Applied to God, the situation is the same, at least metaphorically. Hence the truth of the contention

41 Th. Aquinas, *Summa theologiae*. Iq. 14 a.2 ad 1. On this, see also J. B. Lotz, Person und Ontologie, pp. 341.

42 Cf. R. Goetz, The Suffering God, p. 387

of David A. Pailin: "If...the perfection of the divine is considered to be more akin to that of a person than to that of an abstract ideal or an impersonal object, it is far from obvious that God, as perfect, must be thought to be impassible."[43] Accordingly, the predication of passibility to God could be seen as an affirmation of the perfection of a personal God in relation. Hence the implicit attempt in most contributions to reinterpret the classical divine attributes in terms of love and personal thought, so as to scrape off their substance-ontological scales.

This shift is equally visible in the history of the interpretation of the kenotic motif. As we observed in the third chapter of this study, the major problem that the kenotic motif repeatedly encountered in the history of theology is the tendency to conceive and represent it within substance-ontological categories. The rediscovery of its theological relevance for God-talk in the nineteenth century corresponds exactly with the attempt to explicate it in personal and relational terms. The kenoticists whose thoughts were flourishing at this time were mostly those who attempted to subdue the substance-ontological thinking and promote the relational interpretation of kenosis. They were however not very successful, because, although they were theoretically poised to consider kenosis in personalistic terms, they were in reality tinkering with personalistic categories within a substance-ontological thought-pattern. This seemed like putting new wine in old wineskin. Even in the twentieth century, when it became common to express the kenotic motif in Trinitarian thinking and personalistic categories, the tendency to express kenosis in spatial terms still prevailed. That notwithstanding, the shift from the pure Hellenistic substance-ontology is as obvious as the fact that divine suffering cannot be properly considered in solely substance-ontological terms.

Apart from the contemporary inclination towards the concept of perfection in relational terms, there are several theological reasons why the moderation of the prevalent substance-ontology in theology has become inevitable. With increasing efforts in contemporary theology to fashion our God-talk and God-question in line with the biblical notion of God came the awareness that the biblical view of God is essentially historical, personal and dynamic. This in turn reveals God as a being, who is essentially love (1 Jn 4:16). Understanding God as love leads us of course to reflect upon God's suffering love; it also makes us see that a substance-ontological thought-pattern is not all that relevant. Evidently, therefore, the *reality* of God's historical, personal and dynamic relationship with the world, as revealed in the Bible, seems better expressed in relational, and anthropomorphic metaphors than in substance-ontological categories.

---

[43] D. A. Pailin, *The Anthropological Character of Theology*, p. 46.

10.2.3   *Relational Ontology as a Theological Desideratum*

Although, the departure from the substance-ontological orientation in God-talk is as evident as the desire to replace it with relational thinking, there is no clear alternative to the ontology of substance yet. It is of course one thing to realise the inadequacy of a substance thought-pattern in extracting the biblical message that is cast in historical setting and rendering it intelligible to today's pluralistic theological audience, but quite another to provide an alternative or supplementary philosophical rostrum on which further theological reflections can thrive. Thus, while the departure is evident in all the theologies of divine suffering, the prospective directions of the different models are not always clear.

The liberation theologians, for instance, tend to equate the rejection of substance and static thinking with a denial of the relevance of metaphysics. The danger of substituting metaphysics and ontology with historical and social analysis is evident. Similarly, there are personalistic approaches (Mühlen) which come close to recognising relation as the constitutive meaning of reality and yet stop short at acknowledging its ontological significance. In some others, however, substance-ontological ideas are coated with personalistic and historical categories to produce an admixture of spatial and personalistic conceptions of reality which lack serious philosophical backing (Moltmann and some kenoticists). Only in a few attempts (Balthasar), does one get the impression that metaphysics retains its relevance, despite the attempt to moderate the substance-ontological thinking. But even here, the movement towards the development of a relational or Trinitarian ontology is merely initiated but not consummated.

The question arises, however, whether there can be a theology without a philosophical foundation. Can the metaphor of love be fruitfully predicated of God if it has no ontological presupposition? Can relational thinking be an alternative to substance-ontological thinking, or at least supplement it, if it remains a mere phenomenological reality? We are of the opinion that no theology can forfeit philosophy, neither can any conception of God be consequential if it lacks an ontological foundation. One could say that the locomotive of theological understanding runs on two rails: both on the track of religious experience and on the route of philosophical reflection. If any of these tracks is displaced the theological coach is bound to derail and crash sooner or later.

Not even the biblical notion of God, with all its historical features is without metaphysics. The personal notion of God in the Bible is definitely not conceivable in substance-ontological terms, as the apparent gap between the biblical and philosophical language suggests. Yet, it would be wrong to suppose that the relational image of God expressed within it lacks a metaphysical foundation. To be precise, there must be a relational ontology, an ontology of love, on which the reality of divine dynamism, mutability and passibility are based, and with which the paradoxical tension of the divine attributes could be explicated. One of the things which the issue of divine suffering calls to our attention is the need for and urgency of a relational ontology for theological understanding. It is, strictly speaking, a theological desideratum.

Accordingly, there have been proposals for the development of a relational ontology as implied in the biblical message. This takes the form of a request for the recognition of the relational constitution of being for the ultimate explication of personal realities in the doctrine of the Trinity,[44] Christology[45] and sacramental theology. In sacramental theology, the discussion centres on the issue of the real presence of Christ in the Eucharist.[46] In all, the attempt to see relation in

---

44 Cf. K. Hemmerle, *Thesen zu einer trinitarischen Ontologie*. Hemmerle proposes the adoption of a Trinitarian ontology in all theological understanding. Trinitarian ontology, he contends, underlies the modus of God's self-giving to humankind in Jesus Christ, and the human self-giving to his fellows as a believer. In this case, it is neither a logical abstraction, nor an ontology gained from conventional philosophy, but an ontology that developed out of the Christian message. As such, it provides more for the emergence of what is specific to Christianity than any other type of philosophy (10-35). Hemmerle sees Bonaventure's and Augustine's attempts to conceive love as the ontological kernel of the mysteries of Christianity and the dogmatic conception of *relatio subsistens* and Trinitarian *perichoresis* for the Persons as basic thrusts in the right direction, though they stop short of making love the starting point for their own reflection (36). Love as self-giving must be seen as the "rhythm of being" and "giving", the centre out of which the whole reality should be perceived (38-39). What is new about this ontology, he argues, is that it is derived from God's own self-giving in Jesus Christ (55). Apart from suggesting that God's relation to the world is already implied in his inner-Trinitarian mutual self-giving, formulating ontology relationally would also explain how contingency and contradictions were taken into the kenosis of the Son (56-58). Hemmerle, unlike Balthasar, is however careful not to conceive the generation of the Son as kenosis. Rather, the *missio* is the very kenotic act (58). This point would be best appreciated, if one bears in mind that Hemmerle wrote this book as a birthday present to Balthasar (7).

45 D. Wiederkehr, Entwurf einer systematische Christologie, pp. 477-645, esp. p. 491 f. Wiederkehr sees relational Christology as one of the theological desiderata, which accounts for the apparent gap between the New Testament and traditional systematic Christologies.

46 The departure from substance ontology has been definitive and the call for the development of a relational ontology distinct in this century, especially as theologians show preference for "transignification" over "transubstantiation" in interpreting the real presence of Christ in the Eucharist. Accordingly, a personal ontology is considered most appropriate for the explication of Christ's personal presence. Cf. P Schoonenberg, Inwieweit is die Lehre von der Transsubstantiation historisch bestimmt? pp. 305-311 and J. Ratzinger, Das Problem der Transsubstantiation und die Frage nach dem Sinn der Eucharistie, pp. 129-158. Though Ratzinger does not use the term transsignification, he implies it, especially as he emphasises personal ontology. With reference to Heidegger's philosophy, B. Welte also makes a precise appeal for the use of a relational ontology in the theology of the Eucha-

contrast to its Hellenistic (Aristotelian) interpretation, as a perfection and constituting element of being is evident.

Relation, according to Aristotle, is a category of the accidents, which, by being
neither the substance nor belonging to the transcendentals, is not constitutive of
being. For him, relation is nothing other than "the accidental alteration of a substance".[47] Thomas Aquinas resists the application of this categorial relation of
nature (objects) to God, since this would entail potency or alteration
(imperfection) in God who is pure act. He rather conceives a pure subsistent and
constitutive inter-relation for the persons of the Trinity. The persons are constituted in their relations, though with the full possession of their distinctions. The
question arises however whether the same *relatio subsistens* could be conceived
of the God-world relationship. To this, Thomas' answer is no. For although creatures are related to God *realiter*, there is no *realis relatio*, but only *relatio secun-
dum rationem* between God and the creatures.[48]

Contemporary theologians reject the Aristotelian and Thomistic views. For
William Hill, for instance, the relationality of creatures (relationship to God) must
be "real in a mutual sense" since creatures are images of God and were created to
be capable of "dialogic", inter-subjective, and inter-personal relationship. God
enters into real relationship with human beings and *allows* Himself to be
"determined" by the activities of His "dialogic" partners. To that effect, human
beings are as constituted in their relations as the uncreated persons are in their
Trinitarian subsistence, though analogically.[49] Similarly, Schoonenberg contends
that the subsistent relation - what the Scholastics call transcendental relation - lies
at the heart of every (finite) being. This means that being is not merely self-
possession, or being-in-itself, but "being-with" and "being-for". Self-possession
and relation, in contrast to conventional Hellenistic philosophy, are not inversely
proportional to each other but both constitute being.[50] Thus the main emphasis in
the campaign for relational ontology is the recognition of "being" as "being-in-
relation", and the affirmation of the ontological significance of relation.

This understanding is certainly not new. Series of attempts have been made in
the past both in philosophical and theological circles to conceive being relation-

---

rist. B. Welte, Diskussionsbeitrag, pp. 184-195. See also E. Schillebeecks, *Die eucharistische Gegenwart.* ---, *Christ the Sacrament of the Encounter with God.* For a general
overview see A. Gerken, *Theologie der Eucharistie*, especially p. 173 ff.

[47]   W. J. Hill, *Search for the Absent God*, p. 118.

[48]   Thomas Aquinas, *STh.* I, q. 13, a.7.

[49]   W. J. Hill, *Search for the Absent God*, pp. 117-119

[50]   P. Schoonenberg, *Auf Gott hin denken*, pp. 84-85.

ally, or relation ontologically. This could be seen as the overall goal of social ontology as it is being pursued in transcendental philosophy and in dialogical personalism. Transcendental philosophy, which finds its rudimentary expression in Husserl's transcendental phenomenology of intersubjectivity and its manifest exposition and modification in Heidegger's fundamental ontology and Sartre's phenomenological ontology of intersubjectivity, characterises its discussion on the interhuman through its emphasis on the intentionality of the subjects. Thus the significance of relation for existent beings are recognised, but primacy and originality is given to partners in relation, and not to relation itself. In other words, first there were partners and then later relation, which was effected by virtue of the intentionality and then of the existential praxis of the partners towards themselves.

In contrast, dialogical personalism lays more emphasis on the intersubjectivity, i.e. on the event of the "between" of the subjects, than on the intentionality. This approach to the issue of the relational constitution of being is partly moderate and partly radical. According to the moderate approach, the constitution of the I and the Thou as persons, as "selves" take place in relation. In effect, each of the subjects is an unfulfilled reality prior to the encounter, but can only become a person or a fulfilled "self" in the encounter. Endorsing this view the second approach, which is best exemplified in Buber's ontology, goes yet beyond it to claim that the partners - the I and Thou - are constituted in the "between", in the event of their relations.[51] Hence Buber's talk is about the primacy or the "apriori" of the relation or the between.[52] It is however not always clear what Buber exactly means by the primacy of the relation. Whether he merely means that another relation precedes every being, or that every being is ultimately made up in the event of the very encounter in which it finds itself is a matter of conjecture. However, one thing is clear, and that is what matters for our purpose: For Buber, every being is constituted by a relation. Relation precedes every individuation.

The view that relation is prior to individuation, that "being-from" precedes "being-in-itself", and that "being-in-itself" is realised through "being-for-the-other", is a basic contribution of the dialogical personalism to philosophy. Unfortunately however, this conception stops short at developing into a relational ontology. There are two reasons, why personalism has problems with ontology and metaphysics. Firstly, relations, events and processes with which personalism is preoccupied in contrast to substance elude precise conceptualisation. Secondly, it is something like a philosophical puzzle trying to establish that relation precedes the subjects. There is yet another problem; it is like determining which one is the

---

51 M. Buber, *I and Thou*, pp. 11-34.

52 *Ibid.*, p. 18 f.

first, the hen or the egg. It is apparently impossible to establish the truth of the primacy of relations using philosophical categories, which as we know are mostly substance-ontologically defined.[53] But it is easy to do so in philosophical theology, especially, if the inner-Trinitarian reality is taken note of. That means that the claims of personalism can find their consequent and ultimate development in the realm of a Trinitarian ontology. For if as Buber claims, all "relations meet in the eternal Thou",[54] that is in God, who, according to the doctrine of the Trinity, constitutes Himself in a subsistent relation, the perception of the apriori of relation then becomes a theological possibility. Thus, there can be no doubt that a combination of the ontology of "between" and Trinitarian ontology can prove fruitful for the development of a relational ontology, with which the analogical and metaphorical tension characteristic of the God-talk and God-world relationship could best be explicated.

Relational ontology commends therefore itself significantly in the theological understanding for at least two major reasons. In the first place, as Hemmerle points out in his plea for a Trinitarian ontology, the understanding of being relationally is perhaps one of the major contribution theology makes to philosophy.[55] Secondly, a relational ontology has a better possibility than substance-ontology, for considering historical facts, for mediating between being and becoming, passivity and action, permanence and dynamism, transcendence and immanence, distinction and unity, and not the least, the paradoxical inclusiveness of love and passibility.

In view of the significant role that the concept of kenosis plays in the development of the theology of divine suffering, determining the modus of its interpretation must be a task for future theologies. For one thing, such reflections would entail the examination of the hermeneutic usage of biblical terminologies. Above all, it remains a puzzle, how such a highly disputed concept should be used in qualifying the inner nature of God.

The attempt to interpret the issue of divine suffering with the kenotic motif is, as our study has shown, predominant in contemporary theologies. It is also evi-

---

53 Cf. M. Theunissen, *The Other*. For Theunissen, the apparent impossibility of thinking the precedence of relation over subjectivity must be seen not as a problem peculiar to the philosophy of dialogue, but as a general weakness of philosophy: "I would rather suggest that behind the representation of the unconditioned precedence of the between over subjectivity in all its forms, a determinate truth lies concealed, though one that cannot be reached by philosophy" (377). And as he goes on to say, "It would be philosophically as well as theologically less problematic if one were to address this reality - the 'medium' that links all relations with one another - as the 'domain of God'" (383).

54 M. Buber, *I and Thou*, p. 75.

55 K. Hemmerle, *Thesen zu einer trinitarischen Ontologie*, p. 20 f.

402

dent that the theological significance of this motif shows up fully only when it is interpreted in terms of the doctrine of the Trinity, this means in effect, in relational terms. Since a Trinitarian interpretation is essentially relational, it attains its validity the less spatial and substance-ontological categories are used, and the more the relational and personal categories are integrated.

BIBLIOGRAPHY

Abraham, K. C., (editor), *Third World Theologies: Commonalities and Divergences. Papers and Reflections from the Second General Assembly of the Ecumenical Association of Third World Theologians*, December 1986, Oaxtepec, Mexico, Maryknoll: Orbis Books 1990.

Abramowski, Luise, Die Schrift Gregor des Lehrers 'Ad Theopompum' und Philoxenus von Mabbug, in: ZKG 89 (1978) 273-290.

Ajayi, J. A., *Christian Missions in Nigeria 1841-1891. The Making of a New Elite*, London 1965.

Altizer, T., *The Gospel of Christian Atheism*, New York 1966.

---   & Hamilton, W., *Radical Theology and the Death of God*, Indianapolis 1966.

---   *The New Apocalypse. The Radical Christian Vision of William Blake*, Michigan: University Press 1967.

Appiah-Kubi, Kofi, *Man Cures, God Heals*, New York: Friendship Press 1981.

---   & Torres, Sergio, *African Theology en Route*, Maryknoll: Orbis Books 1979.

Araya, Victorio, *God of the poor. The mystery of God in Latin American Liberation Theology*, Maryknoll: Orbis Books 1987.

Armstrong, Karen, *A History of God. From Abraham to the Present: the 4000-year Quest for God*, London: Mandarin Paperback 1993.

Arnim, Hans von, *Die Entwicklung der aristotelischen Gotteslehre*, (1931).

Assmann, Hugo, *Theology for a Nomad Church*, Maryknoll: Orbis Books 1976.

Awolalu, Omosade J., Sin and Its Removal in African Traditional Religion, in: Journal of American Academy of Religion 44 (1976) 275-287.

Baeta, C. G., *Christianity and African Culture*, Accra 1955.

Baker, D. (editor), *Heresy and Schism as Social and National Movements: Studies in Church History*, vol. ix. (C.U.P.) 1972.

Balthasar, Hans Urs von, *Mysterium Paschale in: Mysterium Salutis, Grundriß einer heilsgeschichtlichen Dogmatik III/2*, (Hrsg.) von J. Feiner & M. Löhrer, Einsiedeln 1970, 133-326.

---   *Theodramatik, Bd. I Prolegomena, Einsiedeln 1973; Bd. II/1 Die Personen des Spiels: Der Mensch in Gott.* Einsiedeln 1975; Bd. II,2 *Die Personen des Spiels: Die Personen in Christus.* Einsiedeln 1978; Bd.

III *Die Handlung*. Einsiedeln 1980; Bd. IV *Das End Spiel*. Einsiedeln 1983.

--- *Theologik, Bd. I Wahrheit der Welt*, Einsiedeln 1985; Bd. II *Wahrheit Gottes*, Einsiedeln 1985.

--- *Das Ganze im Fragment. Aspekte der Geschichtstheologie*, Einsiedeln 1963.

--- *Gott und das Leid*, Freiburg 1984. (Antwort des Glaubens 34).

--- *Herrlichkeit. Eine theologische Ästhetik, Bd. I Schau der Gestalt*. Einsiedeln/Trier 1960; *Bd. III,1/2 Im Raum der Metaphysik / Neuzeit*. Einsiedeln 1965; *Bd. III,2/1 Theologie / Alter Bund*. Einsiedeln/Trier 1966; *Bd. III,2/2 Theologie / Neuer Bund*. Einsiedeln 1969.

--- *Man in History. A Theological Study*, London: Sheed and Ward 1982.

--- *Theologik, Bd. III Der Geist der Wahrheit*. Einsiedeln/Trier 1987.

Balthazar, Eulalio, *The Dark Centre. A Process Theology of Blackness*, New York: Paulist Press 1973.

Barth, Karl, *Church Dogmatics*, transl. by T. H. L. Parker et al., Edinburgh: T. & T. Clark 1957.

Barth, M., Aus einem Brief an Jürgen Moltmann, in: *Diskussion über Jürgen Moltmanns Buch 'Der gekreuzigte Gott', Hrsg. v. M. Welker*, München 1979.

Bastide, R., Color, Racism, and Christianity, in: *Daedalus* 96 (1967) 312-327.

Bauckham, R., Moltmanns Eschatologie des Kreuzes, in: *Diskussion über Jürgen Moltmanns Buch "Der gekreuzigte Gott"*, Hrsg. v. M. Welker, München 1979.

Baur, John, *2000 Years of Christianity in Africa. An African History 62-1992*, Nairobi: Paulines Publications 1994.

Beck, H.-G., Die byzantinische Kirche. Das Zeitalter des Palamismus, in: *Handbuch der Kirchengeschichte III/2*, Hrsg. von H. Jedin, 589-624.

Beinert, Wolfgang, Dogmatik Studieren, Regensburg 1985.

Bennett, Robert, Biblical Theology and Black Theology, in *Interdenominational Theological Centre Journal,* (III, 2, Spring 1976).

Berdyaev, N., *Spirit and Reality*, transl. by G. Bles & co., 1939 and 1946.

--- *The Meaning of History*, transl. by G. Bles & co., 1939.

Bimwenyi-Kweshi, O., *Alle Dinge erzählen von Gott. Grundlegung afrikanischer Theologie*, Freiburg i. Br 1982.

Blancy, A., "Der gekreuzigte Gott" von Jürgen Moltmann, in: *Diskussion über Jürgen Moltmanns Buch "Der gekreuzigte Gott"*, Hrsg. von M. Welker, München 1979.

Bodem, Anton., Leiden Gottes, in: *Veritate Catholicae*, Hrsg. von A. Zeigenaus/ F. Courth/ Ph. Schärfer, (FS L. Scheffczyk), Regensburg 1985, 586-611.

Boesak, Allan, A Holy Rage for Justice, in: *If this is Treason, I am Guilty*, Michigan: Eerdmanns Publ. 1987.

---   Liberation Theology in South Africa, in: *African Theology En Route*, ed. by K. Appiah-Kubi and S. Torres, Maryknoll: Orbis Books 1979.

---   *Farewell To Innocence. A Social-ethical Study on Black Theology and Black Power*, Kampen 1976.

Boff, Clodovis, *Theologie und Praxis. Die erkenntnistheoretischen Grundlagen der Theologie der Befreiung*, München 1983.

Boff, Leonardo, *Jesus Christ Liberator. A Critical Christology for Our Time*, Maryknoll: Orbis Books 1978.

---   *Church: Charism and Power, Liberation Theology and Institutional Church*, London: SCM Press 1985.

---   *Passion of Christ, Passion of the World*. Transl. by Robert R. Barr, Maryknoll: Orbis Books 1987.

Boman, Th., *Das hebräische Denken im Vergleich mit dem griechischen*, Göttingen 1952, 19837.

Bonhoeffer, Dietrich, *Letters and Papers from Prison*, Enlarged Edition, edited by Eberhard Bethge, New York 1971.

Braaten, C. E., A Trinitarian Theology of the Cross, in: *The Journal of Religion*, 56 (1976) 113-121.

Brabant, F. H., God and Time, in: *Essays on the Trinity and the Incarnation*, edited by A. E. J. Rawlinson, London 1928.

Brantschen, Johannes B., *Gott is größer als unser Herz*, Freiburg 1981.

Breuning, Wilhelm, Trinitarische Irrlehren, in: *Lexikon der katholischen Dogmatik*, Hrsg. von W. Beinert, Freiburg i. Br. 1987.

Brunner, Emil, *The Christian Doctrine of Creation and Redemption, Dogmatics*. Vol. II, transl. by O. Wyon, The Westminster Press 1952.

Buber, Martin, Distance and Relation, in: *Martin Buber, The Knowledge of Man*, edited by Maurice Friedman, New York: Harper Torchbooks 1965.

---   *I and Thou*, transl. by Roland Gregor Smith, Edinburgh: T & T Clark 1937, 3rd edition.

Bujo, Bénézet, *African theology in its Social Context*, Nairobi: St Paul Communications, 1992, German original, 1986.

Bulgakov, S. N., The Power of the Cross, in: *A Bulgakov Anthology*, edited by J. Pain & N. Zernov, London: SPCK 1976.

Bultmann, R., *Theology of the New Testament*, Vol. I, London 1952.

Buthelezi, Manas, Black Theology or African Theology?, in: *The Challenges of Black Theology in South Africa*, ed. by B. Moore, Atlanta: John Knox Press 1973.

Cobb, J. B. Jr., *A Christian Natural Theology. Based on the Thought of Alfred North Whitehead*, London: Lutherworth Press 1966.

--- & Griffin, D. R., *Process Theology: An Introductory Exposition,* Belfast: Christian Journal 1976.

--- Panentheism, in: *A dictionary of Christian Theology,* edited by E. Richardson & J Bowden, London 1983.

Cone, C. W., *The Identity Crisis in Black Theology*, Nashville: AMEC 1975.

Cone, John, *Black Theology and Black Power*, New York: Seabury 1969.

--- *A Black Theology of Liberation*, Philadelphia: Lippincott 1970.

--- The Spirituals and the Blues: *An Interpretation*, New York: The Seabury Press 1972.

--- *God of the Oppressed*, New York: Seabury 1975.

--- Black Theology as Liberation Theology, in: *African American religious Studies. An Interdisciplinary Anthology*, edited by Gayraud Wilmore, (Duke University Press) 1989.

--- *For My People. Black Theology and the Black Church*, Maryknoll: Orbis Books 1984.

--- *My Soul Looks Back*, Maryknoll: Orbis Books 1986.

--- *Speaking the Truth. Ecumenism, Liberation, and Black Theology*, Michigan: Eerdmans Publishing Co. 1986.

Copleston, Frederick, *A History of Philosophy. vols. 1 & 2*, N.Y.: Image Books 1962.

Coreth, E, *Was is der Mensch? Grundzüge einer philosophischen Anthropologie*, Innsbruck 1980.

--- Zur Philosophie der Trinität im Denken der Neuzeit bis Schelling, in: J. Möller (Hrsg.), *Der Streit um den Gott der Philosophen*, Düsseldorf 1985, 48-80.

Corwin, V., *St. Ignatius and Christianity in Antioch*, New Haven 1960.

Creel, R. E., Divine Impassibility. An Essay in Philosophical Theology, Cambridge: University Press 1986.

Crenshaw, J. L., The Shift from Theodicy to Anthropodicy, in: *Theodicy in the Old Testament*, edited by J. L. Crenshaw, London: Fortress Press/SPCK 1963.

Crouzel, Henri, *Origène et la "connaissance mystique"*, Paris: Desclée de Brower 1961.

--- La Passion de L' Impassible. Un essai apologétique du IIIe siécle, in: *L'Homme devant Dieu; Mélanges offerts au Père Henri de Lubac, vol. 1*, Paris: Aubier 1963, 269-279.

Dähne, A. F., *Geschichtliche Darstellung der jüdisch-alexandrinischen Religions-Philosphie*, Halle, II (?).

Dassmann, Ernst , *Augustinus. Heiliger und Kirchenlehrer*, Stuttgart 1993.

Davies, J. G., The Origins of Docetism, in: F. L. Cross (Hrsg.), *Studia Patristica VI. Papers presented to the Third International Conference on Patristic Studies held at Christ Church*, Oxford 1959, Berlin 1962.

Dawe, D. G., The Form Of A Servant, A Historical Analysis of the Kenotic Motif, Philadelphia: Westminster Press 1964.

Deneken, M., God at the Heart of Hell: From Theodicy to the Word of the Cross, in: *Concilium, 3 (1993)* 53-63.

DeYoung, James C., "Event and Interpretation of the Resurrection", in: *Interpreting God's World Today*, ed. S. Kistemaker (Grandapids: Baker, 1970)

Dickson, Kwesi, *Theology in Africa*, London/Maryknoll: DTL/Orbis Books, 1984.

--- & Ellingworth, P. (ed.), *Biblical Revelation and African Beliefs*, London 1969.

Diogenes Laetius, *Vitae philosophorum (H. S. Long) 2 Bde*, Oxford 1964.

Dryness, W. A., *Learning about Theology from the Third World*, Michigan: Academie Books 1990.

Dodds, Michael J., *The Unchanging God of Love. A study of the Teaching of St. Thomas Aquinas on Divine Immutability in View of Certain Contemporary Criticism of this Doctrine*, Editions Universitaires Fribourg Suisse 1986.

Dorner, I. A., Über die richtige Fassung des dogmatischen Begriffs der Unveränderlichkeit Gottes, in: *Jahrbücher für deutsche Theologie, 1856-1858, now in Gesammelte Schriften*, Berlin: Wilhelm Hertz 1883, 188-377.

---   *System der christlichen Glaubenslehre II, I*, Berlin 1880.

Downing, Gerald F., Hellenism, in: *A Dictionary of Biblical Interpretation*, edited by R. J. Coggins & J. L. Houlden, London/Philadelphia: SCM/Trinity Press 1990.

Dreyer, Oskar, Begriff des Gottgeziemenden in der Antike. Mit besonderer Berücksichtigung Philons von Alexandrien: Spudasmata 24, Hildesheim-New York 1970.

Dunn, J. D. G., *Unity and Diversity in the New Testament*, Philadelphia: Westminster 1977.

Duquoc, C., 'Who is God?' becomes 'Where is God?'. The shift in a Question, in: *Concilium, 4 (1992)* 1-10.

---   *Christologie, L'Homme Jesus, Vol. 1*, Paris 1968.

Ebrard, August J. H., *Das dogma von heiligen Abendmahl*, Frankfurt 1845.

---   *Christliche Dogmatik*, Königsberg 1863.

Éla, Jean-Marc, *African Cry*, trans. by Robert R. Barr, Maryknoll: Orbis Books 1986 (French Original, 1980).

---   *My Faith as an African*, Maryknoll: Orbis Books 1988.

Elert, W., Die Theopaschitische Formel, in: *Theologische Literaturzeitung*, 75 (1950) 195-206.

---   Der Ausgang der altkirchlichen Christologie. Eine Untersuchung über Theodor von Pharan und seine Zeit als Einführung, in: *Die alte Dogmengeschichte*, Berlin 1957.

Ellacuria, Ignacio, *Freedom Made Flesh. The Mission of Christ and His Church*, Engl. transl., Maryknoll: Orbis books 1976.

Ezeanya, Stephen N., God, Spirits and the Spirit World, in: *Biblical Revelation and African Beliefs*, edited by K. Dickson and P. Ellingworth, London 1969.

Fasholé-Luke, E., Ancestor Veneration and the Community of Saints, in: *New Testament Essays for Africa and the World*, edited by M. Glasswell M., / E. Fasholé-Luke, London 1974.

Feuerbach, Ludwig, Principles of the Future, in: *The Fiery Brook: Selected Writings of Ludwig Feuerbach*, transl. Z. Hanfi, New York: Double-day 1972.

Fiddes, P. S., *The Creative suffering of God*, Oxford: Clarendon Press 1988.

Forsyth, P. T., *The Person and Place of Jesus Christ*, London 1955.

---   The Divine Self-Emptying, in: *God the Holy Father*, London 1957.

Kabasélé, Francois, Christ as Ancestor and Elder Brother, in: *Faces of Jesus in Africa*, edited by R. J. Schreiter, Maryknoll: Orbis Books 1991.

Frankel, Vorstudien der Septuaginta, Leipzig 1841.

Frank, R. S., Passibility and Impassibility, in: *The Encyclopaedia of Religion and Ethics*, edited by J. Hastings, New York 1961.

Fredenthal, J., Are there Traces of Greek Philosophy in the Septuagint? in: *The Jewish Quarterly Review* 2 (1890) 205-222.

Frend, W.H.C., Augustinianism, in: *A New Dictionary of Christian Theology*, edited by A. Richardson & J. Bowden, London: SCM 1983.

Fretheim, Terence E., *The suffering of God. An Old Testament Perspective*, Philadelphia: Fortress Press 1984.

Fries, H., *Fundamentaltheologie*, Graz 1985.

Fritsch, C. T., *The Anti-anthropomorphisms of the Greek Pentateuch*, Princeton N. J. 1943.

Frohnhofen, Herbert, *Apatheia Tou Theou. Über die Affektlosigkeit Gottes in der griechischen Antike und bei den griechischsprachigen Kirchenvätern bis zu Gregorios Thaumaturgos*, Frankfurt a. M. 1987.

Frost, Peter, Attitudes toward Blacks in the Early Christian Era, in: *The Second Century. A Journal of Early Christian Studies*, 8 (1991) 1-11.

Galot, J., *Dieu-souffre-t-il?*, Paris 1976, (Ital. orig., Assisi 1975).

--- Le Dieu Trinitaire et la Passion du Christ, in: *Nouvelle revue theologique* 144 (1982) 70-87.

Gerken, Alexander, *Theologie der Eucharistie*, München 1973.

Gess, W. F., *Die Lehre von der Person Christi*, Basel 1856;

--- *Das Dogma von Christi Person und Werk*, 3 vols., Basel 1887.

Gförer, A. F., *Kritische Geschichte des Urchristentums*, Teil II, Stuttgart.

Ghebremedhin, Manna, The Survival of Christianity in Ethiopia, in: *African Christian Studies*, vol. 6, Nr. 4, 1990.

Goetz, Roland, The Divine Burden, in: *The Christian Century*, 22 (1978) 298-302.

--- The Suffering of God. The Rise of a New Orthodoxy, in: *The Christian Century*, 16 (1986) 385-389.

Goldberg, A. M., *Untersuchungen über die Vorstellung von der Shekinah in der frühen rabbinischen Literatur*, Berlin 1969.

Goodspeed, Edgar J., *Die ältesten Apologeten. Texte mit kurzen Einleitungen*, Göttingen 1914 (Neudruck Göttingen 1984).

Gorodetzky, Nadejda, *The Humiliated Christ in Modern Russian Thought*, London: SPCK 1938.

Grabowski, Stanislaus, *The All-Present God. A Study in St. Augustine*, London: Herder Book 1954.

Grant, Colin, Possibilities for Divine Passibility, in: *Toronto Journal of Theology*, 4 (1988).

Grant, R. M., *The Early Christian Doctrine of God*, Charlottesville: University of Virginia Press 1966.

Gravely, Will B., The Rise of African Churches in America (1786-1822). Re-examining the Contexts, in: *African American religious Studies. An Interdisciplinary Anthology*, edited by G. Wilmore, (Duke University Press) 1989.

Gregor, R., *Secular Christianity*, (1965).

Grenz, S. J., The Appraisal of Pannenberg. A Survey of the Literature, in: *The Theology of Wolfhart Pannenberg*, edited by C. E. Braaten & P. Clayton, Minneapolis 1988.

Greschake, Gisbert, Leiden und Gottesfrage, in: *Geist und Leben*, 50 (1977) 102-121.

---   *Der Preis der Liebe. Besinnung über das Leid*, Freiburg i. Br., 1978.

Grillmeier, Alois, Christus licet uobis inuitis deus. Ein Beitrag zur Diskussion über die Hellenisierung der christlichen Botschaft, in: *Kerygma und Logos - C. Andresen-Festschrift*, Göttingen 1979.

---   Hellenisierung - Judaisierung des Christentums als Deuteprinzipien der Geschichte des kirchlichen Dogmas, in: *Mit ihm und in ihm. Christologische Forschungen und Perspektiven*, Freiburg i. Br. 1975.

---   *Jesus der Christus im Glauben der Kirche, Von der Apostolischen Zeit bis zum Konzil von Chalcedon* (451), Bd.1, 2. Aufl., Freiburg 1979.

Groves, C. P., *The Planting of Christianity in Africa*, 4 vols., London 1948-1958.

Gutiérrez, Gustavo, *A Theology of Liberation. History, Politics, and Salvation*, Maryknoll: Orbis Books 1973, (Spanish original, 1971).

---   *On Job. God-talk and the Suffering of the Innocent*, Maryknoll: Orbis Books, 1987.

---   *The Power of the Poor in History*, Maryknoll: Orbis Books 1983.

Gyekye, Kwame, African Religions and Philosophy, in: *Second Order: The African Journal of Philosophy*, 4 (1975) 86-94.

Hallie, Philip P., Stoicism, in: *The Encyclopedia of Philosophy*, vol. 8, edited by P. Edwards, London / New York: Macmillan 1967.

Hallman, J., Divine Suffering and Change in Origen and Ad Theopompum, in: *The Second Century*, 7/2 (1989/90).

Hankey, Wayne, Aquinas and the Passion of God, in: *Being and Truth, Essays in Honour of John Macquarrie*, edited by A. Kee and E. Lang, London, 1986.

--- Theology as System and as Science: Proclus and Thomas Aquinas, in: *Dionysius* 6 (1982) 83-93

Hartshorne, Charles, *The Logic of Perfection and other Essays in Neoclassical Metaphysics*, La Salle: Open Court 1962.

--- *A Natural Theology for Our Time*, La Salle: Open court, 1967.

--- *Creative Synthesis and Philosophic Method*, London: SCM Press 1970.

Hegel, G. W. F., *Lectures on the Philosophy of Religion*, Vol. III.

--- *The Phenomenology of Mind*, trans. by J. Baillie, London: George Allen & Unwin 1955).

Heinz, H., *Der Gott des Je-Mehr*, Bern/Frankfurt 1975.

Heinze, Richard, *Xenokrates. Darstellung der Lehre und Sammlung der Fragmente*, Leipzig 1892, Nachdr. Hildesheim 1965.

Hemmerle, Klaus, *Thesen zu einer trinitarischen Ontologie*, Einsiedeln 1976.

Heschel, Abraham J., *The Prophets*, New York: Haper & Row 1962.

Hick, John, *Evil and the God of Love*, London: Macmillan Press 1985, third edition.

Hilberath, Bernd J., *Der Personbegriff der Trinitätstheologie in Rückfrage von Karl Rahner zu Tertullians 'Adversus Praxean'*, Innsbruck 1986.

Hill, William J., *Search for the Absent God. Tadition and Modernity in Religious Understanding*, edited by M. C. Hilkert, New York: Crossroad 1992.

Holme, L. R., *The extinction of the Christian Church in North Africa*, New York 1969.

Hood, Robert E., *Must God Remain Greek? Afro Cultures and God-Talk*, Minneapolis: Fortress Press 1990.

Hooker, M. D., Philippians 2,2-11, in: *Jesus und Paulus*, Hrsg. E. E. Ellis und E. Grüsser, Göttingen 1975.

Hudson, W. D., *Philosophy*, Vol. 39, 147 (1964).

Hunter, R. J., Moltmann's Theology of the Cross and the Dilemma of Contemporary Pastoral Care, in: *Hope for the Church. Moltmann in Dialogue with Practical Theology*, edited by T. Runyon, Abingdon: Nashville 1979.

Idowu, Bolaji E., *Towards an Indigenous Church*, Oxford 1965.

--- *Olódùmarè, God in Yoruba Belief* (London: Longman, 1962).

--- *African Traditional Religion: A Definition* (London: SCM, 1973).

--- God, in: *Biblical Revelation and African Beliefs*, edited by K. A. Dickson and P. Ellingworth, London 1969.

Ignatius, Letter to Romans, 6,3, trans. by James A. Kleist, in: *The Epistles of St. Clement of Rome and St. Ignatius of Antioch*, London 1961.

J. S. Pobee, *Toward an African Theology* (Abingdon, 1979).

Jäger, A., *Gott. 10 Thesen*, Tübingen 1980.

Jedin, H. and Dolan, J., (Editors) *History of the Church Vol. II*, (London: Burns & Oates, 1980).

Jeremias, Jörg, *Die Reue Gottes. Aspekte alttestamentlicher Gottesvorstellung*, Neukirchener-Vluyn 1975.

Jones, Major. J., *The Color of God. The Concept of God in Afro-American Thought*, (Macon G. A., USA: Mercer University Press 1987.

Jones, William R., *Is God A White Racist? A Preamble to Black Theology*, New York: Anchor Press / Doubleday, 1973).

Jüngel, E., Das dunkel Wort vom Tode Gottes, in: *Evangelische Kommentare*, 2 (1969) 133-138, 198-202.

--- *God as the Mystery of the World. On the Foundation of the Theology of the Crucified One in the Dispute Between Theism and Atheism*, transl. by D. L. Guder, Edinburgh: T & T Clark, 1983.

--- *Gottes Sein ist im Werden. Verantwortliche Rede vom Sein Gottes bei Karl Barth. Eine Paraphrase*, Tübingen 41976.

--- Das Sein Jesu Christi als Ereignis der Versöhnung Gottes mit einer gottlosen Welt. Hingabe des Gekreuzigten, in: *Entsprechung. Gott-Wahrheit-Mensch. Theologische Erörterungen*, München 1980, 276-284.

--- *Tod*, Gütersloch 1979.

--- Vom Tod des lebendingen Gottes. Ein Plakat, in: *Unterwegs zur Sache. Theologische Bemerkungen*, Münschen 1972, 105-125.

--- Das Verhältnis von 'ökonomischer' und 'immanenter' Trinität. Erwägungen über eine biblische Begründung der Trinitätslehre - im Anschluß an und in Auseinandersetzung mit Karl Rahners Lehre vom dreifaltigen

Gott als transzendentem Urgrund der Heilsgeschichte, in: *Zeitschrift für Theologie und Kirche*, 72 (1975) 353-364.

Kagame, Alex, *La Philosophie Bantu-Rwandaise*, Brussels 1956.

Kamp, J., *Souffrance de Dieu, vie du Monde*, Tournai 1971.

Kappes, Cl., *Freiheit und Erlösung. Untersuchungen zu den Grundlagen zu den Grundlagen der Soteriologie in den Entwürfen von Hans Urs von Balthasar, Karl Rahner und Jürgen Moltmann*, Bielefeld 1986.

Karenga, Maulana, Black Religion, in: *African American Religious Studies. An Interdisciplinary Anthology*, edited by G. Wilmore, (1989), 271-300.

Käsemann, E., A critical Analysis of Philippians 2,5-11, in: *God and Christ, Existence and Promise, Journal for Theology and the Church*, New York 1968.

Kasper, Walter, *Jesus der Christus*, Mainz 1974.

--- Revolution im Gottesverständnis? Zur Situation des ökumenischen Dialogs nach Jürgen Moltmanns 'Der gekreuzigte Gott'", in: *Diskussion über Jürgen Moltmanns Buch "Der gekreuzigte Gott"*, Hrsg. v. M. Welker, München 1979.

--- *The God of Jesus Christ*, London 1984, German original, ---, *Der Gott Jesu Christi*, Mainz 1982.

Kaunda, K., *Letter to My Children*, London/Lusaka 1973.

Kern, W., Gott-Welt-Verhältnis, in: *Sacramentum Mundi* II, 1968, 522-529.

--- Philosophische Pneumatologie. Zur theologischen Aktualität Hegels, in: *Gegenwart des Geistes. Aspekte der Pneumatologie*, Hrsg. Kasper, W., Freiburg-Basel-Wien 1979.

--- Dialektik und Trinität in der Religionsphilosophie Hegels. Ein Beitrag zur Diskussion mit L. Oeing-Hanhoff, in: *Zeitschrift für katholische Theologie* 102 (1980) 129-155.

--- Menschwerdung Gottes im Spannungsfeld der Interpretationen von Hegel und Kierkegaard, in: *Wegmarken der Christologie*, Hrsg. von A. Ziegenaus, Donauwörth 1980, 81-126.

Ki-Zerbo, Joseph, *Die Geschichte Schwarzafrikas*, Frankfurt 1981.

Kierkegaard, S., *Training in Christianity*, transl. by W. Lowrie, Princeton 1941.

Kitamori, Kazoh, *Theology of the Pain of God*, transl. by M. E. Bratcher, London: SCM Press 1966.

Köhler, L., *Old Testament Theology*, Philadelphia 1958.

Kolié, Cécé, Jesus as Healer?, in: *Faces of Jesus in Africa*, edited by R. J Schreiter, Maryknoll: Orbis Books 1991.

Koslowski, P., Der leidende Gott, in: *Theologie und Philosophie* 61 (1986) 562-565.

Krenski, T. R., Passio Caritatis: Trinitarische Passiologie im Werk Hans Urs von Balthasars, Einsiedeln 1990.

Kroll, W., Apathy, in: *The Encyclopaedia of Religion and Ethics*, vol. 1, edited by J. Hastings, New York 1961.

Küng, H., *The Incarnation of God. An Introduction to Hegel's Theological Thought as Prolegomena to a Future Christology*, transl. by J. R. Stephenson, (Edinburgh, 1987).

Kuhlmann, J., *Die Taten des einfachen Gottes: Eine römisch-katholishe Stellungnahme zum Palamismus*, Würzburg 1968.

Kuhn, Peter, *Gottes Selbsterniedrigung in der Theologie der Rabbinen*, München 1968.

--- *Gottes Trauer and Klage in der rabbinischen Überlieferung* (Talmud und Midrasch) Leiden 1978.

Kuitert, H. M., *Gott in Menschengestalt. Eine dogmatisch-hermeneutische Studie über die Anthropomorphismen der Bibel*, München 1967.

Laktanz, De ira Dei / *Vom Zorne Gottes* , Hrsg. von H. Kraft und A. Wlosok, Darmstadt 41983.

Lee, Jung Young, *God Suffers for Us: A Systematic Inquiry into a Concept of Divine Passibility*, The Hague: Martinus Nijhoff 1974.

Lehmann, Karl, Kirchliche Dogmatik und biblisches Gottesbild, in: *Die Frage nach Gott*, Hrsg. von J. Ratzinger, Freiburg-Basel-Wien 21973, 116-140.

--- God im Leiden, in: *Lehmann, K., Jesus Christus is auferstanden*, Freiburg 1975, 24-48.

Liebner, Theodore A., *Christologie oder die christologische Einheit des dogmatischen Systems*, Göttingen 1849.

Lightfoot, J. B., *The Apostolic Fathers*, vol. II/1 1885

Lincoln, C. Eric, The Development of Black Religion in America, in: *African American religious Studies. An Interdisciplinary Anthology*, edited by G. Wilmore, (Duke University Press) 1989.

Lochbrunner, M., *Analogia Caritatis: Darstellung und Deutung der Theologie Hans Urs von Balthasars*, Freiburg 1981.

Lochmann, J. M./ Dembowski, H., Gottes Sein ist im Leiden. Zur Trinitarischen Kreuzestheologie Jürgen Moltmanns, in: *Diskussion über Jürgen Moltmanns Buch "Der gekreuzigte Gott"*, Hrsg. v. M. Welker, München 1979.

Loewenich, W. v., *Luther's Theology of the Cross*, transl. by H. J. A. Bouman, Belfast 1976.

Loofs, F., *Leitfaden zum Studium der Dogmengeschichte*, 6. Aufl., hrsg. von K. Aland Tübingen 1959.

Löser, W., *Im Geiste des Origenes. Hans Urs von Balthasar als Interpret der Theologie der Kirchenväter*, Frankfurt a. M. 1975.

Loth, Heinrich, *Vom Schlangenkult zur Christuskirche - Religion und Messianismus in Afrika*, Berlin: Union Verlag 1985.

Lotz, J. B., Person und Ontologie, in: *Scholastik* 38 (1963), renamed as Theologie und Philosophie.

Maas, Wilhelm, *Unveränderlichkeit Gottes. Zum Verhältnis von griechischphilosophischer und christlicher Gotteslehre*, München 1974.

MacGregor, Geddes, *Introduction to Religious Philosophy*, Boston: Houghton Mifflin Co., 1959.

--- *He Who Lets Us Be: A Theology of Love*, New York: Seabury Press 1975.

--- *Philosophical Issues in Religious Thought*, Washington: Uni. Press of America 1979.

--- (editor), *Immortality and Human Destiny*, New York 1985.

Macquarie, J., Kenoticism Reconsidered, in: *Theology*, 77 (1974).

--- *In Search of Deity, An Essay in Dialectical Theism*, London: SCM 1984.

--- *Jesus Christ in Modern Thought*, London: SCM 1990.

Mantzaridis, G. et al., *Glauben aus dem Herzen: Eine Einführung in die Orthodoxie*, München 1987.

Marbury, Carl H., An Excursus on the Biblical and Theological Rhetoric of Martin Luther King, in: *Essays in Honor of M. L. King Jr.,* edited by John Cartwright, Evanston III: Garrett-Evangelical Seminary 1971.

--- Myth, Oral Tradition and Continuity: A Biblical-Theological Response to 'Roots', in: *The Church and the Black Experience Bulletin*, Evanston, III: Garrett-Evangelical Seminary 1977, 19-22

Martensen, H., *Christian Dogmatics,* transl. by William Urwick, T.& T. Clark, Edinburgh 1892.

Maurer, W., Hellenisierung - Germanisierung - Romanisierung. Bemerkung zu den Perioden der Kirchengeschichte, in: *Kosmos and Ekklesia*, Hrsg. von H. D. Wendland, Kassel 1953, 55-72.

Mbiti, J. S., *Concepts of God in Africa*, London: S.P.C.K. 1969.

--- *African Religions and Philosophy*, New York: Anchor Books 1970.

--- *New Testament Eschatology in an African Background*, Oxford 1971.

--- *Bible and Theology in African Christianity*, Nairobi: Oxford University Press 1986.

McDermott, B., *The Personal Unity of Jesus and God according to W. Pannenberg*.

McFague, S., Metaphor, in: *A New Dictionary of Christian Theology*, edited by A. Richardson & J. Bowden, London: SCM 1983.

McWilliams, W., *The Passion of God. Divine Suffering in Contemporary Protestant Theology*, U. S. A.: Mercier University Press 1985.

Meeks, D., Moltmann's contribution to Practical Theology, in: *Hope for the Church. Moltmann in Dialogue with Practical Theology*, edited by Theodore Runyon, Abingdon: Nashville 1979.

Meessen, F., *Unveränderlichkeit und Menschwerdung Gottes. Eine theologiegeschichtlich-systematische Untersuchung*, Freiburg i. Br. 1989.

Metuh, E. I., Contextualization. A Missiological Imperative for The Church In Africa in the Third Millennium", in: *Sedos Bulletin*, 22 (1990).

--- God and Man in African Religion, London: Geoffrey Chapman 1981.

Michaelis, W., páscho ktl in: *Theologisches Wörterbuch zum Neuen Testament*, 10 Bde. Hrsg. von Gerhard Kittel and Gerhard Friedrich, Literaturnachtrag von G. Friedrich, Stuttgart 1933-79.

Migliore, D. L., Der gekreuzigte Gott, in: *Diskussion über Jürgen Moltmanns Buch "Der gekreuzigte Gott"*, Hrsg. v. M. Welker, München 1979.

Miranda, J. P., *Marx and the Bible*, London: SCM Press, 1977.

Miskotte, H. H., Das Leiden ist in Gott. Über Jürgen Moltmanns Trinitarische Kreuzestheologie, in: *Diskussion über Jürgen Moltmanns Buch "Der gekreuzigte Gott"*, Hrsg. v. M. Welker, München 1979.

Mofokeng, Takatso A., *The Crucified Among the Crossbearers. Towards a Black Christology*, Kampen 1983.

Moltmann, J., *Theology of Hope: On the Ground and Implications of a Christian Eschatology*, transl. by J. W. Leitch, London 1967, (German original, Munich 1965).

---   *The Crucified God: The Cross of Christ as the Foundation and Criticism of Christian Theology*, transl. by R. A. Wilson and J. Bowden, New York 1974, (German original, Munich 1973).

---   *The Church in the Power of the Spirit: A Contribution to Messianic Ecclesiology*, transl. Margaret Kohl, (New York 1977), (German original, Munich 1975).

---   *The Future of Creation*, transl. by M. Kohl, London, 1997, (German original, Munich 1977).

---   *The Passion for life. A Messianic Lifestyle*, Philadelphia: Fortress press 1978.

---   Antwort auf die Kritik an 'Der gekreuzigte Gott', in: *Diskussion über Jürgen Moltmanns Buch "Der gekreuzigte Gott"*, Hrsg. v. M. Welker, München 1979.

---   *The Trinity and the Kingdom of God: The doctrine of God*, transl. by M. Kohl, London 1981, (German original, Munich 1980).

Moser, T., *Gottesvergiftung*, Ulm 1976.

Mozley, J. K., *The Impassibility of God. A Survey of Christian Thought*, London 1926.

Mühlen, H., *Die Veränderlichkeit Gottes als Horizont einer zukünftigen Christologie. Auf dem Wege zu einer Kreuzestheologie in Auseinandersetzung mit der altkirchlichen Christologie*, Münster 21976.

Mulago, V. , Nécessité de l' adaptation missionaire chez les Bantu du Congo, in: *Des Prêtres Noirs s'interrogent*, Paris: Presence Africaine, 1940.

Mutiso-Mubinda, J., *Anthropology and the Paschal Mystery*, (Spearhead, no. 59), Eldoret, Kenya: Gaba Publications 1979.

Muzorewa, G. H., *The Origins and Development of African Theology*, Maryknoll: Orbis Books 1985.

Neill, Stephen, *A History of Christian Missions*, England: The Penguin Books 1964.

Neuner, J. and Dupuis, J., (eds.) *The Christian Faith in the Doctrinal Documents of the Catholic Church*, New York 1982.

Newlands, G., Christology, in: *A New Dictionary of Christian Theology*, edited by A. Richardson & J. Bowden, London: SCM 1983.

Niewiadomski, J., *Die Zweideutigkeit von Gott und Welt in J. Moltmanns Theologien*, Innsbruck 1982.

Nkrumah, Kwame, *Neo-Colonialism: The Last Stage of Imperialism*, London: Thomas Nelson 1965.

Nnamani, Amuluche G., The African Synod and the Model of Church-as-Family, in: *Bulletin of Ecumenical Theology*, vol. 6/2 1994.

Ntetem, Marc, Initiation, Traditional and Christian, in: *A Reader in African Christian Theology*, edited by J. Parratt, London: SPCK 1987.

Nthamburi, Zablon, The Relevance of Donatism for the Church in Africa Today, in: *African Ecclesial Review*, 23 (1981).

Ntwasa, Sabelo Moore, Basil, The Concept of God in Black Theology, in: *The Challenges of Black Theology in South Africa*, edited by B. Moore, Atlanta/Georgia: John Knox Press 1973.

Nwoga, Donatus Ibe, *The Supreme God as Stranger in Igbo Religious Thought*, Ekwerazu: Hawk Press, 1984.

Nyamiti, Charles, *African Tradition and the Christian God*, Eldoret: Gaba Publications 1977.

--- The African Sense of God's Motherhood in the Light of Christian Faith, in: *African Ecclesial Review* 23 (1981) 269-274.

--- *Christ As Our Ancestor. Christology from an African Perspective*, Zimbabwe: Mambo Press 1984.

--- African Christologies Today, in: *Faces of Jesus in Africa*, edited by R. J. Schreiter, Maryknoll: Orbis books 1991.

--- My Approach to African Theology, in: *African Christian Studies*, 7/4 (1991).

--- The Incarnation viewed from the African Understanding of Person, (published in a series), in: *African Christian Studies* (= ACS), vol. 6, March 1990, 3-27; vol. 6, June 1990, 23-76; vol. 7, March 1991, 29-52; vol. 7, June 1991, 41-68; vol. 8, June 1992, 1-28.

Nyerere, Julius, The Churches Role in Society, in: *A Reader in African Christian Theology*, edited by J. Parratt, London: SPCK 1987.

O'Collins, G, Rez. J. Moltmann, Der gekreuzigte Gott, in: *Gregorianum* 63 (1982).

O'Hanlon, G. F., *The immutability of God in the theology of Hans Urs von Balthasar*, Cambridge 1990.

Obi, C. A. & co., (eds.), *A hundred Years of the Catholic Church in Eastern Nigeria 1885-1985*, Onitsha/Nigeria 1985.

Oduyoye, Mercy A., In the Image of God... A Theological Reflection from an African Perspective, in: *Bulletin de Theologie Africaine*, 4 (1982) 41-53

---   *Hearing and Knowing. Theological Reflections on Christianity in Africa*, Maryknoll: Orbis Books 1986.

Oeing-Hanhoff, L., Die Krise des Gottesbegriffs, in: *Theologische Quarterschrift* 159 (1979).

Ogden, Schubert M., *The Reality of God*, London: SCM Press 1967.

Olson, R. E., The Human Self-Realization of God: Hegelian Elements in Pannenberg's Christology, in: *Perspectives in Religious Studies* 13 (1986).

Origen, *Contra Celsum*, transl. by H. Chadwick, Cambridge 1965.

Osborn, E. F., *The Philosophy of Clement of Alexandria*, Cambridge 1957.

Pablo, Richard & co., *The Idols of Death and the God of life: A Theology*, Maryknoll: Orbis Books 1983.

Paczensky, Gert v., *Teurer Segen. Christliche Mission and Kolonialismus*, München: Albrecht Knaus Verlag 1991.

Pailin, David A., *The Anthropological Character of Theology: Conditioning Theological Understanding*, Cambridge: Cambridge Uni. Press 1990.

---   Process Theology, in: *A New Dictionary of Christian Theology*, edited by A. Richardson & J. Bowden, London: SCM 1983.

---   *God and the Processes of Reality: Foundations of a Credible Theism*, London: Routledge, 1989, pp. 42, 466 ff.

Pannenberg, Wolfahrt, *Grundfragen Systematischer Theologie*, Göttingen 1967.

---   *Jesus - God And Man*, transl. by L. Wilkins, Philadelphia 1977, second edition.

---   *Systematische Theologie 1*, Göttingen 1988.

Parrinder, B. G., *West African Religion*, 1969.

Parratt, John, *Theologiegeschichte der Dritten Welt: Afrika*, München 1991.

P'bitek, Okot, *African Religions in Western Scholarship*, Nairobi: East African Literature bureau, 1970

Pelikan, J., *The Christian Tradition. A History of Development of Doctrine*, (1971).

Pénoukou, Efoé J., The Churches of Africa: Their Identity? Their Mission?, in: *Sedos Bulletin*, 22 (1990).

---   Christology in the Village, in: *Faces of Jesus in Africa*, edited by R. J. Schreiter, Maryknoll: Orbis Books 1991.

Pérez-Paoli, Die Menschwerdung Gottes. Apatheia und Veränderlichkeit bei Augustinus, *A paper presented in "Fachtagung der katholischen Akademie Rabanus Maurus*, Wiesbaden 28th to 30th October 1991.

Pfättisch, Ioannes M., *Der Einfluß Platos auf die Theologie Justins des Märtyrers. Eine dogmengeschichtliche Untersuchung nebst einem Anhang über die Komposition der Apologien Justins*, Parderbon 1910.

Philipson, Robert, *Studien zur Epikur und den Epikureern*: Hildesheim 1983.

Pissarek-Hudelist, H., Trinität, in: Wörterbuch der Femisnistische Theologie, Hrsg. von E. Gössmann, Gütersloch 1991.

Pitra, J. B., *Analecta Sacra Patrum Antenicaenorum IV*, Paris 1883.

Plato, *The last days of Socrates*, transl. by Hugh Tredennick, Harmondsworth: Penguin Books 1954.

Pobee, John S., *Toward an African Theology*, Nashville/Tennessee: Abingdon 1979.

Pohlenz, M., *Vom Zorne Gottes. Eine Studie über den Einfluß der griechischen Philosophie auf das alte Christentum*, Göttingen 1909.

--- *Klemens von Alexanderia und sein hellenistisches Christentum*, Göttingen 1943.

--- *Die Stoa. Geschichte einer geistigen Bewegung*, 2. Bde, Göttingen 51978/80.

Pollard, T. E., The Impassibility of God, in: *Scottish Journal of Theology*, 8 (1955) 353-364.

Post, W., Anthropomorphismus, in: *Sacramentum Mundi. Theologisches Lexikon Für Die Praxis*, vol. 1, Freiburg 1967.

Prestige, G. L., *God in Patristic Thought*, London 1952, earlier 1936.

Rackl, M., *Die Christologie des heiligen Ignatius von Antiochien. Nebst einer Voruntersuchung: Die Echtheit der sieben ignatianischen Briefe verteidigt gegen Daniel Völter*, Freiburg 1914.

Rad, G. von, *Old Testament Theology I*, London 1975.

Rahner, Karl, *Der dreifaltige Gott als transzendenter Ursprung der Heilsgeschichte, in Mysterium Salutis. Grundriß heilsgeschichtlicher Dogmatik*. Hrsg. J. Feiner - M. Löhrer. Bd. 2, Einsiedeln 1967, 317-40.

--- On the Theology of the Incarnation, in: *Theological Investigations IV*, (1960).

--- Probleme der Christologie von heute, in: *Schriften 1*, 51961.

--- *Foundations of Christian Faith*, transl. W. V. Dych, Britain: Dtl. 1978.

Ratzinger, Joseph, Das Problem der Transsubstantiation und die Frage nach dem Sinn der Eucharistie, in: *Theologische Quartalschrift*, Tübingen, 147 (1967).

Raven, Charles E., *Apollinarism*, Cambridge: Uni. Press 1923.

Richard, Lucien, Kenotic Christology in a New Perspective, in: *Eglise et Theologie*, 7 (1976).

---   L. J., *A kenotic Christology. In the humanity of Jesus the Christ, the Compassion of our God*, Lanham: Univ. Press of America 1982.

Riedlinger, H., *Vom Schmerz Gottes*, Freiburg 1983.

Ringleben, Joachim, *Interior intimo meo. Die Nähe Gottes nach den Konfessionen Augustins*, Zürich 1988.

Roberts, James Deotis, *Liberation and Reconciliation: A Black Theology*, Philadelphia: Westminster Press 1971.

---   *A Black Political Theology*, Philadelphia: Westminster 1974.

---   *Black Theology Today. Liberation and Contextualization, Toronto Studies in theology, vol. 12*, (The Edwin Mellen Press: N. Y. & Toronto, 1983).

---   *Before Color Prejudice*, (Cambridge: Harvard, 1983).

Roberts, L., *The Theological Aesthetics of Hans Urs von Balthasar*, Washington, D. C. 1987.

Robinson, J. A. T., *The Human Face of God*, Philadelphia: The Westminster Press 1973.

Rolt, C. E., *The World's Redemption*, London 1913.

Rosenzweig, Franz, *Der Stern der Erlösung III*, Heidelberg 31954.

Rossa, Alberto (editor), *The Theology of Liberation*, Diliman, Quezon city: Clarentian Publications, 1986.

Rubingh, Eugene, The African Shape of the Gospel, in: *Impact*, USA 1974.

Rücker, Heribert, *"Afrikanische Theologie". Darstellung und Dialog*, Innsbruck: Tyrolia 1985.

Russell, Bertrand, *History of Western Philosophy*, London: UNWIN 1979.

Rüther, Theodor, *Die Sittliche Forderung der Apatheia in den beiden ersten christlichen Jahrhunderten und bei Klemens von Alexandrien. Ein Beitrag zur Geschichte des christlichen Vollkommenheitsbegriffes*, Freiburg i. Br. 1949.

Ryssel, V., *Gregorius Thaumaturgus, Sein Leben und sein Schriften*, Leipzig: L. Fernau 1880.

Sanon, Anselme T., Jesus, Master of Initiation, in: *Faces of Jesus in Africa*, edited by R. J. Schreiter, Maryknoll: Orbis Books 1991.

Sarot, Marcel, God, Emotions and Corporeality. A Thomist Perspective. *A paper presented in a "Fachtagung der katholischen Akademie Rabanus Maurus*, Wiesbaden 28th to 30th October, 1991.

Sarpong, Peter, *Ghana in Retrospect, Some Aspects of Ghanaian Culture*, Tema 1974.

Sawyerr, H., *Creative Evangelism: Towards a New Christian Encounter*, London 1968.

---   *God: Ancestor or Creator?*, London 1970.

Scharbert, Joseph, *Der Schmerz im Alten Testament*, Bonn 1955.

Schillebeecks, E., *Christ the Sacrament of the Encounter with God*, London: Sheed and Ward 1963.

---   *Die eucharistische Gegenwart*, Düsseldorf 21968.

---   *Jesus, and experiment in Christology*, New York / London 1979.

Schilson, A. / Kasper, W., *Christologie im Präsens. Kritische Sichtung neuer Entwürfe*, Freiburg 1974.

Schineller, Peter, Inculturation and Syncretism: What is the Real Issue?, in: *Sedos Bulletin*, 25 (1993).

Schmaus, M., *Die psychologische Trinitätslehre des Hl. Augustinus*, Münster 1927.

Scholem, G., *Die jüdische Mystik in ihren Hauptströmmungen*, Frankfurt 1957.

---   *Von der mystischen Gestalt der Gottheit*, Zürich 1962.

Schoonenberg, P., Kenosis, in: *Concilium 2* (1966).

---   Invieweit is die Lehre von der Transsubstantiation historisch bestimmt?, in: *Concilium 3* (1967).

---   "Gott ändert sich am andern", in: *Theologisch-praktischen Quartalschrift 133* (1985) 323-332.

---   *Auf Gott hin denken. Deutschsprachige Schriften zur Theologie*, Hrsg. v. W. Zauner, Wien 1986.

Schreiter, R. J., *Constructing Local Theologies*, Maryknoll: Orbis Books 1985.

Schwager, R.,   Der Prozeß um Gott. Zu Jürgen Moltmanns "Der gekreuzigte Gott", in: *Orientierung 37* (1973) 190-192.

---   Rez. N. Hoffmann, Sühne, Kreuz und Trinität, in: *Zeitschrift für katholische Theologie* 105 (1983) 341-342.

--- Logik der Freiheit und des Natur-Wollens. Zur Erlösungslehre Anselms von Canterbury. In: *Zeitschrift für katholische Theologie 105* (1983) 125-155.

--- Der Zorn Gottes. In: *Zeitschrift für katholische Theologie 105* (1983) 406-414.

--- Der fröhliche Wechsel und Streit. Zur Erlösungs- und Rechtfertigungslehre Martin Luthers. In: *Zeitschrift für katholische Theologie 106* (1984) 27-66.

--- *Brauchen wir einen Sünden Bock? Gewalt und Erlösung in den biblischen Schriften,* München 1978.

--- Der Sohn Gottes und die Weltsünde. Zur Erlösungslehre von Hans Urs von Balthasar. In: *Zeitschrift für katholische Theologie 108* (1986) 5-44.

Schweitzer, Albert, *The Quest of the historical Jesus* (?) 1954, 3rd edition.

Sebahire, Mbonyinkebe, Saving the Earth to save life: An African point of view, in: *IDOC Internazionale,* 21/5 (1990) 42-45.

Segundo, J. L., *The Liberation of Theology,* Maryknoll: Orbis Books 1976.

--- *Our Idea of God,* Maryknoll: Orbis Books 1984.

Senghor, L. S., *Prose and Poetry,* London 1956.

Setiloane, G. M., *African Theology,* Cape Town: Blackshaws 1986.

Shelton, A. J., *The Igbo-Igala Borderland. Religion & Social Control in Indigenous African Colonialism,* Albany, New York 1971.

Shorter, Aylward, *African Christian Theology: Adaptation or Incarnation?,* Maryknoll: Orbis Books 1977.

Slusser, Michael, *Theopaschite Expressions in Second-century Christianity as reflected in the Writings of Justin, Melito, Celsus and Irenaeus,* (Oxford Phil. Diss., 1975).

--- Docetism. A Historical Definition, in: *The Second Century 1* (1981).

Snowden Jr., F. M., *Blacks in Antiquity - Ethiopians in the Greco-Roman Experience,* Cambridge: Belknap Press 1970.

Sobrino, Jon, *Christology at the Crossroads: A Latin American View,* Maryknoll: Orbis Books 1978.

--- *The True Church and the Poor,* Maryknoll: Orbis Books 1984, Spanish original 1981.

Sölle, Dorothee, Leiden / Opfer; in: *Wörterbuch der Feministischen Theologie,* Hrsg. von E. Gössmann, Gütersloh 1991.

---   Gott und das Leiden, in: *Diskussion über Jürgen Moltmann's Buch "Der gekreuzigte Gott"*, Hrsg. v. M. Welker, Müchen 1979, 111-117.

---   *Leiden*, Stuttgart-Berlin 1973.

Strauss, D. F., *Life of Jesus*, London: Chapman Brothers 1846.

Studer, Basil, Credo in Deum Patrem omnipotentem. Zum Gottesbegrifff des Heiligen Augustinus, in: *Congresso Internazionale Su S. Agostino Nel XVI Centenario Della Conversione*, Roma, 15-20 settembre 1986, Roma: Institutum Patristicum 'Augustinianum' 1987.

Studdert-Kennedy, G. A., *The Hardest Part*, London 1918.

Stumpf, S. E., Philosophy: *History and Problems*, N.Y. 1971.

Surin, Kenneth, The Impassibility of God and the Problem of Evil, in: *Scottish Journal of Theology*, 35 (1982) 97-115.

Tempels, Placide, *Bantu Philosophy*, Paris: Presence Africaine 1959, French original 1945.

---   *Notre Rencontre*, Leopoldville: Centre d' Etudes Pastorales 1962.

Theunissen, Michael, *The Other. Studies in the Social Ontology of Husserl, Heidegger, Sartre, and Buber*. Transl. by Christopher Macann, Massachsetts 1984, German original 1977.

Thomasius, Gottfried, Ein Beitrag zur kirchlichen Christologie, in: *Zeitschrift für Protestantismus und Kirche*, Neunter Band, edited by G. C. A. Harless, Erlangen 1845.

---   *Das Bekenntnis der evangelisch-lutherischen Kirche in der Konsequenz seines Prinzips*, Nürnberg 1848.

---   *Christi Person und Werk*, 3 vols. Erlangen 1853-1861.

Tinsley, E. J., "Via Negativa" and "Via Positiva", in: *A New Dictionary of Christian Theology*, edited by A. Richardson & J. Bowden, London: SCM 1983.

Tschibangu, Tharcisse and Vanneste, Alfred, Débat sur la 'theologie africaine', in: *Revue du Clergé Africaine 15* (1960) 333-352.

Turner, D., Dialectic, in: *A New Dictionary of Christian Theology*, edited by A.. Richardson & J. Bowden, London: SCM 1983.

Tutu, Desmond, *Hope and Suffering. Sermons and Speeches*, London: Fount Paperbacks 1984.

---   Black Theology and African Theology - Soulmates or Antagonists?, in: *A Reader in African Christian Theology*, edited by John Parratt, London: SPCK 1987.

Ukpon, J. S., The Emergence of African Theologies, in: *Theological Studies* 45 (1984) 501-536.

--- *African Theologies Now - A Profile*, Eldoret, Kenya: Gaba Publications, 1984.

Ullmann, Wolfgang, Die Gottesvorstellung der Gnosis als Herausforderungen an Theologie und Verkündigung, in: K.-W. Tröger, *Gnosis und Neues Testament*.

Unamuno, Miguel de, The Tragic Sense of Life in Men and Nations, in: *Selected Works, vol. 4*, Routeldge & Kegan Paul and University Press 1972, Spanish original 1912.

Uzukwu, Elochukwu E., The God of our ancestors and African unity, in: *African Ecclesial Review* 23 (1981).

Varillon, F., *La Souffrance de Dieu*, Paris 1975.

Vorgrimler, H., Leiden Gottes, in: *ThdG 30* (1987) 20-26.

Walter, Meinrad, Die Fülle des Glaubens geistlich verstehen. Zum theologischen Werk H. U. v. Balthasar, in: *Gott-sucher im Sapnnungsfeld von Christentum und Moderne*. Hrsg. von Jürgen Hoeren, Würzburg 1991.

Weigandt, P., *Der Doketismus im Urchristentum und in der theologischen Entwicklung des zweiten Jahrhunderts*, 2 Bde., Heidelberg Diss. 1961.

Weil, Simone, *Waiting on God*, transl. Emma Craufurd, Britain: Fontana 1959.

--- *First and Last Notebooks*, transl. R. Rees, London: Oxford 1970.

Weischeldel, Wilhelm, *Der Gott der Philosophen. Grundlegung einer Philosophischen Theologie im Zeitalter des Nihilismus*, 2Bde., Darmstadt 1971, Neudr. München 1979.

Welker, Michael, (Hrsg.), *Diskussion über Jürgen Moltmanns Buch "Der gekreuzigte Gott"*, München 1979.

Welte, B., Diskussionsberitrag, in: M. Schmaus (Hrsg.), *Aktuelle Fragen zur Eucharistie*, München 1960.

Wendebourg, D., *Geist oder Energie. Zur Frage der innergöttlichen Verankerung des christlichen Lebens in der byzantinischen Theologie*, München 1980.

Werbick, Jürgen, Prolegomena, in: *Handbuch der Dogmatik I*, Düsseldorf 1992.

--- *Bilder sind Wege. Eine Gotteslehre*, München 1992.

--- Das Leiden Gottes in sich. An sich selbst? Hans Urs von Balthasars sprechen von der Trinitarischen Urkenose als Voraussetzung seines soteriologischen Konzepts". *A paper delivered during a Wissentschafliche Fachtagung der katholischen Akademie Rabanus Maurus, Wies-*

banden am 9.-11. März 1992, zum Thema: Das Leiden Gottes. Ein neues Paradigma der Theologie? II. Systematische und praktische Aspekte.

Westerman, Diedrich, *Africa and Christianity*, London 1937.

Whitehead, A. N., *Adventures of Ideas*, Cambridge: Cambridge University Press, 1933.

Whitehead, A. N., *Process and Reality: An Essay in Cosmology*, corrected edition, edited by D. R. Griffin and D. W. Sherburne, New York: The Free Press, 1978.

Wiederkehr, Dietrich, Entwurf einer systematische Christologie, in: *Mysterium Salutis. Grundriß Heilsgeschichtlicher Dogmatik, III/1*, Hrsg. J. Feiner & M Löhrer, Einsiedeln 1970.

Williams, Daniel D., *What Present-Day Theologians Are Thinking*, (Harper & Row, 1959).

--- *The Spirit and the Forms of Love*, Welwyn: James Nisbet, 1968.

Wilmore, G., *Black Religion and Black Radicalism*, (Maryknoll, N. Y.: Orbis Books, 1883), first published 1973.

--- & Cone, J. (ed.). *Black Theology: A Documentary History, 1966-1976*, Maryknoll: Orbis Books 1979.

--- (ed.), *African American Religious Studies. An Interdisciplinary Anthology*, Durham/London: Duke University Press 1989.

Wimberly, Edward P., The Suffering God, in: *Preaching on Suffering and a God of love,* edited by Henry J. Young, Philadelphia: Fortress 1978.

Yannaras, Rez. J. Moltmann, Der gekreuzigte Gott, in: *Ökumenische Rundschau* 31 (1982).

Young, F., Antiochian Theology, in: *A New dictionary of Christian theology*, edited by A.. Richardson & J. Bowden, London: SCM 1983.

Young, Josiah U., *Black and African Theologies - Siblings or Distant Cousins?* Maryknoll: Orbis books 1986.

Zeilinger, Albert, *Das Alte Testament verstehen II*, Konstanz 1987.

Zeller, E. *Die Philosophie der Griechen, II*, Leipzig 1919-1920.

Zimany, R. D., Moltmann's Crucified God, in: *Dialog 16* (1977).

STUDIEN ZUR INTERKULTURELLEN GESCHICHTE DES CHRISTENTUMS
ETUDES D'HISTOIRE INTERCULTURELLE DU CHRISTIANISME
STUDIES IN THE INTERCULTURAL HISTORY OF CHRISTIANITY

Begründet von/fondé par/founded by
Hans Jochen Margull †, Hamburg

Herausgegeben von/edité par/edited by

Richard Friedli   Walter J. Hollenweger   Theo Sundermeier
Université de Fribourg   University of Birmingham   Universität Heidelberg

Jan A.B. Jongeneel
Universiteit Utrecht

Band 1 Wolfram Weiße: Südafrika und das Antirassismusprogramm. Kirchen im Spannungsfeld einer Rassengesellschaft.

Band 2 Ingo Lembke: Christentum unter den Bedingungen Lateinamerikas. Die katholische Kirche vor den Problemen der Abhängigkeit und Unterentwicklung.

Band 3 Gerd Uwe Kliewer: Das neue Volk der Pfingstler. Religion, Unterentwicklung und sozialer Wandel in Lateinamerika.

Band 4 Joachim Wietzke: Theologie im modernen Indien - Paul David Devanandan.

Band 5 Werner Ustorf: Afrikanische Initiative. Das aktive Leiden des Propheten Simon Kimbangu.

Band 6 Erhard Kamphausen: Anfänge der kirchlichen Unabhängigkeitsbewegung in Südafrika. Geschichte und Theologie der äthiopischen Bewegung. 1880-1910.

Band 7 Lothar Engel: Kolonialismus und Nationalismus im deutschen Protestantismus in Namibia 1907-1945. Beiträge zur Geschichte der deutschen evangelischen Mission und Kirche im ehemaligen Kolonial- und Mandatsgebiet Südwestafrika.

Band 8 Pamela M. Binyon: The Concepts of "Spirit" and "Demon". A Study in the use of different languages describing the same phenomena.

Band 9 Neville Richardson: The World Council of Churches and Race Relations. 1960 to 1969.

Band 10 Jörg Müller: Uppsala II. Erneuerung in der Mission. Eine redaktionsgeschichtliche Studie und Dokumentation zu Sektion II der 4. Vollversammlung des Ökumenischen Rates der Kirchen, Uppsala 1968.

Band 11 Hans Schöpfer: Theologie und Gesellschaft. Interdisziplinäre Grundlagenbibliographie zur Einführung in die befreiungs- und polittheologische Problematik: 1960-1975.

Band 12 Werner Hoerschelmann: Christliche Gurus. Darstellung von Selbstverständnis und Funktion indigenen Christseins durch unabhängige charismatisch geführte Gruppen in Südindien.

Band 13 Claude Schaller: L'Eglise en quête de dialogue. Vergriffen.

Band 14 Theo Tschuy: Hundert Jahre kubanischer Protestantismus (1868-1961). Versuch einer kirchengeschichtlichen Darstellung.

Band 15 Werner Korte: Wir sind die Kirchen der unteren Klassen. Entstehung, Organisation und gesellschaftliche Funktionen unabhängiger Kirchen in Afrika.

Band 16 Arnold Bittlinger: Papst und Pfingstler. Der römisch katholisch-pfingstlerische Dialog und seine ökumenische Relevanz.

Band 17 Ingemar Lindén: The Last Trump. An historico-genetical study of some important chapters in the making and development of the Seventh-day Adventist Church.

Peter Fulljames

God and Creation in intercultural perspective
Dialogue between the Theologies of Barth, Dickson, Pobee, Nyamiti and Pannenberg

Frankfurt/M., Berlin, Bern, New York, Paris, Wien, 1993. IX, 190 pp.
Studies in the Intercultural History of Christianity. Vol. 86.
Responsible Editor: Walter J. Hollenweger
ISBN 3-631-45609-3   pb. DM 64.--*

African Christian theologies aim to contextualise the gospel in African cultures, yet they also have much to offer to the development of systematic theology elsewhere. In this book the responses of Barth and of Pannenberg to the question of how God is related to the world are analysed and then re-formulated. This is done through interaction with the themes of community, life and co-creativity which emerge in interpretation of Dickson, Pobee and Nyamiti. The discussion makes use of Tanner's rules for Christian language about God and creation, and the methods of the African theologies are distinguished in a new classification of models of contextualisation, which is compared with the work of Schreiter and with Frei's typology of modern theology. The concluding development of Pannenberg's theology is shown to be relevant to topics much debated in the late twentieth century: the environmental crisis, the relationship of science and religious belief, the nature of human freedom, and the problem of evil.

Contents: Discussion of methods and themes of Barth, Dickson, Pobee, Nyamiti and Pannenberg.

Peter Lang **Europäischer Verlag der Wissenschaften**
Frankfurt a.M. • Berlin • Bern • New York • Paris • Wien
Auslieferung: Verlag Peter Lang AG, Jupiterstr. 15, CH-3000 Bern 15
Telefon (004131) 9402121, Telefax (004131) 9402131
- Preisänderungen vorbehalten - *inklusive Mehrwertsteuer

DATE DUE

			Printed in USA

HIGHSMITH #45230